75327

+ 30

F/E

A HISTORY OF THE UNIVERSITY OF WALES

VOLUME 2

The University of Wales
1839–1939

J. Gwynn Williams

CARDIFF
UNIVERSITY OF WALES PRESS
1997

British Library Cataloguing in Publication Data

A catalogue record for this book is available from the British Library.

ISBN 0–7083–1436–8

Typeset at the University of Wales Press
Printed in Great Britain by The Cromwell Press, Broughton Gifford, Wiltshire

I
Beryl
ac i holl gyn-fyfyrwyr
Prifysgol Cymru

Contents

Illustrations

Acknowledgements

I thank the authorities of the University for their invitation to write this volume and in particular the present Senior Vice-Chancellor, Professor K. G. Robbins, an old friend and colleague, for his exemplary patience and courtesy, and also Mr J. D. Pritchard, the Secretary General, and his staff for enabling me to explore sources at the University Registry.

My own alma mater, the University of Wales, Bangor, has given me every possible facility throughout the years; I pay tribute to two successive vice-chancellors, Professor Eric Sunderland and Professor Roy Evans, and to my former colleagues in the School of History and of Welsh History. I am much indebted, as are many others, to the College archivist, Mr Tomos Roberts, for his unfailing help in matters large and small, and to the staff of the National Library who have always given me ready, expert advice, notably the Librarian, Dr Lionel Madden, Mr John Graham Jones, Mr Richard Hughes and Mr Richard Lewis.

I am much obliged to the following, some of whom are now dead, for written communications or oral recollections and sometimes both: Mr and Mrs Gwilym Ambrose, Mr T. M. Bassett, the British Broadcasting Corporation (for permitting me to have copies of talks by College Principals in 1938 and also a tape of a talk by Dr Thomas Jones on 'College Principals', 17 December 1953), Mr R. Brinkley, Dr Geraint Bowen, Mr Duncan Cameron, Dr John Cule, Dr B. L. Davies, Dr Elwyn Davies, Professor F. P. Davies, Mrs Haulwen Dodd, Sir Herbert Duthie, Dr David Dykes, Dr E. L. Ellis, Mr R. Wallis Evans, Professor R. Geraint Gruffydd, Dr Eirwen Gwynn, Professor Bryan Hibbard, Dr Christopher Hill, Professor L. E. Hughes, Dr David Jenkins, Professor Geraint H. Jenkins, Professor D. W. T. Jenkins, Dr Emyr Wyn Jones (especially in relation to the Welsh National School of Medicine), Dr Gwilym Arthur Jones, Professor Gwyn Jones (for allowing me to see material acquired in preparing *Fountains of Praise*), Mr John Henry Jones, Mr Moses J. Jones, Mr T. A. Lewis, Professor Alun Llywelyn-Williams, Professor William Mathias, Mrs Huana Morgan and Dr Prys Morgan (for kindnesses at Swansea); Mr John Lancaster,

Dr Dyfnallt Morgan, Miss Nêst Morris-Jones, Mr T. Arfon Owen, Sir Thomas and Lady Enid Parry, Dr D. T. W. Price, Dr G. M. Mitchell, Mr Rheon Pritchard, Mrs Helen Ramage, Mr John Rhys, Dr Enid Roberts (also for allowing me to use the copy she herself made of *Llyfr Aneirin*), Dr Gareth Roberts, Mrs Myfanwy Elizabeth Roberts, Mr O. M. Roberts, Dr Ian Salmon, Dr Isaac Thomas, Sir John Meurig Thomas, Mr Ned Thomas, Revd Lewis Valentine, Mr A. H. Williams, Sir Dillwyn Williams, Dr Gareth Williams, Sir Glanmor Williams (for many invigorating conversations), Professor Stephen J. Williams and Mr W. D. Williams.

I was fortunate to secure the services of Mrs Gwyneth Brindley, who prepared the statistical graph on p. 423, of Mr Douglas Madge, mainly responsible for the illustrations, and of Mrs Moira Thornton, whose typing skills I have long admired and who has helped me in innumerable ways.

At Gwennyth Street itself I was guided in the early stages by Mrs Susan Jenkins and later by Mrs Ceinwen Jones who shrewdly and serenely shepherded this volume through the Press.

My debt to my wife is very great, a debt repaid in part only by a formal dedication.

The illustrations in this volume are reproduced by kind permission of the following:

Cardiff Royal Infirmary: 7, 17, 25
From *Fountains of Praise*, edited by Gwyn Jones and Michael Quinn (Cardiff, 1983): 3
Prys Morgan: 32
Photograph Michael Murray: 2
The National Library of Wales: 1, 15, 16, 20, 21, 22, 35, 36, 37
The National Portrait Gallery: 18
Dr Enid Roberts: 38
The University of Wales, Aberystwyth: 31
The University of Wales, Bangor: 5, 9, 11, 14, 19, 28, 29, 30, 36
The University of Wales, Cardiff: 4, 27
The University of Wales, Lampeter: 8
The University of Wales Registry: 10, 12
The University of Wales Swansea: 6
Lady Irene White: 23
Western Mail and Echo: 33

Preface

To write the history of the federal University of Wales proved more challenging than I had at first supposed. The main problem was to strike an appropriate balance between the University and its constituent Colleges. Quite independently I came to the same conclusion as D. Emrys Evans in *The University of Wales* (1953) for we have both given the same proportionate attention to the Colleges in separate chapters. It may perhaps be urged that since some Colleges later published their own histories it was not necessary even to outline the development of each institution. However, the largest College, Cardiff, has no formal published history and the same is true of the Welsh National School of Medicine. This matter I have considered in the 'Note on Sources'.

There were other factors which weighed with me. Three Colleges were in being before the founding of the University; they had their own charters and endowments; College principals, chosen by the Colleges themselves, were in turn vice-chancellors of the University; teaching and research (apart from extra-mural work) were almost wholly conducted within the College and graduates of the University have mainly identified themselves with the College which was their Alma Mater.

Emrys Evans was in addition 'uneasily conscious' that when students were mentioned in his history 'it has for the most part been as so many heads to be counted'. Since there would be neither university nor college without them, I have ventured to include a sketch of student life. I further believe that it was necessary to give separate treatment to the Great War and also to the Haldane Commission whose report was hailed by Lloyd George as 'one of the most important documents . . . in the history . . . of Wales'. Perhaps I have been rash in attempting to discuss the architecture of the Registry and the 'new' College buildings at Cardiff and Bangor, for I am not at all an expert. Others must judge. It was clear to me that despite some overlap with other sections of this history I should devote two chapters to the links between university and nation. The founders of the University would have applauded the intention.

I should be disingenuous were I not to say that I have hitherto firmly supported the federal principle, a conviction reinforced by my membership of several University Boards. It was also advantageous to me to serve on the Daniel Committee which, though overtaken by the swift turn of events, thoroughly examined the constitutional and financial aspects of the University in its Report (1989), of which I was privileged to write the historical section. I hope, nevertheless, that it will be apparent that I have attempted to be as impartial as the conscious mind allows.

This volume appears in the same year as the University of Wales, Aberystwyth, celebrates its natal day a century and a quarter ago. One hundred and seventy years have passed since the University of Wales, Lampeter, enrolled its first students. It is in a warm federal spirit that I salute them both.

BANGOR, 1997   J. GWYNN WILLIAMS

Introduction

The foundation of the University of Wales was treated in an earlier volume and in this introduction it will be sufficient to draw attention to the principal elements of the story.[1]

Had Wales retained her independence in the late thirteenth century or recovered it under Owain Glyn Dŵr in the early fifteenth, she might perhaps have enjoyed the blessings of two universities, one in north Wales, the other in south Wales. Such certainly was Glyn Dŵr's plan in 1406. Scotland, on the other hand, had three universities before the end of the fifteenth century, St Andrew's (1412), Glasgow (1451) and Aberdeen (1494), and yet another at Edinburgh in 1583. In Dublin, Trinity College, in fact a university, to which other colleges were expected to be added, was established in 1597, a potent instrument, Protestants hoped, in the ceaseless war against popery. In Wales there was a gleam of light when a Monmouth-shire squire in 1600 made plans, alas unfulfilled, to found a college at Tintern in the Wye valley. Failure, too, attended promising schemes after the Civil War and during the stirring years of the Interregnum when all things, it seemed, were to be made new. Nonconformists had academies which flourished in Wales in a modest way in the eighteenth century, but there were no degree-awarding institutions here until St David's College, Lampeter, which received its first charter in 1828, was granted power to confer degrees in theology in 1852 and in arts subjects in 1863. The prime purpose of its founder, Bishop Thomas Burgess, was to educate clergy and to equip them to halt the victorious march of Methodism, which tended to regard the college as an alien institution. In order to graduate, Non-conformists trained in denominational colleges were obliged to proceed elsewhere, usually to Scotland or to London – Oxford and Cambridge being closed to them because of religious tests not wholly extinguished until 1871. Welsh Anglicans of sufficient means, however, had long resorted to the older universities. In 1571 Hugh Price of Brecon founded Jesus College, in time increasingly, though not exclusively, regarded as a college for Welshmen, who also attended several other colleges such as St John's College, Cambridge. The expense of travel and of residence severely restricted opportunities for higher education, genuine talent lay hidden or unburnished, so that in the nineteenth century the conviction spread that within Wales alone could proper provision be made for the penurious. There were persistent cries, too, for an educated democracy, reinforced at each successive extension of the suffrage. Nor was it possible to ignore the pressing claims of a mighty industrial power progressively confronted by determined, inventive foreign competitors, one of the principal stimuli for the planting of colleges in the major cities of England, Manchester, for example, in 1851, Leeds in 1874, Sheffield and Birmingham in 1880. Before the end of the century Hastings Rashdall was to reassure doubters in sheltered cloisters that vocational, non-liberal studies were part of the high tradition of western universities. In Wales, too, the practical wants of society were an ever-present concern. Indeed, as early as 1863 one of the most influential promoters of a Welsh university, Thomas Nicholas, had argued that many of his countrymen, because of lack of education and ignorance of the English tongue, had long been deprived of the inestimable benefits of the industrial revolution. Whereas the ministry of the Gospel had in times past offered the only outlet to an able man, the increase in trade, the spread of railways, the large development of mining and of manufacturing, now 'invite the young men of education . . . to a thousand lines of honourable employment and promotion. The varied and comprehensive course of education which the University would supply would fit our young men for such openings.'[2]

Nicholas's pamphlets struck a responsive chord in Hugh Owen, a civil servant of high repute, less a talker than a doer of the word and the prime motive force in the struggle for higher education in Wales. Both thought mainly of the material advancement of a Welsh middle class and they have been condemned as 'educational technocrats'.[3] Their somewhat philistine pronouncements, however, should not obscure the undoubted fact that the university movement in Wales was part of the late flowering of a robust national consciousness in Wales. Preliminary discussions during the first half of the century were further fuelled by the Blue Book Reports of 1847 which sought to blame the indisputably sorry state of Welsh schools upon Nonconformity and the Welsh language and which inflamed influential Welshmen of diverse persuasions. In 1863 a powerful committee was formed in London composed of Welsh patriots in the metropolis and in Wales to seek the 'immediate establishment'[4] of a university in Wales. The search for a site led to the purchase at a bargain price from its bankrupt owner of a substantial hotel at Aberystwyth. It was there that the University College of Wales was opened in 1872. Hugh Owen's prodigious endeavours to raise funds and to keep the College open without state aid are the stuff of legends. Successive deputations to governments proved useless, but at length, upon the motion of Hussey Vivian, the Liberal member for Glamorgan, a momentous debate in the Commons in 1879 led to the appointment of a departmental committee under the chairmanship of Lord Aberdare, a former Home Secretary, to inquire into the condition of intermediate and higher education in Wales. The report itself, which appeared in 1881, though sometimes ponderously diffuse, is justly to be remembered on several counts. It assembled in an enormous volume the testimonies of many varied witnesses, revealing attitudes of mind and the readiness of the poverty-stricken to seek education in truly dispiriting circumstances. It recommended that there should be intermediate schools, the 'missing link', throughout Wales which had boldly ventured, contrary to the advice of some wise men, to establish first a university college. It further recommended that there should be two colleges in Wales, one in south Wales, either in Cardiff or Swansea, and one in north Wales, either retained at Aberystwyth or moved to Caernarfon or Bangor. Arbitrators had little doubt that the University College of South Wales and Monmouthshire should be at Cardiff (1883), to the natural discomfiture of Swansea. Aberystwyth felt a sense of betrayal when towns to the north of the River Dyfi entered the lists and when the same arbitrators chose Bangor, the home henceforth of the University College of North Wales (1884). Aberystwyth's future appeared desperate, but justice prevailed when the Tory government, much to its credit, responded to the weight of public opinion in many parts of Wales, and agreed that the College should receive the same annual grant of £4,000 given at the outset to each of the other two colleges. A fierce fire at the College in 1885 also helped to rekindle admiration for its heroic tenacity. The University College of Wales survived in fact and in name.

The name was not unimportant. It appropriately recognized seniority and was a reminder that at one time the College had stood for the whole of Wales. The original purpose had been to create a unitary university in Wales. That purpose was not lost sight of until the Aberdare Report effectively snuffed out all hope. It was clear that governments were reluctant to multiply degree-awarding bodies and that the three Colleges would need to act in concert to form a federal university. For some time they would continue to prepare students for the external degree of London University, which in 1859 had acquired the power to grant degrees to suitably qualified persons in any part of the world, whether or not they were attached to a college. The system had proved highly advantageous for, by the application of a common standard by examination, fledgling colleges in England and Wales (and far beyond) were able to build an assured reputation. The service rendered by the University of London to young university colleges was therefore incalculable. Nevertheless, the apprentice stage was bound to be of limited duration. It was not simply a matter of *amour propre*. Teaching and examining were divorced, teachers did not determine curricula, a heavy premium was set upon cramming, and performance in examinations became an end in itself. Thus pressure grew to be liberated from the chains of the London external degree, no more remembered with due gratitude than any other efficient midwife.

The first formal step to be taken was in 1887 at a conference in London when Viriamu Jones, Cardiff's first principal, spoke of the unity of Welsh education and of the leading role of a teaching university. In 1888, however, there was an unexpected setback. An influential body of opinion, mainly associated with R. D. Roberts and with Aberystwyth, always mindful of the sacrificial contributions to the College of the impoverished people of Wales, urged that full-time attendance at any of the three colleges should not be obligatory. The ensuing debate, which lasted nearly three years, threatened the whole university movement. Isambard Owen, one of its main leaders, was disconsolate. If the proposed university were to grant degrees to students not in residence it would be attaching two values to the same degree. To perpetuate the London system within Wales would be disastrous for it would not be countenanced by government. He was certain that failure to obtain a charter at this stage would prompt colleges individually to 'seek federation for University purposes with such English colleges as were nearest their respective seats'. In national terms, he was adamant that 'the passing into law of the University charter was probably a crucial event in the history of Wales'.[5] At last it was agreed to proceed with the original plans but upon a broader basis, for in 1889 the Welsh Intermediate Act had been passed, thus giving promise that future students would be far better prepared upon entry than hitherto. The task of implementing the new act was undertaken by Joint Education Committees whose representatives joined forces with those of the university movement to consider in detail the draft charter of the proposed university. There was such a remarkable degree of consultation throughout Wales that it is difficult to believe that any other university charter was subjected to greater public scrutiny and debate. Everyone, it seemed, was allowed to speak his mind, yet no one could complain of excessive delay. By late August 1893 the charter had arrived on the table of Parliament. A hostile vote in the Lords was ignored by the Liberal government which was fully apprised of the wishes of Welsh members in the Commons where they held a delicate balance. The charter received the royal assent on 30 November and the University of Wales was formally constituted.

The charter of the University has been examined in detail in a preceding volume.[6] It is necessary here only to draw attention to its principal features. The authorities of the University were six in number. The visitor was the monarch who acted through the Lord President of the Council. The chief officer was the Chancellor, appointed by the Court, which by statute appointed two deputies, a Senior Deputy-Chancellor and a Junior Deputy-Chancellor. The Court, the supreme governing body consisting of 100 members, excluding the Chancellor, was considered to be the most democratic of university courts, amply reflecting the popular nature of the university movement in Wales. The proportion of academic members was low by comparison with the Victoria University, 31 per cent as opposed to 65 per cent. Yet it was the ultimate authority on academic affairs for reasons we shall later note.[7] The Court was required to meet twice a year, one of the meetings to be held in a non-collegiate town, alternately in north and in south Wales, thus annually reaffirming the University's links with the whole of Wales. The Vice-Chancellor, selected in rotation from among the principals, was to hold office for one year, later extended to two. One of his tasks was to be chairman of the University Senate, which consisted of the heads of those departments recognized by the University. The Guild of Graduates was not quite the august body at first intended by Isambard Owen, who regarded it as the 'third estate'[8] of the University. All graduates and all teaching members of the University were to be members; it was permitted to make representations to the Court and to collect funds for scholarships and prizes.

Women, as in the newer universities, were given full equality with men for admittance to degrees. Moreover, they were to hold every office in the University and to be members of every authority. It was wisely decided not to seek powers to confer medical degrees at this stage because the opposition of the medical schools would then have obliged the Privy Council to reject the charter out of hand. The circumstances in which the Court might inspect the schools of Wales were so limited as to bear little relation to Viriamu Jones's passionate desire for the educational system of Wales to be a united whole. A clause designed to meet the needs of students in straitened circumstances by exempting them from a portion of the normal period of attendance at a college was never put into effect. As also laid down in the college charters, there were to be no religious tests. Theological disputes were losing much of their virulence, so that it was now possible to admit to a degree in the Faculty of Theology a graduate who had studied in a theological college in Wales. Nevertheless, an unrelenting denominationalism was largely responsible for the failure to include Lampeter in the new University. It was, after all, the first institution in Wales, a 'quasi-university'[9] as it was once called, to grant degrees in arts and in theology. Anglicans were themselves divided. Aberdare, for example, was evidently angered by the tactics of the 'casuistic'[10] bishops during the debate on the charter in the Lords and he also questioned whether all subjects were being taught at Lampeter by qualified specialists. It was a sorry business. The time for accommodation was not yet.

In 1893, therefore, three colleges only joined together in a federal union. Aberystwyth had been independent for twenty-one years. Thomas Charles Edwards had given stout-hearted, selfless service as Principal throughout a tempestuous period. The desire to be free from the claims of administration, often of a petty kind, influenced him in 1891 to accept the invitation to succeed his father as Principal of the Bala Calvinistic Methodist College. He had no part, accordingly, in the hammering out of the university charter, a duty which fell to his young successor, Thomas Francis Roberts, as yet comparatively inexperienced in the arcana of inter-collegiate politics. The chief and perpetual source of inspiration was Viriamu Jones whose vision remained undimmed. He was steadfastly supported by a friend he had first met at Balliol, H. R. Reichel, Bangor's first Principal, who, because of the length of his days, was to see more of the University of Wales in sunshine and in shadow than anyone else.

When O. M. Edwards surveyed the Colleges on the eve of the granting of the charter, he noted that there were 231 students in Aberystwyth, 312 in Cardiff, and 135 in Bangor.[11] The Colleges had their own charters, their own endowments and property, and it was upon their joint petition that the University came into being. Elsewhere, federalism was falling out of favour. What would be its fortunes in Wales?

I

University Development, 1893–1914

One of the most challenging questions to face the young University of Wales was its relationship with London University. A powerful stimulus to secure the charter had been the constant determination to be released from the dreary uniformity of the London examination system. Viriamu Jones never departed from his early convictions and in October 1895 he reminded the Bangor Court of Governors of the virtues of the new dispensation.[1] The charter conferred upon teachers the freedom to give of their best and upon students the opportunity, consistent with wise guidance, to determine their academic courses. There would thus be generated an intellectual atmosphere in which examinations would be less important than a spirit of reverence towards acquired knowledge and towards scholarly endeavours. Viriamu also seized the opportunity to air his objections (widely shared) to the London matriculation examination. Failure in one of six subjects consigned a student to a year's delay, no matter how distinguished his performance in the other five. The relaxation of this oppressive rule by the University of Wales meant that meritorious students need no longer waste valuable time as had often happened in the past. Cardiff rejoiced at the opportunity to break away from the toils of London (apart from honouring existing commitments), for if Welshmen did not believe in their own university, then no one else would.

These remarks were not welcomed at Aberystwyth which proposed to maintain the links with London. Elsewhere, grave men raised their eyebrows for it seemed strange that Wales's oldest university college should lack an elementary sense of duty towards the new university by appearing to quail before the challenge implicit in independence. There were also fierce exchanges in the Welsh press. To be preparing simultaneously for two separate degrees was considered a needless strain upon the resources of the staff and to be academically unsound. Worse still, there was a sense of betrayal. According to an unknown correspondent in the *Manchester Guardian* – it was an age which abounded in anonymous denouncers – there was nothing worse than simulated patriotism; and those who had long 'played the patriotic card'[2] should be brought to task. To perpetuate the old system was simply a device to meet the needs of English students at the expense of the new national degree. *Yr Herald Cymraeg* declared that he who filled his pitcher on both sides of Offa's Dyke would suffer the fate of Reuben: 'unstable as water, thou shalt not excel'.[3] John Gibson staunchly defended Aberystwyth because it could not afford to follow Cardiff's 'bold policy'.[4] Edward Anwyl, the College's Professor of Welsh, agreed that the degree of a new university, however sound educationally, would not be as useful to a student in earning his daily bread as a well-established degree. Until the Welsh degree had won its spurs outside Wales it would only be an object of shame to its possessor and an impediment to self-respect. Gradually, but only gradually, would the superiority of the Welsh degree become manifest. Four years earlier in the College magazine, Anwyl had been equally discouraging. For some time after it was known that a Welsh University was to be founded, 'I felt that there was no great need for one, since every one may enter for the examinations of the University of London.'[5] The initial period was, of course, bound to be difficult and in 1905 the *Welsh Leader* observed that it had been a courageous, costly undertaking to have displaced the University of London by that of Wales: 'There are many graduates of the Welsh University who have suffered in professional standing by their loyalty in taking the Welsh in preference to the London degree. It is only now that the Welsh degree is beginning really to be recognised in the academic world outside the Principality.'[6]

Matters came to a head when the Treasury dispatched a letter[7] on 3 March 1896 to Isambard Owen as Senior Deputy-Chancellor. The message was clear. It was in the interest of the University that students proceeding to a degree should graduate at the University of Wales, not at London or elsewhere. A university or college regulation should state that if a student of a constituent college matriculated at any other university he should then cease to be a member of his college and of the University of Wales. At Aberystwyth the letter caused consternation.

T. F. Roberts wrote to the College President to say that if the proposal were carried out the results 'would be no less than disastrous'.[8] However, it was evident that Aberystwyth could present more than a colourable defence. If students from England were discouraged from coming to Aberystwyth by the discontinuance of preparation for the London degree, the loss of fees would be exceedingly damaging and Aberystwyth, more than any of the other colleges, knew what was meant by acute privation. The majority of women students at the College came from England and women students alone paid no less than £1,000 in education fees, quite apart from maintenance fees. In the 1895–6 session the proportion of students from England at Aberystwyth (including those of Welsh parentage) was 39 per cent, at Bangor 25 per cent and at Cardiff 10 per cent.[9] At Cardiff high principle and solvency apparently marched hand in hand. From the first the college could afford to be more independent of London University than her sister colleges; placed in the midst of a great population, her constituency lay at her very door. Bangor occupied an intermediary position and understood, because she partly shared, Aberystwyth's dilemma.

Reichel was in broad theoretical agreement with his friend, Viriamu, and recognized that it would be 'a disaster of the first magnitude'[10] if the University of Wales were permanently bound to London. At the Bangor Court in 1897 he stated the case with characteristic sagacity. The courses in science in the two universities were closely allied so that it was unnecessary to conduct separate classes for those wishing to take the London degree. The principal reason was that London University was founded in the main by scientists and the London degree in science was thus highly esteemed. In arts the situation was very different; the degree in arts had been established by those who were not so thoroughly acquainted with the study of the classics and of arts subjects. It is not surprising, therefore, that protests against the London degree sprang mainly from arts men. The new science courses in the University of Wales had been largely patterned upon those of London, whereas the arts courses had so widely diverged that it was impossible to prepare for the degrees of both universities in the same class. Loss of fees prohibited a total withdrawal, but educational considerations encouraged discontinuance, especially on the arts side. At Cardiff, Reichel stressed, there had not been a decline in numbers, but he strongly favoured a conference of the three colleges to hammer out a common policy. Aberystwyth, however, thought it inexpedient to embark upon discussions which might end in a result unsatisfactory to all parties, especially since Cardiff was launched upon a course which Aberystwyth could not possibly follow. Any limitation of years which Cardiff and Bangor might wish to impose for the discontinuance of preparation for the London degree would be prejudicial to Aberystwyth.

There were further considerations of importance, as the table indicates.[11] It is clear that in 1896 Aberystwyth was more highly

Comparative statistics of success by individual students, 1896

	A	B	C
London matriculation, January and June	27	8	18
London Intermediate, Arts	23	7	3
London Intermediate, Science	12	3	1
London BA	30	3	6
London B.Sc.	5	3	1
Welsh degree examinations	65	19	58
	162	43	87

geared to the examinations of the University of London than to those of the University of Wales, whilst Cardiff was phasing out its involvement with London. Yet, nearly twice as many students at Aberystwyth had succeeded in the degree examinations of the University of Wales as in those of the University of London; neither Bangor nor Cardiff equalled Aberystwyth's numbers in the degree examinations of the University of Wales. Aberystwyth's most effective reply was the dignified, masterly statement, largely the work of T. F. Roberts, which it presented to the Treasury. Owing to its earlier foundation, Aberystwyth had a longer connection with the University of London than either Bangor or Cardiff, and teaching at the College had won widespread respect. 'A violent breach with the past', it was reasonably argued, 'would press with peculiar heaviness' upon the College, which could not be expected to change the direction of its work 'by one stroke into a new and untried channel'.[12] An eloquent claim was made for freedom to deal with its own problems in its own way and for a period of extended transition during which there would be an annual increase in the number of students preparing for the Welsh degree. The University of Victoria offered an instructive parallel. There the London degree had not been cast aside at once and as late as the 1896–7 session at least 12 per cent were following University of London courses at the Owens College, sixteen years after the creation of the Victoria University. In passing we may perhaps note that Liverpool University College which became a constituent college of Victoria in 1884 continued for some time to prepare students for the examinations of London University, 'perhaps unwisely',[13] says Thomas Kelly, the historian of Liverpool University. To return to the Aberystwyth memorialists, it was urged that if students from England, attracted by the education given by the College, were discouraged, not only would the financial penalties be high, the College would also lose 'social breadth which has in it elements of unquestioned advantage'.[14] Moreover, once English students had discovered the undisputed merits of the Welsh degree they would not be blind to the advantages which lay before them.

The University authorities in turn felt bound to respond to the Treasury letter.[15] They conceded at once that it was vital for students of the University to graduate in their own University. Experience would soon demonstrate the value of the Welsh degree, whereas the Treasury requirement would convey 'an impression of weakness, and be regarded as an attempt to shun comparison with the Degrees of other Universities'.[16] Such a regulation was unprecedented in any university in the land; even at Oxford and Cambridge many outstanding students had taken degrees and won scholarships in the University of London as well as in their own, and such would be the case whilst the University of London acted as a general examining board open to all and offered substantial scholarships and prizes to candidates from many diverse places.

Within a fortnight, the Treasury withdrew its proposal. The question naturally arises as to why, with the full authority of a funding body, it had raised the matter. At Aberystwyth suspicion gave way to conviction. The Tory government would not hesitate to embarrass a college so much esteemed by Welsh Liberal Members of Parliament. Lewis Morris, Vice-President of the College, was certain that 'the enemy hath done this thing',[17] in order to cripple the College. The notion that Bangor and Cardiff were conspiring against Aberystwyth, which had evidently won credence in some quarters, was rightly dismissed by J. Young Evans as 'a childish supposition'.[18] He did, however, suspect Anglican influence in government circles. If Aberystwyth were prevented from preparing students for Oxford, Cambridge and London Universities there would be jubilation in three or four large Anglican schools in Wales whose sixth forms would be undoubted beneficiaries. Rendel considered it an impertinence for a Treasury clerk to dragoon Aberystwyth; to T. E. Ellis it was incomprehensible for the College to be asked to exclude students who wished to take degrees in universities other than the University of Wales.[19] The arguments advanced by Aberystwyth and by the University were certainly powerful but it may well be that the politicians and mandarins caved in the more readily because the Prince of Wales as Chancellor had initialled his approval of the University's submission (only a few months after his installation at Aberystwyth). There is no record of a similar intervention by 'A[lbert] E[dward]'[20] or by any of his royal successors. Aberystwyth and, to a lesser extent, Bangor had cause to be grateful. Even as late as 1914 Aberystwyth was preparing a sprinkling of students for the degree examination of the University of London.[21] A. C. Humphreys-Owen, the Liberal member for Montgomeryshire, was convinced that the conciliatory spirit displayed by the Conservative government in 1889, which made possible the passing of the Welsh Intermediate Act, had been no more than a brief flirtation with Wales. The bishops, he believed, now 'had control of the whole Tory party'.[22] Nor did Treasury officials forget. In response to the severe needs of the University they were not simply parsimonious; they were niggardly and pettifogging, reflecting in ample measure the views of their political masters.

The framers of the charter had wisely deferred a decision concerning the creation of a University Registry, save to say that the office of the Registrar and the records of the University should be kept 'where the Court shall from time to time appoint but always within the bounds of Wales'.[23] That it was a delicate matter may be gathered from the minutes of the University Court in May 1895.[24] A deputation was received from Cardiff offering to provide a suitable office at a cost of £6,000, whilst representatives of Aberystwyth presented a copy of a resolution of its Court of Governors in October 1893 pledging the necessary accommodation if the offices were located at Aberystwyth.[25] O. M. Edwards, in accord with his views in the report of 1893, thought it inadvisable for the University offices to be placed in any University College town.[26] Cardiff was thanked by the Court for its generosity and patriotism, and there was no progress until April 1897. A vigorous debate then took place at Shrewsbury lasting nearly ten hours (with intermissions). According to one speaker there were about twenty contestants; eleven towns certainly evinced serious interest, whilst memorials were presented and deputations received on behalf of eight towns.[27]

Caernarfon's memorial was supported by far more public bodies than that of any other town. Sir John Puleston, constable of the castle, offered to place the university offices within the precincts of the castle.[28] (The *South Wales Daily News* later proclaimed that he had no right to do so since it was a matter for the Commissioner for Woods and Forests.[29]) Lloyd George thought it would be grave indeed if the Registry were given a home in any town where the bulk of the population had no acquaintance with the language, literature, history and traditions of Wales. If people 'wanted to study the finest subjects of nature's architecture they must go to the North, far away from the bustle and commercial environment of the South'.[30] He did not add that the Registry, as planned, would have been a monstrous accretion sorely maiming one of the finest examples of European military architecture. Swansea had already prepared a grander scheme by Henry W. Wills (to whom we must shortly return) to house not only the Registry but a national museum, an art gallery and a record office in Alexander Road. Indeed, *Yr Herald Cymraeg* believed that of all the towns Swansea had made the best impression.[31] Grimaldi Davies, vicar of Welshpool, announced that 'long before other parts of Wales had emerged from the darkness of the past the people of Welshpool fought gallantly in defence of their country against the Roman forces'.[32] Another battle of the sites seemed imminent. G. T. Kenyon, with his happy gift for enlivening a discussion, remarked that whilst seven Greek towns had contended for the honour of being the birthplace of Homer, three times as many were competing for the distinction of providing a residence for Ivor James, the University Registrar.[33] During the debate, conducted not inappropriately in the Shrewsbury Music Hall, some wondered whether it had been wise to exclude by charter sites outside Wales since Shrewsbury was 'so curiously equidistant from the three Colleges'.[34] The fissure between industrial and rural Wales became increasingly marked as the second day wore on. To set up the Registry at Cardiff would be to disturb a necessary balance. Cardiff had not yet justified her claim to be the metropolis of Wales, Thomas Ellis added, contrasting her contribution to higher education with the achievements of rural Wales. R. D. Roberts argued that the Registry should not be in a collegiate town. Viriamu Jones naturally retaliated. Was it right to punish the town which was offering the site simply because the College was there? William Rathbone, always a sound guide, recommended delay.[35] In short, it was decided not to decide for another five years. The Registry remained in the safety zone of Brecon until 1904.

Although the matter could not be determined until 1902, Cardiff's energetic town clerk, J. L. Wheatley, indicated to the University Court at the end of 1901 that the offer of £6,000, to cover the cost of building, and of half an acre in Cathays Park, was being renewed.[36] Cardiff was still a town but with aspirations, fulfilled in 1904, to become a city, and there was a suggestion that a successful presentation of the case for the University Registry would strengthen the larger claim. T. F. Roberts had welcomed the postponement of a division in 1897 because a 'snatched vote' would have been dangerous. He had disliked the 'grasping spirit'[37] displayed by Cardiff, and his opposition was undiminished when the second large-scale debate was held in the University Court in May 1902. On this occasion twelve towns initially wished to be considered. At length Swansea resolved it would prefer to spend its money on technical education; Caernarfon withdrew from the tournament by telegram and there finally remained but three contestants. Welshpool offered a site and the use of the town hall; Llandrindod, later noted as the centre of conferences and assemblies, was proud of its low death-rate but 'we woo you not with gifts as others do',[38] whilst Cardiff brought gifts and a well-argued memorial. R. D. Roberts believed it important for the Registry to be situated in a town where the Vice-Chancellor lived and that there should be university offices in each collegiate town. Humphreys-Owen went further: he objected to aggrandizing one college at the expense of the others; if the Registry were placed at Cardiff, 'one of the most important towns in the Kingdom', Aberystwyth and Bangor would be mere satellites; 'the next step would inevitably be a declaration by Cardiff that it was of sufficient importance to have a university for itself'.[39] Cardiff's Principal did not take kindly to such animadversions. John Rhys was convinced that the University had already taken 'a very good dose of the rotating principle'. Privately he deplored the attitude of Aberystwyth's 'difficult men' and he asked William Jones, the member for Arfon, to tackle them. 'The line to take is that the gift of Ifor bach [the University Registrar] and his office has not made the Men of Brecon perceptibly taller than they were before, so that it really does not matter to Aberystwyth one bit.'[40] Unhappily, it mattered a great deal. The College's first Principal had long cherished an ambition that Aberystwyth should be the local habitation of the University.[41] Such a claim could no longer be sustained. The solution now, it was proclaimed, was either a wholly neutral town (as Brecon had been for the first five years) or rotation from one collegiate town to another. Even when these two proposals had been decisively defeated, Aberystwyth's representatives rejected the Senior Deputy-Chancellor's plea for a unanimous vote in favour of Cardiff. The eight who finally opposed John Rhys's motion to accept Cardiff's offer were all Aberystwyth's representatives, including T. F. Roberts, now Vice-Chancellor.[42] It was an inelegant affair.

Some days earlier Reichel had tried to reason with Roberts. Both shared common assumptions concerning the federal University, but Reichel was more flexible and realistic. He agreed that a rotating registry would be preferable if that were possible. Isambard Owen, however, had convinced him that the original documents of the University should be kept in one place and not carried about; the Registrar was their custodian and 'he must be

where they are'.[43] The experience of the last five years had
dispelled the exaggerated fears of 1897; the real centre of the
university system, it had become increasingly clear, was the Vice-
Chancellor, not the Registry. Again, since Aberystwyth's title was
closer to that of the University than that of Cardiff there was no
serious danger of confusing Cardiff College with the University.
Nor did the choice of Cardiff mean that meetings should be held
any more frequently there than at any other college. If the
alternative was for the Registry to be placed elsewhere, then it
must be at one of the large south Wales towns such as Newport
or Swansea, or 'some out of the way little country town', also in
the south, such as Brecon 'selected as poor Viriamu Jones
remarked because it was equally inconvenient for all three
Colleges'. Reichel's own experience as Vice-Chancellor had not
led him to favour Brecon, whereas of the large towns Cardiff
would be far more suitable than either Newport or Swansea. If
Cardiff were seriously to hearken to siren voices, her withdrawal
would endanger the whole federal structure. A federal university
of two colleges would be as unsatisfactory as a committee of two
persons. Cardiff had been disappointed in 1897; to reject yet
again the best offer presented to the University would appear to
be convincing proof of 'a settled unfriendliness' and would give 'a
dangerous impetus' to the forces of secession. He would not urge
a concession if it injured an academic principle but he foresaw no
such danger, whereas it would be 'wise and politic' to create a
closer bond with a district which had half the population and
wealth of Wales. There was a further consideration. The Treasury
would be bound to look askance if the University chose to go to a
town which provided a site and no building grant. Indeed, if the
University had to provide a building it might have to raid its
fellowship fund, small enough by any standard. Finally, Reichel
urged T. F. Roberts to reflect most carefully before opposing
Cardiff. He himself and Isambard Owen were in entire
agreement on this issue, though Owen could not disclose his
views in Court.

As we have seen, Reichel's reasoned, lengthy plea failed and
Roberts expressed his resentment to Reichel that the Bangor
representatives had strongly supported Cardiff.[44] However, it was
not a defeat for common sense. The right decision had been

made. Occasionally it is said that the Registry is the heart of the University. That is not so and never can be so. It is an administrative centre to deal with certain corporate requirements of the University, and no more, for the fundamental work of the University is almost wholly conducted in its colleges. We may, however, be grateful that the close proximity of the Registry to a constituent college has not affected the impartial, effective administration of university business.

T. F. Roberts and his colleagues at Aberystwyth had acted imprudently, especially in the light of developments in English universities, where federalism was in decline. In 1881 Josiah Mason had expressed the wish that Mason College, Birmingham, should seek admission to the Victoria University or the University of London, but in 1898 the College petitioned the Privy Council to become the University of Birmingham. The prime mover was Joseph Chamberlain, who wielded immense power in Birmingham and far beyond; with the aid of £50,000 from Andrew Carnegie and in expectation of raising £250,000 from various benefactors, Chamberlain presided over the creation in 1900 of the autonomous, unitary University of Birmingham. There were shock waves throughout the university system. This was why John Rhys felt that to concede the Registry to Cardiff would help to allay 'any irritation produced by the Brummagem spirit'.[45] He went on to remark that this selfsame spirit was acting as a 'solvent' in the Victoria University. Since the founders of the University of Wales had paid the closest attention to the federal arrangements in Victoria, especially its charter, it is most germane to our purpose to consider the fortunes of the northern university.

When Owen M. Edwards commented upon Victoria in his report in 1893, he did not detect any signs of tension. He should perhaps have become aware of dissension when R. D. Roberts remarked at the University of Wales Conference in January that at Victoria 'there have been found great difficulties in the working of it'.[46] Sir Henry Roscoe, a former professor at Owens College, had said at Liverpool that preparations were already in train for the time when Liverpool and Leeds would become independent universities. Had Edwards visited Liverpool he might have had a clearer impression of the true situation. An active agent of propaganda was the University Club. 'Its very name', says Thomas Kelly, 'was significant of its purpose.'[47] A century later within the University of Wales, fears were expressed that the title 'university' was being used by the Colleges as a prelude to claims for full autonomy. Be that as it may, the Treasury visitors in 1897 recommended caution because the three constituent parts of Victoria derived much benefit from participation in a large institution; curricula and degrees were thus invested with 'a value and prestige which they would not otherwise possess'.[48] Nevertheless, in 1901 Liverpool sought independent status; Leeds, on the other hand, solidly opposed separation. The arguments presented on both sides to the Privy Council illumined conflicting standpoints within the University of Wales.[49]

Leeds, or the Yorkshire College, as it was often called, argued that dismemberment of the Victoria University would damage the federal principle; henceforth, federal institutions would be regarded as inherently unstable.[50] Only through a federation could a small college extend to its students those privileges derived from a university, a consideration much in the mind of the founders of Swansea some years later. The Leeds petitioners added that only thus could a college in due course demonstrate that it had attained a university standard in order to justify its petition for a charter to become a unitary university. The standard of the best of the federated colleges became the standard for all, urged the Principal of Leeds, and a federal university could aid the weaker without placing constraints upon the stronger. Separate universities could not command the same public confidence or enjoy the same reputation as a federal university which offered 'a much better guarantee of breadth of view and freedom from local or individual prejudices'.[51] Both the number and quality of students would diminish; the standard of the degree would decline by the removal of the 'corrective influence of Boards' composed of members drawn from various colleges, whilst the value of degrees already conferred would be diluted, to the grave injury of existing graduates. Finally, an argument was pressed, familiar enough in the University of Wales, that defects in the system could be dealt with by altering the regulations.[52]

Liverpool presented a redoubtable case, notable for its range and intellectual stamina.[53] The only university of the same type as the Victoria University was the University of Wales. It was idle to make comparisons with Oxford and Cambridge where the colleges were wholly different from federal colleges: in the two ancient universities no college supplied all the required teaching; each college depended on another and upon the resources of the University, and both universities were teaching bodies quite separate from their colleges. To destroy the Universities of Oxford and Cambridge would be an act of the 'grossest vandalism'; to break up a federal university would be no great calamity, for 'it has no equipment of its own and gives no teaching; it is simply a machine for examining and for legislation, and nothing more'.[54] The University of London, reconstituted by the Act of 1898, was not a federal body in any acceptable sense of the term, whilst Durham, in 1902, which had subordinate teaching bodies affiliated to 'a supreme teaching university', could not be compared with teaching colleges joined together to form 'a supreme examining university'.[55] Encouragement was not to be derived either from the remainder of the United Kingdom or from the British Empire at large. The German system was not analogous, whereas France, after her recovery from the stultifying effects of the revolutionary government, provided splendid examples of the stimulus of local independence to her burgeoning universities. Here lay the core of Liverpool's case. That a university should be local involved no contradiction in terms. To appeal to local patriotism was both necessary and rewarding. To respond to local needs was natural, and a university did not thereby become parochial. 'On the contrary', in words which deserve full attention,

> the more truly local a university becomes, the more characteristic its work, the more successfully it develops the study of those subjects which bear most directly upon the occupation and industries of the people of its district, the more certainly will it draw students interested in those subjects from other parts of the world.

In short, 'a period of specialized education requires specialized universities'.[56] Liverpool had particular strengths – tropical medicine is an obvious example – and by concentrating upon them, though it did not say so directly, the University would become a *studium generale*, not a *studium particulare*, for it would draw students from many areas, not from one. Cardiff naturally had cause to reflect upon such arguments, sometimes with a mounting sense of frustration. Nevertheless, if the University of Wales was closer akin to the University of Victoria than any other university, yet there was a significant difference between the two federal bodies, as was clearly expressed in the Liverpool submission. The federal system in Wales 'derives its strength from a national feeling entirely absent in our northern counties. In our great English cities the patriotism of Wales appears as civic and local public spirit. The spirit is the same in both cases, but the basis of unity is different.'[57] Liverpool pressed hard for the abolition of the Victoria University, Manchester followed suit and both received their charters as independent universities in 1903. At Manchester one of the chief protagonists of autonomy was T. F. Tout, the illustrious medieval historian, formerly Professor of History at Lampeter, who had observed the young University of Wales at close quarters. In a characteristically searching paper he argued that the northern colleges had advanced beyond 'the constant compromises inevitable to the federal system. We recognize that the federal University was a useful stage of academic evolution, but we regard it as having fulfilled its work.'[58]

To be sure, members of the University of Wales did not regard federalism as a universal recipe. In 1907 they attended closely to the scheme proposed by Bryce, the Chief Secretary of Ireland, to create a single university for Ireland to include a new college acceptable to the Catholic bishops, Trinity College and the Queen's Colleges of Belfast and Cork in a reconstituted University of Dublin (the colleges of Maynooth, Galway and Magee becoming 'affiliated institutions'). Members of Senate of the University of Wales actively participated in the 'hands-off Trinity' campaign which led to the abandonment of the plan. It is not wholly irrelevant to note that R. B. Haldane, a firm supporter of Trinity and of whom we shall hear much more, was highly influential in discussions leading to the Irish Universities Bill (1908) which ordained that there should be three universities in Ireland. Almost all members of the University of Wales Senate sent a memorial to Augustine Birrell, Bryce's successor, declaring that from their experience of the only remaining federal university in Great Britain none of the ingredients was present in Ireland for the successful working of the federal university envisaged by Bryce. It is not fanciful to discern the influence of 'Irish' Reichel in the attention given to the 'widely-diverging' institutions of Ireland, to their 'dissimilar concepts' of education and to their 'differences in magnitude and traditions'.[59] Union was being strenuously resisted by Trinity College which, like the University of Wales, 'accepts the principle of freedom of study and research from ecclesiastical limitations and denominational supervision'.[60] The proposed Irish federation was totally dissimilar to that of the University of Wales where three colleges differing little in size were of the same educational type, held common ideals and had voluntarily entered into partnership.

As in many partnerships, however, there were reservations. It is striking that in an official history of the University of Wales in 1905 the principal author should express pronounced misgivings concerning the federal system. In words not altogether felicitous and used, it seems, for the first time by Sir Arthur Rücker, Principal of London University, Wales was now 'the last asylum of the federal system in Great Britain'.[61] The writer proceeded to ask: 'will Wales always be able to maintain this type of university, and, even if she is able, is it desirable that she should?' Communications between the colleges were more unsatisfactory than in the north of England where the Victoria University had already been dismembered partly for that reason. The 'expensive experiment' begun in 1893 inflicted a taxing strain on mind and body; those now 'compelled' to operate the system were fully occupied with internal work and additional duties were 'all but proving too heavy'. Temporary expedients could not remove the menace to the federal structure: 'Will the bond of national sentiment', he wondered, 'which now unites the Welsh Colleges prove strong enough permanently to bear the strain?' The likelihood was that Cardiff 'at no distant date' would wish to cast off the 'vexatious bondage' of association with two distant colleges and emulate the great industrial centres of England.[62]

Twelve years only after the grant of the University charter these were frank words. The writer, W. Lewis Jones, Professor of English at Bangor, certainly regarded himself as a sincere patriot.

He was a supporter and confidant of Lloyd George (who stayed with him when he received an honorary degree at Bangor), and he was a close observer of the Welsh scene. When he was preparing *The University of Wales* he knew at first hand that storm clouds were gathering and that there were two immediate causes. In November 1904 the University Senate reported that owing to the growth of the University the direct administration of academic affairs by the Vice-Chancellor was neither desirable nor practicable, the root cause being the unequal division of academic business between the offices of the Vice-Chancellor and of the Registrar.[63] The latter were permanently located at Cardiff but the Vice-Chancellor's clerk was obliged to sojourn, with all his papers and paraphernalia, for two years in turn at Aberystwyth and Bangor. The Vice-Chancellor, moreover, in the absence of an academic registrar, was confronted with a large body of business dealt with in other universities in the registrar's office. In fact, the Vice-Chancellor and his secretary were entirely responsible for the affairs of the Senate and for the conduct of degree examinations, certainly the heaviest administrative work within the University. The Vice-Chancellor was also Principal in his own College and there were times when the weight of work was too much for one man. More than once a Vice-Chancellor's health had broken down; it was said to be common knowledge that Viriamu Jones's early death had been accelerated by excessive strain; T. F. Roberts was never strong, and Reichel, who seems to have suffered several 'set-backs', as he was prone to call them, made it plain in 1904 that he could not again accept such an onerous office under the existing arrangements.[64]

The second cause of contention was the appointment of the Senior Deputy-Chancellor, Isambard Owen, to be Principal of Armstrong College, Newcastle. Many years later Reichel acknowledged that 'there was something anomalous in an arrangement by which the salaried academic head of one university institution acted as the unsalaried lay head of another'.[65] Paradoxically, the great distance was not in practice considered an inconvenience, Reichel and others believing that too much should not be made of a technical reservation amply compensated by the continuance in office of a valued counsellor. This view was not shared by all. Some believed that he clung tenaciously to office and that he arrogated to himself powers similar to those acquired by the Principal of London University. Others thought that he was excessively formal and laborious in the performance of public duties. One critic denounced his 'oppressive courtesy', further declaring that the University of Wales's 'trunk was at Cardiff, its feet at Bangor, its grasping arms at Aberystwyth and its head in the private room of a doctor in Newcastle upon Tyne'.[66]

The perpetrator of this disjointed metaphor was (Sir) Thomas Marchant Williams (1845–1914). Once a Liberal Nonconformist and now an Anglican Unionist, he was a friend of Sir Robert Morant and stipendiary magistrate of Merthyr Tudful. He was also Warden of the Guild of Graduates (1903–7), the first, though not the last, to make a considerable nuisance of himself. The Revd T. J. Wheldon (father of Bangor's third Registrar, Wynn P. Wheldon) thought that the religious revival of 1904–5 had left him with too much time on his hands and it was credibly reported that at a revivalist meeting an old lag, temporarily reformed, had thanked God that he had not seen Marchant Williams for six months.[67] Marchant specialized in outrageous attacks upon estimable men, often prefacing his diatribes with the chill words, 'my old friend'. Sometimes a hawk, sometimes a mocking bird, he had by the end of his days assembled a large company of unrelenting foes. In 1904 he became convinced that the answer to the manifold problems of the University of Wales was to appoint a 'Working Head', as he was called, permanently placed in authority over the College Principals and relieving them of the duties of the rotating Vice-Chancellorship, normally regarded as fundamental to the equitable administration of a federal university.[68] The likelihood is that Marchant modelled his proposals upon arrangements at London University in 1901 when Sir Arthur Rücker was appointed 'Principal' – other titles, such as Rector, had been canvassed - and was given wide powers to administer the university and to advise the senate upon 'all matters relating to the internal and external organization and developments of the University'.[69] This office reached a plenitude of power under Sir David Logan, Principal from 1948 until 1975, but there are clear signs that the University of Wales throughout its history would not readily accept even a modest dose of

Loganization. Rücker, we are told, set about his task at London with a will. Soon he was asking for a third typewriter, then a fourth and possibly a fifth.[70] The Welsh Principals were adamant: an underemployed busybody would become an ungovernable martinet.

The ensuing debate was fierce. Henry Jones was brought down from Glasgow to strengthen resistance in early autumn 1905. No doubt he welcomed the opportunity to place in a broader perspective his remarks at Bangor in July when the College was celebrating its coming of age. He had then hoped that Bangor would develop into a separate university for this was the modern trend. One of the reasons why he had left Bangor for the independent University of St Andrews was to seek greater freedom. Critics soon accused him of wanting to disrupt the University of Wales and of injuring the concept of Welsh unity ('Cymru'n un'). At Cardiff in October, Jones, in a speech lasting two hours, both defended and modified his heady remarks at Bangor.[71] The ideal of three universities was not at war with the ideal of a united Wales. Could anyone point to a single country whose unity was imperilled by having more than one university? An American commission of inquiry in 1901, which had also provided fodder for the Liverpool petitioners, was conclusive on the issue. Napoleon had converted the universities of the provinces into faculties of the University of France, but in 1896 the French government had converted them back again into independent universities, restoring their ancient rights. In 1900 they had more registered students than in 1888; before 1896 more than half of them had fewer students than Cardiff in 1905. Viriamu Jones, he opined, would have sought to give Cardiff independence and Tom Ellis would have wished the same for Aberystwyth and Bangor 'when the time came'.[72] Here was the qualification. The time for three universities in Wales had not yet come, but given a period (unspecified) of 'quiet labour and continued growth . . . the time may come when the conversion of the three colleges into three universities may be the next natural step in their evolution'. Change would come, in characteristic words, 'with matured consent of the whole people, as unconstrainedly as the falling dew'.[73] Concerning the attempt to impose a working head upon the University, there was no qualification whatsoever. Something akin to German 'Barm' had entered the heads of the professors and the scheme was flayed as 'ill considered . . . unnecessary . . . wasteful . . . and mischievous'.[74] Reichel was delighted with Jones's onslaught, telling T. F. Roberts that the effects would be far-reaching and that arrangements were in train for the printed version to be widely circulated within the University.[75]

Marchant was not altogether bereft of allies. There was Charles Morgan, Treasurer of the Guild of Graduates, Thomas Rees of Brecon, later Principal of Bala-Bangor College, A. H. Trow, a future Principal of Cardiff, and E. V. Arnold, acting entirely against the views of the Bangor Senate but whose claws, Reichel said, had been 'partially pared'.[76] Marchant, in concert with these four, issued a circular to members of the Guild of Graduates appealing for 'an enlightened discussion'[77] and for the election to the Court of representatives who would rise above the entanglements of personal, local issues. Shortly before a decisive meeting of the Court in November, Marchant published a lecture disclosing views far from enlightened and the Court was only partially relieved to hear that the Guild's Treasurer had withdrawn a motion to discuss the question of the working head.[78] No more was formally heard of it. The *South Wales Daily News*, to Reichel's great satisfaction, had already opposed Marchant's 'revolutionary programme' and condemned as dangerous any attempt 'to unbridle officialdom'.[79] The *Manchester Guardian* pronounced the matter dead, 'strangled by the violence of its advocates'; dispassionate discussion had been precluded by 'reckless abuse' and 'blazing indiscretions'.[80] For a brief moment Marchant had, however, performed the miraculous: he had united the three Principals in a common cause, for he was more of a thorn in the flesh to the Cardiff Principal than to Reichel and Roberts.

In 1905 the University Court took steps to deal with the serious problem of central administration by pensioning off Ivor James, the Registrar, now sixty-five, though it may be questioned whether it acted as gracefully as the occasion required. Much was made of the need to appoint an 'academic' registrar, by which was meant, not an additional registrar nor one who was necessarily an academic, but a registrar who would deal with academic affairs and relieve vice-chancellors of crushing responsibilities. James, it seems, had long ceased (for whatever reason) to attend meetings of the University Senate. Henceforth many routine matters relating to the Senate and to examinations were transferred to the Registrar. The Vice-Chancellor would continue to preside over the Senate and its committees and deal with doubtful questions, such as the correct interpretation of statutes.[81] The appointment of a new registrar was a delicate matter. Aberystwyth strongly favoured Mortimer Angus, Professor of Latin, who had served the college well as secretary of its Senate and who was generally admired. Reichel concurred, assuring Roberts of Bangor's support; if Angus were ten years younger – he was now fifty-five – there would be no doubt whatsoever, 'if one sets aside a small knot of wire-pullers and anti-academical fanatics who would vote against the Angel Gabriel if he had occupied a Chair in a Welsh College'. As second-string he favoured a James Evans, 'a quite exceptionally strong businessman', who would be 'serenely indifferent'[82] to Marchant Williams. Angus was in fact chosen and by and large gave general satisfaction until his retirement in 1921. He survived until 1945.

The new Registry building was completed in 1904. The Cardiff corporation had agreed to provide 'adequate and dignified accommodation', whilst the University was to hold the land for 999 years and lay out 'gardens and pleasure grounds' on parts of the land not covered by buildings. If there ceased to be a Registry, the Corporation was entitled to repossess.[83] Invitations to present plans were given to Harold H. Hughes, of Bangor, and to Herbert Winkler Wills,[84] of London. The latter was successful. Wills had already been responsible for Aberdare Hall and was therefore well-known to the University authorities. Since 1900 he had been in partnership with John Anderson and together they executed a number of works. Wills later designed many public buildings as well as houses and flats in Harley Street and Portland Place (the home of British architects). From 1913 to 1918 he edited *The Builder*, and from 1918 to 1926, *The Architect*. Wills tells us that work on the Registry was somewhat impeded by the wet winter of 1903–4, which prevented his noticing what would have been apparent in dry weather, that the site itself was especially wet.[85] The building was ready in the autumn of 1904;

in due course the paved forecourt designed by Wills was enclosed by posts and chains, the posts being surmounted with the dragon of Wales cast from models made by W. Goscombe John. By 1921 further accommodation was imperative, and additions were designed by William Kaula, with whom Wills had been in partnership since 1913. T. Alwyn Lloyd was responsible for the extensions of 1930–1, made necessary in part by the demands of the Council of Music.[86] Soon, too, the Glamorgan County Hall had spread to the rear of the Registry.

There is general agreement that the buildings nearest to the city hall and law courts are for the most part superior to later additions in Cathays Park. Percy Thomas thought that the Registry suffered from the proximity of larger buildings.[87] Nevertheless, it has a quiet dignity and well deserves its place in the Park. In reality a three-storey structure, favourable attention has been drawn to the small round windows dexterously inserted in the parapet, in contrast to the tall rectangular windows of the main floor, the *piano nobile*. The Registry was but the third building to be raised in Cathays Park, as the University made clear in its instructions to the competing architects. The park to the east was to be kept as a park, across which was the site of the proposed new College buildings. To the south and south-east were the new law courts and town hall (as it then was) in process of erection in Portland stone 'in a classical or French style'.[88] The competition for those two buildings, won by Lanchester, Stewart and Rickards in 1897, was of great significance because they were the first to be raised at Cathays Park, itself 'the first intentionally planned civic centre in Britain', described by C. H. Reilly as 'a new revelation' and by A. S. Gray as 'a triumph'.[89] Rickards introduced into the city hall strong elements of Austrian and French baroque, whereas the law courts, with their wide recessed Doric portico, are more restrained, as befits their purpose, than the magnificently exuberant city hall. The instructions to H. W. Wills thus called for skilful, sensitive interpretation. The Registry, with its Ionic columns, eschewed Rickards's baroque bravura and reflected a classicism derived in all probability during Wills's period in New York in the office of McKim, Mead and White, who favoured the new classical style originating in Paris. H. B. Creswell wrote warmly of Wills's 'distinguished merit', adding: 'I put myself to some trouble to learn the name of the architect of the Registry building when I viewed the Municipale Grande Place at Cardiff in 1917.'[90] The Registry was fortunate in its architect.

It had clearly emerged during the process of preparing the draft charter of the University that Viriamu Jones's conviction that the whole educational system of Wales should be controlled by the University Court was not widely shared.[91] He had spoken eloquently on the subject as early as 1883 and the University Conference had in 1891 included amongst its guiding principles the desirability of conferring upon the new university the power to undertake the inspection and examination of intermediate schools and other educational institutions, and to grant certificates of proficiency. In the charter itself the principle was so weakened as to be tame and toothless: 'The Court may undertake at the request of any person or persons having authority to make such a request the inspection and examination of any school or schools in Wales and may make report thereon to such person or persons.'[92] In the mean time the Joint Education Committees set up for each county under the Welsh Intermediate Act (1889) had come together to urge the formation of a central education body. By 1896 a bill to create a Central Welsh Board to examine and inspect the county schools of Wales was being considered in Parliament. Viriamu had, however, not surrendered all hope. In the University Court in March 1896 he attached very great importance to unification. If there were to be two bodies instead of one a splendid opportunity would be lost: 'It would be the old mistake – division, division, division – and they [would] have two bodies, each the weaker because their functions were not joined.'[93] He faced powerful opponents in Whitehall and in Wales.

Isambard Owen was convinced that government circles had determined that Wales would have to decide between a separate board and inspection directly from London. The Treasury, he believed, was largely responsible. It was by no means as simple as that. For example, the education committee of the General Assembly of the Calvinistic Methodists at Liverpool in February regretted the 'opposition in some quarters' to the Central Board scheme, by far the best way to look after Welsh Intermediate Education because it would be in close touch with the schools themselves. The University Court had been formed for another purpose and was 'already sufficiently burdened with the care of Higher Education'.[94] Tom Ellis spoke in the same vein. Of those educated at the Welsh Intermediate schools, 75 per cent would not proceed to a university and a distinct body should give its 'whole thought and attention' to their needs. The educational movement in Wales had produced a sufficient number of competent people to deal with educational problems in a 'liberal and generous spirit'. Both bodies would be effectively manned and the conferences of the last ten years had shown that there was 'enough knowledge, co-operation and mutual desire to build up a thoroughly national and coherent system of education'.[95] A. C. Humphreys-Owen, a Liberal member, in turn, thought it would be more wasteful to apply machinery to purposes for which it was not designed than to create 'distinct machinery for doing distinct work'. Privately he told his wife that Viriamu had been 'hammered' at the University Court.[96] This was indeed the case. Viriamu's appeal for 'unity, simplicity and economy' found little favour and the Court in March resolved that every effort be made to secure the passage of the bill through Parliament to establish a Central Welsh Board. It came into being in May 1896. There was agreement to consider within seven years, in the light of experience gained by the Board and the University Court, whether the functions of the Board should be transferred to the Court. It was at best a placebo, for nothing whatsoever was done at the end of seven years.

The first chairman of the Board was A. C. Humphreys-Owen, and the first Chief Inspector, Owen Owen, chosen in preference to O. M. Edwards. In 1907 a Welsh Department of the Board of Education was established at Whitehall, A. T. Davies being Permanent Secretary and O. M. Edwards Chief Inspector. Most Welsh secondary schools were thus subjected to a dual system of inspection which caused friction. The Central Welsh Board, a representative body, operated within Wales whereas the Welsh Department was at Whitehall (where it long remained). Edwards endeavoured to perform all his duties in Wales; not for nothing did he call his Llanuwchllyn home Neuadd Wen ('Whitehall'). Proposals to create a National Council of Education to subsume the functions of both bodies were ineffectually aired from time to time. The Central Welsh Board became familiar to generations of Welsh boys and girls (and not least their parents), but, whereas the University continued to conduct its own matriculation examinations, it agreed in 1907 to recognize the School Certificate of the Central Welsh Board as equivalent, upon certain conditions. The University was thus influential in determining the syllabus of the county schools of Wales.[97]

Principals of the Colleges sat upon the Board, Viriamu Jones was its first vice-chairman and graduates of the University held many of the teaching posts in the secondary schools and in time the headships. Viriamu had, of course, hoped for far more, but in this limited sense he had not been wholly vanquished. We may, however, wonder whether he would have approved of the University's role in strengthening the tendency in the county schools to provide an 'academic, humanistic curriculum',[98] as it has been called, at the expense of practical subjects, a tendency which would have dismayed the authors of the Aberdare Report and which was not liked by O. M. Edwards, who rightly regarded the mastery of crafts and practical skills as ennobling. Edwards was also critical of the Central Welsh Board's policy towards the language, literature and history of Wales, which he considered inadequate, and his onslaught in 1909 caused swells and eddies for years. Meanwhile in London, A. T. Davies was proving troublesome. Known to be difficult to handle, he was prone to take a robust line with superiors and to cave in obsequiously if challenged. When, in 1914, he gave the authorities in Whitehall the impression that he had been authorized to assume responsibility for the Welsh University and its Colleges, he was firmly taken to task by (Sir) Frank Heath, in charge of the new U. Branch, as it was called, which dealt with grants to universities, for Heath was not at all disposed to welcome a rival body in Wales.[99] Davies's frustrations largely stemmed from the dual jurisdiction whereby the Central Welsh Board and the Welsh Department of the Board of Education were both inspecting secondary schools, but his restless schemes for general reorganization, which included the University of Wales and which we shall again have cause to notice, found little favour with the higher authorities.[100]

Swansea understandably felt aggrieved that it had been passed over in 1883 and the University's supplemental charter of 1906 attempted to deal with the question of affiliation. These were the circumstances. Technical classes in some of the pure and applied sciences had been established in connection with the grammar school at Swansea. In 1901, quite independently of the school, they were formed into a technical school maintained by the local authority. Two years later the town council petitioned the University that the technical school be declared 'a College in which students may pursue courses of study of the Degrees of the University in Science and Applied Science'.[101] Early in 1904 the University Court held a special meeting to consider the petition. The outcome was a section in the supplemental charter of 1906 allowing the Court to declare any public body to be an affiliated college provided it was adequately equipped and endowed to promote research, study and instruction in one branch at least of technical or applied science.[102] Swansea's status would be perceptibly less than that of a constituent college, it could not be affiliated except by a two-thirds majority of the Court, whilst the conditions as to equipment and visitation were stringent. Not surprisingly, Swansea made no effort to pursue the matter. Thus it was that certain institutions were in varying relationships to the University. Only the constituent colleges had full academic privileges, and representation on the University Senate was confined to them. But although the University could confer degrees in theology, its Senate had no direct control over university studies, which were jointly supervised by a Theological Board and by a Theological Senate composed of members of 'associated' colleges, but not of 'approved' or 'accepted' theological colleges. The principle of 'affiliation' was recognized in the supplemental charter under strict conditions. In practice the power thereby conferred was not exercised because no request for affiliation was received.

Relations between the Bangor College and the nearby Normal College soon gave Marchant Williams a further opportunity to exercise his malevolent skills. He continued to enrage persons of repute. He had, for instance, recurring battles with John Morris-Jones, himself not averse to fisticuffs upon occasion, and accommodation was no longer possible when Marchant described Morris-Jones's *Caniadau* in 1907 as 'a book of hand-made paper and "machine-made" poetry'.[103] However, it was the University and its Colleges which mostly aroused his wrath. The working head controversy continued to simmer and whenever a difficult problem arose Marchant licked his lips. A dispute between the University and the Bangor College did not escape his notice.[104] As early as 1886, the close proximity of the University College and the Normal College prompted enquiries concerning possible co-operation and the sharing of facilities. At that stage they proved abortive, but the establishment of a Day Training Department[105] at the University College in 1894 in time encouraged government inspectors and the staff of both colleges to consider limited collaboration. For a century and more relations between the colleges were to ebb and flow.

In 1905 the appointment of D. R. Harris, formerly on the staff of the Day Training College, as Principal of the Normal College kindled hope of fruitful joint action. An undoubted spur had been the Board of Education's decision to issue unclassified certificates without division into three parts according to merit as before. Harris determined that a classified diploma, examined by the University College, would encourage his best students to strive for excellence, particularly since the advance of secondary education had equipped an increasing number of training students to tackle degree courses. Harris's overtures were cordially received by the University College Senate which at once agreed that, 'under suitable safeguards', courses at the Normal College should be recognized as equivalent to its own intermediate courses, provided such courses were given by teachers 'subject to the control of the University College', words which later caused trouble. The advantages would be threefold: teachers' training students would be brought 'into closer harmony with University ideals';[106] the door would be open for able students to obtain degrees by completing their degree schemes at one of the university colleges, and the appointment of joint teachers would lead to the increased economy and efficiency of both colleges.

Plans were at once set in motion. One of the joint appointments was that of (Sir) Ifor Williams, then an assistant lecturer in Welsh at the University College, and in 1907 five matriculated students of the Normal College began their intermediate course. The scheme soon struck a rock. Marchant, a former student of the Normal College, who now appeared to be advocating the dissolution of the federal University, pounced upon the Bangor arrangements.[107] If Cardiff acted in this way it could enrol 4,000 students and the situation would become intolerable. Undoubtedly, one of the attractions of the Bangor scheme was that it would appreciably increase the numbers of suitably qualified undergraduates at the College, but the real issue was, not the absurd fulminations of Marchant, but a simple constitutional one, namely, whether the University College was acting in breach of the University charter. The College defended itself with sustained ingenuity. Technically, it was argued, students reading for a degree at the Normal College were not in residence in the University College, but in practice the latter was so conveniently located that its degree work could be brought under University 'control', supervision being almost as direct and complete as if the students were within the walls of the University College. Nevertheless, the University College could scarcely have forgotten that the question of residence had been a source of acrimonious debate before the University charter was granted and that the charter itself clearly stated that a qualifying scheme of study must be pursued '*in* one of the [constituent] Colleges'.[108] It was manifestly insufficient to urge that courses were subject to the 'control' of the University College. The University Court appointed a committee of inquiry consisting of Lord Justice Vaughan Williams, Sir David Brynmor Jones and Sir Isambard Owen, and the College was represented by a King's Counsel. The result was a foregone conclusion.[109] The College was in breach of the University charter and it is difficult to understand why men of the calibre of the Principal and Registrar had pursued the matter to the uttermost. Arrangements with the Normal College were brought to a close, though without injury to the students involved, joint appointments were discontinued, as was the Normal College diploma, and not for two decades did the University attempt to forge new, formal links with Welsh training colleges.[110]

The financial position of the University and its Colleges remained parlous for most of the pre-war period. This was especially true of the University itself. Benefactors usually much preferred to contribute to individual colleges rather than to the University, and then for specific purposes, such as scholarships and buildings, not to the general account from which salaries were paid. O. M. Edwards, in his *Report* on the proposed university in 1893, had recommended that it should receive £10,000 per annum, quite apart from the grants to colleges. He arrived at this figure after considering the financial arrangements in other universities. He was convinced that 'a mere *honorarium*' would not do for external examiners and that it would be wrong to neglect through poverty 'any important branch of inquiry' and 'the higher branches of study',[111] by which he mainly meant the provision of fellowships to encourage postgraduate research. When representatives of the University met the Liberal Chancellor of the Exchequer, Sir William Harcourt, in January 1894, they asked for an immediate grant of £3,000, rising to £8,000 by annual stages within four years.[112] Harcourt seems to have assumed rather a grand air, which came easily to him, questioning the need to pay external examiners more than was done at the Victoria University and quite neglecting the paramount need to secure the services of the best scholars at the outset in order to establish the highest academic standards. He added that Welsh colleges were receiving more from the State than English colleges, though he prudently made no comparison with Scottish and Irish universities. In the event Wales at once received £3,000, but thereafter there were constant skirmishes with the Treasury, as has been already noted.[113] In December 1896 the Treasury wanted to reduce the travelling expenses of those attending University meetings from £825 to £500 and hoped that the University would in future be more self-supporting. Isambard Owen replied that whilst University meetings were held as infrequently as possible it was inevitable that they would be relatively numerous at first[114] (as is, indeed, evident from the records). In fact the University was obliged to pay expenses at a lesser rate to lay members than to academic members, an unhappy discrimination, so that one of the former was heard to protest that the Raven Hotel, where meetings were held at Shrewsbury, could not be expected to emulate the benevolence of the raven which provided for the needs of the prophet Elijah on the banks of the River Cerith.[115] In 1896 a reluctant Treasury agreed to ask Parliament to vote for £3,265, not raised to £4,000 until 1899. In vain did Isambard plead with the Treasury that a deficit could be met in only one of two ways, by reducing the fees of external examiners or by raising the fees of students, both damaging in their consequences. The Treasury was adamantine. The annual grants of £4,000 to the University 'will under no circumstances be exceeded'.[116]

During the next few years all manner of arguments were deployed. Within a generation, a complete system of higher and of secondary education had been created by the Welsh people. College fees in England were twice as high as in Wales, where, if they were raised, there would be a 'choking off',[117] as Reichel put it, of the very people for whom the Welsh Colleges were intended, especially the staff of secondary schools, as also the flower of the teachers in elementary schools. A serious cause of concern was the salaries paid to professors in Wales, the average being £315 and in England £475; the Aberystwyth average was but £295 (including a generous subvention by Rendel); at Liverpool the average was £685. Thus, when it was reported in 1904 that the Tory Chancellor of the Exchequer proposed to double the grants to English universities, the University of Wales judged that the time was ripe for concerted action. Austen Chamberlain, though not entirely hostile, reminded a strong deputation that English colleges on average received from the State half the sums granted to Welsh colleges, that they, too, could increase their numbers if they reduced their fees and that they were in addition subjected to a quinquennial visitation and a sifting of their accounts. He hoped that 'whenever you are coming up again on a mission of this kind, you may be prepared . . . to accept the same kind of inspection and control which is applied to the English Colleges'.[118] Further, it was essential to seek more local support.

The great victory of the Liberals at the polls in January 1906 encouraged prospects of alleviation. Asquith began well as Chancellor by allowing Bangor £20,000 towards its new building. The real issue, however, was an increased annual grant. Asquith seems to have been unduly influenced by Sir George

Murray, Permanent Secretary to the Treasury, who on one occasion floated the madcap notion that the grant to the University would be much better employed if distributed amongst the three Colleges. Reichel had no difficulty in demonstrating that it was 'an absolute delusion'[119] to suppose there would be any saving of scarce resources, for Murray had not even considered the cost of appointing three external examiners instead of one. No more was heard of a 'misconception' which would have had 'disastrous results'. The Treasury, however, was not deflected from its avowed intent, in the interests of economy and uniformity, to bring the University and its Colleges within the purview of the Advisory Committee which determined university and college grants in England. Aberystwyth and Bangor were understandably alarmed because the Advisory Committee applied criteria, rateable value and population amongst them, which would be damaging to rural colleges. Cardiff, on the other hand, similar in many ways to English civic colleges, might readily be tempted to seek an immediate increase in funds. Reichel as Vice-Chancellor (1905–7) was certain that the Treasury would welcome Cardiff with open arms, thereafter placing it on the same plane as the smaller English colleges such as Sheffield or Bristol. Left in the cold, Aberystwyth and Bangor would progressively sink to a lowly status, surrendering all hope of doing for Wales what the Scottish universities had done for Scotland. In short, they would become 'third-rate institutions to which the ablest students of their own districts will not care to commit their University career'.[120]

Reichel, though so badly crippled by neuritis that he could scarcely hobble, took the lead in insisting upon separate treatment for Wales. The matter was not to be resolved by debate with the Treasury but at a political level. He did not think it proper at this stage to seek the direct help of Lloyd George, President of the Board of Trade, who would naturally not wish to interfere with Asquith's conduct of affairs. He found, however, a resourceful ally in Herbert Lewis, now a parliamentary whip, whom he had managed to recruit as Vice-President of the Bangor College. Reichel believed it was time to re-establish the close relationship between the political and academic representatives of the Principality that had rather wilted since the death of Tom Ellis and the retirement of A. H. D. Acland. In the course of correspondence with Lewis, Isambard Owen and T. F. Roberts, Reichel expressed his fears that the Cardiff Principal would sell his birthright for a mess of pottage. He was so alarmed as to write to a number of prominent Welshmen, including Lloyd George on this occasion, 'begging them all', in his words, 'to bring all the pressure they can to avert such a betrayal'.[121] At a meeting of the Guild of Graduates, Marchant Williams, in the unaccustomed role of mediator, urged Cardiff not to denationalize itself for a petty thousand pounds; the colleges should 'sink or swim together'.[122] Already T. F. Roberts had prepared a statement to the Chancellor outlining the financial problems. Reichel was sufficiently impressed to have it widely circulated in order to educate the Welsh public (a favourite theme of his) and to generate the necessary 'political steam'.[123] Asquith in turn acceded to Herbert Lewis's request that he, Asquith, should receive the views of Welsh members (later printed) before he came to a decision. The factors which prevailed upon him to resist the views of the Treasury and to accord separate treatment to Wales were as follows. First, it was acknowledged by the Board of Education that grants to the Welsh Colleges were not adequate. Second, each college had by April 1906 signified its willingness to submit to a quinquennial inspection by an independent *ad hoc* committee, as Austen Chamberlain had suggested in 1904, provided at least one of the inspectors had a sound knowledge of Wales and provided that the special circumstances of Wales were borne in mind. Finally, sustained pressure within his own party convinced him of the unwisdom of caving in to the Treasury on such a combustible issue, especially since the Colleges had in effect placed themselves in his hands. Thus it was that Wales remained outside the writ of the English Advisory Committee. Cardiff, at length resisting the lure of independence, cast her lot with her sister colleges.[124]

The outcome was the Raleigh Committee.[125] Appointed in July 1907, its members were partly suggested by Isambard Owen and Reichel and partly by the Treasury. The chairman, Sir Thomas Raleigh, had been at Balliol with Asquith and at All Souls with Reichel. His radical principles had not immediately commended him to the Irish Protestant but his espousal of Unionist views formed the basis of a long friendship. In India, under Curzon, Raleigh had concentrated upon university development and his knowledge of subject peoples was not considered a disadvantage in dealing with the problems of Wales. Apart from John Rhys, Professor of Celtic at Oxford, virtually the statutory Welsh member, the committee was heavily laced with Scots (including the chairman), one of whom, W. S. McCormick, was for long practically the inspector-general of British universities. Marchant Williams could, of course, be relied upon to speak satirically of Raleigh and his 'Mac this and Mac that',[126] but we may reasonably assume that a conscious effort was made to ensure that the committee was seen to be independent and not an English Advisory Committee in another guise. Scots, moreover, were well placed to examine Welsh educational problems, not wholly dissimilar to their own, whilst a wary Treasury doubtless hoped that North Britons would not make expensive recommendations.

The Raleigh Committee did estimable work, but its report does not stand comparison with the Aberdare and Haldane Reports. The brief was broad enough. It was to examine the nature of the educational work accomplished, the financial position of the University and its Colleges, the lines of future development and the probable staff requirements so as to act effectively. With one exception, to be considered later,[127] it did what was expected of it and the tone of the report is friendly. The matriculation examination in its view was not an efficient sieve to discourage students ill-equipped to profit by university lectures, a defect natural enough in a country where secondary education was not yet fully organized. It should, therefore, be superseded by a system of school-leaving certificates. Performance in all branches of university education was 'very creditable'; the proportion of students who graduated was 'decidedly good'; the quality of independent work produced by teachers and graduates was 'somewhat remarkable'[128] considering the routine duties inevitably undertaken at all levels. Lists of books and papers presented by each college had been carefully examined, confirming initial impressions, whilst graduates of the University were holding their own with graduates of other universities in competition for scientific and educational posts. The Colleges had been very successful in increasing the number of departments, thus attracting more students. However, a price had been paid. The teaching staff was not adequately remunerated. Appeals could be made to erect new buildings but it was less realistic to expect subscriptions in order to augment salaries. As to free studentships and scholarships, Cardiff was demonstrably in the lead with £2,146 at its disposal each year (largely because of scholarships provided by Cardiff, Glamorgan and Monmouthshire, and the Cradock Wells Charity). The Committee was critical of a total expenditure of nearly £2,000 in the three Colleges on undergraduate scholarships out of general income. Indeed, private benefactors might have been deterred from helping needy students because of provision made from college funds. Henceforth, scholarships should be financed by individuals or by local authorities, the latter having especial regard to outlying areas where opportunities were restricted. Awards should normally be for two or three years to protect a student from being left high and dry at the end of his first or second year.[129]

Concerning the nature of the University, it was plain that comparisons could not be made with Oxford and Cambridge, where the University itself was responsible for teaching in many branches of study. In Wales the University taught only through its Colleges, each of which was in a sense a 'local University'.[130] The Committee was therefore not surprised that some looked forward to the creation of three universities. Nevertheless, it rejected such a development. By comparison with the newer English universities the population of Wales could not sustain more than one university and it endorsed the conclusions at Bangor in 1903 of Sir Richard Jebb, the great classical scholar, that the advantage of federation outweighed the drawbacks:

> To represent Wales is not merely to represent a geographical area and a distinct nationality; it is to represent also a well-marked type of national genius, characterised by certain intellectual bents, by certain literary aptitudes, by certain gifts of imagination and sympathy, specially manifested in the love of poetry and music – a type of genius which is peculiarly susceptible to the influence of humane studies. A university which is the one academic expression

of such a national genius holds a position of unique interest and of peculiar strength. It would be a great pity to break it up into two or three Universities, no one of which could have the same prestige. If there were but two Universities – one for North Wales and the other for South – the national sentiment would be divided, the strength which it gives would be impaired, and the unavoidable competition, however generous, might possibly be prejudicial to the interests of Welsh education at large.[131]

The Committee upheld the office of Vice-Chancellor, whose powers would inevitably be diminished by the appointment of a permanent 'working head', thus reinforcing the views of the University Court. Consideration was given to the 'interesting evidence'[132] of David Davies, then member for Montgomeryshire, concerning greater economy of resources. Davies deplored the tendency of each college to be complete in itself and he recommended that advanced work be confined to one institution: mining, metallurgy and medicine at Cardiff; agriculture, law and Celtic at Aberystwyth; geology and forestry at Bangor. He further urged that all scholarships be thrown open to all colleges and that a student at postgraduate level should be able to migrate to another college to pursue his specialism. The Committee speedily recognized a hornets' nest and after a courtly bow declined to 'venture . . . a final opinion on a plan which is as yet only an outline'.[133] It did, however, utter a note of warning, to which one member of the Committee, W. S. McCormick, was later to give close attention. If a college wished to create a new department it should explain the financial implications to the Treasury. In short, 'the funds voted for the assistance of existing departments should not be depleted by additions to their number'.[134] The work of the University and its Colleges should be referred to a committee 'somewhat in the same manner'[135] as the English Advisory Committee.

The requirements of the colleges as stated by the Raleigh Committee may be briefly summarized. Professors should be paid £500 on average; there should be a superannuation scheme; tutorial assistance needed to be extended, and libraries and laboratories to be better equipped; the training of teachers should continue to be financed and postgraduate studies encouraged by fellowships. As to the University itself, the Report was somewhat tepid. Additional income was not 'actually necessary',[136] but higher education would be fortified if the University received additional revenue to further research. The Committee noted that the Welsh Colleges had enjoyed appreciably greater financial support than English colleges of comparable size, so much so that they had been able to establish a large number of departments and that more of their students had proceeded to a degree. Nevertheless, the Committee agreed that the Welsh Colleges had special claims. First, Wales was not a rich country, it had few large towns and it was ill-provided with educational endowments. Second, local authorities in Wales bore educational burdens disproportionately heavy in relation to their income. Third, the demand for higher education in Wales was 'more active and more widespread than it is in most parts of England'.[137]

Since the Committee had been asked to ascertain the 'probable requirements'[138] of the Colleges to enable them to perform their duties effectually, it is curious that the Committee did not feel obliged to present specific financial recommendations when it reported in June 1908. Not until March 1909 did the government announce an additional grant of £15,000. There was further delay when the government asked Raleigh to state precisely how the money was to be distributed, and only in December 1909 did detailed instructions reach the Colleges, nearly six years after the interview with Austen Chamberlain. With few exceptions, such as Ellis W. Davies (Caernarfonshire), Welsh members were rebuked for pusillanimous inactivity in not exerting constant pressure upon the government. It was, however, not reasonable to assail Lloyd George, appointed Chancellor of the Exchequer in April 1908. When Raleigh presented him for an honorary degree at Oxford in June (thus anticipating the University of Wales by some months), he had found him generally 'well-disposed' to the Welsh colleges. Soon, too, he was to face bitter contests over the Dreadnoughts and the People's Budget.[139]

Of the further grant of £15,000 to the University, £12,000 was to be equally divided between the three Colleges.[140] Half of the remainder was wisely given to Cardiff College's Medical School, the only instance of preferential treatment; the other half was set aside for fellowships. As to the grants to the colleges, there were unequivocal prohibitions: they were not to be used for scholarships or buildings of any kind; hostels and residential halls were specifically excluded as proper charges upon private donors or local authorities. On the positive side, each college was to devote £1,000 to departmental libraries and museums, to the expenses and equipment of laboratories, though it was hoped that a substantial portion would be spent on the main library; £500 was to be used to extend tutorial assistance; half the sum to each college was to raise the salaries of the principal, professors and heads of departments, and a further £500 to establish a super-annuation scheme. Lloyd George would certainly have welcomed the last two provisions, for when receiving his honorary degree at Bangor he had said: 'You cannot hope to retain the services of the very best men at the really very inadequate remuneration we give them at present.'[141] Reichel rejoiced especially at the sums set aside for fellowships for postgraduate work, which he later attributed entirely to Raleigh's 'foresight and initiative',[142] though it is evident that T. F. Roberts had brought the matter to the attention of Austen Chamberlain in 1904. What cannot be reasonably disputed is that the adoption of the Raleigh Committee's recommendation, in Reichel's words, 'virtually transformed the higher work of the Colleges'. Hitherto there had been but the 'scantiest provision'[143] for postgraduate studies, as T. F. Roberts noted. The 1851 Exhibition Research Scholarship in Science was awarded once to each college every three years. There was also a fellowship of the University, open to competition, which from 1898 to 1909 had been given to twelve students only (for varying periods). We need scarcely be surprised, therefore, to learn that students later eminent in the life of Wales failed to receive a fellowship, J. F. Rees, for example, to undertake research into Wales under the Commonwealth, and R. T. Jenkins, also in 1904, to study the Arthurian cycle in Iceland.[144]

The annual sum provided by the Treasury in the wake of the Raleigh Report was supplemented by an unexpected windfall. J. Eyton Williams, a chemist of Pepper Street, Chester, who had lived a quiet, unostentatious life, determined that his small fortune (of perhaps £30,000) should, after various bequests, be divided between the College at Bangor and the University to provide scholarships. He had, however, hedged in his bequest by leaving a memorandum restricting awards to those who believed 'in the existence of a Supreme Being' and who accepted 'the tenets and principles of the Protestant faith'.[145] Apart from excluding genuine unbelievers and an increasing band of honest doubters such a requirement ran counter to the charters of the University and the Colleges which all eschewed religious tests. Moreover, the bequests were confined to Welsh-born males, an unjust, offensive restriction. The College acted with some dispatch. The matter was tested at law. The President of the Probate, Divorce and Admiralty Division declared that the memorandum should be treated as part of the will. The bequests would thus be invalid. The College won on appeal, the Master of the Rolls ruling that the intention of the testator was not to be found in the existing memorandum but in a future, unexecuted memorandum. There was great thanksgiving both in the College and in the University, the latter receiving £10,000. It should not escape notice that Bangor won another victory at law when the Inland Revenue appealed against a ruling of the High Court that the College should be exempt under schedules A, C and D to the Income Tax Act. The Court of Appeal dismissed the appeal, thus deeming the College to be in the same position as other charities. The immediate gain to Bangor was not great, but university institutions throughout the land benefited so that they willingly and gratefully contributed to the payment of Bangor's legal expenses in pursuance of a common cause.[146]

The Eyton Williams Bequest, taken in conjunction with the annual Treasury grant of £15,000 in consequence of the Raleigh Report, made available to the University each year the sum of £2,000 for research purposes. It was thus able to offer three fellowships of £125 each year, tenable for two years (extended to three years in cases of unusual merit). Between 1910 and 1916 it was reported that twenty-nine students had received fellowships under this scheme. The University also henceforth offered twelve postgraduate studentships of the annual value of £65, tenable for two years. It should perhaps be added that in 1900 the University received a legacy from the estate of Price Davies of Leeds which brought in an annual income of £200 to provide entrance scholarships at either Aberystwyth or Bangor. In 1916 the

University believed that the income would be better devoted to postgraduate scholarships. On the eve of the Great War, then, the higher work of the University had indeed, in Reichel's words, been transformed. The number of graduates had increased perceptibly, if not uniformly, between 1897 and 1907, 1,200 in all, of whom 297 were scientists.[147] A significant development was that the University of Wales had in 1898 instituted the MA degree by research some years before London and indeed before any other university in the United Kingdom. In 1914 the Senior Deputy-Chancellor felt sufficiently emboldened to have printed a brief survey of the original works of staff and students between 1909 and 1914.[148]

Standards of admission and of examinations were a constant preoccupation. There was one acutely unhappy affair which billowed out monstrously. In June 1910 news reached the Vice-Chancellor, E. H. Griffiths, that there had been leakages in the University examinations in French.[149] It was soon evident that 'tips', 'hints' and 'suggestions' had been transmitted by Cardiff students in a cordial federal spirit to Aberystwyth and thence to Bangor. The examinations, deemed to have been vitiated, were at once cancelled and fresh papers set. Fully aware of the gravity of the situation, the University instituted an inquiry at the highest level. The conclusion reached was that the responsibility lay with Paul Barbier, Professor of French at Cardiff. There was no evidence that he had acted with intent, but it was impossible to acquit him of negligence 'of so grave a character as to make it undesirable that he should again act in the capacity'.[150] Others went further, saying that Barbier's disclosures in lectures had been preceded by readily discernible gestures which today would be called 'body language'. Students, about 350 it is believed, were obliged to sit papers decidedly less familiar than on the first occasion, at some expense and inconvenience. Pleas were made that further study would impose an especially heavy strain upon women. The calamity was compounded when Marchant Williams intervened. He and others had always opposed allowing internal staff to act as examiners and here was public proof that they were right. In a series of letters to the *Western Mail* he denounced the system whereby professors examined their own students as 'an imposture' for it ignored 'the infirmities of the human race'[151] (upon which he himself battened). For years, he claimed, there had been leakages, which in legal language meant 'fraud'. Moreover, it had been alleged, he continued, that other departments were guilty, namely Latin, Welsh, political science and mathematics. Not surprisingly, a Professor of Latin, E. V. Arnold, responded vigorously to Marchant's pieces in the *Western Mail*, entitled 'The University on the Rocks'. He also published a well-argued pamphlet, *The University of Wales and the Nation* (1910), refuting Marchant's charges but insisting on a most rigorous investigation.[152] The University did not consider that the allegations in the *Western Mail* justified an inquiry for they were withdrawn in August, but the report upon the French 'leakages' was a scrupulous, impressive document which, whilst condemning Barbier's grave negligence, gave a reasoned exposition of the examination system.[153] During the Court meeting at Aberystwyth in November 1910, S. N. Jones of Newport re-echoed Marchant's criticisms. (Sir) Henry Lewis of Belmont, Bangor, recalled the occasion in the privacy of his diary. Reichel, though still lame and in pain despite treatment in London, had come down to participate in the discussion. Arising from his 'shawls and wrappers' he asked S. N. Jones whether he realized that the system adopted by the University of Wales was adopted by every university in the United Kingdom except London and that in no other university in continental Europe or in America were external examiners allowed. Lewis added: 'He spoke with great concentration and looked at Mr Jones as if he would spring at him.'[154]

In the short term an unhappy occurrence of this kind was bound to damage a young institution. Such had been the case, though more serious, at Nottingham in the same year. Unintentional errors in computing student numbers, upon which the Treasury grant depended, led to the arrival of eighteen inspectors and to the departure of both Principal and Registrar, the former finding refuge as chaplain to English communities at Seville and elsewhere.[155] Barbier was allowed to remain at Cardiff, for although he had been culpably foolish he had otherwise given good service. It must also be added that the University dealt with the matter with exemplary swiftness. It was right to do so, for nothing could be more injurious to its welfare than the remotest suspicion that its academic standing was inferior to that of other British universities. It is fitting, therefore, to consider the efforts made to attain and to maintain the highest academic standards.

In the early days many entrants were painfully ill-equipped to pursue the most elementary courses. Cardiff had in fact soon dispensed with written entrance examinations in favour of oral tests.[156] Even after the passing of the Welsh Intermediate Act of 1889 it took time to establish secondary schools, to appoint good staff and to reach modest standards. Matriculation long remained a grievous stumbling-block. In October 1896 the University Court, perhaps a little shamefacedly, decided that the number of passes only at matriculation should be released to the press, always ready to publish bad news.[157] As late as 1910 the Matriculation Board reported that the failure rate in the June examination was 66.1 per cent and in September 72.8 per cent.[158] There were inevitable consequences. During their first year at college students were obliged to prepare for either the whole or the uncompleted part of matriculation requirements. Then again, university teachers of the highest calibre intellectually had no option but to teach at a frustratingly low level. Upon appointment in 1902 E. H. Griffiths declared that entrance standards were well below those of England, though it may be doubted whether this was true of all English provincial colleges before the effects were felt of Balfour's Education Act of 1902. In any case, no one could question his statement that 'it was not right that the energies of professors should be employed to remedy the deficiencies of schools'.[159] In 1907 Cardiff's Professor of Engineering was gratified that during the previous two years as many as half his students had matriculated before entry.[160] Generally speaking there had been a marked improvement, for in the same year T. F. Roberts noted that 93 per cent of full-time degree students had matriculated before coming to Aberystwyth, whereas only 25 per cent would have done so fifteen or twenty years earlier.[161] In fact in 1910 the examiners to the Matriculation Board thought that the time had come to stiffen standards which in the past had been 'somewhat low in consequence of the exceptionally poor quality of a certain proportion of the candidates who not only know little but appear to be of insufficient capacity to profit by a University course'.[162]

These were timely words, but there was more to come. Each examiner upon appointment should be told that 'it is the intention of the University that the standard of knowledge required should be at least as high as that of any other university and that this standard should be maintained without regard to the percentage of passes'.[163] We must therefore conclude that, from its inception, the standard of the 'Welsh matric' had not been wholly satisfactory and that large concessions had been made to the growing pains of intermediate schools. Strangely absent from such assessments are references to language problems, which appear frequently in the departmental reports of the three colleges.

We turn now to consider the standard of achievement at degree level. We have already seen that pleas to the Treasury for grants in the 1890s largely hinged upon the paramount need to appoint external examiners outstanding in their field. A glance at lists published in successive calendars gives firm assurance that this was done. In 1899 Isambard Owen spoke of 'the academic credit which examinations of the University have just succeeded in winning'.[164] During the next two years the University received congratulatory messages from its Chancellor, in 1900 as Prince of Wales and in 1901 as monarch wishing to relinquish his office and to assume the title of Protector. Pleasure was expressed that 'so large a proportion of the candidates, out of those who went up for Science, have gained First Class Honours',[165] and that it was especially gratifying to him to notice the progress made in the scholarly study of Welsh and in the scientific teaching of theology, tributes which were well deserved, if somewhat un-expected from this quarter. More significant for our purpose is the testimony of Vice-Chancellors of the University. Giving evidence to the Raleigh Committee, Reichel outlined the role of the external examiner, appointed by the University. After consulting the internal examiners and requesting suggestions he drew up draft papers later considered by all examiners. Thus teaching and examining went hand in hand (as far as possible), thereby avoiding the inevitable evils of examining when examiners were all external, as under the London system. Secondly, the external examiner brought in 'light from outside',[166] helping to provide unity of standard between the three colleges and also between the University of Wales and other universities. In correspondence with Herbert Lewis, Reichel developed this point:

> At the second meeting of each Board of Examiners I have always as Vice-Chancellor asked the External Examiner whether in marking the papers he had adopted the same standard as he would in marking in degree examinations at Oxford or Cambridge. Most of them have at once replied that they marked on exactly the same standard. In the few cases where the answer was that they had not marked quite so strictly I have insisted that this should be done. In the technical subjects two examiners informed me that they marked *more strictly* in the University of Wales than they would venture to do in the old universities.[167]

To the Raleigh Committee Reichel gave a further illustration. When an external examiner in Greek was recommending two candidates for first class, Reichel asked, 'Would you think that on their papers, so far as quality was concerned, you could recommend them for first class in Moderations?' He replied: 'No, not quite, because their composition is hardly good enough.'[168] The Examining Board placed them at once in the second class. T. F. Roberts praised the freedom given to the colleges to initiate courses of study, though, as we shall see, the Senate of the University later came under fire because of its cumbersome machinery. He drew attention to the pass degree of the University which he considered superior to the pass standard at Oxford and Cambridge and resembling more the MA degree in Scotland or the standard of the London ordinary degree.[169] At honours level he placed the highest value on the presence of the external examiners who, if anything, were more indulgent to candidates than internal examiners. In 1910 E. H. Griffiths, as Vice-Chancellor, declared that the standard enforced by the University of Wales was equal to any in the kingdom. The Examining Boards were especially vigilant and their verdicts 'had probably been given against rather than in favour of the candidates'.[170] Not long before the outbreak of war, it was reported that an outstanding feature had been 'the work submitted for higher degrees in the faculties of Arts and Science, which, both in quality and quantity, had been remarkable'.[171] Kenyon, in his quinquennial survey, 1909–14, wrote in a similar vein. All things considered, 'the University of Wales does not fear comparison nor shrink from criticism'.[172] In so far as we are able to judge, the authorities of the University were not whistling in the dark.

II

The Colleges, 1893–1914

Aberystwyth

In 1895 Aberdare decided to relinquish the office of President of the College which he had held for twenty-one years. He had given time and energy to its affairs in trying days. Yet there was a residual feeling that he had not always defended the just interests of Aberystwyth, either in the report which bears his name or upon other critical occasions. His successor, Lord Rendel, went so far as to speak of 'betrayal', though he freely acknowledged that Aberdare was 'a charming personage and a delightful companion'[1] and that his enthusiasm for Welsh education was entirely genuine. In writing thus he scarcely did justice to a major figure in the university movement in Wales. Stuart Rendel, an Etonian and an Oxonian, was managing director of Armstrong Whitworth which manufactured armaments. A Liberal, he had broken the Wynnstay hegemony in Montgomeryshire in the election of 1880 and he remained a Member of Parliament until his elevation to the Lords in 1894. For the college at Aberystwyth he had early shown a deep, enduring concern, because it represented for him the aspirations of the extraordinary common people of Wales. In 1892 he convinced Gladstone to include in his programme for Wales a University charter.[2] His relations with T. F. Roberts, the College's second principal, were infinitely warmer than Aberdare's ragged association with Thomas Charles Edwards and much more akin to the cordial relations at Bangor between Kenyon and H. R. Reichel. True, Rendel was frequently plagued by ill health, drearily magnified by hypochondria; he once apologized to T. F. Roberts for his 'cold, captious, caustic remarks', freely acknowledging on another occasion that Roberts's 'touch is the gentlest I have ever experienced'.[3] Rendel's commitment to Aberystwyth was exemplary. From 1901 until his death in 1913 he subscribed £750 yearly to raise

the salaries of staff; income from his legacies helped to endow the
Rendel chair of English language and literature at the College,
which in a hundred years, it was said, 'never had a truer friend'.[4]
He was succeeded in 1913 by Sir John Williams, baronet, who,
with the constant help and encouragement of his widowed
mother, herself fired with 'a great hunger for learning',[5] rose from
a humble home in Carmarthenshire to enjoy the patronage of the
royal family on account of his eminence as an obstetrician. In
1903 he retired to Plas Llanstephan, Carmarthenshire, in order
to be intimately associated with cultural movements in Wales. As
a lover, collector and donor of Welsh books and manuscripts, he
has a lasting place in the affections of his countrymen.

Sir John would have understood the early struggles of T. F.
Roberts, born at Tywyn, Meirionnydd, the son of a devout
Baptist policeman. Educated at Aberystwyth and at Oxford,
where he excelled in classics, he was at twenty-three appointed
Professor of Greek at Cardiff; here his skill and unremitting
industry, amply confirmed by a quiverful of testimonials, led to
the Aberystwyth principalship in 1891. Those who took a surface
view were sometimes critical. His air of pensive sadness incited
the venomous Marchant Williams to say that 'he always wears the
appearance of a monk who has broken his vows'.[6] Lloyd George
was never prepared to include him even in the longest of honours
lists, mainly because he considered that he lacked zest and fire.
Roberts, however, was perfectly capable of acting fearlessly, with
determination and dispatch; no one who has read his
correspondence, especially with Rendel, can fail to be impressed
by his qualities. He was a man of high principle, an unwavering
Christian and a noble patriot. It was wholly characteristic of him
that he should have accompanied a student, sent down for a
serious offence, to explain the circumstances to his parents. Not
many would have contemplated, far less undertaken, such a
lugubrious journey.

Roberts's principalship was often interrupted by ill health. The
College Registrar since 1892, T. Mortimer Green, was also often
unwell. Upon his retirement in 1905 he was followed by J. H.
Davies, who was later frequently called upon to deputize for the
Principal. All officers, whatever their circumstances, were
confronted by persistent financial problems. It is true that the

government in 1894 gave a grant of £10,000 towards the reconstruction of the 'Old College'.[7] The implementation of the Raleigh Committee's recommendations was also an undoubted amelioration. Individuals responded with a will, particularly Rendel and the Llandinam family. Yet, the College's scant seed-corn was in the main annually devoured. Cardiff and Bangor had from the beginning received state grants, whereas Aberystwyth had perforce depended for years upon voluntary subscriptions. In 1909 it was noted that the average salary of professors at Aberystwyth was 'considerably less than the corresponding figure for the other two Colleges'.[8] The heroism of the early days has in the popular mind been rightly celebrated; the heroism of the period 1893–1914 has seldom received the attention that it deserves. In a government report upon universities in 1914 there is a pitiful footnote to the Aberystwyth accounts: 'the Professor of Music received no salary during the year, being indisposed'.[9] In 1915 David Jenkins was dead.

The structure of the main building required prompt attention. Although the early history of the 'Old College' lies beyond the strict limits of the present volume, yet it would be unrealistic not to outline its architectural development. The first building upon the dagger-shaped site was Castle House, raised by John Nash in 1795 for Sir Uvedale Price. It was to be the nucleus of one of the substantial hotels which Thomas Savin, once an Oswestry draper and later an impetuous railway entrepreneur, proposed to erect on the coast of Cardigan Bay. Convinced that regular trains would bring to Aberystwyth a limitless number of 'people in the higher ranks',[10] he turned to J. P. Seddon to construct for him a grand hotel. Seddon, deservedly commemorated in one of the College's finest rooms, began his career as a committed 'Goth'. Indeed, he has been described as 'a major theorist of the High Victorian Gothic movement'.[11] His links with Ruskin, William Burges and the Pre-Raphaelites convinced him that by blending past styles he could fashion an individual, 'sublime' style worthy of the nineteenth century. At Aberystwyth, despite endless frustration, he left a lasting memorial. In 1866 a severe banking crisis led to the bankruptcy of Thomas Savin and to the sale of the Castle Hotel, then no more than an empty shell but nevertheless the most romantic building in Wales before Burges's creations at Cardiff Castle and Castell Coch. To the College fathers this was a heaven-sent opportunity; the hotel reputed to have cost £80,000, was bought for £10,000. Seddon was again employed, though there are still signs of labour suspended, such as unworked capitals and brackets abandoned as plain blocks of stone in the Old Hall.[12] In 1885 fire badly damaged the north wing, a catastrophe which tested the nerve and loyalty of the College's supporters. Proposals to raise a new building on another site happily collapsed and Seddon was allowed to proceed. The south wing was now razed to the ground and replaced by a firm, clean-cut science block which derives its inspiration from the architecture of thirteenth-century France, as is evident from the steep roof and towers with conical spires reminiscent of Castell Coch. In the arts wing he created the unique quadrangle covered by the ornamental roof with coloured glass panels. Other memorials to his work are the grand staircase, the Old Hall, the library extending across the width of the building, the triangular carriage porch, the double tower and the fine bowed section on the sea front. In an obituary to Seddon it was said that he was the most original of the Gothic revivalists because he renounced slavish imitation and 'sought to look behind the reasons that prompted medieval form'.[13]

C. J. Ferguson, much influenced by the Queen Anne style frequently reflected in educational establishments of the time, was responsible for the central block, which when completed in 1898 gave the College its present appearance. In addition to various changes within the College – the library, for example – his most successful venture was to enclose the bar of the hotel with a screen to provide a room for the growing collection of manuscripts and books, the core of the future National Library. It must be added that in close proximity to one another the styles of Seddon and of Ferguson do not blend well.

One external feature which attracts much attention was not the work of either. On the south wing, compared to a figurehead facing the prevailing south-westerly blast, there is a triptych by C. F. A. Voysey. A major architect and designer, it is said of him that he remained true to the Gothic ideal, that he designed from first principles and that 'fitness for purpose was his watchword'.[14] The exact purpose of the coloured mosaic has long prompted hesitant speculation, but Roger Webster in a recent and, alas, posthumous, study, has placed the matter beyond reasonable doubt.[15] The figure in the centre (no longer the supposed Archimedes) is a representation of 'Science'. Beside him there is a globe and above him two stars, symbols of the earth and of the heavens. On the right-hand page of a book on his lap there is a drawing of a skull and on the other page a triangle; the one represents the study of man, the other mathematics, the indispensable key to scientific knowledge. The figure in the left panel holds a locomotive and the figure on the right, described as 'epicene' (thus combining both sexes), holds a ship powered by sail and steam. Both kneeling figures are here reverently presenting pure science with the products of applied science whose triumphs were made possible only by the unimpeded study of man, the heavens and all around him. Voysey was here conveying a potent message to all universities, a message which the industrialists of south Wales signally failed to comprehend,[16] to the mounting dismay of E. H. Griffiths and his colleagues at Cardiff.

Little remains of the original building. It is likely that the marble pillars of the central staircase off the quadrangle were rescued from the old hotel dining-room. The oldest survival, not normally seen, a relic of Nash's Castle House, is the handsome, carved fireplace in the Principal's room, perhaps the work of Thomas Banks, then in the employ of Thomas Johnes of Hafod. The architecture of the 'Old College' has not received universal approbation. To one writer it has a 'bizarre' appearance; another observer was reminded of marzipan, whilst H. V. Morton considered it to be like the illegitimate offspring of the London law courts.[17] But of this we may be certain: both within and without, in the eyes of generations of staff and students it has a 'personality' which is matchless. They would doubtless applaud the judgement of H. R. Hitchcock, an authority on European architecture of the nineteenth and twentieth centuries: 'certain aspects of the building, the bowed section on the sea-front . . . and the entrance and stair tower on the rear are amongst the grandest and most boldly plastic fragments produced in this period. Neither Oxford nor Cambridge have anything of comparable quality!'[18]

The other major building involved the rehousing of the chemistry department. The breach in 1886 with David Davies, the College's first treasurer and head of the wealthy family of Llandinam, was soon repaired after his death. Edward, his son, was also treasurer and although he lived only until 1898 the links with Aberystwyth were handsomely maintained by Gwendoline and Margaret Davies, his daughters, and by his heir (Lord) David Davies. Their generous, early act of filial piety enabled the College to raise the splendid Edward Davies Laboratory, eventually to cost £23,000 and opened in 1907 by H. H. Asquith, then Chancellor of the Exchequer. David Davies later bought a hotel (adjoining the College) which was converted into a college for the Calvinistic Methodists, a purchase fully in harmony with plans to attract denominational colleges to University College towns. An ambitious proposal by Davies to make the College entirely residential foundered, however, for reasons which are somewhat obscure but which may have stemmed from the failure of the seven county councils affiliated to the College to co-operate. A decade earlier it had been possible to provide a purpose-built hall of residence for women, under the effective command of E. A. Carpenter. It was opened in 1896, when the Prince of Wales was installed Chancellor, by the Princess of Wales, whose name, 'Alexandra', it therefore bore. More than two decades later a Carpenter Hall was established.[19]

The determination to secure a National Library for Wales and to place it at Aberystwyth was part of the same national movement which had led to the creation of the University of Wales. The success of the enterprise affected both the College and the University. Little progress could be expected, as in the case of the University, unless pressure was exerted on the floor of the House of Commons. Here in 1892 came Herbert Lewis, who eagerly sought for Wales a due share of the museum grants of the United Kingdom. The term 'museum' included both art galleries and libraries and Lewis was indignant that whereas Scotland in 1893–4 was to receive £16,636 and Ireland £22,208, Wales was, as before, wholly excluded. No European country, he claimed, apart from Russia and Turkey, was in this respect so badly treated.[20] To convince many English members that Wales was not a region of England required persistence and patience. Indeed, many years elapsed before it was recognized that Wales should receive a museum and a library grant. The ensuing problem was that of location; to this we shall presently return.

The College at Aberystwyth had as early as 1873 formed a steering committee to establish 'a National Library of Wales',[21] some years before the Aberdare Report had apparently crushed all hope that Aberystwyth would be a unitary university and thus the principal centre of national studies in Wales. This was in response to a speech of Gladstone's at the Mold National Eisteddfod upon the importance of safeguarding the cultural inheritance of Wales. In the hardest of times the College set aside sums, inevitably small, to acquire books and manuscripts which were to be the nucleus of a national library. No great progress was made until 1896 when, after the collapse of the Liberal government in 1895, Thomas Ellis, always a source of inspiration, was able to intervene decisively. Under his influence the College Council agreed that a site should be secured and plans made 'for the erection of a Library *apart from the College* for Welsh books, manuscripts and records relating to Wales'.[22] There were further developments. First, the Principal launched a national appeal for volumes and manuscripts, which arrived in impressive numbers and which in 1899 were set apart to form a Welsh library.[23] Second, Sir John Williams, indicated that he was prepared to give to the College his library, soon to include the incomparable Hengwrt-Peniarth treasures, conditional upon the acquisition of a suitable site. Four members of the College Council, in a private capacity, speedily snapped up fourteen acres of Grogythan lands on Penglais hill, a superb site, for £2,000. At first Rendel, who had not been consulted, was highly critical of costly ventures at a time when the College was crushed by debts as if by leaden weights. To the Principal, privately, he even spoke of 'megalomania'.[24] Soon, however, he recognized the wisdom of the course and bought the land himself for the original sum, leasing it to the College at a peppercorn rent. The consequences were momentous, though not at once. During the next few years the College made another public appeal and acquired further collections (those of Gwallter Mechain and of Owain Myfyr amongst them).

Thus it was that Aberystwyth was able to present an eloquent case for the library grant reluctantly promised by the government. It was generally and justly assumed that the grant for a museum would be given to Cardiff, but Cardiff hoped to acquire both a national library and a national museum, further proofs of its claims to city status. Although the Lord Mayor acted with disagreeable pertinacity, aspirations were legitimately fostered by the presence of the Cardiff Free Library, housing items of importance, and by the fine Salisbury collection purchased by the College in 1886 against fierce competition. Curiously, the first owner, E. G. R. Salisbury, who suffered the turmoils of bankruptcy, had as early as 1873 spoken of the need for a Welsh national library. Viriamu Jones, shortly before his death, had consulted the College Registrar as to whether it would be proper to transfer the Salisbury collection to a national library if both a national library and a national museum were located at Cardiff. James fully agreed, provided the collection was returned to the College if the two national institutions were dissolved. On no account, however, was it to be handed to the Cardiff Free Library, any more than the University of Oxford would contemplate leasing the Bodleian Library to the City of Oxford.[25] In order to avoid another protracted, unpleasant 'battle of the sites' the matter was resolved by arbitration. The National Library went to Aberystwyth, the National Museum to Cardiff.

The wisdom of the decision has sometimes been questioned by those who take a bleak view of placing a national institution upon a distant shore. Nevertheless, apart from calamities which especially damage cities and towns, seldom even in peacetime free from impurities injurious to man and all his works, we should perhaps consider the opinion of the National Library's real founder, Sir John Williams. To him the Library was 'not intended for the amusement of those who compass sea and land'.[26] He had at an early stage favoured Cardiff but soon came to feel that the great desideratum was a small town with cheap, quiet, comfortable rooms, not 'a large commercial town with its noise and hurry, high rents, and expensive living'.[27] At all events, his role was decisive. The one great sadness in the life of the famous obstetrician was that he himself had no children. The National Library of Wales and the Aberystwyth College became his beneficiaries, from generation to generation. Throughout the tortuous proceedings T. F. Roberts had acted with tact and wisdom. He had seen that it was necessary to hand over the College Library to the National Library, provided the latter remained in perpetuity at Aberystwyth. 'It may not be agreeable altogether to flesh and blood', he told Rendel in 1904, 'but to succeed in getting the Library at Aberystwyth will mean that we have the substance if we lose the name of possession.'[28] In 1907 the National Library received its charter of incorporation; in 1909 it was housed in the Assembly Rooms at Laura Place; in 1911 the foundation stone upon the hill was laid by George V and Queen Mary and in that year the Copyright Act gave the Library the privileges enjoyed by five other libraries in Great Britain.[29] The presence of the Library has been of inestimable benefit to the College and it was entirely fitting that the University's Centre for Advanced Welsh and Celtic Studies, which the College had done most to promote (sometimes in discouraging circumstances), should in time be raised in close, comely proximity and on land belonging to the National Library of Wales.

We turn now to examine the principal academic developments, first on the arts side. When M. W. MacCullum resigned from the chair of English at Aberystwyth in 1886 it seemed that he might be succeeded by Owen M. Edwards, who, however, succumbed to the persuasions of Benjamin Jowett, amongst others, that he would do more for Wales at Oxford than at Aberystwyth.[30] The successful applicant, C. H. Herford, described as 'the most accomplished English scholar of his age',[31] ranged widely in the literatures of Germany, Italy, Norway and Russia, specializing in the ideas and characters of authors. In time he was elected a Fellow of the British Academy. He left a lasting mark upon his better students. R. T. Jenkins wrote: 'To me, until I die, the *meaning* of the name "Aberystwyth College" will be "Charles Harold Herford".'[32] The two who followed, G. C. Macaulay, in 1901, and J. W. H. Atkins, in 1906, were notable scholars, though not of Herford's rank. Several languages, ancient and modern, were long taught by one man, Hermann Ethé. A voluntary exile from his native land, he rejected the spiked helmet of the new Bismarckian state, which to him disfigured the Germany of

Schiller and Goethe. At one period he taught French language and literature, Italian, German, Hebrew, Arabic and Sanskrit, further adding, with refreshing optimism, that he would 'be happy to read with students in other oriental languages'.[33] From 1909 to 1944 the department of French was in the charge of André Barbier whose animated wife brought new life to the department of music during the declining years of David Jenkins and also a whiff of scandal to the Aberystwyth scene. T. F. Roberts, highly thought of as a professor at Cardiff, taught Greek until 1909 when he handed over his duties to J. W. Marshall, for long an immensely popular Vice-Principal. When the Professor of Latin, J. M. Angus, was appointed Registrar in 1905, he was succeeded by E. Bensly. Joseph Brough's tenure of the chair of philosophy from 1883 until 1911 has been commemorated by a postgraduate university prize in logic or philosophy.

John Edward Lloyd, responsible for history, Welsh language and literature from 1885, left for Bangor in 1892. Not for the last time, he was replaced by two persons. Edward Edwards, brother of O. M. Edwards, became lecturer in history and in 1895 professor; he remained at Aberystwyth for thirty-eight years, contributing more to the administration of the College than to research. Edward Anwyl was appointed Professor of Welsh Language and Literature and later Professor of Comparative Philology as well. Educated at the King's School, Chester, and at Oxford, Anwyl was called 'a great scholar'[34] by his successor (Sir) T. H. Parry-Williams, who also praised him for his encyclopaedic knowledge. Anwyl, in addition, attached great importance to the study of theology. His chief administrative post was that of chairman of the Central Welsh Board (1896), thus further strengthening the links between the University and the secondary schools of Wales. His contribution to Welsh education was recognized by a knighthood in 1911. Two years later he was appointed first Principal of Caerleon Training College, but he died in 1914 at the age of forty-eight before entering office.[35] Aberystwyth had stolen a march on Bangor when it received Board of Education permission to establish a Day Training Department in 1892 under a vigorous Master of Method, Henry Holman.[36] By 1914, 32 per cent of full-time students were training to be teachers in elementary schools. The departure in 1913 of Foster Watson,

Professor of Education since 1896, was a serious impoverishment. An authority on the history of education, he is especially remembered for *The English Grammar School to 1660* (1908) written at Aberystwyth. His successor, C. R. Chapple, remained in the chair until 1939.

The resolution in London in 1899 to found the Aberystwyth Law School was both enlightened and brave. More than half a century had elapsed since a Select Committee on Legal Education had reported upon the grave inadequacy of legal education in Britain. It recommended that universities should teach law, emphasizing broad philosophical principles, and that the Inns of Court and the Incorporated Law Society should concentrate on professional training. In the densely populated cities of the north of England, the new unitary universities taught students already articled to solicitors. To place the Law School at Aberystwyth rather than at Cardiff was a deliberate act to break away from urban patterns and one which was not liked in the commercial centres of south Wales. As Lord Justice Vaughan Williams observed in 1899, the 'object is to teach, not the practice of the law, but the principles of the law'.[37] Undeterred by grievous financial problems and the inveterate hostility of T. Marchant Williams at Cardiff, the College proceeded to fill the chair of English law. Indeed, with remarkable boldness it appointed two professors in 1901. The first was W. Jethro Brown, formerly the holder of a chair in Tasmania and now Professor of Law at University College, London. The second was T. A. Levi, son of the Revd Thomas Levi, 'King of the Methodists'[38] in Cardiganshire. Levi, nevertheless, owed nothing of consequence to local influence. His academic career at Oxford had been outstanding. A. V. Dicey and other scholars urged him not to apply 'as his chances as a lawyer are so good'. Owen M. Edwards, on the other hand, wrote to T. F. Roberts to say that 'I impressed upon him the truth that every Welshman is bound to offer his services to Wales first, at whatever sacrifice',[39] advice curiously at variance with his own decision not to apply for the chair of English at Aberystwyth in 1887.

The early years were unusually demanding, for it was necessary to deliver extension lectures, at Swansea most frequently, to prepare articled clerks for examinations of the Law

Society whose help was essential to the development of the school. Levi enjoyed the struggle and the lecturing, at which he was *non pareil*. Not so Jethro Brown, primarily a scholar who overcame difficult circumstances to write his celebrated work *The Austinian Theory of Law* (1906), before returning in 1906 to Australia. By then, however, the Law Society's generous grant had provided a secure platform for further advance. Henceforth, Levi ruled the roost and legends abounded, some of them fostered by himself, so that it was often difficult to determine whether he was a confirmed or an unconfirmed bachelor.

On the science side, two Aberystwyth students graduated on the same day in 1901 with first-class honours, Herbert John Fleure in zoology and Owen Thomas Jones in physics. Both held chairs at Aberystwyth and Manchester, both became Fellows of the Royal Society, both were noticed in the same volume of the *Dictionary of National Biography* (1961–1970). Fleure's grandfather had shaken hands with Napoleon (though in what circumstances is not entirely clear); despite delicate health, Fleure survived to the age of ninety-two (1967). The time-span is remarkable. From his home in Guernsey, Fleure proceeded to Aberystwyth with an open scholarship. After research in Wales and at Zurich, he was in 1910 appointed Professor of Zoology and lecturer in Geography. O. T. Jones, a Dyfed farmer's son who spoke only Welsh until he was fifteen, studied at Aberystwyth and at Cambridge. His mapping of the western portion of the south Wales coalfield established his reputation; in 1910 he was the first holder of the chair of geology at Aberystwyth, where he taught with authority upon all branches of his subject. Tall, fair and undisturbed by convention, he flitted to the hills when term ended. By 1912 'he had mapped 1,800 square miles of west mid-Wales, and in so doing, had discovered the central Wales syncline . . . the key to a new and deeper insight into the evolution of geosynclines'.[40]

The department of mathematics was divided into two parts in 1908. R. W. Genese, called a 'stormy petrel', continued as Professor of Pure Mathematics. Applied mathematics was in the hands of G. A. Schott from 1900 to 1933; a specialist on the classical theory of electromagnetism, he was elected a Fellow of the Royal Society in 1922. The department of chemistry prospered under H. Lloyd Snape and its teaching and research resources were immensely strengthened by the building of the Edward Davies laboratories during J. J. Sudborough's later tenure of the chair. John Lloyd Williams, appointed to the chair of botany in 1914, had the distinction of receiving a doctorate of science at London for his work on marine algae and a doctorate of music (honoris causa) of the University of Wales for his service to ethnomusicology.[41]

The study of agriculture and its practical application derived great benefit from advances in these allied disciplines. Bangor, as we shall see, was the first college to establish a department of agriculture. It had also conducted classes in Meirionnydd and Montgomeryshire, two counties which had rendered more than yeoman service to Aberystwyth. It seemed unreasonable that Bangor should claim in perpetuity the whole of north Wales as its province; in order to avoid unseemly controversy, the problem of demarcation was resolved by bringing Meirionnydd within the sphere of Aberystwyth, whilst Montgomeryshire was shared by both colleges (partly in recognition of the authority in the county of Bangor's president, the Earl of Powis). The year 1890 is rightly lauded as the *annus mirabilis* in agricultural education, for it was then that local authorities received with gratitude the so-called 'whisky money' to subsidize technical and agricultural education.[42] Aberystwyth elicited £1,170 from the seven counties associated with it to enable the department of agriculture, under the direction of Tom Parry, to deliver 175 extension lectures in the 1892–3 session alone. Much of the technical instruction provided, it must be conceded, was of an elementary kind, well below university standard, but it was a practical expression of the College's concern for the chief industry of an area which had sustained it in dark days. Unhappily, in 1901, Tom Parry was accused of giving undue attention to dairy maids in his care and of having embraced a number of them *seriatim*. He had to leave, though with a golden handshake. The ensuing atmosphere of muddle and disintegration was not dispelled until C. Bryner Jones was appointed to the chair of agriculture in 1907. For ten years on the staff of Bangor, and latterly at Armstrong College, Newcastle upon Tyne, he was highly recommended by Isambard Owen (Head of the College) who predicted that he was 'destined to take a high place among the teachers and organisers of agricultural education'.[43] At once learned and courtly, dynamic and decisive, his work both within and without the College prompted the government to persuade him to become the Agricultural Commissioner for Wales in 1912. Later, as a distinguished Welsh Secretary at the Ministry of Agriculture, there was scarcely any branch of agricultural activity which he did not promote.

On the eve of the Great War, apart from the Exchequer grant of £8,000, the largest single source of income from the state came from the Board of Agriculture. Rather less than a third of income was derived from fees. Of the 65 members of staff, 19 were professors. Of full-time students 264 were men and 173 women.

Bangor

The College's first President, the Earl of Powis, died in 1891. He had served the College with wisdom, dignity and fidelity. In his place came William Rathbone, Liberal member for Caernarfonshire in 1880 and for the northern division of Arfon after 1885. Rathbone's roots were in Liverpool and his experience as one of the principal progenitors of that city's University College was of the utmost value to the College at Bangor. He was 'in a special degree'[44] its founder, Reichel believed, and he had a share, too, in the foundation of the University of Wales. He retained to the end a warm, unabated attachment to the quarrymen and small farmers of north-west Wales. He was succeeded in 1900 by Lloyd Tyrell-Kenyon, fourth Baron Kenyon of Gredington, Shropshire, Vice-President since 1897. It would be hard to point to any peer in north Wales (Rendel alone excepted) who had a keener sense of the importance of higher education in Wales.

The College's first Principal, Harry Rudolf Reichel, the son of an Anglican who successively became professor at Queen's Belfast and Bishop of Meath, had at Balliol taken four firsts, excelling the performance, Benjamin Jowett thought, of any living person. Jowett added that he was energetic, that he was 'quite a gentleman' and that he had 'good sense',[45] a quality which did not always accompany outstanding educational achievements.

The fact that he was unusually reserved was not mentioned and it may at first sight seem strange that when many conventional avenues of advancement lay open to him he should have sought the principalship of an infant college in a land of which he was almost entirely ignorant and of whose language he knew nothing. He was certainly influenced by his Oxford friend, Viriamu Jones, and he had a high sense of public duty. In an obituary tribute to Kenyon in 1927 he employed the motto of Toc H: 'Service is the rent which we pay for the room we occupy in the world.'[46] It was the light which guided his own steps.

The College's first Registrar, W. Cadwaladr Davies, though deprived of the early educational advantages of his colleagues, was admirably qualified to discharge the duties of his challenging office. He spoke fearlessly to Churchmen and Nonconformists, and earned the qualified applause of even T. Marchant Williams, who declared that he was 'in all *essential* respects an ideal registrar'.[47] Called to the bar, he resigned in 1892 and was followed by John Edward Lloyd, the son of a Liverpool draper. Lloyd's parents, he tells us, made it a point of honour to bring him up to speak Welsh.[48] A member of a remarkable band of early students at Aberystwyth, he thereafter proceeded to Oxford where he distinguished himself in classics and in the growing School of Modern History. For seven years he had taught at Aberystwyth, as we have seen, before beginning his life's work at Bangor. Primarily remembered as a scholar, his period as Registrar from 1892 to 1920 prompted Bangor's second Principal to say that 'if Reichel was the captain, Lloyd was the pilot, steering with steady hand and clear purpose'.[49]

Such qualities were much called upon when Lloyd arrived, at the age of thirty-one, to face a nasty squall. The affair of the women's hall has already been adequately treated elsewhere, but it is necessary to draw attention to the main elements.[50] The Lady Principal of the hall, her very title indicative of a rival authority, had acted in an unduly authoritarian fashion towards a woman student, and a Professor of Philosophy was alleged to have made tentative advances to two women students. In tranquil circumstances the College need not have been exposed to high drama, but at a time when the education of women was still at a sensitive stage there were perils ahead, further fuelled by religious and political divisions during the election year of 1892. The lower press, ever attentive to the possibilities of scandal, magnified the issue beyond reason; there was vigorous correspondence in *The Times* and elsewhere; the participants included Hugh Price Hughes, champion of the 'Nonconformist Conscience' and also of his own sister, the Lady Principal, and educationists such as Frances Buss and Sophie Bryant; there was a libel case at Chester Assizes, and the dispute was brought to the floor of both Houses of Parliament when the charter of the University was being considered. At one point all the College professors were on the verge of resigning and such prominent men as the Duke of Westminster and Lord Penrhyn severed their association with the governing body of the College. If we are to judge from the volume of newspaper cuttings regularly kept by the College, this baleful episode consumed the energies of its chief officers during the lengthy period when the charter of the University was being subjected to widespread discussion and debate. It may be that cautious men thereafter became even more cautious, but on the whole the loss of members of Court and Council not deeply committed to the welfare of the College was richly compensated by the presence of new members more truly representative of the community which the College was established to serve.

The problem of accommodation was becoming annually more acute. Upon their foundation, colleges could scarcely expect to occupy buildings raised for the purpose. Aberystwyth, as we have seen, had been fortunate enough to secure a substantial hotel; Cardiff began life in an old infirmary, the Yorkshire College of Science (later Leeds) in a disused bankruptcy court, Liverpool and Leicester in a lunatic asylum. In any case, the oft-proclaimed priority was to attract the best staff; buildings would follow in due course. Bangor's first home was in the Penrhyn Arms, an old coaching house, designed by Benjamin Wyatt at the end of the eighteenth century. Outside Bangor on the coach road to Holyhead, it derived its name from the powerful family which dominated the area. The arrival of the railway in mid-century deprived the Penrhyn Arms of most of its clientele and the first baron was ready enough to lease it to the College at a rent of £200 per annum, half the yearly sum paid by Cardiff for the Old Infirmary. The site overlooking Beaumaris Bay excited much admiration and contemporary prints display attractive gardens reaching down to the water's edge. Staff and students who occupied the building always spoke of it with affection. By the end of the century it was evident that further structural changes and extensions could not realistically be contemplated and the search began in earnest for the best site upon which to raise a new college. By common consent the crown of the Aethwy Ridge overlooking parkland and the cathedral was pre-eminently suitable. Other towns in north Wales were ready to make gifts of land but there was no sign that the second Baron Penrhyn, the owner of the Penrallt estate, was inclined to act generously towards the College. It was in 1902 that the city of Bangor, in a spirit of enlightened self-interest, determined to buy Penrallt from Lord Penrhyn and six acres of the Bishop's Park, in all ten acres, and to present them to the College. The cost to the corporation of Bangor was £15,000, equal to a levy of 30s. per head of the population.[51]

An assiduous canvass for funds followed, akin to the earlier campaign in the 1880s. The government gave £20,000 and the subscription list amounted to nearly £63,000 (though there were defaulters, including Edward VII). In 1907 the foundation stone was laid by Edward VII, Harry Reichel was knighted and below Penrallt 1,200 children formed a living Union Jack. It was an imperial occasion. So also was the opening of the College in 1911 by George V in the presence of a large assembly of notables. The fleet in the Straits fired salutes and there were enthusiastic demonstrations of loyalty. The total cost of the building was £106,000.[52]

The quest for the best architect had been conducted with great care. The choice fell upon Henry Thomas Hare (1861–1921). A native of Scarborough, he had studied at Paris before establishing his practice in London. From 1917 to 1919 he was President of the Royal Institute of British Architects where his portrait may now be seen. Hare, influential in the planning of public libraries, moved easily from one style to another. His Stafford County Buildings (1892–5) have been described as free Baroque, the Oxford Town Hall (1892–7) as Jacobean, the Westminster College (1899–1902) as pure Elizabethan and the College at Bangor as monumental Free Style. He was much influenced by T. G. Jackson, who initiated a free Jacobean style in university buildings at Oxford, especially his massive University Examination Schools in the High Street and the Jacobean front quadrangle buildings of Trinity College.

Hare's original plans were not adopted. All the competitors had planned a building to be placed upon a level site after costly excavation. Not one had taken full advantage of the lie of the land. It was Isambard Owen who, in a committee, suggested an alternative. Reichel recalled the occasion:

> 'The kind of thing I had in mind', he remarked, 'was something like this', sketching rapidly a smaller quadrangle, with several stories [*sic*] in front, the number of which diminished as the ground sloped towards the back, and with a somewhat withdrawn extension to the right (looking across the valley). We all felt that he had probably hit on the true solution, and the . . . architect . . . was at once struck with the idea, and, frankly adapting it in preference to his own, worked out the plans of the beautiful building which now crowns the Upper Bangor ridge.[53]

The original intention had been to include certain science departments upon the Penrallt site, whilst others would be on the level land. Thus, there would be ample provision for 'the ultimate College of 640 to 700 students'.[54] However, owing to shortage of money, the main quadrangle was not completed until well after the Second World War, and then in a manner (particularly the library extension) which would scarcely have pleased Hare and his clients. It was only at an advanced stage that it was possible to include the main hall, an essential element in the corporate life of the College. His hope was that a wealthy man would associate his name in perpetuity with such a laudable enterprise. There were good precedents. At Aberdeen there was the Mitchell Hall, at Glasgow (always much in the minds of Bangor men), the Bute Hall, at Edinburgh, the McEwan Hall, and at Manchester, the Whitworth Hall, all of which had brought added dignity to their institutions. At Bangor, the initiative of Herbert Lewis and of Lloyd George was decisive, for they were able to prevail upon one of the princes of Regent Street, (Sir) John Prichard-Jones, to shoulder the entire cost of the hall which bears his name, to the tune of £17,000.

As to the style of the building, there have been varied attributions. Hare himself thought that 'technical terms are apt to have very vague impressions', but it seems that he had in mind a time 'when our forefathers were fighting for their liberties',[55] probably the struggle against Spain in the late sixteenth century and for the rights of Parliament in the seventeenth century. We may not be far astray if we describe the style as Jacobethan, the blend of the Elizabethan and the Jacobean. The only other plan in Hare's portfolio was that of Jesus College, founded in 1571. In 1906 he said that his design was greatly influenced by the colleges at Oxford and Cambridge, 'our typical national collegiate style'.[56] His aim, we may be certain, was to link the College architecturally with the older universities, where learning had been transmitted from generation to generation.

Hare evidently took account of the cathedral below and of the castles in the vicinity, which encouraged him to indulge his partiality for towers. Indeed his plan for the National Museum of Wales was probably rejected because his proposed tower would have competed with nearby buildings to the discomfiture of the city fathers. At Bangor, the tower, with its gently tapering sides, gave a sense of dignity to the whole, especially in relation to the 'wonderful outline of firm, horizontal lines'.[57] The tower is perhaps best viewed not from the main quadrangle but upon entry into Bangor, near the site of the old College. Partly to avoid expense and partly to avoid monotony, he chose sandstone from Cefn, near Ruabon. Delicately varied in hue – some stones were tinged with orange – the College in its early years, when the sun was bright, bore the aspect of warm cane. Hare also steadfastly refused to use the blue Caernarfonshire slate, which, in disagreeable conjunction with the red brick of Ruabon, had travelled far and wide. Instead, and in the teeth of local protest, he chose Pembrokeshire slates of mixed, broken colours, in pleasing harmony with the sandstone from Cefn. Probably the most attractive building is the upper (Shankland) library, given to the College at a cost of £15,000 by the Drapers' Company, with its barrel ceiling of plaster and its wainscot ribs. The most ornate is the Council Chamber where Hare was apparently not restrained by financial considerations.

It must be conceded that Hare was not uniformly successful. Acoustics in the Prichard-Jones Hall were for long unsatisfactory, so that one aged well-wisher of the College remarked wryly that the hall would do excellently well for banquets or as 'the nave of a cathedral where people did not preach to be heard'.[58] His choice, too, of sandstone, admirable on aesthetic grounds, has been severely questioned, for it has weathered badly in those portions exposed to the buffeting of the rain-bearing south-westerly winds. Nevertheless, Hare's work at Bangor has been widely applauded. C. S. Lewis spoke of 'the strange and beautiful hillside College at Bangor', and John Betjeman of Hare as one 'whose detailing was always admirable, whose plans were practical and clear, and whose sense of perfection never failed him'. Alastair Service, an authority on Edwardian architecture, speaks of the College as a major building of the time, a splendid example of its kind, especially in its disposition of 'large, simple, but broken masses'. In an obituary by one who knew him well, it was said that the College was Hare's finest achievement and the one which Hare valued the most highly: 'the future will assign him an important place in the history of his time'.[59]

The trials of teaching mathematics to matriculation students was an understandable strain upon successive heads of department. The first professor, G. Ballard Mathews, retreated to Cambridge in 1896 but returned to Bangor in 1911 having been elected a Fellow of the Royal Society for his contributions to the higher arithmetic. A man of broad scholarship it was wholly fitting that the Ballard Mathews Lectures at the College should treat both arts and science subjects. George Hartley Bryan, who became professor in 1896, was a brilliant eccentric whom Reichel regarded as one of his mistakes. It is true that he was wayward, causing unpredictable turbulence, and that it was difficult for a small college to accommodate a thoroughly incompetent teacher, at elementary levels at least. In the upper realms of mathematics, however, he often soared alone above his fellows. He received the gold medal of the Institute of Naval Architects in 1901 and of the Royal Aeronautical Society in 1915; he was a Fellow of the Royal Society and President of the Mathematical Association. In 1903 he informed the College Council that his discoveries held the clue to the problem of artificial flight; his paper to the Royal Society, jointly with William Ellis Williams, was described in *Nature* in 1928 as 'epoch-making'.[60] After the establishment of aeronautics at the National Physical Laboratory, his theory of stability became a fundamental part of aeroplane design. In the *Proceedings of the Royal Society* it was said that his 'maturity . . . coincided with the birth of aviation and provided an opportunity for the exercise of his mathematical genius'.[61]

The practical aspect of flight was explored by William Ellis Williams, joint author of the paper in 1903 and later Professor of Electrical Engineering at the College. In the summer of 1911 he achieved short flights above the sands near Llanddona, Anglesey, in a plane constructed by himself to his own specifications and upon which he reported to professional journals, particularly the *Aeronautical Journal* in October 1914. Earlier his advice had been sought concerning Blériot's views upon the staying of overhead wires on monoplanes.[62] An outstanding product of the department of mathematics, Robert Jones, was the first student in the University to qualify for a higher degree in aerodynamics (in 1913). He and D. H. Williams, a fellow student, later had a major role in the commission of inquiry into the loss of the ill-fated dirigible, R101.

The department of physics had prospered under Andrew Gray, 'a solid Roman pillar of the state',[63] as Reichel called him. In 1896 he was elected a Fellow of the Royal Society and in 1899 he received an irresistible invitation to succeed his old chief, Lord Kelvin, in the chair of natural philosophy at Glasgow. At Bangor he had collaborated with Ballard Mathews to produce *A Treatise on Bessell Functions* (1895) and his *Gyrostatics and Rotational Movement* (1919) was described as 'the fullest treatment of the subject in any language'.[64] He was followed at Bangor by one of the College's own students, Edward Taylor Jones, a beneficiary of the old North Wales Scholarship Association, who later succeeded him at Glasgow.

James Johnston Dobbie, educated at Glasgow, Edinburgh and Leipzig, was the College's first Professor of Chemistry. The true creator of the department of agriculture, as we shall see, he was able during the last twelve years of his period at Bangor to devote most of his energies to investigating the structural and stereo-chemical relationships of alkaloids, which led in 1904 to his election to a Fellowship of the Royal Society. In 1911 he became government chemist and was knighted in 1915. He was in

academic terms one of the founding fathers of the College. In his
stead came K. J. Previté Orton, who, at Heidelberg in 1896, was
the first Englishman to be placed in the highest class of the Ph.D.
For the great work of his life, conducted at Bangor, on the
halogen components of aniline, he was elected a Fellow of the
Royal Society. He also had a passion for geology, music and bird
life, especially the hawk tribe. It is unusual for a lecture to be
endowed to celebrate a professor's extra-mural pursuits, but such
is the case with the Kennedy Orton Lectures, delivered biennially
by a prominent naturalist.

The opportunities for the head of the department of zoology to
pursue research were exceedingly limited. P. J. White, appointed
in 1895, was obliged to devote twenty-four lectures a week to the
intermediate class alone. Nevertheless, he built up a more than
serviceable museum. His zest for bones bordered upon the
rapacious, and after his death, to avoid the charge of sacrilege,
R. Alun Roberts was asked by the College Registrar to return a
cranium, perhaps that of St Seiriol himself, to Ynys Seiriol; he
long remembered rowing by moonlight to perform this pious act.
White's laudable ambition to establish a marine station was not
fulfilled for several decades. R. W. Phillips, Professor of Botany,
was caught up in the toils of administration, a decision firmly
defended by Reichel on the ground that the times were critical,
'while Botanical research is always going on'.[65]

The energy and initiative of J. J. Dobbie had ensured that the
College received a government grant in 1888 to further
agricultural education and dairy farming. It was the largest sum
received for the purpose by any institution. The new generation of
farmers, he believed, should be persuaded to attend courses at
universities, but he urged, in a letter published in Welsh and
English newspapers, that it was necessary to carry education to the
very doors of those actively engaged in agricultural work by
establishing classes 'in every considerable market town'.[66] Mindful
of German and French precedents, he was so successful in
promoting extension classes, especially in dairying, that by 1891
the Board of Agriculture reported that the College had organized a
complete system of agricultural education which might profitably
be extended throughout the kingdom. The Bangor model was in its
main features adopted by Aberystwyth, Leeds, Durham, Newcastle

and Nottingham. Dobbie's lead was faithfully followed by Thomas Winter, appointed to the new chair of agriculture in 1895. The department evidently enjoyed the confidence of the Board of Agriculture, the original grant being soon augmented to £1,200, together with a further grant for the college farm, which at length found a lasting home at Aber, near Bangor. The government's decision in 1911 to provide technical advice of a high order to the farming community enabled the College to appoint two advisers, G. W. Robinson in agricultural chemistry and J. Lloyd Williams in botany. The one became professor at Bangor, the other at Aberystwyth. A natural development at an earlier stage had been to encourage the teaching of forestry in north Wales, and Bangor was one of two institutions selected by the Board of Agriculture to provide instruction. Under Fraser Story, lecturer in 1904 and professor in 1910, the department of forestry prospered.

In the Faculty of Arts, W. Rhys Roberts, formerly a fellow of King's College, Cambridge, had been in charge of Greek since 1884. In 1900 he urged influential College governors to ensure that every child of literary promise in an intermediate school had the opportunity to learn Greek. In 1904, when he left for Leeds (where he helped to found an Honours School of Classics), he remarked, somewhat optimistically, that 'the University of Wales is destined to do much to quicken the love and further the study of Greek literature'.[67] He was an authority on Greek literary criticism and it was said of him that 'to know him was a liberal education'.[68] His successor, Thomas Hudson-Williams, was one of the small band of British scholars who made a name for themselves in classical studies without having attended Oxford or Cambridge. Educated at Friars School, Bangor, and at the University College, he took the old London degree. Appointed to the staff of the College he soon showed a mastery of many languages. Apart from contributions to his own discipline, such as *Elegies of Theognis* (1910) and *Early Greek Elegy* (1926), he had lectured in French and German and in the course of a long life he published an Irish text in a German journal, a history of Polish literature, a grammar of Old Persian, Welsh translations of Russian plays and novels, as well as original works in Welsh, amongst them *Y Groegiaid Gynt* (1932). E. V. Arnold was Professor of Latin for forty years. His principal study was *Roman*

Stoicism (1911), by no means confined to stoicism at Rome. Students remembered him mainly for his elementary Latin textbooks, particularly *Forum Latinum* (1898), which earned him the nickname 'Forum'. Something of a gadfly, he was a formidable debater on issues large and small.

H. R. Reichel was from the first in charge of English language, literature and history. In 1894 he relinquished the headship of the department of English. His successor, W. Lewis Jones, had won an open scholarship at Queens' College, Cambridge, from Friars School, Bangor. For a time a journalist in the United States, he contributed regularly after his return to the *Manchester Guardian*, bringing University and College matters to the attention of a wide public. In collaboration with W. Cadwaladr Davies he produced the first history of the University of Wales in 1905. As a scholar his principal contribution was to the study of the Arthurian Legend. Reichel remained head of the department of history until 1899 when John Edward Lloyd became professor. Lloyd had already, at his own request, lectured on the history of Wales, to which he now gave increasing attention although he continued as Registrar. In 1911 there appeared *A History of Wales from the Earliest Times to the Edwardian Conquest* in two volumes. Such sober history was not to everyone's taste, for some found it disconcerting to have a scalpel applied to hallowed legends which had sustained their countrymen for centuries. Archaeological investigation has naturally transformed the earliest portions of the book, but the main body, the framework of 'political' history, has weathered the scrutiny of over nine decades and is a landmark in Welsh historical writing. Probably the last substantial work to be written in Wales in 'the grand manner', its measured periods cannot disguise the love of country, most evident in the concluding section upon the death of Llywelyn ap Gruffydd in 1282. To Saunders Lewis, J. E. Lloyd was 'the lantern-bearer of lost centuries'[69] ('llusernwr y canrifoedd coll').

(Sir) John Morris-Jones became head of the minuscule department of Welsh in 1889.[70] Born in 1864, he was educated at Friars School, Bangor, Christ's College, Brecon, and Jesus College, Oxford. Although he had graduated in mathematics, his explorations in the Bodleian Library stirred in him a passion for Celtic studies. His early years at Bangor were depressing until emancipation from the London system enabled Welsh to be included amongst subjects examinable for the degree of the University of Wales. In 1894 he was appointed professor and although Bangor was the smallest of the three colleges, the number taking Welsh in 1907 (as reported to the Raleigh Committee) was 108, compared with 55 at Aberystwyth and 48 at Cardiff. His major scholarly work, *A Welsh Grammar, Historical and Comparative* (1913) may at first have surprised the uninitiated, for symbols were so widely distributed that some wondered whether the mathematician was in the ascendant. His etymological explanations have not always found favour, but the main part, on descriptive grammar, remains a masterpiece. To describe the language as it once was and to demonstrate its development is a task of great complexity. Before Morris-Jones there had only been two grammarians of the front rank, Gruffudd Robert, the Catholic exile, who published a Welsh grammar in two parts in the sixteenth century, and Dr John Davies of Mallwyd, Meirionnydd, who published his Welsh grammar in Latin in 1621. Morris-Jones excels them both. Again, in his translations and in his own poetry, he stressed purity of diction. As scholar and critic he dominated the scene. The ablest of his pupils at Bangor was unquestionably his successor (Sir) Ifor Williams, already engaged in 1906 upon a study of *Y Gododdin*, the poems attributed to Aneirin, the sixth-century poet, the core of his life's work.[71]

When Frederick Spencer vacated the chair of modern languages in 1903 it was resolved to create two departments. O. H. Fynes-Clinton, a former Taylorian scholar in Spanish at Oxford and an outstanding linguist, became Professor of French and of Romance Languages. The creation of a separate department of German and Teutonic philology (though without a chair until 1909) was a recognition by the College of German 'as the language of the most powerful and, in some respects, most progressive European nation'.[72] Very few students studied German, or were likely to do so, until the Welsh colleges trained teachers of German for the new intermediate schools. By 1912, however, the number of students taking German almost equalled those taking French, to the considerable credit of the College's first professor, E. Milner-Barry, who, like the pursuit of German itself at the College, fell victim to the Great War.

Following Bangor's lead, the framers of the University charter had agreed that theology, initially excluded from the curriculum of the colleges by their charters, should be formally recognized so that the degree of BD could be pursued as a postgraduate study at one of the 'associated' theological colleges, at Bangor the Bala-Bangor and Baptist Colleges. In furtherance of this aim some subjects studied for the BD were to be taught by the staff of the University College, thus relieving the theological colleges of the responsibility for branches of study which they were normally not well equipped to provide. In this way the Bangor Joint School of Theology came into being. Central to the success of the school was Thomas Witton Davies, appointed tutor in Hebrew at the Baptist College in 1898 and first head of the department of Semitics at the University College in 1899. Born in Monmouthshire, the son of largely illiterate parents, he had struggled hard in order to be educated in London and Germany. He had mastered Hebrew, Arabic (which more than any other Eastern language, he believed, had a value of its own), Assyrian and Syriac. He was a doctor of Jena and Leipzig universities and received honorary doctorates at Geneva and Durham.

When the chair of philosophy fell vacant upon the departure of Henry Jones for Glasgow in 1891, a somewhat unsavoury election led to the appointment of E. Keri Evans. Circumstances conspired against a long stay and his duties were for a time performed by a young Scot, (Sir) Robert Horne, Chancellor of the Exchequer in 1920. Keri Evans was succeeded by James Gibson, a reserved Ulsterman of great integrity, who had been fellow of St John's College, Cambridge. His volume on *Locke's Theory of Knowledge and its Historical Relations* (1917) was described in *Mind* by A. E. Lindsay as 'a rare contribution to the stock of historical studies of eminent philosophers which may fairly be called classics'.[73] It is thus a misfortune that he did not publish more.

Bangor did not establish a Day Training Department until 1894, the delay probably caused by the hall of residence controversy. The number of students rose from 152 in 1893 to 278 in 1897, of whom 100 were Day Training Students. The first head of department was John Alfred Green, educated at Firth College, Sheffield, and at the Borough Road Training College, the best training college in the land. He dealt sternly with undisciplined 'Normal' students in his 'model' lessons, but he could coax into speech a shy, inarticulate child with a skill far removed from the crude catechetical tyranny of the ordinary classroom. His *Educational Ideas of Pestalozzi* (1904) and his editorship of the *Journal of Experimental Pedagogy* were a stimulus to the growth of educational science and of educational psychology. In his stead came Richard Lawrence Archer who had taken two firsts at Oxford and had been on the staff of the Cambridge University Day Training College. 'Daddy' Archer, as he was popularly known, was Professor of Education at Bangor for thirty-eight years. It was of inestimable advantage to the College that Thomas Shankland, in charge of the Welsh Library, was acquiring important collections, including a peerless array of Welsh ballads, at a time when it was possible to discover rarities in farmhouse lofts, local auctions and in the open bookcases in the Charing Cross Road. This he did before and after the founding of the National Library of Wales (1907), with whose librarian he was on excellent terms, thus avoiding unseemly competition. Although the College had been fortunate to receive a handsome legacy of £47,000 in 1890 from Evan Thomas of Manchester, it had an accumulated deficit on the general fund of £5,000 in 1907, and despite the adoption of the Raleigh Committee's recommendations it was still difficult in 1914 to balance accounts, in part because of a decline in full-time student numbers to 296, of whom a third were women. If full-time and part-time students are taken into account, Bangor had in 1913 a more favourable staff–student ratio than the other colleges, 1:6, as opposed to 1:8 at Cardiff and 1:10 at Aberystwyth.[74]

Cardiff

Cardiff's first President was Lord Aberdare, who had rendered such service that he was regarded as the 'Commander-in-chief of the Welsh educational Army'.[75] He was followed in 1889 by the third Marquis of Bute, a Roman Catholic, remembered for many munificent benefactions in Cardiff and Scotland; he completed the Bute Docks and rebuilt Cardiff Castle; of scholarly inclinations he was closely associated with the cultural life of Wales.

From 1894 to 1896 Dean C. J. Vaughan was President; formerly headmaster of Harrow and Master of the Temple, he had refused more than one bishopric and was now Dean of Llandaf; Jowett, somewhat generously, considered him to be 'the wisest man I know and the wittiest'.[76] He was succeeded by the first Viscount Tredegar, who rode in the Light Brigade in the Crimea and had been Conservative Member of Parliament for Brecon; his benefaction helped the College to acquire 'the island site', bounded by Newport Road (the main entrance), West Grove, the Parade, and the old Rhymney Railway. His successor in 1901 has been described as 'the staunchest supporter of the college since before its foundation'.[77] He was Sir Alfred Thomas, created first Lord Pontypridd in 1912. Son of a Cardiff contractor, he spent a lifetime in the business and he knew Cardiff intimately well. From 1895 to 1910 he represented East Glamorgan as Member of Parliament and he was chairman of the Welsh Parliamentary Liberal Party. He was followed in office by the first Earl of Plymouth, a wealthy landowner and lord lieutenant of Glamorgan for thirty-three years. The last to hold office before the First World War was the coal magnate Sir William Thomas Lewis, raised to the peerage as Lord Merthyr in 1911. By 1890 he had control of pits later known as Lewis Merthyr and it was upon his early initiative that the South Wales and Monmouthshire Coalowners' Association was formed to combat trade unionism and strikes.

Cardiff's first Principal was chosen from amongst thirty applicants. The College and later the University could not have been more fortunate. Born at Pentre-poeth, near Morriston, in 1856, Viriamu Jones lived from 1859 to 1870 in the modern Babylon, as he relates,[78] his father holding Congregationalist pastorates at Regent's Park and later at Camden Town, where one of the worshippers was Robert Browning, a close family friend. Thereafter at Swansea he prepared himself for an illustrious career at University College, London, by coming first out of 500 in the matriculation examination. Distinctions and honours came easily to him both at London and at Balliol, particularly in the natural sciences. At twenty-five he was Principal of Firth's College, Sheffield, and in 1893 patriotic zeal spurred him to seek the Cardiff principalship and, associated with it, the professorship of physics. He greatly welcomed the opportunity to promote scientific and technical knowledge in an area now increasingly industrialized. Only ten years earlier James Clerk Maxwell had published his *Electricity and Magnetism* which, according to Einstein, 'changed the axiomatic basis of scientific thought'.[79] Viriamu, however, was more intrigued by the practical application of Maxwell's discoveries, notably electrical engineering. Whilst principal he seized every opportunity to continue his own research, but his main energies were directed to the broad educational needs of his countrymen. Born and bred a Nonconformist, he fully understood the disabilities under which they had suffered and was appalled that true merit had been neglected throughout the centuries. He had, moreover, at Oxford associated with men who rebelled against a laissez-faire liberalism and a view of life at once utilitarian and pseudo-scientific. T. H. Green, the first layman to be a fellow of an Oxford college, was a deeply formative influence. Green's intense preoccupation with social questions attracted many of the ablest undergraduates, Arnold Toynbee, Asquith and Milner amongst them. The noble concept of responsible citizenship within a full democracy appealed to Viriamu, heart and mind. Thus it is not surprising that he was an unequivocal, unswerving advocate of the equality of women, of extension lectures and of university settlements to bridge the gulf between the educated and uneducated. It is certain, too, that he helped to influence the social attitudes of his Balliol friend, the conservative-minded H. R. Reichel, to whom the headship of the Bangor College was also a high calling.

It seems probable that Viriamu accepted most of the cardinal principles of the Christian religion, but whispering tongues, as in the case of Henry Jones, hinted at unorthodoxy, suspicions reinforced by Viriamu's Sunday visits to the laboratory. He remained on the best of terms with men of varying religious convictions. He may have known more Welsh than any other Cardiff Principal, but his wife thought it unlikely that he had ever held a conversation in Welsh. That certainly could not be said of Reichel, however arduous the process of communicating. Viriamu possessed unusual charm. To Reichel he was an enchanter who held others in thrall. Only those who had fallen under his spell could fully comprehend his compelling power to enliven, to persuade and to inspire. Reichel considered that he had 'one of the most versatile minds I have ever come across, and, along with this, a real streak of genius'.[80] All saw in him a tough, formidable fighter who believed that social justice was to be achieved through education. The Education Act of 1870, he announced in 1881, in a somewhat rhetorical effusion, assured that 'no child in all the land is left without the key with which, if he wish, he may unlock the portal of the treasure house of human thought, and take possession of a rich reward'.[81] The older universities were trembling with new life for 'they have been dipped in the cauldron of Medea and are young again',[82] and infant institutions, such as the Firth and Cardiff Colleges, were springing up throughout the land. It was not an age of peace, nor of faith, but of education. Under his guidance scientific and technical studies were unlikely to suffer, but he also intervened at an early stage to amend the proposed, stereotyped syllabus of the University's Faculty of Arts to allow teacher and student as much freedom as possible to devise schemes of study. He was the main driving force in the creation of the University. Where many counselled caution in a land destitute of intermediate schools, he could not abide delay. Isambard Owen, more than anyone else the architect of the University charter, believed that the demand for the charter in the 1880s was a 'hardy proposition to put seriously forward – one that needed rare confidence and courage to advocate'.[83] He added that Viriamu's hardiness was the 'hardiness of genius'. It was no small achievement to enlist by 1887 the wholehearted support of his fellow Principals, the officers, governors and staff of his own College and the townspeople of Cardiff. During the process of fashioning the charter for presentation to the government, Viriamu had the most challenging task of all, that of persuading the industrial areas of south-east Wales that they should not stand aloof but should cast their lot with the rural areas to found a national, federal university. Isambard's considered opinion many years later was that no other person could have performed this task so well. 'The unity of Wales', he believed, 'was really at stake.'[84] In 1901 Viriamu Jones was overwhelmed by a mysterious disease which defeated the skills of Swiss doctors. He was forty-five. There was widespread grief and tributes flowed from high and low. Nearly a century later he remains the foremost educationist Wales has produced.

Isambard Owen, by general consent, was first approached to succeed Viriamu, but he declined. Out of thirty-two applicants, Edward Howard Griffiths,[85] a physicist, was chosen. Born in 1851, he was the son of Henry Griffiths, tutor at Brecon Independent College. His mother traced her ancestry to the Cromwellian Admiral Robert Blake and E. H. Griffiths himself did not entirely eschew the quarterdeck manner. He was educated at Owens College, Manchester, and Sidney Sussex College, Cambridge, of which he was fellow. From the proceeds of his large coaching fees he built a laboratory in his own grounds. He and a colleague, H. L. Callendar, determined the boiling point of sulphur (correcting Regnault's value as being 4 degrees too high) and converted the crude resistance boxes of the day into instruments of precision. Griffiths later submitted the fruit of one of his other investigations, on the latent heat of evaporation of water, which he considered his best work, for the degree of D.Sc. of the University of Wales. He was elected a Fellow of the Royal Society in 1905 and, shortly after he came to Cardiff, Lord Kelvin paid public tribute to his experiments which were 'of the highest and most searching accuracy in developing the techniques of high-temperature measurements'.[86]

Before long Griffiths was tackling with gusto the manifold financial problems of the College, concluding, for instance, that zoology was the most expensive department and history, not unexpectedly, the cheapest. Such statistics, however, bordering at the time upon the arcane, availed him nothing for several years, indeed not until the Raleigh Committee began its work in 1907. Soon after arrival he was drawing blood on a wide front. The Welsh, he said, worshipped mediocrity, caused in part by the multiplicity of eisteddfodau; the Central Welsh Board was too reliant upon examinations; manufacturers and employers of labour in Wales had not learnt, as their counterparts in America had, that prosperity and education went hand in hand; only four Welshmen were Fellows of the Royal Society, and, finally, his own father had been hounded out of Wales for advocating state aid for education.[87] Candid observers would have conceded that there was truth in most of these assertions, but whether Griffiths was wise to trumpet them vigorously was another matter. Ahead lay many challenges, mainly the planning and erection of the new building, the need to establish a School of Mining and to develop the Medical School. These most laudable aims he always expounded with force and clarity. (Sir) Percy Watkins believed that his long period in the inner circles at Cambridge – he was fifty when appointed – had not prepared him well for the leadership of a democratic institution in Wales. We gather that he was no democrat, that he kept students at arm's length and that he did not suffer fools gladly. Lloyd George did not care for him, nor did his fellow Principals, and it is evident, on good authority, that for some time he lacked the respect and support of the College Council. He had few relaxations, apart from playing billiards on Saturday nights 'for money',[88] as Thomas Jones tells us. His inability to enlist the anticipated aid of south Wales industrialists was acutely frustrating, but where Viriamu had failed, Griffiths was unlikely to succeed. Nevertheless, not every Principal has received the plaudits of his Registrar, and we may fittingly quote the words of Percy Watkins, who said of him that 'he brought to his task a great ability, a fearless regard for truth, and distinct independence of judgement'.[89]

The College's first Registrar was Ivor James who had acted as joint secretary of the conference which had prepared the University charter. As has been noted elsewhere, the College was indebted to him for his exertions in acquiring the Salisbury Library in 1886. Later, we are told, he 'attained some notoriety as a minor literary forger'[90] when he invaded Coleridge studies. Austin Jenkins, the second Registrar, did not enjoy good relations with E. H. Griffiths, who much welcomed the appointment in his stead of Percy Watkins. It was an excellent choice. Watkins did not last long, but he had sufficient knowledge of his chief clerk, D. J. A. Brown, to rejoice that he was to succeed him. Brown served from 1911 to 1936, 'leaving behind', Watkins tells us, 'a most fragrant memory among all who knew him, as well as a record of quiet, effective and wise service of which any man might well be proud'.[91]

The major undertaking during this period was the building of the new College. The need was great. Temporary premises in Newport Road and around the Old Infirmary, the College's first home, were hopelessly inadequate and the cramping conditions could no longer be borne. In 1893 a magnificent opportunity presented itself when the Marquis of Bute offered to sell to the Cardiff Corporation thirty-eight of the fifty-nine acres of Cathays Park for £120,000, provided they were used for municipal and public buildings and for a pleasure park. In response to the Corporation's invitation to state its needs, the College Council at once indicated that it wished four to six acres to be reserved for a new College building. During 1895–6 the Corporation and Lord Bute each agreed to pay the £10,000 they had hitherto promised; the Drapers' Company offered a similar sum; the Treasury made a grant of £20,000 conditional upon raising the same amount locally, and a public appeal was launched. In October 1900, only seven months before his death, the ailing Viriamu Jones successfully appealed to the Corporation of Cardiff to make a free gift to the College of five acres of the Park. His speech, happily preserved, is justly regarded as a masterpiece of eloquence.[92]

Thus it was that, twenty years after the founding of the College and after public competition, four architects were invited to prepare plans for the new buildings, amongst them John Belcher and Basil Champneys. The successful contestant was William Douglas Caröe,[93] son of the Danish consul at Liverpool. Educated at Ruabon Grammar School and Trinity College, Cambridge, he had a wide practice and was consultant architect to both Canterbury and Durham cathedrals. In order to tackle this 'austere and intricate'[94] problem, he betook himself to the Lake District, where, favoured by incessant rain, he completed his plans in a fortnight. Although the architecture of the older universities which Caröe loved was not wholly suitable for a modern non-residential institution devoted in large measure to technical instruction, nevertheless, since arts studies had a prominent place in the University of Wales, 'some attempted flavour of the later Oxford and Cambridge scholarly manner was not to be gainsaid. The problem was to secure stateliness without the formality of the somewhat stereotyped Town Hall style, some element of the picturesque without the domesticity of the ancient college building.'[95] Caröe regarded it as a 'precious privilege'[96] to design a building in Cathays Park.

The externals of the building were to conform with the civic buildings in Cathays Park. Thus, all frontages were to be faced in Portland stone. Further, the height of the plinths and cornices was to be in accord with those of the city hall. After acceptance of his application, Caröe insisted that the main cornice be raised because he believed the city hall to be too squat, as if it had 'sunk its own weight into the ground'[97] and that the prescribed low cornice would diminish the effect of the whole west front. At length, with the aid of the College Principal, with whom he was on friendly terms, he was allowed to raise the cornice over the main entrance, but only here. Otherwise, the long elevation would have been exceedingly monotonous. Not everyone approved of his other devices. (Sir) Percy Thomas regarded the elevations as 'restless';[98] *The Builder* considered the two intermediate pavilions on either side to be 'needless projections'.[99] Jennifer M. Freeman, on the other hand, argues that 'the whole composition reaches a crescendo in the central section where the 3–5–3 rhythm generates an astonishing sense of movement inward to the entrance arcade and upwards to the cupola'.[100] Although Caröe, as we have seen, was anxious to avoid the town hall style, *The Builder* believed that there was rather too much of it in his plan. The most pleasing feature, it added, was the north elevation, with its 'long row of rusticated arched windows below and mullioned windows above'.[101] A detached Great Hall was to have closed the quadrangle on its east side. In length the quadrangle was only a few feet less than that of Trinity College, Cambridge, Caröe's own college; it was appreciably longer than the courts of King's College, Cambridge, or of Tom Quad, Christ Church, Oxford; in width it was much greater than the length of the second and largest court of St John's College, Cambridge. Cardiff's Great Court, with its fountain, was, when completed, to be 'sacred to the collegers themselves'.[102]

   Projecting into the Great Court was the handsome barrel-vaulted library; the gift of the Drapers' Company (as at Bangor), it had echoes of the library of Trinity College, Dublin. One member of staff thought that the Council Chamber, with its handsome coved roof and its wood carving so reminiscent of Grinling Gibbons, relieved the tedium of Academic Board meetings more than any other room employed for the purpose in the whole University.[103] In response to the needs of the age adroit arrangements were made to segregate men and women. As elsewhere, professors were grouped together in private rooms;

there was no privacy for lecturers, granted two common rooms, and individual departments were thus not recognized. In the entrance hall, most appropriately, was placed a striking effigy of Viriamu Jones by W. Goscombe John, born in Canton, Cardiff.

A few of the exuberances in Caröe's original plans were toned down, otherwise there was little change during his lifetime. The £200,000 set aside by the Building Committee was soon seen to be insufficient, especially since all the frontages were to be of Portland stone. The whole building was two feet lower than Caröe wished; the Great Hall to enclose the quadrangle was never built and the University's first Professor of Architecture spoke of a 'bruised Great Court'.[104] The horizontal division of the library by a mezzanine floor has not been universally applauded. Further additions in immediate proximity to the main building have proved injurious. Thus, the north front, much praised by *The Builder*, as we have noted, is so dominated by a tall neighbour as to discourage inspection. Both on the 'ranch site' and in Park Place the piling up of buildings had in the view of Dewi-Prys Thomas (not given to understatement) 'reduced W. D. Caröe's loving handiwork to the status of a frilly petticoat'.[105] He was, of course, speaking in righteous indignation at the failure of public bodies to measure up to their responsibilities as he saw them. Yet, later generations cannot altogether detach themselves from the dilemmas of hard-pressed planners severely restricted by financial and physical considerations. Again, those who contend that the grand buildings in Cathays Park do not reflect the nature of the popular national movement in nineteenth-century Wales cannot elude the hard fact that there was not in Wales a tradition of vernacular collegiate architecture to which Caröe could turn. It was natural that both he and H. T. Hare (at Bangor) should draw much of their inspiration from the colleges of Oxford and Cambridge. There was also the spirit of the age. Indeed, Dewi-Prys Thomas, after animadverting at large upon buildings raised in the late nineteenth century and especially upon the redbrick variety, rejoiced that 'sanity returned to promoters and their architects around 1900, just in time for our Civic Centre'.[106] He described his first visit at eighteen to Cathays Park. Brought up in a sooty northern city, he marvelled when he saw that 'the city of man' could be white. Centuries earlier his ancestors had marvelled at the whitewashed splendour of the Edwardian castles of north Wales. Caröe had created a '*mélange* of effects' and his 'complex orchestration' was carried out with 'astonishing panache'.[107] Caröe, it is true, said that he had prepared a design in the classical manner and that 'a monumental symmetry had been in the main preserved but not slavishly'.[108] A recent interpreter of his work, however, argues that '"Classical" is . . . too broad and too reassuring a description for the highly individualistic and idiosyncratic Mannerist Baroque style which he adapted for the complex'. She adds that he 'drew heavily on 17th-century metropolitan and provincial classicism and laced it with well-honed elements from continental Baroque models, Spanish flourishes, touches of Greek revivalism and Jacobean motifs'.[109] Despite qualifications here and there, the writer in *The Builder* of 1903 confidently predicted that Caröe had planned 'a fine building'.[110] As such, it merits, like Bangor, more than a passing mention in any survey of the University of Wales. Fortunately, both were raised before 1914.

Cardiff's 'New College' was declared open on 14 October 1909 but it is sad to reflect that less than half the £160,000 sought in 1905, when the appeal was launched, had in fact been received. 'In short', wrote S. B. Chrimes, 'New College was built, not indeed on sand, but on a pile of debt (equal to about four times the then annual general income) which was to burden the College finances for many years to come.' In practice the College had no alternative but to build and Chrimes further pertinently remarked that 'it could not in 1905 have reasonably been predicted that such a weak response would be made to its appeal to the local public for aid to the institution which had been inaugurated with such enthusiasm almost a quarter of a century earlier'.[111]

Viriamu Jones had set his heart on the development of technical education in Cardiff and in south Wales. The usual forerunners of technical colleges in Britain were mechanics' institutes. This was not so at Cardiff.[112] Here classes in science and arts were first held in 1866 under the auspices of the town library in St

Mary's Street and thereafter, from 1882, in the Hayes. The Science and Arts Schools were thus securely based before legislation enabled a technical school to be founded in the borough. These were the circumstances. The passage of the Technical Instruction Act of 1889 authorized county and county borough councils to levy a rate for technical education. The Local Government Act in the following year placed 'whisky money'[113] at their disposal and Viriamu saw at once that significant income would now be available for schemes of high importance, namely the teaching of applied and technical science in every large centre of population. In 1890, without ado, he came to terms with the Cardiff Borough's Technical Education Committee to establish a Technical School within the College. Accommodation and teaching, library facilities and the use of scientific apparatus were to be provided by the College in return for an annual sum of £2,500, plus fees and grants, together with a further £2,600 for building, maintenance and salaries. The nineteen courses made available were to include commerce, modern languages and advanced art. These arrangements, extended beyond the initial period of ten years, prospered exceedingly. The counties of Glamorgan and Monmouth participated and it was soon seen that a School of Mines was needed and that metallurgy and agriculture should be actively promoted. Technical classes were established throughout south Wales and Monmouthshire and several towns made frequent requests for lectures. As early as 1894 many classes were held in Cardiff's old proprietary school in Dumfries Place, later the College's students' union. By 1903–4 there were 2,010 students in the Technical School, all attending in the evening. Howard Spring recalled in *Heaven Lies About Us* that early in the century he was a member of one of those classes in the University College, 'a hotch-potch collection of wooden shacks surrounding a building that had once been an hospital'.[114] They were good classes, he thought, many of them conducted by professors who sought to supplement their income. He remembered receiving in the city hall a prize of £3, riches indeed in those days, and collecting sixty volumes of the Everyman Library at a shilling apiece.

If the buildings were a hotch-potch the same could also be said of the administrative arrangements. In 1907, therefore, Sir Philip

Magnus was invited by the Cardiff Corporation to report upon the provision of evening technical instruction in the city.[115] He did not mince matters. No place stood out prominently as the Technical School, there was no proper control or co-ordination and he recommended the adoption of an entirely new scheme. When this was done in 1908 it was urged that the agreement with the College be terminated. Not until 1916 was effect given to the proposal, the College then losing income which it could ill afford. In the mean time the Technical College, as it was now known, was granted a site in Cathays Park. The Technical School which had begun its days within the University College grew after transplantation into a sturdy oak. In 1967 it became the University of Wales Institute of Science and Technology, and in 1988 it entered into partnership by royal charter with the University College as the University of Wales College of Cardiff.

Physics from the outset had been in the hands of Viriamu Jones, though illness later interrupted his work so that the heaviest responsibility lay with A. H. Selby who was made professor in 1898. The most significant research in physics at Cardiff before the Great War was conducted by the College's two first Principals. One of Viriamu's chief concerns was the determination of the ohm by his modifications of an apparatus devised by C. V. Lorenz of Copenhagen. Viriamu and W. E. Ayrton, an eminent electrical engineer and physicist, worked together on the Ayrton–Jones current weigher, as it was called, later presented by the Drapers' Company, which had financed the project, to the National Physical Laboratory as a memorial to Viriamu.[116] When we consider the demands upon his time, it is remarkable that E. H. Griffiths was at all able to pursue research, in his case into the thermal capacities of metals from liquid-air temperatures up to 100 degrees centigrade. It must also be remembered that he presented his personal laboratory to the College, that he gave the minutest attention to the new Viriamu Jones Memorial Research Laboratory, insisting that it should be built entirely of non-magnetic materials, and that he himself, in the absence of laboratory assistants, devoted his leisure hours to equipping the laboratory. Not the least of Griffiths's contributions was the encouragement he gave to Ezer Griffiths, a student of the College, who, having first studied the problem of magnetism, came under the influence of the Principal with whom he began his work on the theory of heat. It was during this period that 'the abnormal specific heat of substances at deep temperature was the most exciting subject in physics'.[117] The fruit of their investigations which tested the theories of Einstein and F. A. Lindemann (later Viscount Cherwell) was published in 1913 and 1914 in the *Transactions of the Royal Society.* Ezer Griffiths, who wrote the piece on E. H. Griffiths in *The Dictionary of National Biography,* became a Fellow of the Royal Society. His most important work was at the other end of the temperature scale, namely refrigeration, upon which he was a world authority.[118]

The Professor of Chemistry, Claude Metford Thompson, held the chair from 1883 to 1921. At London, where he formed a close friendship with Viriamu Jones, and at Cambridge he had a distinguished record. He gave much time to investigating 'rare earths', at first believing they could be used for illumination. He served the College in a variety of ways and when he received an honorary degree of the University in 1930 it was largely for his ungrudging contribution to the cause of university education in Wales. The department of biology included in the first instance zoology and botany. It was presided over by W. N. Parker, for two years an instructor in T. H. Huxley's laboratory. His application for the chair was supported by twelve prominent scientists; in essence he was a vertebrate zoologist. For years the pressure upon him was unrelieved until A. H. Trow was appointed lecturer in botany in 1892, head of a separate department in 1900 and professor in 1905 when it was evident that a far greater number of students were taking botany, increasingly taught in schools, rather than zoology. Trow for many years provided apparatus for essential experimental work out of his own pocket. He remained head of department until he became Principal. The appointment of A. A. Read in 1894 marked the beginning of teaching in metallurgical subjects. The main impetus was the decision of the Dowlais and Iron Steel Company to move to a coastal site and to open at East Moors a large iron and steel works. Theoretical and practical instruction was provided for full-time and part-time students. It seems that the student in 1903 who qualified for the B.Sc. degree of the University of Wales with metallurgy as a Final subject was the first to do so in Great Britain. In 1907 Read was made professor, continuing with his researches into the chemical relations between carbon and iron. In 1914 the School of Mines at Trefforest recognized the College as 'the desirable authority to give the whole of the necessary instruction of all kinds of Mining other than Coal Mining'.[119] For this purpose the coalowners gave £5,726 to erect a building (including a large laboratory) on the Newport Road site to teach certain branches of metallurgy.

In 1886 Viriamu Jones had made a special appeal to the government to establish a medical school in the College and also a department of engineering. The fortunes of the former, to which Viriamu would have given precedence, are considered elsewhere.[120] He certainly believed that the development of engineering 'is an experiment which it is most important in the interests of the country to make'.[121] He did not succeed at this stage, but in 1889 the Drapers' Company offered a gift of £1,000 and an annual grant of £300, subject to certain conditions. By 1890 sufficient funds had been acquired to establish a new department under Professor A. C. Elliott. When the buildings were opened on the Newport Road site by the Master of the Drapers' Company in 1896, he declared them 'worthy of a great commercial centre'.[122] At the beginning there was a department of mathematics and astronomy, headed by only one member of staff, H. Lloyd Tanner, who became a Fellow of the Royal Society in 1899. His early published papers on differential equations were regarded as an important advance in mathematical physics. Thereafter he studied 'the purest of the pure'[123] in mathematics, that is, the number theory, which later became one of the principal interests of the department. For a time he fell foul of orthodox Anglicans because he once had a slight connection with the National Secular Society, but he was much respected by his colleagues and served the College well as acting Principal during Viriamu Jones's illness. In 1909 he retired on health grounds and was succeeded by R. H. Pinkerton. Shortly before the war, honours in applied mathematics drew closer towards mathematical physics rather than to astronomy.

Even at the outset, providence did not smile upon the department of mining. The first professor, Sir William Galloway,[124] appointed in 1891, was a well-known mining engineer. He had at first accepted the orthodox view that explosions were caused by the combustion of fire-damp, but in papers to the Royal Society, 1875–7, he argued that floating coal-dust was responsible for extending the area of explosions. His views, initially regarded with profound scepticism, were confirmed in 1886 (and later by evidence to a royal commission). The College's first historians were fully entitled to say that, since the south Wales coalfield was the most important in Great Britain and its coals 'unrivalled in quality and . . . of world-wide reputation', there might have been a reasonable expectation that the department 'would speedily have built up the foundations for the successful establishment of the most important School of Mining in the whole country'.[125] On the surface the auguries were propitious. Galloway, however, because of his consultancy work, was unable to give due attention to the department, and the authors, in a splendid understatement, observed that the attempt to combine the two responsibilities 'did not prove to be a complete success'.[126] The fundamental problems, however, were deep-seated and must be considered later. Central to the development of mining studies was a thriving department of geology. The first professor, W. S. Boulton, despite cramping conditions, firmly believed in applying geographical knowledge to the needs of society. Sibly, a gifted geologist, followed him in 1913 and during the war was able to conduct important research into the location and nature of carboniferous limestone.[127]

The first generation of staff at Cardiff spoke of the College with great affection. Although few in number, 'we were all young', said T. F. Roberts, Professor of Greek, 'and the friendships I formed among my colleagues on the staff there can never, I feel, be equalled'.[128] W. Paton Ker, first head of the English department, looked back upon Cardiff with keen pleasure. When Roberts became Principal at Aberystwyth he pressed Ker, by now professor at University College, London, to serve upon the College Council where his pointed contributions to discussion helped to uphold standards.[129] R. M. Burrows, the third holder of the chair of Greek, seemed to symbolize in his own person the conviction that the study of Greek enriched the whole man and was not to be confined to linguistic discipline. At Cardiff Burrows helped to found a branch of the Workers' Educational Association, he won the men's singles College championship at tennis and, as we shall see, at East Moors he and his wife created and directed the Cardiff University Settlement.[130] His teaching was so inspiring that the number of Greek students doubled; his best book, *The Discoveries of Crete* (1907), was written whilst he was at Cardiff. He later became Hulme professor of Greek at Manchester and Principal of King's College, London. Gilbert Norwood, who followed him, was a prolific scholar who also managed to remain in the forefront of discussions relating to the College; he was one of those who gave evidence on behalf of Cardiff to the Haldane Commission.

The first Professor of Latin, J. R. Wardale, had been at Shrewsbury with his successor, G. Hartwell Jones, a considerable scholar, who regarded his Cardiff days as 'the happiest of my adult life'.[131] R. S. Conway, professor from 1893 to 1902, believed that the English pronunciation of Greek and Latin in schools and universities should be discarded because it led to confusion and concealed 'the musical and rhythmical beauties of the two languages'.[132] He and E. V. Arnold of Bangor jointly published an erudite pamphlet, *The Restored Pronunciation of Greek and Latin* (1895), approved by the Senate and the Court of the University, thus demonstrating a fruitful measure of federal co-operation and also that the authors were in the van of organized reform in Britain as a whole. D. A. Slater (1903–14), reserved and gentle, a 'lover of beautiful words and of felicities of rhythm',[133] was later elected a Fellow of the British Academy, mainly because of his study of Ovid's *Metamorphoses* (1927), written when he was in Liverpool.

W. P. Ker, in charge of English, faced hard pioneering work. His celebrated, influential *Epic and Romance* (1897) appeared after he left Cardiff. 'He spoke seldom, and then always briefly, but with extraordinary effect',[134] wrote R. W. Chambers. For forty-four years he was a Fellow of All Souls. C. E. Vaughan, nephew of Dean Vaughan, was more fortunate than his predecessor because freedom from the London examinations enabled him to devise a syllabus, enlightened in the 1890s, requiring all his students to read literature from 1580 to 1870 and allowing honours students to study in detail either Beowulf or Shakespeare's Comedies or a special author. One student spoke of Vaughan's brilliance as a teacher and of his 'poignantly keen' sense of truth which awoke hundreds of Welshmen from their 'dogmatic slumbers'.[135] Later in his career, after leaving Cardiff, he became a recognized authority on Rousseau. Vaughan's successor, Harold Littledale, after consultations with various colleagues, extended the study of literature 'to the present day'.[136] Paul Barbier, a Frenchman, reigned over the department of French for thirty-seven years, not all of them glorious.[137] The stress on grammar, syntax and accidence was somewhat relaxed by the beginning of the century. The teaching of German did not prosper under Frank T. Arnold at Cardiff for forty years. The number of students 'stubbornly refused to rise'[138] beyond single figures (as they had done dramatically under Milner-Barry at Bangor before 1914). Prose composition and unseen translations were the order of the day and students in examinations were annually expected to translate an extract from the preface to Motley's *The Rise and Fall of the Dutch Republic* first published in 1855.[139] The scene is one of dreary inadequacy. Hebrew made its appearance early in the College, but it was not until 1905 that the title 'Semitic Languages' was given to the department headed by D. Tyssil Evans, son of a Pembrokeshire farmer, who came late to academic life and who wrote the substantial *Principles of Hebrew Grammar* (1912).

Cardiff was the first of the University Colleges to create a chair of Celtic. This it did in 1884 and Thomas Powel was the first professor. Powel had graduated in classics at Oxford and although he did not receive formal education in his chosen discipline he early demonstrated scholarly talents in his edition of the medieval prose work, *Ystorya de Carolo Magno* (1883), followed by other volumes before the end of the century. Attractive both in appearance and personality, he was not endowed with robust health and he felt obliged to choose between research and teaching. He chose teaching, and generations of students, said Henry Lewis, 'have every reason to know how fortunate they were'.[140] The arrival of William John Gruffydd as a lecturer in 1906 was a major event in the history of the College and indeed of the University (which he later represented in Parliament). At the interview he had appeared in a silk hat and tails, an unwonted obeisance to authority, but his academic performance at Oxford had been less than lustrous, a third in classical moderations in 1901 and a second in English – a fourth had been feared – in 1903. However, his supporters were well aware of his scholarly and literary promise. This he amply fulfilled.[141]

For several years the teaching of English language, literature and history at Cardiff was the responsibility of one professor, as in many other university institutions (Bangor included). In 1892 A. G. Little was appointed to lecture exclusively in History and C. E. Vaughan now omitted 'history' from the title of his chair. Little had to wait until 1898 before he became a professor. In 1900 he was teaching 159 students with very little assistance; his resignation in 1902 may partly have been on this account. He was a historian of the front rank and when twenty years later he was elected a Fellow of the British Academy it was mainly in recognition of his fine studies on the Franciscan movement. Herbert Bruce was at once made head of the department and professor in 1908. A cultivated man, he had two slim volumes to his credit but it seems that he was not committed to research. By 1900 the Council of the College was expressing concern that adequate provision was not being made for the teaching of Welsh history. The major problem was that the history of Wales, as the Senate remarked, 'has yet to be written'.[142] Nor was there anyone on the staff preparing a major work, such as J. E. Lloyd at Bangor who was giving to students the first fruits of his scholarly investigations. At honours level, pertinent medieval texts were 'recommended'; popular lectures were also delivered, some of which were included in *Medieval Wales* (1902), produced by Little himself, by no means unmindful of the claims of Welsh history in a Welsh college. The most encouraging sign before 1914 was that a Cardiff student, William Rees, was laying the foundations of his many systematic contributions to Welsh medieval studies.

The first four holders of the chair of philosophy, all Fellows of the British Academy, were men of unusual distinction. Andrew Seth Pringle-Pattison, educated at Edinburgh and Germany, was at Cardiff for four years. Here he wrote two volumes, *Scottish Philosophy* (1885) and *Hegelianism and Personality* (1887), which at length enabled him to achieve his ambition of becoming Professor of Logic and Metaphysics at Edinburgh. He was not lacking in candour: after delivering the first of his Gifford

Lectures on *The Idea of Immortality* (1922), he remarked privately that immortality was 'an unpleasant subject'.[143] W. Ritchie Sorley, his successor, had enrolled at Edinburgh at fifteen to study theology, which he also pursued in Germany. His record at Cambridge, when he became Professor of Moral Philosophy in 1900, was outstanding. His chief work, *Moral Values and the Idea of God* (1918), was highly influential in the education of students of philosophical theology. At Cardiff he was active in conferences leading to the foundation of the University of Wales. John Stuart Mackenzie, rejected in disquieting circumstances for the Bangor chair in 1892,[144] came to Cardiff in 1894 from Cambridge where he was a fellow of Trinity College. As a student at Glasgow he had been persuaded by Edward Caird to take up social philosophy rather than the study of Hegel, which he would have preferred. His *Manual of Ethics* (1893), somewhat to his surprise, had apparently 'made his name familiar almost wherever ethics were taught and English was spoken'.[145] His principal works, as he would have regarded them, were written after his departure from Cardiff in 1915.

The department of political science was established in 1899 when (Sir) Sydney J. Chapman, an extension lecturer at the Victoria University, was appointed lecturer. Two years later he returned to Manchester as Stanley Jevons Professor of Political Economy. The economic element so developed after the arrival of Henry Stanley Jevons, who followed C. J. Hamilton, a political scientist, that the title of the department was changed to Economics and Political Science. Shortly before he left, Jevons was made professor (in 1910) and in 1915 he published *The British Coal Trade*, influenced by his work and experience at Cardiff, thus following in the footsteps of his father after whom the Manchester chair was named and who in 1865 had predicted the exhaustion of British coal supply.[146] The study of economics was making an increasing appeal. W. J. Roberts, a man of wide-ranging talents, who became professor in 1911, taught single-handed at all levels until 1922, without disturbing the balance between the academic and practical aspects of his discipline. Although it was Aberystwyth which had taken the lead in delivering lectures in law in south Wales, initially at Swansea in 1905, their popularity with articled solicitors and bar students was so great that representatives of the Cardiff College and of the towns in south-east Wales established in 1911 the Joint Board of Legal Education in Wales, upon which the three colleges were represented. In co-operation with local law societies, budding solicitors were prepared for the examinations of the Law Society.[147] Music, taught at the College from the outset, was invigorated when Joseph Parry became head of department in 1888. His years as Professor of Music at Aberystwyth had not been entirely happy; after his departure in 1880 he worked at Swansea, as organist and head of a music college he had established, much as he had once done in Dannville, Pennsylvania, and yet again at Cardiff. The courses he introduced in the College were patterned on those at Oxford and Cambridge and more rigorous requirements paved the way for the University's Mus.Bach. degree. During his lifetime he was Wales's leading musician and his romantic, stirring career captured the imagination of his countrymen. He wrote Wales's first opera, *Blodwen*, and 400 hymn tunes; his anthems marked a great advance in Welsh sacred music. When he died in 1903 at the age of sixty-one, in his stead came David Evans, made professor in 1910. His contributions to the musical development of the College before the war were considered enterprising. An outstanding soloist at the concerts of the Choral and Orchestral Society was Morfudd Llwyn Owen, who proceeded in 1912 to the Royal Academy of Music where she gave further proof of her promise as a composer.[148]

Since Cardiff was the first of the three colleges to provide for the training of teachers, it is as well here to consider the broad background. The rapid expansion of elementary education following the Forster Education Act of 1870 and of compulsory education in 1880 led to an unprecedented demand for teachers, especially in Cardiff's large urban area. In Wales as a whole, where Nonconformity greatly predominated, two of the three training colleges, Swansea and Carmarthen, were Anglican foundations, whilst Bangor Normal College was for men only at a time when there was a desperate shortage of women teachers. In 1885 Viriamu Jones's proposal that Queen's scholarships should be held at the College was warmly supported by the Cardiff School Board, whose case was effectively presented by

Lewis Williams to the Cross Commission, inquiring into the Education Acts. Lewis Williams, aptly described as 'an unsung hero of Welsh educational history',[149] was not only chairman of the Board, he was a member of the College Council, and later a Vice-President. He was an unyielding supporter of the 'Day Training College',[150] a somewhat unsatisfactory term which requires explanation. The intention was that prospective teachers should live at home or in lodgings (by contrast to students in residential training colleges) and receive instruction within university institutions. Day Training Colleges, however, were not all non-residential and none was a 'college' in the common usage of the word. They were an integrated part of a university or university college, in fact harbingers of departments, schools and faculties of education. This was their distinguishing mark. In addition to the clamant need for trained teachers, it was urged that if lawyers, clergy and doctors were trained in universities, it was wrong to exclude teachers. Better-qualified teachers would enhance the profession, and education was 'a distinct academic subject which also had a practical discipline'.[151] The Cross Commission, though not unanimous, recommended the creation of Day Training Colleges, to which grants were given by the government in 1890. Cardiff in that year was amongst the first to take advantage of the scheme whereby Day Training students received their general education in the classes of the College and their professional training in a special education department. For a time the standard at entry did not approach that of the Bangor Normal College. As late as 1899 the University Colleges together had but one-third of the number of first-class students admitted to the Normal College. Throughout the period the role of Viriamu Jones was crucial, and alone amongst the Welsh Colleges, a separate department was established at Cardiff in 1892 for the training of women teachers for secondary schools. The first Master of Method, as he was called, was Thomas Rayment, formerly a tutor at the Borough Road College, who became professor in 1904, the year before his departure to the Goldsmiths' College, London, where he was Vice-Principal. H. Millicent Hughes (who married J. S. Mackenzie) was the first head of the women's department and its first professor in 1904. Allied to these advances was the determination of the College, in co-operation with the Local Education Authority, to establish a Training School of Cookery and Domestic Arts in 1891 to prepare students for its own Teacher Diploma in Cookery.[152] Hitherto Welsh women had been obliged to study in London or Liverpool. The new school also took the initiative in convening a conference in London in 1895 which successfully promoted necessary reforms in Training Schools. The College continued to administer the Cardiff School until 1912 when the management was entirely transferred to local authorities. Two decades elapsed before the College resumed control of this, the only Training College of Domestic Arts in Wales, the responsibility for the final examination of students lying with the University of Wales Training Board.

On the eve of the Great War Cardiff's income was nearly £25,000. Of parliamentary grants, £9,500 came from the Exchequer. Fees accounted for a third of the income. There were seventy-two members of staff, of whom twenty-three (including the Principal) were professors. There were 497 full-time students; a third were women.

III

War

When war broke out in 1914 Reichel was not taken unawares. He had long been convinced of the German menace. Though of German extraction, though his father had studied at the University of Berlin and was as much at home in German as in English and though he himself had favoured Prussia in the war of 1870, he had become disenchanted two decades before 1914, partly because of 'relentless propaganda'[1] in the universities, especially by Heinrich Treitschke, Professor of History in the University of Berlin. The German attack was an unparalleled example by a civilized nation of 'cold-blooded wickedness',[2] based on intellectual training and scientific efficiency. John Morris-Jones in turn believed that Germany had sold its soul to the devil and in an appeal in Welsh and English to the people of Wales he declared that the war was being fought not only against military aggression but against the most extreme form of ungodliness ever to possess a nation.[3] His colleague, Ifor Williams, translated into Welsh C. A. McCurdy's *Revelations of Prince Licknowsky*, the German ambassador to the Court of St James from 1912 to 1914.[4] To Henry Jones it was the 'moral splendour' of the sacrifice which appealed: 'Never had the history of the world shown so much spirit of Christianity.'[5] J. E. Lloyd believed that German education had 'deified the state . . . as the sole good of all its citizens and the criterion of all their actions'.[6] After the war, the Cardiff Principal discerned in Earl Haig, upon whom an honorary degree was conferred, 'the spiritual descendant' of Belisarius, Scipio, Alfred, Garibaldi and others mighty in battle who had preserved 'the European idea'[7] against barbarism. The voice of moderation, however, was not wholly stilled. At Aberystwyth, T. F. Roberts, though firmly supporting the war, had no wish to disparage 'what Germany has achieved, and yet under happier auspices will achieve'.[8] At Cardiff, Gilbert Norwood, Professor of Greek, asked an audience in 1914 to 'remember that every nation, whether it is Wales or England, or France, or Belgium, or Russia, or Germany, forms, so far as it really is a nation, one note in the voice of God'. That it was difficult to remember this patiently in time of conflict made war 'so profound an evil'.[9] In the following year a colleague, J. S. MacKenzie, discoursing upon the meaning of *Kultur*,[10] held that in cultivating individual culture one should understand that it was not the property of the few and that it should be extended as far as possible to the people as a whole. On the other hand, it should not be imposed by force on others. Britain had tended to stress the individual aspect rather narrowly, Germany the national aspect, also narrowly. One-sided views were in need of correction. Such an enlightened discussion, worthy of a wartime university, was a welcome antidote to the frenzied attacks upon German *Kultur*.

Few had the remotest conception of the consequences of total war. In October 1914, Kenyon, the Senior Deputy-Chancellor, praised students who had responded to the summons: 'All honour to them. Their studies may be delayed, but their minds will be enlarged.'[11] The delay was a good deal longer than anticipated. Lieutenant William Thomas, later of Trefloyne and one of Aberystwyth's greatest benefactors, was among the first students to be wounded and captured. Writing from his German prison in April 1915 he wished good luck to students in their sessional examinations, adding that he hoped to be home before the end of the summer vacation.[12] Not until 1915 did the Bangor Senate resolve that a free copy of the College *Calendar* should no longer be sent to the University of Berlin.[13] In Cardiff's college magazine in December one writer said that 'though many of us would like to spend the next few months at the pastime of killing Germans, circumstances are too much'.[14] Another remarked: 'Yes, this is a terrible War, but unfortunately it's the best we have at present.'[15] Odious flippancy was soon dispelled.

The Colleges adjusted themselves as best they could to war conditions. Rooms were set aside as military hospitals at Bangor and two acres of playing fields turned into allotments. In 1917 women at the hall of residence unpatriotically developed German measles and the College had to close early. In the interests of economy, heavy long hockey skirts disappeared, so that henceforth knees were to be seen in peace as well as war. Refugees from Belgium were received at the beginning of the war and from Serbia at the end.[16] A goodly number of Belgians, sponsored by the Llandinam family, were welcomed at Aberystwyth and there were expectations, largely unfulfilled, that they would augment a small ensemble at the College as part of the development of music so close to the heart of Gwendoline Davies.[17] A substantial decline in numbers led to a corresponding decline in fees. As early as October 1914 the Cardiff Principal, Registrar and senior members of staff offered to surrender a portion of their salary and the administrative staff basic increments.[18] Financial privation at Cardiff prompted the second Lord Aberdare, the newly elected President, to opine, with disestablishment in mind, that some would also have to find money for their church in Wales 'which had been very little better treated than Belgium',[19] a remark so lacking in balance that he was roundly rebuked in the *South Wales Daily News*. Applications for fellowships on the eve of war had been unusually impressive, but postgraduate ambitions were inevitably disrupted. For example, D. Emrys Evans's study of the Greek inscriptions of Phrygia, Asia Minor, requiring research in Germany, was a casualty. Henry Lewis's edition of *Chwedleu Seith Doethon Rufein* was delayed for years by military service.[20] P. Mansell Jones's first postgraduate venture was a comparison between Walt Whitman and the Belgian poet, Emile Verhaeren, whom he had met in pre-war Paris and whom he next saw as a refugee in Wales 'driven like a leaf before the full blast of war'.[21] At Oxford, Jones encountered a young visitor, Morfydd Owen (1891–1918), then studying at the Royal Academy of Music. One of the few 'apparitions'[22] he ever saw in his life and a product of the Cardiff College, her 'brilliant promise' had persuaded the University of Wales to award her the comparatively large sum of £100 to examine 'the elements in Folk Music which permanently influence the musical development of a nation',[23] especially Russia, Norway and Finland, and to enquire into similar possibilities in Wales. Research in the old Petrograd was part of her plan, extinguished by the war and by her tragic end in 1918, the victim of a wrong anaesthetic. It was a calamity for Welsh music.

Courses were modified according to circumstance. At Bangor

military history, much favoured by Reichel, was considered a suitable substitute for the study of German. Lewis Valentine would have been excused intermediate Greek had he shown a decent competence in military training which he abominated. Students of engineering at Cardiff were encouraged to devote two days to munitions without detriment to their studies. The University recognized two days' weekly training by members of the Officers' Training Corps as part of their degree course. No one, however, appears to have gone to the same lengths as T. A. Levi at Aberystwyth who indicated to his law students that 'if they enlisted he would guarantee that their examination would be passed for them'.[24]

As numbers dwindled there was talk of closing the Colleges. In May 1915 the Aberystwyth Vice-Principal, Edward Edwards, announced that he would serve in a civilian or military capacity, whichever the authorities chose, as soon as the College shut its doors. Shortly after Lloyd George became Minister of Munitions the Edward Davies laboratories were placed at his disposal. In the same year E. V. Arnold at Bangor did not see why the College should be kept open; every man and woman would be better employed in workshop or field. Later he volunteered for work in the Ministry of Munitions, but bounced back after a term, describing his duties as 'futile'.[25] Others were profitably employed in the national interest. Departments of mathematics, physics, agriculture, forestry and especially chemistry were badly hit; by the end of the war many courses were discontinued and some departments closed. Heady recruitment during the volunteer period deprived the country of talent better directed to scientific war work, an error not repeated in the Second World War. The absence of research students in mathematics at Bangor retarded Bryan's fundamental aeronautical studies but he fortunately joined Selig Brodetsky at Bristol where their joint endeavours on the mathematics of aircraft structure led to the superior stability of British planes, enabling them to swerve, swoop and often outclass the enemy in aerial combat. At the core of these exploits lay Bryan's classic *Stability in Aviation*.[26] Departments of agriculture at Aberystwyth and Bangor had made their contribution to the sinews of war before 1914. As we shall see, Stapledon's work at Aberystwyth won golden tributes after the

Second World War.[27] In 1916 Bangor's services to agricultural practice between 1885 and 1914 were officially praised in the Commons. In north Wales the yield of crops had greatly improved, oats, for example, by 7 bushels per acre; sheep had increased by 840,000 and cattle by 50,000.[28] Practical classes in chemistry had early been greatly modified because Germany was the principal source of 'fine chemicals'. Nevertheless, the method devised by a Bangor student of determining the exact degree of purity in 'toluol', the 'mother substance' of high explosive, was adapted by the Department of Explosives Supply and the college presented annual reports to the Ministry of Munitions.[29] In 1920 the *Western Mail* recalled 'with a sense of shame'[30] that because of lack of equipment the Cardiff College, unlike other British universities, was unable at the outbreak of war to participate in research relating to munitions. Late in 1915 it was reported that the College's Professor of Engineering was engaged in the vital work of preparing shell gauges.[31] There was naturally a major role for the Medical School. Indeed, General Sir Ivor Herbert had said before the war that the school would prove equivalent to the addition of a whole army corps to the future fighting strength of the country. David Hepburn, Professor of Anatomy, was as surgeon-colonel the officer commanding the Third Western General Hospital, whose headquarters at Cardiff dealt with thousands of cases. In October 1917 the premier congratulated him upon the splendid work of the hospital.[32]

Before we consider the central question of recruitment, it is as well to be reminded of the anger directed at those believed to be enemies of the national cause. In the case of Kuno Meyer there could be no doubt. At one time honorary professor in Celtic languages and literature at Liverpool, Meyer belonged to the heroic age of Celtic scholarship. In recognition of his merit the University of Wales had conferred upon him an honorary doctorate in 1909, two years before he became Professor of Celtic at the University of Berlin. During the early months of the war he bitterly attacked Great Britain in America. He also caused trouble among Irishmen in America and in German prison camps. This was not to be countenanced. In July 1915 the University Court regretted that under the powers given by charter it could not revoke the degree conferred upon him. Thus it is that Meyer's name appears in each successive *Calendar* of the University of Wales.[33]

The University in its corporate capacity bore no responsibility for the maltreatment of Hermann Ethé, another eminent German scholar. One of her colleges, however, did not escape censure, some of it unjust. As we have noted earlier, developments in Germany had depressed him and since 1876 he had been professor at Aberystwyth.[34] He had made no effort to blend into the restricted society in which he found himself, nor to become a British citizen. In fact he was a nonconformist, though not of the kind generally applauded in Wales. After forty years he still spoke with a heavy German accent; Martin Luther on his lips became Martin 'Loser'. In a largely teetotalitarian town he drank openly and with relish. He made no effort to learn Welsh and according to T. Gwynn Jones he claimed that the only necessary Welsh word was *cwrw* (beer), which would lead one to the nearest pub, where English was spoken.[35] Such characteristics, whilst they throw light on subsequent events, scarcely exonerate his persecutors. It was Ethé's custom to visit Germany each year. There, in August 1914, he was trapped until the College sought government permission for him to return to his academic work. In the heated atmosphere of the times, the Principal prudently resolved to meet Ethé at the station to counsel caution. He was accompanied by the Registrar, and also by three students in order to show that the student body were ready to receive him back. The three were David Hughes Parry, Archibald Rowlands and William John Pugh, each of whom was later knighted. The episode was interpreted by an inflamed public as an official 'welcome' to a German. Next day an ill-humoured crowd of 2,000 assembled outside Ethé's home to hear fiery, irresponsible speeches by prominent local men. That evening Ethé and his wife left for Reading. He was given a small pension by the College and he died in 1917, laid low by the bitterest blow he had ever received. Rightly has it been said that he was 'a casualty of war just as certainly as any young soldier killed at the Front'.[36] War fever had unhinged men who should have known better. A former student of the College, by then a prominent lawyer in north Wales and a Council member, joined the hunt. F. Llywelyn Jones, styled 'Cromwell' in college, was so enraged by the loss of the *Lusitania* and the use of poison gas that he demanded the withdrawal of a wholly innocent man who had discerned the nature of the German menace at least two decades before Reichel and who was employed by the wartime government to translate and to crack the codes of the German Navy. T. F. Roberts was largely correct when he told R. T. Jenkins that 'it was *not* the hooligans; it was the responsible leaders of the town who did this'.[37] It is also doubtless true that the College acted far better than the town worthies whose vengeful spite was not for years quenched. Nevertheless, the College was injured and through the decades some have felt that it should have fought with greater tenacity to defend the rights of Hermann Ethé.

Women students seldom contributed directly to the war effort, though some became part-time nurses in the Voluntary Aid Detachment. This they were fervently urged to do by Elizabeth P. Hughes, who reminded students at Alexandra Hall, Aberystwyth, in 1917 that 'women were being treated by the country more seriously than ever before; they were on their trial and it behoved them to show the best possible public spirit'. Moulded by the Red Cross into disciplined women they would become 'far more useful in every sphere in post-war Britain'.[38] It is evident that they had by no means detached themselves from the struggle. Early on, the Cardiff Principal had given an unqualified assurance that women students were 'preparing all kinds of comforts for the troops'.[39] Here and there they flourished a white feather at unenlisted men, the traditional sign to the spurned that they were not true gamecocks. In December 1914 'Cadet' wrote an open letter to women students at Aberystwyth to express disapproval of their behaviour. The ancient and laudable custom of 'quadding', whereby men and women perambulated separately on either side of the quad, was being disrupted by the growing habit amongst some women who had developed an 'ecstatic super-patriotism' of walking 'on our side of the quad as if to show us that our place is no longer here'.[40] In reply two members of Alexandra Hall proffered an 'unqualified apology to all men in College for the wholly indefensible attitude of certain lady students towards those men whom circumstances have prevented from joining the army'.[41] About the same time it was reported that the more ardent women students had 'casually rebuked'[42] unenlisted men. The knitting of khaki socks during meetings of college societies was resented, the loud clicking of needles being perhaps grimly reminiscent of the *tricoteuses* of revolutionary France. By the end of 1917 there was bad feeling at Aberystwyth between men and women, the latter being charged with arrogating to themselves privileges and rights that 'belonged exclusively to the men of pre-war days' and of taking advantage of their superior numbers to set up a 'petticoat government'.[43] Throughout the war Cardiff and Aberystwyth persisted in electing male presidents of the Students' Representative Council. Bangor was the exception. In the 1916–17 session the College and the University were well served by Marion C. Soar, who before the Haldane Commission gave a spirited defence of the medieval universities of Italy where student power allowed the survival of only the ablest of their professors. Several decades later her pertinacity on this occasion, and that of her followers, won the warm admiration of Lord Ashby.[44] At the end of the war both sexes were attacked without discrimination by a virulent influenza virus. Amongst the women who succumbed in 1918 was the recipient of a loan from a University fund. Shortly afterwards her brother, who had agreed to act as guarantor, was killed in France. In 1923 the University Council was informed that this was the only loss sustained by the fund, repayments having 'always been regular and complete'.[45]

The coming of conscription in 1916 intensified the pressure upon unmarried men to enlist in January and upon married men in April. Those who could not reconcile the taking of life with the principles of the Christian religion or with the claims of individual conscience faced ignominy. Theological students were not exempt. Middle-aged deacons were ready to tell them that there were 'plenty of men in all the churches, of non-recruitable age, who can keep the lamps of the Temple burning while the war lasts'.[46] If they had serious reservations about fighting they were encouraged to serve in the Royal Army Medical Corps, the Army Service Corps or the Young Men's Christian Association. The principal chaplain to Welsh soldiers, the Revd John Williams, Brynsiencyn (who also served on the Bangor College Council), persuaded the War Office to create a Welsh Students' Company, Royal Army Medical Corps, in which ministerial students could perform non-combatant duties. It was originally understood that they would not be transferred to a combatant branch, a pledge not later honoured. Among students who joined the RAMC was Lewis Valentine, whose wartime diary has been published; David Ellis, a poet of promise who disappeared in mysterious circumstances in Macedonia, and A. E. Jones (Cynan) whose war poem 'Mab y Bwthyn' won him a National Eisteddfod crown in 1921. The Welsh Students' Company was called 'God's Own' and Sheffield, where it was centred, 'the Holy City', though not for long.[47]

Those who suffered most were the 'absolutists', determined not to hand the smallest morsel to the dogs of war. 'I will make their path as hard as I can',[48] said Lloyd George (who had readily championed the Boers). It may well be that it was the 'absolutists' who were the first to undermine Lloyd George's reputation as a Radical. 'Do not incur this man's wrath'[49] was the advice of the Revd John Williams, and a vindictive spirit may be seen in the Representation of the People Act of 1918 which disfranchised conscientious objectors for five years after the war.[50] The *North Wales Chronicle* saw fit to misinterpret Shakespeare by informing its readers that 'conscience doth make cowards of us all'.[51] In fact 'conchies' bravely faced tribunals, imprisonment and public scorn. A correspondent to Aberystwyth's *Dragon* in 1917 referred to the custom of listing in its columns the students in the Armed Forces. He now proposed that a new list be opened of students who had entered His Majesty's Prisons in the service of the human race. One day it would be recognized that conscientious objectors had followed 'the more excellent way, and chosen to suffer rather than fight'.[52] One of them was George M. Ll. Davies, in 1923 the University of Wales's representative in Parliament. At the height of the war he was in prison and when he and others were being transferred from Knutsford, Cheshire, to Dartmoor it was necessary to change trains at Cardiff, where Lloyd George was being formally received with great pomp by the station master. As soon as the

Premier's wife saw Davies she at once left the party and warmly greeted him, dressed as he was in prison uniform.[53] In presenting her for an honorary degree of the University Ifor Williams later said that though raised on high she had not become grand ('wedi codi ond nid ymgodi').[54] Conscientious objectors were thus not wholly friendless. At Aberystwyth they had defenders amongst the staff. T. H. Parry-Williams had studied before the war on the continent. At Freiburg the martial customs of German students, their pride in duelling scars and their arrogant patriotism filled him with distaste. His resolve to be a conscientious objector was further stiffened upon hearing sermons by religious leaders at Aberystwyth on behalf of the just and holy war, a repugnance fully shared by Thomas Gwynn Jones who sensed a growing distance between himself and zealous promoters of the crusade against Germany whom he had deeply admired, O. M. Edwards and Henry Jones amongst them.

Both Parry-Williams and Gwynn Jones gave their unqualified support to *Y Wawr*, a student publication (with the aid of a few members of staff), which in fact went beyond religious and humanitarian opposition to the war. O. M. Edwards believed that such violent pacifism was 'plain treason'[55] ('teyrnfradwriaeth amlwg'). A fierce contribution by D. J. Williams in 1916 and numerous attacks against the government were held by the College authorities to be so subversive that the student editor, Ambrose Bebb, and his committee, having refused to retract or reform, were required to resign. At Bangor, Thomas Rees, once a farmhand and now Principal of Bala-Bangor Independent College, stood as a rock in defence of conscientious objectors. His frequent appearances on their behalf at tribunals provoked petty, vengeful men to exclude him from the new Bangor golf course, though a more ludicrous sanction can scarcely be imagined. On a wider scene he is remembered for his editorship of *Y Deyrnas* which provided an essential forum for conscientious objectors. W. J. Gruffydd, who regularly read the news-sheet when he was on naval service in distant parts, believed that Thomas Rees's *Y Deyrnas* was one of the principal reasons why the spirit of Wales was not totally overwhelmed by wartime madness.[56] When Gruffydd returned to Cardiff ill-feeling towards conscientious objectors persisted for some time, the

Daily Herald, for example, having to be protected from destruction in the students' common room in 1921. No one did more to champion the cause of conscientious objectors in the College than Gruffydd. In his case the salt had not lost its savour.[57]

Widespread euphoria at the outbreak or war manifested itself in various ways. A Bangor correspondent of Aberystwyth's magazine declared that 'the war-fever has attacked us rather savagely'.[58] Men were wavering between various paths of duty. E. V. Arnold aroused understandable resentment by suggesting that many were restrained from enlisting by their mothers. The city authorities forbade the usual student speeches at the town clock after matches and a Bangor tradesman with a penchant for synonyms proclaimed that he was 'ashamed to pass these great, big, tall, stalwart fellows in the street'.[59] Dominated by the Cathedral and the Penrhyn family, lower Bangor in a narrow valley, with its small retailers and its masonic lodge, was not a nursery of large-minded views. In May 1915 the city fathers, believing that students were favourably treated, considered the position of shirkers and resolved that the Bangor War Emergency Committee should meet daily to hear the explanations of those who had not enlisted and to distribute badges to those who could show good cause.[60] Such slights were less effective than the eloquent advocacy of members of staff, convinced that the barbarians who had invaded Belgium were striking at the vitals of the British Empire.

Many students responded with alacrity. At Bangor Hugh Lloyd Williams, later a lieutenant colonel (DSO, MC), confessed to conflicting emotions when he heard that war was declared. There was a sense of the 'awful possibilities of the future . . . the vague fear of torture of mind and body which all of us were presently called upon to endure'. There were also 'the patriotic thrills that surged in the breast'; to enrol was for him 'the only right and proper course'.[61] Soon Lloyd George was exhorting his countrymen to fight with every nerve and sinew in united action against the common enemy of Wales and of England. E. H. Griffiths was later to rejoice that Welshmen sang 'Land of my Fathers' when they went 'over the top'.[62] In Lloyd George, it has been well said, 'the nation's moral and emotional capital was invested',[63] as seemed evident from his speeches at national eisteddfodau, at Bangor in 1915 (deferred from 1914) and again at Aberystwyth in 1916 where he urged his hearers to sing in the depth of a dark night.

Rhetoric, sometimes shameless, played its part, the Officers' Training Corps rather more. At Aberystwyth and Bangor the OTCs were offsprings of Volunteer Companies formed in 1899 at the beginning of the Boer War which had aroused outbursts of intemperate patriotism unequalled until 1914. Haldane's army reforms in 1907 (basely forgotten in the Great War itself) led to the creation of a Territorial Army and to the extinction of the old Volunteers. Before long there were khaki uniforms bearing the shoulder-flash 'University of Wales OTC', proficiency certificates A and B becoming familiar to generations of students. There was better equipment because no longer was it necessary to polish guns retrieved from the Crimea, and there were annual summer camps, for the artillery at Trawsfynydd – the home of the poet, Hedd Wyn, slain at Pilkem Ridge but 'Tin Town' to regular soldiers. A few members of College staff were commissioned, partly because they were attracted by the trappings of military authority and partly to defend the vast realm when duty called.[64] It is remarkable that Cardiff, the largest of the colleges, did not have an OTC, mainly because it had not formed a Volunteer Company, and that in military affairs the 'highland' colleges were in the lead. In 1910 Cardiff took issue with the government.[65] According to Haldane (as Secretary for War) the College had promised everything except an engineers' training corps, adding that the matter had gone to sleep for three years. In May 1914 it was reported that there was no money in the army estimates for a Cardiff OTC. In December the student president ironically remarked that they had the satisfaction of knowing that a corps would be one of the fruits of peace.[66] It is certain that its absence in 1914 was an impediment to recruitment at Cardiff. Those who remained weighed the matter gravely, we are told, some concluding that 'to the undergraduate enlistment means a sacrifice greater than that entailed on [sic] the ordinary man'.[67] Such remarks were not well received by the Cardiff Principal. The College had 'felt a blow by enlistment and it is hoped that the blow will be felt still more severely'.[68] Seventy-eight students were in the forces but by the test of Oxford and Cambridge 250 should have enrolled. Because of the absence of an OTC only 12 per cent had been commissioned, but Griffiths drew limited comfort from the fact that more members of staff were serving than at Aberystwyth and Bangor. The small church hostel at Llandaf had closed, four-fifths of its occupants having responded to the call of country.[69]

By March 1915, 140 out of 170 men students at Bangor belonged to the OTC, together with 80 students of the Normal College. According to one military commander Bangor had 'done splendidly';[70] of those in residence at the beginning of the war and who had joined the forces, two-thirds had been commissioned. Aberystwyth's Principal was initially angry that many student recruits were not commissioned, whereas commissions were 'freely given'[71] to students of the older universities and to public school cadets. If snobbery was the cause, as has been suggested,[72] it soon withered away following the high casualty rate amongst subalterns. The *Windsor Magazine* in June 1915 reported in a survey of recruitment at British universities and colleges that the 'learned world' of Wales was 'inspired with the ancient martial spirit of the Principality'. It added that in September 1914 the Principal of St David's College, Lampeter, had sent a circular to all students stressing 'the paramount need of men and the urgency of the country's call'.[73] When the College reassembled, all members were regularly drilled. By 1916 the annual admissions had fallen to eleven. In the following year the cast of *The Merchant of Venice* performed at Lampeter consisted of twenty-four girls, mostly domestic servants and wage-earners.[74] The readiness of Aberystwyth men to join the colours was further reflected in the *Windsor Magazine* where it was demonstrated that the College had by far the best figures by comparison with Bangor and Cardiff; 230 were on service, of whom 68 per cent held commissions. It seems too that, in the peaceful surroundings of the College, the array of armed might created an illusion of irresistible power. In April 1915 the inspection of the Welsh Territorial Division on the Vicarage Field at Aberystwyth was a brilliant spectacle. In splendid weather 12,000 troops passed the saluting base at the south end of the gymnasium, the white building of the National Library towering above the scene.[75]

Most of the staff and students, past and present, of the University served in the army. The 'Kitchener' battalion, raised in Rhyl in September 1914, was later known as the 'North Wales Pals Battalion' with which the undermanned University of Wales Battalion was amalgamated. Several joined the University and Public Schools Battalion of the Royal Welch Fusiliers at Epsom. In November 1915 OTCs at universities were commanded to stand down. In their stead came Officers' Training Battalions. R. Silyn Roberts, Secretary of the University's Appointments Board for Wales, was already persuaded that Welsh graduates were at a disadvantage. When OTC selection courses were held in London he had successfully proposed the formation of a Welsh branch of the Inns of Court OTC, he himself acting as secretary for Wales. Before conscription most Welsh graduates were commissioned through this branch. The University's *Roll of Honour*, published at the end of the war, showed that the majority had served in the Royal Welch Fusiliers, the Welsh Regiment and the South Wales Borderers. The total roll of service and the number commissioned were as follows: Aberystwyth 631 (63 per cent), Bangor 554 (56 per cent) and Cardiff 734 (53 per cent).[76]

Many had faced the full fury of the most ferocious war in British history. True, there were occasional respites and reunions. In May 1915 came news that Lieutenant Clayton of Garthmyl, Montgomeryshire (later a lieutenant-colonel bearing the Military Cross), had met fellow Aberystwyth subalterns during the fighting around Hill 60. There they gave the College yell and sang the College song 'under the most exceptional circumstances that one could imagine',[77] thus in their minds for a fleeting moment further demoralizing the Boche. In 1916 a group of officers, formerly at Aberystwyth and mostly on leave from Gallipoli, spent a merry, reminiscing evening at the Savoy Hotel, Port Said, where, we gather, they had more than glanced at the cocktails when they were yellow.[78] Lewis Valentine recalled that the yells of the Baptist College and of the University College, Bangor, were heard at a concert for the wounded at Walton-on-the-Naze. R. Williams Parry had been refused a commission because of inefficiency in conducting drill and for lacking 'bounce'. Indeed, he was ill-suited for military service in any of its myriad forms. 'I cannot, like Chaucer', he once said, 'be a soldier *and* a poet.'[79] It was therefore a happy day when Captain Richard Williams, a former adjutant of the College OTC, having come across him attempting to clean a large gun by the wayside, immediately had him transferred to his office as clerk. Lieutenant-Colonel Hugh Williams, whom we have already met, recalled that when the battle of Ypres was at its fiercest in late April 1917 an abandoned farmhouse became the headquarters for his battalion. After inspecting the whole line he returned to find an artillery battery in the farmyard:

> This I ordered to clear out, and truculent messages passed between myself and its commander. He presently made his appearance 'to have it out with me', no doubt, but when we met face to face we almost fell on one another's shoulders, for he was Major A. S. Carr, secretary of the Students' Representative Council at Bangor. We at once compromised, the battery being put in a position well away from my H.Q., but its H.Q. being joined to mine. Three young pigs and some fowls were that evening sacrificed on the altar of friendship.[80]

Many years later Edward Povey, having read the account in the College history, was inspired to include the scene in his striking mural in the Powis Hall.

To be a prisoner in Germany was infinitely preferable to the horror of the trenches. Gwilym Davies, a future Professor of Latin at Cardiff, who had a brilliant academic record at Aberystwyth and Oxford, was visiting sites on the Danube when war broke out. At first placed in internment camps, he was later granted milder conditions in Vienna and its neighbourhood because his historical and archaeological researches were held in high esteem by Austrian scholars.[81] Lieutenant William Thomas, a wounded prisoner in Germany as early as October 1914, appears to have been humanely treated. He found freedom in January 1918 in Scheveningen: 'This is a lonely spot: I christen it the Aber of Holland.'[82] Like many prisoners he used his time to advantage. In a letter to O. M. Edwards in August 1917 he said that he had studied French, German and a little Russian and Spanish. He also taught a variety of subjects to others and he had applied for a fellowship at Aberystwyth.[83] It is evident that boxes of books were regularly sent out by the National Library to servicemen in German prison camps and on active service. Cynan recalled seeing such a box in Salonika. In one camp a future head of the German department at Aberystwyth, David Evans, taught Welsh to a group which included his future Principal, Ifor L. Evans, who in 1936 had the satisfaction of welcoming 'Dai Deutsch' to the Senate as professor.[84]

It had not taken long for the first intoxicating flush to be followed by a sober realism. The process may be seen in a letter of a Cardiff student from France early in 1915. 'I have somehow every confidence of returning' (mercifully not misplaced). 'I have always got into scrapes, and have always disentangled myself with but little effort'; henceforth he would 'act with circumspection, for . . . I am going through a purifying crucible'. War was not a purifying crucible for everyone.[85] As late as 1928 an Aberystwyth graduate said of his fellow ex-servicemen that they 'had killed cheerfully and lasciviously.'[86] No man can write such words in jest. They serve to remind us of the brutalizing consequences of the descent into hell. One of the fullest accounts in Welsh of the carnage was by another Aberystwyth man, D. Cynddelw Williams, a chaplain decorated with the Military Cross, who retained to the end a devout, unswerving sense of duty to serve God and his countrymen.[87] His diary may lack the artistry of the works of Robert Graves and Siegfried Sassoon and of Llewelyn Wyn Griffith's *Up to Mametz* (1931), but its value stands high as a direct, unadorned record of unsparing service at the worst of times.

Some were filled with foreboding. Thomas Roberts, a graduate of the University, drew up his will on the battlefield, leaving his transcripts of Dafydd Nanmor's poems to Ifor Williams to use as he thought fit in preparing his series of editions of works by masters of the *cywydd* (one of the divisions of Welsh strict metres). Roberts died of wounds before the Armistice. In 1923 there appeared *The Poetical Works of Dafydd Nanmor*, revised by Ifor Williams, who, in the words of Idris Foster, 'performed this moving act of *pietas* with delicate care'.[88] The University's one Victoria Cross was won by a former Bangor student, Arthur Moore Lascelles, who had proceeded from Uppingham to Bangor in 1899. Returning to Britain from South Africa in 1915, he was commissioned; at Cambrai in 1917 he acted with 'most conspicuous bravery, initiative and devotion to duty when in command of his company in a very exposed position'.[89] He was killed four days before the Armistice. Several in each college were highly decorated. The proportion of servicemen killed was as follows: Aberystwyth 16 per cent, Cardiff 15 per cent and Bangor 17 per cent. The heaviest loss had been amongst junior officers.[90] There was also the great company of those mangled in mind and body consigned to stumble as best they could for the remainder of their days. Poison gas had been a new torment. Not many survived its onslaught as long as Barnett Janner (1892–1982), a young Cardiff graduate, later a champion of worldwide Jewry and a persistent, successful campaigner in Parliament for British ratification of the United Nations' genocide convention.[91]

Beyond all computation was the appalling price of victory. Western man, it seemed to many, had become insane, bent on his own destruction. The words of Pericles were often repeated: 'When the young men are taken out of the city, spring is taken out of the year.'[92] But to what end – a grave in a foreign field, a name on a brass memorial and a fading sepia photograph? 'Was it for this the clay grew tall?',[93] asked Wilfred Owen. Yet the thought of futile sacrifice was not to be borne. Anger, pride and grief were intermingled. One student remembered seeing the name of a friend in the columns of *The Times*: 'A wave of indignation swept over me . . . I knew Watkin, and by knowing him, loved him.'[94] It was a daily preoccupation to read the long lists in *The Times* of the fallen, 'last seen as fresh-faced young men going with apparent cheerfulness to war'.[95] Another woman student recalled that 'in those highly strung times the thought of peace was still traitorous, and victory was the password'. As the casualty lists became longer and more frequent 'our secret prayer was for it to be stopped somehow . . . Some of us could only see the stupidity, the senselessness, the horror of it all.'[96] Within the narrow compass of the *englyn* R. Williams Parry came nearest in Welsh to voicing a nation's sorrow in the 'wrenching times'. A line of his is engraved upon the Welsh National Memorial in Cathays Park, Cardiff: 'dros fôr fe droes i farw'[97] ('across the sea he turned to die'). It is said that when the Principal of the Baptist College at Bangor came to chapel to see the oak memorial upon which was carved his son's name 'none durst speak unto him', for, like Job of old, 'they saw that his grief was very great'[98] ('canys gwelent fyned ei ddolur ef yn fawr iawn').

IV

The Haldane Commission

It was natural in time of war to look expectantly to the future. Out of the Second World War came the Beveridge Report and Butler's Education Act of 1944. It is true that Lloyd George's extravagant promises during the First World War of a land fit for heroes later led to bitter taunts; no one, however, could doubt that there were substantial achievements, amongst them the Fisher Education Act of 1918. Lloyd George had often told his countrymen that the nightingale's sweetest notes were heard at night. In fact the nightingale was no frequent visitor to Wales, but of the Haldane Report upon the University of Wales, prepared in the depth of the war, it could fairly be said that it was more than a tremulous thrush in a dark hedge.

Towards the end of 1913 the Chancellor of the Exchequer asked the standing Advisory Committee on University Grants, under the chairmanship of Sir William McCormick, to visit the University of Wales and its Colleges. The Committee, which included two members of the Raleigh Committee, had before it the Raleigh Report and was able to say that a 'distinct advance' had been observed in the efficiency of the colleges and in achieving a 'true university spirit'.[1] It added that the work should be of a university standard and should not descend to the level appropriate to a secondary school. Apart from considering the needs of individual colleges, certain general observations were made. The paucity of endowments was a 'conspicuous weakness', indeed, a 'source of instability'.[2] Each college had on the capital account a deficit of £20,000, which should be eliminated by sinking funds. The average salary of a professor should be no less than £500, the minimum no less than £400, and grants should be given to junior staff to encourage research and to compensate for the loss of extraneous work. Colleges should join the Federated Superannuation System for Universities and provide for members of staff too old to benefit from the new arrangements. An additional £20,000 was needed. The University should receive £2,000, Aberystwyth and Bangor £4,500 each and Cardiff £9,000 because it had expensive departments.

Two matters required special attention. The first concerned government and organization, the second the Medical School. As to the first, the Colleges had outlived their purely local and municipal status and now 'collectively form the national provision for university education in the Principality'.[3] The Committee, however, was not certain that the authorities of the University and of the Colleges fully appreciated this fact. True, there was a measure of co-operation and the University 'recognized' departments for degree purposes, but once a department had been so recognized at one college, the other two colleges were free to establish a similar department without recourse to the University. There was thus wasteful duplication, a serious concern in a federal University financed almost entirely by the State. The University did not act as a co-ordinating authority and it was doubtful whether it was capable of assuming such responsibility. The Committee spoke plainly:

> We were at first disposed to suggest that questions as to what new activities should be undertaken by the several Colleges should be decided by the University. It was represented to us, however, that if the allocation of the general grant to the College were placed at the discretion of the University, and power given to the University Court to decide such questions, the result might be to raise difficulties so serious as even possibly to lead to the dismemberment of the Federal University as at present constituted. The opinion was strongly expressed, not only by representatives of the Colleges, but also by members of the University Court, that an impartial outside authority, acting on the advice of this Committee, should decide such questions.[4]

An allied question concerned local government assistance for university education. In the course of its inquiries the Committee, at the express wish of the Chancellor, prepared a supplementary memorandum on the subject. Local support usually took the form of gifts of capital sums for building purposes by private benefactors, gifts which, of course, involved annual expenditure on maintenance, and the Committee expressed concern at the total absence of support from local authorities for the direct maintenance of Aberystwyth and Bangor (while Cardiff received only £2,000). It was now proposed that the Treasury should supplement the income of the University and its Colleges by a sum equivalent to the product of a farthing rate to be contributed by local authorities. If £20,000 were raised in this way from both sources, the proportion of the total Exchequer grant to that of local authorities would in Wales be nearly 4:1, whereas the proportion in Scotland was about 3:1, in England nearly 2:1. Two points need to be noted: first, the principle of pound for pound for university education in Wales was enunciated for the first time, and second, that although the richer industrial areas would naturally be more directly interested in Cardiff, the Committee gave as its opinion that grants from local authorities should be for the University as a whole.[5]

The proposal to institute a complete National School of Medicine in Cardiff can only be touched upon here.[6] The great generosity of Sir William James Thomas had brought within the range of possibility the creation of a school which taught the last two years as well as the first three years of a medical course. Its proper maintenance, however, would require substantial additional grants, as became clear when a deputation headed by Kenyon and Reichel saw Lloyd George, as Chancellor, in February 1914. A departmental committee of the Board of Education, asked to advise the Treasury, recommended that half the necessary sums should be derived from the Exchequer and half from local authorities and private donors. The thorny problem of the government of the school need not now detain us, save to say that the Committee, aware that its proposals were not ideal, declared that 'short of a reconstitution of the University and of fundamental changes not only in the University Charter but those of its constituent colleges, it would be impossible in the opinion of the Committee to devise a completely satisfactory scheme'. Should the Treasury conclude that 'a stronger and more logical organisation'[7] was essential before making grants, then the whole university structure would need to be examined by a suitable body.

The Treasury could scarcely ignore the views of two powerful committees. In a crucial minute of 9 February 1915, the Treasury argued that further financial assistance was necessary, but that money alone would not place university education in Wales upon 'a permanently satisfactory basis'.[8] A competent inquiry was 'an essential preliminary', and in a covering letter the University, in consultation with its Colleges, was invited 'to consider the steps to be taken with a view to altering the constitution of the University'[9] and to make known its views as early as possible. In response representatives of the University and of the Colleges held several barren conferences from March 1915 onwards which it would be tedious to pursue in detail. There was an inauspicious beginning. The University Registrar, Mortimer Angus, deemed it inexpedient to release the text of the Treasury letter (which was not published in its entirety until 1916), thus exposing himself to charges of needless secrecy. 'Wales must know the truth and know it now',[10] said the *Western Mail*, which in April announced that the University of Wales had as much influence over the Colleges as had the Khedive of Egypt over the British campaign in Egypt. Some believed that the Treasury minute was minatory (a 'nasty job',[11] in fact), whereas Reichel in particular thought the tone 'most friendly'[12] because the Treasury was actually acknowledging that financial assistance was needed.

It soon became clear that successive conferences were unlikely to tackle the fundamental question of reorganization as required by the Treasury. Moreover, a case could be made for deferring a radical overhaul until after the war and a resolution to that effect was unanimously carried by the Central Welsh Board. Again, elder statesmen of the University, Isambard Owen and D. Brynmor Jones, who tended to venerate the charter of 1893, largely fashioned by them, as a masterpiece of draftsmanship, would be disinclined to welcome substantial, necessary changes which could not be dealt with by statute.[13] Indeed, the conviction grew amongst acute observers that attempts to deal with a serious problem without altering the charter were from the outset doomed. Attention was largely concentrated upon constructing a constitution for the Medical School which gave the Cardiff College far more general authority over a National School of Medicine than the Treasury would ever have considered desirable. The proposals to allow Cardiff a large say in the management of the Medical School were perfectly acceptable to the Councils of both Cardiff and Aberystwyth. Bangor's Council did not dissent, provided it was distinctly understood (in the unmistakable tones of Reichel) that the scheme was provisional and might be reopened at a suitable time to consider the larger question of university reorganization.[14] When, therefore, the University appealed to the Treasury for increased interim grants to meet urgent financial needs, without presenting a plan for reorganization, the response was predictable. The national interest would not allow a great increase in grants 'before a satisfactory scheme of reorganisation has been effected or fully guaranteed', but the Treasury would provide additional funds as recommended by the Advisory Committee upon the clear condition that the University and Colleges agreed to request 'the immediate appointment of a Royal Commission on the University and to accept the decision which His Majesty's Government may arrive at, based upon the findings of that Commission with regard to the reform of the University, including the government of the National Medical School'.[15]

The Cardiff Principal had always disliked the Treasury's association of university reform with the establishment of the Medical School, but he nevertheless welcomed the opportunity to receive immediate grants, imprudently, even impudently, adding that he did not care whether the Royal Commission lasted ten years.[16] Henry Jones, who had always opposed procrastination, wrote to Reichel in typical vein:

> Reichel, it has just struck me that your safest way is to *push* on and get your *Commission* appointed without any delay. Evidently folk that matter are in the right mood just now. Heaven knows who *also* may have their innings if you postpone. *Strike*, Reichel, and get the others to strike while the right mood is dominant amongst the authorities.[17]

By the end of the year the University and its Colleges had formally asked that a Royal Commission be appointed. The correspondent of *The Times Educational Supplement* thought that the conference had wasted valuable months only to find itself obliged to accept a Royal Commission which it might earlier have accepted without ignominy as a free agent.[18] William George in turn expressed keen regret that the initiative of setting into motion a systematic inquiry had been left to the Lords of the Treasury. He felt humbled and rebuked; conferences had failed because of the notion that the situation could be remedied by a stitch here and a stitch there, whereas the government had determined not to tolerate 'a thing of shreds and patches'. In offering a Royal Commission it had shown that it 'meant business and meant to do something substantial for the Welsh people'.[19]

At this point it seemed that prominent Welshmen were embarking upon a demoralizing bout of self-immolation. Yet it is just to remember that institutions seldom find it easy to reform themselves. External intervention had been necessary at Oxford and Cambridge, at the Scottish Universities, at London, and in Ireland it was the Irish Universities Act of 1908 which had brought in radical changes. Between 1896 and 1909 the whole system of 'modern' universities had been transformed; the Universities of Birmingham, Bristol, Durham, Leeds, Liverpool, Manchester, Sheffield, and the University Colleges of Nottingham, Reading and Southampton had either been created or reconstituted. In Wales thirty-five years had passed since the Aberdare Committee's report and twenty-two years since the granting of a charter to its University. A properly conducted inquiry could lead to beneficent reform and to solid progress. It was time to take stock.

Misgivings arose as to the composition of the Commission. Would an outside body understand the needs of the national University and would there be too many Scottish members? Upon this latter point one Principal (probably E. H. Griffiths) injudiciously aired his prejudices in the *Western Mail*. 'We generally find', he observed, 'that a Royal Commission of that kind is constituted of Scotsmen who will bring to bear upon Welsh education their experience of Scottish institutions. We do not want any of that.'[20] Neither he nor Reichel can have objected to a Scot as chairman for they had initially favoured Lord Bryce, and T. F. Roberts seems to have concurred. Bryce was a celebrated jurist, historian and statesman (and 'notorious for his integrity',[21] according to Arnold Toynbee), but his age may have told against him, for he was now nearly seventy-six. Henry Jones was not averse to Bryce but favoured Sir William McCormick, chairman of the Treasury's Advisory Committee. Lawyers as a whole he thought too rigid to be good heads of commissions, yet he readily advanced the claims of Richard Burdon, first Viscount Haldane, both a former and future Lord Chancellor, presumably because he had the saving grace of being a philosopher who was at his best in dealing with legal principles rather than in interpreting facts. 'He has a large intellect', said Henry Jones 'somewhat loosely packed, but he would not do too badly at all.'[22] He had certain disadvantages, a piping voice, penguin-like gestures (for he was rotund) and an untamed tendency to prolixity upon public occasions which exposed him to ungenerous criticism. More serious, his education in Germany, his deep attachment to German philosophy (Lotze in particular), his abortive mission to Germany in 1912 – on behalf of the government and never satisfactorily explained – led in the early months of the war to a virulent attack by the press which hounded him out of office in 1915. For a time, too, he fell out of favour with Lloyd George but by 1915 the two were evidently reconciled. In June 1916 William George spoke of meeting 'your friend Lord Haldane. He was very sincere and cordial and appears to be very keen on making a good job of it.'[23] It was an excellent appointment. According to Henry Jones, Haldane had the great merit of actually believing in education. Nor had he disqualified himself in the eyes of Nonconformists by presenting the case for Welsh Church disestablishment in the House of Lords in 1913.[24]

Even if the Commission did not include such Olympian figures as had served on the London Commission (Lord Milner, for example, or Sir Robert Romer), yet it was a distinguished body.[25] There is no evidence of an initial reluctance to appoint a woman member or a medical expert as had been the case at London in 1908. Emily Penrose, Principal of Somerville College, Oxford, the largest of the women's colleges, was, we may be sure, in part appointed to safeguard the interests of women but she was much more than the 'statutory woman'. As has been well said, Emily Penrose not so much asserted as assumed the equality of women.[26] The Welsh Medical School had been a major cause of the inquiry, which was to benefit from the contributions of Sir

William Osler, Regius Professor of Medicine at Oxford and earlier Professor of Medicine at Johns Hopkins University. W. H. Bragg, Quain Professor of Physics at London University, was, with his son, awarded the Nobel Prize for Physics in 1915. W. H. Hadow, Principal of Armstrong College, Newcastle upon Tyne (University of Durham), recognized authority on music, had in addition co-operated with his gifted sister, Grace E. Hadow, to produce the *Oxford Treasury of English Literature* (3 vols., 1906–8). Equally welcome was A. D. Hall, a commissioner under the Development Act, the first Principal of Wye College, Director of Rothamsted Experimental Station and an eminent scientific agriculturalist. W. N. Bruce, second son of the first Lord Aberdare, an administrator at the Board of Education, had earlier as an assistant examiner to the Charity Commission taken part in implementing the Welsh Intermediate Education Act. Sir Henry Jones and Sir Owen M. Edwards, outstanding Welshmen of their generation, could be counted on to represent Welsh educational aspirations. A. H. Kidd, the secretary of the Commission, was exceedingly able and was trusted by the Treasury. Herbert Lewis could not imagine a better appointment: 'he is made for it'.[27]

There were notes of dissent, mostly in private. Reichel thought that Owen Edwards was 'faddy',[28] that he lacked the power of weighing evidence and had alienated most of those who were organizing Welsh secondary schools, an obvious reference to the 'expensive report' of 1909. Lewis confided that Edwards was anathema to the three Principals, who solemnly predicted a minority report.[29] The somewhat angular M. F. Rathbone judged him to be 'decidedly impractical', too limited, and not deeply interested in university education and that elementary education was for him 'the ideal brand'.[30] An impartial reading of the minutes of evidence of the report does indeed suggest that his interrogation of witnesses was not always impressive. On the other hand, during his membership of the Commission his health was not good, he was heavily overworking (compounded by an inability to delegate) and he was the only member to have attended every meeting of the Commission, including one, as has been noticed elsewhere,[31] which coincided with a Congregation of the University of Wales at which he was to have received an honorary degree. Most of all, no one, as editor and writer, had

given greater delight and encouragement to the younger
generation, and for this reason alone T. F. Roberts was right to
say that his membership of the Commission 'would give great
confidence throughout Wales'.[32] One of the highest tributes ever
paid to Edwards was by a schoolmaster in the course of his
evidence to the Commission: 'You taught us that Wales was a
nation'.[33] Herbert Lewis came nearer the mark than most:

> The greatest honour I have at the Board of Education is that of
> being at any rate the nominal 'chief' of the greatest living
> benefactor to Welsh literature. I often say that when those of us
> who are now working for Wales are forgotten dust, two names will
> survive – those of Lloyd George and O. M. Edwards. Ceir gweled.
> [Time will tell].[34]

All the principals had asked for the appointment of Henry Jones
(and if not Jones, then John Rhys, who was, in fact, too old and
beyond recall). Jones, in turn, came under fire. T. Gwynn Jones
considered him to be but a remnant of his former self and to have
succumbed to mere verbiage.[35] Whilst it may be conceded that
Henry Jones had from his early days developed a declamatory
style and was often given to rhetorical surges, nevertheless,
Gwynn Jones's strictures cannot be sustained by a reading of the
minutes of the Haldane Report or of his wartime
correspondence. The truth is that Gwynn Jones (not always the
best judge of men) was mortified, as were others, by Henry
Jones's reiterated claims that the Great War was a spiritual
crusade against the powers of darkness.

E. T. John, a former Middlesborough industrialist, now Liberal
member for East Denbighshire and a fervent advocate of home
rule for Wales, wondered whether Henry Jones and O. M.
Edwards were rather too detached from the realities of industrial
life and whether they lacked the 'stability of intellectual poise'[36]
to withstand the demoralizing pressures of an international
conflagration. John's views may have been coloured, however, by
his ardent wish to have served on the Commission himself. The
most benighted attack upon the Commission came from
Anglesey. Apart from Edwards and Jones, it was said, the
members of the Commission were 'absolute failures',[37] a view

exceeding in imbecility the castigation by the *Celt* of certain members of the Welsh Land Commission in 1893.[38]

Temperate opinion was generally favourable, but there were residual doubts. The *Welsh Outlook* had once thought that a small commission of five members, rather than nine, would have sufficed.[39] More serious was the ineradicable suspicion that Haldane was in thrall to Germanic ideas. The well-informed thought otherwise. It was agreed that Haldane had long studied Germany's educational system, but it was evident from his *Education and Empire* (1902) that he had a large knowledge of the organization and spirit of American, French and Swiss universities as well as those in these islands:

> Our notions are entirely different from those of Germany. There everywhere is done by the state right through . . . What we want is to take the British principle, which is local administration and control fostered and assisted by the State. That to my mind is the keystone to which our educational system must conform, having regard to what is the genius of our people.[40]

Some drew comfort from the fact that his constructive philosophical work was entitled *The Pathway to Reality* (1903). Haldane would have welcomed the comments of E. T. John, who praised Haldane's catholicity of temperament, which 'with all its continental implications arouses no prejudice in the Principality'.[41] Others were impressed by the composition of the Commission, skilfully balanced and representing vital interests. There was also a fitting degree of continuity: Emily Penrose and William Osler were both members of the Advisory Committee on Grants to Universities and Colleges which had reported in 1914 on the University of Wales, whilst W. N. Bruce, through his father Lord Aberdare, reached back to the early days of the colleges at Aberystwyth and Cardiff. The Welsh correspondent of *The Times Educational Supplement* thought that there was 'general satisfaction'[42] concerning the Commission, which the *Welsh Outlook* declared was 'in every way a strong and worthy one'.[43]

Matters did not proceed altogether smooothly. Unwarranted suspicions of secrecy were aroused when it was bruited that the Commission's proceedings were to be conducted behind closed doors, a perfectly reasonable decision in the light of experience at the Welsh Land Commission's open sessions where the presence of the public sometimes raised the temperature beyond the level of frank exchange.[44] More serious was William George's report in *Y Beirniad* that Haldane during one of his visits to the Colleges had suggested that it might be advantageous if an official body of ten persons were appointed to control the University and its Colleges and to advise the crown as to their needs.[45] William George had evidently become convinced that Haldane's aside was now a settled item of policy, whereas it cannot have been other than a testing of the waters. Haldane, however, was soon to find that he had caused more than a ripple. The brother of the Prime Minister went beyond the columns of *Y Beirniad*, for in January 1917 he and others summoned a number of influential persons to the Raven Hotel, Shrewsbury, and appointed a committee to organize a widespread protest in Wales against dangers now supposedly revealed. Resolutions were passed thick and fast in several areas and the inhabitants of Waunfawr, Caernarfonshire, were informed by their Member of Parliament that a democratic system would be transformed by 'the Germanisation of the University'[46] whose governing body had agreed to accept the Commission's findings. By March tempers had cooled and the *Western Mail* thought that the campaign begun in north Wales had been premature, a view confirmed by a perusal of the appendix to the Commission's first report, newly published, where there was no suggestion in the questions put to witnesses of an authoritarian government by decemvir.[47]

At all events there were few signs of that apathy which the *Welsh Outlook* had feared in 1916.[48] Indeed, always bubbling below the surface, and sometimes erupting, was the ardent ambition of a group of Cardiff secessionists to dismantle the federal University. Aberystwyth and Bangor were convinced that E. H. Griffiths had resolved to achieve university status for Cardiff before he retired. In early 1916 Reichel told Henry Jones that a conference of the three colleges had failed because Cardiff had strongly argued that freedom of teaching was impossible in a federal university, firmly rejecting arguments based upon the system then operating at the new Catholic University of Ireland where each college had a separate syllabus, the internal examiner setting the examination paper which was merely revised by the external examiner.[49] Influential figures at Aberystwyth and Bangor sometimes responded by declaring privately that the two colleges 'should together be *the* University of *Wales* (Welsh Wales)'.[50] Joint action, however, was seldom favoured even when it was seriously initiated. A planned meeting of Bangor and Aberystwyth scientists foundered because four Bangor scientists were 'laid up',[51] according to Mary Rathbone, who condemned certain members of the Bangor staff for not being sufficiently energetic. There was further disquiet when John Morris-Jones heard that Aberystwyth nourished ambitions to concentrate advanced Welsh studies at the College. He expressed himself freely to J. H. Davies, the Aberystwyth Registrar:

> Some of our people here are disturbed by a suspicion . . . that you at Aberystwyth intend to press your claim to be the only College at which Welsh should be studied to an advanced stage, basing it on the fact that the National Library is situated at Aberystwyth. I trust there is no truth in this. I do not think Welsh should be sacrificed in Wales in the interests of any supposed retrenchment to be gained by doing away with overlapping. Each of the three centres has its own advantages for the study of the subject, apart from the fact that it should be represented as worthily as possible at each College. Welsh sentiment will revolt against a proposal to degrade the subject at any College. That is what makes me feel sure there can be nothing in the supposition that any College would put it forward.[52]

Again, was there a danger that the magnanimous Llandinam gifts to Aberystwyth might encourage notions of independence?[53] At about the same time Thomas Jones – often known as T.J. – was preparing a memorandum (privately circulated in the first instance, though later published) concerning the future of Aberystwyth.[54] Of all College documents prepared with the Royal Commission in mind it is probably the most impressive both in breadth of view and in its detailed proposals. At Bangor it was bound to raise hackles. T.J. agreed that the college in Snowdonia should have a chair of geology, but its case for a chair of economics was 'less strong'. An 'advanced' agricultural department should be placed at Aberystwyth, though 'valuable advisory work' should continue to be done at Bangor, whilst a Social Studies School, so it seemed, was to be at Aberystwyth alone. Mary Rathbone could not assent to such propositions,[55] much as she admired Thomas Jones, who was chided also by Henry Jones for his apparent wish to limit the reasonable claims of both Bangor and Cardiff. Jones addressed T.J. as only he could:

> I approve of everything you want for Aberystwyth so long as you neither express nor imply *limitations* to the other two Colleges . . . Your *confinement* of the Social School to one College is horribly onesided and your implied opposition to a School of Economics at Bangor . . . I *would* like to see the leaders in Wales rise above this sort of thing, – is there any chance of arresting this damnable snatching . . . *Tom*, I adjure, I command you if I may, to qualify yourself by your *impartiality* and wide sympathy and outlook to lead education in Wales as a whole after the Commissioners (yours truly included) have turned to dust.[56]

By 1919, Jones was writing to T.J.: '*Every one of you stick to Wales*, and not mainly to Aberystwyth. That will *never* be a fine College, so long as it is in the power of the *Cardis* and the people who make religion do instead of rectitude.'[57] Such animadversions were not conducive to high thoughts concerning the common good, but for the most part they were set aside during the hectic preparation of submissions to the Commission.

The commissioners soon found themselves confronted by many critics of the University of Wales. William George thought that the Welsh colleges had far from exhausted 'their possibilities for good for the people of Wales',[58] who, in turn should take their share of the blame for the failure of the Colleges to fulfil the aspirations of the early pioneers. Richard Price, a Dowlais headmaster, feared that the University was not even a name to many local primary teachers.[59] J. C. Davies, Director of Education for Denbighshire, believed he reflected the views of local authorities in saying that 'the tendency of the University at present is not in a national direction'; he had detected amongst Senate members at Bangor 'a very distinct cleavage'[60] in their attitudes towards national issues, a remark which earned him a sharp rebuke from Henry Jones who said that he never knew a body more loyal to the community than his colleagues there twenty-five years before.[61] J. H. Davies, the Aberystwyth Registrar, feared losing touch with the Welsh people: 'that is, I think, our danger'.[62] The Cardiff Senate (apart from the Principal) favoured autonomy as soon as possible, a view reinforced by south Wales industrialists who had indicated in uncompromising terms that they were more likely to support applied science departments in a local rather than in a federal university.[63] Principal Griffiths, at best a reluctant federalist, pronounced emphatically that unless the College authorities were assured that they had sufficient powers 'to make their own arrangements with men of business in the district they would be bound to press for a separate university in South Wales'.[64] It should, perhaps, not escape attention that the unanimous Cardiff Senate included A. H. Trow and T. F. Sibly, both soon to become heads of University Colleges in Wales, and Thomas Powel, the ailing Professor of Celtic.

The role of the University Court was widely assailed. During discussions preceding the grant of the University charter two opinions had emerged. Some wished the Court to be the prime architect of Welsh education. Others, mindful of the autonomy of the colleges, believed it wiser to confine the powers of the Court to narrow limits pertaining to curricula and examinations. The second view had prevailed, and Brynmor Jones indicated to the Commission that he had been told in 1893 that 'the University was not to have any control (other than in regard to the granting of degrees) over the management of the Colleges, and not even in the appointment of Professors or other teachers therein'.[65] With the passage of time the question arose as to the wisdom of entrusting the Court with academic matters. Isambard Owen defended the decision on the ground that, for many years to come, the teachers of the University were unlikely to have been born or trained in Wales and that therefore they would not understand 'the special mental characteristics'[66] of Welsh students, whose interests were best protected by the Court representatives of Welsh thought and opinion. For fifteen years or so these arrangements had worked comparatively well – Owen thought that in the early days the Court was 'a public body of a remarkably good type'[67] – but new members, less equipped to deal with academic matters, accepted in supine fashion the recommendations placed before them by the University Senate. Soon there were complaints that it was a waste of time to attend meetings where business was 'cut-and-dried' and where hands were raised as if members were compliant freeholders at a pre-reform election. Principal Harris, of the Bangor Normal College, felt that when he was absent from a meeting of the Caernarfonshire Education Committee he had missed something of consequence but that the same could not be said of the University Court, which 'lacks vitality'.[68] Then again there were doubts concerning the quality of some members of the Court. Kenyon, for instance, was not satisfied with all county council representatives, of whom there were 'heaps' on the Court (twenty-seven in all); often old 'so-and-so'[69] was elected casually and knew no more about education than the local grocer (and no more, perhaps, than Kenyon himself knew of local grocers). There was a widespread suspicion that county councils were sending their ablest men to the Central Welsh Board rather than to the University Court, which had not fulfilled Tom Ellis's confident hope of 'the hundred best men in Wales for university purposes'.[70] The Executive Committee of the Court was not attacked, for it performed efficiently the tasks deputed to it. Although the Registrar's office was in Cardiff, the Committee met regularly in London, a practice defended by the Senior Deputy-Chancellor on grounds of general convenience, a view which prevailed for many decades.

The academic governance of the University was widely considered to be unsatisfactory, indeed, intolerable. The Cardiff Senate complained that the scope and efficiency of its teaching was seriously hampered, the Aberystwyth Senate condemned the complexity of regulations and procedure, whilst the Bangor Senate, though fully recognizing the measure of freedom enjoyed after casting away the bonds of London University, was deeply aware of 'certain cramping conditions'.[71] It is evident that students were in fact allowed a considerable range of options in constructing their degree schemes but that complicated, unsuitable choices were not sufficiently discouraged in the colleges. A. H. Trow of Cardiff thought that a number of combinations were unsatisfactory, though we have no record that Hebrew and electricity were fused together as in one university.[72] A student representative told the Commission that 'we should not be held responsible for getting our course into a muddle when we first come to college'.[73] There is evidence that courses were not always properly covered and that incorrect information was occasionally given concerning set books.[74] Some believed that since 1893 teachers had simply exchanged one tyranny for another; a common examining body for the three Colleges inevitably consigned the individual teachers to a subordinate position in the preparation of examination papers, whilst no account was taken of a student's work during the year. The main charges, however, were levelled at the University Senate, the breeding ground of entangling regulations. Once again, geography exacerbated the problem. All heads of departments were members of the peripatetic University Senate which met twice a year and which periodically involved absences of four to five days. Arcane rules were drawn up and two, sometimes three, years elapsed before they were printed. In such circumstances, E. H. Griffiths averred, it would have been difficult to promulgate the Ten Commandments.[75] It was said that only three mortals understood these stultifying regulations, the University Registrar, E. V. Arnold of Bangor, and the Secretary of the Senate, Miss Pearson, whose formidable boxes in the Registry have hitherto deterred even the most dry-as-dust historian.[76] Arnold did his best to defend the system, but it became increasingly clear that the Senate's executive committee had infrequently exercised executive powers. Isambard Owen might well plead that neither the charter nor the statutes were responsible for such calamities; nevertheless, under the federal system as it had developed during twenty years, the University was in one sense principally a board responsible for examinations and curricula in Colleges far apart, thus encouraging hard-pressed staff to save time and to avoid contention by submitting to compromise and uniformity. A proper balance had not been attained between the due freedom of teacher and student, on the one hand, and the reasonable requirements of central control, on the other.[77]

Inevitably, too, the commissioners had in the forefront of their mind the criticisms of the Advisory Committee on University Grants in 1913, especially the doubt expressed as to whether the

University and its Colleges were as aware as they should be that in combination they were a national institution, not simply local or municipal bodies, and that the University as a whole was apparently unable to prevent the creation of new departments and costly duplication, especially in applied science. Again, early inquiry into the formation of a National School of Medicine had seemed to suggest that the University was not well suited to assume responsibility for educational plans involving the whole of Wales. Such misgivings on a broad front boded ill for the future of the University. Yet the Commissioners unanimously recommended reform, not defederalization. Why was this so?

First, it was at once apparent that Cardiff Senate's desire for independence was not supported by Cardiff's own College Council, nor indeed by any public institution, educational or otherwise, represented before the Commission. Haldane was later to say that 'there was a greater place than Cardiff, and that was the Principality of Wales, in which Cardiff was included'.[78] Whilst it may be conceded that the prospect of an autonomous Cardiff was not wholly unrealistic even at this stage, yet it was doubtful whether Aberystwyth and Bangor, 'the northern Colleges',[79] as Kenyon called them, could face the future with confidence, either together or independently. Moreover, the Cardiff Senate was in no way opposed to a substantial measure of co-operation with the other two colleges in such matters as fellowships, postgraduate studies and uniform standards for matriculation and entry. Isambard Owen took it as self-evident that when a single college had reached the size of Manchester (barely exceeding 1,000 students by 1914) it could reasonably expect to become a separate university.[80] But there were others, such as E. T. John, who would not countenance the disintegration of the national university on grounds of numbers. D. Lleufer Thomas believed that there could be no finality upon a matter which a future generation would need to determine in the light of its own experience, but 'the time in my opinion is certainly not ripe now'.[81] Such was the general view. Percy Watkins thought that too much had been made of the trials of travelling long distances to University meetings, and when the chairman wondered whether the tranquil reflections of 'the professorial mind'[82] were not unduly disturbed by tedious interruptions,

Watkins replied that to leave the cloister occasionally was advantageous, particularly to confer with those engaged in similar pursuits in other parts of the Principality. Further, the splitting up of the old Victoria University offered no real parallel because conditions in Yorkshire and Lancashire differed markedly from those in Wales which he regarded as a convenient unit for administrative purposes and which needed *'unification* of effort and purpose'[83] in order to heighten an awareness of national identity. Another witness, Elizabeth P. Hughes, believed that the University of Wales could bind together the various parts of the country, thus helping to maintain Welsh nationality.[84] Representatives of students reinforced the argument. The distinguishing mark of the University of Wales was its national character and the Welsh people would give a larger measure of support to a national institution than to an agglomeration of local units. It is noteworthy that students pressed for the representation of the University in Parliament.[85] The Commission was also influenced by other arguments to which it drew attention: 'a single university affords the best security for freedom as against external interference, and for a due appreciation of the value of the degree outside Wales'. Moreover, 'it enables Wales collectively to confer honour on distinguished men; and . . . it is in accordance with the trend of other recent popular movements in Wales which has been in the direction of unity'.[86]

The commissioners were attracted by certain practical proposals for the reconstruction of the University. Individual colleges should enjoy larger freedom in their dealings with students, from matriculation to graduation, thus recognizing the essential bond between teacher and taught. External authority, most apparent in matters pertaining to examinations, sometimes discouraged, in Haldane's words, a 'joint voyage of discovery in search of truth'.[87] In relation to appointments, Isambard Owen had greater confidence in College rather than in University authorities, for the former would have to live with their errors.[88] Nevertheless, there was general agreement that the University should be given clear, if limited, powers over a wide area of administration. On the vexed question of recognition of new departments, the Bangor Senate and Council had given a firm lead, for they explicitly stated that a department should not be

recognized by the University unless sufficient evidence was produced that it would be adequately staffed, equipped and maintained, and, secondly, that the University should have authority
to refuse to recognize a new department even if such a
department had been recognized in another College.[89]

These proposals, amongst many others, convinced the Commission that necessary criticisms levelled against the University
were in the main presented in a constructive spirit. Equally
evident were the qualities of heart and mind of the commissioners themselves. They had assuredly listened to many
charges and criticisms. Nevertheless:

> . . . the impression we have received from these utterances is not at
> all that of a series of confessions of failure. On the contrary, these
> witnesses were all proud of the University, and full of hope for its
> future . . . What strikes us is the fearless undoubting assumption
> that the University and its work should be a subject of constant
> and lively concern to all men and women in Wales, and should
> bring a potent and recognised influence to bear upon their lives. It
> is the presence of this spirit which has so constantly lifted the
> subject of our Reference out of the dull atmosphere with which its
> technicalities too often surround it.[90]

Despite all the difficulties and drawbacks the commissioners
were persuaded that 'Wales desires – and is right in desiring – a
single national University'.[91]

The next question to determine was what kind of federal
university it should be. There were some similarities between the
colleges at Oxford and Cambridge and those of the University of
Wales, for each recognized a central University organization, and
in each the College was the real bond between the student and
the University; Wales could also look with advantage to the
tutorial system at the older universities. Yet it was unrealistic to
compare the two types of colleges in the hope of deriving many
profitable lessons. For one thing, they were the products of a
vastly different history. In Oxford and Cambridge the University
had preceded the foundation of Colleges; in Wales the reverse
was the case. The colleges of the University of London, on the
other hand, had a strong resemblance to those of Wales, but there

were two manifest differences. On the one hand, the London colleges were in a comparatively compact area, while, on the other, they were troubled by the dual aim of meeting the needs of both internal and external students. If Wales was to have a federal university it must look elsewhere for exemplars, if such indeed were to be found. The federal system, 'an invention of British origin',[92] had been created in order to confer upon a group of individual colleges, too frail to stand alone, the privileges of university status in the expectation that they would grow into fully fledged institutions. At first the Victoria University was considered a fitting model, and O. M. Edwards, as we have seen, was misled into believing that the northern light was brighter than it was.[93] The functions of the university, those of examining and of awarding degrees, had imposed upon the colleges a wooden uniformity leading to resentment rather than to a true sense of common purpose. New Zealand's federal university was again primarily an examining body and the discontents voiced in the Antipodes at length led to an invitation to Bangor's Principal to inquire and to report.[94] The University of Durham comprised three institutions whose intricate system of government was eased by the considerable freedom enjoyed by the colleges and by their close proximity allowing frequent communication impossible in Wales, which might at most derive some 'useful hints'[95] from Durham but scarcely a constitutional model. Scotland and Switzerland had long demonstrated that small countries could nurture a handful of universities without injury to patriotic ideals of unity and the commissioners were wise to consider whether important lessons might be learnt from a close inspection of the Scottish scene. After legislation in 1858 and 1889, The Universities (Scotland) Acts, there were certain restrictions upon university independence in relation to entrance examinations, for example, and the creation of new chairs, but it was difficult to discover important advances in fashioning a united policy or in fact any serious measures which could profitably be adopted elsewhere.[96]

The sober conclusion was that there was no system which Wales might usefully emulate. The one essential prerequisite of reconstruction was a keen awareness of the strength of national feeling. A University of Wales should be able 'to enlist a patriotic energy and fervour in its service such as perhaps no other University in the Kingdom has inspired',[97] and the challenge to the commissioners was to harness that spirit in the service of higher education to create an organization which would give it full, constructive expression. In pursuance of this aim the distinction between legislative and executive functions must ensure that the decisions taken were swift and soundly based and that administrators acted in accord with university policy after consulting well-informed, capable advisers. If the 'national element' was to be reinforced in the government of the University, it must not be at the expense of the local autonomy of the Colleges, which should be greater than hitherto. The University should realize more than ever before 'the illimitable field of its duties towards every section of the community'. Institutions capable of reaching university standards in some aspects of their work should be encouraged and guided by the University. Finally, it should 'send out its graduates to carry the light of knowledge to the very doors of those whose daily avocations do not allow them to enter its Colleges'.[98]

It is easy to say that fine words butter no parsnips, but no one can justly question the sincerity of the commissioners. To convert high aspirations into hard, clear recommendations, however, was another matter. The core of the Commission's proposals was as follows. The University Court was to be 'a Parliament of higher education . . . thoroughly representative of the proper elements'[99] in Welsh life, a factor of far greater importance than the size of the Court, now almost doubled, from 108 to 213 members. It was no longer thought necessary to have thirteen crown representatives, henceforth reduced to three, but there was a mighty increase in the representation of local authorities, from twenty-seven to ninety-one, and upon this decision we must for a moment dwell. Since the granting of the University's first charter, local education authorities had been given large powers by Parliament to make provision for higher education and there was a reasonable expectation that they would in concert grant a substantial annual sum to the University whose fortunes they would thus view with the keenest attention, preferably from within the University. Criticisms that local authorities in England had impeded the progress of the younger universities and

colleges stemmed from the fact that they were in origin 'civic'
institutions and could not easily claim the full allegiance of local
authorities whose responsibilities extended well beyond the area
in which universities and colleges had been established. The
territorial consideration was not so significant in Wales (except
perhaps to a limited extent in Cardiff) because the University was
deemed to belong to the whole country. There was a further
recommendation of more than passing interest. Since representation of local authorities was dramatically increased and since
some of their ablest members might be appointed to the Court
by another body, local authorities were encouraged in such
circumstances to nominate a suitable person outside their own
ranks so that the University might indeed draw upon the 'proper
elements'[100] in Welsh public life. It was normal that Glamorgan
and Monmouthshire should contribute nearly one half of the
members and that national institutions, such as the National
Library and the National Museum, should be represented.
Members of Parliament were to choose three out of their own
members, on the whole a sensible decision because other
national bodies which have included all Members of Parliament
have found that their attendance has been at best fitful. The
commissioners had evidently listened intently to the evidence of
William George who had spoken of the reconstituted Court as

> a real high festival for education so as to make it worth the people's
> while going from home and making a sacrifice to go from home to
> attend it, and a sort of meeting which teachers and people engaged
> in education would like to attend – a sort of purple day to relieve
> the monotony of their lives – something really fine.[101]

In short it was to be a great national gathering, an eisteddfod in
its own right. The commissioners echoed these sentiments and
we cannot fully appreciate the temper of the report without a
lengthy quotation upon this theme:

> We commend earnestly to the Welsh people and to the
> reconstituted Court the plan, suggested to us by one of the
> witnesses, for a yearly or half-yearly meeting of the court which
> should not hurry through its formal agenda in one day with its

attention divided between the business and the clock or railway-guide, but should set out deliberately to spend four or five or six days on the discussion of both the practical affairs and the broader aims of higher education. Its members, or many of them, are in other capacities accustomed to attend long sessions of the National Eisteddfod or the British Association, and to listen, to discuss, to judge, to enlarge their knowledge and taste, to launch schemes for the good of their country at such meetings. Why should this not be possible for the great meeting of the National University Court? . . . The gathering need not be confined strictly to university business. It would afford an opportunity for lectures and addresses by eminent persons on appropriate subjects, and there would be many occasions on which the public might be admitted to attend the proceedings, or even to take part in some of the discussions . . . Great projects of reform and development might be discussed, and even if there were no immediate result these discussions would be at once the outcome of public opinion and the means of bringing it to ripeness. We believe that if educational leaders and workers in Wales will take this adventure upon them with the zeal and spirit they have so often displayed in educational movements, an immense impulse will be given to the cause of higher education, and that the University will gain a new footing as a national institution and awaken interest in numbers of people it has never yet reached.[102]

Whether such eloquence bore close relation to reality is a matter which must be deferred to a later occasion. This much, however, is certain. The commissioners (or most of them) can scarcely have been exposed previously to such enthusiastic pleas for higher education expressed in national terms.

The prescribed functions of the Court,[103] which was to elect its Chancellor and which was normally to be presided over by a Pro-Chancellor, included the making of new statutes, the conferment of honorary degrees upon the nomination of the University Council, the approval of the admission of a new constituent college and of the institution of any new degree, diploma or certificate, in each case upon the recommendation of the University Council. The Council[104] of eighteen members was a new executive body, mainly, but not entirely, the creation of the University Court. At least one third of the members of the Council were to be elected from among the representatives of local authorities on the Court. At one stage it appeared that there would be no College representatives, so as to avoid the danger of distracting rivalries. E. H. Griffiths of Cardiff preferred to have an entirely impartial tribunal, but Reichel believed that such a body would not work effectively in the absence of knowledge of College affairs. In the end there was a compromise, each college being allowed one representative, in practice its Principal.[105] The Council's chief duty was to determine the allocation of funds. Hitherto government grants had been paid separately to the University and to its Colleges and a portion of such grants had been 'earmarked' for specific purposes in order to ensure the speedy remedy of defects. Henceforth 'earmarking' was to be discontinued, as had already happened in England, and the whole of the state grant paid to the University in one sum to be determined by the Advisory Committee on University Grants (as was also the case in England). In pursuance of this exacting duty the Council would confer regularly with the College authorities and receive the advice of an Academic Board but it would not need to have its decisions confirmed by the Court. It also had a wide range of functions relating, for instance, to honorary degrees, the appointment and tenure of the officers of the University, and the admission of new constituent colleges. Attention should especially be drawn to the power to approve the establishment of a new department in any college and to withdraw approval of an existing department. We should note, too, the unlamented passing of the old University Senate of over sixty members, now replaced by an Academic Board of seventeen members which, as we have already seen, was to advise the University Council and which in addition had the right to make direct representations to the Council and to appoint outside experts upon committees which it might wish to create.[106]

As to the constitution of the constituent colleges the commissioners were disposed to leave the matters to the Colleges themselves in the expectation that they would implement certain recommendations.[107] On Councils there should be at least three Senate representatives and also representatives of employers and of employees where there were strong local industries; councils should not normally exceed thirty-five members. Senates should include all professors and heads of departments, two representatives of other teaching staff and at least one woman academic member since there were so many women students and since the charter of the University had so stalwartly asserted the equality of the sexes as a fundamental principle. Standards for the admission of students were to be determined by the University in consultation with secondary school authorities, whilst the University itself would test students who had followed a stony, circuitous path. The University was to prescribe the period of residence and study for both pass and honours degrees and approve combinations of courses. Advice and guidance concerning courses should be given by the Colleges, and in a brief, pregnant sentence the report quenched much smouldering discontent: 'The approval of syllabuses should be a matter lying entirely between the teacher and his College.'[108] Again, once students had been admitted, the University should not intervene in their examinations until the initial degree. At this stage, witnesses had generally agreed, there should be an external examiner, if only 'to give the public confidence',[109] as Sibly of Cardiff had said. Reichel had been more positive: 'he performs a real function'.[110] Atkins of Aberystwyth felt that 'we as internal examiners welcome the assistance of another in arriving at our decisions'.[111] The commissioners had no doubts. In the final examination for the initial degree, a single external examiner should represent the University on each body of internal examiners. He was not to set the examination papers, in future to be prepared by internal examiners after considering his suggestions. He retained the right of veto upon the passing of candidates.

There followed several recommendations relating to the teaching staff.[112] Professors and heads of departments were to be recognized by the University, which should have a say in their appointment. 'While their appointment should continue to rest with the College, it should be made on the recommendation of expert Standing Committees appointed jointly by the College and the University.'[113] Tenure needed to be more secure, the commissioners favouring *ad vitam aut culpam*[114] ('for lifetime or until fault'), a concept which has been under fire in more recent times. But if such fixity could not be contemplated, then dismissal should be preceded by full inquiry and right of appeal.

The perennial problem of salaries next engaged their attention. They entirely upheld the recommendations of the Advisory Committee that a firm demarcation be drawn between the emoluments of present and future teachers in a manner strangely reminiscent of the parable of the workers in the vineyard.[115] Henceforth, professors would receive a minimum of £500 upon appointment, speedily rising to £650, and perhaps more for special merit; the minimum could be exceeded to attract scientists and technological experts. Independent lecturers should receive no less than £300 and rise incrementally to £500 at the very least. Assistant lecturers, the curates of the profession, were to begin at £150 and proceed by unexciting stages to £200, at which point, if they were not promoted to lecturer, their services were to be discontinued; otherwise they could expect a final salary of £450. All members of the permanent staff were encouraged to join the Federated Superannuation System for Universities. Routine teaching should not become excessively burdensome, otherwise independent investigation would inevitably suffer, to the hurt of the nation, especially its scientific needs. Sabbatical leave, a necessary refreshment allowed elsewhere, should be introduced whenever possible. The creation of University Faculties presented difficulties in a federal University but the commissioners hoped that College Faculties would act jointly on occasions and elect joint committees for special purposes. The tutorial system, badly neglected, would invigorate teaching, and teachers and students would be less harassed if the complicated division of courses into successive hurdles were substantially modified. A large purse would be needed to deal with these proposals and the financial implications were deferred to the end of the report.[116]

Two recommendations led to the creation of new institutions. In the case of Swansea the matter was dealt with expeditiously, the new-born College receiving its charter in 1920. The commissioners urged the independence of the National School of Medicine at Cardiff, but, as we shall see, a long, troubled *accouchement* preceded delivery. These major developments are of such importance that they must be treated separately.[117] Technological studies in the University were to be based on the co-operation of the University College at Cardiff with the proposed College at Swansea; a University Faculty of Technology and a Board of Technology should be established and a degree in Technology awarded; upon certain conditions advanced work in recognized post-secondary institutions should count towards a degree.[118]

Proposals relating to agriculture were revived periodically, if not with the regularity of a rotating crop; they aroused controversy which has not yet been wholly resolved to the satisfaction of disinterested observers. Both Aberystwyth and Bangor had presented plans to transform their agriculture departments upon a scale exceeding that of any other agriculture department in the realm. The commissioners found it difficult to justify, and especially to finance, two such departments designed to enable a student to pursue advanced scientific courses.[119] At the heart of the debate lay the differences in soil and farming between north and central Wales which called for specialized inquiry. The commissioners concluded that existing degree courses were unsuitable for both the practising farmer and the prospective teacher, and should in future consist of more economics and history than of pure science. At an advanced level a postgraduate course was needed, highly scientific in content and provided in one college only which should be suitably staffed and equipped. Perhaps the commissioners were prudent not to indicate whether this department should be at Aberystwyth or Bangor, doubtless judging that such a divisive question was best settled by the reconstituted University. In the event, upon this particular issue, Aberystwyth and Bangor became allies in adversity and the proposals faced a two-pronged attack. As to forestry, it would have to wait upon a declaration of national policy concerning afforestation.[120]

That Celtic studies in the University needed to be thoroughly organized and to receive a substantial injection of funds was evident after a mere perusal of an excellent paper presented by J. H. Davies, then Registrar of Aberystwyth.[121] In Celtic studies Ireland had preceded Wales; at University College, Dublin, a former Bangor student was professor, and nearer at hand, Liverpool had a chair of Celtic and a lectureship in Welsh. In order to pursue studies in Celtic, Welshmen had gone to Oxford, Freiburg and Berlin, Paris and Rennes. The commissioners drew attention to the collection of Welsh books at Bangor and especially to the National Library which had given a pronounced stimulus to Celtic studies. They also noted an undue concentration upon the history and philology of language (a criticism often directed against other universities) which did not meet the needs of the majority of students. J. H. Davies thought that such specialization was due to two factors. The first occupant of the chair of Celtic at Oxford, 'the father of modern study in Welsh',[122] was Sir John Rhys and students who later became teachers of Welsh in colleges and schools tended to follow his philological bent. Secondly, the scant attention given to the literature of Wales after 1400 and to history after 1300 was largely due to shortage of printed material. The commissioners readily accepted J. H. Davies's main proposals.[123] A University Board of Celtic Studies should be established; it should co-operate with the National Library and National Museum; it should be largely composed of persons most competent to supervise such studies; it should not have direct control over College courses and it should be principally concerned with postgraduate studies, the organization and publication of research, and it should receive a grant from University funds. Substantial financial aid would certainly be necessary 'for some time at least'[124] to implement an allied proposal, the creation of a University Press Board. Too often the work of scholars either did not appear at all in print or found its way to comparatively obscure journals. It could also do much to encourage able persons outside the University, teachers, for example, and outstanding members of tutorial classes, to pursue and publish significant studies. Not surprisingly, there was to be a University Extension Board whose main function was to assess the needs, co-ordinate the activities and supplement the work of the colleges. The commissioners noted with gratification that the extra-mural movement (so close to the chairman's heart) owed little to the student's supposed ambition to graduate and that 'there is in Wales a great desire both to give and to receive instruction conceived in the true university spirit'.[125]

The sections of the report which deal with music, we may reasonably suppose, bear the imprint of W. H. Hadow. No people in Europe found in song 'a more intimate means of expression' than the Welsh people, and it was proclaimed 'without exaggeration' that Wales was 'a land of singers, and that she has the power of making, in music, a contribution to the art of the world which is comparable to the highest achievements of painting or poetry or sculpture'.[126] However, a necessary note of realism was soon introduced. Choral performances of Handel and Mendelssohn were in themselves splendid, but there was a reluctance to leave well-trodden paths. Instrumental music had been seriously neglected. At the eisteddfod of 1916 there was only one string quartet; in most parts of Wales hardly anyone had ever heard an orchestra, let alone played in one. To be deprived of symphonic and concert music was akin to studying English poetry without ever reading Shakespeare. The commissioners therefore urged that in each university college there should be a department of music, fully staffed, to teach music to degree level and to act as a centre of music for its district; the University should co-operate with educational bodies, the Central Welsh Board, for example, and with the National Eisteddfod. There followed an imaginative proposal that the office of Music Director be created. Preferably he should be a professor at one of the colleges and be responsible for work in his own college district, but as Director he should be *primus inter pares*, and act as chairman of the new Council of Music for Wales, 'the supreme consultative body on all matters with which the musical education of Wales is concerned'.[127]

Theology had long been a vexed question, though public opinion was clearly moving by 1893. A Faculty of Theology had been established and a candidate for the degree of Bachelor in Divinity, who had first graduated in arts and science, could follow at a theological college a course recognized by the University. The commissioners were convinced that the time had come for closer co-operation, partly because it was wrong to make 'an absolute divorce'[128] between teaching and examining, partly because a knowledge of Semitic languages was essential to other disciplines and partly because Hebrew was taught both in university colleges and theological colleges, a wasteful duplication. They concluded that the University and its Colleges should now be given unrestricted freedom to provide instruction and to undertake research in theological subjects. The national University was to be the sole judge of the use made of the new freedom. On the subject of St David's College, Lampeter, the commissioners were properly circumspect, but since most students of the College did not proceed to Oxford or Cambridge they expressed the view that it was 'a real loss both to their Church and to Wales that young Welshmen should spend these precious years of mental and moral development segregated from their contemporaries in the University Colleges'.[129] These were wise words.

There were other matters of comment rather than of recommendation. The relationship between the University Colleges and training colleges had not been examined in detail, but the commissioners believed that closer co-operation was highly desirable.[130] One suggestion for exploration was whether the whole of a prospective teacher's professional training could be pursued at a training college. An experiment of this kind, so it seemed, was possible at Bangor because of the close proximity of the Normal College, but those well acquainted with both Principals did not anticipate serious progress on this front. There was approval for Bangor's proposal that peripatetic teachers appointed by the university should for limited periods, visit two or more colleges when continuous teaching was not essential.[131] In practice not much came of it, but there have been echoes from time to time. As to law, a creditable beginning had been made at Aberystwyth; each college would in time wish to make provision for the subject, but the most advanced work should preferably be concentrated in one populous centre having ready access to courts of law.[132] Again, Wales was virgin ground for the teaching of commerce. Cardiff and Swansea had obvious claims, but care would be needed to strengthen the study with intellectual content to avoid a superficial empiricism. The social sciences could do much to humanize administration and implant in the minds of men a new awareness of the duties of citizenship.[133]

The immediate *raison d'être* of the Commission was finance. Its members were clear in their minds that the country should no longer be content with the low rate of state aid to universities. The war had fully demonstrated 'the folly of starving higher education'.[134] In some matters 'parsimony is inexcusable. Not only is expenditure upon education the most remunerative of investments, it is also the most necessary of all forms of insurance.' Yet there was much to be said for the Treasury view that state grants should 'supplement and encourage local effort',[135] a principle clearly enunciated by Lord Cranbrook and G. J. Goschen when grants were first made to English universities in 1889. Wales had received grants because the Aberdare Report had persuaded the government that Wales was too poor to support colleges by its own efforts, but since then there had been rapid industrial development in south Wales, now rich and prosperous, whilst local authorities had long been responsible for education and had substantial powers to levy rates. The commissioners did not mince matters. Local education authorities had 'in general shown little sustained interest in the work of the University and even less inclination to contribute financially towards its expenses', but there were signs that a 'profound modification'[136] was at hand.

Henry Jones, who believed that he had scotched the idea of a 'Super-Principal' for all the Welsh colleges, wished also to claim, and retain, the credit of having introduced the idea of a penny rate in Wales for university purposes.[137] He remembered persuading a hesitant William Rathbone nearly thirty years earlier to test public opinion to see whether it would support a rate for intermediate education. Having done so, Rathbone returned on the morrow to the Penrhyn Arms. 'I remember yet', said Jones, 'how your face beamed with joy as you told me on the College stairs of the successful meeting.'[138] Thereafter matters went from strength to strength and at length a long-delayed bill became the Intermediate Act of 1889. Fortified by this experience, Jones raised with Haldane the possibility of a penny rate for the University throughout the whole of Wales. He did so as both walked in the garden of a hotel on the Menai Straits (probably the George Hotel) during the Commission's Bangor visit. Haldane, as sceptical initially as Rathbone had been, advised Jones to speak to W. N. Bruce and W. H. Hadow. Bruce was cautious, but observed that a penny rate in Wales would produce about £50,000 and that a self-imposed rate would induce the Treasury to respond with an equal amount. Hadow warmly favoured the proposal, but may have had reservations. Soon Jones was closely questioned by his fellow commissioners who raised many objections, all of them valid, thought Jones, but surmountable. What Wales had done in 1889 Wales could again do. Leadership was of paramount importance and Welsh Members of Parliament, like the wild pigs Jones had seen in Burma, would run excitedly before a forest fire.

The commissioners were won over, gave the proposal their blessing and appealed 'with all possible earnestness'[139] to the Welsh people to place the product of a penny rate at the disposal of the University. The State in turn should provide grants on the basis of one pound for every pound of fresh local support, and, under certain conditions, grants in aid of capital expenditure. The state grant was to be fixed for a period of five years after receiving a report from the standing Advisory Committee on University Grants appointed by the President of the Board of Education. The University of Wales was in future to be paid by the Board of Education, rather than by the Treasury, as hitherto. Of this more must be said later.[140] As to private benefactions, generous individuals had tended to provide buildings and scholarships, which were immensely valuable, but it would be particularly advantageous if donors were to endow chairs or add to the general income of the University and its Colleges. The abolition of students' fees had been widely canvassed and whilst the effect on the revenues of the Welsh Colleges would not be as adverse as elsewhere because fees were lower, yet it would be considerable, and if the poorest students were to derive benefit a widespread system of scholarships would be essential.

Acceptable arrangements for the distribution of University funds was, of course, vital. E. H. Griffiths of Cardiff disliked entrusting the allocation of grants to a representative body, for it would lead to wire-pulling. As he rather inelegantly put it, 'you get to the state of throwing coppers amongst boys to scramble for'.[141] Kenyon was inclined to agree that it was difficult to allay Griffiths's misgivings and he did not at all care for the idea that Colleges should submit budgets to a central body. William George recommended that commissioners be appointed for five years to distribute funds until the Colleges had settled down to the new system; afterwards a statutory committee (including nominees of the crown) should be established for this purpose.[142]

The commissioners concluded that the University Council should deal with moneys at its disposal, namely grants by the State, the rate fund made available, it was hoped, by local authorities, and other income provided for university purposes. The constituent colleges were to present estimates, preferably annually, as were University Boards, and after due consultation and consideration the University Council was to determine the allocation of university funds. [143]

When the report was finally published there was general approval of the spirit in which the Commission had approached its task. From the first, Henry Jones had been anxious that it should stay in the neighbourhood of each college and become 'saturated'[144] with information and with every point of view. The Commission certainly did visit each college, but almost all its meetings were held in London and few of its members were so urgently anxious as was Jones when he wrote to Reichel for press clippings, opinions, plans, 'anything that you can believe will make me a better man for this job', and inviting him also, for full measure, to 'blow me up when needed'.[145] If surviving letters are a fair reflection, Jones was rather too much in touch with one college (Bangor), but we cannot reasonably question his conviction that 'a more eager Commission to help Wales could not have been invented'.[146] William George, at a time when he was wary of the chairman's intentions, praised the kindness and courtesy accorded him when he appeared before the Commission; indeed, he had greatly enjoyed being cross-examined for an hour and a half and he later had the satisfaction of seeing that his views had influenced the recommendations of the Commission.[147] It was not in Haldane's nature to trap or browbeat witnesses. As he explained to one of them: 'Sometimes when we put suggestions I am afraid that people run off with the idea that we are putting preconceived views. We are of course only testing opinion and trying to bring out points which people have overlooked.'[148] So it had been on the London Commission, the salty questions coming from others, Sir Robert Morant, for example.[149] On the Welsh Commission it was left to Henry Jones to rebuke certain Flintshire representatives who were unable to substantiate their strictures upon the standards of the University of Wales.[150]

Haldane deserved praise, too, for his deductive approach. He established first the broad governing principle in the light of which he tackled particular problems. At London he was not content to seek a practical solution to an immediate predicament – the future of Imperial College – and then propose consequential changes. His commission early determined what were 'the essentials of a university in a great centre of population'[151] at the heart of a vast Empire before applying the principles to the special needs of the University of London. In Wales the occasion of appointing the Royal Commission was the pressing need to determine the future of the Medical School and to establish an efficient method of distributing moneys. Haldane knew that the real issue lay far deeper: how was the University of Wales as an instrument of higher education to give effective expression to the national aspirations of the Welsh people? Other questions, no matter how important, were to be considered in the light of this grand, guiding principle. We need not be surprised, therefore, that although the University was barely twenty-five years old in February 1918 the report included a historical retrospect (nearly a quarter of the whole report) and was itself the culmination of intense activity. Haldane's own enthusiasm was conspicuous and he later told the House of Lords how moved he and his fellow commissioners had been by their experiences.[152] As we know, they had held thirty-one sittings to hear oral evidence and had examined 156 witnesses; they had held thirty-six sittings to deliberate amongst themselves; the report of over 100 pages was accompanied by three stout, double-columned volumes of 961 pages of evidence, which included 14,304 questions and answers and forty-two appendices. If it be thought pedantic to record such bare details, the purpose is to indicate the scope of an inquiry which is of immense value to historians.

The report itself, like the London report, is wonderfully lucid and bears the clear imprint of Haldane himself. Its spirit is friendly and helpful and there could be no greater contrast with the Blue Books of 1847. In analysis, tone and presentation it is undoubtedly superior to the Aberdare report. Kenyon, as Senior Deputy-Chancellor, spoke of the 'vision splendid'[153] and the general view was well expressed by the correspondent of *The Times Educational Supplement*: the evidence had been 'sifted and tried in the balance of expert knowledge and experience with studied fairness and impartiality', adding that 'throughout the report there run, as golden threads, notes of intimacy and sincerity, a desire to render service, and a consciousness of potentialities which will not be lost upon the Welsh people'.[154] True, the Colleges had certain reservations, to which we must presently turn; it was also true that the Treasury had extracted a promise from the authorities of the University before the Commission was appointed that they would accept the decisions which the government might reach, based upon the findings of the Commission. It was characteristic of the temper of the report that Haldane and his colleagues did not rely upon such coercive power but rather upon the good sense of the University, the Colleges and the local authorities.[155]

Matters were not allowed to stand still. On 14 August 1918 a powerful delegation of forty, headed by Kenyon, the Senior Deputy-Chancellor, and Reichel, the Vice-Chancellor, met the Prime Minister at 10 Downing Street.[156] It is ironical to reflect that in early 1916 Mary Rathbone had feared that Lloyd George was 'worked to death'[157] and had no time for the University and its Colleges. This may, therefore, be a convenient point to pause and to consider his relations with these national bodies, one of which lay within his constituency.

The College at Aberystwyth was opened when Lloyd George was nine years old. Many years later, when he was still Prime Minister, he declared at the College's jubilee celebrations that as a young man at Cricieth he had looked across the bay with wonder: 'I envied those who could travel to it. I envied still more those who could remain for three years within its portals. That was all I could do at the time.'[158] He had been obliged to struggle without any of the aids and privileges which would have been conferred upon him by Aberystwyth's first Principal, the teacher, the preacher, and the fighter who had refused to be humbled by cruel adversities. Had he been educated at Aberystwyth, 'that great institution',[159] he would have been more grateful than many who had been there. A generation earlier he told Liverpool Welshmen that he owed nothing to universities; his debt was to the 'little Bethels'.[160] When he received an honorary degree at Bangor in 1908 he amused the students by telling them: 'It has taken me thirty years of hard work to become a graduate of your University.'[161] Some of his hearers, alas, never became graduates at all. It was natural that Lloyd George should have a special interest in the Bangor College, situated as it was in the only one of the Caernarfon boroughs which had the 'unenviable distinction',[162] as he put it in 1900, of having a Tory majority. Acutely aware of the pervasive influence of Lord Penrhyn, the upstart attorney from Cricieth did not hesitate to declare publicly that Penrhyn Quarry land had been filched from the people. In April 1900 Lloyd George had been man-handled after a tempestuous meeting at the Penrhyn Hall, Bangor, and was obliged to seek refuge at the home of a prominent friend of the College.[163] Six years later he had a comfortable majority in Bangor, though this was later reduced to ten against a strong local candidate, Hugh Vincent, in January 1910. In both elections in 1910 it is beyond question that 'we Liberals',[164] as a Bangor professor put it, staff and students alike, helped to tilt an uneasy balance in Lloyd George's favour. Students delivered blows outside the Conservative Club and an influential Liberal member of the College Council, Henry Lewis, later knighted, addressed workmen from a box in a newly built College classroom in the light of naphtha lamps.[165] Some years earlier Lloyd George recalled that his first experience of public finance was in raising subscriptions at Cricieth for the College; he was then barely twenty. He hoped that 'before I have parted with the Exchequer to do something to carry on my work'.[166] During the public scandal concerning the women's hall of residence in 1892–3, which threatened the well-being, even the future, of the College, he loyally defended the Principal and his colleagues against scurrilous, unfounded charges. We may reasonably surmise that the President of the Board of Trade was active behind the scenes when Asquith as Chancellor gave Bangor College £20,000 for its building fund. He also believed that he had been largely instrumental in unlocking the substantial coffers of John Prichard-Jones when the College was bereft of funds to build the Great Hall which later bore the donor's name. In 1931 he endowed the Lloyd George Scholarship, thus enabling a succession of students to undertake postgraduate work in Welsh history at Bangor.[167]

As might be expected, he cast a vigilant eye upon the affairs of the University as a whole. Purely local considerations, however, darkened counsel when he supported Caernarfon's claim to become the seat of the University Registry.[168] On financial matters he was watchful. In 1896 he attacked Sir Michael Hicks Beech, the Chancellor of the Exchequer, for contemptuously refusing the request of a united Wales for an extra £3,000 per annum 'to keep the University going'.[169] When he became Chancellor in 1908 he announced during a public dinner at Bangor (after he had been given an honorary degree) that he was convinced that the Colleges deserved a large support from the government and that he was ready to make substantial additions to the present grants 'when the time came'.[170] But the time was not yet ripe. A month earlier he had said privately that he wanted to appeal to Carnegie to help the Welsh Colleges because it was impossible for the government to do anything at this stage. Waiting for governments to act, he said in 1907, was like 'waiting for sunshine in a summer like ours'.[171] In any case, Lloyd George was unable to act before 1909 because the Raleigh inquiry into the University of Wales had not published its report and because he himself was soon busily engaged in vehement battles over naval estimates. Herbert Lewis was adamant that, whenever Lloyd George was free to turn his attention to the University of Wales he displayed great courage and determination in dealing with Treasury officials. Thus, when Lewis informed him in 1909 that Sir George Murray, the Permanent Secretary, was recommending an extra grant of £1,000, George Barstow, secretary of the Raleigh Committee and another Treasury man, £9,000, and Lewis himself no less than £12,000, Lloyd George said, 'Take thy pen and write fifteen', precisely the sum Asquith had in mind before the Treasury prevailed upon him to appoint the Raleigh Committee. When Barstow warned that such an award would cause trouble with English universities and colleges, Lloyd George told Lewis: 'We'll stick to 15 and stand the racket. What's the use of being a Welsh Chancellor of the Exchequer if one can do nothing for Wales?'[172] To speak thus in private was one thing, but we may wonder whether Kenyon had been the soul of discretion when he said publicly in 1908 that Welshmen 'felt that they had a personal friend at the Exchequer who might be extremely useful to them'.[173] In 1910 Reichel recognized that Lloyd George might be exposed to 'unfriendly criticism' because of his Welsh connections, gratefully adding that it was not too much to say that the Chancellor had 'not only assured to the university and the colleges of his native land a longer and fuller life, but had done much to create in political circles a truer conception of what its universities meant to a nation'.[174] In public, as we might suppose, Lloyd George was more circumspect. In 1918 he did not hesitate to tell a large delegation which waited upon him to discuss the Haldane Report on what was virtually a public occasion, that he must constantly bear in mind the claims of British society at large: 'whatever grant is given here is a grant which can be demanded as a right by every other area in the United Kingdom'. The government had to consider 'principles of general application'.[175]

Informal relationships were another matter. Neither before nor afterwards have Welshmen found a Prime Minister so readily accessible, as Professor J. Lloyd Williams of Aberystwyth discovered when he called, by invitation, to see Lloyd George, then Minister of Munitions, concerning a proposed Cymanfa Ganu (Singing Festival) to be held at the Aberystwyth National Eisteddfod of 1916. Lloyd George at once left an important meeting, sang hymns with Lloyd Williams for half an hour and upon his return startled the committee by talking with animation of Welsh hymns 'before they had been Prussianized'[176] and by singing one himself. Amongst Welsh professors he had a sprinkling of friends, mostly at Bangor, but he was not enamoured of the College Principals. Not unexpectedly, he spoke with two voices. In public he praised Reichel for his 'hard, earnest and self-sacrificing service' to his adopted land which he had made every effort to understand, for he had not contented himself with a 'sort of schedule of Welsh peculiarities'.[177] In private, during a car trip to Llyn Ogwen, he told Henry Lewis and C. F. Masterman that only Henry Jones came up to his idea of a Welsh Principal, that he did not like Reichel 'and advised us to get rid of him as soon as we could'.[178] On another occasion he remarked that if the Welsh University were to be properly organized 'the first thing would be to hire somebody to anaesthetise the three Principals',[179] for they were not blending into the Welsh scene. To John Williams, Brynsiencyn, the reverend recruiter, he observed (in Welsh) that he could do nothing for the Welsh

Colleges whilst Reichel and Griffiths were heads of two of them, that T. F. Roberts was not quite in the same category but that not much could be said of him either. In short there was 'not a single man who could inspire the youth of the country at the head of affairs'[180] and the Colleges' educational achievements were unsatisfactory. To an extent he was sharing the views of certain witnesses, including his own brother, who appeared before the Haldane Commission as constructive critics.

Lloyd George believed that reform was necessary and possible. That it was necessary must have become increasingly apparent when, as Chancellor, he had not only received a deputation concerning the Medical School but had in fact instructed McCormick's Advisory Committee to produce a supplementary memorandum on local support; the Treasury's forthright minute of February 1915 would have been familiar enough to him.[181] Indeed, Herbert Lewis in January 1916 consulted Lloyd George (at the latter's request) concerning the choice of commissioners, adding that 'the whole matter was originally opened by your direction',[182] a clear reference to the steps taken by the Treasury in 1914 during Lloyd George's chancellorship. In January 1916 Lloyd George indicated that he 'favoured a Commission of *great* and *independent* men, and not men from Wales alone or even chiefly from Wales'.[183] When the report appeared, he was profoundly impressed. It was 'one of the most important documents . . . in the history, not merely of education in Wales, but of Wales itself'.[184] Twice as premier, 'the nearest thing England has known to a Napoleon',[185] thought Haldane, he set aside time to discuss the future of the University of Wales. On the first occasion, 14 August 1918, it was immediately after a meeting of the Imperial War Council. The German lines were not then broken, though Ludendorff was later to call 8 August the blackest day of the German army. The Prime Minister felt a wave of optimism and he was, as H. A. L. Fisher, President of the Board of Education, noted in his diary, in sparkling form.[186] The delegation which met him included representatives of the University, its Colleges and important Welsh institutions, as well as Members of Parliament.[187] The Premier was accompanied by Fisher, Herbert Lewis and Alfred T. Davies. He treated Reichel with the courtesy due to a Vice-Chancellor, but he was inclined to be impatient with

Griffiths, who irritated him; T. F. Roberts was too ill to be present.

The discussion inevitably centred upon finance. The Royal Commission had estimated the cost of its recommendations at £100,000, but £120,000 was now thought to be nearer the mark. The Commission, however, had not agreed to abolish student fees, though urged to do so by the counties which had agreed to pledge a penny rate for the University. After stressing the traditional poverty of the Welsh student, Reichel spoke of the challenges from abroad which would have to be countered if Britain was to retain its position as a world power.[188] Griffiths argued strongly against the Commission's proposal for a complete separation of the Medical School to create a new constituent college, a recommendation wholly at variance with various resolutions passed by authorities in Wales, including the University Court and Senate. In reply the Prime Minister at once conceded the need to improve opportunities for higher education in the United Kingdom:

> Amongst the many useful lessons that have been taught us by this War has been the lesson that education is not a mere luxury for those who can afford it but that it is essential to national well-being, and, what no one quite realized before, to national security . . . [We] have to make up a good deal in grit for what we lacked in training.[189]

The question of grants would be approached in a spirit totally different from that which had prevailed before the war. Wales would, of course, understand that the general principles now being enunciated would apply to the whole of the United Kingdom; there would be equal rights and equal obligations. He was adamant that the Commission's recommendations must be accepted by the Welsh education authorities and Herbert Lewis much admired his courage in protesting strongly against earmarking for local purposes.[190] Great nations had pooled their resources in defence of weak nations and the rich counties of Wales refusing to share their wealth with the poorer counties would be out of touch with the spirit of the times. Mindful of recent unrest in the south Wales coalfield, he said that harmonious industrial relations depended upon the recognition by the strong of their responsibilities to the weak. To claim for oneself the wealth provided by Providence in any area was 'the theory of extreme Syndicalism', whose motto was, 'It belongs to us';[191] for his own part he no more wanted syndicalism in county councils than in any other sphere. He had clearly not forgotten the rupture between industrial and rural Wales which had undermined Cymru Fydd's political aspirations. Counties economically poor had one essential gift, 'a virile population' which had done so much to develop the mineral resources of Wales:

> I never go to South Wales without being addressed in good North Wales accents. I know at once where it comes from; there is no doubt it has come from Anglesey, or it has come from Carnarvonshire, and I also detect the Cardiganshire accent; I am quite accustomed to them all by now.[192]

Earlier he had rounded on Griffiths of Cardiff: 'This is a Welsh University, and not a sort of little local show.'[193] There was to be no divisive particularism and if assets were pooled, then the Treasury would match rate aid and private benefaction (including contributions from workmen) pound for pound. As to a proportionate grant for building purposes (not necessarily pound for pound), he was not altogether hostile, for he recognized that the 'Highland Universities'[194] of Wales (Aberystwyth and Bangor) were a special case, but at this stage he preferred to reserve judgement. He stressed that continuity of financial provision was vital. As he prophetically remarked, 'there is nothing that kills a University so much as never being sure from year to year what will be its income'.[195] He was angered by the stupidity and cruelty of the low salaries paid to professors, exacerbated by the absence of pensions. The Scots had lured good men by offering financial inducements, whilst in Wales an ageing teacher faced the prospect of being 'flung on the dung-heap without anyone to keep him, after doing his best to train the brains of generations of people essential to the life of the nation'. It was 'bad business as well as being inhuman'.[196] He also made a brief but pregnant reference to the waste of effort when uncoordinated bodies ran the Welsh educational system.

In order to understand the full significance of this observation we must glimpse behind the scenes. A month or so before Lloyd George met the deputation, a memorandum[197] had been handed to him by Alfred T. Davies, Permanent Secretary of the Welsh Department of the Board of Education, established in 1907 in an attempt to placate widespread discontent at the failure to create a National Council for Wales with autonomous powers to deal with Welsh education as a whole. Davies argued that education in Wales suffered from duplication of effort, dissipation of energy and factious rivalries. An excellent opportunity now presented itself to fuse the Central Welsh Board with the University Court into one 'thoroughly democratic national body, of University rank and status'.[198] Fisher recorded in his diary that he had strolled with Lloyd George in the garden of 10 Downing Street some time before the delegation was to assemble and had persuaded him not to accept Davies's suggestion.[199] Fisher in turn had been admirably briefed by A. H. Kidd (secretary of the Haldane Commission) who urged that it would be imprudent to offend the local education authorities with 'an educational coup d'état'[200] at the very time when they were asked to contribute handsomely to the University. Lloyd George told the delegation that desirable though co-ordination might be, to pursue the matter now would generate dangerous controversy, and Davies was obliged to sit in silent discomfiture. As to the appropriate action to implement the report, welcomed by the delegation with slight modifications, the Premier could have appointed an executive commission to draw up charters and statutes. Instead, he wisely followed Kidd's advice to allow the University to submit proposals according to the Commission's recommendations.[201] He ended the meeting, as Welshmen of the day not infrequently did, upon a resolute imperial note:

> I hope you will produce a scheme which will be a real Charter for Welsh education, and which will enable Wales to make an even greater contribution to this Empire, and through this Empire, and through the Empire to the world, than it has made in the past'.[202]

The representatives of the University did not meet Lloyd George again until March 1920. In the interval there had been developments. During the early months of 1919 the local education authorities indicated that they wished to receive and examine the University's detailed annual financial estimates. The *Welsh Outlook* expressed alarm.[203] Kenyon feared that the local education authorities regarded University officers as reactionary and antagonistic to popular control, whilst 'we look on them as narrow minded and too exclusively national'.[204] Fisher agreed that estimates should be submitted for information only and should not be subject to revision.[205] The local authorities further declared that public money should not be devoted to the teaching of 'subjects usually confined to theological schools'.[206] The University Court adopted M. F. Rathbone's amendment that moneys should not be spent on the teaching of 'Dogmatic Theology'.[207] The fat was in the fire. Bad news came from Brecon County Council and from Newport Town Council: the penny rate would be withheld unless the original words were adhered to with the utmost strictness. The University Court at once capitulated and a relieved Reichel sent the good news to the Prime Minister.[208] Lloyd George would also have been pleased that the University, contrary to the wish of the Haldane commissioners, would continue to receive moneys from the Treasury, not from the Board of Education which had hitherto distributed grants to other universities. Henceforth, state grants to all universities would come from the Treasury, via the University Grants Committee established in 1919. He would naturally recall his days as Chancellor when he had strenuously and successfully resisted the attempts of Sir Robert Morant to transfer the rate for the Welsh Colleges from the Treasury to the Board of Education because he imagined that the Board had a clerical bias inimical to the interests of Nonconformity. The details of the protracted controversy as to which government department (Treasury, Education or Agriculture) should administer university grants has indeed some of the elements of a Whitehall farce. The victory of the Treasury, however, in taking the University Grants Committee under its wing, had less to do with the safeguarding of the autonomy of the universities than with the staid constitutional reason that the Board of Education's authority did not extend to Scotland, whereas the Treasury's writ ran throughout the United Kingdom.[209]

Attention must also be drawn to an unseemly wrangle in the caverns of officialdom. It concerned the grants to be given to the

University of Wales, for they appeared to be disproportionately smaller than those given to the Scottish universities. The chairman of the University Grants Committee, Sir William McCormick, was somewhat haughty with Herbert Lewis, now Member of Parliament for the University of Wales, testily refusing to be questioned concerning the large Scottish grant 'on any national ground' but adding that 'the Scotch universities were five centuries old, whereas the Welsh Colleges were only thirty years old'. Aberdeen and Edinburgh each taught more subjects than the three Welsh Colleges together; the antiquity and dignity of the Faculties of Philosophy, Law and Medicine had made the Scottish universities 'celebrated throughout the world', and the University Grants Committee had manifestly borne this in mind: 'To maintain a great reputation great expenditure is necessary.'[210] No attempt was made to explain how a great reputation was achieved and maintained with exiguous resources, a perpetual discouragement to such truly committed teachers as O. T. Jones and H. J. Fleure at Aberystwyth, who, less concerned with their salaries than with the development of their departments, had been obliged at length to leave for Manchester.[211] 'To those who have shall be given' was a Gospel maxim which appealed to the University Grants Committee, heavily peppered, it seems, with Scots who had not meekly entered into their inheritance. It therefore did no harm when Herbert Lewis was able to inform McCormick that the Prime Minister was dealing with the Welsh Colleges 'on his own account'.[212] On 4 March 1920 Lewis added that the Prime Minister would probably arrive at a settlement within a few days, whereupon McCormick replied: 'Very well, let the P.M. issue his commands and we will obey them.'[213]

Exactly a fortnight later, Lloyd George met representatives of the University and of local authorities at Downing Street. He had before him a printed statement prepared by Kenyon and Reichel for reconstituting the University in accordance with the Haldane Report.[214] Reichel explained that there were three principal departures from the Commission's recommendations. They related to the role of local authorities, to the School of Medicine and to agriculture. Local authorities now had their representation increased so that they had an absolute majority on the University Court. The University had further acquiesced to their proposals that the Secretary of the University Council should be expert in finance and in academic matters, and that annual statements of accounts should be furnished to each county council and county borough for information. Lloyd George had no objection to the provision of information, which would inevitably lead to discussion, but the Treasury would not countenance a referral back of university estimates by local authorities. He agreed that the University had wisely bent to the wind by conceding that public money should not be spent in teaching theological subjects 'defined as subjects the teaching of which is confined to theological schools'. The penny rate would soon disappear 'if you had a theological row on the five points of Calvinism; or if you had the Baptists quarrelling about your interpretation of some Greek words'.[215] In response to Reichel's plea that the implementation of the Commission's recommendations, originally assessed at £100,000 and which Reichel in 1918 estimated to be £120,000, had now swollen to £224,000, Lloyd George declared that he could not concede any substantial increase, despite depreciation, because of mounting burdens upon the community. Reichel was understandably anxious that the penny rate should be made compulsory, a view supported by Herbert Lewis, and based upon the dismal spectacle of the Welsh National Memorial Fund's dependence on cap-in-hand appeals. Lloyd George appreciated such fears (for as we shall see they were not groundless). A county might well sulk if large sums were spent in another county, wrily adding, with perhaps a glance at Fisher, that 'we must not give ourselves away too much in the presence of foreigners'.[216] The Minister, he continued, could not bring in a bill for compulsory rates and Fisher added that the experience of English universities was that once rates had been given (and English universities largely depended upon them), local pride would effectively deter withdrawal. Lloyd George felt impelled to say that Wales had been the pioneer of local rates and that with a little coaxing the penny rate for the University of Wales would become permanent, especially when it was fully appreciated that an additional penny would come 'down from London to our part of the world'.[217]

That financial considerations lay at the heart of the matter may be further illustrated. The University's proposal to traverse the Commission's recommendation concerning the Medical School by maintaining an organic connection between the School and the Cardiff College prompted the Premier to warn that great care should be taken not to direct substantial sums to the school at the expense of other long-felt needs.[218] Behind the scenes, W. N. Bruce firmly supported the Commission's recommendations concerning the Medical School. It was simpler administratively and would cause less friction. Kidd agreed, but did not think it should be insisted upon, especially since Sir William Osler had used language implying strong sympathy with Cardiff's case. Fisher felt that Lloyd George should give way since it was not an essential element in the report. As to agriculture, there was a distinct unwillingness to accept the Commission's adjudication that postgraduate work should be conducted in one college only. Reichel noted that agriculture was the only subject rejected for development by the Commission on grounds of economy. Bruce believed that Bangor's criticisms had been presented with much ability and would require very careful consideration. Kidd was less sympathetic. Sir David Hall, a member of the Commission, had greatly opposed more than one postgraduate centre and it would be regrettable if the vested interest of Cardiff in medicine and of Aberystwyth and Bangor in agriculture were to lead to two departures from the best academic policy. Fisher advised that the question of agriculture should be determined by the reorganized University; he and Lloyd George agreed that if money were available both colleges could pursue advanced work at the highest level.[219] In fact, when asked whether the proposals now submitted by the deputation were 'practically accepted', Lloyd George replied succinctly: 'That is so.'[220]

There remained the question of the charter. The Commission had not thought that a new charter was necessary, but whilst allowing that much could be done by statute (so elastic was the existing charter), Reichel did not believe that the Council could be constructed without one. Brynmor Jones, one of the architects of the first charter, thought that drastic changes would be needed.[221] Upon this subject Lloyd George declined to pronounce. In practice, there was little choice and on 20 September 1920 the University of Wales was re-formed. To what extent there was a reformation, however, is a matter to be considered in a later chapter.

V

The Founding of the University College of Swansea and the Welsh National School of Medicine

The University College of Swansea

In 1882 the arbitrators appointed by the government determined that the University College for South Wales and Monmouthshire should be placed in Cardiff. All factors considered, it was a sensible choice. Swansea was naturally downcast that the decision had 'put a night-cap on what might have been a brilliant luminary for South Wales'.[1] Unhappily it was less than constant in defeat and its mayor, believed to have been ineffectual in pressing the town's claims, was given a severe drubbing. Worse still, the town council made the most of hostile criticism of Aberystwyth in the Aberdare Report and derived further encouragement from the *Western Mail*'s odious advice to the people of Swansea to pull hard together 'and the College is theirs'.[2] The attempt to persuade government to transfer Aberystwyth's grant to Swansea was never likely to succeed and the surge of sympathy with Aberystwyth, following the calamitous fire, ensured its survival. In 1916 (Sir) Richard Martin, a powerful figure in the community, said that for many years it had seemed that Swansea would be 'for ever'[3] without a college of university rank.

Nevertheless, important preliminary steps were soon taken. In accordance with the Technical Instruction Act of 1889 and benefiting from the 'whisky money', the town council in 1896 began evening science and commercial classes at the grammar school; in 1898 day technical classes were opened in six science departments. By 1901 the Swansea Technical College was in being and in 1903, as will be recalled, the town council petitioned the Court of the University of Wales to declare it a college where students might study for the degrees of the University in science and applied science.[4] The University Court resolved a month later to alter its charter, but the cumbersome procedure was not completed until the arrival of the supplemental charter of 1906 which authorized the Court by statute to declare a college suitably endowed and equipped to be 'affiliated' to the University in the Faculties of Science and Applied Science, provided the statute was passed by a two-thirds majority of the Court. The term 'affiliation' implied a decidedly subordinate position and later Haldane, somewhat playfully and doubtless thinking of affiliation orders and suchlike, said that it had 'rather an evil flavour in the law; it implies something which is not quite legitimate'.[5] In any case, Swansea representatives felt that a two-thirds majority was an unreasonable requirement bearing in mind the composition of the Court. And there the matter rested until the middle years of the Great War.

In December 1916 Swansea's advocates appeared before the Royal Commission well equipped with arguments and statistics.[6] The town had also displayed pertinacity in directly petitioning the Privy Council for the creation at Swansea of a constituent college of the University of Wales. It was not difficult to demonstrate that here was the thriving centre of a large, expanding industrial area in west Glamorgan and east Carmarthen with an increasing population believed to be about 400,000. The tinplate industry, dating back to the seventeenth century, had in the record year of 1913 exported tinplates and black plates valued at £8,000,000, mainly from Swansea, the chief shipping port of the trade.[7] The anthracite coalfield, which differed from its south-eastern counterpart, also had easy access to the port. Chemical and engineering works added to the wealth of the district. The alert, energetic W. M. Varley argued that few areas as populous as Swansea were without a university college and here at hand was a technical college, of which he was the first Principal and which had proved its sterling worth. Since 1910, 139 students had passed through day courses and eleven had graduated in science and engineering, despite the interruption of the call to arms.[8] T. J. Rees, 'Superintendent of Education' in Swansea, the 'Metallurgical Capital of Great Britain',[9] as he called it, indicated that eligible students from the locality would be deterred from enrolling at Cardiff. By the same token, the increasing number wishing to prepare for the London external degree in applied science, particularly metallurgy, could scarcely be expected to face regular laboratory work and supervision far from home. An institution unable to prepare students for degrees would inevitably suffer: 'Degrees are not only certificates, they are also distinctions; and the hope of academic distinction excites emulation and rivalry, which, though not the highest motives, are powerful incentives to sustained effort and self-denying exertions.'[10] The pressing needs of local industry called for systematic inquiry into the efficient use of electrical power in engineering processes and into the problems of mill-roll breakages, an exceedingly expensive item in tinplate manufacturing.

Whilst the essential role of pure science was acknowledged by Sir Alfred Mond (who also appeared on behalf of Swansea), classes in applied science were usually given primacy. Doubts arose as to the readiness to include humanistic studies in the proposed college. Richard Martin held that a man could be 'as perfect a thinker as it is possible for a man to be without the humanities',[11] and he was not to be dislodged from his position by Haldane who attributed the intellectual freshness of the Imperial College of Science to its proximity to great arts institutions and the primacy of the Massachusetts Institute of Technology to the requirement that its students should take courses in the humanities.[12] Swansea's reluctance in this instance to swim with the tide may now appear strange, but a partial explanation is that when affiliation was sought before 1906 great efforts were made to convince Aberystwyth, Cardiff and Bangor that Swansea would not compete with them by introducing arts courses.[13] In January 1917 a Swansea doctor, G. Arbour Stephens, was quite ready for the proposed college to assume work already performed by other colleges. He now wanted to include agriculture and music and to move Professors of Law at Aberystwyth to Swansea because Welsh people, especially in an industrial area, were 'rather fond of litigation'.[14] At one stage the Cardiff Principal told the commissioners that the population of Wales could hardly support three constituent colleges, let alone four.[15]

Isambard Owen, when questioned concerning Swansea's claim, placed stress on the amount of its endowment (and its proposed mode of government), and here the commissioners were impressed upon hearing that £71,000 had been raised within a few weeks (soon likely to rise to £85,000), not for buildings, land or scholarships (as was so often the case) but in order 'to attract the best professors we can get for the chairs'.[16] No professor was to receive less than £600, no reader less than £300. The apparent support of local industrialists seemed crucial. The Haldane Commission was presented with letters from twenty-two companies (directed originally to the town clerk of Swansea) enthusiastically applauding the town's endeavours.[17] Amongst them was one from W. Gilbertson and Company, whose managing director was F. W. Gilbertson. Aptly described as 'the acknowledged leader of the movement to create a university college in Swansea',[18] he not only sought to persuade steel and tinplate manufacturers to contribute to the appeal but he also became chairman of the important committee to advance the cause of the University College. Officers of the University Grants Committee in 1920 thought that Swansea's fees were low, bearing in mind that the metallurgical industry had attracted investment of £50 million into the area. If local industrialists responded as their counterparts had done in Birmingham and Manchester the future would be safe. The Mayor of Swansea, David Davies, increased the target of the endowment fund in each successive speech.[19] By 1918 it was £150,000, whereas in reality the fund never reached the claimed £71,000. The expectations of Swansea's first Principal that the College's School of Metallurgy would be the best in Britain, and probably in Europe, thus seemed unlikely to be fulfilled. Swansea industrialists had also given their initial blessing to an ambitious scheme grandiloquently entitled 'the South Wales and Monmouthshire Business Committee on Scientific Research and Technology'[20] which presented to the Haldane Commission a scheme for the organization of technological studies. The purpose of the plan, far too complicated to be considered here, was to seek co-operation between Cardiff and Swansea and the technical institutions in their neighbourhood. It did not prosper.

In fact, Swansea's ambition to transform its Technical College into a constituent college composed of a technological faculty did not commend itself to the Haldane commissioners. They were

ready to raise the status of the Medical School at Cardiff, which
had but a single faculty, into a constituent college: 'the new
College at Cardiff will find itself in a city in which a University
tradition is already well-established, and next door to a
University College which will take an active part in its government', adding that there were 'many less formal ties and
associations which will, we may hope, unite the teachers and
students of the two institutions'.[21] In Swansea, however, this
advantage was lacking: 'There is no university tradition, no
university atmosphere, very little even of pioneer work in the field
of higher education and scientific research.'[22] Nor was there any
prospect in the immediate future of developing 'higher humanistic studies' which would broaden the training and outlook of
those who pursued technical and practical vocations. On the
other hand, the advancement of higher education and scientific
research was 'a crying need' at Swansea, the heart of industrial
development in south-west Wales. A university college should be
established there 'and brought into the inner life of the University',[23] provided satisfaction was given concerning vital
matters: the constitution of Council and Senate, the numbers,
qualifications and conditions of employment of the teaching
staff; full courses in pure and applied science and technology;
buildings, equipment and the maintenance of the College, and
higher education in arts subjects, 'pending the establishment of a
complete Faculty of Arts'.[24]

The commissioners firmly stated that the Privy Council should
not consider any proposal for a charter unless it was submitted
through the University Court and that it should seek advice from
the Court or from the Advisory Committee on University
Grants. At length, after extensive negotiations with bodies in
Whitehall it was resolved that a committee of five scientists be
appointed, of whom only one, the Principal of Cardiff, came
from within the University of Wales. No sooner had this been
done than it was realized that the question of a Faculty of Arts
had been neglected; the Provost of University College, London,
and the Regius Professor of Greek at Oxford were then invited to
give their opinion. The appointment of the committee was a
further stimulus to the College promoters to review their plans,
otherwise failure to give due attention to the humanities might

prove disastrous. Thus, renewed consideration was given to the incorporation in the College of the Swansea Training College for Women as the core of the Arts Faculty. Men and women would be admitted to pursue courses of university standard in line with the Education Act of 1918.[25]

The science experts were not convinced that existing arrangements for advanced study and research were sufficient to justify the conversion of the Technical 'School', as they termed it, into a constituent college. In the interests of economy it was recommended that engineering work in the third and fourth years at Swansea and Cardiff should be co-ordinated (an unlikely outcome). A substantial increase in teaching staff was needed to implement plans now unfolded with energy and devotion, but staff should not be expected to undertake evening teaching which would discourage original research.[26] The arts committee of two discerned 'a new spirit' which would encourage the teaching of the humanities and provide 'a wider outlook and an influence . . . beyond the reach of a College confined to purely technical education'.[27] Although a Faculty of Arts was not at present proposed, the future merging of the Training College into the University College clearly pointed in this direction. A department of education would at the outset be the strongest in the College, though the committee questioned whether its professor should receive a salary twice that of the other two professors, of English and of economics. There was unease as to the provision for classics, history and modern languages. In contrast to the science committee's report, it counselled that

> in a town like Swansea, where we are satisfied that there is zeal for education and a desire for knowledge, the members of the Arts staff should regard it as an essential part of their duties to provide courses, not merely single lectures, for the general public.[28]

Both reports were considered favourable, though at the University Court the curiously tepid references to Celtic prompted R. Silyn Roberts, J. E. Lloyd and D. Lleufer Thomas to move that 'ample recognition'[29] be given to the language, literature and history of Wales. The reports, blessed with the Court's strong recommendation, were forwarded to the Privy

Council which responded with unwonted celerity. In July the University Court was able to congratulate the Mayor and Corporation of Swansea 'on the consent given by the Privy Council'.[30]

The Welsh National School of Medicine

An extended treatment of the origins of the Welsh National School of Medicine may be justified on several counts. The process was so long and tortuous that a bald summary would be misleading. The heated controversies affected the fortunes of Cardiff University College and led to the foundation of another separate institution within the University, which itself became so embroiled as to present a stark illustration of the perils inherent in a federal system of government when there is absent a broad measure of goodwill and, at times, of ordinary discretion.

The first attempts to establish a medical school at Cardiff were briefly outlined in an earlier volume.[31] It will be recalled that Viriamu Jones had set the greatest store upon developing medical education in Wales, where there were no facilities of any kind and 300 of the 1,686 doctors practising there had been educated in Scotland. In 1886 he presented a persuasive case to the government, predicting that Cardiff would 'shortly develop into one of the best of the Provincial Schools'.[32] The study of engineering was also to be promoted, but it would not be felt by the Welsh people as a whole to be so great a boon as a medical school which would bring the College into close touch with the agricultural as well as the manufacturing districts of Wales and 'act throughout the whole country as a most important stimulus to Higher Education'.[33] The Treasury, however, was inflexible; £12,000, 'a very liberal contribution',[34] had already been made from imperial funds to the three Colleges and no more could be expected. Nevertheless, Cardiff raised a sufficient sum to accommodate the departments of anatomy and physiology by adding a storey to the building in Newport Road. In 1893 two full-time professors were appointed, Alfred W. Hughes in anatomy and J. Berry Haycroft in physiology, the twin subjects which provided preliminary training for medical students. A complete medical school had been ruled out by the charter of the University, mainly because it was feared that the charter would otherwise be rejected by the Privy Council which disliked multiplying degree-awarding medical bodies. Nevertheless, even though students after their preliminary training were obliged to proceed elsewhere for further instruction, there was at Cardiff the nucleus of a medical school which was highly esteemed. Hughes had set the department of anatomy upon secure foundations before he moved to London in 1897. During the Boer War he administered the Welsh Hospital in South Africa; shortly before leaving Pretoria he contracted enteric fever of which he died upon his return home. He was in his fortieth year.[35] There was widespread sorrow and a memorial to him may be seen where the widened road bends at Corris, Meirionnydd.

In 1906 the supplemental charter permitted the University to award degrees in medicine,[36] but for years students were still obliged to migrate in order to complete their studies before passing the MB and B.Ch. degree examinations of the University of Wales. The appointment of E. Emrys-Roberts in 1910 as head of the department of pathology and bacteriology was soon followed by the promise of an anonymous donor, later discovered to be Sir William James Thomas, to house a complete school of medicine at a cost, initially, of £90,000. As we have seen, the financial problems relating to the proposed school were a major reason for the appointment of the Haldane Commission. Its report recommended that the school be organized as an independent constituent college of the University, governed under the University by its own Council and Senate, and that it should adopt the 'hospital unit system', to which we must shortly return. The recommendation concerning the status of the School of Medicine did not find favour with the University authorities, who supported the College's resolution in July 1918 that, 'subject to the supremacy of the University',[37] the Cardiff College Council should be the chief governing authority of the School of Medicine assisted by a Board of Medicine and a Faculty of Medicine. Attention was drawn to the support of fourteen local authorities in south Wales and especially of Glamorgan County Council, which went so far as to insist that it would not raise funds for University education unless the School was constituted as an integral part of the Cardiff College and was adequately financed. At Downing Street in 1920 Lloyd George, whilst insisting that the School should not have preferential treatment, accepted the University's proposal.[38] The College, therefore, was entitled to proceed with its plans for a complete medical school and to put into effect the Commission's recommendation concerning the hospital unit system.

The hospital unit system had been introduced with variants in Germany and America. Evidence concerning its operation had been given to the Royal Commission on University Education in London, of which Haldane was chairman, by Abraham Flexner (a close friend of Thomas Jones) and by Sir William Osler who had initiated the scheme at Johns Hopkins University in Maryland. Flexner's basic premise was that 'university teaching can be given only by men who are actively and systematically engaged in the advancement of knowledge in the subject they teach'.[39] It followed that an appropriate hospital should be brought within the ambit of the University and so organized as to provide facilities for the thorough study of disease and for the training of students in as rigorous a manner as was done in other fields of university study. In each clinical subject the professor would be allotted a number of beds, staff, both clinical and educational, laboratories, lecture rooms and all necessary facilities for teaching and research. The head of each unit would be assisted by hospital staff; practising surgeons and physicians would be offered University appointments with an appropriate title. At the Cardiff Royal Infirmary, as it became in 1923, four hospital departments were organized into units, namely, medicine, surgery, obstetrics and gynaecology, and pathology. The adoption of the unit system, the concept of a medical school for the whole of Wales, the readiness of the local authorities to contribute and of the Royal Infirmary to allocate beds prompted the Rockefeller Foundation in 1924 to grant £14,000 to build laboratories and improve clinical facilities. Further signs of progress included the endowment by Emily Talbot of Margam of a chair of preventive medicine and by the Davies family of Llandinam of a chair of tuberculosis, and the recognition of the Medical School by the University of London, the Conjoint Board of the Royal College of Surgeons and the Royal College of Physicians.[40]

Until early in 1923 the sky had to most observers appeared cloudless. The College had appointed staff and planned the erection of new buildings, the chief being the new Institute of Preventive Medicine in Newport Road. It also presented, in common with other colleges, a draft supplemental charter to the Privy Council. In Cardiff's case article xiv recognized the Welsh National School of Medicine as 'a distinct unit' of the College. In February 1923 the Privy Council responded with a thunderbolt.[41] Its considered view was that the School should become a separate constituent college to be governed as recommended by the Royal Commission, thereby removing unnecessary administrative obstacles threatening the future of the School. Cardiff could scarcely be expected to submit tamely. Feelings were further exacerbated when the Council of the University (which had been consulted by the Privy Council) indicated that it favoured, not the creation of a constituent college, it is true, but a completely independent School of the University.[42] The Privy Council concurred and informed the Cardiff Council early in 1925 that it could not advise the government to accept the College's revised supplemental charter. When the Court of the University met at the Grand Pavilion Theatre at Llandrindod Wells in October 1925 it had before it a resolution in the name of William George that the best interests of the School would be served by constituting it an independent School of the University. Once a telegram of greeting had been dispatched to the University Chancellor, the young Prince of Wales, safely home from South America and South Africa, the Court turned its full attention to the contentious resolution.[43]

To many it seemed exceedingly unjust that the Cardiff College should be faced with the loss of the Medical School which it had brought into being, nursed in infancy and for whose needs it had provided as best it could. Wisely the College had at first created a preliminary school only, leaving until later the provision of clinical teaching. Isambard Owen paid high tribute to the standard of medical training at Cardiff, far in advance of that provided at the other provincial schools, so much so that students sent from Cardiff were 'marked men'[44] in the metropolitan schools of medicine, not only because of the excellence of their preparation but because they won prizes and scholarships altogether disproportionate to their numbers. Owen's own school, St George's Hospital, had in fact founded an additional entrance scholarship in order to attract them. Of the Cardiff School's early days, Isambard once observed that 'it may not be far wrong to say that it was the most brilliant single piece of work ever done in the University of Wales'.[45] However, Isambard's view of the future of the Medical School underwent a change. When he appeared before the Haldane Commission he gave the decided impression that he favoured organizing the School as a constituent College of the University, so that the commissioners in their report indicated that they had been influenced by him.[46] Later, however, Owen announced that he firmly opposed 'such drastic treatment as an amputation at the hip-joint'.[47] Circumstances had changed. Before the war the College had asked the Treasury for a direct grant to finance the School, but after the war the government required the pooling of grants, both state and local; thus there was now no question of a separate grant to the Medical School. Assuming, therefore, that the Commission's recommendation had lapsed, Isambard saw no obstacle to the continued close association of the School with the College. Others did not interpret matters in this light and rounded upon him for changing his mind.[48]

The College in turn, making the most of support from a former Senior Deputy-Chancellor and an acknowledged authority on medical education, marshalled powerful arguments. Unity of academic life must be preserved and there were no signs that medical education had been stultified within the Universities of Glasgow, Edinburgh and those of northern England.[49] According to the Vice-Chancellor of Liverpool, separation had a pernicious effect on medical students (and an even more pernicious effect on theological students).[50] Isambard considered it wrong to insulate them from regular contact with arts and science men; they considered themselves a class apart, 'an aristocratic body',[51] in fact, and the General Medical Council was well aware that the poison of class could infect relationships. Cardiff's second Principal urged that students of all disciplines should mingle together to their mutual benefit; they belonged to one regiment, not to different armies.[52] Separation, moreover, would encourage costly duplication of such departments as chemistry and physics whilst it would be damaging to deprive the parent body of anatomy and physiology, increasingly seen as essential to a science faculty; administratively, it would be highly undesirable to have two institutions in close proximity in Newport Road; to transfer to another body the property and endowments directly given to the College would discourage further benevolence; the moneys already spent by the College Council on the School would amount, so it was averred, to an uncompensated donation of £100,000; the loss of medical staff would impoverish the College Senate and lead to a narrowing of academic outlook. Again, it was not necessary for a national school to be independent. All the University Colleges were 'in their integrity'[53] national institutions, according to the Cardiff Council, and the same could be said of the Medical School at Cardiff as of the Law School at Aberystwyth and of the Theological School at Bangor. The *South Wales Daily News* said that separation would mutilate the strongest constituent college and jeopardize the whole federal structure, a view supported by the *Western Mail.*[54] Cardiff's Council believed that the draft scheme it had submitted to the Privy Council was entirely in conformity with the University charter, whereas the University Council's proposal appeared to be illegal, for the University charter gave no authority to its Court or Council to create and support teaching institutions of its own other than constituent colleges.

The College was here touching a sensitive nerve and the University Council felt bound to reply. In recommending the constitution of University Boards for Celtic studies, music and extra-mural work, the Haldane Commission clearly thought that under certain conditions it was proper for the University itself, quite apart from its constituent colleges, to 'exercise some educational and teaching functions'. Moreover, the University intended the Welsh National School of Medicine to control its teaching 'as far as the special circumstances allow',[55] as if it were a constituent college. In any case the University was prepared to amend its charter if it were deemed desirable and expedient.

This response was not considered satisfactory by the Cardiff protagonists. The University, however, was now fully determined upon complete separation which would lead to a simpler organization. The question of endowments and of buildings was

by no means insuperable, whilst the central funding arrangements of the University Grants Committee meant that the
Medical School would depend for its maintenance upon funds
under the entire control of the University Council. Ominously,
too, the School's Board of Medicine and the Faculty of Medicine
firmly favoured separation, as did the authorities of the Cardiff
Royal Infirmary whose chairman, Sir William Diamond, officially
declared that existing arrangements made co-operation impossible.[56] The University Council was convinced that if the
hospital unit system (still a tender plant in these islands) was to
have a fair chance of success, 'freedom of action and concentration of purpose and effort'[57] were essential. The College naturally
could not give undivided attention to a School which needed an
unfettered opportunity to work out its own salvation. Moreover,
the University authorities were increasingly convinced that
independence was vital if the School was to be truly identified
with the Welsh nation. In fact David Davies of Llandinam had
early in 1914 suggested that it would be advantageous if Sir
William James Thomas were to make his gift to the University,
not to the College. Moreover, if it were established that the
University could constitutionally accept gifts of this kind, he
himself would be prepared to act likewise with his proposed
endowment of colonial history at Aberystwyth. The principle
would thus be enshrined that special subjects would be within
the province of the University, thereby avoiding the dangers of
overlapping.[58]

It was indeed unfortunate that the University had not cleared
its mind much sooner, for at first, as we have seen, it had agreed
to preserve the organic connection between the Medical School
and the College, which naturally felt a sense of betrayal. The
truth seems to be, as Reichel put it to W. N. Bruce at the Board
of Education, that the details of the scheme had not been
'sufficiently worked out by the University . . . amidst the hurry
and pressure involved in our reconstruction'.[59] In the short
history of the Cardiff College which appeared in 1933 there is a
reference to those who 'allied themselves to the authorities in
Whitehall'.[60] Bruce was convinced that the Haldane Commission's plan was 'simpler administratively and was less likely to
produce friction than any other'. The Cardiff College had already

a heavy burden of new work and could not give sufficient time to the affairs of the Medical School which needed to be freed from the old conventional academic approach if the hospital unit system was to succeed. Finally, it was necessary to guard against a 'premature revival in South Wales of the movement for the disruption of the Federal University'; if the College retained control of the Medical School, 'its temptation to claim complete independence will be greatly strengthened'.[61] A. H. Kidd, the secretary of the Haldane Commission, was in entire agreement. Reichel had been too much concerned with the problems of agriculture at Bangor: 'In fact I am inclined to think that his belated doubts are not really a sign of grace and that his fears are more for Bangor than for the future of medical education in Wales.'[62] A. T. Davies, not designed by nature to be peacemaker, further stirred the pot. A recent appointment to a newly established chair at the Medical School had been made by the College, 'in the teeth of the available expert opinion'.[63] Lord Kenyon, the first chairman of the Medical Board which assisted the Cardiff Council, made it clear to the University Grants Committee in 1923 that the majority opinion in the University Council and in Wales generally favoured the recommendation of the Haldane Commission.[64] It was evident, too, that the Privy Council was in cordial agreement.

We need not be surprised, therefore, that William George's resolution to constitute an independent School of Medicine of the University was passed by 71 votes to 41 at the University Court in 1925.[65] Preparations were then made to fashion a draft charter. The Cardiff Principal, A. H. Trow (E. H. Griffiths's successor), recognized that his room for manœuvre had now severely contracted and indicated as much to the Cardiff Council. But he was determined to rescue all that he could. D. Emrys Evans said that the Cardiff College, led by Trow, 'fought a stubborn rearguard action'.[66] Consultations in 1926, though not wholly abortive, were time-consuming and injurious to both the College and the University. The College wished to retain the property and endowments of the School, in particular the departments of anatomy and physiology which the University understood to be included in the School when its future was determined at the Court in 1925. The opinions of four acknowledged experts were at length sought.[67] Sir Charles Sherrington, an ex-President of the Royal Society and a former external examiner at Cardiff, said unequivocally that anatomy and physiology should be an essential part of the independent School, a view reinforced by the President of the General Medical Council who had consulted 'some of my wisest colleagues'[68] and who stated plainly (though misleadingly, in the event) that if these departments were not included in the Welsh National School the General Medical Council would be obliged to oppose the proposed charter before the Privy Council. W. A. Sheen, the Provost of the Medical School, declared that the retention by the College of anatomy and physiology would be a judgement of Solomon, cutting the School in half.[69]

It was clear, however, that Cardiff, the undoubted mother of the School, had no intention of following scriptural precedent. In December 1926 it was reported that contributions had not been received from four south Wales county councils and one county borough (Swansea).[70] Early in 1927 Kenyon received one of those arch letters in which the Privy Council specialized, expressing the hope that 'the right construction has been placed upon the restraint during 1926 of the Privy Council Office'.[71] In 1927 W. N. Bruce, the new Pro-Chancellor, was extremely displeased that the Cardiff Council had not presented a compromise in tune with the Court's resolution in 1925.[72] At this point Trow fired a loud cannon. His College was so perplexed by the attitude of the University, he told the University Court, that it had sought legal advice. Alexander Grant, KC, did not hesitate to say that the University was acting illegally. Trow announced that if the University were so ill-advised as to defy the constitutional rights of the College, the deplorable necessity would arise to take legal steps to defend those rights. He successfully moved to refer the question back to the University Council.[73] The Court had wavered because it had little time to digest the legal opinion with which it had been starkly confronted.

Matters went from bad to worse. The Cardiff College found itself in fierce combat with the Royal Infirmary. From the outset it was evident that the hospital unit system could only succeed upon the basis of mutual trust and goodwill. The Haldane Report had perceptively observed that 'a system, in which the Hospital physician or surgeon is a Professor and the University Professor is on the staff of the Hospital, obviously necessitates great care in the making of appointments'.[74] Ivor J. Davies, who taught at the hospital for many years, believed that disagreements began when E. Emrys-Roberts, a graduate of Liverpool, was appointed in 1910 to the newly created chair of pathology and bacteriology tenable at the Infirmary, over the head of the existing pathologist to the hospital who had been an applicant.[75] Emrys-Roberts was not well received by most of the staff and the two men responsible for pathological work of the Infirmary did not speak to one another. The canker grew. Complaints that attempts were made to carry on clinical training at the Infirmary without the co-operation of the honorary members of staff led the Conjoint Board of the Royal College of England and the University of London to refuse recognition unless members of the honorary staff were invited to become recognized clinical teachers.[76] A crisis was averted on this occasion, but discontent simmered. Personal factors obtruded and *arriviste* professors were said to have gained ascendancy. A former distinguished student of the School, Sir Thomas Lewis, said that the highest success was not possible so long as the School was dominated by the College, whose Council did not include 'a sufficient number of men fully conversant with the needs of medical education and research'.[77] A first-class man could not conceivably do his best work in such an atmosphere.

At the Infirmary the cauldron continued to froth and bubble. Lurking in the background and never brought into the open was the question of the fees and emoluments of the honorary staff, whilst the decision to raise the retiring age to sixty-five kept in post senior members rancorously opposed to the Medical School. In May 1928 it was reported that five members of the honorary staff would no longer teach unless the administration and clinical work of the Infirmary were reorganized.[78] In September seventy students were given one month's notice that they would not be allowed to enter the Infirmary for clinical studies. The consequences were dire. According to Dr D. Llewelyn Williams, the action was 'cruel and callous'.[79] In early October at Pembroke Terrace Calvinistic Methodist Chapel the congregation bade farewell to students whose parents were forced to send them to London.[80] Some parents were placed in severe financial difficulties and appealed in vain to the Infirmary. In December it was said that 'we now have no Welsh National School of Medicine'.[81] There were significant resignations: Lord Aberdare, honorary treasurer of the Infirmary, who at one time before its incorporation had been responsible for its overdraft of £100,000, Professor H. Dibble, Professor of Pathology and Bacteriology, who had only come to Cardiff in May, attracted by the handsome buildings erected by Sir William James Thomas, and three other members of staff, two of whom had been educated at the School.[82]

There were shafts of light. The London medical schools gladly received the Welsh students, convinced that they were excellently prepared for clinical studies, and some London schools, greatly to their credit, were ready to meet the parents in their financial distress. One parent successfully sought legal redress on the grounds that the students' composition fee covered the whole of his training, and it appears that the parents of all students were adequately compensated by the College and the Infirmary.[83] But it was a disgraceful episode; public opinion was justifiably outraged and county councils with few exceptions were withholding their grants from the School which had a deficit of £2,000 in 1929 and the likelihood of £7,000 in the following session. In July 1929 the University Court was told that prompt action was necessary by October so that the University Grants Committee could make its assessments for the 1930–5 quinquennium. By then, however, there were no further threats of legal action and representatives of the University, the College and the Infirmary evolved a settlement of twenty-five clauses.[84] The essence of the agreement was that the School should continue to be organized on the basis of the unit system, beds being allocated to the Professors of Medicine, Surgery, Obstetrics and Gynaecology, that a Board of Clinical Studies should be established composed of all recognized clinical teachers who were honorary members of staff of the Infirmary, together with the three professors and also the Professor of Pathology. The University agreed to finance the pre-clinical departments of anatomy and physiology which were to remain departments of the College. The clinical departments of medical study (the fourth, fifth and sixth years) were to be separated from the College and incorporated by charter; a Joint Academic Committee representing the old and new schools was to control common academic matters. There were further exchanges between College and University before an exhausted Privy Council finally gave approval to the charter of the Welsh National School of Medicine, dated 5 February 1931, which created a School of the University, a constituent unit, not a College, with a Provost as its principal academic and administrative officer, and with its own Council and Senate. It differed from the Colleges in an important respect for the Court of the University was its Court of Governors.

Thus ended a prolonged war of attrition. When W. N. Bruce became Pro-Chancellor in 1927 he declared that it had already lasted longer than the siege of Troy.[85] The generous, wholly blameless donor, Sir William James Thomas, was heard to say in the following year that 'if my life is shortened it will be because of this controversy'.[86] Reichel was led, perhaps in an unguarded moment, to attribute the death in 1927 of Kenyon (at the heart of the proceedings) to the 'acrimonious vehemence with which the *perfervidum ingenium celtorum* [the perfervid spirit of the Celts] is apt to pursue controversies'.[87] When a settlement was finally reached great care was necessary not to fan the smouldering embers.

VI

University Development, 1920–1939

The first meeting of the Court under the new supplemental charter was held at the Albert Hall, Llandrindod Wells, on 25 November 1920. Since heavy duties prevented the Prime Minister from attending, he appropriately asked Haldane to deputize for him. Upon arrival, Haldane was in jubilant, even effervescent mood. As he told his mother in one of his almost daily letters, 'They treated me like a prince. This extravagant government sent me down from Euston the sole occupant of a magnificent saloon. The superindentent of the line was sent with me, and a cook and an attendant.'[1] In his message to the Court, Lloyd George said that the national University was a creation of the people 'known throughout the world for their devotion to learning and their sacrifices for the cause of education'. A new era had been inaugurated and the constitution had been remodelled to bring its administration into direct association with elected local authorities, whose ready contributions were to be distributed in the interests of Wales as a whole. 'Cash and control are inseparable',[2] he said, and he appealed to merchant princes to endow chairs and departments, for there was no more enduring memorial than to be associated with a generous educational endowment in perpetuity. The three pioneers whom he selected for remembrance were Hugh Owen, Thomas Charles Edwards and Viriamu Jones. Kenyon, the new Pro-Chancellor, read a message from George V, now relinquishing the office of Chancellor and assuming that of Protector.

The sovereign was succeeded by the Prince of Wales who was installed Chancellor in the early summer of 1921. He had a certain boyish charm which both students and greybeards found affecting. They approved of his delight in pronouncing the Welsh formula when he conferred an honorary degree on Balfour, indicating that Balfour could no more understand the Welsh words than he, the Prince, could understand the Latin words when he received an honorary degree at Balfour's hands a week earlier at Oxford.[3] Herbert Lewis thought it especially fitting that the new Chancellor, who during his recent tour of the Dominions had won the hearts of the New World, should preside over 'the most democratic university in the world'.[4] Some months later Kenyon informed the Honourable Society of Cymmrodorion that the young Chancellor had taken up fox-hunting, a sport which brought out the best characteristics of the British race; there was nothing more democratic than a fox-hunting field, 'where there was no place for the jealous rider',[5] nor indeed, we may suppose, for an anxious fox. The Prince of Wales gave ample satisfaction at the level expected of him until 1936, when he became a very short-lived Protector of the University. He was succeeded as Protector by his brother, George VI, and as Chancellor by another brother, the Duke of Kent. The royal connection with the world's most democratic university continued unbroken, and so remains.

Kenyon, who had served as Senior Deputy-Chancellor, an office now extinguished, was the inevitable choice as the University's first Pro-Chancellor. As may already have been gathered, he was a *grand seigneur* and his contacts with the royal court were advantageous to the University. A devoted Conservative and Anglican, he nearly caused turbulence within the University by his opposition to church disestablishment in Wales. The range of his sympathies, however, was far wider than might at first seem. He was equally at home in distributing prizes at small schools throughout Wales as in welcoming royalty; he spoke warmly of Labour men, he was on good terms with Lloyd George, he regarded himself as a Welshman and he was proud to work unsparingly on behalf of the University. Thomas Jones, recalling the ancient fissures in Welsh society, said that Kenyon was

> an outstanding example of a man who did more than any nobleman of his time in Wales to bridge this social cleavage – to restore the old friendly relations. He brought to the service of the Welsh people the qualities which in the past made leadership easy and natural to aristocracy.[6]

Kenyon, who died unexpectedly in 1927 at the age of sixty-three, was succeeded by W. N. Bruce,[7] whom we have already met as member of the Haldane Commission; later he was chairman of the Departmental Committee on the organization of secondary education in Wales (1919–20) and deputy-chairman of the Departmental Committee of Inquiry into the Welsh language, which reported in 1927. As Pro-Chancellor he displayed tact and dignity, especially during the dismal dispute relating to the Medical School; he shared many of the ideals of his countrymen, but he had a shrewder appreciation than most of the limits of the possible. He was followed in 1934 by G. C. Joyce, Bishop of Monmouth. Said to be descended from a family of Rugby brewers, he became Principal of Lampeter in 1915. A steadfast bachelor, he has been described as 'genial', 'ethereal' and 'seraphic'; the junior clergy, as is their wont, went further and called him 'the Holy Ghost'.[8] Such immoderate tributes caused unease for he was known to have hated his successor at Lampeter, but all in all we cannot do better than rely on D. Emrys Evans, who knew him well and who praised his penetrating mind, his capacity to master administrative details, his eloquence and his 'fine Christian character'.[9]

In concluding this brief section on personnel, it must be noted that Mortimer Angus's tenure of the office of Registrar now ended. Even if he was still as erect as a youth and could read his newspaper without spectacles, this good and faithful servant of the University was in his seventieth year and a further extension could not decently be contemplated. He was succeeded, not by R. Silyn Roberts as some had hoped, but by D. Brynmor Anthony, an Aberystwyth graduate who had won the Military Cross (to which was later added a bar) at Mametz Wood, where many of his countrymen had fallen. At this stage, too, it was deemed advisable to appoint a Secretary to the new University Council. The first holder of the office was Jenkin James, also in his mid-forties, director of education for Barnsley (formerly for Cardiganshire), to whom Thomas Jones was to dedicate his *Leeks and Daffodils* (1942). Duties overlapped at the edges, accommodation at the Registry was restricted – indeed Secretary and Registrar shared the same room – and the system of dual appointments was not always wholly successful.[10]

The Court was the supreme governing body of the University as it had been from the beginning. The Haldane Commission had recommended that its membership should be almost doubled, from 108 to 213. By charter it was further increased to 243. The Commission proposed to augment the representatives of local authorities from 27 to 91; by charter they were now to number 122, thus allowing them as a body a majority of one over all others (apart from the ten to be co-opted by the Court, which when complete, would consist of 253 members). Moreover, a clause in the charter entrenched their majority irrespective of any additions which might thereafter be made. The reason for this enormous increase in the representation of local authorities reflected the expectation that a penny rate would be levied by every Welsh county for the benefit of the University. Membership was upon the basis of four for each county and county borough council and one additional member per 40,000 of the population (a slight variant upon the Haldane proposals). Thus Glamorgan had seven more representatives than all the six north Wales counties combined. The number of those appointed by the Lord President of the Council was reduced from thirteen to three, a change not always beneficial because the power of nomination in prudent hands could achieve a better balance of interests than was always reached through the processes of 'pure' democracy.[11]

Normally the University Court met twice a year, in one of the constituent colleges in July and in one of the non-collegiate towns of Wales in December. In 1936, however, by a thin majority, it was resolved to hold all meetings at one of the Colleges, apparently because of accommodation problems in some towns. Usually they lasted two days and occasionally there were special meetings to deal with such critical matters as the fate of the Medical School during its first decade. In November 1923 it was resolved that a collegiate graduation ceremony be held in July in each constituent college for the admission of graduands to the degree of baccalaurius in all faculties except divinity. For this purpose the title of Pro-Vice-Chancellor was conferred upon the Principals of constituent colleges. An inter-collegiate graduation ceremony was to be held in July at each college in rotation to admit graduands to the degree of Baccalaureate in Divinity and to higher degrees.[12]

As to the work of the Court, much would depend upon the representatives of local authorities, now placed in a majority in the hope that the people's university would be the beneficiary of a penny rate. Their record of attendance, fluctuating between 30 and 40 per cent, deserves neither praise nor censure. Haldane and William George had hoped, as we have seen, that the Court would deliberately set out to spend several days, perhaps six, discussing the practical affairs and the broader aims of higher education. Parallels were drawn with the extended sessions of the National Eisteddfod and its sectional discussions, and it was hoped that advantage would be taken to launch schemes and initiate large projects of reform. It is true that there were contributions during the Court's proceedings, by the Duchess of Atholl, for example, on Scottish education and by (Sir) Clough Williams-Ellis on the cultivation of a sense of beauty.[13] But in practice Haldane's high expectations were unlikely to be fulfilled. D. Emrys Evans, normally temperate to a fault, spoke with impatience of such grand sentiments.[14] The University could not usurp the function of the Eisteddfod or of preaching meetings which had an accepted place in Welsh life. Again, if the University ventured beyond its proper province it might incur the hostility of other educational bodies such as the Central Welsh Board. Nor was it likely that lectures on highly specialized topics would fire the imagination of those wholly untrained in demanding disciplines. Nevertheless the Court received and considered reports on a wide variety of matters concerning Wales and her people, not simply the work of statutory boards, with which we shall later deal, but also the reports of committees set up to consider such questions as broadcasting and the plight of rural industries. As to the quality of members, doubt was sometimes expressed. Kenyon believed that the method of appointment by local authorities was haphazard.[15] Moreover, it is usually the case that busy men are disinclined to devote a day or two to matters which appear 'cut and dried'. Haldane's attempt to deal with this problem had not really succeeded.

The Council was the executive body of the University, in effect its linchpin. There were nineteen members: three were *ex-officio*, the Chancellor, Pro-Chancellor and the Vice-Chancellor, three were nominees of the crown, four were to be elected by the Court to represent the Colleges, seven were representatives of local authorities, and two, as we have seen, were to be elected without restriction. At the outset, in November 1920, the Court had been urged to make the best appointments possible. The composition of the Council has been criticized as being too restricted inasmuch as it reflected the composition of the Court, itself determined by local authorities not sufficiently aware that they were in effect choosing potential representatives to serve upon the Council. Further, since College Principals were in practice (and appropriately) chosen to represent the Colleges, it followed that experienced, accomplished lay members of College Councils found no place on the University Council. When, in addition, the Court did not exercise its right to elect two representatives 'without any restriction' to the Council we may perhaps question whether the Council always enjoyed the benefit of the 'best brains', as Kenyon had hoped.[16] There are signs that at first, at least, the central authority of the Council was resented in some quarters as 'an intolerable tyranny'. The Colleges, it was alleged, could 'hardly call their souls their own, let alone their purses'.[17] Such an initial response to a wholly new body was perhaps to be expected for the Council had wide powers and functions: to make regulations; to approve of the creation of new departments and to withdraw approval, subject to the right of appeal of the Colleges to the University Court; to determine College fees; to conduct the executive business of the University and to negotiate with government departments; to report to the Court; to promote and encourage research, and to distribute equitably the various funds at its disposal. This last duty was perhaps the most delicate and difficult of all its tasks.

The problems of distribution were legion. On the one hand each college had common overhead charges – the salaries of a principal and a registrar, for example – which had to be met irrespective of size. On the other, the number of students, circumstances and special needs varied constantly so as to preclude a simple mathematical division. The Bishop of Monmouth, before and during his period as Pro-Chancellor, demonstrated a remarkable mastery of financial complexities. Indeed, the ingenious formulae devised were of such exquisite intricacy as to prompt the question whether they were the handiwork of man alone. Early on it had been resolved that 60 per cent of the Pool Fund, as it was called, should be applied to the Equal Fund, 30 per cent to the Proportional Fund, which took account of the number of students, and 10 per cent to the Adjustment Fund designed to meet the 'proved commitments' of the four colleges. The Pool Fund was initially divided in the following proportions: Aberystwyth 5, Bangor 2, Cardiff 5, Swansea 2. The Adjustment Fund, as may be imagined, aroused much debate, but the sums were arrived at after close scrutiny of College accounts, empirically, in fact, 'and not upon any mysterious principles of distributive justice', as the bishop sagely explained, adding that 'it is only natural that each College should feel that in strict justice it ought to be receiving more than it does'.[18] The reactions of the Colleges ranged between satisfaction and resignation. In a federal university no more could be expected.

The principal income of the University and its Colleges was derived from the State which had in addition agreed to pay a further sum, pound for pound, for contributions from local government by the levy of a penny rate and also for private benefactions. We shall in the first instance consider the main state grant. It was distributed by the University Grants Committee, established in 1919.[19] The UGC recognized that resources were needed in order to restore pre-war standards; it did its utmost to strengthen existing university institutions by encouraging them, for example, to provide better libraries and to place the superannuation scheme for staff, begun in 1913, upon a sound footing. On no account, however, did it favour the creation of new institutions, not merely because the influx of ex-servicemen would soon abate but because proliferation might endanger standards. More than forty years were to elapse before the State gave its blessing to the rapid expansion associated mainly with Lionel Robbins.

At first the fortunes of the University of Wales seemed appreciably brighter. The Treasury had increased its contribution from £36,000 in 1918 to £95,000 in 1920–1. In the following year, too, the penny rate was paid in full for the first time. Alas, the fall of the 'Geddes Axe' reduced the income of universities on mainland Britain from £1,500,000 to £1,200,000. In the summer of 1922 the University Council was obliged to state that 'even after the exercise of the strictest economy'[20] income did not meet expenditure and that it was necessary to increase the fees of students. In Wales this was an especially sensitive issue. There had been talk of abolishing them altogether – a wonderful ideal but chimerical at the best of times – and had this been done in 1922 college deficits would have increased by £40,000. The Board of Education would thus be relieved of the payment of tuition fees for nearly a thousand students in the teachers' training departments and local authorities of the burden of tuition fees for those who had won scholarships. The Carnegie grant of £60,000 to help pay the fees of Scottish students had no counterpart in Wales, where fees bore little relation to the cost of training full-time students. They were also far below those of English universities. For example, a pure science student paid £16. 0s. 0d. per annum at the University of Wales (apart from a registration fee of £1. 15s. 0d.), at Birmingham £32, at Liverpool £34 and at Leeds £41. Even when due allowance is made for the fact that fewer students were able to live at home in Wales (especially at Aberystwyth and Bangor) than in Scotland and England, the case for increasing fees could no longer be resisted. In 1923 they were raised by 25 per cent but as late as the 1938–9 session the proportion of income derived from fees was well below the average for Britain as a whole. Immediately before the Second World War the recurrent Treasury grant (increased to £111,000 in 1925–6) stood at £158,000.[21] One of the Treasury's acts, however, was considered to have been base. When representatives of the University saw Lloyd George in August 1918, he said that a pound for a pound would be given for private benefactions provided they were given for a period of five years, a perfectly reasonable condition so as to avoid the consequences of sudden discontinuance. The Treasury now interpreted this clear intention to mean that the government commitment did not extend *beyond* five years, 'a distinct perversion' of Lloyd George's words, according to one college treasurer, 'in a sense entirely foreign to the spirit in which they were spoken and meant'. When the question was raised in the Commons the Secretary to the Treasury affirmed that 'during the war the then Prime Minister made a promise of the kind referred to, but it is obvious that he cannot bind Parliament in perpetuity under quite different conditions'.[22] There remained a festering sense of injustice.

This dispute, however, was as nothing by comparison with the protracted and often dispiriting negotiations with local authorities concerning the penny rate. The full amount of £51,000 was paid by county councils and county borough councils in 1921–2; until the end of the decade it remained at about £52,000. In 1923, however, there were signs that all was not well. Montgomeryshire County Council notified the University Council that it had decided to reduce its contribution to the product of a halfpenny rate for the financial year 1923–4 and that thereafter it would discontinue all contributions to the University. This it had done despite the recommendation of its Education Committee, which had received a deputation consisting of Major David Davies and of the Aberystwyth Principal, that a penny rate should be levied. The University Council, naturally disconsolate, indicated that if such an attitude persisted the consequences for the University would be most serious.[23] It was indeed a decision startling to those who had often heard its natives speak of 'mwynder Maldwyn' ('the gentleness of Montgomeryshire') but who were unaware of the curious duality which for centuries had characterized the county and indeed other Marcher areas, fortunately less rebellious on this occasion. After further representations the original decision was rescinded, partly because the county council appeared now to be satisfied that responsible, constructive use was made of University revenue, and to a greater extent, perhaps, because it was convinced that a reduction in the grant would strengthen the hands of those who wished to make compulsory the contributions of local authorities. Fissures in Wales became more apparent in the wake of the Local Government Act of 1929, sometimes called the Derating Act, which reduced the value of a penny rate by one third. Local authorities appeared to be unanimous that the total contribution to the University should now be the product of a rate of $1\frac{1}{3}d$. The catch lay in the inability to agree as to the share to be borne by each authority. During the years of economic depression, 1929–32, the University agreed to abate 10 per cent of the sum due from the authorities, on condition that they agreed amongst themselves. The University was thus losing £5,000 per annum, a severe diminution of income had it not been able to draw upon the dwindling Reserve Fund. A few authorities had also withheld their contribution of one-eighth of a penny rate to the Welsh National School of

Medicine. At a conference in 1935 local authorities reached a compromise whereby three-quarters of their contributions would be based on rateable value and the remaining quarter upon population. Other variants were subsequently proposed but it is unnecessary to pursue every shift and change from conference to conference, not lacking in expressions of cordiality, but persistently ending in disagreement.[24] The University was thus losing thousands of pounds each year. The Pro-Chancellor was entitled to say in April 1939 that, whereas a proposal to make the penny rate statutory had been rejected when the University was reconstituted, yet local authorities had at the time 'pledged their word' to provide a penny rate. At the same meeting the Cardiff Principal regretted that local authorities 'should go back on a principle they had always enunciated, namely that they did not wish the University to suffer from derating'.[25] Moreover, it could not be forgotten that local authorities had a majority of members on the University Court and seven members out of nineteen on the University Council. There was also a tendency to suppose that the University was in a better financial posture than was in fact the case. When the Treasury increased its grants the new money was for new purposes to fund developments fundamental to a young university. Again, tithe money, as we shall see, was intended to meet the needs of poor students and not to supplement professorial salaries only recently increased to a minimum of £850 per annum. Nor should it escape notice that the contribution by the authorities in 1922–3 was 10s. 6d. for every pound contributed by the Treasury and that in 1938–9 it had been reduced to 6s. 9d.[26] On the other hand, local authorities were obliged to make painful economies and were directly answerable to questioning, watchful ratepayers. Although income from local authorities was perceptibly diminishing it could not be gainsaid that in 1938–9 the proportion of total income from this source was twice that for English and Scottish universities as a whole.[27]

Tithe money was in time to prove a useful supplement. The University did not benefit before 1939, but the distribution of funds had already been determined. The story is a complicated one in all its ramifications, but the essence of the matter is this. In 1914 the Welsh Church was disestablished and partially disendowed (although the date of disestablishment was postponed until after the Great War). The year 1662 was chosen for the purpose of disendowment as indicating the broad division of the Welsh people into Anglicans and Nonconformists. Endowments before that date were to be secularized. According to the Welsh Church Acts of 1914 and 1919, parochial tithes were to be transferred to the county and county borough councils in Wales and Monmouthshire for charitable purposes, whilst estates belonging to cathedrals (usually known as capitular estates) and the tithes belonging to them and to episcopal properties were granted to the three Colleges, the University and the National Library of Wales. It appears that the National Museum of Wales, founded like the Library in 1907, chose not to benefit from arrangements only made possible, it was held, by plundering the Welsh Church.[28] Two members of the University played a vital role in these proceedings. One was Sir John Edward Lloyd, a member of a royal commission whose recommendations led to the passing of the Tithe Act in 1936, enabling distribution of moneys to be made some decades earlier than had once seemed possible. The other was the Aberystwyth Principal, Ifor Evans, whose financial acumen was invaluable. According to the initial apportionment, each of the three Colleges was to receive one-quarter, the University and the Library one-eighth each. However, since the passing of the Welsh Church Acts a new constituent college had been founded, and it was an admirable expression of a fraternal, federal spirit when the councils of the three Colleges agreed to place Swansea upon an equal footing by a redistribution which gave each of the Colleges a three-sixteenth share. It was fitting that the University Court at Swansea in July 1938 should express satisfaction at the 'cordial co-operation'[29] of the other Colleges. It was evident, too, that each College would readily fulfil the requirement of the Welsh Church Acts that the moneys should be used to meet the needs of poor scholars and also for new purposes concerning student welfare, notably hostel accommodation for men and capital payments to established hostels for women. An attempt by Sir William Jenkins to impose a uniform system upon the four Colleges was resisted, again in accord with the sound federal principle that when moneys had been assigned absolutely to each College 'it was entirely within the competence of each college how it should use the money'.[30]

Of benefactions there were comparatively few. The most substantial gifts were usually given to individual colleges for special purposes. Unconditional donations to the University were especially welcome. Dan Radcliffe's handsome gift of £50,000, presented to the University Chancellor at St James's Palace in May 1923, enabled the University to deal with needs which might otherwise have been neglected. Again, a donor, anonymous until his death in 1932, gave £20,000 to the University. He was Dr Samuel Williams of Llanelli. The income from this capital sum enabled the University Council, after consulting the Academic Board, to award postgraduate scholarships and fellowships. Yet the bald truth is that the percentage income derived by the University and its Colleges from endowments was a great deal less than the average for British universities.[31] Indeed, it will be useful at this stage to tabulate for comparative purposes the income derived from various sources by English, Welsh and Scottish universities during the 1938–9 session:

Income to Universities in £, 1938–9

	Endowments	Donations and sub-scriptions	Grants from local authorities	Parliament-ary grants	Fees	Other income
England	838,837 (15.7%)	141,489 (2.7%)	454,174 (8.5%)	1,809,725 (33.9%)	1,635,853 (30.7%)	453,822 (8.5%)
Wales	21,994 (5.6%)	4,496 (1.1%)	70,604 (17.8%)	205,881 (51.9%)	74,768 (18.9%)	18,644 (4.7%)
Scotland	174,926 (17.8%)	26,634 (2.7%)	81,179 (8.3%)	384,796 (39.2%)	288,212 (29.4%)	26,033 (2.6%)

These statistics are self-explanatory. Parliamentary grants constituted more than half of the University's income and, as has been noted earlier, grants from local authorities were a far higher proportion of income than in England and Scotland, whereas income from fees, and especially endowments, was appreciably smaller.[32]

The Council was one of two new central bodies created as a result of the Haldane Report. The other was the Academic Board of twenty-one members which replaced the old, unbewailed Senate which had swollen to over sixty members. When he first read the Haldane Report, W. Rhys Roberts, formerly of Bangor but now at Leeds University, wondered whether teachers, 'the lifeblood'[33] of a university, were to be given sufficient voice in academic matters. He may have been partly mollified by the provision in the charter that the Board 'shall advise the Council on all academic matters and shall be entitled to make representations to the Council and request conference with the Council'.[34] But he would not have been pleased to see that members of the teaching staff were not represented on the Council. Indeed, he feared that they would come to regard the huge Court and the small Council 'as external bodies with which they are in no very direct or living relation'.[35]

How effective was the Academic Board? It normally met five times a year for two consecutive days. Most matters it took in its stride. It usually gave clear, considered advice to Council concerning the creation of new departments and of chairs, as, for example, when it appointed two visitors to examine the accommodation and equipment in the department of zoology at Aberystwyth before R. D. Laurie was appointed professor.[36] Nor should it perhaps be blamed for hedging when asked by the Council of the University to report on the relative merits of establishing a chair of philosophy at Swansea and of a chair of geology at Bangor. Both sides were carefully presented to Council, for the claims of the two colleges were manifestly strong, but the Board was 'unable to pronounce uncondition-ally'[37] and confined its attention to purely academic aspects. The immediate result was that the Council temporized. Two years later the Council acceded to a request from Swansea for the philosophy chair whereas Bangor was yet again left to nurse vain hopes of a geology chair.[38] The Board was wise enough to enlist the services of the retired John Edward Lloyd at its meetings, for he was heavy with case law. Unhappily, his deafness was only partially relieved by a brass trumpet, and he was once heard to call out to the chairman of the Board, J. F. Rees, the Cardiff Principal (once on his Bangor staff): 'Rees, I cannot hear a word they are saying, but I am certain that they are wrong!'[39] Wrong they certainly were in their dealings with the grade of reader. The

Board had in 1932 agreed that readers should be appointed 'on grounds of special distinction and responsibility'.[40] Three years later, having considered five applications, including one from Saunders Lewis, it recommended that the title of reader be revoked. One of the reasons given for this astonishing reversal was that in matters of academic distinction it would be very difficult to form a judgement 'without serious risks of creating anomalies and grievances within the University'.[41]

Such an episode, though deplorable, was scarcely typical. Emrys Evans, who had an intimate knowledge of the workings of the Board, believed that the presence of the College Principals provided a 'durable core',[42] and that the practice of changing representatives gave most Senate members of each college direct experience of the complexities of federal government. The Board was no more than an advisory body, but the Council in practice almost always adopted its recommendations. The verdict must be that the Board trod a middle path between a dangerous invasion of the rights of Colleges and a limp acquiescence in the interest of a spurious federal harmony. Yet there were already portents of decline. The Board was customarily asked to nominate persons to represent the University on Joint Selection Committees for chairs and the headships of departments. However, in May 1935 the Board was unceremoniously bypassed when the Cardiff Principal successfully moved that in relation to two appointments, 'in view of the urgency of the matter, the Council should proceed at once, without waiting for a recommendation from the Academic Board'[43] to appoint representatives on the Selection Committee. In short, the Board's views did not greatly matter. By 1945 W. J. Gruffydd was thundering eloquently against the Board's total inability to co-ordinate the work of the Colleges.[44] It is difficult to avoid the conclusion that the Principals were not much enamoured of the Academic Board. (Indeed by 1964 not one of them was ready to support the retention of the federal University.) In time the full Academic Board met in the afternoon, when it received reports on individual cases predetermined by a small group in the morning and delivered with a bewildering rapidity. Not often were matters of high academic principle bruited, let alone discussed. Dismayed by such tendencies, the majority report of an inquiry into the

University proposed in 1964 to make the Academic Board 'the *ultimate authority* in all academic matters'.[45] It was not to be. The Board subsided little by little into a 'demure'[46] body, as it has recently been called. It seemed that the 'durable core' was becoming a soft centre.

Doubts again emerged concerning the rotating office of Vice-Chancellor. Writing privately to Emrys Evans in 1943 and surveying his period as principal, Ifor L. Evans said that 'the duties of Vice-Chancellor of the University and Principal of a Constituent College cannot properly be performed by the same person'. They were 'an intolerable burden' upon a Vice-Chancellor who attempted to perform his work conscientiously (though of course he had long been relieved of teaching duties which had taxed the early holders of the office). Most of the suggestions for strengthening the University at the centre were 'doomed in advance'. A proposal to appoint a permanent Vice-Chancellor would not be acceptable. Regular meetings of the four Principals would be admirable, but when such meetings were held in the past they were regularly attended by the Aberystwyth and Bangor Principals but not by the Cardiff and Swansea Principals. The only practical answer was to maintain the present arrangements with minor simplifications; 'it is a rotten system, but the only feasible alternative might well be worse'.[47]

It is perhaps against this background that we should read the remarks of the Cardiff Principal in the jubilee number of the College magazine in 1933. He amused himself, and doubtless others, by reflecting upon the possible state of the College in the 1980s. The editor of the magazine would have at his disposal the fruit of research into the archives of the 'former' University of Wales, archives by then at the National Library of Wales, as he erroneously surmised. One researcher might have dealt with 'The Fallacy of supposing that because Educational Institutions are linked together by Joint Committees their contribution to the life of the Community is more "national" than it would otherwise be'. The editor would also be able to ask 'one of the men in the seminar class on obsolete institutional terminology to ascertain (if possible) what was meant by a federal university'.[48] J. F. Rees can hardly be blamed for not foreseeing that federalism in its diverse forms would be a highly controversial issue in 1983, at home and abroad, but whether it was wise to raise the question in this fashion so soon after the costly dispute concerning the Medical School is another matter.

The University's responsibility for adult education (to be considered in chapter X) largely lay with the Colleges, as the Haldane Report properly noted. Yet the University had a role, recognized in the constitution of the University Extension Board, 'to review, co-ordinate and assist and if necessary supplement'[49] the work of the Colleges which should annually submit reports to the University authorities concerning their activities. Again, the Haldane Report, deeply mindful of the need to develop the musical talents of the Welsh people, recommended the appointment of a Music Director, preferably a professor at one of the colleges, who should be chairman of a University Council of Music. In the charter of 1920 this Council was called 'the supreme consultative body in all matters relating to musical education in Wales'.[50] The Director's duties, defined by statute, were 'to promote, in consultation with the authorities of the constituent Colleges and without prejudice to their autonomy, a general co-ordination of musical activities and musical education in Wales'. The first director was Sir Walford Davies, to whom we shall return.

Two boards require extended treatment, namely, the Board of Celtic Studies and the Press Board of the University. The first, in receipt of an annual grant from the University Council, was

> to draw up and direct the working of a comprehensive scheme for the development of Celtic Studies in Wales, including a survey of material available for the study of (i) the Celtic languages and their literature; (ii) the history, laws and customs of the Celtic peoples; and (iii) Celtic archaeology and art.

In pursuit of these objects the Board was to 'organise and employ a body of skilled workers'[51] and to publish the fruit of research and exploration. Membership of the Board included representatives of each of the Colleges and of major national institutions, such as the National Library and the National Museum, with whom the Haldane Commission had deemed it essential for the Board to co-operate. The association with the National Library has been especially close. By 1921 J. Bodfan Anwyl had been installed there (together with typewriter and desk) as Dictionary Secretary to the Board. A year later Anwyl reported that from virtually nothing he had now assembled 'a copious and varied vocabulary . . . contributed by a company of faithful and diligent readers'.[52] To prepare a standard, scholarly dictionary of the Welsh language was a mighty undertaking and we need not be surprised that Anwyl a year later reported that 'the task is still very far from completion',[53] the first of many similar announcements through the decades. There are encouraging signs that the majestic *Geiriadur Prifysgol Cymru*, at first appearing as fascicules, is now near completion. A magnificent example of Welsh scholarship of the twentieth century, it owes much to the advice of a succession of scholars, from C. T. Onions of Oxford and Sir John Morris-Jones to Professor J. E. Caerwyn Williams. Attention must also be drawn to the *Bulletin* of the Board, from 1921 onwards, divided into three parts, Language and Literature, History and Law, and Archaeology, corresponding to the three main sections (for many years) of the Board itself. The *Bulletin* enabled the scholar to communicate his findings in a manner seldom hitherto possible. A disappointment was that the systematic study of place-names, as opposed to excellent individual ventures, was not placed on a secure footing throughout the period of our inquiry, nor, indeed, far beyond.

The Haldane Commission had recommended the creation of a University of Wales Press. Based upon twelve years' experience the Press Board in 1934 defined its policy. It was to publish Welsh texts for the use of University students in Welsh, books in Welsh for the use of the Welsh reading public 'on the lines of the Home University Library', works of research on the history of Wales and standard readers for use in schools. It was satisfied that this was a wise policy, adding that the kind of book published by the Board would seldom, if at all, be 'a paying proposition'. It followed that 'a University Press in Wales must of necessity be a subsidized press'.[54] There was no serious hope that it would ever print its own works. True, there were preliminary negotiations in

1929 with Rowland Thomas of Hughes and Son, Wrexham, who wanted his firm to print, publish and distribute books and journals in the name of a 'University Press of Wales'.[55] The University Council, expected to contribute £5,000, could not contemplate such expenditure, and the Press Board itself concluded that whilst it might be possible in the future to set up a university press, the work would be more economically performed by contract, a view that still inevitably prevails. The University Council made annual grants, initially of £250 and increased to £1,200 in 1939. In 1929 and 1930 the University Grants Committee gave two special sums of £500 to assist the publication of Welsh texts for university and other students.[56]

The problems facing the Board may be illustrated by considering the case of A. H. Dodd who presented in March 1930 the manuscript of his impressive study of the industrial revolution in north Wales, later described by Sir John Clapham as 'an admirable piece of work'.[57] Since it would have cost a guinea in the shops, the author was asked to reduce the size of the work, advice he prudently declined. After fruitless attempts to publish it elsewhere he turned again to the Board. Largely because of a grant of £100 from the Thomas Ellis Memorial Fund (and another of £50 from the Board of Celtic Studies) it at length saw the light of day, priced 12s. 6d. Three years had elapsed between submission and publication. Thomas Ellis would have rejoiced that the fund established to commemorate him frequently tipped the balance in favour of publishing works of unquestioned worth. Again, only a subvention of £1,000 from the Dan Radcliffe Fund made it possible to produce John Lloyd-Jones's indispensable *Geirfa Barddoniaeth Gynnar Gymraeg* (1931–63), a glossary of early Welsh poetry. A natural cause of concern was the inability to publish the original research of staff in subjects other than in the field of Welsh and allied Celtic studies, the Board's first charge. There were one or two exceptions, H. R. Rowley's *Darius the Mede and the Four World Empires* (1935), for example, but Ifor L. Evans was right to complain that the £100 granted by the University Council for this special purpose was too small to administer. He successfully persuaded the Board to ask Council for the sum to be quadrupled in order to subsidize the publication of articles (particularly in the sciences) as well as books. No progress, however, was possible and following the outbreak of war the Council's grant to the Board was halved.[58]

Some important works were long maturing. Morgan Watkins's edition of *Ystorya Bown o Hamtwn*, first brought to the attention of the Board in 1922, did not appear until 1958. W. J. Gruffydd in 1939 advised the Board not to allow the Clarendon Press to publish an Oxford book of Welsh verse, possibly because it would compete with his own *Y Flodeugerdd Gymraeg* (1931).[59] Book production seems to have touched a peak of 20,858 in 1931–2; in 1934–5 it was down to 13,307 and did not again reach 15,000 before the war. Between 1922 and 1939, 250 titles appeared. The Board published on behalf of the Board of Celtic Studies and it also had a special responsibility towards the University's Council of Music. The publishing of cheap Welsh classics was strongly advocated in a forthright memorandum to the Board by R. T. Jenkins, who maintained that they were more readily available a generation before, though often in bad type and on bad paper.[60] The project, however, though much favoured, did not gather momentum until after the war. From the outset it was the avowed purpose of the Press Board to set an example to printers and publishers in Wales of high standards of book production. Members of the Board included Sir Frederic Kenyon, Director of the British Museum, and Sir John Ballinger, Librarian of the National Library. Naturally, scholars within the University were well represented and it was one of them, Sir John Morris-Jones, who devised the press mark which appears on all the University Press publications. It is somewhat noteworthy that the four lions of Gwynedd are allowed to stand for the whole of Wales. Sir T. H. Parry-Williams regarded his long membership of the Board as one of the greatest privileges of his academic life, a view echoed by many.[61] It is now increasingly recognized, even by the more advanced marketeers, that a press in large measure designed to publish specialist works relating to Wales cannot survive without a realistic subsidy.

The Guild of Graduates, one of the authorities of the University, elected fourteen representatives to the Court. Even so, it was not the majestic body envisaged by Isambard Owen, who deplored the failure of two charters to give ample recognition to his cherished hopes. He had originally wanted the

Guild to appoint trustees 'to hold property independently of the University' in order to promote research. By the first charter the Guild was allowed only 'to collect' money for scholarships and prizes and by the second merely to 'receive' moneys for educational purposes.[62] Again, as to membership, the Guild at first included the teaching staff of the University who were not graduates of the University of Wales; in 1920 they were excluded. The first Warden of the Guild, O. M. Edwards, believed that the Guild had three principal functions: first, to bring the 'united opinion' of graduates to bear upon the advancement of education; second, to keep them 'in life-long touch' with the University, and third, to publish manuscripts largely inaccessible to students.[63] Thomas Ellis, the second warden, was in entire agreement. In view of its limited resources, the Guild's publishing programme, which began in 1899 with Ellis's first volume of the works of Morgan Llwyd, was promising. After 1920 this responsibility was transferred to the Board of Celtic Studies and to the Press Board of the University (which received the Guild's unsold stock of books). The Guild's Scholarship Fund to allow graduates to undertake particular studies was never large, but in 1938–9 two awards were made, one of them to enable P. H. Burton of Port Talbot (the adoptive father of Richard Jenkins, who took his name) to study the theatre and broadcasting in America.[64] The *Transactions* of the Guild, extending from 1901 to 1926, were succeeded by the *Guild Annual*, first published in 1928. Both included reports from the various subject sections set up to further research. By 1936 there were seven sections, almost all concerned with arts subjects. The two most active were the theological and philosophical sections. Publications of the Guild included *The Bibliography of Welsh History* (1931), *Y Geiriadur Beiblaidd* (1924–6) and the excellent journal, *Efrydiau Athronyddol,* produced by the philosophical section. The task of keeping in touch with graduates proved formidable. In 1928 the Guild *Annual* said that the 'vast majority' of members did not know what the Guild was doing. The problem had been in part anticipated after the Great War by Ernest Hughes of Swansea who, in response to the large influx of ex-servicemen, suggested the formation of branches in 'Wales and the Borderland', whereas in fact graduates outside Wales were mainly to be found in the north of England, the Midlands and, of course, in London.[65] In 1939 the total membership was 13,132, of whom only 8,713 wished to receive notices. The Guild has always been ready to act as a pressure group when it judged that Welsh interests were imperilled. Thus in March 1936 it resolved to protest against the establishing of bombing facilities in the Llŷn peninsula because of likely harm to the cultural life of the area. On this occasion, however, there were unexpected difficulties. When Henry Lewis, the Warden, asked J. E. Lloyd and R. T. Jenkins to prepare a memorandum, both, it seems, were 'too busy' and had 'no clear vision' on the subject. Far greater success attended the Guild's efforts to give prominence to the plight of unemployed graduates.[66] The wardens, democratically elected, have usually acted wisely and Guild representatives on University bodies have been firmly committed to the best interests of the University.

We have seen that an early attempt to associate the Bangor College with the Normal College had failed ignominiously.[67] In consequence of the Burnham Report of 1925 plans were afoot to link the University and the training colleges in Wales. By 1929 there was created by statute a University Board for training colleges, replacing the Board of Education as the examining body for training colleges in Wales. The new Board, which reported annually to the Court, had an equal distribution of members representing the University and the training colleges; it was responsible for schemes of study, for appointing examiners and for establishing Boards of Study composed of teachers in the University and in the training colleges. At best this body was but moderately successful. Its influence on the curricula of training colleges was slight. It has been justly criticized for failure to speak out on the retrenchment in teacher training in the 1930s (apart from the financial aspects), for rarely referring matters to school-teachers, none of whom was represented even on its committees, and for its reluctance to take the initiative. On the other hand, it was responsive to certain Welsh needs (such as the teaching of Welsh history and of religious knowledge) and the staff of training colleges welcomed the opportunity at Boards of Study to meet university teachers and external examiners. By the end of the decade, too, there were tendrils of hope that it would not become the creature of either the Board of Education or of the University itself. After 1939 it preserved the existing order as best it could, but, following the McNair Report of 1944 it was put to rest in 1948, to be replaced by the University School of Education which profited from the experiences of its predecessor.[68]

The University's relations with Lampeter must on no account be passed by, and it is perhaps permissible to employ yet again the words of D. Emrys Evans who likened them to 'those of a moth to the flame – an alternation of darts and retreats as its wings were threatened with singeing'.[69] It was not surprising that a later Principal of Lampeter, recalling in 1980 the events of the 1960s and 1970s, entitled his book, *Moth or Phoenix?* There were times earlier in the century when survival seemed uncertain, even improbable. At first the Lampeter authorities hesitated to be represented before the Haldane Commission, and the Principal of the College, C. G. Joyce, confined himself to a severely factual statement, an informed survey of the past rather than a confident declaration of policy.[70] The chairman made it clear that he was anxious that Lampeter (empowered to grant the degrees of BD in 1833 and of BA in 1865) should come within the University system in Wales 'as a college permeated by the same spirit of general educational idealism which we begin to see signs of in other places'. Joyce's reply was tepid: 'I am not able to give any information as to the coming in or staying out. I come to voice the words of the Council, and the Council has said nothing about that at all.'[71] The Commission's Report referred to the reluctance of the College and its Principal to commit themselves upon this central issue. Lampeter would be greatly the gainer and would render larger service to the nation if, on the one hand, it 'put itself in a position'[72] to become a constituent college of the University, open to all classes of students, or, on the other, if it were to depend upon the University for the general education of its students, concentrating itself upon the BD as a postgraduate degree and upon ministerial training.

Joyce soon addressed himself to the second proposal with some vigour – he had already aired these views as far back as 1909 –

and his reticence before the Commission we must attribute to his loyalty to the College Council which had not come to terms with such a development. Reichel's paper to a Manchester conference in 1908 had probably left its mark upon Joyce's recommendations that every ordinand should pursue a six-year course composed of a three-year course leading to a BA degree, a two-year course of professional education in theology and a final year of practical training. For a student to spend six years in one college is seldom intellectually emancipating, and Joyce's solution contained some intriguing ingredients. Lampeter was to be divided into two parts: at the proposed St David's College at Aberystwyth students would be supervised whilst they followed at the University College the BA degree of the University; after three years they would return to Lampeter to take the BD degree in two years, and then proceed for a sixth year at St Michael's, Llandaf. Thus, it was hoped, the presence of 120 church students might in time help to replace the barren rivalry between Lampeter and Aberystwyth by the healing spirit of understanding. There were several objections: the improbability that the St David's College at Aberystwyth could attract at least forty students each year; a host of legal impediments, according to learned counsel, and amongst some Anglicans more than a vestige of disestablishment dejection.[73]

In 1922 Joyce presented to the College Council an emasculated version of his original scheme. There was no longer mention of a St David's College at Aberystwyth; to maintain an arts side at Lampeter would be 'a piece of incredible extravagance'[74] and he now proposed to transform Lampeter into a postgraduate theological college offering a two-year vocational course for more than eighty ordinands. Joyce was defeated and departed for Pembrokeshire, where, in 1927, he arose, phoenix-like, as Bishop of Monmouth, indeed the only Lampeter Principal to become a bishop in the twentieth century. He was succeeded in 1923 by Maurice Jones, an appointment widely welcomed by both Nonconformists and Anglicans. Described by Bishop Gore as 'a strong thinker', he brought dynamic energy to the office of Principal and his dramatic sermons were compared to 'a Christmas pudding catching fire from brandy sauce'.[75] No man was better equipped to dispel the encircling gloom, but his task was not an easy one. He could not count on the loyalty of all his staff, the Bishop of Monmouth hated him and he had no cause to like the new Archbishop of Wales ('the old brute',[76] as he was known in the Jones household). But no discouragement made him once relent. The centenary celebrations of 1927 attended by the Archbishop of Canterbury were a great success and we are authoritatively informed that the College could soon afford to send down students for less than satisfactory work. By 1938–9 Lampeter had 200 students, appreciably more than Hull (162) and Leicester (82), and standards were apparently maintained throughout the late 1920s and the 1930s. It was considered a special mark of confidence in the future when Jones restocked the College cellar in 1933.[77]

The links between Lampeter and the University remained tenuous. There was a growing feeling amongst some, including T. F. Tout, the celebrated medieval historian, long a luminary at Lampeter and now at Manchester, that the College should surrender both its degrees (the BA and the BD) provided the University granted an *ad eundem* BA degree to Lampeter graduates, that is, to admit them to the same degree of the University, thus making them eligible to be presented for the University's MA degree, after due preparation.[78] Jones was under the impression that a special statute of 1923 had opened an untrammelled path for Lampeter graduates to be recognized by the University but in 1924 the University Court, acting upon the recommendations of the Academic Board and University Council, agreed to grant the *ad eundem* degree to Lampeter graduates 'if and when St David's College, Lampeter, ceases to grant degrees in Arts'.[79] This was not at all acceptable and tedious discussions led nowhere. The Lampeter Principal, however, pursued the matter relentlessly, protesting 'most earnestly against the treatment which it is proposed to mete out to this College by the University of its own country'. Oxford and Cambridge, on the other hand, had always given it every encouragement and it would be 'a deplorable tragedy'[80] if the University of Wales did not recognize the College's century of service to higher education in Wales. In 1928 an impression was given that Lampeter was prepared to accept the University's condition and the College, with a somewhat disingenuous tenacity (for the University's views had not changed) applied for recognition as an associated theological college. The request was seriously entertained by visitors appointed by the Academic Board, Sir Harry Reichel and Professor W. B. Stevenson of Glasgow, who, however, upon arrival at Lampeter were discomfited to find that the College was not willing to surrender its BA degree, a fundamental requirement. In 1938 the College Council, contrary to the advice of its College Board, raised the question again, only to be rebuffed in like fashion.[81]

In urging that the arts degree be discontinued the University was in fact confirming the views of prominent churchmen, Principal Joyce and Archbishop Edwards amongst them, but the University's policy was a constant source of irritation. Both Liverpool and Bristol recognized the Lampeter BA as qualifying candidates to pursue their respective MA courses, whilst London allowed Lampeter's arts graduates to prepare for its BD degree. Yet, in reinforcing Lampeter's resolve to retain its arts side the University paradoxically pointed the way to the College's ultimate salvation. Shorn of its BA degree, Lampeter would have declined into a lonely Anglican seminary attended by a diminishing band of ordinands for whom there would be adequate provision elsewhere in Wales, at Bangor and Cardiff (and, if need be, at a college established at Aberystwyth). To return to Emrys Evans's metaphor, the moth would have been shrivelled in the flame, not singed. The retention of the BA degree, on the other hand, enabled this attractive College to survive post-war vicissitudes and to be welcomed in 1971 as a valued constituent institution of the University.[82]

By the end of the period surveyed in this chapter the fortunes of the federal University were more securely based. The largely demoralizing peregrinations of the early years to seek funds from the Treasury were now long past and the new University Grants Committee was increasingly seen as an effective link between government and universities. The first chairman, Sir William McCormick, formerly chairman of the Advisory Committee on University Grants, represented an element of continuity, and his successors, such as Sir Walter Moberley, generated confidence. The war years had demonstrated the folly of inadequate provision for higher education and from 1920 to 1938 the total parliamentary grant for the University of Wales more than doubled to £205,881. Funds, however, were inadequate and vigilant husbandry was vital, especially during the aftermath of the First World War and during the years of depression. Happily the federal atmosphere in the 1930s was pacific, certainly by comparison with the restless 1920s. Solidarity was a prime ingredient of survival and a natural rivalry between colleges was not allowed to sour relations. Thus, the Haldane Commission's expectation that advanced work in agriculture should be confined to either Bangor or Aberystwyth was amicably settled when the University Court rejected the recommendation. The division of state moneys by the University Council seldom satisfied all parties, but it was generally recognized that wise men had struggled to be just. In the 1930s, too, all the heads of colleges were at least formally committed to the federal principle and were rarely given to unguarded public statements. Resources were never sufficient for them to embark upon adventurous policies, even had they so wished, but they had a genuine concern for the common good. That was no small matter; they served the University well both before and for some years after the Second World War.

VII

The Colleges, 1920–1939

Aberystwyth

During the war Thomas Jones was preparing imaginative plans for his old college. It was to be a powerful 'engine of social progress',[1] specializing in Celtic studies, music, art and the social sciences. In these four branches the College was to be unsurpassed in Britain and its extra-mural activities would regenerate life in rural Wales. The ladies of Llandinam, captivated by his ideas, were the anonymous donors reported to the Haldane Commission as being ready to give the College £100,000 in instalments of £20,000 over five years. Indeed for a decade or so Aberystwyth appeared livelier, more constructive than Cardiff, obsessively immersed in the Medical School dispute, or Bangor, believed by some to be governed by a gerontocracy.[2]

The main fruits of the new spirit were the appointment in 1919 of (Sir) Alfred Zimmern to the Wilson chair of international politics and of (Sir) Walford Davies to the chair of music. T. F. Roberts, the College's second Principal, who died in that year aged fifty-eight, had viewed these developments from a sick-bed. Administrative duties he had always tended to find burdensome – no small disadvantage in a principal – and his health steadily deteriorated during the war years. It was not easy to know him well, but those who had access to the innermost man spoke of him in the highest terms. True to his working-class origins, he lamented the inadequate educational opportunities for the poor. Welshmen should be rooted in the traditions of their country; to be divorced from one's background was a calamity; a mature nation should discover her own natural leaders, for only thus could Wales contribute significantly to a wider world.[3] A profoundly religious man, he did not readily respond to the implications of scientific discoveries. The significance of the year 1859 in his eyes was the religious revival in Wales, not the publication of Darwin's *Origin of Species*. David Williams perceptively observed that Roberts 'in himself combined a Hebrew passion for social righteousness derived from his Biblical upbringing with a Greek love of truth and beauty derived from his study of the Classics, and he applied both within the framework of the Welsh cultural heritage'.[4]

The search for a successor led to unseemly contention, not unknown at Oxford and Cambridge but less public there. Metropolitan opinion unanimously favoured Thomas Jones, since 1916 at the heart of government in the cabinet secretariat.[5] If appointed his would be a central role in implementing the Haldane recommendations. Amongst his advocates were H. A. L. Fisher, R. H. Tawney, Sir William McCormick and William Temple (who wrote in reassuring tones to the Welsh bishops). As we have seen, he had drawn up stimulating plans for the development of Aberystwyth, particularly on the arts side, and he was largely responsible, with the firm support of David Davies, Llandinam, for the appointment of Walford Davies and Alfred Zimmern. However within Wales there were several who believed him to be too closely allied with David Davies and who were suspicious of the plutocratic embrace. Further, his religious credentials were questioned and he was asked to give satisfaction to a Carmarthenshire archdeacon concerning the eternal verities.[6] In the event three candidates were interviewed: Thomas Jones, J. H. Davies, the College Registrar who had acted as Principal during Roberts's disabling illness, and J. E. Lloyd, Bangor's distinguished medieval historian who had sought the post as far back as 1891. Lloyd was interviewed for five minutes, Jones for slightly more than fifteen minutes and Davies, the successful candidate, for forty-five minutes, an invidious allotment of time. The failure to appoint Thomas Jones baffled and amazed his supporters. Fisher was despondent concerning the future of the University; the Master of Balliol expressed 'indignation and contempt' and R. Silyn Roberts was certain that the College had 'sinned against the light'.[7] T.J. was understandably cast down, but to his credit he did not allow himself to be embittered. In 1953, when he surveyed the University scene since 1893, he calculated in a fit of whimsy the average expectation of life of Welsh College Principals. He concluded that had he been appointed to Aberystwyth he would have died in 1933 and he thanked the College Council for an extension of at least two decades.[8]

The new Principal, John Humphreys Davies (1871–1926), was by no means a cipher. True, his early career had not been spectacular. At Oxford he acquired the somewhat comic degree of honours in the fourth class (which Evelyn Waugh, predictably, would have much preferred to his well-deserved third). Called to the bar, he entered public life; soon he was a justice of the peace and treasurer of the General Assembly of the Calvinistic Methodists, an effective power-base, especially in Cardiganshire. An adroit, affable conciliator, he was generally respected as Registrar and students warmly applauded his appointment. In youth he had happily rejected his mother's advice to be 'more careful in small things such as buying books'[9] for in time he built up the splendid Cwrtmawr collection, now at the National Library, which he had done much to establish. His term as Vice-Chancellor was interrupted by an unusual misfortune. Unscathed in rural Cardiganshire, he was struck by a falling tree on Haverstock Hill, North London, the direct cause of his premature death.[10]

The search for a principal in 1927 was decorous by the standards of 1919. Thomas Jones canvassed the claims of (Sir) David Hughes Parry, a former student of the College and an academic lawyer of great promise. It is strange to reflect that the former had much to do with the appointment of Aberystwyth's sixth Principal and the latter with his departure. In the event, once the merits of Hughes Parry and J. F. Rees (soon to become Cardiff's Principal) had been weighed, the choice fell upon Henry Stuart Jones.[11] Of Cornish extraction, he had early shown his supremacy as a classical scholar. At Oxford he was placed in the first class in classical moderations (1888), and in *literae humaniores* (1890); he won the Hertford, the Ireland and Craven scholarships, and the Gaisford Prize for Greek prose with a Platonic dialogue. He was elected fellow of Brasenose when he became Camden Professor of Ancient History in 1919. Why, at the pinnacle of his professional career and at the age of sixty, he chose to respond to the challenge of Aberystwyth is not now easy to determine. It is possible that he is to be included in the ever-lengthening procession of scholars unduly seduced by the lure of administration and who would have been happier had they remained where they were. T. Gwynn Jones, with a poet's eye, thought that when the time came for him to retire he would leave no greater impression 'than does a stick when it is drawn through water'.[12] Thomas Jones said that as a speaker he was 'rapid and indistinct' with very little small talk; he further described him as 'learned, retiring and without subtlety'.[13] Yet it is clear that Stuart Jones, who had learnt, though not mastered, Welsh, enjoyed the esteem of students, for he was ready to travel overnight from London in order to cheer them on in an important rugby match on the Vicarage Field. Above all, staff and students rejoiced in his high international reputation and it was evident that he had not deserted research, for it was common to see him perched perilously on a tall ladder in the classics section of the library.[14] Although plagued with ill health (like his two predecessors) he was able before his death in 1939 to see through the press the long-needed revision of Liddell and Scott's *Greek-English Lexicon* (1925–40). Nor did it harm a college long taunted as a Nonconformist academy to have at last appointed a devout Anglican as its principal.

Upon Stuart Jones's departure in 1934, the College interviewed four candidates for the principalship, including the best internal candidate, W. J. Pugh, before it unanimously pitched upon Ifor L. Evans, fellow of St John's College, Cambridge. A native of Aberdare, he was in Germany at the outbreak of war. Interned at seventeen for the duration, he had learnt Welsh. Ivor became Ifor. It was no small transformation. At Cambridge he excelled and was elected Whewell scholar in international law. Soon he was publishing authoritative works on the agricultural revolution in Romania and on African affairs. In 1927 he was seriously considered at thirty for the Aberystwyth principalship. Harold Temperley cannot have advanced his cause by privately and preposterously stating that he had 'no liking for administration'. H. D. Henderson, editor of the *Nation*, thought otherwise. Evans would make 'an exceptionally good administrator'; he would not be weighed down by routine duties and attendant worries so as to lose his 'spring and zest'.[15] During the intervening seven years, it was said, he had ripened. In fact he

1. The University College of Wales, Aberystwyth, opened in 1872.

2. The triptych on the turret of the south wing of Old College
building, Aberystwyth, added after reconstruction. Science in
the centre is presented with symbols of modern inventions.

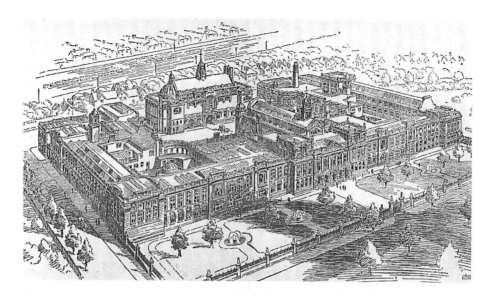

3. W. J. Caröe's plan of Cardiff's new College. The proposed Great Hall was never completed.

4. The entrance to University College, Cardiff.

5. H. T. Hare's building at Bangor (1911).

6. Singleton Abbey, Swansea's first home.

7. The original Medical School building in Newport Road, Cardiff, given by Sir William James Thomas and opened in 1921.

8. St David's College, Lampeter, the first degree-awarding College in Wales.

9. Disaster for the University averted. Caernarfon's proposed site for the University Registry within the castle precincts.

10. The University Registry, Cathays Park, Cardiff.

11. Sir Isambard Owen, Senior Deputy-
Chancellor, 1895–1910. Bust by W.
Goscombe John.

12. Lord Kenyon, Senior-Deputy
Chancellor, 1910–1920, and Pro-
Chancellor, 1920–1927.

13. John Viriamu Jones (1856–1901), the
University's first Vice-Chancellor,
1895–1896.

14. Sir Harry Reichel (1856–1931).

15. Thomas Francis Roberts
(1860–1919).

16. Sir Thomas Franklin Sibly
(1893–1948).

17. A. W. Sheen (1869–1945).

18. Lord Haldane (1856–1928).

19. Lloyd George, after a doctorate had been conferred upon him at Bangor in 1908, and John Morris-Jones.

20. Ivor James, the University's first Registrar, 1895–1905.

21. Owen M. Edwards, first Warden of the Guild of Graduates, 1895–1896.

22. Sir Herbert Lewis, the University's first Member of Parliament, 1918–1922.

THE CALL.

24. Women students were called to contribute to the war effort.

23. The Prince of Wales visits Coleg Harlech in 1934 accompanied by Thomas Jones and Ben Bowen Thomas, both of whom had close links with the College and the University.

25. Lt. Col. Hepburn, Professor of Anatomy, and Matron Montgomery Wilson visit the war-wounded at Cardiff Royal Infirmary.

26. The first issue of *Y Deyrnas* ('The Kingdom'), a forum for conscientious objectors.

DON'T CRUSH!

[It is announced that at least six professors at Bangor University have married lady students.]

28. The *Morning Leader* on 7 July 1905 drew attention to extra-curricular opportunities at Bangor.

27. The Cardiff Festival, 1931.

29. The tennis team at Bangor, 1897.

30. Aberystwyth cricketers and tennis players welcomed at Bangor in May 1906.

31. Aberystwyth's soccer team, 1924–1925, which won the British Universities Championship.

32. Swansea, outstanding in rugby, included in its 1929 team three future captains of Wales.

33. Cardiff's Jim Alford winning the mile at the Commonwealth Games in New Zealand in 1938.

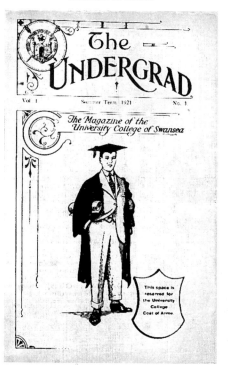

The UNDERGRAD

Vol 1   Summer Term 1921   No. 1

The Magazine of the University College of Swansea

This space is reserved for the University College Coat of Arms.

34. College magazines were immensely popular from the outset. Swansea speedily followed suit.

STUDENTS' JOKE.

SIR AUSTEN TAKEN TO WORKHOUSE.

'SEASIDE LANDLADIES' AS GUARD OF HONOUR.

"BACK TO LOCARNO" SPEECH.

DARK PROSPECT OF DISARMAMENT CONFERENCE.

Sir Austen Chamberlain found himself on Friday afternoon in a strange land among people who spoke a strange tongue. He came to Aberystwyth to deliver his address as president of the Debates Union of the University College of Wales.

When he stepped from the train he was greeted by strange yells from the men and women students who gathered round the platform gates. They were in peculiar costumes, but there was something which was familiar to Sir Austen, for nearly every student wore a monocle.

A guard of honour was formed by students who were dressed as seaside landladies, each armed with a broom. Sir Austen enjoyed the scene, and when he left the platform the landladies presented arms with their brooms. The college yell rent the air, and amidst the din Sir

SIR AUSTEN CHAMBERLAIN.   Austen was escorted to a motor-car.

The officials of the Debates Union, who should have welcomed Sir Austen, had been kidnapped earlier and locked up in one of the college boathouses.

The students, who impersonated them, went with Sir Austen to the Poor-law institution, where he spent a few minutes with the aged inmates.

In company with Mr. Ernest Evans, M.P. for the Welsh University, he was received by the matron (Mrs. Lloyd), and was amused at a placard near the entrance which announced that the building was "the home for broken down professors."

35. Pranksters at Aberystwyth, 12 February 1932.

36. At the inter-college Eisteddfod at Bangor in 1921, a *Gorsedd* ceremony was bravely held within grapeshot of John Morris-Jones, fiercely hostile to the *Gorsedd* of Bards.

37. Participants in an inter-college debate (in Welsh) at Aberystwyth in 1913. Seated are the burly Professor Anwyl (centre), Kate Roberts (second from left) and Griffith John Williams (extreme right).

38. Specialist textbooks were scarce. One student made her own copy of J. Gwenogvryn Evans's *Llyfr Aneirin* (1900).

39. Called to account.

had matured earlier than most. He was soon to display an unusual skill in financial affairs. Within the College he had inherited a debt of over £60,000 which he succeeded in removing. Agricultural development, in turn, gave him great satisfaction. As chairman of the University's Estates Committee his role was especially valuable when scattered properties were acquired under the Tithe Act of 1936. The cultural side of his nature found expression in promoting Welsh hymnology and folk songs, and T. H. Parry-Williams paid the highest tribute to his discriminating judgement as chairman of the University's Press Board.[16] His death at the age of fifty-five was a tragedy. D. Emrys Evans, who dedicated to his memory his history of the University, discerned in him the colourful, the artistic and the practical: 'somehow, he managed to blend them all, not without much inner tension, into a very rich and constructive whole'.[17] Believed by some to be masterful, though not oppressively so, his combative instincts served the College well in opposing a mettlesome, meddlesome benefactor.

The retirement of Sir John Williams from the presidency in 1926 at the age of eighty-six prompted the College to turn to David (later Lord) Davies. Its debt to members of the Llandinam family was immeasurable. They had demonstrated through the years that there was no necessary antagonism between wealth and social conscience. Their Saviour's words concerning the camel and the eye of a needle held no terrors for them. David Davies moved easily through all ranks of society – he was a hero to his chauffeur, who dubbed him 'Double Diamond' – and his wartime experiences had planted in him a profound belief in the League of Nations as the salvation of humankind. However, like many lesser men, he disliked having his authority challenged. After the rejection in 1919 of Thomas Jones as Principal, whom he had fervently supported, he withdrew into his tent. His election to the presidency seven years later enabled him to cast an eagle eye upon the administration of the College. Complications arose in an acute form in 1936 when the chair of international politics which he had generously endowed was offered to E. H. Carr. He immediately resigned because the College Council had not accepted his view that the holder of the chair should be 'wholehearted in his devotion to the cause of international co-operation'.[18] At the core of the conflict lay the high academic principle that appointments should not be made because of commitment to a particular doctrine, however noble. David Davies's judgement was further darkened by his attempt to force the issue, thus endangering another principle, that of democratic control. It was much to Ifor Evans's credit that he was resolute. The College was indeed shaken to its foundations. An attempt was made to repair the damage. David Davies at length resumed office, but his detachment from the affairs of the College indicated that, admirable though he was in many ways, he could not forget his sad, though necessary, defeat. Disaffection between President and Principal was inevitably injurious to the best interests of the College, as it had been in the days of Lord Aberdare and Thomas Charles Edwards. Even earlier his views had not prevailed. When J. H. Davies became Principal, the College decided not to appoint a successor as Registrar, partly because Davies had long mastered the arcana of administration which he had no wish to surrender, partly because two experienced secretaries were deemed sufficient and partly to save money. David Davies did not care for these arrangements and in 1929 he received the concurrence of the Council to fill the office. He approached the Bangor Registrar, (Sir) Wynn P. Wheldon, who was hard-headed enough to resist his absurd blandishments of public recognition in the honours list. There was even mention of being made a Companion of Honour. The very notion that the honours system could be employed in this way is a further indication of serious debasement. Within three months Wheldon was able to tell Davies that Bangor had increased his salary and that he would remain there (though not for long as it emerged).[19] Only in 1936 was J. Morgan Jones (A. W. Ashby's able assistant) appointed Registrar.

Amongst departmental developments, one of the chief was the creation of the chair of international politics, which David Davies had originally intended to found at Oxford. It was to be associated with the 'illustrious name' of President Wilson. An idealist at heart, Davies believed that a small nation such as Wales could thus contribute to an understanding of the world's gravest problems by enlisting the services of 'the best international scholar'.[20] Circumstances and personalities so conspired that within the College there was not always that spirit of concord which Davies had hoped to promote in the larger world. The first holder of the chair was Alfred Zimmern, whose Jewish father had migrated from Germany to England after the collapse of the revolution of 1848. A fellow of New College, Oxford, Zimmern's best work, *The Greek Commonwealth* (1911), had won general acclaim, but the war and its consequences led him increasingly to the study of international affairs and especially of the new League of Nations. Alert and vigorous in discussion he was immensely popular with students who roared their approval of his strictures upon the lecture system and the spoon-feeding of adult minds. His more insensitive remarks, however, made him several enemies and he was soon in an impossible situation for he had formed an attachment to the powerful, determined Madame Barbier, wife of the Professor of French. Trained at the Paris Conservatoire, she was long remembered for arranging remarkable concerts at Aberystwyth. She now asked for a divorce in order to marry Zimmern. Small colleges are at best ill-equipped to deal with such irregularities and a defiant speech by Zimmern to a hostile Council was the inevitable prelude to his departure to wider fields of endeavour, notably at Geneva where he was director of the School of International Studies.[21]

The morning sun was but briefly overcast. From the chair of modern history at Liverpool came C. K. Webster, deeply committed to the League of Nations and already an authority upon the international relations of the post-Napoleonic era. The terms of his appointment were enlightened: one term of each year at Aberystwyth, another at any university which sought his services (Harvard from 1927), and a third in study abroad. Webster's main work at Aberystwyth, *The Foreign Policy of Castlereagh, 1815–22* (1925), firmly established his reputation and equally firmly restored that of Castlereagh. In appearance large and rather untidy, he was a man of transparent honesty who made no enemies, at Aberystwyth or elsewhere. When he left for London in 1932 David Davies reviewed the position. Webster had set an example to occupants of similar chairs throughout the world. He had 'laid the foundations and mapped out the territory; it is for them to build and to explore'.[22] Webster's successor, however, Jerome Green, a most agreeable American and a former secretary of the Rockefeller Institution, had early ruffled the feathers of Lord Davies and left after two years. There was no immediate search for a replacement, for the depression had led to a substantial diminution in the value of the stocks upon which the chair depended. Nevertheless, in 1935 fifty-seven names were considered, some of them not lightly to be dismissed, Geoffrey Barraclough, D. W. Brogan, Herbert Butterfield, E. H. Carr, and A. J. Toynbee amongst them. At length Carr was chosen in 1936. After a distinguished academic career at Cambridge he rose to the rank of first secretary at the Foreign Office. Composed of conflicting characteristics, both utopian and realist, it is realism which prevails in his influential volume *The Twenty Years Crisis, 1919–1939: An Introduction to the Study of International Relations* (1939), written at Aberystwyth.[23] The appointment, as we have seen, led to an unhappy conflict between the President and Council, for Davies had favoured W. Arnold Foster, an enthusiastic supporter of the League of Nations.

The Haldane Report recommended that the post of Music Director and Chairman of the Council of Music for Wales should be established by the University and be held at one of the colleges. The ladies of Llandinam had no doubt that the College appointment, including the chair, should be at Aberystwyth, although the case in favour of Cardiff, which served a densely populated area, seemed to some unassailable. Many believed that D. Vaughan Thomas was eminently suitable. Not only had he endeavoured to set new standards for the National Eisteddfod, he was accounted 'a pioneer in the movement to lead Welsh music forward from a limited choralism to a more sensitive practice and appreciation of other musical forms'.[24] It seems that Thomas, who died in Johannesburg in 1934, never fully recovered from the shock of rejection. From Gregynog came the firm message that only one candidate measured up to the requirements of both posts, an opinion shared by powerful persons. Walford Davies, organist and director of the choir at the Temple Church, was well known to Lloyd George who was so impressed by his services to the armed forces in France that he had him knighted in 1922, and also to Henry Hadow (a member of the Haldane Commission) who discussed the project with Davies during a blow on Hampstead's breezy heath. A visit to Aberystwyth clinched the matter.[25] T.J. was delighted with the coup. Not everyone agreed. Some thought Davies to be frothily exuberant, others that elementary economics were alien to him. His gifts of communication and of evangelical zeal, however, were not to be measured by the gill but by the imperial gallon. Soon he had won the affection and attention of rumbustious post-war students who learnt to sit still in College concerts conducted not only by him but by Elgar, Holst, Vaughan Williams and Henry Wood. It is not too much to say that he transformed the musical scene at Aberystwyth. His heavy duties outside the College exhausted him and he was finally convinced that the directorship of the Council of Music should not be publicly associated with any college.[26] In 1926 he was succeeded as Professor of Music by David de Lloyd.

In 1930 Edward Edwards ('Teddy Eddy', as he was affectionately known by students), who had never regarded systematic research as his first charge, relinquished the chair of history, though until 1932 he clung like a limpet to the office of Vice-Principal, thus completing forty years in the service of the College. His social gifts were many and varied, he was popular with students and he had furthered town–gown relations during difficult, querulous days. He was succeeded in the chair, at the age of twenty-eight, by R. F. Treharne whose *The Baronial Plan of Reform, 1256–63* (1932) signalled further, solid achievements. When Stanley Roberts retired in 1934 it was clear that the potentialities of the chair of colonial history had not been fully explored and a reluctant Lord Davies was persuaded to allow his endowment to be used to finance two lectureships, one in the department of history and one in the department of colonial history. The preliminaries to the appointment of a professor of Welsh history were so convoluted as to preclude discussion here. Public disquiet at the long delay in establishing chairs of Welsh history in the University had been partially placated by the appointment of William Rees to the Cardiff chair in 1930 and of R. T. Jenkins to an independent lectureship at Bangor in the same year. In 1931, upon terms considered favourable by him, E. A. Lewis, Professor of Economics and Political Science, accepted the invitation to fill the chair of Welsh history which bore the name it still retains, that of Sir John Williams, whose further generosity to the College was thus fittingly recognized. 'Doc Lewis' – he was the first D.Litt. of the University of Wales – was now able to concentrate upon his main interest, manifest since the publication of *The Mediaeval Boroughs of Snowdonia* in 1912. He also taught palaeography and diplomatic, indispensable to the serious study of medieval and early modern history. He was succeeded as Professor of Economics and Political Science by R. B. Forrester, Reader at London University, one of two recommended to the Council by J. Maynard Keynes.[27]

In 1913 Sir Edward Anwyl, Professor of Welsh Language and Literature for over two decades, was appointed Principal of Caerleon Training College but died before taking up the post. The College, largely because of wartime constraints, did not replace him and was bitterly criticized. In 1919, however, the prospect of Llandinam moneys prompted the Council to make full amends. There were to be two chairs, one in Welsh language and one in Welsh literature. Thomas Gwynn Jones, reader since 1913, became convinced that there were forces at work to exclude him, for he was an uncompromising pacifist and anti-imperialist.[28] If he were passed over he had contemplated emigrating to South America. In August 1919, however, the phantoms of the night were dispelled. He was appointed to the first, and indeed the only, separate chair of Welsh literature. Gwynn Jones's other colleagues had clear claims upon the chair of Welsh language, but the issue was muddied because T. H. Parry-Williams, the stronger of the two candidates, had held conscientious views during the war, whereas the other contestant, Timothy Lewis, was an ex-serviceman who made the most of his experiences in his application and who was supported by many members of the 'Comrades of the Great War', the forerunner of the British Legion. The College Council temporized and not until 1920 was Parry-Williams justly elected to the chair, Timothy Lewis being appointed Reader in Celtic Philology and Palaeography. Lewis in the course of time became withdrawn and entertained speculations which did not command the wholehearted assent of his peers. Parry-Williams remained in the chair until 1952. 'It is doubtful', says R. Geraint Gruffydd, 'whether any Welsh scholar, before or since, received such a thorough preparation for his life's work in so many countries and at the feet of so many world-renowned scholars.'[29] He excelled in two fields, the English element in Welsh and the popular free-metre verse of the sixteenth to the eighteenth centuries. A large public, at the Eisteddfod and especially after the advent of radio, delighted in his felicitous intonation of the more softly sonorous of Snowdonia's sounds. Gwynn Jones, with whom he had worked in complete harmony, retired in 1937. Thereafter, there was a reversion to the previous title, namely, the department of Welsh language and literature. Gwynn Jones had received few educational advantages. He never attended a college and at one time there was a serious danger that he might subside into the police force. A fertile scholar, he was considered by some to be the foremost poet of his age. He enriched the literature of Wales and the lives of his students, as many eloquently attested. They remembered his passion and his eloquence, the flashing eye and the half-mumbled oath, all, it seemed, to promote the best of causes.

Further developments on the arts side included the departure in 1932 of the Professor of Latin, J. F. Mountford, for Liverpool where in due course he became a highly valued Vice-Chancellor. In 1938, since neither department had many students, Latin and Greek were amalgamated under E. D. T. Jenkins. In 1932 the young R. I. Aaron (who for long achieved his wish to remain first in *Who's Who*) was appointed Professor of Philosophy; later he became Fellow of the British Academy for his authoritative study of John Locke. Amongst those whose academic careers were drawing to a close were J. W. H. Atkins, Professor of English Language and Literature (1906–40) and Thomas Levi, professor for thirty-nine years. Levi had created the department of law. He cannot be accounted a scholar in the strict sense, but he was able to communicate the central principles of the laws of England to generations of Welsh students with panache, a sense of theatre and a curious nasal twang which usually eluded his many imitators. After the First World War, especially, the department became a nursery for lawyers who reached the topmost branches of their profession and who gratefully remembered the 'irresistible and irrepressible'[30] Tommy Levi.

In 1919 the long reign of R. W. Genese over the department of mathematics came to an end. He was succeeded by a brilliant mathematician, W. H. Young, already a Fellow of the Royal Society. Equally impressive in classroom and Senate, his desire to import foreigners described as 'exotic'[31] to the department and his persistent requests for leave of absence caused inevitable tensions. Such resources as were available to the professor of international relations (independently funded) were not forthcoming and it is sad that a small college was unable to retain the services of one who later pursued his studies in Göttingen, Geneva and Lausanne. E. J. Williams, however, resisted temptations to wean him away from Aberystwyth, except for essential absence during the Second World War. Appointed Professor of Physics in 1938, he may well have been the ablest scientist at any of the Welsh colleges during this period. Educated at Swansea, he had worked with W. L. Bragg at Manchester, with Rutherford at Cambridge and with Niels Bohr at Copenhagen. His distinction in experimental and theoretical physics led to his election to the Royal Society at the age of thirty-six. Of his contributions during the war, P. M. S. Blackett said that they had been of 'decisive importance'[32] in the victorious struggle against the U-boat. After the war he returned to Aberystwyth, but died of cancer in September 1945, aged forty-two.

The appointment of H. J. Fleure to the new chair of geography at Manchester in 1930 was a grievous impoverishment to the College. At the centre of events at Aberystwyth, Fleure was a fine scholar and had occupied the first chair of geography and anthropology since its foundation in 1918, an ambition he had long nursed. For the first time at a British university it was now possible for a student in the faculties of arts and science to prepare for initial and higher degrees in geography. The academic study of geography was then at a formative stage and faced opposition. To Fleure it was a subject 'wherein he could best express his philosophy, investigating the full environment of nature underlying man's progress towards the mastery of nature itself'.[33] The Aberystwyth school under him became famous and his departure caused him some distress. Although the financial inducement was not insignificant, the prime determinant was Manchester's undertaking to create a chair if Fleure would accept. The opportunity to spread the gospel of geography was not to be refused. Eleven years earlier, O. T. Jones had left Aberystwyth to fill the chair of geology at Manchester; in 1930 he became Woodwardian Professor of Geology at Cambridge. The rocks of Wales continued to be his main study. One of his major contributions was to establish the Llandovery series as a standard measurement of geological time; it was internationally recognized. At the age eighty-eight he wrote his last paper, in Welsh, on the distribution of the blue stones of Carn Meini in Pembrokeshire.[34] In 1919 he was succeeded at Aberystwyth by his favoured candidate, (Sir) William Pugh, newly returned from the war, who served the College with distinction until he, too, was enticed to Manchester. In the 1940s O. T. Jones and Pugh collaborated upon climactic studies which led to the identification of an early Ordovician shore-line in the Builth-Llandrindod Wells area. Upon the death of Wilfred Robinson in 1930 Lily Newton was appointed to the chair of botany. Under her fostering care the number of students increased and the reputation of the department was enhanced within and beyond Wales. Her knowledge of the College, her acumen and courtesy proved invaluable when she served as Acting Principal during the difficult days which followed the death of Ifor L. Evans. In 1920 R. D. Laurie was invited to fill the chair of zoology. Resourceful, importunate and indefatigable, he is also justly honoured as a founder of the Association of University Teachers.

It is natural that special attention be given to the College's contribution to agriculture. In January 1919, C. Bryner Jones, the Professor of Agriculture, was able to give the Principal news of first importance. Laurence Philipps (later Lord Milford) had agreed to give the College an endowment of £10,000 and an annual income of £1,000 to establish a plant breeding station at Aberystwyth to be modelled on the National Institute of Agricultural Botany at Cambridge which had rendered excellent service to English agriculture. It was at once resolved to invite R. G. Stapledon to become Director of the Station and also Professor of Agricultural Botany. A Devon man and educated at Cambridge, Stapledon had taken long to discover his true bent, somewhat to the impatience of his mother, wont to call him 'shilly-shally'. During the hot, dry summer of 1911, however, he had intensively studied the wild, white clover on the Cotswolds. Fascinated by his discoveries he became 'not only a scientist, but a philosopher'.[35]

The College, to its great credit, acted speedily and bought a ninety-two acre farm at Frongoch, near Aberystwyth. Mistrustful of extravagant promises and working with limited resources, Stapledon created the Plant Breeding Station which became renowned throughout the world. By 1927 Aberystwyth was chosen as the centre for the Imperial Bureau of Plant Genetics; in the following year the Empire Marketing Board enabled Stapledon and his colleagues to extend the range of their inquiries. Ahead lay the years of depression. Stapledon and the Principal wrote to *The Times* in 1932 to appeal for £20,000 to maintain the Plant Breeding Station. Agricultural progress in Britain, they said, depended on livestock production; grasslands were a vast underdeveloped asset both at home and in distant parts of the globe. Almost immediately, Sir Julian Cahn responded with £7,000 annually for seven years. His benefaction enabled sheep to winter on upland farms far higher than before. Many of the new varieties of grasses, clovers and oats, designated as the 'S' strains, became widely known throughout the temperate zones of the Commonwealth, especially in New Zealand. Stapledon's international reputation as the authority on grassland development was recognized in 1937 when research workers from thirty-eight countries assembled at Aberystwyth to elect him president of the International Grassland Congress. In 1939 he was knighted and elected a Fellow of the Royal Society. L. S. Amery, a forceful Colonial Secretary, paid a handsome tribute to the work of the Plant Breeding Station in the development of grass, 'by far the most important of all Empire crops'. At the end of the war, Reginald Dorman-Smith, a former Minister of Agriculture, believed that without Stapledon's victories in the arts of peace 'we most certainly would have been starved of food and there would have been no military victories about which our generals now may argue'. In the same spirit Stapledon's biographer held that 'the names of Aber-Stapledon should join in the public mind in the same way as El Alamein-Montgomery'.[36]

There were, of course, others whose contribution Stapledon readily recognized. There was T. J. Jenkin who succeeded him in the twin appointments in 1942, and A. W. Ashby (son of the celebrated Joseph Ashby of Tysoe) who became Professor of

Agricultural Economics in 1929, indeed, the first in Britain. Born in a Warwickshire village, the eldest of eight children, Ashby well understood the hardships of rural life and speedily won the respect of Welsh farmers by his manner and mastery of his subject. A prolific writer, his best work is to be seen in the published proceedings of the Agricultural Economics Society and of international conferences. A strong believer in co-operation, he had a large share in creating the Milk Marketing Board for England and Wales; as a member of the Agricultural Wages Board he sought to improve relations (frequently frayed) between master and man. It is an ironic reflection upon the Labour administrations of the day that they took so little advantage of his experience and knowledge.[37]

Although the number of students at Aberystwyth declined from its inter-war peak of 1,088 in 1920 to 663 in 1938, it had long been clear that serious development could not be confined to the lower reaches of the town, particularly between Laura Place and Pier Street. A substantial wooden structure had been raised on land adjacent to Queen's Road. It had admirable acoustics and could hold 2,500. Lloyd George spoke here during the Jubilee celebration in 1922 and Walford Davies could always fill it. In 1933 the College suffered its second visitation by fire; the hall was totally destroyed and for forty years the College was deprived of a building of its own to accommodate large congregations. Upon the hill, however, above the National Library, opportunity beckoned. In 1929 eighty-seven acres on Penglais had been purchased to enable the College to prepare elaborate plans for expansion. The generous donor was Joseph Davies Bryan, a former student of the College, who, with his brothers, had prospered in Egypt. In Cairo and Alexandria they owned large stores, with branches in Port Said and Khartoum; they were so widely trusted that Arabs preferred to deposit substantial sums of gold with the firm, even without written security, rather than in banks.[38] David Davies had discovered in 1921 that the College was in debt to the tune of £100,000, so that a realistic building programme was out of the question. Nevertheless, there was ready acceptance of Thomas Jones's proposal to invite Sidney Greenslade, the architect of the National Library, to prepare plans for the Penglais estate.

Greenslade responded with alacrity, but was obliged to withdraw because of nervous exhaustion; much had been expected of him. The commission was finally entrusted to Percy Thomas. It was not until the 1960s that the College on the Hill displaced the Old College by the Sea as the main centre of activities.

Soon after the Great War, Aberystwyth had 1,088 students, more than at any other college. Decline then continued until a gradual rise from 721 in 1929 to 835 in 1935, a reflection of the years of depression. In the session immediately before the Second World War there were but 663 students, of whom 31 per cent, still ahead of all other colleges, were women, though Cardiff at 30 per cent had nearly closed the gap.[39]

Bangor

The Haldane Report led to various changes. The composition of the Court, Council and Senate of the College was altered, though only marginally. Two fundamental matters required a supplemental charter, granted in 1922. Henceforth restrictions were removed upon the teaching of theology and upon the acceptance by the College of endowments or gifts for purposes theological. Further, students were no longer prohibited from residing in College buildings, thus enabling the College to own and to administer hostels for students.[40]

There were changes, too, in personnel. Kenyon, the College President and the University's Senior Deputy-Chancellor, had suddenly died in 1927. It was a grievous loss to the College, which he had served as President since 1900, and also to the new Principal. (In 1947 the College was to turn to Kenyon's thirty-year-old son to carry on the tradition of his father. Lloyd Kenyon, the fifth baron, was President for thirty-five years and Chairman of its Council for almost the whole of that period. In sum, father and son served the College for over six decades, a record scarcely paralleled elsewhere.) W. E. Gladstone's third son, Henry Neville, first baron Gladstone of Hawarden, became the College's third President. Despite advancing years (he was now seventy-five), he displayed genuine concern for the welfare of the College. Upon his death in 1935 he was succeeded by Lord Howard de Walden who presided at the meeting of the College Court in 1936, but not thereafter. In 1940 he was followed by Lord Harlech, another regular absentee. It is against this background that the College must measure and recognize the remarkable services of the Kenyon family from English Flintshire (as it is traditionally called).

The sadness of impending retirement was further deepened for H. R. Reichel by the death of Isambard Owen, the prime architect of the University's charter (1893) and her first Senior Deputy-Chancellor. He was also a Vice-President of the College, and it is wholly appropriate that a bust of him should have been placed both in the University Registry and near the Council Chamber at Bangor. Isambard requested that he should be buried near to W. Cadwaladr Davies, the College's first Registrar, in Glanadda Cemetery, within sight of 'the College on the Hill', which Isambard had helped to design but which Cadwaladr did not live to see.

In 1927 H. R. Reichel retired in his seventy-first year.[41] Had he departed earlier his reputation might have been higher. Subdued and saddened by the war, to outward appearances austere and withdrawn, he was not suited to deal with ex-servicemen contemptuous of petty rules and little impressed by their Principal's peacetime reputation as a crack rifle shot and as commanding officer of the Officers' Training Corps. We gather that students saw little of him in his declining years. He was in fact approaching an age when it is not uncommon to dwell more in the company of the departed than of the living. His colleagues, however, had pressed him to extend his term in the unfulfilled expectation that he would preside at the birth of the Bangor Joint School of Theology upon which he had set his heart. Such a precedent unhappily discomfited colleagues who later unsuccessfully sought an extension.

From the outset Reichel had suffered certain disadvantages. An unjust resentment long remained that an Irish Anglican Unionist had been appointed Principal instead of Henry Jones, a craftsman's son, whose triumphs over early adversities had passed into folklore. Reichel was also exceedingly reserved and his unrelieved silences perplexed the uninitiated. With characteristic frankness he acknowledged that he had no natural power of speaking, a disability in a land which prized, and perhaps unduly prized, the oratorical arts. These shortcomings, however, were seen as trifles by those who knew him best. Beneath the forbidding demeanour lay an unyielding devotion to the welfare of the College and of the University of Wales. In his speeches, lectures and articles, whether on the Welsh Intermediate Act of 1889, university education in New Zealand and in the United States (both of which he had visited) or upon manual education, his analysis was lucid and searching, grounded in principle and guided by practical needs. In his tribute to departed colleagues there is more than elegiac melancholy; there is warmth and affection. No Principal has equalled his record of service to the University – he was six times Vice-Chancellor – and it is a substantial loss that in retirement he was unable to tackle a projected survey of the educational scene in Wales during his lifetime. From the first, Reichel was determined to learn the language of his adopted land. By 1886 he was writing recognizable Welsh on the Meath line in Ireland (and on his lap) to a Bala correspondent. When he died a former student telegraphed the College from South Africa: 'Welshmen abroad lament the death of a great Welshman.' He had come to Wales 'a doubting Thomas', as he told William Rathbone in 1900, because he had direct, personal experience in Ireland of the harrowing effects of social, religious and national divisions, but he now had 'a steady faith' in the future of the educational movement in Wales. From London he wrote upon the same theme to Hastings Rashdall, the authority on the early history of universities: 'I cannot say how much I feel when I come into England the elevation of the society I have left behind me on this mighty question.' James Gibson, a colleague of long standing, said that Reichel's greatest gift was his capacity to reconcile 'apparently divergent aims' and conflicting ideals, 'the severest and final test of academic statesmanship'. There was another quality which transcended all the others: he was, in the words of a former student, 'absolutely straightforward'. His integrity was never questioned.[42]

It is curious that so many founders of the University died abroad, Hugh Owen in Menton, Tom Ellis in Cannes, Viriamu Jones in Switzerland, Isambard Owen in Paris and Reichel in Biarritz in June 1931. Reichel was buried in the family grave at Whitechurch, Rathfarnham, near Dublin and within the Pale.

When the memorial service was held at Bangor Cathedral, the College and the city were shrouded in a silvery mist.

In seeking a successor to Reichel, the College Council ensnared itself by adopting an invidious procedure. The selection committee (including two members of the University Council) was to submit either one name to the Council or not more than three names, accompanied by a reasoned statement as to their qualifications. Common prudence ordains that a retiring principal should not participate in the choice of his successor. Reichel, however, was a member of the selection committee. The details of the proceedings have been fully treated elsewhere.[43] J. E. Lloyd was convinced that his own son-in-law, W. Garmon Jones, would have been master of the field but for Reichel's opposition. Only one candidate was recommended, but when it became clear that two persons whose names were submitted by members of the Council had not withdrawn their candidature, the committee of selection felt bound to explain why they should not be appointed. In the case of the College Registrar, Wynn P. Wheldon, it was said that he did not 'possess high academic distinction and teaching experience'. Age was against John Morris-Jones, administrative work would be uncongenial to him and it would be a 'national loss' if he were diverted from Celtic scholarship. Paternalistic recommendations that appointment would not be in the professor's own best interests enraged Morris-Jones, who took Reichel to task in a series of mordant letters. It is sad to reflect that two colleagues of nearly forty years did not long survive the encounter.

It cannot be doubted that the College, by wayward paths, had chosen the best candidate, David Emrys Evans. Born at Clydach, Swansea, in 1891, the son of a Baptist minister, he was educated at Bangor, where he excelled in classics and was president of the Students' Representative Council. During the war he completed research at Jesus College, Oxford, served in the YMCA and taught in a south Wales school. After lecturing at Bangor, he was appointed Swansea's first Professor of Classics. He soon displayed exceptional gifts as an administrator. Some believed that he would have flourished in one of the less flamboyant branches of the legal profession, perhaps in the Chancery Bar. Emrys Evans held that Bangor was 'the most national of all the colleges'.[44] Of patriotic inclinations, he attended a summer meeting of the new Welsh Nationalist Party in 1927 and was photographed in riding breeches sitting next to Saunders Lewis. The early flirtation did not last long. Subsequent developments, especially the fire at Penyberth, were a severe jolt to him as to others of like mind, and he soon returned to conventional Liberalism. Like Reichel, he saw to it that little of his University and College correspondence was allowed to survive, to intrigue and to illumine a curious posterity. At once cautious and alert, he was a sure pilot in well-charted coastal waters. Not for him, had it been possible, the deep-sea ventures which injured Cardiff in the 1980s, and in consequence the whole university system. Entirely characteristic was his remark in 1927 that he was not going to Bangor 'to make drastic changes or formulate new schemes'.[45] It was generally recognized that Emrys Evans found it difficult to enter into warm relationships with colleagues, as F. W. Rogers Brambell rightly noted, partly because, upon his entry into office, there were members of Senate who remembered him as a student.[46] The rapid expansion of universities in recent decades would have appalled him, as is evident from his observations in *The University of Wales* (1953), a slim survey which he was better equipped to write than any person then living. He remained a scholar; from his study there flowed erudite translations into Welsh of the masterpieces of antiquity. Contemporaries regarded him as an academic statesman. Tall, dignified and judicious, he was an impressive figure in Senate, in the Court and Council of the University, and upon ceremonious occasions, indeed upon all occasions where clarity of mind and felicity of speech were most needed and esteemed.

John Edward Lloyd had for twenty years been simultaneously Registrar and Professor of History (and for a lengthy period, librarian). It was, therefore, not surprising that in 1919, after unflagging devotion, he should seek leave to vacate the office of Registrar. In his stead came a wounded and much medalled veteran of the Great War, Major Wynn P. Wheldon, a former student, a Calvinistic Methodist and now a qualified lawyer. He had progressed greatly since the bleak day at the century's turn when, because of transgression at a picnic, the College Senate resolved that he 'be not allowed in future to be an officer of any

College Society'.[47] Upon his departure to be Principal Secretary to the Board of Education in 1933, he was followed by Elias Henry Jones, the son of Sir Henry Jones. One of the few Welshmen to have entered the Indian Civil Service, he served in the army until captured by the Turks. His adventurous escape was vividly unfolded in *The Road to En-dor* (1920), long familiar on the bookshelves of the reading public in Wales.

The most clamant academic need was the provision of new science buildings. The original intention was to include both science and arts faculties upon the crown of the hill. Financial considerations dictated otherwise. The scientists displayed great generosity of spirit. Kennedy Orton, Professor of Chemistry, argued that since the arts faculty was unlikely to attract funds from industrialists it would be proper to give priority to arts, administrative and library buildings. In the mean time, science laboratories in the old college were steadily deteriorating. When the war was at its fiercest, 'The North Wales Heroes' Memorial Fund' was launched to provide a memorial to the dead, bursaries for the children of the fallen and new buildings for the science departments of the College. The fund had been initiated by R. J. Thomas, an Anglesey man who had prospered in shipping at Liverpool and who now offered £20,000, his own services and paid secretaries. By 1918, £61,000 had been promised. Kenyon's suggestion to place the Memorial Arch at the upper entrance in College Road was carefully weighed, but was at length set aside because it would injure Hare's original concept, particularly the fine tower. Instead it was raised in the south-west corner of College Park, where in time it suffered from disharmonious additions. After Hare's death in 1920, the new architect was chosen by competition at the National Eisteddfod at Caernarfon in 1921. He was D. Wynne Thomas of Bolton, who sensitively interpreted his delicate task in relation to Hare's building. The Memorial Arch was opened on All Saints' Day 1923 by the Prince of Wales as Chancellor, watched by 10,000 people in College Park. In the upper chambers of the Memorial were inscribed the names of the 8,500 who were slain, county by county, parish by parish. On Armistice Day in later years buglers on the Arch played the 'Last Post' which preceded the two minutes' silence. The whole College then filed through the upper chamber in remembrance of 'the men of the North' ('Gŵyr y Gogledd').[48]

During his visit the Prince of Wales laid the foundation stone of the new science buildings. In order to reduce delay and costs (a perpetual concern) it was decided to raise four 'transitional' inexpensive structures for agriculture, botany and zoology, chemistry and physics, not on the base of the hill, clearly unsuitable for such buildings, but to the west of Glanrafon Hill. The architect was A. E. Munby, a specialist in laboratory building and a former pupil at Cambridge of J. J. Thomson, the greatest living physicist. Upon opening the new buildings in 1926 Thomson called them 'palatial' (somewhat surprisingly) and 'admirably fitted' to participate in the great work of scientific inquiry.[49]

We must now consider briefly the main departmental developments during the post-war period. After absence from Bangor on aeronautical research, G. H. Bryan returned in 1920 and remained for five years. A mathematician of outstanding ability but with an inability to count pennies correctly, his eccentric behaviour caused both mirth and irritation, and it was with relief that the College heard of his final departure for the Italian Riviera. His successor was W. H. Berwick, whose *Integral Bases* (1927) was considered an important contribution to algebraic theory. He soon, alas, became the victim of a progressively deteriorating disease and the efficiency of the whole department was soon affected. One of the College's most distinguished alumni, E. Taylor Jones, an authority on the classical field of electromagnetism, left the department of physics to follow Andrew Gray, also a former professor at Bangor, in Kelvin's old chair of natural philosophy at Glasgow in 1926. Another Bangor student, Edwin Augustus Owen, now succeeded Taylor Jones. Highly thought of by J. J. Thomson, his work on X-rays led to the Röntgen Award and to the formulation of Owen's Law. The development of applied electricity encouraged the College to establish an independent department under the headship of W. E. Williams, in the hope that the rural industries of north Wales, as in Switzerland, would be reanimated by hydro-electric power. The study of chemistry had from the outset prospered exceedingly. In 1921 Kennedy Orton was elected a

Fellow of the Royal Society in recognition of his work on chloramines and their application to the study of halogenation of anilines and ethers. In 1925 four of the seven honours candidates were placed in the first class. Five of his pupils became professors of chemistry. Orton was followed by (Sir) John Lionel Simonsen who had spent eighteen years in India. His strength as a chemist was on the experimental side, for theory did not much interest him. He became the expert on *terpenes* of which he gave a comprehensive account in six volumes. In 1932 he was elected a Fellow of the Royal Society. He left Bangor in 1942; he was knighted in 1949 and received the Davy medal in 1950. His assistant at Bangor, F. G. Soper, later became Vice-Chancellor of the University of Otago.[50]

Unremitting, selfless service to the College had impeded R. W. Phillips's algological studies which he partially resumed after retirement in 1922. He was followed by David Thoday, a trim, modest Devonian educated at Cambridge. At the time of his appointment, he held the chair of botany at Cape Town where he had seized the splendid opportunity to study the xerophytic plants which flourished in South Africa's seasonally dry climate. He displayed much ingenuity in designing simple apparatus of great value to his fellow botanists, such as the Thoday potometer and the Thoday respirometer. His ideas on plant tissues were ahead of his time and his contributions to research and teaching were recognized by his election to a Fellowship of the Royal Society.[51] P. J. White, long Professor of Zoology, continued to acquire specimens by land and sea for the museum which he had lovingly created. Rogers Brambell, who succeeded him at the age of twenty-nine, remained in Bangor for the rest of his life. He had been educated at Trinity College, Dublin, and at University College, London. In 1930 he published *The Development of Sex in Vertebrates* and in 1949 he was elected a Fellow of the Royal Society. He served upon a variety of scientific bodies, but his chief loyalty was to the College and to his department which he ruled with 'a firm but benevolent hand'.[52] He had early developed a course in marine biology from which grew the Marine Sciences Laboratory at Menai Bridge. His celebrated Easter vacation courses at Bangor on marine biology determined the dates of the vacation, and Brambell's 'tides' were the subject of jocular comment in a College where he became a father figure.

The Haldane Report's recommendation that advanced research and teaching in agriculture should be confined to one college was stoutly resisted. Research at Rothamsted concerned Britain as a whole, whereas the farmers of north Wales had special problems. The Welsh breed of sheep provided an excellent opportunity for genetic study and R. G. White, Bangor's Professor of Agriculture, argued forcefully that since a plant breeding station had been endowed at Aberystwyth, a natural complement would be a Research Institute in Animal Biology at Bangor. Both colleges wisely acted in concert and successfully retained their independence and individual specialisms. Out of the department of agriculture there branched two new departments after the war, agricultural chemistry and agricultural botany. Agricultural chemistry had already been placed upon a sound foundation by Gilbert Wooding Robinson, appointed to the College in 1912. His influential volume, *Soils, their Origin, Constitution and Classification: An Introduction to Pedology*, was published in 1932. Whereas 'pedology' was a term common enough on the continent, this was its first use in Britain where 'soil science' held sway, a barbaric term, according to Robinson. Barbaric or not, it later became familiar enough at Bangor. The significance of Robinson's study lay in the fact that it was 'the first English book dealing with soil simply as a physical entity and not in relation to the growth of plants'.[53] Robinson was appointed professor at Bangor in 1926 and thereafter a Fellow of the Royal Society. Agricultural botany had also been recognized by the College in 1912 upon the appointment of John Lloyd Williams, who, however, left for the chair of botany at Aberystwyth in 1914. After the war the work of the department was extended when the new Ministry of Agriculture sponsored an adviser in plant pathology and another in entomology. In 1926 R. Alun Roberts became an independent lecturer in the department of agricultural botany, though he was not appointed professor until 1945. He is chiefly remembered for his gift of interpreting the world of nature in lectures and broadcasts in Welsh. The fortunes of forestry were decidedly insecure until 1932 when additional grants made the finances of the department somewhat less hazardous.[54]

On the arts side classics were affected by the decline in the study of Greek in schools. The head of department, Hudson-Williams, was already urging the value of studying translations, otherwise the Greek mind would be permanently closed to almost everyone. E. V. Arnold, who had taught Latin from the early days, relinquished the chair in 1924. He was an editor of the *Classical Quarterly* for many years. A born fighter, usually in a good cause, he sniffed the smoke of battle from afar. In the *Welsh Leader* he claimed that 'the privilege which a professor most prizes is that of differing from everyone else'.[55] His successor, H. J. Thomson, was a mild-mannered scholar remembered for his sustained labours on medieval Latin glossaries and on the Christian poet Prudentius. J. Whatmough, a distinguished member of the department who had competed against him, became professor at Harvard in 1927. W. Lewis Jones long served the college in a variety of ways until, borne down by ill health, he was obliged to retire from the chair of English in 1919. He was followed by H. G. Wright, an authority upon the influence of Wales on English writers. John Morris-Jones's magisterial career, somewhat darkened by disappointment, drew to a premature close, for he died in office in 1929. His true deserts had already been widely recognized by other universities, though, strangely, not by the British Academy. He was knighted (and acquired a hyphen) in 1918, the year in which he published his *Taliesin*, a work of remarkable, if not of serene, scholarship, in origin a devastating rebuke to J. Gwenogvryn Evans who had unwisely entered choppy waters in a flat-bottomed boat. The year before his death Morris-Jones was responsible for the draft of *Orgraff yr Iaith Gymraeg* (The Orthography of the Welsh Language), a lasting boon to imperfect, hesitant writers of Welsh. There is a bust of him by R. L. Gapper, a former student of the College, in the main library. His inevitable successor was (Sir) Ifor Williams, in 1920 appointed to the newly created chair of Welsh literature, but who now became Professor of Welsh Language and Literature. Ifor Williams was probably more responsible than anyone else for launching the *Bulletin* of the Board of Celtic Studies, regularly enriched by the erudition he also effortlessly carried into the lecture room, where he sparkled and enchanted. His *magnum opus*, *Canu Aneirin*, appeared in 1938, the year in which he became a Fellow of the British Academy. Knighted in 1947, he retired with some reluctance. His successor (Sir) Thomas Parry, a lecturer in the department since 1929, had already given proof of high scholarly attainments and of his gifts as a teacher who spoke with an authority seldom questioned. He, too, became a Fellow of the British Academy. Both he and R. Williams Parry helped to correct the undue attention (as many thought) given to the study of philology and grammar.[56]

Having been relieved of the duties of Registrar, J. E. Lloyd was now able to direct his energies to the demands of post-war expansion in the department of history. In 1919 A. S. Turberville was freed from the forces and remained at Bangor until 1926, when he left for Manchester (and thereafter to the chair of modern history at Leeds). Before retirement in 1930 J. E. Lloyd had delivered the Ford Lectures at Oxford, which appeared as *Owen Glendower* in 1931. After the war he guided the new Board of Celtic Studies of the University; he had drawn up its draft constitution in 1919, he was general editor of its *Bulletin* until 1937 and chairman until 1940. Elected Fellow of the British Academy in 1930, he was knighted in 1934. The appointment of A. H. Dodd to the chair of history gave Lloyd great pleasure. One of the illustrious sons of a Wrexham schoolmaster, Dodd was educated at New College, Oxford. After war service he reconsidered his intention to enter the Civil Service and, much influenced by R. H. Tawney's tutorial class at Wrexham a decade earlier, he found it congenial in 1922, according to College policy, to share his duties between extra-mural work and internal lecturing. His investigations into the industrial revolution in north Wales appeared in a valuable volume in 1933, as we have seen.[57] A change of direction, regretted by some, led to important pioneering studies in early modern Wales, which preoccupied him for the remainder of his long life. His lectures, superbly delivered, were models of clarity.

Lloyd's departure encouraged the College to establish a department of Welsh history and to make an imaginative appointment. Robert Thomas Jenkins, educated at Aberystwyth and Cambridge, now forty-nine, had hitherto been a schoolmaster. No eyebrows were raised by anyone aware of his writings and personality. He wrote mainly in Welsh and his works cannot be properly judged, as they sometimes are, by those with an imperfect grasp of the language. He was a good deal more than a belletrist, though he often chose to write in essay form. He was the outstanding interpreter of Methodism in Wales; he understood its inner spirit and as a scholar of wide learning, not least in the classics, he viewed the movement in broad perspective. He deserves the chief credit for the appearance of *Y Bywgraffiadur Cymreig* (1953), followed by the English version, *The Dictionary of Welsh Biography*, in 1959. Those who had the privilege of following his lectures cannot forget the experience. Goronwy Rees said that he had a 'gift for treating history as if it were something one had just read about in the morning paper . . . He was the best teacher of history I have ever known.'[58] The inability of the College to create a chair of Welsh history for R. T. Jenkins until 1947 is not to be viewed with equanimity, for at Aberystwyth there has been an uninterrupted occupancy of the chair from 1930 until the present day. Indeed, for a time, Aberystwyth was able to sustain two such chairs. Financial circumstances were the prime cause, and the College has good reason to be grateful to the endowment of Sir John Williams.

Fynes-Clinton retired as head of the department of French and of Romance philology in 1937, to be succeeded by Percy Mansell Jones, whose legendary career at Bangor belongs to a later period. War memories did little to promote the teaching of German, and not until 1953 was proper recognition given to a major European language by the creation of a chair. T. Witton Davies surrendered the headship of the department of Semitic languages in 1921, after an unsuccessful appeal in his seventy-first year for a year's extension because of inadequate super-annuation arrangements. Tribute was paid to him for his devotion to teaching and learning which had inspired his students and established a 'strong and important department'.[59] He was followed by Edward Robertson, a Scot who had studied at St Andrews. In 1926 he was able to say that the number studying Hebrew at Bangor was larger than in any university college in the United Kingdom. After leaving Bangor he was, in turn, Professor of Semitics and John Rylands Librarian at Manchester. In his stead came Harold Henry Rowley, who in 1945 also moved to Manchester. Apart from a passion for philately, he was so totally immersed in his work that he professed not to know that there were mountains in Wales.[60] He is remembered more as a scholar of immense thoroughness than as an innovative thinker. The principal development in this field during the inter-war years was the founding of the Bangor School of Theology. The College had submitted an impressive plan to this end to the Haldane Commission, involving not only the existing chair of Semitics but an additional four, in the history of religion, church history, Hellenistic Greek and the philosophy of religions. Economic contraction and the questioning of traditional beliefs were formidable impediments. Nevertheless, the College's supplemental charter of 1922 had removed a major obstacle. After consulting T. F. Tout concerning arrangements at Manchester, where there was a Faculty of Theology, it was agreed that the theological colleges at Bangor and the University College should jointly provide the necessary courses for the degree of BD. Teachers in the denominational colleges became 'special lecturers' in the University College and all the staff engaged in this common purpose became members of the new Faculty of Theology. The two architects of the enterprise, Thomas Rees of Bala-Bangor and H. R. Reichel, were dissimilar in almost every way. The spirit of reconciliation, however, prevailed. Sadly, the Bangor School of Theology did not come into being until 1934, after the death of both.[61]

The College had also pressed the Haldane Commission to be enabled to include in its range of subjects the study of economics, in its social aspects now increasingly popular. First taught by Robert Richards in 1921 as independent lecturer, it suffered a reverse upon Richards's election as member for Wrexham in 1922. The appointment in 1925 of Henry Higgs, an able former Treasury official, non-Welsh, ageing and partially deaf, precipitated a grim public controversy.[62] Higgs was right to protest that to confine the study of economics to two years, and in harness with philosophy and history, was tantamount to planting an acorn in a flower pot. Upon his departure in 1929, the College fortunately enlisted the services of J. Morgan Rees, who established a full three-year course and who became professor in 1937, some years before a tragic breakdown in health.

In 1932 James Gibson, Professor of Philosophy since 1895, was followed by a Scot, Charles Arthur Campbell. Invalided out of the army in 1917, he resumed his studies at Glasgow before treading the path to Balliol and becoming an accomplished exponent of the Idealist school. R. L. Archer of education, with prospective teachers in mind, had quite failed to introduce geography into the Faculties of Arts and Science. He had, however, been largely instrumental in establishing a civics course, a development outlined in his book, *The Passman*, in 1918. The new pass course, of which philosophy, history and economics were the principal ingredients, was designed, and succeeded in its aim, to give a student 'an insight into the life of the society in which he has to play a part'.[63] As to music, the Haldane Report had somewhat exceeded the College's own proposals by recommending that there should be 'a full-staffed' department of music, including a professor to prepare students for university degrees. An independent department was in fact established in 1920 under E. T. Davies, an experienced choirmaster, but it was not possible to create a chair until 1943.

Library facilities caused constant concern. It is true that the library contained more bound volumes, although the College had fewer students, than the other colleges. In the 1938–9 session, for example, Bangor had 111,600 bound volumes, Cardiff 76,300. Moreover, 4.1 per cent of its expenditure was devoted to the needs of the library; by contrast Cardiff spent 3.5 per cent and Aberystwyth 2.5 per cent.[64] However, staff and students at Cardiff were able to take advantage of the city's Central Library, those at Aberystwyth of the peerless resources of the National Library, whereas the Cathedral Library at Bangor was of little practical value. Nevertheless, none of the other colleges had manuscript collections approaching in importance those at Bangor, importunately garnered and scheduled in racy fashion by the College's librarian, Thomas Richards, an authority on the history of religion in Wales in the seventeenth century. His imperious rule, occasionally enlivened by a puckish grin, lasted from 1921 to 1946. One of the main rooms in the library appropriately bears his name.

The jubilee of the College in 1934 was an occasion to take stock and to raise funds for future developments. The celebrations at Bangor seem to have been more modest than those at Cardiff. The highlights of the two days of commemoration were addresses by Lord Sankey and the Bishop of Monmouth and a lunch. A well produced brochure drew attention to the needs of the College. Geology made a further forlorn appearance: 'It has always been acknowledged', eloquence by now evaporating, 'that the College will not be serving North Wales satisfactorily so long as it is without a department of Geology'. Near the Memorial Arch was to be a Museum and Art Gallery 'to take its true place in the scheme of education'. An imperative requirement was a new hall of residence for men to replace Plas Menai. But times had changed and times were hard. The appeal in the 1880s to set the College on its feet had been followed at its coming of age in 1905 by a further campaign to raise the new building, whilst in 1920 both the losses and the lessons of the war (especially the neglect of science) had made possible the erection of the Science Memorial Buildings. By 1934 the community was drained of resources. The call for the hall of residence, never popular with local, vocal landladies, was stilled and it was resolved to concentrate upon the department of music which for fourteen years had suffered 'peculiar financial disadvantages'.[65] Even so, the target of £20,000 was soon seen to be unrealistically high; barely a quarter of this sum was raised. Towards the end of our period there was a gleam of hope when news came of the moneys to be released under the Welsh Church Acts and intended to benefit students. The College was thus enabled in 1937 to begin the construction of a new hall of residence for men (Neuadd Reichel) in the neo-Georgian style. Inescapable retrenchment had obliged the acceptance of a flat, rather than a sloping roof, as at Pantycelyn, Aberystwyth, with the loss of something of the intended country-house character. Finally, it may be noted that after the immediate post-war bulge of 637 in student numbers in 1921–2, the next peak was 598 in 1934–5, declining to 485 immediately before the Second World War. The proportion of women students in 1923–4 was 43 per cent, falling to 23 per cent in 1938–9, lower than that of any College, apart from Swansea.[66]

Cardiff

When Henry Campbell Bruce, the second Baron Aberdare, retired from the office of President in 1919, he was succeeded by William James Tatem, first Baron Glanely, a wealthy shipowner with large interests in docks and railways, and a generous benefactor of the College. In 1925, Sir David R. Llewellyn held office; he was chairman of several collieries, a director of many industrial concerns and the only former student of the College to become President. He was followed in 1929 by John Caradoc Herbert, the first Baron Treowen, a wealthy Monmouthshire landowner, a professional soldier and a Liberal Member of Parliament. Upon his death in the year of the College's jubilee, Lord Glanely returned to office.

E. H. Griffiths indicated in 1916 that he wished to retire, though wartime conditions obliged him to remain until 1919. It had not been an altogether happy principalship. Griffiths had an unusually clear mind and he was probably at his best in analysing the financial problems of the College. A close collaborator with him in his scientific work, Ezer Griffiths, believed that the change from the groves of academe at Cambridge to the industrial surroundings of Cardiff were not to his liking. Ezer Griffiths added that 'the problems of administration in the College of a democratic university were strange to him, and to one of his temperament must have proved irksome'.[67] He constantly urged that a university was charged with extending the bounds of knowledge at a time when several still believed that teaching was its prime purpose. 'It was an opportune moment in the life of this college', we are told, 'for its new Principal to give a strong and unwavering lead in favour of research in all branches of learning.'[68] His last address to the College Court was wholly characteristic. He smote the industrialists of the area hip and thigh, and told the Court itself that libraries and laboratories at Cardiff were well below the standard of those at English provincial colleges and that, in view of the low salaries, 'you have a much better staff than you deserve'.[69]

The task of seeking a suitable successor was not well handled. The Council was told in February 1919 by the committee of selection that it was impressed with the qualifications of Thomas

Jones and that it also wished to submit the names of (Sir) Thomas Franklin Sibly, (Sir) Ernest Barker and S. J. Chapman. The Council, having rejected Thomas Jones's candidature by 25 votes to 10, proceeded to advertise. Thomas Jones had received powerful support from prominent Englishmen, R. H. Tawney, Sidney Webb, (Sir) Robert Morant and (Lord) Hankey, and from Welshmen, Percy Watkins and Sir Henry Jones. Indeed the latter, in the role of unofficial agent, was not as diplomatic as the circumstances required, for he challenged a number of people to drive T.J. out of Wales as he himself had been driven out decades earlier. Much was made of T.J.'s supposed irreligion – Lord Pontypridd, for instance, had asked 'Why isn't the fool religious?'[70] T.J., too, had offended Cardiff doctors who held him responsible for a clause in the Insurance Act of 1911 allowing workmen to choose their own doctors. Moreover, businessmen and industrialists of the area found his political views intolerable and Lord Merthyr's newspapers were ranged against him. Many moderate men were disconsolate, for there was little hope that advertisements would reveal unknown talents. W. J. Gruffydd, newly appointed to the chair of Celtic at the College, declared himself available in a printed application of seven pages which he affected to present 'with great diffidence', adding that he 'was not intensely desirous of having this unequalled opportunity of serving the College and the Nation'. His real purpose was to inform the Council that the College was detached from 'the deeper concerns of the nation',[71] and this he did *con brio*. The Council doubtless turned with relief to promote A. H. Trow to the office. He had already served as Acting Principal.

Born in Newtown, Montgomeryshire, in 1863, Albert Howard Trow was educated at the Bangor Normal College, Aberystwyth, and Freiburg. In 1904 he became associate Professor of Botany at Cardiff and a full professor thereafter. His years as Principal severely restricted opportunities for scientific inquiry, though he never lost a lively concern for his subject. A student was surprised to see the Principal, whom he did not know to be a botanist, bending low outside the main entrance to the College, to remove a weed and to caress a flower. During the war he had given evidence to the Haldane Commission on more than one matter and his administrative experience prepared him for the fierce contests of the 1920s. He was not perhaps as flexible as the circumstances demanded; some thought that he fought rearguard actions when victory was not possible. He was a firm supporter of the Welsh language and was twice Warden of the Guild of Graduates. In his retirement speech to the College he foresaw the time when the University of Wales would follow the example of the northern universities, separating into its component parts.[72]

Pressure was again put on Thomas Jones in 1929, upon Trow's retirement, to allow his name to be placed before the College Council. Jenkin Jones, secretary of the University, was impassioned. No Welshman had received a clearer call to return to live among his own people. There was a hint of a higher mandate: 'If this is not the voice of God, what is?'[73] Another correspondent, Mabel Howell of Cardiff, hoped that T.J. would not feel too old (he was born in 1870): 'We so badly need a leader with vision and faith and courage.'[74] T.J. listened to the voice of duty, but finally declined, partly, we must gather, because Cardiff 'had never engaged his affection as its sister college at Aberystwyth had done'.[75] It seems that over forty contestants entered the lists. Some were easily eliminated, including one Owen Richards, who, having worked in Egypt, claimed that he would be unlikely to make the mistake of treating his countrymen 'on the lines appropriate to Egyptians'.[76] W. J. Gruffydd was seriously weighed in the balance, though not by Morgan Watkin who spoke skittishly of 'our bardic colleague who appears to think he has special claims upon the office'.[77] Gilbert Norwood, former Professor of Greek at Cardiff and newly elected to a chair at Toronto, spoke eloquently of him. Percy Watkins thought that Gruffydd was the kind of Welshman who was bitten by 'the lack of appreciation complex' rather than by an inferiority complex and that he would 'mellow and improve in the sunshine of recognition'.[78] Gruffydd, however, was not appointed, for the choice fell upon James Frederick Rees.

Raised in the new County Intermediate School at Milford Haven, J. F. Rees proceeded to the Cardiff College and then to Lincoln College, Oxford, where he became O. M. Edwards's favourite pupil. His striking achievements at both colleges paved the way to a lectureship in history at Bangor. Thereafter he specialized in economic history at Belfast, at Edinburgh and at

Birmingham, where he was Professor of Commerce. He had thus a wide experience of the British Isles before returning to Cardiff. Sir William Beveridge believed that no one known to him was better qualified to move from academic to administrative work. Richard Lodge considered that all he needed to be an ideal principal was a few inches of height; 'after all he is not shorter than my old contemporary, Viriamu Jones'.[79] Ernest Barker, who had taught Rees and who had a tougher mind than O. M. Edwards (as David Williams once noted), was unwontedly enthusiastic: 'I find it hard to refrain my pen in writing about him.'[80]

Rees certainly knew more of the history of Wales than most of his countrymen, but as a true native of south Pembrokeshire he was inclined to view the fortresses of the language and culture of Wales with detachment. His father, a shipwright, once went to visit his own grandfather, a small farmer in the vicinity of Trefgarn. They could not converse; the one spoke only English and the other was a monoglot Welshman. This divide J. F. Rees made no discernible effort to bridge. In recommending this 'splendid little fellow' to Bangor in 1910 O. M. Edwards said that his only fault was an imperfect knowledge of Welsh which he had strongly counselled him to correct whilst at the northern college. South Pembrokeshire, however, remained in the ascendant. The tragic plight of industrial south Wales touched him deeply. At Cardiff he was remembered for his calm authority wholly free from the pomposity which in others he rejoiced to puncture with gentle raillery, and also for his constant solicitude for the welfare of staff and students. To the end he remained a scholar; his writings were crisp and spritely. After retirement in 1949 he became visiting professor to the University of Ceylon and for two years afterwards head of the department of economic history at Edinburgh. In recommending him to Cardiff Ernest Barker drew attention to the old proverb, 'Rule will show the man', predicting that Rees's tenure of office would reveal a man of 'quiet manner, good temper, gentle consideration and firm purpose'.[81]

The conclusion of the ferocious debates concerning the Medical School and the appointment of J. F. Rees appeared to inaugurate a new era. Rees, it seemed, had entered office upon a rising tide. The visit of the Prince of Wales as Chancellor of the

University to the College in May 1930 quickened popular imagination, for he had flown to and from Splott in a day. One of his duties was to open the new Tatem chemistry and physics laboratories in the west wing of the College. Lord Glanely, whose natal name they bore, contributed a further £20,000 to clear the building of debt. From Sir William James Thomas the Prince received the deeds of gift of the Institute of Preventive Medicine. During the summer of 1931 there was a fête and a pageant in the castle grounds. Staff and students presented five dramatic episodes in the history of Cardiff, the medieval period, for instance, being in the capable hands of William Rees, who knew a great deal about the Norman period – rather too much, some students thought – whilst the Principal did not count it an indignity to appear as Ralph, Archdeacon of Llandaf. At a Congregation of the university in 1933 it was estimated that 2,500 were in attendance; later that day twenty-five representatives of universities and colleges presented addresses of greeting. The former Principal A. H. Trow and the Registrar D. J. A. Brown (who retired in 1936) wrote *A Short History of the College, 1883–1933*, still useful in a modest way.[82]

The profit from these varied proceedings was used to reduce the debt on the new extension to the students' union building in Park Place, where a refectory for 250 students was planned. A new athletic ground at Caerau was purchased; the triangular site called the 'ranch' to the north of the College was leased from the city at a peppercorn rent, and in 1936 Aberdare Hall, the second largest women's hostel in Britain, was handed over to the College. A section of the west front of the College was set aside to meet the needs of the Agricultural Advisory Board which gave valuable advice to farmers. The south side of the main building remained an unfulfilled plan and there seemed no prospect of a great hall on the east front to complete the quadrangle.[83]

On the science side, the opening of the Tatem laboratories was a deliverance to the chemistry and physics departments after their long constriction upon the old Infirmary site. C. M. Thompson had been succeeded in 1921 by W. J. Jones who had worked with Lapworth in Manchester. In 1938 S. T. Bowden published a standard text, *The Phase Rule and Phase Relations*. As to teaching methods, there were significant changes. Until the

early 1930s demonstrations were an essential part of a chemistry
lecture, but thereafter the lecture became more conceptual,
demonstration experiments being seldom conducted on the
lecture bench. The inter-war period has been modestly described
as 'relatively undistinguished'[84] in the history of the physics
department. The foundations were, however, laid for crystallo-
graphic work, the department's main specialism which
burgeoned after the war under A. J. C. Wilson, a future Fellow of
the Royal Society. The botanists were not so fortunate. Trow's
successor, R. C. McLean, had to make do with the ramshackle
building in Newport Road throughout the inter-war years, thus
adding to the accumulating lore of 'shoe-string' science. He
recalled that on a winter's day the forty incandescent burners
caused several faintings. The unquenchable human spirit,
nevertheless, sustained him in his wooden ghetto; above the door
of the lecture room were the words: 'It is not the cage that makes
the bird sing'[85] (translated from the German). McLean specialized in plant fossils and in the 1930s the department's
mycological studies, we are told, won international recognition.
Despite dishearteningly adverse circumstances, W. M. Tattersall
built a flourishing zoological school. He laid great stress upon
fieldwork, not only locally but at Port Erin and Lough Ine,
County Cork; he himself was an authority upon the various
groups of crustacea.

The College, as we have seen, managed to retain the
departments of physiology and anatomy in 1931. The
appointment in 1919 of T. Graham Brown to the chair of
Physiology caused much subsequent misgiving. His work on the
physiology of the nervous system led to a Fellowship of the Royal
Society in 1927, but thereafter he lost a sense of direction,
though not in the Alps where he fulfilled an all-absorbing
ambition to climb Mont Blanc by a new route up the Brevna
face. It is worthy of note that the piece upon him in *The
Dictionary of National Biography* (1981) is by Bangor's third
Principal, internationally renowned as a climber.[86] In time,
Brown's uncontrolled addiction to mountaineering in and out of
term led to demands for his dismissal, but in Cardiff he
remained. Indeed, after retirement he resided in a departmental
room where he was waited upon by a technician. Some praise,

however, is due to him for inviting (Sir) Tudor Thomas to work in the department for here Thomas in 1922–30 mastered the technique of cornea transplantation. In anatomy virtually no research was done before the late 1920s. In fact we are reliably informed that it was not until after the Second World War that the subject 'entered technological realms undreamed of by the earlier anatomists'.[87]

Although it was said that the College diplomas in engineering were almost as acceptable to the engineering profession as the degrees of the University pursued in the three subdepartments of mechanical, electrical and civil engineering, nevertheless, none could doubt the significance of instituting an honours degree in 1925, already available in all other universities of the United Kingdom. Hitherto, Welsh students had been seriously handicapped by the absence of the degree when they competed with graduates of other universities for government and other appointments in engineering, especially those involving research. After the Great War, financial assistance from the Drapers' Company came to an end. Originally given for a limited period, it had twice been renewed, but it was felt that the initial purpose, that of stimulating local incentive, had been fulfilled. We may perhaps question the College's claim to have had 'unbroken' success in meeting the needs of the engineering profession in south Wales. What cannot be questioned is the achievement of A. J. Sutton Pippard, Professor of Engineering 1922–8 and later a Fellow of the Royal Society. Cardiff's department differed little from those of other provincial institutions of higher education. It was understaffed and its laboratory facilities were inadequate. Yet Pippard was principally responsible for a radical transformation, 'turning the teaching of the theory of structures into a scientific discipline, actively promoting and participating in research, and generally raising the intellectual level of civil engineering courses in the country'.[88]

In its jubilee year, the College observed that 'further attempts' had been made to deal with mining education 'on a scale commensurate with the importance of the subject, and its relation to the industrial and commercial prosperity of South Wales and Monmouthshire', bleakly adding that a grant of £30,000 from the Miners' Welfare Fund to further these aims was 'definitely promised a few years ago'.[89] Some improvement seemed in prospect for the College felt sufficiently confident in 1935 to appoint T. David Jones to the chair of mining. In 1928 the coalowners had given up their School of Mines at Trefforest, which was taken over by the county council for more general work and which became in time the Polytechnic of Wales and thereafter the University of Glamorgan. In 1936 they agreed to provide scholarships for at least five students recruited from schools and industry. In the following year they promised £5,000 per annum to finance new developments. They had also established the South Wales and Monmouthshire Coal Owners' Research Association, under the direction of T. D. Jones, and useful inquiries were conducted into the hazards of airborne dust. It was, however, late in the day. Slender though it was, such a spirit of co-operation fifty years earlier would have been an immeasurable blessing to the College and to the south Wales coalfield. The same is true of the department of metallurgy and fuel technology, as it was called after 1933, when a major extension was completed, planned by Professor A. A. Read and financed by the coalowners. W. R. D. Jones, who followed Read, specialized in light-weight metals, magnesium and aluminium, of considerable significance to the expanding motor vehicle and aircraft industries.[90]

The department of geology sustained two substantial losses at the end of the war. (Sir) Thomas Franklin Sibly left for Newcastle and, soon afterwards, for Swansea. His field research on the lower carboniferous strata of south Wales and elsewhere placed him in the first rank of British geologists. (Sir) Arthur Elijah Trueman, a lecturer at Cardiff in 1917–20, began the study of the Liassic rocks and fossils of south Wales which he was to continue at Swansea. A. Hubert Cox was a worthy successor at Cardiff to Sibly; when he retired in 1949 his outstanding contributions were recognized by the award of the Murchison Medal of the Geological Society of London. Many Cardiff graduates held important positions in the five continents and Cox was not idly boasting when he said in successive departmental reports that the demand for Cardiff students exceeded the supply. The department was in the van of exploration geophysics; it also encouraged the study of geology in Welsh schools. One disappointment was the failure to form a department of geography, which Cox had urged upon the College in 1924. Nearly half a century elapsed before geography became a Part One subject in the College.[91]

Amongst academic developments in the arts to be observed during the inter-war years was the continued relaxation of the rigid, oppressive insistence upon philology as a central requirement in the honours degree courses. H. Littledale, the Professor of English, had argued for a change long before his retirement in 1921, confidently relying upon the support of Cyril Brett, his successor. Both had been influenced, like W. J. Gruffydd (Welsh) and Herbert Bruce (History), by the extended debate on the establishment of a chair of literature at Oxford and also by the needs of secondary schools. In 1933–4 the honours class in English, which never greatly exceeded thirty, had phenomenal results, ten firsts being awarded. Two of Brett's students became Professors of English at Cardiff, E. C. Llewellyn in 1936 and Gwyn Jones, scholar, critic, a creative writer prominent in the Anglo-Welsh movement and an international authority on the history and civilization of the Vikings, who returned from the chair of English at Aberystwyth in 1965.[92]

Dogged by ill health for many years, the gentle Thomas Powel, Professor of Celtic, retired in 1918. He was succeeded by a former lecturer in the department, W. J. Gruffydd, newly returned from naval service and full of reforming zeal. As has already been indicated, he was in rebellion against the domination of degree studies by language and philology. He wished to make courses in his department 'a means of genuine culture and of obtaining a large knowledge of life and a wider sympathy and humanity'.[93] Language teaching was placed in the hands of the battle-scarred Henry Lewis, soon to leave for a chair at Swansea. The gradual substitution of 'Welsh' for 'Celtic' in official publications was symbolic. Gruffydd rejoiced that his college had a larger share than any other body in the preparation of the notable departmental report on Welsh in the educational system, *Welsh in Education and Life* (1927). The task of translating the volume into Welsh was undertaken by his colleague, G. J. Williams, an inspired teacher and unceasing researcher to whom a holiday was but a further opportunity to pursue his life's labour of love. Gruffydd himself was a poet of distinction, an editor of anthologies and a scholar whose studies ranged from the *Mabinogion* to early modern prose. His *Hen Atgofion* (1936), an autobiography, and *O. M. Edwards* (1937), a biography, are classics. As editor of *Y Llenor* (1922–51) he was a formidable figure in the cultural life of Wales.[94]

In 1915 J. S. MacKenzie retired at the comparatively early age of fifty-five in order 'to have time to write'. His chief works were published during and after the Great War. MacKenzie was third in a remarkable succession of four Professors of Philosophy at Cardiff who became Fellows of the British Academy. On the science side there was no such sustained record of achievement. MacKenzie was followed by (Sir) Hector James Hetherington, much influenced by his teacher at Glasgow, Henry Jones, whose biography he wrote. Later as head of Glasgow University he won plaudits as a university administrator; Yale formally recognized his 'marked distinction in the art of government'.[95] J. W. Scott, who remained in the chair from 1920 to 1944, kept alive the social conscience of the department especially during the 1930s.

The notable reign of Gilbert Norwood (1908–26), Professor of Greek, ended when he left for Toronto. His output was said to be 'legendary'. H. J. W. Tillyard, who succeeded him, remained for two decades and earned a widespread reputation as principal editor of the series *Monumenta Musicae Byzantinae*. Kathleen Freeman, a member of the department, an accomplished popularizer of Greek themes, was better known as a writer of detective novels, under the pseudonym, Mary Fitt. L. R. Palmer, who graduated in the 1920s, became Professor of Greek at King's College, London and later Professor of Philology at Oxford. In 1919 the department of Latin lost O. L. Richmond to Edinburgh. Latin studies at Cardiff received a severe blow upon the death from war wounds of G. A. T. Davies (1919–23). W. W. Grundy, who held the chair in 1925–6 and who was known as a bon vivant, treated his own works lightly in *Who's Who*; they were 'not worth reading'. The achievements of R. G. Austin (1936–54), however, were no jesting matter. We are told by a sure judge that 'Austin perhaps, beyond all other Latinists associated with University College, Cardiff, displayed a wealth of scholarship and literary sensitivity which was greeted with critical acclaim from all his peers'.[96]

When Paul Barbier, the Professor of French, retired in 1920 he had served the College for thirty-seven years. From 1904 to 1920 he had but one assistant, who regularly changed. Barbier's main concerns were philological, but his successor, Morgan Watkin, had a broad range of interests reflected in the altered name of the department in 1935 to French and Romance philology. His early career was cast in a heroic mould. Rooted in rural Carmarthenshire, he practised the craft of stonemason until he was 'rescued' by Barbier during one of his forays to west Wales. It has been said of him that

> in many respects he remained a country craftsman at heart all his life; and his students and colleagues, who associated him above all with the pursuit of knowledge, would have been surprised to learn that for the gamekeepers of West Wales he was more associated with the illicit pursuit of trout and salmon.[97]

He had two main passions, Wales and France, especially the medieval inheritance. Italian had been introduced as an option for students of French in 1931, but thirty-five years were to elapse before a full department was formed. The study of German, impaired by the outbreak of the Great War, was further injured by the reluctance of the lecturer-in-charge to travel frequently from his home in Bath. Under his two successors, Idwal Lloyd and Oliver Edwards there was a decided improvement. Despite J. F. Rees's plea for the teaching of Spanish, 'one of the greatest commercial languages of the world'[98] – advocacy which won the warm thanks of the Spanish and South American consulates – no progress was made until 1954.

Theodore H. Robinson, already head of the department of Semitic languages, was appointed to the newly created chair in 1927. Educated at St John's College, Cambridge, where there was an august tradition in oriental studies, he added to Hebrew at Cardiff the study of Aramaic, Syrian and Assyrian. Two of his assistants became Fellows of the British Academy, H. H. Rowley (later Professor at Bangor and Manchester) and Aubrey R. Johnson, who followed him in the Cardiff chair in 1944. During the 1931–2 session a School of Theology was established in association with the South Wales Baptist College. It followed the

Bangor pattern, Robinson and his colleagues teaching Hebrew within the new Faculty of Theology. The misleading impression was thus given that the department of Semitic languages was a 'quasi-theological department',[99] an impression which impeded the full blossoming of Semitic and Near Eastern languages in the college during the 1940s.

Herbert Bruce remained in the chair of history until 1935. He did not publish a good deal but he was remembered in the college as a highly cultivated man, much esteemed by staff and students. When Ernest Hughes departed for Swansea in 1920 he was replaced by William Rees, a native of Brecon and a former student of the College. Both before and during the Great War Rees had acquired a mastery of original sources at the Public Record Office, the British Museum and elsewhere, thus laying the foundation to two remarkable works, both casting penetrating light upon the complex social and economic organization of Welsh society between the Edwardian conquest and the Glyn Dŵr rebellion. The first was *South Wales and the March, 1284–1415: A Social and Agrarian History* (1924), and the second, a historical and cartographical triumph, his map of *South Wales and the Border in the Fourteenth Century* (1933), half an inch to the mile in four sheets, described by Marc Bloch as the work of 'un savant du premier mérite'.[100] He seemed an obvious candidate for a chair of Welsh history but the College temporized a great deal, even in the teeth of public pressure, before financial alleviation enabled it to deal with a matter of 'primary urgency',[101] as the Council called it in 1925. Rees was at length appointed professor in 1930 and head of the department of Welsh history. He was fortunately given a new assistant, David Williams, a distinguished young historian who remained at Cardiff until 1945 when he became the Sir John Williams Professor of Welsh History at Aberystwyth. Upon Bruce's retirement in 1935 it was resolved to invite Rees to act as head of the department of history, as well as of the department of Welsh history; this he did until his retirement in 1953. The arrival of Christopher Hill, a future Master of Balliol, though he remained for only two years, and of Dorothy Marshall, greatly strengthened the teaching of history.

When (Sir) Mortimer Wheeler burst upon the Welsh scene in 1920 it was a significant moment in the history of the university teaching of archaeology in Britain. Hitherto scant attention had been given in British universities to British archaeology, an omission Wheeler was soon to repair upon his joint appointment as lecturer in archaeology at the College and as keeper of archaeology in the National Museum of Wales, of which he became director in 1924. His *Prehistoric and Roman Wales* (1925) was immediately recognized as a pioneering study. The examination of the Roman fortress at Segontium is regarded as a classic demonstration of modern analytical and stratigraphical techniques. Here, and elsewhere in Wales, he trained a small band of pupils. Wheeler's six years in Wales set a pattern for the remainder of his career, at the London Museum, in India (the closest parallel) and at the British Academy.[102] He was followed as lecturer by (Sir) Cyril Fox, who relinquished the post upon appointment to the directorship of the National Museum. He had, however, already begun the mighty task of investigating Offa's Dyke, at first a real and at length a symbolic boundary between the Welsh and the English. In his steps came one of Wheeler's most brilliant pupils, Victor Erle Nash-Williams, who, between 1926 and 1939, excavated sites of first importance in south Wales, particularly the legionary fortress at Caerleon. On his return from the war, he was not again able to give such uninterrupted attention to field investigation.[103]

During the inter-war years the number of students in the department of economics increased fourfold. Until 1922 W. J. Roberts was obliged to teach economics and political science single-handed. In his day he had lectured in the departments of classics, German, Welsh and mathematics. Indeed, the mathematics professor said that Roberts was the only person he had ever known who had taught himself mathematics. His teaching burden, only partially relieved by a single assistant, was so heavy that he was entitled to say in 1938 on behalf of his department that the 'rapid prosecution of research'[104] was impossible. Nevertheless, Roberts did give some assistance (not easily assessed) to Hilary Marquand in preparing his survey of industrial South Wales. The study of industrial relations in south Wales came to fruition at Cardiff, not by the prudent benefaction of a local industrialist, but by the generosity of a north-country Jew of Lithuanian parentage who had made his fortune in Britain by becoming the nation's tailor at 50*s.* a time. He was Montague Burton. This admirable, self-effacing man had two main concerns, industrial and international relations. Leeds, Cardiff and Cambridge (in that order) benefited from the first; Jerusalem, Oxford, Edinburgh and Nottingham from the second. In view of the lamentable industrial strife in the south Wales coalfield, Cardiff was a clear candidate for the creation of a chair of industrial relations, and it appears that Alfred Zimmern, who had long left Aberystwyth, was influential behind the scenes.[105] The first occupant of the Montague Burton chair was Hilary Adair Marquand, educated at Cardiff High School and at the University College where he took firsts in history (1923) and economics (1924). A period of study in America and a lectureship at Birmingham, preceded his appointment to Cardiff in 1930. His American experience enabled him to write *The Dynamics of Industrial Combination* (1931), a significant contribution to a subject hitherto largely neglected in Britain. He had long renounced the traditional Conservatism of his own family; in 1929 he married the daughter of the owner of *Llais Llafur* (The Voice of Labour), the first Labour newspaper in Wales. It is not surprising that he was invited by the government to prepare two important surveys of the economy of south Wales.[106]

The long association of David Evans, Joseph Parry's successor as head of the department of music, drew to a close in 1939. A fine teacher within the College, he devoted much energy to two Welsh institutions, the *cymanfa ganu* and the eisteddfod. He specialized in religious music and some of his works are included in both Welsh and English hymn books. He edited *Y Cerddor* (1916–31), an influential Welsh musical journal, and (in large measure) the hymn book of the two Welsh Methodist denominations.[107]

The College had from the first arrival of Viriamu Jones readily and fully recognized its duty to train women for the teaching profession, a view reinforced by a perusal of the Raleigh Report (1909).[108] For years there was separate, though equal, provision for women and men. H. Millicent MacKenzie (wife of James Stuart) became associate Professor of Education in 1904 and professor in 1910, to be succeeded in 1915 by Barbara Foxley, who was in turn followed ten years later by (Dame) Olive

Wheeler. In charge of the men's department was William Phillips, who retired in 1932. The College found this dual arrangement advantageous for it ensured the necessary presence of an able woman on the Senate. The other colleges, however, dissented and were even fractious, on the grounds that education, of prime importance to every institution, was thereby enjoying an unduly privileged position at Cardiff. In 1932, upon the retirement of Phillips, it was resolved to amalgamate the two departments, happily under the headship of Olive Wheeler, a vigorous defender of the rights of students during her undergraduate days at Aberystwyth, a specialist on nursery and adolescent education and for long a prominent figure in the life of the University.[109]

In January 1931 the College received its supplemental charter, which dealt with the new circumstances concerning the Medical School. The College Court was allowed to remain large, but the Privy Council insisted upon reducing the College Council from sixty-one to forty-five members. In June the College's overdraft was £39,657; despite heroic endeavours, income (£96,253) did not match expenditure, though the disparity was not nearly as alarming as it became in the 1980s. In 1920 there were 1,061 students, in 1934 a peak of 1,292 and in 1939, 970; the proportion of women students steadily declined.[110]

Swansea

In 1920 the *Welsh Outlook* declared that the foundation of Swansea marked the close of a struggle characterized by 'faith, patience and persistence', qualities still needed in the years ahead but to which must now be added 'wisdom, statesmanship and vision'. The new college had many advantages. It was situated in an area which had great educational traditions whilst the rapid development of industry presented exceptional opportunities to pursue technological and scientific studies. It was to be a 'University' College and the editor praised the provision of 'full facilities' for arts subjects (a decided overstatement). The first Principal was an idealist as well as an organizer. All in all the prospects were bright.[111]

When George V, as Chancellor of the University of Wales, came to Swansea in July 1920 to lay the foundation stone of the college to the north of the archery lawn at Singleton Park no one knew for certain where the site of the College would be. The stone was removed after the ceremony and did not return until 1937 when it was incorporated in the newly built library. Only in 1919 had the estate of 250 acres, the home of the Vivians, come on the market and the Swansea Corporation pondered hard before making a formal gift. The College, however, had no time to lose and opened its doors to science students at Mount Pleasant in October 1920. Arts students had to wait another year for admission. At the outset, therefore, the authorities were obliged to concentrate upon personnel rather than buildings. Viriamu Jones and H. R. Reichel had always believed that this was the correct priority. The first chairman of the University Grants Committee had in any case hoped that the new college would be built on practical lines, not in the old quadrangular and Gothic style, advice reminiscent of Lewis Morris's remarks to the government shortly before Cardiff was chosen in 1883 as the south Wales college.[112]

The College in embryo which received its charter on 21 January 1920 had reason to be grateful to its first officers, and indeed to others, notably (Sir) Richard Martin, rightly called 'the father of the University movement in Swansea'.[113] The first president, Frank W. Gilbertson, a humane, shrewd man of business, was a major figure in the steel and tinplate industry and was chairman of the South Wales Siemens Association, 1918–25. His death in 1929 at the age of fifty-six was an acute loss to the College. It was fitting that upon the acquisition of Clyne Castle as a hall of residence in 1955 it should be called Neuadd Gilbertson. He was succeeded in 1930 by Sir George Barstow. A former civil servant, he had two decades earlier learnt far more concerning the Welsh colleges than is generally realized, for it was he who was secretary of the Raleigh Committee. Upon leaving the Treasury in 1927 he devoted himself to business interests, particularly in the Middle East. He was a man of acumen, probity and wit.[114]

No more important task faced Gilbertson and his colleagues than the selection of the College's first Principal. During the course of the usual informal feelers, he had told Haldane that the College needed an 'organizer'. Haldane, presumably with tongue in cheek, observed that if this were the case he could recommend General von Donnop, Commandant of Woolwich Arsenal.[115] It was clear that the College needed not simply an administrator but a leader capable of upholding university values and of guiding the young institution into the mainstream of university life. It seems that six candidates were shortlisted, but it is not known who they all were. Thomas Jones was apparently offered the post, having been told by Gilbertson that 'the soil is prepared for the seed here' and that 'the conditions are much more hopeful than in the purely colliery districts'. However T.J. declined, in part because of 'the dearth of money to run a College properly'.[116] Nevertheless, he had earlier persuaded Lloyd George to recommend that Swansea be granted a charter. He later freely gave advice to the first Principal on the recruitment of staff. The committee of appointment inclined thereafter towards Charles Alfred Edwards, but he indicated that he preferred to become the College's first Professor of Metallurgy. At length, and thereupon without hesitation, the College chose Thomas Franklin Sibly. After entering the University College, Bristol, he graduated externally, as so many Welsh students had done, at London University (in 1903) and he was placed in the first class in experimental physics. His further studies at Birmingham, however, led him to examine carboniferous limestone and it was as a geologist that he first made his name. In 1913, as we have seen, he became professor at Cardiff where, we are told, 'he proved a teacher of fine quality, clear and stimulating in exposition, and exercising over his students a firm control which they willingly accepted'.[117] He impressed the Haldane Committee more than any other academic. We may surmise that the failure of his application to become Principal at Cardiff prompted him to move to Armstrong College, Newcastle upon Tyne, in 1918. Two years later he returned to Wales and at Swansea he discovered his true profession. At once far-seeing and a master of detail, he was at times ruthless; generally, however, he was benevolent and unselfish. One who knew him well spoke thus of him: 'He bore a very formidable dignity when business was in hand', but he would 'joyfully divest himself of it, as if taking off a garment, when the business was ended'. He had a strong personality, and his staff, 'who felt some awe in public affairs, turned eagerly to him as a friend when they needed advice on either academic or personal problems'.[118] His friendship was unfailing. In 1926 he became Principal of London University, an office he did not much enjoy, in 1929 Vice-Chancellor of Reading University and in 1938 chairman of the Committee of Vice-Chancellors and Principals.

Upon Sibly's departure considerable pressure was exerted upon Thomas Jones to accept the principalship. There was general agreement that Sibly had laid sound foundations, having accomplished, as Sir Lewis Jones remarked in a somewhat ungainly phrase, 'the commercial traveller's part'. Swansea, he believed, now had 'its proper place in the University of Wales'.[119] His successor would have the pleasanter role of concentrating upon internal development. T. J. Rees, director of education for the borough, thought that the College no longer needed men of 'the Sibly type'. Writing to Jones he said that the College was free from disruptive devilry (*cythraul canu*, as he called it), adding, rather blandly, that there were 'no cliques as far as I know'[120] on Senate and Council. Various interests were, of course, represented on College bodies and T.J. was the person to keep them together, as they had not always been kept together in less fortunate institutions. F. W. Gilbertson indicated that it was the unanimous wish of the College to invite him. T.J., however, though flattered, declined. 'Some years ago', he said, 'an educational post of this kind in Wales would have had great attractions for me, but I have now "burnt my boat".'[121]

One of those who had unfeignedly urged acceptance was C. A. Edwards, Sibly's successor. It will be recalled that seven years earlier he had clearly indicated that he preferred to be Professor of Metallurgy rather than Principal. His first decision may have been the wiser. He was a remarkable man. At sixteen he was an apprentice in the Lancashire and Yorkshire Railway's foundries. Quite without formal education in a university or college, he was by 1914, at the age of thirty-two, Professor of Metallurgy at Manchester. It was at once recognized at Swansea that he was 'pre-eminently the man for our Chair'[122] and that it was the duty of the College to create a department of metallurgy outstanding for its teaching and research. It was in a sense understandable that when Edwards became Principal he should wish to retain an eager interest in the fortunes of the department; he remained its formal head until retirement in 1947, administrative duties being performed by an assistant professor. A heavy price was paid, for it became increasingly difficult for a Principal to engage in substantial research. Thus, in the early 1930s Edwards delivered admirable lectures on the theory of alloys, later known as metal physics, but they were never published. At the same time, too much power slipped into the deft hands of the Registrar, Edwin Drew. Such situations are never desirable. For brief periods during the present century they also arose at Bangor and Aberystwyth, though not, it appears, at Cardiff. The voice of Swansea, therefore, was not always effectively heard in the inner councils of the University, especially if we are to judge from the caustic remark of a fellow Principal after an important University meeting: 'There goes Edwards back to Swansea to report to Drew and be told what he should have done.'[123] Edwards, however, is not to be dismissed with a quip. In days when it was not easy to embark upon fresh ventures he had a significant role in raising the new neo-classical library in 1937, designed by Venner A. Owen Rees, the architect of the London School of Hygiene and Tropical Medicine. Edwards was much liked by staff and students to whom he was readily accessible. He regularly joined in tea at four in the afternoon in the department, everyone sitting on stools around a bench in the assay laboratory, 'outrageous theories and explanations becoming tempered by argument and student problems resolved by free discussion'.[124] Three years after becoming Principal, Edwards was elected a Fellow of the Royal Society; he conducted fundamental research in collaboration with his postgraduate students, many of whom later held high positions, and he brought the College into close association with industry at both local and national levels.

Although the corporation of Swansea had petitioned for a charter in 1918 to enable the new University College, consisting of the training and technical colleges, to be concentrated at Mount Pleasant, it was soon evident that this was by no means an ideal solution. The first scientists appointed were dismayed by the inadequate facilities. It was not until 1923, and after hectic

controversies amongst members of the corporation, that Singleton Abbey and nineteen acres of land to the south and west
(together with fifteen acres to the west of Sketty Lane as playing
fields) were made over to the College. Two years were to elapse
before the whole College was brought together at Singleton. The
corporation retained certain rights until the 1960s, such as the
use of the land to the south for fêtes, agricultural shows and
sheep-dog trials, colourful additions to the academic scene which
were long remembered. The value of the gift was £90,000 and
the site itself overlooking Swansea Bay was incomparably better
than any other in the area. Sibly considered it 'the finest site in
the country', adding that the Abbey and the park 'made an
inspiring habitation'.[125] The science buildings, especially the
metallurgy building, were considered to be of high standard.
Despite the fact that these 'pavilions', as they were called, were to
be replaced within a decade, they survived for over fifty years, as
is often the case with 'temporary' erections. Buildings for physics,
chemistry and metallurgy were opened in 1923 by Sir Alfred
Mond and for arts departments, the library and the department
of engineering by Lord Eustace Percy, President of the Board of
Education, in 1925. The industrialist, Roger Beck, gave six large
houses in Gwydr Gardens for a women's hall of residence as a
single unit, known as Beck Hall.[126]

The science faculty began with four professorial departments.
J. E. Coates, the Professor of Chemistry, a former Bangor
student, had been commended for his work on smoke-screens
during the war. One of his students, D. H. Hey, became a Fellow
of the Royal Society. E. J. Evans, Professor of Physics, was an
expert on spectroscopy. E. J. Williams, a brilliant product of the
department, became professor at Aberystwyth.[127] The work of
P. M. Davidson and W. G. Price on the quantum mechanics of
the hydrogen molecule was amongst the best in the international
field in the inter-war years.[128] A. R. Richardson, Professor of
Mathematics, a future Fellow of the Royal Society, was an
authority on hydromechanics. Frederic Bacon, the Professor of
Engineering, had held a chair at Cardiff since 1913. Sibly was not
free to teach geology, but he had brought with him from Cardiff
Arthur Trueman as independent lecturer. Trueman continued his
studies of the Liassic rocks of south Wales and his work on the

stratigraphical palaeontology of the coal measures enabled him in time to establish a zonal classification applicable not only to Wales but to other British coalfields.[129] Before leaving Swansea in 1931 he had been appointed Professor of Geology and head of the department of geography. He was succeeded by one of the College's first students, T. Neville George, also to become a Fellow of the Royal Society. In 1947 George followed Trueman to the chair of geology at Glasgow. Two years later Trueman became chairman of the University Grants Committee. Florence Mockeridge's independent lectureship in biology was not converted into a professorship until 1937. Her studies on the water relations of the *bryophyta*, supplemented by the work of two lecturers in allied disciplines, led to the development of marine science at Swansea.[130]

In his inaugural address Sibly remarked that 'we have started as a Science College, with only the nucleus of our Faculty of Arts'. He added that the College was urgently providing for subjects in that Faculty 'not only because we are alive to the strong and widespread demand for them, but also because we recognize that a one-sided institution would have no full title to University work',[131] though he should perhaps have recalled that the title was not denied to the medieval universities of Bologna and Salerno, specializing respectively in law and medicine. The Haldane Report, as we have seen, clearly envisaged 'the establishment of a complete Faculty of Arts'.[132] Sibly fully acknowledged the demand for arts graduates, but there was an additional factor. 'Poets, philosophers and preachers, who can express their ideals, their achievements, in a language intelligible to a great public, who can show them in obvious relationship to human affairs, human aspirations, are recognized as humanists.'[133] The scientist, on the other hand, in order to convey his findings employed a technical tongue understood by very few. For diverse reasons, then, arts subjects were to be planted and carefully cultivated at Swansea.

The first beginnings were modest. The head of the department of history, which was to have an illustrious future, was Ernest Hughes, not made a professor until 1926. Partial blindness impeded original research, but his inspiring lectures to extra-mural classes in all parts of south Wales created a 'public' for

Welsh history. He was to receive valuable assistance from Glyn Roberts, later Professor of Welsh History at Bangor, whose untimely death was a severe deprivation, and from W. N. Meddlicott, appointed in 1953 Stevenson Professor of International Relations at London. In 1921 Henry Lewis, wounded in France and thereafter recruited from Cardiff by Sibly (so it seems), became Professor of Welsh Language and Literature at thirty-two. Tough and tenacious, he cast his net wide, but he is especially remembered as a pioneer of comparative Celtic linguistics and for his exploration of the syntax of the Welsh sentence. From the outset he had followed W. J. Gruffydd's revolutionary lead at Cardiff by making the Welsh language the medium of instruction and of examination. In this respect Aberystwyth and Bangor dawdled. It is certain that his energy and enthusiasm were largely responsible for the status of Celtic studies at Swansea, where he also contributed most effectively to the administration of the College. W. D. Thomas, a brilliant teacher, was Professor of English Language and Literature. The failure to merge the Swansea Training College with the University College Training Department was a disappointment to both Sibly and to the new Professor of Education, F. A. Cavanagh, succeeded in 1934 by W. Moses Williams, then only twenty-eight and who had displayed much early promise.[134]

The first Professor of Classics, D. Emrys Evans, was appointed Principal at Bangor in 1927. After him came S. K. Johnson, later Professor of Classics at Newcastle, and then R. B. Onians, thereafter Professor of Classics at Bedford College, London. Benjamin Farrington, who followed Onians in 1936, is mainly remembered for his much acclaimed *Greek Science* (1944) in the Penguin series. The appointment of Mary Williams to be head of the department of modern languages was steadfastly resisted by G. Arbour Stephens, a member of the College Council, who did not think that a woman could possibly fill such a demanding post. Subsequently, Stephens, a consultant cardiologist, surrendered to the claims of the heart by marrying her. The initial attempts to establish a chair of philosophy were frustrated by the University Council's reluctance to proceed, partly for financial reasons and partly on the tenuous ground that the subject had not been included in the petition of the promoters of the Swansea charter. Five years elapsed before the College was able to obey Haldane's categorical imperative in his inaugural address: 'you must have a Chair of Philosophy. It is the widest of all subjects.'[135] In 1925 Archie Heath was appointed. His main preoccupation was the philosophy of science and he did more than any other teacher to bridge the gulf between arts and science. Economics was the victim of even more protracted delay, surprisingly so since the College lay at the heart of an industrial area. The first occupant of the chair, K. S. Isles, remained but two years before departing for Adelaide in 1939, apparently before completing a systematic study of unemployment in the tinplate industry. Six important monographs, however, on the industrial and economic background of Swansea were sponsored by the corporation and published before the end of 1940.[136]

In 1936–7 the College was rocked by an event which injured its reputation and which reverberated throughout Wales. Saunders Lewis, a member of the department of Welsh and an outstanding figure in the life of Wales during the twentieth century, together with two other members of Plaid Genedlaethol Cymru, Lewis Valentine, a Baptist minister from Llandudno, and D. J. Williams, a schoolmaster at Fishguard and a well-known literary figure, had tried to set fire to the Royal Air Force Bombing School at Penyberth, near Penrhos in Llŷn, considered to be an economic and cultural threat to the local community. The three regarded the act as largely symbolic and immediately surrendered to the police. When the jury at Caernarfon failed to agree, the authorities imprudently transferred the case to the Old Bailey, where the three were sentenced in January 1937 to nine months in prison after refusing to give evidence in English. On legal advice Swansea College Council at once suspended Lewis, on the technical ground that he had terminated his appointment. It then declared the post vacant.[137] Lewis Valentine, on the other hand, returned to his pastorate and D. J. Williams to his teaching post in the anglicized portion of Pembrokeshire. The refusal to reinstate Lewis caused uproar far and wide. Within the College he had many supporters, Archie Richardson, the mathematics professor amongst them, but most notably Stephen J. Williams of the department of Welsh. Beyond the College came protests from

Nonconformist ministers in Llanelli, for example, from adult education classes, from individuals such as the young Gwynfor Evans of Barry and Lady Artemus Jones of Llanrwst.[138] There were many cross-currents. Lewis admittedly did not much care for teaching at an elementary level, especially if the classes were largely composed of 'new girl undergraduates at the whispering and giggling stage of life';[139] hard-pressed colleagues were sometimes dismayed that his lectures did not always last the statutory fifty minutes. On the other hand, he rejoiced to teach the ablest students. Nor had he ever disguised his political views which had nearly cost him his post at the initial interview; to his wife he said that 'they examined me nearly an hour on Sinn Fein in Wales. I was never so flattered in my life.'[140] For fifteen years there had been no hint of dismissal. Yet when the crisis came he could not count on the sympathetic understanding of Henry Lewis, his head of department. The College Council stood firm on the mistaken grounds that it did not wish to enter the political arena. In the teeth of protestations and public meetings it remained resolute or, as many thought, intransigent. When the predominantly Labour corporation came out in support of Lewis, the leaders of industry on the College Council believed that the corporation was fishing in troubled waters.[141] A request to hold a special meeting of the College Court to sound opinion was refused. The temperature was further raised when a successor to Lewis was appointed without public advertisement. He was Melville Richards, later a noteworthy professor at Bangor, who incurred undeserved odium for accepting the post. As one surveys the sorry scene it is difficult to avoid the conclusion that the College had offended the spirit of natural justice. It is to be regretted that almost all the records relating to the controversy have disappeared. We must presume that they were either the victims of so-called 'salvage' during the war or of wholesale destruction upon the retirement of the registrar, Edwin Drew, in 1952.[142]

Relations between Swansea and her sister Colleges and the University were on the whole cordial, particularly since Cardiff had not greatly welcomed the prospect of another University College in south Wales. In 1925 there was a baseless rumour that Sibly, who had changed his mind concerning federation, now also wanted a separate medical school so that he could weaken the Cardiff College by offering courses for the first three years of the medical degree of the University at Swansea.[143] Earlier Sibly had been praised for resisting the temptation to seek financial aid, following the Sankey Committee's recomendations, to establish a mining department at Swansea, thus properly recognizing Cardiff's prior claims. The University, in turn, as we have seen, had fittingly agreed that Swansea should have an equal share of the tithe moneys.[144] When Swansea applied to the Board of Education for an increased number of teacher training students, the Board asked the University whether it could arrange a redistribution amongst the Colleges so as to avoid adding to the number of such students. The University wisely replied that it could not offer advice without injuring the autonomy of the Colleges and that it was far better for the Board to accede to Swansea's request.[145] Membership of the federal University was a source of strength to the new institution during the inter-war years which presented intractable problems for all educational institutions, as indeed for the community at large. A young college seemed especially vulnerable. Swansea suffered because of the decline in the tinplate industry which it had long dominated. Yet there were ameliorating factors. The production of anthracite coal actually increased during the 1930s, whereas the mining valleys to the north and east were maimed. The challenge facing Swansea was not as severe as for Cardiff and Bangor during their early days, and particularly Aberystwyth which then had no grant from the state. Quite apart from the Board of Education fees for the training of teachers, Swansea received two-thirds of its moneys from the government. Income from endowments compared favourably with Cardiff, 6.4 per cent as opposed to 2.9 per cent. In 1920 it had opened its doors to eighty-nine students, of whom only eight were women. In 1928 C. A. Edwards reported that Swansea's progress had been phenomenal and had never been equalled in the history of university education in Britain.[146] In that year there were 413 students and in 1933 a peak of 751 (appreciably more than at Bangor at any time during the 1920s and 1930s). In 1939 seventy-five graduated in arts subjects and forty-five in science, a proportion which would probably have surprised Haldane twenty years earlier. True, there was a smaller selection of arts subjects than in the other colleges, but a solid basis had been laid for future development. Extra-mural work flourished and there was a successful Old Students' Association. Edwards spoke enthusiastically of the invigorating influence of the staff in encouraging postgraduate work. Not all, naturally, were equipped by temperament or ability to undertake research, but 'quite a number of our young men do possess outstanding ability, original attitudes of mind, and the keenest possible desire to take up research work for which they show real aptitude'.[147] The department of physics alone nurtured in these years six students who later became Fellows of the Royal Society. It was no small achievement.

The Welsh National School of Medicine

The Welsh National School of Medicine received its charter on 21 February 1931, thus becoming a separate institution of the University, though not a constituent college. The School's Court of Governors, as we have noticed, was the Court of the University. The Council of the School reported annually to the University Council and Court. The School gave instruction in the last three of the six years of medical instruction, that is in clinical and associated subjects, and also in pharmacology. The first-year course in the preliminary sciences was taught in the four Colleges of the University, but in practice most of the first-year students came to University College, Cardiff, where in the second and third years they were taught anatomy, physiology and organic chemistry, as well as pharmacology (in the School itself). By the charter a Joint Academic Committee was created. It consisted of the academic officers of the College and the School, including the Principal and Provost, who was chairman, and it had charge of medical students during their first three pre-clinical years. The Provost was a member of the College Council to which he presented the reports of the Joint Academic Committee. It seemed that the wit of man had at length devised the best constitution imaginable to safeguard the interests of two separate, but closely linked, institutions.[148]

The first President, Lord Stanley of Alderley, who did not long survive his election, was succeeded by G. C. Joyce, Bishop of

Monmouth, followed in turn by the third Lord Aberdare in 1938. The first Provost was Alfred William Sheen, son of a surgeon at the Cardiff Royal Infirmary. Educated at University College, Cardiff, and at Guy's Hospital, he was the second man in south Wales to become a surgical consultant without doing general practice; his sole predecessor was (Sir) John Lynn Thomas. Sheen, like W. A. Hughes, had served in the South African War, thus gaining experience of field hospitals, which stood him in good stead during the First World War. In 1913 he was amongst the earliest to reach the pit-head at Senghennydd, where 439 men lost their lives. Highly praised for his work in directing rescue parties, he had a lasting concern for the rehabilitation of the victims of industrial injury. In 1921, he was the new School's first Professor of Surgery and director of the surgical unit. He was the natural choice as Provost in 1931. Somewhat brusque in manner, 'the Colonel', as he was known, was in fact friendly and hospitable, enlivening conversation with a host of entertaining anecdotes.[149] Although the School did not receive its charter until 1931, it was a complete School in 1921. Opened in that year, it was from 1 October known as the Welsh National School of Medicine. The year before, the Prince of Wales had opened the Institute of Physiology, also the gift of Sir William James Thomas. We have already considered the turbulence to which the School was exposed in the 1920s, and it is thus refreshing to outline the progress of the School from 1921 to 1939. As we have seen, two pre-clinical subjects, anatomy and physiology, remained within the University College. David Hepburn's tenure of the chair of anatomy ended in 1927; he was succeeded by C. McLaren West. In 1919, T. Graham Brown was appointed to the chair of physiology vacated by J. Berry Haycraft. The vexed question of differentials between pre-clinical and clinical professors did not smooth relations. Thus, whereas the Professor of Medicine, for example, received £1,500 per annum, Brown and McLaren West were paid £900 per annum. The differentials persisted, doubtless accounting for the reluctance of the medically qualified to contemplate pre-clinical teaching.[150]

The School itself comprised seven departments, together with other specialisms. A. M. Kennedy, appointed to the chair of medicine in 1921, was in charge of the medical unit. Educated at

Glasgow, he remained at Cardiff until 1950. Here he acquired his expert knowledge of cerebro-spinal fever and meningitis. A. W. Sheen, the Provost, remained responsible for surgery until the appointment in 1935 of Lambert Rogers, an Australian who had joined the School in 1926 and who in time became the acknowledged authority in Britain on spinal tumours. The head of the department of obstetrics and gynaecology was (Sir) Ewen John Maclean; of Highland parents, he was reared at Carmarthen and Haverfordwest and received his professional training at Edinburgh. In south Wales he built up a considerable consulting practice. He has been described as a 'keen clinician, a conscientious and conservative surgeon and a teacher of marked ability'.[151] In 1926 he gave £3,000 to fund a postgraduate scholarship to promote research in the School into 'the factors which constitute and the conditions which vary resistance to disease, specially as regards Midwifery'.[152] Gilbert I. Strachan, the next occupant of the chair, was educated at Glasgow and became deeply attached to Wales. His *Textbook of Obstetrics* (1947), embodying much of his direct, personal experiences, was widely known. The sum of £37,500 given by Emily C. Talbot of Margam endowed the Talbot chair of preventive medicine; the Institute of Preventive Medicine, facing the Parade, the gift of Sir William James Thomas, was occupied in 1927. The first holder of the chair was E. L. Collis, a specialist in industrial diseases and director of health and welfare at the Ministry of Munitions, 1917–19. He was succeeded by R. M. F. Picken, a Glasgow graduate, whose high integrity was widely respected both before and during his period as Provost.[153] The chair of tuberculosis was made possible by the generosity of the Llandinam family who, when the endowment became insecure, remedied the position in 1937. The first holder of the chair was S. Lyle Cummins, a native of Cork and much decorated in several wars. A gift of £14,000 to the School by the Rockefeller foundation in 1924 provided a laboratory for the medical unit at the Royal Infirmary. Scholarships were endowed to promote research into medicine, medical pathology and cancer. The department of pathology and bacteriology had been created in 1910 under the headship of E. Emrys-Roberts, who died in 1923, a casualty of war. E. H. Kettle, who succeeded him, was a major figure in British pathology. His three years at Cardiff (1924–7) called for diplomacy and hard work, particularly in obtaining from the Royal Infirmary those pathological supplies fundamental to teaching and research. An eponymous lecture is still given in his honour in Cardiff every third year.[154] The chair was not filled until the appointment of John Bright Duguid in 1933. Born at Black Dog, Aberdeenshire, and educated at a Quaker school, he was an authority on atherosclerosis. There was no chair of materia medica and pharmacology until the appointment in 1938 of R. St A. Heathcote. Three years earlier the University Court approved proposals to institute a new degree of Bachelor of Pharmacy. Amendments were needed in the charters of both University and School so that courses could be pursued in the department of pharmacy of the Cardiff Technical College. The arrival of A. G. Watkins in 1932 from Great Ormond Street augured well for the development of pioneering methods in the treatment of sick children in Cardiff hospitals. Harmonious relations with the hospitals of the city were, of course, fundamental. In 1938 Sheen disclosed plans to extend the School at the Royal Infirmary. A little earlier the Llandough Hospital of the Cardiff Corporation and the Lord Pontypridd Hospital for Children were associated with the School as clinical institutions; there were several others, including the hospitals and laboratories of the Welsh National Memorial Association for the purpose of tuberculosis teaching.[155]

Lack of accommodation obliged the authorities to restrict by selection those entering upon the first three years at the University College; there was also the fear that the profession might become overcrowded because of lack of appointments in industry and commerce. Indeed, the new Institute of Preventive Medicine was obliged to house several other departments. Yet, in the School 'proper', as it was termed, numbers increased steadily, from 67 in 1932 to 173 in 1938, whereas in the University itself after 1933 there was a sharp decline. Women students, a mere 9 per cent in 1932 rose to 24 per cent in 1938.[156] Concern was expressed that the 'national' School was not attracting more students from north Wales,[157] where there was a long-established tradition of proceeding to Liverpool. It is good to record that the School admitted seven German medical graduates of 'non-Aryan ancestry' who, obliged to leave their native land, duly obtained registrable British qualifications and who were 'very satisfactory . . . in every respect'.[158] The ceaseless need to acquire expensive medical books and journals understandably prompted the School to appeal to the National Library of Wales to transfer its stock to Cardiff 'as an out-lying section'[159] of the Library, which replied courteously and sympathetically. Problems relating to the privilege of copyright enjoyed by the Library, however, proved insurmountable, though hopes of a satisfactory arrangement before the end of the century have not yet been wholly extinguished.

The School was scarcely affluent, but it was solvent. There had been a great change from the early days of the century when E. H. Griffiths complained that students had to be sent to London two or three weeks before examination so that they could see ordinary apparatus in use in ordinary laboratories.[160] In 1935 it was encouraging to hear that every rating authority had again agreed to contribute to the School, whose proportion of income from endowments was appreciably higher than that of the College, 7.5 per cent in 1938 as opposed to 2.9 per cent.[161] In 1933 a high tribute was paid to the School by Lord Horder, the outstanding clinician of his day. In a speech at Cardiff, reprinted in *The Lancet*, he spoke of his experience as external examiner for the degree of MB and MD at the School. The standard was 'very satisfactory indeed'. Not even in London, with its peerless facilities, was better work done so that 'when I meet a graduate in medicine of the University of Wales, my attitude is one of entire respect'.[162] After the hammer-blows of the 1920s it was now possible to face the future with robust confidence.

VIII

Student Life

We shall first examine the geographical origins of students. During the early years the number of students from England and abroad at Aberystwyth far exceeded those at Bangor and Cardiff. Aberystwyth had clung more resolutely than the sister colleges to the London external degree examinations. In 1896 the College informed the Treasury that the proportion of students from beyond Offa's Dyke (mostly women) was as high as 39 per cent. The reasons, it claimed, were highly creditable, reflecting tendencies which also attracted Welsh students to the universities of Scotland and England, and English and American students to German universities. For the College there were substantial financial gains, as we have seen.[1] In addition, it was urged, the College derived 'real advantages' from the presence of English students. Since the Welsh language held 'undisputed sway' in the heart of Welsh Wales there was no danger that English influence would impair Aberystwyth's 'strongly marked Celtic impress'. English students were brought into touch with Welsh ideals and in turn contributed 'a social breadth . . . of unquestioned advantage'.[2] The Welsh degree would thus be widely recognized both in England and Wales, to the benefit, it was implied, of the other colleges as well. Nevertheless, early in the next century there was a perceptible decline in the numbers of students from England and abroad, a change of fortune attributed to the establishment of the universities of Manchester, Liverpool, Birmingham, Leeds and Sheffield. In 1903 the proportion was 31 per cent, further reduced to 16 per cent on the eve of the Great War. Thereafter the proportion of English students outside Wales pursuing degree courses at Aberystwyth was no larger than 13 per cent, but sufficiently high for Iorwerth Peate to say that the College partook of the nature of a *universitas*, not in the sense, of course, that it taught all subjects but because it approximated to the old *studium generale*, 'a school of general resort'. By 1938 it was less than 8 per cent. Cardiff never attracted many students from outside Wales before the Second World War, in 1938 only 3 per cent. Bangor's 15 per cent in 1906 was reduced to 9 per cent in 1938, but it was then the highest proportion in the whole University, a matter which gave considerable satisfaction to D. Emrys Evans. Swansea in this connection was not statistically significant, for in 1938 it had one student only from beyond Wales.[3]

As to the distribution of students from within Wales, the following pattern emerges from a study of one typical year immediately preceding the Second World War.[4] Proximity to a college, as Matthew Arnold had long ago heralded, was the prime determinant. Of all Cardiganshire students in the University of Wales, 88 per cent went to Aberystwyth; of Caernarfonshire students, 85 per cent were at Bangor; 87 per cent of students from the Cardiff county borough went to Cardiff (and the Medical School) and 87 per cent from the Swansea county borough to Swansea, thus reinforcing the prediction of a witness before the Haldane Commission that Swansea's young people were unlikely to travel to Cardiff for their education.[5] Moreover, not a single student from Cardiff was at Swansea. Students at Aberystwyth were far more representative of Wales as a whole than those at the other colleges, 33 per cent from Glamorgan and Monmouthshire, 21 per cent from north Wales and 37 per cent from Cardiganshire and Carmarthenshire. If Bangor had proportionately more students who habitually spoke Welsh, as is most probable, it had attracted not one student from the county boroughs of Cardiff, Merthyr Tudful, Newport and Swansea and but one from Cardiganshire. Cardiff and Swansea in turn had very few students from north Wales. Thus Aberystwyth had a claim, in addition to that of seniority, to be considered the University College of Wales. Not for nothing did the College decorate the ends of the beams supporting the roof of the quadrangle with the crests of all the Welsh counties.[6]

We shall next consider briefly the number of students who came to the national University from the counties of Wales in proportion to population. Cardiganshire's record was out-standing and in accord with its educational tradition. In the 1936–7 session 33 per 10,000 of the population were at the

University of Wales. During the inter-war period it was ahead of all other counties, apart from the 1934–5 session when Caernarfonshire, which normally came second, headed the list. The counties on the western seaboard (Pembrokeshire excepted) sent proportionately more students on average than the other counties. In the early 1920s between 9 and 10 students per 10,000 came from Glamorganshire, increasing to 16 by 1934, at a time when student numbers were at their peak. The county boroughs as a whole were always below the average for Wales. In assessing the general pattern, a committee of the University Court in 1928 was therefore entitled to say that the geographical distribution of students was more extensive than if there had only been two Colleges in Wales.[7] We may further surmise what would have been the position had the University of Wales been a unitary university, and thus in one location.

As to access to higher education, Lewis Williams of Cardiff believed that the 1889 Act had enabled children of the poorer classes to proceed from the gutter to the College.[8] Poverty is, of course, a comparative term often eluding precise definition. In 1913 Reichel told the Royal Commission on the Civil Service that the educational system made it 'absolutely impossible' for original talent not to proceed from elementary schools to the Welsh University Colleges because 'the meshes of the educational net are so close'.[9] When questioned by Philip Snowden as to whether there were any amongst the 300,000 in the primary schools of Wales who could have profited from higher education had they been given a chance, he replied that the number was negligible.[10] The chairman of the Welsh Insurance Commission said that it was 'quite possible for a boy to enter the first standard of an elementary school and proceed to his degree at a Welsh university without any cost to his parents'.[11] In 1930 it was said that university training was 'now within the reach of nearly every capable Welsh boy and girl'.[12] There are many still alive who know that this was not the case.

Circumstances had, of course, vastly changed since the days recalled by Henry Jones in 1880: 'I thank God for the struggle, but would not like to see a dog try it again. There are scores of lads in Wales that would creep up, but they cannot. Poverty has too heavy a hand for them.'[13] Nine years later the Welsh

Intermediate Act offered unprecedented opportunities. In 1907 the chairman of the Raleigh Committee expressed surprise at the number of students at Bangor whose fathers were working men.[14] The College Registrar replied: 'That, of course, we take here as the most natural thing in the world, but I have no doubt it does appear remarkable.'[15] By 1911 there is evidence that 'the effective accessibility' of university training was almost twice as high in Wales as in England. The number of boys proceeding to universities from Welsh intermediate schools was 4.3 per cent, from English 'council' secondary schools 1.9 per cent.[16] In 1938–9, the University Grants Committee noted that the percentage of students with homes in the United Kingdom who began their education in a public elementary school was 38.6 in England, 65.7 in Scotland and 92.0 in Wales.[17] It could not be gainsaid either, as Emily Penrose remarked in 1917, that 'the Welsh colleges seem to be the least expensive'.[18] To live 'on the very cheapest scale'[19] at Oxford and Cambridge, said J. E. Lloyd, would cost three times as much. A former Aberystwyth student at Cambridge wrote to the *Dragon* in 1897 to say that 'a fellow does not relish overmuch having to pay for one day at Cambridge sufficient money to satisfy his landlady at Aberystwyth for a whole week'.[20] Fees were from the first kept to an absolute minimum. Indeed, after the Haldane Report there were fanciful hopes, as we have seen,[21] that fees could be abolished altogether in response to the expected product of a penny rate promised by the local authorities. No government providing grants would ever have countenanced such a proposal and it was difficult in 1904 to resist Austen Chamberlain's argument that if the new English university institutions kept their fees as low as those in the Welsh colleges then they too would have a higher proportion of the sons and daughters of working men.[22] When fees were revised in the University of Wales it was with a heavy heart. Even so, the proportion of income received in fees by the Welsh colleges remained decidedly less than in English universities and colleges.

Yet there was no cause for complacency. Many were defeated in their attempts to enter a college. The novelist, Howard Spring, presents a melancholy account of his brother's feverish efforts at Cardiff in the early 1900s. Having missed a scholarship to the Higher Grade School he was later fired by the sight of his contemporaries in the streets of Cardiff with mortar boards and 'gowns fluttering in the wind':

> The thought of all they were getting and all we were missing gnawed him, and suddenly he hurled himself with what can only be called passion into the acquiring of knowledge. With his day filled by the earning of his living, with a wretched physical constitution that was the bequest of our childhood, he nevertheless drove at learning with sustained frenzy. I have come home late at night and found him asleep with his head on the table amid a pile of books and with a penny bottle of ink upset at his hand. It killed him in a few years. He took a trip round the world on a cargo boat in the hopes that a wrecked body might be repaired, and he died at sea.[23]

Whether the reach was greater than the grasp we cannot tell, but Howard Spring was always haunted by his brother's unslaked thirst for knowledge. In 1903 the Cardiff Principal said that he knew a young collier who went down the pit at six in the morning, returned home at five, had a meal, tramped five miles to Cardiff to study for two hours, then tramped back. Caradog Prichard, poet and journalist, prevented in youth from entering a college, enrolled as a full-time student at Cardiff. At night he worked on the *Western Mail*, from which he escaped for three unpaid months before graduating in 1933 to the tumultuous applause of his fellow students on capping day.[24] (Sir) David Hughes Parry, a future Vice-Chancellor of London University, failed to win a modest entrance scholarship at both Bangor and Aberystwyth, thus imposing a heavy strain upon his farming parents.[25]

In 1916 T. F. Roberts took a more realistic view than Reichel a few years earlier of the financial support available to students during their college career. In the large populous areas of Glamorgan and Monmouthshire it was possible to offer a large number of free studentships, further augmented by the Cradock Wells maintenance scholarships of at least £20. The counties of Cardigan, Meirionnydd and Montgomery, on the other hand, provided few county exhibitions and ranging only from £10 to £15.[26] The headmaster of Hawarden Grammar School, Flintshire, commented in 1914 on the great disparity between counties. Glamorgan, he calculated, devoted 39 per cent of a penny rate for county exhibitions to university, Denbighshire only 5.7 per cent.[27] Prospects for boys and girls depended less on ability than on the county of domicile. At Aberystwyth there was a further problem. Practically all students were obliged to live in lodgings or hostels, their homes being at a distance from the college.[28] In 1907 it was reported that at Bangor two-thirds of the students held some kind of award, though at times as low as £5, and Reichel conceded that the Board of Education grants for prospective teachers did 'not pay their way by any means'.[29] It is true that a man could find lodgings of the lowest grade, without board, for as little as 3s. 5d. a week in the beginning and for no more than 4s. 6d. before the Great War. Even after the war some students seem to have managed on 15s. a week (board and lodging), but fees and other expenses were additional. An official view was that before 1914 an arts student (male) could manage, with some privation, on £38. 12s. 6d. per annum and a science student (male) for £42. 12s. 6d.[30] Women in a hall of residence needed more. In the early 1930s, it was formally stated that on average the total cost of living, including lodgings and tuition, lay somewhere between £75 and £90.[31] State scholarships had by then been introduced, £80 in value, so that a state scholar with other scholarships lived comfortably; a 'swell' could easily follow the fashion and sport plus-fours.

State scholarships, however, were few. During the last pre-war year for which we have reliable evidence 5.7 per cent of candidates at the Higher School Certificate level received an award, one-third of whom went to the University of Wales.[32] Nor was there anything comparable to Carnegie's splendid benefaction to pay the fees of Scottish students, 95 per cent of whom were beneficiaries at St Andrews in 1907–8.[33] Curiously, Reichel was not much in favour of the Carnegie bounty, preferring instead the American system he had seen at first hand in 1903 of working one's way through college, though he did not suggest practical methods of introducing such a scheme in Wales. In fact, it was not customary for students to work during the vacations and there were hardly any opportunities to do so. In 1922–3, 7.8 per 10,000 of the population were university students in England, 12 in Wales and 21.1 in Scotland.[34]

Evidence submitted to the Consultative Committee on Examinations in Secondary Schools indicated that in view of the poverty of scholars, Wales was inadequately provided with exhibitions. A committee in 1918 which inquired into the position of natural science concluded that there was a grave wastage of good material. Because of 'the insufficiency of maintenance allowance' many boys in secondary schools in industrial areas were leaving prematurely, attracted by the comparatively high wages in industry.[35]

By 1920 Reichel was ready to acknowledge that 'a certain amount' of leakage took place between secondary school and university. 'All the best talent does not get through', he told the Cymmrodorion Society, adding ruefully that 'some of the material that does had better have been left behind'. Having witnessed and indeed promoted educational advances during his lifetime, he had been at first reluctant to admit that there were flaws in the structure. Now he was readier to take into account 'the vagaries of mental growth'[36] and to allow for the late developer. Coleg Harlech, established in 1927, was to demonstrate amply that the educational mesh was not as close as Reichel had once supposed. Student numbers reached their peak in the University of Wales in 1933–5 because the general depression in trade prompted many students to avoid unemployment, as in more recent times. The decline from 3,521 in 1934–5 to 2,779 in 1938–9 was considered unavoidable following an abnormal increase. At the University Court the Pro-Chancellor viewed the situation with philosophic calm. There had been an 'overproduction' of graduates and a dimunition in numbers was 'not altogether a bad thing'; classes were now of a reasonable size. Some disapproved of the bishop's resort to the language of the market-place. 'The University and its Colleges', said J. Morgan Jones, 'were not out to produce articles on demand or to satisfy a demand like a business house.' Their purpose was 'to create an educated community'.[37]

Without the sacrifice of parents many would not have remained in college. Having closely analysed the occupations of parents in readiness for the Raleigh Committee in 1907, J. E. Lloyd concluded that five-sixths would need to struggle to keep a student in college. Kate Roberts could never forget during her

time in college that a railwayman earned only 18s. a week (and
his clothes) and a quarryman between £3 and £4 a month. Dilys
Glynne Jones related after the Great War that 'really
extraordinary efforts'[38] were being made by Welsh parents to give
higher education to their children. It was in recognition of such
devotion that the Aberystwyth Court at its Llanelli meeting in
1930 paid a graceful tribute to Fred Jones, a tinplate worker, and
his wife, who were invited to attend. They had given university
education to three sons and a daughter at Aberystwyth out of
very slender means. Idris played rugby for Wales and later held a
high position in the Coal Board. Gwyn was in 1930 the manager
of a firm in Rio de Janeiro, Winifred was an inspector under the
Ministry of Labour in the Midlands. Elwyn, the youngest, had
not yet finished his course and he had only a scholarship of £10.
In 1974 he became Lord Chancellor.[39]

There were many cases of hardship. In 1902 the attention of
the Prince of Wales (later George V) was drawn to the penurious
student obliged at end of term to walk home from Bangor, a
distance of twenty-seven miles. Cardiff's first student magazine
had to be read in manuscript in the common room because
students had no funds to have it published. It was accounted a
great merit in T. F. Roberts when he was on the Cardiff staff that
he saw to it that on cold days there was always a bright fire in the
room where he lectured. In 1907 the Cardiff Registrar reported
that many poor students unable to afford fire and light in their
lodgings resorted to an upper room in the College to work in the
evenings.[40] R. S. Thomas recalled that he was sometimes chosen
to play for Bangor's second rugby fifteen, but more frequently in
away matches because he could afford to pay the fare. A Swansea
student of poor parents remembered that her mother removed
the red badge from her school cap, thus converting it into a hat,
and tailored a coat for her out of a grandfather's blanket. The
daughter of a middle-class family at Cardiff which had fallen on
bad times recalled that she often had to make do with toast and
hot grapefruit juice. Two generations earlier Viriamu Jones and
his wife were concerned that women students were tempted to
survive on tea and macaroons.[41] In 1911 Thomas Rees said that
if ministerial students did not preach on Sundays they would be
reduced to starvation. An Aberystwyth student of the inter-war

years, Jack Griffiths, recalled that he 'saw more dinner-times than dinners'.[42] During the depression years the Theophilus brothers from Merthyr Tudful marked on a loaf with an indelible pencil their ration of bread for the day. Many who travelled daily to Cardiff from the mining valleys did not eat until they returned home. One student maintained himself and his unemployed parents at Pontypridd for four years on a state scholarship. He further supplemented his income by humming a tune for 5s. in Sunday evening religious broadcasts from Cardiff ('Silent Worship') and then walking home in all weathers. In 1934 the Bangor Registrar begged the Denbighshire Society at its London meeting not to run away with the notion 'that everything had been done for the humble students of North Wales'. He could cite cases of men who were 'struggling to get enough to eat while pursuing their studies'.[43] A marked social division became apparent when evacuees from University College, London, arrived at Aberystwyth following the outbreak of the Second World War. The number of students of both colleges was about equal at Aberystwyth and initial impressions were not propitious. The guests tended to be patronizing. More important, perhaps, was the middle-class tendency to embrace theoretical Communist views which seemed extreme to their hosts who had known at first hand, in the words of an Aberystwyth student, herself of English middle-class parentage, 'not just the pinch, but the grip of poverty in their childhood years'.[44]

Poor parents were encouraged by Viriamu Jones to consult him concerning the education of their children. They may have at first approached him in trepidation but he always received them with great courtesy.[45] Staff frequently helped the truly indigent. Thomas Charles Edwards was said to have given freely of his money in this way. R. L. Archer, warden of a Bangor hostel for men, could be depended upon in emergencies, refusing to accept IOUs and relying instead upon a sense of honour. There were usually small loan funds, though they cannot have been more than temporary palliatives.[46] Early attempts to provide a meal for 8d. or so at Aberystwyth failed when it was found necessary to raise the price by a penny. In 1907 the College's Registrar remarked that those who daily ate one very good, plain meal looked 'altogether, in better condition'.[47] Serious anxieties

concerning malnutrition among men students prompted the
authorities there to form a men's dining club, of which the
president for many years was R. I. Aaron, always concerned for
the welfare of students. Other colleges had already made similar
arrangements, though the charge at Swansea in the 1920s of 1*s*.
4*d*. for a meal including meat deterred the needy. At Bangor there
was clear evidence that many students were unwilling to impose
such a daily impost upon their parents. Aberystwyth, it seems,
was to the fore amongst universities and colleges in introducing a
comprehensive medical scheme for students, for men only, on a
voluntary basis in 1923 and made compulsory in 1931, when
women were also included. For a fee of 12*s*. 6*d*. students were
entitled to medicines and all hospital services. The scheme
flourished because of the devoted labours of the Professor of
German and because of the readiness of Aberystwyth doctors to
charge the smallest of fees.[48]

The advantages of residential accommodation were generally
recognized. In 1907 T. F. Roberts told the Raleigh Committee
that hostels would be 'much more educative'[49] than lodgings for
men. A short-lived experiment for men at Plynlymon,
Aberystwyth, demonstrated, as did other halls of residence, that
academic achievement was higher than for students in lodgings.
In 1909 it seemed for a moment possible that Aberystwyth could
become wholly residential within six years if it could put into
effect the generous, imaginative proposals of David Davies and
his sisters who were prepared to contribute £8,000 in the first
instance. For reasons that are not wholly apparent, the College
was unable to measure up to the challenge and the offer was
withdrawn. Had the bold venture succeeded it is not too much to
say that 'it would have transformed the quality of university life in
Aberystwyth, and may well have given the College an indisputable primacy among the Welsh colleges'.[50] Substantial halls for
men were not opened until after 1939, Neuadd Reichel (Bangor)
in 1942 and Pantycelyn (Aberystwyth) in 1951. On the eve of the
war, 26 per cent of full-time students lived in hostels at
Aberystwyth, 37 per cent at Bangor, 11 per cent at Cardiff and 4
per cent at Swansea. Those living at home amounted to 12.7 per

cent at Aberystwyth, 22 per cent at Bangor, 60 per cent at Cardiff and a remarkable 83 per cent at Swansea. The young Roy Jenkins, who spent a year at Cardiff before proceeding to Oxford, was not untypical, as he later observed, travelling, in all, two and a half hours daily to and from Pontypool, in his case by bus.[51] Nearly nine out of ten students at Aberystwyth were living in lodgings, almost six out of ten in Bangor. In these small towns, then, there developed a boarding-house subculture and Stephen Leacock's 'Boarding House Geometry' in *Literary Lapses* (1910) struck a responsive chord. In the early days, some landladies, unduly fearful of being struck off the official College Register, reflected the prevailing puritanism, even objecting to chess on Sundays and encouraging their guests to attend religious meetings on weekdays as well as Sundays, partly, it was noised, to economize on coal and light. Generally speaking, they were indulgent, in some cases long-suffering. Waldo Williams was struck by their infinite variety. The same could be said of a fellow lodger. If one were fortunate, 'to co-dig is to marry a little'.[52]

One thing was certain: digs were not for women students. During the uncertain period following the Aberdare Report there were serious suggestions that the Aberystwyth College should become a girls' school, that even Ashford School in Kent might move here.[53] Happily this did not come to pass. The College had admitted women in the 1870s, a development viewed by Hugh Owen with consternation, but the first woman to pursue a complete degree course was not enrolled until 1884, as at Bangor. For some years women students were of a superior social status to that of men students. Usually they were of English, middle-class parents who saw the opportunity to have their daughters prepared at less expense for the degree examinations of London University than at Bedford College, for example, or at the Royal Holloway College, London, and in the main in salubrious surroundings. The financial advantage to the colleges was evident enough. There was also a social cachet. The early ruminations of Dean H. T. Edwards and Isambard Owen that prosperous parents would settle down near the colleges, as they had done at Cheltenham, Clifton and Bedford, whilst their offspring were being educated, came to nothing. The notion, however, long persisted that young ladies taught at fashionable English schools would confer a desirable *ton* upon the people's colleges. Cardiff was the first Welsh college to provide a hall for women: 'Aberdare Hall of Residence for Female Students' opened in 1885, the second university hostel for women in Britain. Both Aberystwyth and Bangor were highly praised in the *Baner* for speedily following Cardiff's example, in 1885 and 1886 respectively.[54] These halls, compulsory for almost all women undergraduates not residing at home, normally provided a higher standard of living than for men in lodgings. The halls at Oxford and Cambridge were to be the pattern. Aberdare Hall was opened by the Principal of Newnham, Mrs Sidgwick, and University Hall, Bangor, two years later by Helen Gladstone who brought the good wishes of Newnham to Bangor, her 'younger sister'.[55] At Cardiff, Isabel Bruce, daughter of Lord Aberdare, was the first of many Oxford women to serve Aberdare Hall. Women closely connected with the Colleges identified themselves with the halls, Lady Verney and Lady Reichel, for example, at Bangor and Mrs Viriamu Jones at Cardiff. The early titles of 'Lady Principal'[56] and 'honorary Principal' (later replaced by 'Warden') conveyed a spurious sense of grandeur, reinforced by the spectacle at Aberystwyth of one maid standing at table to every two students.[57] The weakness was that the strict rules smacked of English boarding schools and were frequently a source of discord. The distinct impression conveyed is that at Aberdare Hall there was a more relaxed atmosphere than in other college halls. When officially opened in 1895 it was remarked that a motto on the fireplace at Cefn Mably (a Glamorgan house dating back to the sixteenth century) was exceedingly apposite: 'A good fire, a clean hearth and a merry maiden' (Tân da, aelwyd lân a merch lawen).[58] Such spritely remarks would not have found favour at Aberystwyth or Bangor.

What cannot be questioned was the determination in all the Colleges to provide good facilities for women within the bounds of rigid budgets. Women from Wales gradually exceeded in number those from England, especially after the discontinuance of preparation for the London degree; at Aberystwyth as late as 1906 there were somewhat more women than men students, a phenomenon not remotely matched at Bangor or Cardiff at any time (apart, of course, from the war years). Thereafter, until the 1930s, the proportion of women to men in the colleges usually varied from one-third to two-fifths. Relations between the sexes were unduly complex in the early years. Solemn, well-meaning members of staff who considered that they were *in loco parentis* often found the responsibility perplexing, even daunting. Still in thrall to the illusion of the ages, sanctified by religion, that woman was indeed the weaker vessel, they were persuaded that she needed special protection from the rigorous challenge of life. Physiological factors, it was darkly hinted, caused nervous strain at examination time, for instance, a point more than adequately disposed of before the Aberdare Committee by Frances Hoggan. A native of Brecknockshire, she was in the forefront of the movement to extend educational opportunities for women. Drawing upon her rich experience of advances in Switzerland, she told the Committee that examinations were strenuous for males as well as females.[59] Yet over thirty years later O. M. Edwards was wondering whether women 'can stand the physical and the mental strain' of higher education. He concluded that 'the tendency always is for the academic side, which is tested by examinations, to encroach on the domestic side'.[60] Mixed tennis had been allowed at Bangor before 1914, but the privilege was not extended to 'sinister winter games', such as hockey. As late as 1919 the Bangor Senate rejected a request for joint sports for men and women on the ground that 'the question of Athletic Sports for women under any circumstances required very careful consideration from the medical point of view'.[61] The subsequent triumphs of women in the Olympic Games would have astounded such august bodies. The propriety of allowing women to row became in 1917 a subject of general concern throughout the university system. 'Sliding seats', for instance, were not considered appropriate. Isambard Owen, now at Bristol, took a hand in the discussion. The river there was not suitable, but in any case he felt obliged to add that in his view, 'as a physician', rowing was not a decorous exercise for young ladies. Sibly, having left Swansea for Reading, firmly stated in 1931 that 'under no circumstances' should a crew of women compete with a crew of men.[62]

Little mixing of the sexes was at first allowed. Picnics were strictly chaperoned by wardens of women's halls, though not always successfully it appears, for a visit of Cardiff students to

Caerphilly Castle was marred in the eyes of the authorities because couples wandered freely and unseen among the ruins.[63] A 'Romeo and Juliet' affair at Aberystwyth in 1895 began when a spirited woman student (already under the surveillance of the Warden) spoke from an open window at Alexandra Hall to a man student who had drawn her attention by whistling. The woman was mildly punished but the man (later a headmaster of repute) was sent down for two terms after eight Senate meetings lasting thirty-three hours. The students now in uproar derived no small satisfaction when the Principal was fined half a crown by local magistrates for cycling without lights from a late Senate meeting.[64] The expulsion from Bangor of a man and woman in 1901 for comparatively minor transgressions led to a serious student strike. Many years later the woman became the wife of the Professor of Semitics at the College and mother of a future Archdeacon of Oxford, a happy reversal of fortunes. The College, which had until 1901 relied upon an 'honourable understanding' to govern relations between the sexes, now felt obliged to be specific. We may be sure that the words were not misunderstood at the time:

> Reasonable intercourse between men and women students is permitted –
> (a) at authorised social meetings within the College;
> (b) on the College field during the progress of matches;
> (c) in the College itself for business connected either with College societies or with class work.[65]

These rules chafed and were frequently broken. In 1912 there was a renewed outburst of ill-feeling (fully shared by the young Kate Roberts) when a woman student who had arranged to meet a man student (killed in the Great War) at Valley, Anglesey, arrived slightly late at University Hall. Immediately placed in purdah, she was soon withdrawn from the College. Thereafter she took a first in Tout's History School at Manchester.[66] Cardiff was far less troubled by such episodes because of the city's cloak of anonymity. The College, however, was no less severe when the occasion arose. Gwyn Jones recalled that in the 1920s a prankster seen by the Principal to have entered the Women's Common Room was immediately sent down.[67]

If the presence of women at the colleges of the University led to indiscipline, there were certainly other causes of friction. The bounds of the permissible were never clearly understood, but, as in the twelve days of misrule, legitimized disorder was reluctantly winked at, the authorities in this respect aping the long, indulgent tradition of the Scottish universities. Not unexpectedly the cauldron frequently boiled over. Students at Aberystwyth, punished for excessive rowdyism during the visit in 1907 of the Raleigh Committee, from which substantial financial amelioration was expected, took their revenge at the degree ceremony shortly afterwards. Such was their unruly behaviour that the authorities were obliged to move from the Coliseum Theatre to complete the ceremony in the relative privacy of the College. Apologies from the Registrar and the students were received by the University Court at its next meeting.[68] Not to be outsmarted, Cardiff students gave their version of unseemly conduct two years later. At the degree ceremony they convincingly performed a Maori war dance, a member of the Welsh Church Commission was assaulted with flour and around the dignified Isambard Owen squibs danced like marionettes, at length extinguished, not inappropriately, by the principal of a Baptist College. These were heady days and the stage was set for an intervention by Marchant Williams, who announced that he knew of people who had emphatically declined to contribute to the Colleges because of the disturbance. The splendidly named Miss Rule, representing Newport, further declared to the University Court that the ringleaders should be dealt with, adding for good measure that she herself was a firm believer in punishment.[69]

Students, as the need arose, were also quite ready to deal with their own kind. A future historian, J. Conway Davies, who had caused offence by remarks in a local paper concerning the Aberystwyth rugby team, was tarred, feathered and wheeled around the town.[70] Initiations for entry into the education department at Bangor were relentlessly continued until the end of the Second World War. The most elaborate jape hitherto discovered was at Aberystwyth in 1932. Gwynfor Evans recalled that he and his contemporaries were sent invitation cards stating that Lord Davies of Llandinam would be pleased to welcome all first-year men to dine at his residence, evening dress being optional. Upon the appointed evening they were taken by charabanc (for which they themselves had to pay) to what purported to be the entrance of a mansion and marched down the drive to a large farmhouse. The charabanc then returned home speedily, leaving the disconsolate 'guests' to walk back fifteen miles on a wintry, howling night.[71] When he went to Cambridge in 1933 Gwynfor Evans reflected disapprovingly upon the noisier manifestations of social life at his old college. Too many entered Welsh colleges with the sole aim of getting a degree 'with as much pleasure as possible thrown in', adding, indeed, that 'they might be Zulus for the interest most of them take in their own country'.[72] It must be allowed that 'college spirit' and noisy customs such as rags and yells did not appeal to everyone. On the whole there was little anti-social behaviour, few took to drink (and not only because they could not afford it) and at Cardiff and Swansea there were usually no more exotic excitements than coffee at the Kardomah and perhaps Russian tea.[73] 'Medics', who usually kept to themselves, tended to be rumbustious, untidy and not averse to pipes and tankards. Generally students acted a good deal more responsibly than Evelyn Waugh and his companions at Oxford and there was nothing comparable to the 'sit-ins' at Bangor in 1976 and 1979, albeit in a good cause and to teach the senators wisdom, nor to the six-week suspension of normal work at the London School of Economics when the author of the Robbins Report was chairman of the Court of Governors.

Rules universally considered harsh by students were substantially modified upon the return of ex-servicemen in 1918. It was inevitable. Petty restraints were at once cast aside and large concessions extracted from middle-aged professors who had seen nothing of the carnage. An ex-serviceman later wrote that the academic staff were 'rightfully alarmed at setting loose in a co-educational college those men who had so valiantly wiped German Kultur off the face of the map'.[74] None in fact durst say them nay. At Aberystwyth staff who resorted to such risible tactics as to 'cut' the unruly on the street and promenade were regarded with amusement. When students at Bangor spent the night drinking in the Principal's room it was idle to talk of sanctions, as Lewis Valentine, the student president, recalled.[75]

Social regulations which were not changed after discussion were ignored. Gradually the presence of ex-servicemen brought about wholesome reforms, later extended, after their departure, in a co-operative spirit by principals and student presidents. At Aberystwyth it was observed with satisfaction in 1928 that but few pinpricks remained. Freshers were not to chat with the opposite sex after seven in the evening; men and women were forbidden to pass beyond a limit of three miles outside the town and some wags wondered how the rule could be enforced westwards and skywards.[76] If ex-servicemen were unwilling to bend the knee to authority without ample cause, their maturity and experience were invaluable, nowhere more so than at the University's youngest College. They were the men who mattered most. In 1924 a correspondent to Swansea's student magazine, the *Undergrad*, wrote: 'It meant that we were able to take our stand by the side of our sister colleges and make ourselves almost immediately a factor in the inter-collegiate life.'[77] More important was their contribution to internal matters, for Swansea's Students' Representative Council was given backbone at its foundation. In the other colleges the early development had tended to be uneven.

Individual societies and clubs long preceded the formation of Students' Representative Councils. There were already such councils at Edinburgh and Glasgow. In Wales the initiative was taken by a Cardiff medical student in the 1896–7 session. Bangor followed suit in 1899, the first president being elected in December, and Aberystwyth in 1900. Hitherto members of staff had guided student affairs, rather too closely, it was increasingly felt. As is not uncommon, a mild devolutionary measure did not slake the thirst for a further extension of power. Student representation on College Senate was long resisted, an unduly cautious response as subsequent events have shown. In general such changes have been advantageous to senates and students, though it must be conceded that the SRC, as it was popularly known, was not always able to exercise decisive control over the student body when tempers ran high. It did, however, command broad assent when amalgamation fees were introduced to finance recognized student societies, a significant advance. Most of all, it gave valuable experience at a modest level in the processes of self-government. The students' estate was by no means to be despised. Inevitably, there were constitutional changes. The most drastic was at Cardiff in the 1926–7 session when the SRC was transformed into the Students' Union Society, following the acquisition of 51 Park Place to house the students' union to commemorate students killed in the war. At Bangor the common rooms in the main building were refurbished when the University Grants Committee set aside moneys for the purpose in 1924. Aberystwyth had long suffered from inadequate facilities, its common room being described in 1915 as resembling 'a third-rate waiting-room, dingy and comfortless'.[78] In 1921 it was resolved, as a memorial to the founders of the College and to students who had fallen in the war, to buy the assembly rooms in Laura Place as a students' union. For decades they were the robust, vivacious centre of social life. At Swansea, despite constant pressure from students, it was not possible to provide a union building before 1946, when Maes yr Haf was purchased near Beck Hall. In 1913 Bangor successfully proposed the formation of a Central Students' Representative Council which, it was hoped, 'will have a great influence towards cementing the three colleges with a closer bond of fellowship'.[79]

Sport was encouraged for several reasons, not least because the health of students caused alarm. Reichel from the outset believed that the physique of Welsh students compared unfavourably with that of public-school pupils, a view corroborated by examination of volunteers during the Boer War (much as the Second World War, followed by national service, revealed a disconcerting degree of illiteracy). Undernourished bodies fell prey to the unsparing ravages of tuberculosis, Bunyan's 'captain of the men of death'.[80] At length in 1910 war was declared on *y dycáe* (consumption) when David Davies, MP, launched the Welsh National Memorial Association, soon to confirm in stark terms that bad housing, poor hygiene and malnutrition were especially prevalent in the rural counties of Wales. In 1939 the three north-western counties were the very worst. Thirty-five years earlier a Glasgow doctor had established that there was indeed a link between tuberculosis and overcrowding. The case for fresh-air activities appeared unanswerable. Outdoor games had long been neglected in Wales, partly because of puritan opposition to an apparently prodigal use of time, often in undesirable assemblies, so that it was not surprising that Aberystwyth's first Principal, when asked by students for permission to hold an athletics meeting, gave his consent only after seeking divine guidance.[81] Fifteen years later Reichel proffered moral reassurance to honest doubters. Games generated self-confidence, self-reliance and a love of truth, 'Half the lying in this world', he confided, 'came from want of nerve.'[82] Swansea's first president, F. W. Gilbertson, believed that the cultivation of games and sports would raise the public spirit of the College and help to produce gentlemen. The older universities, not those of America, would teach them most. There were also imperial considerations. Students of the University of Wales who proceeded to Oxford and Cambridge discovered at once that sport was vastly more important than in their alma mater. Muscular Christianity had worked wonders in post-Arnoldian public schools and was performing the like service in controlling savages overseas. Sudan, the colonial show-piece, was so well provided with Oxford athletes as to be called a nation of blacks ruled by blues. Such thoughts were not far from Reichel's mind and to promote *esprit de corps* he was ready to bay encouragement from dank touchlines. Thomas Jones held it a merit in Stuart Jones that he travelled overnight to support Aberystwyth in a Saturday match.[83] Such contests were popular, both sexes being allowed to mingle in the interest of College spirit. Good manners did not always prevail. P. H. Burton recalled that when he was defending the honour of Cardiff against an unnamed theological college, both teams were sent off after ten minutes for bad language.[84]

One of the advantages enjoyed by the Welsh Colleges was that their playing fields were more readily accessible than was possible in the great industrial cities. When suitable fields were acquired – and this was no easy matter – they became nurseries of talent. Towards the end of our period, too, advantage was taken of the National Fitness Council's comparatively generous capital grants to provide gymnasia and swimming baths. Of the various sporting activities, soccer and rugby were the most popular. Bangor defeated Aberystwyth in soccer during five successive seasons,

1898 to 1902, and Bangor men won four international caps
between 1919 and 1922. Aberystwyth seldom lost at home and
after the war won the British universities soccer championships.
Rugby was for long a frail plant at Bangor (for it was never
seriously a north Wales game). The College did, however, win the
inter-varsity championship in 1926, as did the women's hockey
team, in that *annus mirabilis*. Aberystwyth did not lose a single
rugby match for twenty years against the other colleges until the
late 1920s. Amongst the College's triumphs in 1927–8 was to win
the British universities rugby cup and to have contributed five out
of seven runners to the Welsh harriers team which became British
champions. The Cardiff men's hockey team won the British universities championship five times between 1922 and 1928. At the
Commonwealth Games in New Zealand in 1938 the College's
Jim Alford was victorious in the mile race. Six Cardiff students
were capped, including Percy Bush who represented Wales in the
celebrated victory over the New Zealand All Blacks in 1905.[85] The
palm, however, must assuredly be given to Swansea. The following
captained Wales: Watcyn Thomas, first captain of the University
of Wales Rugby club when formed in 1926 and who led Wales in
the first victory at Twickenham in 1938; Claud Davey, captain of
Swansea and Wales in 1935 when both sides beat the All Blacks;
Haydn Tanner, capped twenty-five times between 1935 and 1949,
considered to be one of the greatest scrum halves of all time, and
Idwal Rees who played in the 1933 and 1935 matches and who
became headmaster of Cowbridge Grammar School at the age of
twenty-seven. Their rugby careers extended, of course, beyond
their student days, but they may rightly be regarded as products of
the University of Wales.[86]

Part of the attraction of sporting activities was that they
enabled men and women to assemble and mingle together. The
same was often true of the meetings of the Literary and Debating
Societies, which also tended to encourage swashbuckling
speeches and comic turns, scarcely satisfying after the war to
students passionately concerned to debate issues of the day,
capitalism, socialism, international relations and imperialism. At
Aberystwyth a Political Union was formed and at one of its
debates in 1925 between Sir Alfred Mond and Frank Hodges, the
trade-union leader, a total of 620 votes were cast, 88 per cent of

the number of full-time students then at the college.[87] At Cardiff a Political Union Society was founded after the war as a non-party society, but within it in 1922 was formed the Socialist Group which, by 1924, was attracting speakers such as Bertrand Russell. It later became affiliated to the Cardiff City's Trades and Labour Council. Earlier there was a Socialist Society at Aberystwyth to which an infant branch at Bangor appealed for support in December 1915. The driving force at Cardiff was Hilary Marquand who had arrived at the College from Cardiff High School with a state scholarship. In 1922 the University of Wales Labour Party was formed, composed of Socialist groups in all the Colleges. One of its purposes was to advance the fortunes of Labour candidates in the University of Wales elections, in which, apart from the briefest interlude in 1922–4, traditional Liberalism held sway amongst graduates. In 1925 it was reported that Marquand, formerly chairman of the University of Wales Labour Party, was at Oxford elected chairman of the University Labour Federation. Yet it is evident that at the outbreak of the Second World War the main political parties were not effectively organized at the Colleges. We must ask why this was so.[88]

As early as 1923 Marquand was convinced that 'the number of students genuinely interested in politics is continually decreasing',[89] largely reflecting the exodus of ex-servicemen. It must be added that his own exodus deprived the College of a vigorous, influential leader of opinion and of action. When he returned to his old college in 1930 he was, at twenty-nine, the youngest professor in Britain. Two years earlier a former president of Cardiff students remarked that the political clubs throughout the University were 'in their origin, in the time of the ex-service student . . . spontaneous creations'. They had, however, changed, merely serving 'the purpose of collecting, as appendages of the outside parties, those persons who prefer one political label to another'.[90] By the mid–1920s the Political Union at Aberystwyth had merged with the old 'Lit. and Deb.' to form a new Debates Union. It is also clear that annual mock-elections, in no sense a true guide to political allegiance, consumed in a boisterous, somewhat immature, fashion those energies which might profitably have been devoted to genuine political action. Nevertheless, it cannot for a moment be doubted that several students at

Cardiff and Swansea fiercely repudiated an economic system held responsible for the widespread, demoralizing unemployment in the depressed areas. Yet a Marxism more than tinged with atheism was to many an unpalatable solution to the woes of society. Again, the absence of a convincing Tory presence at the Colleges meant that Liberals were unable to confront their traditional antagonists. Steel was not whetting steel. Indeed, if we are to judge from the contents of college magazines and the standard of college debates in general we might be tempted into believing that tormenting developments in Europe largely passed unheeded. This would be misleading. Idealism had by no means evaporated. For a time it hinged upon the question of disarmament, in purely college terms upon the continuing existence of the Officers' Training Corps.[91]

The question of OTCs did not concern Cardiff (apart from the Medical School) and Swansea, both free from controversy on this issue. In all Colleges a substantial body of opinion supported the League of Nations as the only hope of preserving peace in a distracted world. A number of students went further. At a general meeting at Aberystwyth in 1930 it was resolved to abolish the OTC, 'an adjunct to militarism'.[92] The Council declined to do so, but the great debate ('y ddadl fawr') had begun. Early in 1933 the Oxford Union passed its famous resolution that 'this House will not fight for King and Country'. It may not have had much effect on foreign governments, even if they noticed it at all, but there was a stiffening of resistance among a younger generation. A few months later Aberystwyth students were carrying placards bearing a similar affirmation. In May 1934 Aberystwyth's Court asked its Council to state that 'preparing for war was not one of its functions'. Lord Davies, a fervent supporter of the League of Nations, did not see matters in such simple terms. Nations needed to defend themselves and '"negative" disarmament carries us nowhere'.[93] The Council agreed that it would be as wrong to disband the OTC as to compel students to enrol. The following year there were storm clouds at Bangor. William George, voicing the views of many students, proposed in the College Court that the College should have no official connection with an organization having for its object the training of young men in the art of war. The OTC was a recruiting ground for the War Office.

The Principal replied in jocund, even taunting, manner, that William George in his recent biography of Richard Lloyd, his uncle, had written of Lloyd George's membership of the old Volunteers and of William's successful efforts to conceal 'the awful fact'[94] from his uncle. Emrys Evans added that Lloyd George's brilliance as a war leader had revealed nothing to suggest that membership of the Volunteers had corrupted his character. There was no compulsion, he proceeded, to join the OTC. Indeed moral compulsion came from the greater number of students who opposed the OTC. During the last eight years only two had joined the regular army so that the militarizing influence was slight. Membership of the OTC was a condition of entry to many professions, particularly the colonies. Should the College, therefore, deprive students of appointments in the service of their country and empire? These arguments prevailed by a comfortable margin.[95] Nevertheless, there was a residual feeling that they were not best presented by one who had not been received into the service of the Young Men's Christian Association until the last stages of the Great War. Criticisms that he was a link between the War Office and the student body during the Second World War were less than fair for as Principal he was acting in an *ex-officio* capacity. Matters were not allowed to rest. At the University Court William George was soon applying a bellows to live coals. His motion in 1935, fully supported by the student representative, that the University should have no connection with a military organization, was passed by a two-thirds majority. There was much impatience in official circles. The question was put to counsel who concluded on good constitutional grounds that the OTCs at Aberystwyth and Bangor were a domestic concern in accord with the chartered rights of the Colleges. Thus, these small military contingents remained intact and continued to enjoy until the outbreak of war their annual training camps.[96]

Genuine religious convictions persisted in an increasingly sceptical age. It is true that the rationalist press had won converts in industrial south Wales. A young Cardiff student, Cathrin Huws (later Daniel), was appalled to discover during an inter-college debate at Coleg Harlech in 1935 that Antichrist had come to Wales. The Swansea speaker's blasphemies were 'terrible to hear'[97] as he endeavoured to prove that Christ was a materialistic Communist. From time to time an occasional Nonconformist minister gave the impression that the Colleges of the University were breeding a plenteous supply of agnostics, charges which could not reasonably be sustained. The religious life of the Colleges centred in the first instance upon the Christian Union, affiliated to the British Colleges Christian Union, a branch of the Student Christian Movement, the usual title after the Great War. It had no intention of being a substitute for any branch of the Christian Church, it avoided damaging doctrinal disputes and presented a broad ecumenical approach which many found attractive, especially in the dolorous aftermath of the War. Wary of sudden outbursts, such as the Revival of 1904–5, the SCM encouraged in a questioning age a more thoughtful conviction through publications and conferences and under the influence of such men as William Temple, C. E. Raven and C. H. Dodd. P. H. Burton tells us that he had reacted against conventional churchgoing, but at Cardiff his mathematics lecturer helped him to find a genuine faith so that he became a student president of the College's branch of the SCM, 'a liberal body acknowledging that a religion can and should face all questions and try to find answers'.[98] In 1921 there appeared the first number of *Yr Efrydydd*, the Welsh organ of the SCM. Its appeal was not only to students 'but also to the Welsh nation outside the colleges',[99] for it would be calamitous to stand aside from the external world.

An awakening social conscience had early prompted students to consider the plight of the underprivileged. At a working men's institute in Mill Street, Aberystwyth, there was a reading room and a games room where students held concerts; in 1905 there was a branch at Trefechan. The keenest sense of social commitment was at Cardiff, where the noble experiment of Ronald Burrows at East Moors was long remembered. One aspect of the work was well recalled by P. H. Burton. During his four post-war college years (and for several thereafter) he took a leading part in camps for grammar school boys 'started by a group of idealistic university men, many of them pacifists as a legacy of their war experiences'. The purpose was to enable boys (inevitably boys) to come under the stimulus of vigorous minds:

Such men as Professor Dodd came to the camps, which were held on beautiful sites along the seashores or amid the mountains of Wales. Living conditions were invigoratingly primitive: bell tents and ground sheets, not even sleeping bags. Every night there was a sing-song and chapel, but the sing-song was much more than that; it was an entertainment often requiring a deal of preparation, and here I found full vent for my propensities as performer and storyteller.[100]

Eyes were turned to wider horizons. In 1903 at the Manchester Congress of English and Welsh inter-varsity students, Welsh representatives derived satisfaction, perhaps immoderate satisfaction, when, amongst those of other University Chancellors, greetings were received from the Prince of Wales, Cambridge having to rest content with the Duke of Devonshire and Leeds with the Earl of Ripon.[101] At first hesitant in their relations with the National Union of Students, it was not long before J. E. Meredith, Bangor president of SRC, became president of the National Union, whose official organ gave occasional attention to Welsh matters. At the beginning of the Great War many Belgian refugees found succour at Aberystwyth and at Bangor. In 1923 students at Swansea launched a campaign to relieve their comrades in Germany and Russia. At a meeting of international students at Geneva in 1925 it was reported that 12,000 Russian, Georgian and Ukrainian refugees were distributed throughout Europe 'almost all in a state of great distress'.[102] It is sad to reflect that the University was obliged to conclude in 1933 that it did not have resources to provide posts for displaced 'non-Aryans' as German teachers. Spanish Communists were welcomed at Caerleon, where they received the attention, amongst others, of a young history lecturer, Christopher Hill.[103] Students from the United States and Germany visited Swansea in 1937, but the arrival at Cardiff of 'students' from Germany at Easter of the same year caused bad feeling. The student president was roundly attacked by the Socialist Society (mainly Communist) for permitting the visit. Although he was wholly innocent of any intention to play into the hands of the Nazis, it emerged that the visitors were older than the average student, that they distributed pamphlets with swastika markings and that their cameras were extensively used to photograph the docks which they had especially asked to see.[104]

In general we may say that there was an increasing concern amongst the leaders of student opinion for public affairs at home and abroad. An outstanding example was W. Moelwyn Merchant. Born and bred in Port Talbot, he had as secretary of the student union at Cardiff participated in social work in the devastated coalmining valleys of Rhondda and Cynon. The example of the Quakers and the Maes yr Haf Settlement greatly moved him and he was admirably suited to organize a conference at the College on 'The Problems of a Depressed Industrial Area'. Senior and junior members of several British universities attended and saw at first hand the suffering of the mining communities. Merchant contributed an essay on 'The Undergraduate and the Crisis' to a volume, *Young Minds for Old* (1936). Many years later he recalled that amongst his fellows 'there were few theorists of left or right', but that there was a 'fixed determination to see the betterment of society and the alleviation of immediate despair'.[105] In his essay he repudiated the idea that universities erected 'insurmountable barriers' between classes. The University in a depressed area had been the first to abandon the notion: 'Where a University is in the closest daily contact with the needs and problems of a community, academic segregation becomes an impossibility.'[106] At Cardiff there was a wholesome habit of sending the president of the union to the conferences of the International Student Service and the World Student Christian Federation, from which Merchant greatly profited. It is evident, too, that he brought a sharpened awareness to bear upon the fearful crisis, economic and moral, facing German, Italian and East European students. First, his experience in south Wales had made him 'more receptive to these matters than many of my fellows from Britain, from more affluent parts of the country'. Second, the British delegation was guided by a distinguished churchman, Canon Tissington Tatlow of St Paul's, both cheerful and saintly. He tells us that Tatlow's 'ability to relate the grief of the German students at the death of their ideals to the quite different but equally tragic plight of the British unemployed, prepared us, at least in part, for the traumatic wakening to holocaust for Europe in 1938–9'. Merchant adds that Tatlow and the International Student Service Conference 'were for many of us our second and profoundly important university'.[107] Ten years earlier Bangor students had looked forward to a time when all students, wherever they might be, would feel that they were members of one 'World University', that 'then and not till then can we be called a University in the true sense of the word'.[108]

As time passed an increasing number of students argued that only from a basis of strength was it possible for Wales to stand upright amongst the nations. That Welsh interests were not adequately secured within the national University was apparent from the first beginnings and a number of students challenged their seniors with an uncompromising zeal, especially after the Great War. Since English was exclusively employed for educational and administrative purposes throughout the University it was natural for students to urge that the language of Wales should not be injured by neglect in its own home. One of the first signs was the founding of *Y Wawr* at Aberystwyth before the First World War. There were serious discouragements. The editor of the College magazine, the *Dragon*, in part perhaps suspicious of a rival publication, did not see why the cause of Welsh nationalism should be advanced and further committed himself to the astounding statement that 'by far the greater majority of the students do not understand Welsh sufficiently well to read it (if they understand any at all)'.[109] Welshmen, he vouchsafed, were regarded with suspicion in England and anglicization was the only remedy. Something of the same spirit prevailed at Bangor. Before 1914, said Ifor Williams, there were at the College 'many greenhorns, young men from the countryside who had no experience of life in towns, and a handful of young Englishmen could dominate College life'.[110] The founders of *Y Wawr*, however, had no intention of being muzzled by either students or staff. The new journal owed its existence to 'the intense feeling on the part of the more patriotic students at the College that the University should be brought into closer touch with the nation'. Moreover, it was 'an attempt to repay the people of Wales for their efforts in establishing the University'.[111] This 'interesting little periodical',[112] as it was archly called in the *Dragon*, was more than a squib. Its wartime attacks on the government's war aims were considered so subversive by the College authorities that the

editor, Ambrose Bebb, and his committee, having refused to
retract or reform, were obliged to resign. After the war there was,
as we have seen, a sturdy sense of independence. Before long,
Iorwerth Peate, as editor of the *Dragon*, hoped that the University
acting as a body corporate would 'impart to our countrymen a
breadth of outlook and a sympathy of understanding'.[113] More
Welsh articles were to be seen in the magazine. Indeed, the vigour
with which Welsh issues were expounded caused antagonism and
in 1929 the *Dragon* conceded that relations between some English
and Welsh students had deteriorated.[114]

At Cardiff progress was fitful. In 1903 it was pronounced in
the College magazine that 'ours is a distinctly and essentially a
Welsh College'.[115] The implications of this encouraging
declaration were not always understood. The Welsh language was
evidently proving a stumbling-block, for in 1910 the editor of the
magazine protested against so much Welsh in the College
Eisteddfod: 'We firmly believe that in the interests of the *esprit de
corps* of the College, less emphasis should be placed on the
language.'[116] His remarks elicited a lucid, tough response from
Henry Lewis, then a student. Soon after the war attempts to
secure for Welsh the same status as English in the Students'
Representative Council failed.[117] By now non-Welsh-speaking
students were tolerant enough in relation to the Eisteddfod and
the Gorsedd, but not when their own position appeared
threatened, as it must have done, long before the advent of
instantaneous translation. In 1925 there were ineffectual protests
at Swansea against the absence of Welsh in the Students'
Representative Council. During the next decade Alun Llywelyn-
Williams included Welsh sections in his editorial in *Cap and
Gown* and when these were discontinued by his Welsh-speaking
successor, he reminded his fellow students in 1935 that Cardiff
was not a provincial English college and that *Cap and Gown* had a
duty to perform towards the Welsh language. In the following
year Geraint Bowen, a future archdruid, deplored the ebb and
flow in the fortunes of the language in student publications.
Nevertheless, there had been some progress, as was evident in
subsequent numbers of *Cap and Gown*. T. M. Bassett, later the
historian of the Welsh Baptists, did not fully comprehend what it
was to be Welsh until he became a student at Cardiff.[118]

After the Great War a handful of students became increasingly convinced that a firm basis for Welsh aspirations could be secured only by political action. Bangor was the main seed-bed. Ifor Williams noted the change when young Welshmen came back from the war. He tells us that 'they took their rightful places in the college'.[119] If one of the purposes of the great carnage had been to defend the rights of small nations, as Lloyd George constantly affirmed, especially in Wales, then Wales was certainly one of them. 'Returning from the war, I was an out-and-out Welsh Nationalist',[120] said Lewis Valentine, president of the Students' Representative Council. Building upon the tradition of a pre-war society, *Y Macwyaid* was reformed with the proclaimed purpose of making the College more Welsh. Three further societies followed, of which a Welsh Nationalist Society founded in 1921 was the chief, Y Gymdeithas Genedlaethol Gymreig (or Y Tair G, as it was popularly known). It may well be that events in Ireland were the prime stimuli in developing a new political awareness, as J. E. Jones, the first formal organizer of the future Plaid Cymru, believed.[121] The government's policy towards the Irish had inflamed opinion, particularly after the execution for complicity in an ambush of Kevin Barry, whose fellow students at the National University College, Dublin, thanked the students of Bangor in May 1921 for their support: 'It is a source of pleasure to us to know that the news of Ireland's struggle is being heard in Wales . . . Nothing would afford us greater joy than that the natural friendship between Wales and Ireland should continue to increase.'[122] Several members of staff of the University informed its representative in Parliament that the Welsh nation was deeply concerned for Ireland, adding that 'there is a vigorous unanimity among Welsh University students on this question; their grief is second only to that of Ireland itself'.[123] Students prominent in the future Plaid Cymru were in entire accord, amongst them Lewis Valentine and Moses Griffith, the party's astute first treasurer. In the late 1920s J. E. Jones, then a student, did not discern hostility amongst English contemporaries to Welsh aims. In 1927 it was agreed that Welsh might be spoken at meetings of the Students' Representative Council, minutes henceforth to be kept in both Welsh and English. Thomas Parry thought that Welsh students at Bangor lived their lives as naturally as English students at Bristol and free from gloomy introspection.[124] D. Tecwyn Lloyd, a student at Bangor from 1934 to 1938, went further. Under firm leadership and given a Council less old-fashioned in a 'British' way, it would have been possible to have transformed Bangor into an 'all-Welsh College without much difficulty'.[125] That, however, was to beg the question. Principal and Council believed they were reflecting public opinion and such a proposal would have been instantly, not to say coldly, dismissed as a quaint flight of fancy.

In the 1930s there were fissures. Representatives of Mudiad Gwerin (the People's Movement) founded by Goronwy O. Roberts, a Bangor student, though of brief duration, challenged the leaders of the Welsh Nationalist Party at Swansea in 1938, arguing for state control of heavy industry and municipal control of small industries. However, the attempt to fuse socialism with Welsh nationalism, much opposed by Saunders Lewis, was almost unanimously vanquished. Meanwhile, in each of the Colleges small groups dedicated to political action derived encouragement from members of staff, notably R. Williams Parry at Bangor and T. Gwynn Jones at Aberystwyth. Gwynfor Evans did not become a member of Plaid Cymru until he had left Aberystwyth, but it was here that he resolved to join. At Cardiff, Griffith John Williams and his wife, Elizabeth, were a source of inspiration, as also was W. J. Gruffydd until his departure, or defection, as some thought, to more traditional pastures. Amongst students there, Cathrin Huws passionately espoused the nationalist cause and spoke eloquently on its behalf. When Saunders Lewis was obliged to leave Swansea, the small College branch was nurtured by Stephen J. Williams, long remembered for his constancy in difficult days. Students, though naturally voteless, strongly supported Lewis.[126]

It is scarcely surprising that students often recalled the teaching which they had either enjoyed or endured. They tended to be immoderate in both praise and stricture. Occasionally stricture was justified. W. H. Bryan at Bangor, a mathematician of outstanding gifts, was wholly unskilled in the arts of pedagogy. In a just world he should have remained with his illustrious peers in the rarefied atmosphere of higher mathematics. Instead, he was obliged to teach matriculation classes which, in response to his incompetence, resorted to buffoonery and even riotous behaviour. A. N. Whitehead once remarked that 'the study of mathematics is apt to commence in disappointment'.[127] This was certainly the case at Bangor for many years. Venerable figures were not spared. Kate Roberts and others detected traces of indolence in John Morris-Jones, prone to cancel lectures when contrary northern winds impeded his progress by cycle from Anglesey. The earlier Professors of History were in the main severely criticized by a cloud of otherwise amiable witnesses. H. R. Reichel was one of the exceptions, his lectures being 'as clear as a mountain rill'.[128] The eminent J. E. Lloyd, mechanically and aloofly reading from a yellowing manuscript (kept in the Registrar's safe), was said to drain the past of all excitement. Moreover, since his magisterial volumes published in 1911 ended in 1282, it was considered unfair to proceed no further than the Statute of Rhuddlan (1284), thus requiring his shepherdless flock to wander as best they could through the three succeeding centuries upon which they were also examined. Indeed, failure to survey the whole course was a frequent complaint in other subjects. Across the Dyfi, Edward Edwards was censured for never rewriting his lectures, considered unimpressive upon first delivery and to be further desiccated by endless repetition. H. A. Bruce, who had come to Cardiff full of Oxford promise, seems not to have bothered with facts at all, whilst William Rees's acknowledged erudition was impaired in the eyes of students by prolixity and an idiosyncratic accent. At Swansea, T. J. Morgan, having sampled the resources of the history department, resolved that his future lay in other branches of inquiry. Few, it seems, in any department were ready to follow the example of C. E. Vaughan, the English professor at Cardiff, who, if tradition is to be relied upon, burnt his lectures after delivery and studied intensively before preparing a further set.[129]

For a lecture at its consummate best there is no substitute. Unhappily, it often became the sole, dull vehicle of communication, lecture notes being handed down from one generation to another so that attendance at classes became for students an empty formality leaving them free, like Keats before them, to play

with sunbeams. Hywel Davies, a leader of the ex-servicemen at
Aberystwyth, arranged to have printed in the *Dragon* of 1921
Henry Sidgwick's 'Lecture against Lecturing' in which he
denounced 'the ordinary expository lecture . . . as an antiquated
survival'.[130] College teachers should print their lectures and
devote their time to supplementary enunciation, informal
discussion and conversation. This was much in tune with Lord
Kelvin's remarks at Bangor when he opened the science
laboratories. The catechetical method employed in language
classes differed greatly from the lecture as a *conférence*, the French
concept warmly commended by Kelvin: 'Professors and students
must speak to one another. One of the greatest things is to
promote freedom of conversation in such classes, to cultivate the
power of expressing ideas in words.'[131] Such was certainly Alfred
Zimmern's view at Aberystwyth, where he attracted large
numbers to his weekly survey of great international issues.
Writing to the Principal, he said that Welsh boys and girls
matured later than their English counterparts (in itself a good
sign, he thought) and it was clear that they needed 'the most
elementary guidance in intellectual habits' and that 'the present
system of getting up subjects almost entirely by means of lecture
notes and small text books does them . . . more harm than good'.
He was horrified to discover that 'freshers' sometimes appeared
more intelligent and interested than third-year students. 'I am
sure that there is only one cardinal remedy, more individual
attention', adding two or three months later that he preferred to
throw 'my main strength next year into tuition and personal work
rather than lecturing'.[132] Alas, Zimmern, to the infinite regret of
students, did not last sufficiently long at Aberystwyth to put his
plans into operation, but he had drawn attention to a common
defect. Those who came from good schools where they had
received personal attention – Alun Llywelyn-Williams[133] at
Cardiff, for example – were dismayed by the dismal fare at first-
year level. Nor was it common to set essays at any stage. The
widespread absence of tutorials seemed all the stranger since
many professors and lecturers had been brought up on the
tutorial system at the older universities. It was also a curious
anachronism that students both before and during their college
courses frequently participated more in the process of learning by

discussion in Sunday schools than within their own academic departments.

Over-reliance on lectures was in part the consequence of ill-stocked libraries. In 1900 a contributor to Cardiff College's magazine said that 'our library is so poor that if all the College borrowed from it there would be little of any value left'.[134] In order to borrow a book a deposit of £1 was required, thus striking hard at those who could not afford to buy books and who most needed to borrow. In the 1930s the only copy of R. L. Nettleship's standard work on Plato had to be shared between thirty. Inevitably there were thefts. Donors in turn tended to unload on colleges those books they did not want (Bibles in some numbers) and which were of little direct relevance to university studies. By the end of the Great War, College libraries were badly run down. Bangor felt aggrieved in 1931 because the number of students for each member of staff was 8.8, the highest in the University of Wales, whereas the average for Bristol, Reading, Sheffield, Durham (Armstrong College) and Nottingham, taken together, was only 6.7.[135] Today it would not be thought that Bangor had legitimate cause for complaint, but such statistics mask the problems of two or three members of staff in small departments obliged to provide complete courses from matriculation, in the early days, to the honours degree. Again, it is important to note that criticisms of the lecturing system were by no means confined to Wales. Glasgow began to agitate in 1932, Birmingham in 1936 and Liverpool during the 1937–8 session, as Bruce Truscott (Allison Peers) was to remind wartime readers of *Red Brick University*.[136] The National Union of Students in 1937 'emphatically endorsed' the University Grants Committee's views in 1936 that there should be more tutorials and seminars and that lectures should be reduced to 'an absolute minimum'.[137] In 1920 the forthright ex-servicemen at Aberystwyth were but anticipating widespread discontent.

In retrospect it is evident that students of the University were privileged to have been taught by scholars at the height of their powers. They might indeed have preferred John Morris-Jones to have lectured in Welsh, but since examinations were in English there were practical advantages. To some his rendering of Welsh poetry and prose in the course of a lecture delivered in English seemed all the sweeter, to others like diamonds on a necklace. At his splendid best his lectures were rapturously received. If W. J. Gruffydd and Saunders Lewis did not greatly care for teaching elementary classes they left a lasting impress upon the best students at advanced levels; both were intellectuals who travelled freely in the realm of ideas. The teaching of mathematics may often have been purgatorial, but W. H. Young at Aberystwyth succeeded, we are told, in communicating a 'rare intellectual excitement to his students',[138] and P. H. Burton paid unqualified tribute to a mathematics lecturer at Cardiff who influenced him in manifold ways. Before proceeding to Cambridge, Glyn Daniel spent a year in the geology department at Cardiff. Here, he said, 'I received . . . some of the best teaching in my life; when I eventually came to teach in Cambridge, I modelled myself consciously and deliberately on the Department of Geology at Cardiff as it was in 1931–2.'[139] T. A. Levi sometimes made law appear more simple than it actually was, but his superb oratory, no less compelling than that of great preachers at dramatic religious festivals, drove his spellbound hearers to examine leading cases for themselves, at the College or at the National Library. It is certain that during our period tutorial teaching had not much prospered, but within narrow confines there were experiments. W. J. Roberts, a lovable eccentric, turned lectures in economics at Cardiff into large seminars, to the dismay, admittedly, of those who needed precise compass points and who had been taught to receive knowledge by the spoon. At Aberystwyth, under C. H. Herford, the Professor of English, there were early shoots of the tutorial system, but he had left in 1901. More enduring were A. H. Dodd's efforts at honours level at Bangor, where he had long taught extra-mural classes, an admirable preparation for full and frank exchanges, not favoured by timid, sheltered scholars. The real obstacle was financial. In 1936 J. F. Rees told the University Court that Cardiff had considered instituting the tutorial system but that progress was impossible, not from lack of goodwill but because of the inadequate numbers of staff. On the science side there was regular supervision in laboratories. A visiting Japanese professor declared himself much impressed at the close contact between staff and science students at Swansea, in complete contrast to universities in his homeland where numbers were far greater.[140]

We must next consider the relation between training and achievement. Students were sometimes accused by their fellows of devoting their whole energies to the acquiring of degrees instead of cultivating mind and body in non-academic pursuits. That social life was by no means neglected is apparent in the preceding pages, but it was clear that formal qualifications were indispensable for those obliged to make their way in the world without prospect of private income. To take their ease like the well-heeled at Oxford and Cambridge was not a recipe for those unlikely to forget the unremitting sacrifices of their parents. In the subjects chosen for study there were changing fortunes. In the years between 1907 and 1915 the numbers of those graduating in Greek had halved to fifty-three, further reduced by 1930 to nineteen. German was gradually gaining ground at the expense of French before the Great War which, not unexpectedly, had such adverse effects that in 1924 there were only two graduates in German throughout the University. The most impressive rise was in science. In 1900 honours graduates in science were barely 10 per cent of the total number of honours graduates in both arts and science. In 1939 the corresponding figure was 35 per cent.[141] The neglect of science was gradually being repaired, though in Reichel's view the tendency had proceeded too far, for he was not convinced that the study of science was as humanizing as the study of the arts. At the final or pass degree level in 1939, marginally more science students were presented for examinations, the success rate being slightly less than in the arts departments. Nearly twice as many were presented for honours degrees in arts, an indication that science departments took more readily to the necessary process of winnowing. J. F. Rees thought that not all who came to College were 'by nature' honours 'men'. The Burnham scale (by paying more to teachers who were honours graduates) had performed a disservice to the pass degree: 'a criticism that I would make privately is that the Colleges are already nominally too much Honours Colleges'.[142] In fact the good pass degree man was considered a worthy product of the University. In 1918 R. L. Archer, of Bangor, extolled the virtues of the new pass degree in *The Passman*, which attracted attention far afield.[143] The demise of this degree in a later generation was to be regretted by zealous guardians of the old school who feared that the standard of the honours degree would be diluted if opened to all and sundry. At first, graduation seemed to many a distant, unattainable goal, but even a failed BA felt that he could display honourable scars. Gradually, matriculation ceased to be a major barrier because of the spread of intermediate schools. An imperfect grasp of the English language long remained an obstacle. As late as 1907, Reichel told the members of the Raleigh Committee that it would be difficult for them to realize 'how entirely English is a foreign language to most of our students'.[144] Between the Raleigh and Haldane inquiries, however, there was a perceptible advance in some subjects, as may be illustrated by the table:[145]

Total percentages of passes at all levels

	1907	*1915*
Latin	59.6	68.9
English	72.4	85.7
Welsh	88.0	83.3
French	73.9	73.9
History	70.4	75.3
Pure mathematics	72.3	69.1
Applied mathematics		74.5
Physics	73.1	70.0
Chemistry	66.4	74.5
Botany	68.3	68.3

On the eve of the Second World War 21 per cent failed the final or pass degree in science as a whole, 17 per cent in arts. At honours level almost everyone was classified. In arts 19 per cent were placed in the first class, 27 per cent in science. Chemistry usually had a higher percentage of firsts than other science subjects, economics more than other arts subjects. Of all graduates (final and honours) in 1939, 12 per cent were placed in the first class. Improved performance is attributable to various factors. Preparation in the secondary schools became increasingly effective as more graduates were appointed. In the 1920s and 1930s keen competition for posts brought to the schools teachers of high ability who often kept in touch with their old College. Within the University liberation from the London system had given promise of independence in the shaping and teaching of courses, a change nevertheless injured by bureaucratic demands of the University's own making. Rejuvenation followed the Haldane Report which conferred upon staff and students the freedom which had often eluded them. Not least, the printed word became less inaccessible, though still not sufficiently accessible.[146]

Graduate unemployment, especially in the 1930s, prompted morose speculations which came to a head when a senior lecturer in botany at Swansea, Kenneth Rees, presented a motion to the University Court.[147] On the surface it was innocuous. It requested that a permanent committee of the Court be set up to inquire into the academic, social and physical needs of students. Rees did not question the academic standards of the University which he considered, without evidence, to be higher in some cases than in other universities. What concerned him was the general comportment of graduates. Looming in the background was the ancient charge of 'provincialism'[148] which had troubled Aberystwyth's first Principal. Decades later Sir Henry Lewis confided in his diary the disquiet he felt when a ministerial student arrived at his Bangor home on a Saturday evening without an overnight bag preparatory to conducting Sunday services in Lewis's largely middle-class chapel.[149] That a prospective minister, doubtless fresh from the plough, quarry or mine, had so blundered was no great offence. Still, rough places had to be made plain and Reichel persisted for many years with his alarming breakfasts for men students, partly to follow the example of Jowett at Balliol but mainly to introduce the uninitiated to the customs of polite society.[150] Some had a lighter touch. In 1922 a former student at Cardiff, before the end of the old century, remembered an invitation to dine with C. E. Vaughan (English) and J. S. Mackenzie (philosophy), both then bachelors at Llanisien. The fear of committing a social error at the table of professors filled the erstwhile collier with alarm, which, nevertheless, speedily vanished during the dinner of six or more courses. Vaughan in particular was as genial a host as he was a brilliant lecturer. 'Discussion', we are told, 'waxed hot over coffee and cigarettes.'[151] Such individual acts of kindness cannot have had much general effect and it is understandable that in the 1930s pressure grew to establish halls of residence for men. Women had been well provided for and had benefited from the civilizing influence of lady principals and wardens. It seems that Kenneth Rees had touched a nerve by raising the question of acceptable demeanour, particularly in interviews. True he had not spoken of strong accents, of Gallic trills and of explosive sibilants, but he did assert of Welsh students that 'too frequently there are sneering taunts at their lack of poise, of "savoir faire", their lack of general culture, extending even to more personal matters' (unspecified). Something was lacking in 'the final equipment of our graduates'.[152]

Rees was formally and frostily thanked for having moved the motion, but there were hints that he himself had lacked *savoir-faire* in bringing the matter to the attention of the University Court. It was more than a breach of etiquette, it was like shouting in church and it would have been much better to have discussed the problem in his own college. Moreover, these issues were common to other universities, particularly the newer ones. The Vice-Chancellor, J. F. Rees, believed that 'in the mass students everywhere were much the same'. As a member of the Miners' Welfare Fund Committee he had interviewed candidates from Scotland, the West Riding, the Midlands and Wales. His colleagues had told him 'how delighted they were with the appearance, bearing, conduct, and accent of the candidates from Wales'.[153] Rees, in any case, disliked self-deprecatory noises which led to touchiness, on the one hand, and to boastfulness on the other. His constant concern was the readiness of so many graduates to enter, indeed, to retreat into, the teaching profession without seriously considering other professions, notably the civil service, though he recognized that Welsh students could not afford to stay an additional year to prepare for the examinations of the administrative grade. At Swansea, P. S. Thomas, tutor in extra-mural studies, did his utmost to persuade students to consider occupations other than teaching, but there was a decided 'reluctance on the part of students and their parents to show initiative, create opportunities and possibly take some risk'.[154] In 1936 *The Times Educational Supplement* observed: 'A university training in South as in North Wales is still an avenue of escape, of freedom from the grim conditions which the parents have had to face', adding that 'it is not surprising that when the latter risk their savings on the higher education of their children they should not be inclined to venture upon further uncertainties in the hope of quick returns'.[155] Moreover, grants from the government to prospective graduate teachers were a strong incentive to enter the profession and for many there was thus a moral duty to honour the obligation. The most detailed analysis of vocations of students over a number of years was prepared at Bangor in 1907. Of 1,303 students, 59 per cent were engaged in various branches of education, whilst 16 per cent were clergy and ministers. In 1937, the student president at Swansea, D. Andrew Davies, concluded after a survey that 65 per cent of arts students and 55 per cent of science students had not contemplated any other career.[156] In 1939 the University Appointments Board reported that of the 478 who had registered with the Board, 59 per cent had been placed in various educational posts. The statistics of the Board are incomplete because they do not include those who had made their own arrangements, such as ministerial students hardly likely to seek the offices of the Board in determining which 'call' to accept. Of the 170 non-teaching posts, 47 were in engineering, 2 in the colonial service and but 1 in the home civil service. Marginally more found situations in England (220) than in Wales (215).[157]

Associations of former students were established to keep them in touch with each other and to promote the interests of the colleges. They were usually called Old Students' Associations, but Cardiff formed an Association of Past Students – though neither title managed to avoid a hint of decrepitude. Aberystwyth was the first to act, in 1892. The prime mover was Thomas Ellis, the first president, who remained in office until his death in 1899. Cardiff and Bangor followed suit in 1898, and Swansea soon after its foundation. Reichel had been impressed by the role of alumni in American universities, without appreciating that the wealthiest of them were sometimes oppressively interfering.[158] The Welsh colleges were, however, free from these hazards and were indebted to former students for moral and financial support. Bangor set aside a special room in the new building for the OSA (as it was popularly called) and at Cardiff the APS was actively engaged in providing for a students' union after the Great War. Members of the OSA at Aberystwyth were represented on a committee of staff and students 'to consider any matter relating to the general well being of the student body'.[159] In Wales, at least, it was a pioneering step in joint consultation. Annual reunions were not at first successful. At Bangor they were considered too stiff 'to be really pleasant',[160] perhaps due to Reichel, seldom given to merry sallies. Soon, however, they were prospering, but nowhere as much as at Aberystwyth, which in the 1900s attracted 200 to the Easter Reunion. Other colleges founded branches in dispersion, but again no college more successfully than Aberystwyth. In 1910 a branch was formed in Switzerland and in 1915 news came via the British Embassy bag that two Aberystwythians had performed a like service in Tokyo.[161] This latter exploit we should not perhaps take too seriously, but it is nevertheless true that when a handful of former Aberystwyth students gathered together there was a gleam of expectation. Why was this so?

Devotees of Aberystwyth would not be at all surprised. Thomas Jones, for instance, before he was seriously rebuffed at his old college, held that there was no comparison between the Old Students' Associations at Bangor and Cardiff and the flourishing association at Aberystwyth. Reichel, in characteristically frank fashion, allowed that Bangor's former students were 'somewhat behind their compeers of Aberystwyth'. Sibly at Swansea hoped that his students would nurture something akin to 'the Aber feeling', a 'strange thing',[162] as he called it with evident mystification. The reasons, however, were ready to hand. The campaign to establish the College in 1872, the ensuing struggle to survive and the destructive fire of 1885 had stirred the public imagination. It was the first of the Colleges which later united to form the University and it had captured the unyielding loyalty of students, ever ready to spring to its defence and who were more geographically representative of Wales as a whole than those of the other Colleges. However, it was neither easy to reach nor easy to leave. A former student declared: 'Who goes to Cardiff goes there as a passenger. Who goes to Aberystwyth should go there as a pilgrim and the Cambrian railway sees that he does.'[163] Some frail souls did not adjust themselves with ease to the Aberystwyth scene, believing, often unjustly, that they were under scrutiny. Here undoubtedly were the main ingredients of a close community before the days of the post-war settlements on the hill. Indeed, the restricted area of the College prompted Lord Davies in the 1930s to say that whereas 'it may be impossible to exercise sufficient supervision in a great city like Cardiff, where the students are scattered about in the midst of a large population', it would, however, be possible at Aberystwyth 'to exercise a certain amount of control, just as it is in Oxford and Cambridge'.[164] Had he been given a free rein, and the College usually saw to it that he was not, there might have been proctors and bulldogs in Chalybeate Street and in Llanbadarn Fawr.

Bangor, Aberystwyth's closest counterpart, was much more accessible by rail, for the motor car was not for years a realistic competitor. After 1911 it was divided into two distinct parts. The 'College on the hill' did not include scientists, who remained at the old Penrhyn Arms until the move to Deiniol Road in lower Bangor in the 1920s. In fact there was a fissure, which, amongst other reasons not easily identifiable, led to the formation of secret clubs which would have been hooted out of existence in Aberystwyth's 'open' society. Bangor students enjoyed a vigorous social life and travellers by day, such as Kate Roberts for a time, felt deprived of active membership of College societies.[165] At Cardiff and Swansea there were ready-made entertainments for those who did not commute so that College groups tended to rely on a core of enthusiasts who lived, or who were in lodgings, close at hand. One of these was Gwyn Jones, from Blackwood, Monmouthshire, well stocked with scholarship moneys, whose outstanding Viking studies later led to membership of the Icelandic Order of the Falcon and who always spoke of his life at Cardiff in the 1920s as 'pure magic'. None the less it was a minority, and a privileged, view. In the *Welsh Outlook* for 1924–5, which included reports from the colleges, Aberystwyth appeared under 'Multitudinous Activities',[166] whereas from Cardiff came a lamentation at the failure of most societies to flourish. Perhaps, as was once remarked, the 'Aber spirit' was at times so intense and flamboyant as to become parochial, so that students felt it a duty to attend all kinds of societies that jostled with one another for attention. Be that as it may, when students of the 1920s and 1930s published their recollections they entitled them *The Golden Years* (1972), a perusal of which enables us to understand the better the phenomenal success of the OSA at Aberystwyth.[167]

A final question remains. That there was a 'College spirit' we cannot doubt, but was there a significant sense of belonging to the University of Wales? T. F. Tout, who had at first fully supported the federal Victoria University (of which Manchester was the first member) soon became a dauntless advocate of an independent university for Manchester. Those who opposed a federal university 'do not believe', he said, 'that students dwelling in places thirty to sixty miles apart, with no opportunities of mutual association and no personal knowledge of each other can ever be in a real sense the students of the same University'. He added that they could not feel 'a proper pride in so intangible and unreal an *alma mater*'.[168] Welsh students were well aware of the challenge. As we have seen, a Central Students' Representative Council, with a president from each college in turn, was formed before the Great War, and performed a useful co-ordinating service. It was at a meeting of CSRC at Aberystwyth in 1924 that it was resolved to prepare a *University of Wales Supplement* to the magazine of the National Union of Students, called *The University*. It first appeared in 1925 under the editorship of H. A. Marquand, who dismissed it with airy impartiality as 'a dull publication'. However, a beginning had been made and the Prince of Wales, as Chancellor, on the eve of his departure for South Africa, expressed the hope that it would develop into 'a real University Magazine'.[169] A somewhat larger *Supplement* appeared in 1926, and in 1928 it emerged for the first and apparently only time as *The University of Wales Magazine*. Subsequent developments are not easy to disentangle, but it seems that Welsh affairs were later reported occasionally in the National Union of Students' magazine, *The University*, which became in 1932 *The New University*. In short, neither the separate *Supplement* nor *The University of Wales Magazine* prospered. H. A. Marquand had certainly done his best to promote the concept of a university amongst students of the four colleges. In common with others, he wanted an exchange of teachers and of students, and it became customary for teachers to deliver a short series of lectures at other Colleges. A further means of fostering good relations was the inclusion of letters and greetings from other Colleges in each College magazine. Thus Marquand urged Swansea readers to join those of Cardiff to encourage every form of close contact. A Bangor correspondent, however, struck a plaintive note: 'We must remember that we really are one University.'[170]

Marquand's departure undermined a sense of solidarity at Cardiff. In its jubilee year of 1934 W. Moelwyn Merchant remarked that the very need to have a Central SRC was proof of organizational difficulties in a federal university.

> On but very few occasions can the 'Varsity spirit be felt in Wales, since it is inevitable that each College will develop a tradition of its own, which is probably all to the good, particularly if Cardiff, as is to be sincerely hoped, is to become a University.[171]

He was more than echoing the words of the Cardiff Principal in the jubilee number of *Cap and Gown*. One of the few occasions to which Merchant referred was the annual inter-college week, including sports matches in each of the Colleges and culminating in an eisteddfod at one of them in turn. They generated feverish enthusiasm which spilled over into boisterous behaviour often viewed with alarm by the authorities. In private D. Emrys Evans fiercely attacked the inter-college week as 'the annual plague'[172] and the Bangor Senate invited the other Colleges to do away with the eisteddfod considered disruptive of good order, especially since it went on until the early hours of the morning. This autocratic spasm led to vehement, united opposition. The inter-college week remained untouched, a sturdy demonstration of student power.

It may be added that the Guild of Graduates performed a valuable role in linking graduates of the University together, a role formally recognized in the constitution of the University. Yet, even members of the Guild, when they looked back upon their student days, inevitably thought primarily of their own college. In 1916 Kenyon, not at all in favour of disrupting the federal system, said that at Bangor 'we feel that we are a little university ourselves'.[173] As in other matters we cannot lightly set aside the considered views of T. F. Tout. In 1953 D. Emrys Evans quoted the words of A. H. Trow before the Haldane Commission in 1916: 'If one student meets another and says "Where are you trained?" and he says Cardiff, if the questioner comes from Aberystwyth he is as much a stranger as if he came from Bristol. They do not say "University of Wales".' Emrys Evans, who had an unsurpassed knowledge of student opinion during these years, did not consider Trow's picture 'overdrawn'. However he affirmed that 'no such bold statement' could be made in 1953, adding that 'the University looms larger in the mind of the student today than forty years ago'.[174] Nevertheless, it could be said that students of the Welsh University Colleges from the outset had more in common with each other than with students of colleges outside Wales. W. Rhys Roberts, formerly Professor of Greek at Bangor and subsequently at Leeds, understood well the difference between membership of the old University of Victoria and of the University of Wales. In 1917 he wrote: 'There is no distinctive bond of nationality uniting Lancashire and Yorkshire. In population, the two counties number some nine million souls, as compared with some two and a half million in Wales (including Monmouthshire).' He went on to ask: 'in the way of a common *title*, have they anything to point to except the Lancashire and Yorkshire Railway?'[175] Welsh students had a good deal more to point to than a leisurely railway system and could feel proud to belong to a national, federal university.

IX

University and Nation 1

To what extent may we reasonably speak of the University of
Wales as a national institution and to what extent did it depend
upon the resources and loyalty of the Welsh people? (Sir) Thomas
Parry, a Welsh scholar of distinction and a former Vice-
Chancellor of the University, believed that there was a deplorable
tendency to survey the last half of the nineteenth century in
Wales, and thus the founding of the University, through rose-
tinted spectacles. His articles in Welsh on the subject in 1964
were, it is true, somewhat polemical, for he was justifying his
inability to join forces with those who wished to preserve one
federal, national university. Nevertheless, his views command
attention. There were no grounds, he thought, for supposing that
the ordinary people had established the University. Only a
handful of far-sighted men were behind the movement, none of
them 'of dazzling inspiration'.[1] Wales had nurtured a flourishing
middle class and he portrays the Nonconformist minister as 'a
minor overlord who lived in a handsome house and who had his
own carriage to carry him, silk hatted, to the services'.[2] Material
success and religious conviction were closely allied in a pervasive
atmosphere of philistinism. The early impulses were all derived
from the middle classes who wished to place their sons on the
ladder of advancement, after exposure to 'fairly elementary
education',[3] at a university college where scarcely any attention
was given to the study of Welsh. The founders of the University
had a single purpose: it was to bring three colleges together into
one degree-awarding institution, and he quoted in support and
with relish the remarks of D. Emrys Evans, to which we shall
presently turn.[4] The founders, Parry proceeded, had certainly no
intention of creating a university 'which incorporated Welsh
aspirations and which stressed her separate identity'; it was not to
be 'a fortress for Welsh nationalism'. Had this been so, an
'enlightened nationalist',[5] such as Emrys ap Iwan, would have

taken pride in it. Instead, he was wholly silent on the subject, whereas he set great store by having a capital for Wales as a symbol of Welsh independence. The defederalization of the University, Parry concluded, would not be for Wales a disaster unsurpassed since 1282.[6]

It must at once be allowed that Thomas Parry made potent points. Education provided at Aberystwyth during its early days, as in other young institutions, was of an elementary character, inevitably so in the absence of intermediate education. One of the College's principal benefactors, David Davies, had not remotely supposed that it would offer anything else. In fact, it took several years to educate many well-wishers as to the true purpose of a university. The Liberal member for Cardiganshire, however, saw matters differently on the opening day of the College, or of the University, as he called it. The promoters of the movement had intended 'to establish here a centre of intellectual life', adding that 'we do not expect to grow into manhood all at once, nor can we build up a University in a day'.[7] Again, we must agree with Parry that the new university was not regarded as a 'fortress of Welsh nationalism',[8] particularly if this implied the need to protect its occupants from outside influences. It is true, too, that some were indifferent, like Emrys ap Iwan, or actively hostile, because the new university had failed to make provision for capable men impeded by poverty to prepare themselves for degrees at home as had long been possible under the London system.

Thomas Parry considered it strange that claims were made in 1964 that 'the University Movement is a movement of the people',[9] for he believed that the early impulses were all of middle-class origin. It is incontrovertible that during the third quarter of the nineteenth century appeals were constantly directed to the needs of the middle class in Wales. After Forster's Education Act of 1870 it seemed to Thomas Nicholas, one of the chief advocates of university education, that the working class had received adequate attention, but not so the 'better-conditioned and most gifted sons'[10] of the middle class. The philosophy of such 'educational technocrats' has been understandably stigmatized as 'repellent', for in the interests of a 'hard, calculating utilitarianism'[11] they were ready to sacrifice language, tradition and history. In this sense, Parry was right to denounce the philistinism of the age, although it must be added that little progress in the teaching of Welsh was likely in the Welsh colleges so long as they were tied to the London curriculum. In fairness to Nicholas he did not entirely dismiss the possibility of a professorship of Welsh but he had no intention of alarming his middle-class audience by diminishing the force of his message that the wide diffusion of English was the key to prosperity. Nicholas's notions were much in accord with those of Hugh Owen, the *primum mobile* of these transactions. The dominant tone of the Aberdare Report, to which Owen gave valuable, first-hand evidence, is decidedly middle-class.[12] When questioned concerning the usual social origins of students during Aberystwyth's first eight years, he replied 'middle class'. It was natural that Parry should examine the occupations of the parents of students as listed in an appendix to the report. They were, he said, as follows: 'Farmers, Clergymen, Merchants, Master Mariners, Managers of Works, Surgeons, Solicitors, Ship-brokers, Architects, and the Indian Civil Service. Every one of them from the middle class.'[13] In fact the report lists not ten occupations but forty-five, including labourers, five times as numerous as architects, or ship-brokers or Indian civil servants.[14] We may be certain, too, that the great majority of the seventy-four farmers (by far the largest group) were small farmers. It is also necessary to add that the class most favoured by Owen was generally less wealthy than its English counterpart, and that the Nonconformist minister portrayed by Parry, with his horse and carriage, was scarcely typical. Indeed, it has been persuasively argued that politicians and reformers were resolved to create a middle class in Wales to bridge the social gulf between high and low.[15] Nevertheless, even the Aberdare Report observed that most Aberystwyth students belonged to the 'humbler and less opulent classes' and that it was not uncommon for those who eventually arrived at the College to have acquired their slender means 'by the labour of their hands'.[16] By 1893 it had become increasingly common to refer to students of the Welsh Colleges as coming from the lower middle class and the working class. It may be said with some assurance that more than a fifth of the students who had attended the three Welsh Colleges before 1893 were firmly of the labouring class. The base was being constantly broadened so that it was proper to speak of the 'people's University'.[17]

Parry was undoubtedly right to stress that a fundamental purpose in seeking the charter in 1893 was deliverance from London University and to establish a degree-awarding body. He applauded as 'completely correct' the following words which he attributed to D. Emrys Evans: 'Certainly the champions of the University idea were less influenced by the desire to create a national sentiment than by their solicitude for the colleges.'[18] Evans's actual words were as follows:

> Certainly the champions of the university idea were less influenced by the desire to create *a national institution to satisfy a national sentiment* than by their solicitude for the colleges, which they wished to strengthen by breaking down their isolation and giving their teachers the greater scope and opportunity they would obtain when set free from dependence on the University of London. The petitioners expressly stated that their object was 'the development of the higher or university education given in these Colleges' by incorporating them in a degree-giving University.[19] [my italics]

In short they were concentrating upon the immediate business on hand. Evans, however, tended to draw a needless antithesis. It was natural that the petitioners should speak of 'the same need'[20] for independence by incorporating the College in a University of Wales as had been felt by colleges recently incorporated in the Victoria University. It was to be expected, too, that a formal petition would eschew the language of a manifesto. In any case the petitioners stated plainly that Welsh educationists 'had with one accord expressed a desire for the establishment of a University in and for Wales'.[21] What required to be said had been clearly said, and by able men. The notion of *creating* a national sentiment in 1893 would have surprised them. Convinced, however, that the founders of the University lacked a true sense of national consciousness, Parry appealed for a 'searching analysis' by a 'perceptive historian'[22] of the nature of Welsh society in the last half of the nineteenth century. In fact in the year preceding the publication of Parry's articles there had appeared K. O. Morgan's *Wales in British Politics, 1868–1922* (1963), an excellent study by a young historian who placed the university movement in its historical perspective. In the following year Morgan declared that '"the People's University", *Prifysgol y Werin*, is a product of nineteenth century democracy. It forms perhaps the most glorious monument to the national revival which revitalized Wales in the late Victorian era.'[23]

Limited though his concepts were of Welsh educational needs, and of a separate national identity, Thomas Nicholas had spoken of the injustices suffered by Wales in comparison with other parts of the British Isles. The Scottish universities, London University and the Queen's University had enjoyed the bounty of the state: 'Wales, alone, though contributing towards the outlay, remains unvisited by their generosity.'[24] Statistics were endlessly brandished to illustrate the measure of deprivation, most authoritatively perhaps in the Aberdare Report which devoted a section to consider Wales's 'distinct nationality'.[25] Members of Parliament who had pressed for the appointment of the Aberdare Committee constantly and eloquently canvassed the claims of Wales. Leaders of the movement echoed the words of Thomas Charles Edwards that Aberystwyth was 'Wales writ small'.[26] To Viriamu Jones, the University of Wales meant 'national self-realization on the intellectual side'; it was 'an organ of the national life' and the charter recognized by its democratic character that the University was 'a matter of concern to the community as a whole'.[27] T. F. Roberts detected in the University 'the reawakened principle of nationality'.[28] Thomas Ellis held that 'the best minds of the nation' looked upon Aberystwyth as the 'embodiment of national unity in education' and that the desire for unity, 'at first centred on Aberystwyth College alone, is now embodied in a University for Wales'.[29] At an International Eisteddfod at the World Fair in Chicago 5,000 Welshmen resolved to thank Gladstone and his government 'for acceding to the demand of the Welsh people for a National University'.[30]

It would, of course, be foolish to disregard Thomas Parry's warning against a sentimental view of the early years of the university movement. It had not been possible to include in the University the first degree-awarding institution in Wales, St David's College, Lampeter. Denominationalism remained a blight, a substantial proportion of the population did not darken a place of worship, and drunkenness, for example, was a disfiguring vice. Yet one cannot doubt that Welsh middle-class Nonconformity drew much of its inspiration from the lower ranks of society. Sharp observers, Englishmen as well as Welshmen, were profoundly impressed, and often moved, by the readiness of a significant portion of the nation, usually members of chapel communities, to make heavy sacrifices to further religious and educational causes. They were the *gwerin* of Wales, often portrayed at their upright best, but by any reasonable standard uncommon, common people, as they have been more than once described. In 1869, when many Welshmen assembled in London to celebrate the Liberal victory of 1868, there was also a meeting of supporters of the Welsh university movement. Its second secretary, David Charles, declared that the movement could not rely upon the aristocracy and the wealthy and that henceforth the poorer classes would be its 'great strength'. Once the matter was presented to them they would see the value of the institution and 'readily come forward with their mites'.[31] One of the merits of the Aberdare Report was to assemble evidence of the heroism of ordinary people. In addition to other burdens, chapel-building, establishing and maintaining theological colleges, churches and chapels made special congregational collections on the last Sunday in October in 1875, 1876 and 1877. It was called *Sul y Brifysgol* (University Sunday). Hugh Owen's careful analysis of various appeals was a revelation: 4,034 persons had given over 2*s.* 6*d.* each, 4,938 exactly 2*s.* 6*d.* each and at least 100,000 sums below that amount. The disastrous fire at Aberystwyth in 1885, dramatically recalled in penny readings, provided further testimony that calls for support from those in lowly circumstances were not in vain, as was further demonstrated when Cardiff and Bangor were founded.[32]

Such shining examples of self-help, in tune with the spirit of the age, did not pass unnoticed. There was also the remarkable capacity of ordinary people to organize their activities, religious and secular. In Sunday Schools, for adults as well as children, the 'opening' and expounding of the Scriptures were followed by close questioning concerning doctrine, criticism, the meaning and etymology of the words of the Welsh Bible. Abstruse theological points were aired and a taste acquired for abstract discussion often continued on weekdays. It was reliably reported that in the 1870s an English Professor of Theology and a Welsh preacher were taking their ease in a very Welsh county when they heard two labourers arguing vigorously. The preacher assured his companion that, far from quarrelling, they were debating whether Christ had two wills or one (the Monothelite controversy, as it is known). He proceeded to translate the conversation, the professor at length declaring that the opposing arguments were 'as subtle and absurd as any of those to be found in the old books'.[33] Others had similar experiences, apparently well-authenticated. It was common to hold reading meetings, singing meetings, literary and debating societies and eisteddfodau and for members under their natural leaders to form themselves into committees, to elect officers, move resolutions and amendments, using their own language, and to 'handle the terms of public business with the familiarity of old parliamentary hands'. When Henry Jones returned for a visit to Wales from Scotland, he spoke with admiration of the manner in which 'a crowd of rustics' at a local eisteddfod listened intently to the recital of a number of *englynion* (the most ancient recorded Welsh metrical form). They had, he said, 'shown themselves *worthy* of higher education'.[34] He might have added that they were the inheritors of an ancient oral poetic tradition. In 1919 a brief account was given of the social life of Cardiganshire labourers. The older men were very attached to the chapel, especially the Sunday School where most of the teachers were farm labourers who prepared themselves thoroughly for their classes and where 'book-shelves are well stocked with theological works, and especially with Bible commentaries'. One labourer, given a heifer after seven years' service, sold it in the market and bought books with all the proceeds; a shepherd, winner of several bardic chairs, had a good library and was 'well versed in the current literature and monthly periodicals published in the Welsh language'; another shepherd was a conductor of choirs; a crofter, who specialized in folklore and history, had undertaken research work at the National Library.[35] Two festivals were especially popular: the *cymanfa ganu* (singing festival) and *cymanfa bwnc*, held to catechize the Sunday School on a specified part of Scripture. Both festivals, extending for the whole day, were attended by men and women servants, given a holiday for the purpose.

The way of life outlined here was largely, if not entirely, the creation of Welsh Nonconformity which, Viriamu Jones insisted, had given his countrymen a veneration for education. Though in danger of losing its vigour after the First World War, it had persisted side by side with the University and in many ways independently of it. Nevertheless, it was from within this tradition that the university movement had sprung, as also several of its middle-class leaders wholly convinced from their own experience, like Henry Jones, that the *gwerin* of Wales had earned a full entitlement to the benefits of higher education.

The question naturally arises as to the treatment of women within the University of Wales. Part of the resentment against the Blue Books of 1847 sprang from the odious comments upon Welsh women. The widespread conviction that they had been traduced had two consequences. First, there was a tendency to idealize the 'angel in the house'. Second, there was a firm resolve to repair the educational injustice of the past. Welsh women such as Dilys Glynne Jones and E. P. Hughes were in touch with leaders of opinion in England and amongst their activities was the founding of the North Wales Scholarship Association which would, amongst other aims, provide scholarships to enable a few, at least, to attend endowed schools for girls, at Denbigh or Dolgellau. Although there was but one woman on the body which fashioned the charter of 1893, there was total agreement that women should be granted complete equality.[36] This was the one clause that was never questioned or amended. There were to be no restrictions of any kind and membership of every authority within the University was to be open to women as to men. There were no half-measures and *The Times* ventured to say that 'in this important respect the new University was in advance of every British University'.[37] These unequivocal affirmations were held to be sacrosanct.

Quite apart from issues of principle, women were needed as teachers, especially after the passing of the Intermediate Act of 1889. The government was ready to assist both sexes with grants, so much so that W. H. G. Armytage remarked that the civic universities in their struggling years and the university colleges all along, owed the very existence of their arts faculties and in many cases their pure science faculties to the presence of a large body of intending teachers whose attendance at degree courses was almost guaranteed by the state.[38]

In addition to financial considerations, satisfaction was derived from the fact that women students at first were usually of a superior social status.

It was to be expected that in wartime women should have a larger share in the running of affairs, but only in one college was a woman elected president of the Students' Representative Council, indeed, the only instance throughout our period.[39] After the war there was a backlash against even modest advances. Women, it appeared, had arrogated too much to themselves. According to one Bangor ex-serviceman, a future president of SRC, speaking of the 1918–20 sessions, 'I really do not think that some of the women students . . . were ever able to grasp what had happened to the quiet, cloistered college they knew.'[40] At Aberystwyth, where joint consultation between Senate and the SRC was conceded in 1919, women students were specifically excluded from drawing up rules which affected returning servicemen. Women were separate but not equal. A woman student recalled that in the 1930s when she was waiting to be examined in practical physics in the laboratory at Bangor the external examiner brusquely passed her by as one who had no business to be studying the subject.[41] Following the exodus of ex-servicemen, women in the Welsh Colleges reached 40 per cent in 1924, exceeding the proportion in Scotland (34 per cent) and in England (29 per cent). In 1933, at the depth of the depression, there was a decline in Wales to 28 per cent and a further descent to 27 per cent in 1938. Aberystwyth still headed the list at 31 per cent, whereas Bangor was as low as 23 per cent and Swansea a mere 17 per cent.[42]

There were few women professors in the University between 1893 and 1939: three successively in the women's education department at Cardiff; two at Swansea (one of them in the teeth of opposition), one at Aberystwyth and none at Bangor. According to one analysis, the proportion of women on the staff of British universities, with the exception of Oxford and Cambridge, was 10.7 per cent in 1931; in London colleges 11.7 per cent, in Scotland 7.2 per cent, in Wales 12 per cent, in the older civic universities 10.2 per cent, in the younger civic colleges 19.4 per cent.[43] Here and there one detects unpleasant undercurrents. At Swansea women were not permitted to be members of the senior common room until after 1945. Gwyn Jones, at Cardiff in the 1930s, recalled that not everyone favoured a mixed common room. 'We men had a splendid one; women staff had one less splendid', adding that 'when the experiment of a small one for both sexes was tried in a reasonably inaccessible corner no man to the best of my knowledge ever set foot in it'.[44] The situation at Liverpool was not dissimilar. In the 1930s Mary Stocks found that women 'could not even lunch with their academic colleagues'[45] except as occasional guests.

The principle of equality may be further tested by examining the composition of two University bodies, the Court and Council (after its creation in 1920). In 1916 E. H. Griffiths, in evidence to the Haldane Commission, ventured to say that there was 'a very considerable representation of women on the University Court'. He had not counted how many there were, 'but I should say from roughly looking around the room quite one-third of those present at a Court meeting are women'.[46] It is difficult to account for this absurd remark on a responsible occasion by a Vice-Chancellor who must have known that only eight women were members of a Court of 101 members and that although their attendance before 1914 was superior to that of men, the eight could not always simultaneously divest themselves of other duties. The proportion of women on the Court remained at the end of our period what it had been at the beginning, namely 8 per cent. As to the University Council of nineteen members, there was but one woman member, Mary F. Rathbone, from 1922 to 1937, appointed by the Lord President of the Council in order to redress, however slightly, an otherwise wholly male dominance. From 1937 there was not even a whiff of 'tokenism' until the wartime appointment of Megan Lloyd George.[47] On College Courts and Councils the situation was perceptibly better.

The record was not impressive. The Haldane Report spoke out on the issue. The 'absolute equality of the sexes in the University has always been a fundamental principle of the Charter', and it expressed disappointment that the promoters of the movement for the admission of Swansea as a constituent college had 'shown in the construction of their plans so little regard for the needs of women'. It added that 'if the new University College is worthily to discharge its responsibilities to the great and growing community of which it is the centre, it must spare no pains to remove this defect in a scheme which is otherwise so hopeful'.[48] Further, it was disappointing that it had not been found practicable to give greater effect to the principle of equality in appointing teaching staff, especially since women formed so high a proportion of the student body in Wales. One witness representing the Welsh County Schools Association thought it incredible 'that it is not possible to get one or two women of high academic standing for each University College'. The report, however, felt that the 'operation of time'[49] was a better solution than the passing of regulations suggesting special protection. There was to be nothing approaching 'affirmative action', as Americans say.

Traditional attitudes long persisted. When the question of having a new officer at the University Appointments Board was being discussed Cardiff specifically stated that a man should be appointed. Women were not at first invited to adult education classes at Blaenau Ffestiniog. According to Robert Richards, 'unfortunately, there was rather a prejudice against having women in', but 'gradually the prejudice broke down, and we had women in the class in later years'.[50] The failure to elect women as presidents of the SRC was less a deliberate slight than a blissful acceptance of the preordained role of man. The sharp decline in the number of women students during the 1930s may in part be attributed to the reduced grants for teachers in training, increased competition for posts and the readiness of local authorities to terminate appointments upon marriage. There were other factors. To take Bangor as an example, the fees in the women's hall of residence (where undergraduate women were obliged to live, unless they were day students) ranged from £51 to £61 per session and for men at Plas Menai (decidedly inferior, it must be allowed) a standard £43. State grants to prospective teachers in hostel were £43 for men and £34 for women, a revealing example of discrimination. Finally, parents who could not afford to educate both sons and daughters of promise in bad times often accorded preference to sons. As was laconically noted in 1933, 'girls are expected to stand aside in order to allow their brothers to proceed to further education'.[51]

Even those who championed the cause of women did not always express themselves felicitously. Elizabeth P. Hughes in 1917 spoke of 'the great want of discipline throughout the country, a want more acute where women were concerned even than in the case of men'. Mary F. Rathbone deplored the 'distraction of weaker women students, especially Welsh girls from the country, by any notice on the part of the men'. M. O. Davis, the Bangor warden, hoped that her charges would not sink 'into that squalor and apathy which so easily besets literary and scholastic females'.[52] The 'new woman' in turn was chastised for being deliberately unfeminine. When a new hall was opened at Cardiff in 1897, the 'lady-correspondent' of the *Western Mail*[53] drew attention to the severe coats and collars and to the austere felt hats, sure signs, we are to suppose, of the importance of being earnest. Olive Wheeler did nothing to placate male chauvinists in 1925 by announcing that women were more intelligent than men.[54] These outpourings, however, need not detain us. Staff and governors of the Welsh colleges were mostly in favour of extending the franchise to women. True, T. J. Wheldon, a member of Bangor's College Council, gave a severe pastoral warning to his Bangor flock that they were not on any account to involve themselves in the suffrage campaign. Nor can it be denied that men students who were Liberals tended to take their cue from Lloyd George, who, like Asquith, was not on the side of the angels. Nevertheless, the stand taken by William Rathbone, the College's second President and father of Eleanor, the most influential of British feminists, in favour of votes for women strengthened the resolve of several members of staff and their wives to support and indeed to confer respectability upon the National Union of Women's Suffrage Societies in the locality. A former student in the College's Day Training Department (1896–8), Charlotte Bell (later Price White) became secretary of the Bangor branch of the NUWSS and saw to it that suffrage literature was translated into Welsh and distributed throughout Wales. In south Wales Eirene Lloyd Jones, a former Aberystwyth student and Thomas Jones's wife, was secretary of the Barry branch before 1914. At Cardiff College's settlement at East Moors the equality of the sexes was honoured in word and deed. Two sisters, Lilian and Mabel Howell, nieces of the founder of Howells department store in the city, were prominent in the area. The former was a leading light in the settlement. The latter, for long a member of the College Council, was one of Thomas Jones's valued correspondents upon college affairs.[55]

The older universities were remarkably reactionary. Women were allowed to graduate at Oxford in 1920, but not at Cambridge where they faced opposition, from subtle innuendo to stentorian ribaldry. In 1939 Sir Charles Grant Robertson, like Reichel a fellow of All Souls and indeed his executor, wrote that women graduates were 'as plentiful as tabby cats, in point of fact too many'.[56] That he was repeating a quip concerning bishops in *The Gondoliers* scarcely exempts him from the charge of mockery. Others were rooted in an ancient monkish tradition sometimes bordering on misogyny. When it was decided at Oxford's Sheldonian in 1927 to limit the number of women students by statute (to 840), it was a sad day for Margery Fry, Principal of Somerville, fervently supported by H. A. L. Fisher and Gilbert Murray but not by Stuart Jones, one of her chief opponents and *en route* to the principalship at Aberystwyth, where the proportion of women was then 46 per cent. It is scant wonder that the *South Wales Daily News* found the situation rather piquant, but Stuart Jones does not appear to have repeated his Sheldonian performance at Aberystwyth.[57]

The opening of the women's hall at Bangor in 1897 was regarded as 'a new sign of the life and growth of the Welsh educational system'. The older universities had had 'to face in one form or another, the sex problem', whereas 'it was the distinguished glory of the University of Wales that from the first she determined that men and women should be alike, human, within her borders'.[58] Needless to say, this was a gilded version of reality. College authorities knew that many, as in the older universities, were ready to pounce gleefully at the slightest sign of scandal. The *cause célèbre* at Bangor in 1892–3 had demonstrated that comparatively minor matters could swell to ungovernable proportions. The result was to resort to pernickety, stifling regulations, roundly condemned by students within the Colleges themselves and beyond. Those at Aberdeen berated the authorities in Wales for their 'grandmotherly legislation', whilst a Welshman from Warwick who had sent six children, in all, to English, Welsh and Scottish universities wrote to the *Manchester Guardian* to say that matters were better ordered in Scotland, where students led a 'thoroughly happy and healthy life, free from all espionage and suspicion' and whose chaperones did 'just sufficient to satisfy Mrs Grundy'.[59]

Most students in the Welsh colleges supported women's suffrage and found attitudes at Oxbridge hard to comprehend. In 1904 a former Aberystwyth student, then at Cambridge, wrote back to his old college to say that 'the first thing that struck me was the very subdued, and, I might say, humbled air, with which ladies came to classes. They seemed to feel that they were there on sufferance, and that I regret to say a very unwilling sufferance.'[60] Professors were refusing point blank to recognize that there were any women students at all in the University. Such marked hostility, he considered, was a matter for anthropologists and psychologists. In fact, women at Cambridge were not granted full membership until 1948. In 1920 a former Aberystwyth student at Oxford heard vague rumours that women he had known at college were 'immured in some of the women's colleges, but the maternal discipline of this place has so far prevented us from finding out exact particulars'. In the 1930s Mervyn Jones contrasted the 'complete equality of the sexes for all academic and social purposes' at Aberystwyth with the monastic atmosphere of Cambridge which he found 'far less moral'.[61] When C. A. Edwards discovered that women were not welcome in the common room at Swansea, he at once refused to enter it himself.[62] In presenting Kate Hurlbatt, warden of Aberdare Hall, for an honorary degree in 1933, J. F. Rees said that she had lived through the transition from blue stockings to bare legs.[63] It was from the mixed universities, Gilbert Murray told Aberystwyth students in 1908, that he expected 'the greatest real advance towards some reasonable solution of the difficulties that now lie between the sexes'.[64] If progress in the colleges of the University of Wales sometimes seemed fitful, even paltry, it was never easy to take giant steps ahead of public opinion. In a broad sense we may justly say that the University of Wales opened windows which faced the light.

Welsh students were from the outset encouraged to look beyond the confines of their own country. Thomas Charles Edwards said that they should associate fully with English and Scots for 'this will make them gentlemen in the best meaning of the word'.[65] Reichel pressed Welsh students at Oxford to emulate the Scots, of whom he had seen a number at Balliol. They should cease to be a 'peculiar people', who formed enclaves. Indeed similar criticism was heard of Welsh medical students at Edinburgh. The Scot, Reichel proceeded, threw himself confidently into English life, whereas the Welshman seldom took 'the decisive plunge'. Speaking within three years of his appointment at Bangor, he attributed such defects to inadequate education at secondary level (soon to be repaired by the Intermediate Act of 1889) and to an imperfect grasp of the English language. Until Welshmen mastered the imperial tongue they could not serve 'the finest, most widely expanded, and most beneficent Empire in the world'.[66] The answer, he maintained, lay not in the renunciation of Welsh but in bilingualism which had several merits beyond a monoglot's ken.

Religious oppression and economic privation had prompted Welshmen from the early seventeenth century onwards to seek a new life beyond the seas, but they had little sense of imperial destiny. Indeed, when Sir George Baden-Powell had in 1892 ventured to speak on 'Welshmen and the British Empire' to a Liverpool audience he was hard put to it to say anything of consequence.[67] Times, however, were changing. In 1887, at a decisive stage in the history of the university movement, Viriamu Jones was urging Wales to set aside all narrowness of spirit and act in close alliance 'with all portions of the great empire of which she may well be thankful and proud that Providence has willed she should form a part'.[68] Reichel was certain that Wales should influence England, as Scotland and even 'backward' Ireland had done. England, justly renowned for concepts of toleration and fair play, had grievous faults, and he did not think it amiss, as late as 1921, to inform Manchester Welshmen that 'there is probably no white race that has so little respect for the intellectual side of

life'.[69] Earlier he had said that each 'province' of Britain had its
own mental and moral contribution to make to the 'national
universities' of Oxford and Cambridge, and Englishmen were
further encouraged to believe that the Welsh had distinctive gifts
which would enrich the Empire.[70]

Supposed 'racial' characteristics had long been listed by
Giraldus Cambrensis, whilst the views of Matthew Arnold had
been repeated with variants by Thomas Ellis and O. M. Edwards.
Reichel who regarded himself as 'North Irish by birth and
breeding' – he was writing in 1921 – 'but Welsh by life-work and
adoption', sailed confidently into these perilous waters. The
English by their sense of justice held the Empire together; the
Scots, 'rather severely logical', were an indispensable ingredient;
whilst the Welsh were generously endowed with 'imaginative
intuition'. Thus was formed 'the national amalgam'. The
Welshman also had a 'caution and sanity which nature or history
has denied to his brilliant but wayward and irresponsible Irish
kinsman'. He applauded the judgement of Ernest Renan, of
Breton parentage, who had often visited Wales and who spoke of
the Welshman as 'the Teuton of the Celts'.[71] Appealing for funds
for his College, he asked the rich men of London at the Mansion
House not to neglect Wales, one of the 'seed plots where the men
of Empire are grown'.[72] Was Lloyd George, who had spoken of
Wales's secondary school system as 'the wonder of the Empire',
he enquired of the Mold Cosmopolitan Society, 'less a patriotic
Welshman because he has become an Imperial statesman?'[73]

To Alfred Zimmern, who spent a brief period at Aberystwyth
and who later boldly challenged Lloyd George in the 1924
election in the Labour interest, 'the tree of Empire had many
roots and Wales was one of the oldest and toughest'.[74] Elizabeth
P. Hughes deplored Welsh isolationism. The British Empire, she
said in 1904, was now cosmopolitan and her countrymen, long
dominated by a stronger race, had developed gifts of adaptability
and of understanding: 'We ought to find it easier than the English
to get in touch with other races and with those of different
conditions to our own.'[75] The Celtic peoples, so ready to respond
to national patriotism, should respond also to imperial patriotism
for it was probable that the white man would rule the tropics for
centuries. Such considerations were much in the mind of Reichel

when at the Imperial Conference at Toronto in 1921 he urged the teaching of the British Empire. He had doubtless frequently discussed the question with his colleague, J. E. Lloyd, who, as far back as 1897, had said that national history (upon which he was deeply engaged) 'should be a preliminary to that study of the Empire which is needed to make us realize our responsibilities as heirs of a vast inheritance'.[76] Reichel did not hold out much hope for a League of Nations. Speaking ten years before the creation of the Commonwealth of Nations, he believed that the British Empire, as a member of a permanent group of great powers, had a vital role. It was a confederation of peoples and a thorough knowledge of their history was a 'paramount' unifying force. At Aberystwyth, he proceeded, a fine example had been set by Major David Davies, as he then was, in endowing a lectureship in colonial history. It was the university which ultimately determined the character of a nation's education, for it was there that 'the élite . . . acquire their intellectual equipment and ideals'.[77] Davies himself told T. F. Roberts in 1906 that he wanted Empire Day (24 May) to be celebrated at Aberystwyth in a fitting manner. Students should have a holiday and in the evening listen to a distinguished colonial governor. In the colonial colleges 'the occasion is not allowed to pass without some sort of recognition'.[78] In wartime, a member of the Aberystwyth Council and chairman of the Royal Colonial Institute, Sir C. P. Lucas, hoped that universities would present, particularly to the working classes, a more accurate view of the Empire than might be derived from 'highly coloured popular lectures'.[79] Even in the official *Report on the Position of Welsh in Education and Life* (1927), it was firmly stated that loyalty to Wales did not imply lack of sympathy or of co-operation with the United Kingdom and the Empire 'in which Wales has a vital share'.[80]

Thus it was that Welsh students and their mentors were encouraged to contribute to the Greater Britain beyond the seas. The frenzied jubilation following the relief of Mafeking constrained Rendel to protest against jingoistic intemperance at Aberystwyth.[81] Few could be wholly impervious to the determined imperialism of Ellis Griffith, Brynmor Jones and Beriah Gwynfe Evans. Yet students were seldom deeply touched by the spirit of jingoism. In his reply to Rendel in 1900 concerning the Mafeking celebrations, T. F. Roberts said that Welsh students 'detest beyond everything the grasping materialistic temper of some of the gunfire-mongering of the day. Their interest in the British Empire is as different from this, and also from militarism, as the east is from the west.' He added that 'the Empire is to them an ideal – and as such is exercising a wonderful fascination – which means broader standards, vaster brotherhood, purer democracy'.[82] One suspects that T. F. Roberts, the most honest of men, was being carried aloft by his own eloquence. In any case the fascination did not last long. Missionary and educational activity apart, not many Welsh Nonconformists responded eagerly to the challenge of imperial service under palm and pine. For Reichel, as we might imagine, the glow of idealism remained, to soften the darkness of his declining days. By then, however, Lloyd George's wartime rhetoric seemed increasingly threadbare and his advisers in Wales would more readily have applauded his speech to the Cymmrodorion of Cardiff in 1906. His theme then was that small nations remain and that proud empires fade away. Caernarfon was the Bulawayo of Rome, the outwork of the greatest empire the world had ever seen. The walls were still there and small children at a nearby school learnt the language of the dead empire: 'But they play and talk and laugh in the language of the conquered savages.' He added, in a sadly prophetic vein, that 'the time will come when the last truckload of coal will reach the wharves of Cardiff';[83] the riches of the language and literature of Wales, however, were inexhaustible.

Close involvement in the British Parliament was an entirely different matter. Welsh members had played a crucial role, particularly between 1868 and 1893, in bringing the educational needs of Wales to the attention of the House of Commons. Thereafter their record had been less impressive in university matters. Student representatives appearing before the Haldane Commission had firmly spoken in favour of a representative for the University, but the report did not pursue the matter. Nevertheless, there was a strong feeling in some quarters, though by no means all, that the University of Wales should have its own Member of Parliament under the Representation of the People

Act (1918) which allowed a second vote to be cast in a university constituency. As initially proposed, Wales would be linked with seven other universities and Herbert Lewis cogently argued that it would thus be impossible to secure the services of a parliamentary representative who could speak with authority not only on university matters but on broad educational questions relating to Wales. He further asked Lloyd George to bear in mind that the contribution of Wales to the armed forces had in proportion exceeded those of her partners in the United Kingdom and that therefore she should not be 'meanly treated'.[84] Sir Herbert Roberts (West Denbigh) in one of his rare remarks in the Commons noted that the University of Wales stood on a different footing from all other universities in the kingdom: 'It represents the whole of Wales.'[85] Nevertheless, when David Davies moved in November 1917 that the University be given independent representation, especially since the Scottish universities had three members, he had but twelve supporters. Salvation came from an unexpected quarter, the government accepting in the Lords the motion of Lord St David's that the University of Wales be granted a member.[86]

The search for a suitable candidate proceeded apace. Many appealed to Lloyd George to accept nomination, but having no wish to leave his constituency he recommended Herbert Lewis, widely canvassed in university circles. H. J. Fleure unsuccessfully tried to persuade Millicent Mackenzie, the Labour candidate and a former Professor of Education at Cardiff, to withdraw in Lewis's favour. O. T. Jones, also of Aberystwyth, managed to convince the Revd Joseph Jones, a Liberal, not to stand. At Bangor Ifor Williams had cycled for days seeking signatories for Lewis, but it was hard work, he said, because the feeling against the coalition government was very bitter, ministers of religion being particularly hostile.[87] Lewis won a decisive victory in 1918 and was succeeded by another National Liberal, T. A. Lewis, in 1922. Conscientious objectors, scandalously deprived of a vote for five years after the war, doubtless helped to give a tenuous majority in 1923 to a Christian Pacifist, George M. Ll. Davies, who for his beliefs had suffered harshness and ignominy with a nobility which should have shamed his tormentors. His two successors, Ernest Evans and W. J. Gruffydd, were both Liberals.

From 1918 until the disappearance of the seat in 1950 there had thus not been a single Conservative member, contrary to the bold prophecy of Lord St David's in the Lords in 1918. University members generally were deemed by A. J. P. Taylor to be reactionary.[88] The University of Wales was more fortunate. It is, none the less, ironical that a university which took pride in its democratic origins and constitution should at the election of 1918 have a constituency of only 1,066 and that in 1922 the member returned received less than 500 votes. W. Llywelyn Williams, though not enamoured of university representation, told the Commons in 1917 that had Glyn Dŵr succeeded in founding his two universities there would have been a constituency of 10,000, a flight of fancy which cannot have carried much weight.[89] In the 1918 election Flint alone had a constituency of 46,528. Eleven years later Labour members were agitating for the abolition of university representation.[90] The second vote, an unjustifiable anachronism, was swept away in 1948.

The University was from its inception empowered to confer honorary degrees. On the first occasion, in 1896, it had acted with remarkable restraint. Not a single Welshman was honoured, though it was scarcely fitting to have passed by Thomas Charles Edwards, Aberystwyth's first Principal, who had left office five years earlier. Without him the College might not have reached its twentieth birthday. As might be expected, the annual list was received with mixed reactions, a sniff of approval here and an irate remonstrance there. In May 1906 attention was drawn to the degree of magister conferred upon Elvet Lewis (Elfed) for 'very moderate services to his native land' – he later received two doctorates from the University – whereas O. M. Edwards had been 'contemptuously ignored'.[91] Like T. C. Edwards, 'O.M.' was honoured two years before his death. He was then only sixty, but it frequently happened that degrees were conferred upon the feeble and the ancient of days whose merits were seldom greater than they had been a decade or two earlier. The question of good judgement was often raised. Was it seemly that T. C. Edwards received a majority of but two or three votes in the Distinctions Committee whereas Joseph Chamberlain was unanimously supported? In 1928 D. Lleufer Thomas complained that not a single doctorate in arts or science was conferred.[92] The Guild of Graduates did not fear controversy. Henry Lewis, as warden, contended that the degree of magister should be given on academic grounds alone and the degree of doctor solely for pre-eminence in learning and scholarship. William George thought that the operations of the Distinctions Committee were too narrow and that the Committee 'was not conversant with a great class of people who were doing important work and who deserved to be recognised by the University'.[93] In his opinion the recommendations of the Guild would only intensify dissatisfaction. According to a Newport alderman not one of Christ's disciples would have been entitled to a doctorate in divinity if subjected to the opinions of the Guild. J. F. Rees averred that 'it would be better if we were all treated with the plain mister',[94] doubtless in good conscience until he was knighted in 1951. Thus it was that arguments ebbed and flowed. The abiding impression is that well-intentioned, if not always well-informed, men did their best to act justly. At least no one could question Stanley Baldwin's words in acknowledgment of the degree conferred upon him in 1938: 'You are the only University that can offer an honour from a nation.'[95]

The maintenance of proper academic standards is, of course, fundamentally important to any university worthy of the name. It must be at once allowed that they were inevitably low at entry before the Welsh Intermediate Act (1889) began to bear fruit. After entry the failure rate was high and remained so for many years. Care was taken to recruit the best scholars as external examiners, a policy involving a heavy charge upon the University's exiguous resources. It is a striking fact that the external examiner in physics during the first decade of the century received £90 for his services and an assistant lecturer an annual salary of but £120. From the outset external examiners reported that they were well satisfied with standards reached and with the evenness of standards among the Colleges, said by the Vice-Chancellor in 1930 to be as high as those of other British universities.[96] Periods of high graduate unemployment prompted gloomy fits of introspection as to the comparative value of the Welsh degree and it was reassuring to hear Sir Charles Grant Robertson, chairman of the Committee of Vice-Chancellors, declare in 1934 that 'there is little or no difference between the standard of a first-class degree of any university'.[97]

The divisive effects of denominationalism aroused suspicions that justice was not always done. Old animosities between Anglicans and Nonconformists still simmered, and sometimes seethed, below the surface. During the mid–1920s the University had not handled as sensitively as it might the question of admitting graduates of St David's College to the higher degree of the University. The Principal complained that the proper procedure had not been followed, but it was evident that the University under charter, and in accord with a resolution of 1924, could not accede to Lampeter's request. Its Principal, however, pursued the matter relentlessly, protesting 'most earnestly against the treatment which it is proposed to mete out to this College by the University of its own country'. Oxford and Cambridge, on the other hand, had always given it every encouragement and it would be 'a deplorable tragedy' if the University of Wales did not recognize the College's century of service to higher education in Wales. We gather that at the Academic Board 'he allowed himself to threaten the University with the displeasure and even boycott of the Church',[98] a remark which angered many, including some churchmen. Sibly, however, handled the matter delicately. Disestablishment and disendowment naturally angered devout churchmen and the knowledge that tithe money was to be mainly used to meet the needs of students, many of them indigent, failed to mollify those who commented rather sourly that the inherited wealth of a despoliated church was being employed to buy billiard tables, seen by some as a seductive distraction from life's larger purpose. Difficult situations were sometimes solved by a skilful sleight of hand. When W. D. Caröe contemplated placing a statue of St David in the central niche at the east end of the Drapers' Library at the Cardiff College, some interpreted the proposal as expressing approval of the established Church. The patron saint was allowed to appear only after a cantankerous debate in the College and upon condition that he did not wear a mitre. Since tall mitres were not common until the late Middle Ages, Caröe gave him a low hat as seen in the earliest representation of mitres. Nonconformists were never heard to object, remaining either in gracious or in ignorant silence.[99]

Appointments were sometimes the occasion of sharp protests. It is difficult to pronounce upon such matters, for in the nature of things one can usually see but through a glass darkly. Yet it would be unduly timid to evade a subject which sometimes aroused fierce controversy affecting the standing of the University and its Colleges. A distinction must clearly be drawn between decisions which caused disagreement and those which involved the undue exercise of influence. The former not infrequently generated bad feeling, fuelled in private by disappointed candidates and their friends and in public by a hostile press alert to each hint of discord. The decision not to appoint W. J. Gruffydd to a lectureship in English at Bangor in 1903 provoked an unjustifiable outcry and in private the fast-flowing rhetoric of T. Gwynn Jones. In this instance the necessary evidence is available and it is difficult to question the College's decision.[100] It is, of course, understandable that when Colleges were largely staffed by Scots, English and a sprinkling of Irish it was bracing to be able to welcome a Welshman. In 1915 Aberystwyth's Registrar was informed that at Cardiff only 21 per cent of chairs were held by his countrymen and that it was 'practically impossible'[101] for a Welshman to get a chair. Cardiff's second and third Principals, however, believed that the College Council's system of appointment worked admirably.[102]

It has recently been stated that it was Reichel's aim to pattern Bangor upon the provincial English colleges. This is not so, for although he was envious of endowments enjoyed by many civic universities he knew that the rural colleges of Wales differed in character and aims. If he were ever drawn to emulation, he would have wished Bangor to become 'a little Balliol'. It has further been said that it was his policy not to appoint a Welshman 'as a matter of principle'.[103] This is a baseless calumny which cannot be allowed to stand. He unequivocally believed that only the best-qualified should be chosen and that if that person were Welsh, so much the better. A Bangor committee's choice of an artist to paint Lord Kenyon's portrait fell upon Allan Gwynne Jones, 'not because he was Welsh, but because he was in their judgement the best man available. But they were gratified that their unbiased choice had fallen upon a young Welshman.'[104] In 1925 the College formally stated that it was a great advantage if the holder of a post in the College had a command of Welsh for it would help him to a sympathetic understanding of students. Nevertheless, academic considerations were paramount for academic posts.[105] At Cardiff in 1915, at the laying of the foundation stone of the Welsh National School of Medicine, Lord Pontypridd said that the nationality of candidates for positions on the professorial staff 'did not count'.[106] It was their efficiency that mattered. In this spirit men of brilliance had been appointed to the chair of anatomy, first a Welshman, Alfred W. Hughes, followed by A. E. Dixon, an Irishman, and then by David Hepburn, a Scot. As we shall see, the rigorous pursuance of this policy was sometimes questioned.[107] The prevailing atmosphere at Aberystwyth was considered by many to be more Welsh than at the other Colleges, though at all times the proportion of Welsh-speaking students at Bangor seems to have been higher. A. C. Humphreys-Owen, a doughty defender of Aberystwyth, once remarked rather savagely that Cardiff was a washpot of peoples (*colluvies gentium*), that Bangor was Tory-ridden, whilst its nationality was the 'note' of Aberystwyth, 'really and truly the Welsh college'.[108]

The extent of local influence in the making of appointments is not easy to determine. Percy Watkins knew for certain that it was no small factor when he was a candidate for the post of Registrar at Cardiff in 1911. Since he appeared to be indifferent to 'the usual way in South Wales', he received 'frantic letters' from friends urging him to spend a week 'showing himself' to members of the College Council. He capitulated to the extent of spending two rather wretched days visiting Council members to explain his 'strong inhibition'[109] against asking for support. Although he had not quite played the game as expected, he was nevertheless appointed. His fate might have been otherwise had he applied for a post in the teaching profession, where canvassing was often a *sine qua non*. The correspondence of the period leads inexorably to the conclusion that local influence helped J. H. Davies in 1919 in his contest with Thomas Jones for the Aberystwyth principalship. On the other hand, it was possible to argue on perfectly conscientious grounds that J. H. Davies would cause less disturbance than Thomas Jones to the established order. The distasteful aspect was the readiness to rake up unworthy, petty matters to defeat Jones. In late 1922 A. T. Davies (at Whitehall) wrote that local influence had led to a very unfortunate appointment to the first of the newly established chairs at the Medical School, 'in the teeth of the available expert opinion',[110] a view confirmed by the severe condemnation, separately and privately communicated, of three eminent surgeons. In May 1922 A. H. Kidd, secretary to the Haldane Commission and well-disposed to the University, spoke of local and unacademic considerations which had 'too frequently'[111] determined appointments in the Welsh Colleges. At the time he was in correspondence concerning the proposed Wilson chair at Aberystwyth, but doubtless he had in mind the rejection of Thomas Jones which had dismayed leading men in government, in the civil service and in academic life. This episode had done untold harm.

Although denominationalism was losing much of its splenetic force by 1893, sectarian allegiance was not to be disregarded, as Reichel early discovered when a successor to Henry Jones was being sought at Bangor. The claims of E. Keri Evans were zealously canvassed by W. J. Parry, 'the quarrymen's champion', in opposition to those of a superior candidate, J. S. Mackenzie, recommended by the selection committee. 'If a Welshman is not elected this time', Parry told a fellow Congregationalist, 'the feeling will get stronger than it is against Bangor.' More significant for our present purpose was his remark to the candidate himself, another Congregationalist: 'One has to be careful to keep from view the sectarian aspect of the question.' In Council, Keri Evans was elected with a handsome majority and Parry was soon writing to Thomas Gee to thank him for his strong recommendation on behalf of Evans in his newspaper, the *Baner*, which appeared the same day as the Council meeting. 'It was a crushing defeat for the Principal',[112] he observed. At about the same time a Scot at Aberystwyth, J. W. Marshall, was assiduously promoting his own interests as a candidate for the chair of Greek at Cardiff. He informed his confidant, J. E. Lloyd, of plans to canvass members of the Cardiff Council. His most spectacular proposal was 'to get at' the Marquis of Bute through a Roman Catholic priest at Kilmarnock who knew Marshall's father and who had 'a sort of spiritual oversight over the Marquis's Scotch

Estates'. Hitherto he had hesitated for fear of offending Protestant consciences, but 'it is not likely to be known how I got at him: and it would be natural enough to have the countenance of a Scotch peer'.[113] J. E. Lloyd evidently did not restrain his well-wishers from actively intervening on his behalf when he was an applicant for the Cardiff principalship in 1901. The secretary of the East Glamorgan Association of English Congregational churches promised to employ his influence 'to the last ounce'.[114] The campaign manager was Ainsworth Davies, an Aberystwyth professor and a relative through marriage. In October he told Lloyd that the Aberystwyth Registrar was writing on his behalf to four members of the Cardiff Council, 'mostly Calvinistic Methodist ministers', all with votes, adding for good measure that 'I am seriously tackling the Baptists upon whom I hope to make an impression'.[115] Earlier, Davies had advised Lloyd to keep his preaching engagements 'in the dim background. I fear they may tell against you in the ungodly south. I will look up the Cardiff Calendar and see about influence: you are no doubt looking well after this chief essential.'[116] In a highly unpleasant letter in November, Davies wrote that 'Alderman Saunders is a tower of strength with far more influence than the miserable little Jewish-looking scoot who is backing the oleaginous Darlington'. In the same month a relative urged that 'we must not relax in our wire-pulling'.[117]

Attempts by individuals and external bodies to control and to undermine the free expression of opinion were naturally to be resisted. The sole recorded attempt to harass a member of staff on religious grounds was by members of the College Council at Cardiff in the 1880s, when Lloyd Tanner, the Professor of Mathematics, came under fire. Suspicion of free-thinking and of links with the declared atheist Charles Bradlaugh prompted Dean Vaughan to demand his dismissal, an act neither in accord with the clause in the College charter forbidding religious tests nor with Jowett's immoderate tribute to Vaughan's wisdom. The proposal was lost by thirteen votes to eight (six of which were cast by clerics). Vaughan threatened to resign but thought the better of it when presented with a mollifying letter from Aberdare, Henry Richard and the Principal. The pulpit of Bangor Cathedral became a 'Coward's Castle'[118] on this occasion, as

Hartwell Jones, himself a cleric, later declared, because it was the centre of attacks upon the Cardiff College as the home of infidelity. Earlier still, Aberystwyth's first principal, a Calvinistic Methodist, faced furious criticism in the press because in services for students he read from the College's *Manual of Prayer and Praise* which included a prayer 'for the good estate of the Catholic Church'.[119] Further, the use of Lent and Michaelmas for College terms was held to be a betrayal of the true spirit of the Protestant Reformation. It was thus rather hard when one of Bernard Shaw's characters later spoke of 'Nonconformist holes in Wales'.[120] From time to time it was not uncommon to hear attacks upon a college because students were said to return home as self-proclaimed agnostics.

Attention is drawn elsewhere to the efforts of the coalowners to control the curriculum of the School of Mines at Cardiff.[121] As a young Principal Reichel was anxious to placate the powerful men of Gwynedd. He even attempted to muzzle his colleagues from delivering speeches on political issues. Henry Jones and others stood their ground.[122] Reichel wisely did not repeat the prohibition, although he knew by instinct, and soon from experience, that landlords and quarryowners bared their teeth if members of staff spoke out on matters affecting their interests. To be an avowed Liberal in Bangor, dominated more by the Penrhyn family than the cathedral, could lead to unpleasantness. When three 'professors' accompanied Lloyd George in a carriage during his triumphal progress through Bangor in 1892, Penrhyn refused to contribute to the memorial fund to the College's first President, the Earl of Powis, the noblest of true Tories, thus making it impossible to establish a much-needed travelling scholarship for students. A lecturer in agriculture, bold enough to speak in Welsh to tenant farmers at Beaumaris after the departure of the chairman, Sir Richard Williams-Bulkeley, found himself in peril. Lord Penrhyn insisted that unless the College Council apologized and dismissed the lecturer the Landlords' Defence Association would draw public attention to 'Welsh-speaking professors of this sort'.[123] The outcome was that the lecturer, John Owen, was obliged to write a submissive letter. Penrhyn also attempted to dissuade Kenyon from becoming a governor of the College, advice which he happily disregarded to the College's great gain. Relations were further injured by the manifest sympathy of the preponderating majority of staff and students with the quarrymen during the Great Strike of 1902–5.[124] At Aberystwyth, Lord Davies, an enlightened Liberal and a considerable benefactor of the College, found it difficult not to interfere. W. P. Wheldon thought that he was often 'imperious and impatient'.[125] Perhaps the interests of Cardiff and Bangor may have been better served by the disengagement rather than by the interventionist attentions of the opulent to whom cash did indeed mean control.

The fact that J. E. Lloyd, an august man with a reputation for probity, should have allowed his supporters to act on his behalf in a somewhat tribal fashion is the best indication imaginable that canvassing was customary a century ago. Nor should it be regarded as a peculiarly Welsh infection. Percy Watkins found canvassing rampant in the West Riding (where he worked before moving to Cardiff), though he was exceedingly impressed by the county authority's determinedly successful measures to stamp out the practice.[126] It is significant, too, that neither Lloyd nor Marshall were in fact appointed. Canvassing, it seems, like patriotism, was not enough. When he appeared before the Haldane Commission J. Gwenogvryn Evans was asked whether 'purely local interests'[127] affected the appointment of professors. In reply Evans agreed that there was a danger in a body largely composed of local men, but in a Council drawn from a wide area there would be no opportunity for conspiracy. Evans further advanced the view that from his own experience of both Aberystwyth and Oxford, petty, personal considerations determined elections at Oxford in a manner 'impossible'[128] at Aberystwyth where the large Council was composed of members resident in distant places in both England and Wales. Evans's opinions are an interesting anticipation of those expressed later by H. A. L. Fisher, who believed that one of the main dangers confronting academic life in the civic universities was 'unintelligent municipal control'.[129] Whether he was primarily thinking of Sheffield where he had been Principal he did not say. In passing, it may also be noted that the historian of Nottingham University said that in its early years the College 'was in effect one of the many activities of the Corporation'.[130] A. H. Kidd saw the advantages of the federal structure of the University of Wales. An English university concentrated in a single town was 'liable to domination by the local municipality', whereas a large group of local education representatives from all parts of Wales would exert 'a less narrowing influence' upon the University because they would have 'the national aspect of the matter clearly before them'.[131]

Denominationalism in its unattractive form was long a-dying. In the 1930s A. H. Williams, a postgraduate student seeking a testimonial from J. E. Lloyd, asked that the subject of his substantial research on Welsh Wesleyan Methodism (one of the smallest denominations in Wales) should not be disclosed in case of possible injury to his career prospects. Lloyd replied pensively that in Cornwall he might find it a distinct advantage.[132] Gradually, however, attitudes altered. Provision in the University's founding charter for the teaching of theology at postgraduate level was a welcome harbinger of change. The presence of theological colleges close to university colleges and harmonious co-operation within the University and its Colleges contributed fruitfully to a new awareness of shared beliefs. Staff and students progressively recognized that firm convictions need not be an obstacle to the common pursuit of intellectual ideals. In time Councils and Courts were influenced by a similar spirit, whilst former students in churches and chapels throughout Wales 'acted as a wholesome leaven of conciliation and harmony'[133] in public and social life. After the representatives of the North Wales Calvinistic Association had appeared before the Haldane Commission, Henry Jones said that 'I didn't expect such breadth and insight. I think that all the Commissioners were greatly pleased by their large-minded liberality.'[134] Anglicans had played a larger part in the university movement than is often acknowledged. Under the new dispensation the first two Pro-Chancellors, Kenyon and W. N. Bruce, were Anglicans. The third, G. C. Joyce, Bishop of Monmouth, a former Principal of Lampeter, was elected unopposed, a symbolic act of no small significance. The appointment of another Anglican as Principal at Aberystwyth in 1927 would scarcely have been possible two or three decades earlier. It must be allowed, too, that post-war disillusion and the spread of secularism led to the loosening of religious ties. In the densely populated areas of Wales, especially, political affiliation was counting for more than denominational allegiance.

With the passing years the University and its graduates helped to establish proper standards of behaviour. Percy Watkins's reluctance to doff his hat before his Cardiff interview may have prompted members of Cardiff Council to review the habits of a lifetime. Thomas Jones spoke in 1934 with contempt of the absurdly eloquent testimonials upon which it was not possible to place any reliance, even upon those written by ministers of the Gospel. 'The desire to be kind', he thought, 'drove out the desire to be honest.'[135] Instead of producing two men of worldwide significance in a century – he had in mind Robert Owen and Lloyd George – Wales, in its own estimation, was producing two a week. W. J. Gruffydd in *Y Llenor* in 1933 created a necessary stir by castigating, as only he could, the gross canvassing for posts in many of the schools of Wales and the *pour boire*, not infrequently expected thereafter, in some instances even a slice of the salary.[136] It was wholly right that university men should mercilessly condemn corrupt practices which demeaned public life. Reichel in 1920 recalled an occasion during his first years at Bangor – he may well have been thinking of the rejection of J. S. Mackenzie – when he urged, as he always did, that the post should be given to the better man. A member of Council, a chairman of a county governing body, who 'had some reputation as an educationalist, asked me with a frankly puzzled air: "But, Mr. Principal, if the other can do the work satisfactorily, why should you want a better man".'[137] Such attitudes could not be tolerated. In acceding to his own Registrar's request for a testimonial for the Cardiff principalship in 1901, Reichel wrote: 'The fact is that I cannot say I know of anyone except Isambard to whom I could give an unqualified testimonial for this particular post. The requirements are so formidable.'[138] It cannot under the circumstances have been easy to speak with unflinching directness. Such a quality was bound to leave its mark upon the institution and in some measure upon the wider society.

The notion that the state should invest in universities on purely prudential grounds was only reluctantly accepted. There had long been danger signals that advances of fundamental importance in pure science were not being applied to industry and commerce as on the continent and in America. Britain's poor performance in the Paris Exhibition of 1867 was a clear warning, to thinkers such as Matthew Arnold and Mark Pattison, that the neglect of higher education amounted to a state of national destitution.[139] The Imperial College of Science at South Kensington, the direct counterpart of the much admired Physical Technical Institute at Charlottenburg, was not established until 1907. Lloyd George in 1918 described as 'very interesting'[140] the information given him in Downing Street by Reichel that the income of American universities was ten times that of universities in the United Kingdom and that the University of Berlin alone received in annual grants the total annual grants to universities and colleges in England and Wales. Scotland and Ireland had both been handsomely treated, it was held, the one protected by the terms of the Act of Union (1707) and the latter by its stormy history. The Welsh Colleges did indeed receive state grants, the first being Cardiff in 1883, whereas English colleges had to wait until 1889 and for lesser sums. In 1905 the authors of *The University of Wales* quoted with understandable approbation the remarks of Sir Norman Lockyer to the British Association that if the Welsh University and its Colleges were put on an equal footing with the best universities of Germany and America a capital sum of four million pounds would be needed.[141] Such an astronomical proposal – Lockyer was, in fact, an astronomer – would have been received with derision by governments, Liberal and Conservative alike. It was, of course, incontestable that the Welsh University and Colleges must look for the bulk of their income to the state, which, in turn, insisted that it would normally help only those who had helped themselves.

What, then, of the world of commerce and industry? It was tempting to look beyond Offa's Dyke. T. H. Huxley had in 1879 threatened the great companies of the City of London that if they did not disgorge some of the inherited riches of the ages to promote technical instruction they would 'deserve to be taxed down to their shoes'.[142] The more enlightened companies at once recognized that it was wise to invest in Britain's industrial prosperity. Thus the Clothworkers' Company created the Textile and Dyeing Department at Leeds to which it had given a quarter of a million pounds by 1924. The Fishmongers' Company was kind to Hull; the Goldsmiths' Company founded in London the college which bears its name, and the Drapers' Company gave £400,000 to the polytechnic in East London. Aberystwyth, mindful of the plight of the ailing industries of rural Wales, was therefore cast down upon the failure of its appeal to the Clothmakers to support a School of Dyeing and Weaving at the College. A similar petition to the Drapers' Company was also rejected. Such, too, was Bangor's fate when it sought help from the Plumbers' Company to train operatives for the improvement of the sanitation of the north Wales seaside resorts. Reichel entertained vain hopes of the Goldsmiths, and the £50 from the Fishmongers, though welcome, was a mere droplet. The Drapers' Company, prompted by its ancient and profitable associations with the Welsh woollen industry, gave timely, generous assistance to Cardiff and to Bangor, mainly by providing them with new, handsome library buildings.[143]

Andrew Carnegie, endlessly pursued by the impecunious, declined an eloquent invitation by Rendel to contribute to Aberystwyth's depleted coffers. It is more than a shade ironical that when Rendel, former director of Armstrong Whitworth, was asked to assist Armstrong College, Newcastle, he unblushingly replied: 'Self-help is the best help.'[144] Cardiff's second Principal understood this well enough. In 1902, not long after his appointment, E. H. Griffiths said that it was undesirable for Wales to go cap in hand to her neighbours: 'I believe that outside help *is* to be got if necessary, but not until we have shown ourselves capable of self-help.'[145] Disillusionment had not yet set in. A quarter of a million pounds, Griffiths thought, was needed to erect new, majestic buildings: 'If the employers . . . within our sphere of action were alive to their interests, we should get it within six months.'[146] This was also one of Lloyd George's recurrent themes. In response to Kenyon's request for help to Bangor, Balfour courteously replied that he was busy collecting funds for Edinburgh and Cambridge, adding that: 'I take a strong view as to the financial straits from which our Universities suffer, and which I think the rich people of this country ought to do much more to relieve than at present they seem inclined to undertake.'[147] Another Conservative, Austen Chamberlain, then Chancellor of the Exchequer, thrust his poniard more directly when in 1904 he addressed representatives of the University. The 'natural condition' of Wales indicated that Welsh colleges should include a School of Mines and one or more professorships of geology, and he clearly thought that 'the great Mining and Quarrying Industries of Wales ought to be ashamed to come outside Wales and to look to others than themselves to make provision for this purpose'. He went on: 'I think they ought to be well able to afford to establish a School, and that you must direct your efforts to educating these people in the value which University training may be to the future prosperity and development of Wales.'[148]

In north Wales the prospects were not bright. The criticism has been made that, while Bangor was more aware of the needs of industry than Aberystwyth, it had neglected the industries of north-east Wales. Michael Sanderson found it difficult to avoid the conclusion that in hindsight it was wrong to have recreated another Aberystwyth-type college in north Wales and that 'some location further to the east might have resulted in more varied industrial benefits for the Welsh economy'.[149] The arbitrators who considered petitions from various contestants in 1883 decided, however, against Wrexham, by far the strongest candidate in the north-east, possibly because it was rather too close to Liverpool and Manchester and probably because the quarrymen of Gwynedd had demonstrated unbounded enthusiasm to have a college in their midst. It is true that the College authorities felt fully justified in regarding agriculture as the main industry of north Wales, mining and quarrying as secondary, thereby prompting D. R. Daniel, secretary of the North Wales Quarrymen's Union, to remark wryly that whereas quarrymen had contributed magnificently to the college, they had 'ever since had the pleasure of seeing the College educating farmers'.[150] Reichel and his colleagues, however, were well aware of the importance of setting up a School of Quarrying and Mining to provide for the wants of the coal and slate industries of north Wales, in which 36,274 were employed and which were still hampered by antediluvian methods. Evidence showed that the initial investigation in the barren Highlands of Scotland had led to the enormously successful exploitation of the goldfields of the Transvaal. North Wales had at hand rich resources of coal, slate and stone. In Caernarfonshire there was one of the best slate quarries in Britain, Meirionnydd did not lag far behind Cornwall in mining, whilst in Flintshire and Denbighshire there were valuable coal, lead and zinc mines and substantial open workings for stone. It was therefore unreasonable that a lad of parts had to be trained at Cardiff, Redruth, Camborne or London, since mining studies could equally well prosper at Bangor. The elimination of ancient methods would lead to improved working conditions for quarryman and collier, who, like the owners themselves, would benefit from enhanced profits. Reichel, always alive to developments on the continent, knew that mining schools flourished where industry was strong. More than once he spoke of the advice given him by Professor Louis of Newcastle upon Tyne who encouraged him to establish at Bangor a School of Mines concentrating upon quarrying, for no such school existed anywhere. Reichel, however, did not think that he should develop quarrying at the expense of an existing department, and it was natural for him to look expectantly to the industrialists and landlords of north Wales.[151]

He looked in vain. The minor gentry were happy to cluck around the College's first President, the Earl of Powis, on a grand occasion, but they did little else, whilst the fifth Marquess of Anglesey (1875–1905), a jewellery fetishist, could not be relied upon. The key figures were the redoubtable second Baron Penrhyn (1836–1907) and G. W. D. Assheton Smith (1848– 1904). It is true that declining rents and industrial disputes had diminished the income of quarry owners, but neither had ever warmed to the cause of higher education in Gwynedd. Assheton Smith declared that 'I have no interest in Bangor'. His wife spoke like a latter-day Marie Antoinette. It would be better if Welshmen went to English universities: 'they have far too good an opinion of themselves and the more Colleges they have in this country the more self-opinionated they will become'.[152] Political contro- versies had seriously marred relationships. Penrhyn refused to present a site to the College or to make possible a School of Mining or a chair of geology. The failure to enlist the support of a rich benefactor proved fatal. Families who had derived great wealth from slate, land and labour stood aloof. The disengagement was total. It is not surprising that the College, with one brief interlude, has sought its presidents from north-east Wales and its borders.

It would be grossly unjust to suggest that all industrialists in other parts of Wales averted their gaze from the just claims of the Colleges. In south Wales Lord Glanely, a wealthy shipowner, set a magnificent example: his gifts, including the Tatem Laboratories, amounted to £100,000. A similar sum was given by Sir William James Thomas, coalowner, who made possible the Welsh National School of Medicine. Sir David Llewellyn, a College President, contributed £32,000 to the appeal fund of 1921. The Davies family of Llandinam and Gregynog responded with a discriminating liberality to the high challenge of inherited wealth, also derived from the coal industry.[153] Yet, the role of south Wales industrialists in general, especially the coalowners, was dismal. The person best placed to survey the scene was E. H. Griffiths. Soon after his arrival at Cardiff he had initiated an amendment to the Mines Regulation Act of 1887. Henceforth it would be possible to qualify as a coal manager or surveyor after academic study of two years for a diploma, followed by practical training of three years in a mine. In 1903 he said that if the coalowners of south Wales were now ready to emulate the assistance given by their counterparts to Birmingham (where mining was of secondary importance) and to the Wigan Mining and Technical School, an annual expenditure of £1,000 would be repaid tenfold.[154] In 1918, at the end of his principalship and cast down by successive reverses, Griffiths reminded the College Court that the provincial universities of England regarded it as both a special duty and a privilege to assist the industries and manufacturers of their immediate districts. Leeds had attended to the cloth-making interest, Newcastle had a school of naval architecture, Sheffield served the steel industry, whilst the study of tropical medicine was natural at the great port of Liverpool. 'Hitherto, unfortunately', said Griffiths, 'we have not been able in this College to produce evidence of a like satisfactory nature.'[155] The laboratories and libraries of the Welsh Colleges did not give Welsh students equality of opportunity with those of England and Scotland. Yet south Wales was so favoured by nature as to be one of the wealthiest parts of the kingdom. The College could not fulfil its mission unless the industrialists turned to the College for help in solving the problems of industry.

The department of mining had stumbled badly from the beginning and attempts to invigorate it, initiated in 1902, proved unsuccessful. The coalowners then determined to set up their own Mining School at Trefforest in Glamorgan, lavishing upon it between 1912 and 1916 no less than £250,000, the sum Joseph Chamberlain had hoped to raise at the outset for the University of Birmingham.[156] There was a measure of co-operation between the College and Trefforest in preparing for diploma purposes, but a diffusion of energy and resources was not in the best interests of the mining community. There are solid grounds for believing that before the First World War mining and engineering students trained at Cardiff and who found a career in Wales were a small proportion of those required in managerial posts. In fact it is likely that about 70 per cent of engineering graduates left Wales before 1914.[157] When the College resurrected in 1935 the chair of mining (vacant since 1902) it was very late in the day. Further, the failure of the College to involve itself in the tinplate industry before the founding of Swansea was deplorable. On good authority it was said in 1917 that there was no trained chemist in any tinplate works in south Wales. A partial explanation is that the industry consisted of many small unenterprising employers. It is clear, too, that when Mond Nickel was established in 1902 its founder preferred to have links with Cambridge, not with local colleges.[158]

A wide appeal shortly before the war to establish a department of commerce was a grotesque failure. Only £15 were raised, three banks having each given £5.[159] Two prominent men in the commercial life of Cardiff announced that they opposed the development. Joseph Shaw, chairman of the Powell Duffryn Steam Coal Company was forthright: 'You will not get any money from me for a faculty of commerce.'[160] Again, bearing in mind the strife in the south Wales coalfield, the case for a department of industrial relations seemed unanswerable, yet it was not founded by the magnates of the area. In 1902, Aberystwyth derived £304 per annum from endowments, Bangor £1,699 and Cardiff a paltry £20. It is scarcely surprising that K. G. Robbins should have drawn attention to the absence of a single reference to the College in an authoritative study of Cardiff as a coal metropolis from 1870 to 1914.[161] In 1933 it was noted ruefully within the sedate confines of the College's celebratory *Short History* that in relation to endowments 'the history of the College is disappointing, one might say not creditable, and certainly not proportionate to the wealth and the industrial and commercial importance of South Wales and Monmouthshire'. Five years later James Griffiths said that Cardiff 'prided itself on being the capital of Wales and was asking Welsh people to say so'. However, 'when there was any money to be paid Cardiff was the odd man out . . . It was losing the respect of Wales.'[162]

Why were the coalowners loath to be associated with the Cardiff College? Lewis Williams in 1907 believed that the capital of the great works was absentee capital. One of the main companies had capital of £5,000,000 and another of £3,000,000. The chairman of a south Wales company lived in the Midlands; he had given £5,000 to Birmingham University but not a penny to the Cardiff College, in which he had no personal interest.[163] In 1918 E. H. Griffiths said that those concerned in the glass industry in south Wales were contributing to the University of Sheffield and had set up glass-making tanks there without having made any approach to the Cardiff College.[164] It seems, too, that businessmen did not properly appreciate the importance of pure science as the necessary basis for advance in applied science. Nor was it thought useful to turn to the College to train their managers in modern languages. One industrialist said that his best men came from English public schools, adding that the railway companies would say the same, their men never having received training 'in any commercial place, such as Birmingham or the like of that'[165] (cheering words, indeed, for J. F. Rees, later Professor of Commerce at Birmingham). The study of economics was not to be contemplated by industrialists, probably because it touched upon matters considered subversive. Socialism was, of course, anathema. When Lord Glanely opened the Cardiff College's new playing fields at Caerau, he asked: 'Why is it that so many of your students think it a sign of superior intelligence to be on the side of Socialism . . . The need of our times is not Socialism, but a sterner interpretation of the rules of life.' Sir David Llewellyn, as we have seen a substantial benefactor to the College, had gone further in 1923. In words which arouse profound unease and which only the captive of the capitalist can fully comprehend, he remarked that 'if the result of teaching certain textbooks on economics were to leave men tainted with Socialism the sooner those books were burned the better'.[166]

Joseph Shaw clearly regretted having had any connection with the College's School of Mining in the early days. It had soon emerged that the coalowners insisted upon control of the curriculum, of funds and of staff appointments. Businessmen, as F. W. Gilbertson put it succinctly, 'want not only control of the money, but control of the results'.[167] The College was apparently prepared to be concessive to the extent of being ready to alter the College statutes, but legal opinion was firm that the proposed changes were contrary to the College charter. Thus it was that eleven companies began their own school at Trefforest in 1912.[168] Co-operation was further frustrated by the attitude of industrialists generally to the University of Wales. The 'bedrock principle' of most of them, according to E. H. Griffiths, was 'that they will not contribute their money if they think it is to be disposed of in North and Mid-Wales'.[169] In order to discover their views we need not dig deep. It is sufficient to hearken to their unabashed, artless disclaimers to the Haldane Commission. Hugh M. Ingledew, secretary of the Trefforest school, believed that if there were a separate university at Cardiff, 'freed from association with North Wales',[170] the College would receive greater support. A man of commerce looked upon Cardiff 'as a local part of an institution in North Wales for the training of divinity students. Naturally that type of education does not very much appeal to him.'[171]

F. W. Gilbertson believed that the industrial spirit throughout south Wales differed from that of north Wales, 'where there is not the same spirit in the people at all'.[172] It was much easier, he added, for north and south Wales to communicate with London than with each other. Shaw thought that the headquarters of the University was at Aberystwyth 'or somewhere in that direction'. He and his fellows knew 'nothing about Aberystwyth or mid-

Wales, and we do not want gentlemen from there interfering with us'.[173] Businessmen, it seems, did not care to serve on popularly elected bodies, in no small measure because they did not care to be heckled, said a prominent industrialist.[174] In fact, it is likely that the democratic nature of the University of Wales deterred several wealthy men from contributing. Not without cause did Thomas Jones urge the Haldane Commission to remember the 'great resources of idealism among our people' and not to be misled by the 'apparent materialism' of life in south Wales or by 'the philistinism of some of our public men'. In private Henry Jones said that the Cardiff industrialists who appeared before the Commission had given him a shock from which he would never quite recover. He saw no redeeming virtue: 'There were not enough good men in Sodom and Gomorrah to save them.'[175] The notion that the Colleges of the University wished to hold themselves aloof from industry, both in north and south Wales, cannot be sustained. Their best endeavours were for the most part endlessly thwarted. The chief responsibility for disengagement lies with the captains of industry.

Some prosperous Englishmen of the middle class in London, Manchester and Liverpool (virtually the capital of north Wales), as well as in Wales, supported the Colleges, though not as many as had been hoped. Beyond these islands little was forthcoming. As generation followed generation and *hiraeth* wore thin, Welshmen in dispersion attended more to their genealogies than to the needs of the homeland. True, a Melbourne man provided an ornamental roof to create the inner quad at Aberystwyth and Thomas Charles Edwards's American tour in 1890 brought in moneys to equip the new library, but later missionaries failed to arouse expatriate zeal.[176] In 1929 J. F. Rees, on his first day as Principal, hoped that Thomas Jones who was accompanying the Prime Minister to the States would be waited upon by his fellow countrymen 'with bursting pockets' asking 'what they may do to be saved'. He surmised that T.J. would suggest an endowment for adult education. He himself ventured to hope for 'a Great Hall (with organ)'[177] to complete the college buildings in Cathays Park. Welsh Americans, however, sought salvation from other directions, so that it is difficult to discover a significant benefaction before the Aberfan disaster in 1967.

The allegiance of the humbler classes could be counted upon in many parts of Wales. The main challenge which faced them was to maintain their sons and daughters in the colleges which they had struggled to establish. In realistic terms it must be acknowledged that the pennies of the colliers, the quarrymen and farm labourers were but a minute portion of the necessary sums at length contributed. Yet, their ennobling example of self-sacrifice excited admiration and emulation. In addition, Cardiff and Bangor were obliged to raise new college buildings during the first decade of the century, a challenge to which Aberystwyth was not obliged to respond until after the Second World War. There are signs of the readiness of workmen in the south Wales counties and in Monmouthshire to contribute a farthing a week for ten years to the Cardiff College, but the historian of the College, at his best in dealing with financial matters, has exceedingly little to say on the subject save to remark that the scheme was perhaps 'utopian'.[178] We do know that by 1894 scholarship funds had been set up in some collieries and that hundreds of colliers in the Ocean collieries in the Rhondda Valley continued to subscribe small amounts to the David Davies Memorial Scholarship Fund in 1907. When the College Registrar appeared before the Raleigh Committee in that year it was apparent that the precise number of contributors had not been kept, in marked contrast to the detailed evidence submitted by Hugh Owen to the Aberdare Committee.[179] It is also remarkable that in the College's *Short History* (1933) no reference whatsoever was made to colliers in its survey of gifts to the College save to one sum 'definitely promised a few years ago'.[180] On the other hand, Bangor, in preparation for its fiftieth year, delighted to draw attention to moneys raised for the New Building.[181] Anglesey had given the equivalent of 30*s.* for every household in the island; in Penisarwaun, north Caernarfonshire, there were forty-five houses, fifty-six persons having subscribed a total of £31. 2*s.* 0*d.*; in Llanuwchllyn, Meirionnydd, there were 163 houses, 186 persons contributing a total of £42. 15*s.* 6*d.*[182] In sum, it is difficult to avoid the conclusion that Aberystwyth and Bangor took infinitely greater pride than Cardiff in their relationship with local communities.

It was wholly natural that the University and its Colleges should endeavour to attend to the needs of the Welsh economy and of Welsh society. Jaroslav Pelikan in his impressive *The Idea of the University* (1992) applied the words of Edmund Burke, in another context, to the duties of a university, namely 'to be attached to the subdivision, to love the little platoon we belong to in society, [as] the first principle (the germ as it were) of public affections'. Burke added that 'it is the first link in the series by which we proceed towards a love to our country and to mankind'.[183] In Wales, because of the initial and continuing links with the small platoons, this duty was especially compelling. Notice has already been drawn to Michael Sanderson's work in which he says that 'the Welsh university colleges are . . . a pathological example of the dangers of disengagement between the universities and industry'.[184] At an important conference at Edinburgh in 1983 this view was refuted by Robert Anderson. Sanderson, he said, had missed the point: 'In creating a university which would turn out ministers and schoolteachers, and safeguard a distinctive literary and religious culture, the Welsh had aims and preoccupations of their own.' He cautioned against 'letting our own preoccupations with science, economic growth, or industrial decline distort our understanding of a university history which often centred on problems of a very different kind'.[185] It is, of course, true that the University was providing teachers in considerable numbers; in 1937, for example, as many as 66.6 per cent entered the teaching profession, in England as well as Wales (via the Appointments Board).[186] It is also true that many of them would not have entered the University at all but for state grants to enable them to become graduate teachers. Nevertheless, as we have seen, the Colleges had no wish to detach themselves from industry and were in fact hindered at almost every turn by owners of mines and quarries. Metallurgy, on the other hand, began promisingly at Swansea under C. A. Edwards, and on no account should the efforts at Cardiff to tackle industrial and social problems be disregarded. The School of Medicine attacked the diseases of those pent up in dark conurbations and healed the injuries so common in the mining valleys of south Wales. There was also the settlement movement, to which we shall presently turn.[187]

Members of the Cardiff College were much influenced by the Garden City Movement which led in the early years of the century to the creation of the Rhiwbina Garden Village. Already a new estate had been established at Letchworth and also at Hampstead, whose Garden Suburb was the model for the Cardiff project. In essence the movement was a reaction against the degrading conditions of urban life. At Cardiff a group led by Stanley Jevons, Professor of Economics, proposed in a spirit of brotherhood to provide comely housing conditions for workers and also for members of the middle class. Land was bought at Rhiwbina and in 1912 the Cardiff Workers' Co-operative Garden Village Society, under the chairmanship of D. Lleufer Thomas, issued its first prospectus, in 'Reformed Spelling',[188] which gave an added flavour to the venture. In 1914 Jevons left for India to become professor at Allahabad and W. J. Gruffydd spoke of his 'deep regret at the great sacrifices he [Jevons] had made in pursuit of his objectives',[189] for Jevons had lost much money in attempting to establish similar communities in south Wales. Gruffydd himself was at the centre of the Garden Village Society. He gave Welsh names to streets in the new estate, and when the affairs of the Society appeared hopelessly entangled he dealt with them, said a Cardiff businessman, in a manner 'worthy of any chartered accountant'.[190] True, the vision splendid of raising hundreds of houses was not fulfilled. Nor was it possible to provide many houses at a rent which the very poor could afford. After 1945 co-operative ownership was no longer practicable, yet members of staff, at least, formed a close community at Rhiwbina which long retained the spirit of a garden village.

The most systematic study of the economic plight of south Wales in the desperate days of depression was undertaken by Hilary Marquand during his period as Professor of Industrial Relations. He was principally responsible for *An Industrial Survey of South Wales* (1930), prepared for the Board of Trade by the Cardiff College. Thereafter, at the invitation of the Commissioner for Special Areas and under the active encouragement of J. F. Rees, he directed an inquiry into the industrial potentialities of south Wales, particularly the special areas, for expanding existing industries and for establishing new ones. *The Second Industrial Survey of South Wales* appeared in 1937 in three volumes of 1,200 pages and maps. Much influenced by Alfred Weber's classic study of the location of industry, Marquand presented not only a fine descriptive account (of great value to historians) but a penetrating examination of possible pathways to recovery, inevitably obstructed in the short term by the outbreak of war. Meanwhile his *South Wales Needs a Plan* (1936), which pointed to Keynesian intervention by government, was recognized by a wider audience as a significant contribution to the analysis of urgent economic problems.[191] If the results were predictably meagre, it was not Marquand's fault. Unemployment in Wales caused profound dismay to University authorities. By 1934, for example, it had reached the appalling figure of 73.4 per cent in Dowlais, where the steel works had closed. In 1936, Henry Lewis, warden of the Guild of Graduates, and R. I. Aaron, in a moving submission, appealed to the University Council on behalf of unemployed graduates. Unemployment was always bad, 'but unemployment of the finest product of our schools and colleges is surely unspeakably bad'.[192] It was also unspeakably bad amongst juveniles in the south Wales coalfield, and the University Press published an authoritative study in 1936 by Gwynne Meara[193] and supervised by Marquand. Alas, the remedies proposed in both instances involved the expenditure of moneys which were not to be found.

The Appointments Board of the University, set up before the war and served by an energetic secretary, R. Silyn Roberts, did its best in discouraging circumstances. Primarily designed to channel suitable candidates from Welsh schools and University Colleges to positions in the civil service, industry and commerce, it succeeded most in assisting graduates to enter the teaching profession. After the war, the Board came under the direct control of the University Registry.[194] Its best endeavours were not always applauded. The young Caerwyn Williams, for instance, believed that whilst Wales had refused to conform to the Anglican Church it was sad that she had not also renounced the true religion of the English, that of 'getting on' in the world, for the Board was instrumental in transplanting professional men from Wales.[195] He was indeed touching upon a sensitive issue.

In 1934 C. A. Edwards reported that half Swansea's graduates were finding appointments outside Wales.[196] The agricultural depression which set in during the late 1870s was of international dimensions and its impact upon Wales was given remarkably detailed scrutiny in the volumes of the Royal Commission on Land in Wales and Monmouthshire published three years after the founding of the University. If we examine a wider span, from 1851 to 1911, it is true that the net loss of 388,000 out of rural Wales was nearly offset by migration to the Welsh coalfields and laterally to Liverpool, the west Midlands and London. Wales before the First World War did not suffer the catastrophic fate of Ireland. Nevertheless, the decline caused growing alarm. In 1851, 35 per cent of males were engaged in agriculture, in 1911 only 12 per cent. In one decade alone, 1881 to 1891, when Aberystwyth was still struggling for its very existence, 21.7 per cent migrated from Montgomeryshire and 16.5 per cent from Cardiganshire.[197] It has rightly been said that the exodus between 1881 and 1911 cannot be described as dramatic, but it is equally right to speak of the 'beginning of a long-run process' and of a 'creeping depopulation'[198] which continued between the wars. For Aberystwyth and Bangor rural depopulation was a cloud larger than a man's hand.

The antithesis of town and country has a long ancestry. The quip that God made the country, man the town (with the further embellishment that the devil made the suburbs) is not of recent origin. It was easy to sentimentalize country life, to praise the herbs and flowers in the cottage garden and to forget, not only the rats in the rafters, but the indisputable fact that tuberculosis was far more common in rural than in industrial Wales.[199] Newcomers to Wales such as Reichel and Rendel were profoundly impressed by such figures as Thomas Ellis, the authentic son of rural Wales, and were early concluding that the *gwerin* of Wales far excelled the clodhoppers of rural England whom they regarded as the despair of educationists. Baring Gould remarked that 'the Welsh of the labourer and small farmer class are brighter, quicker, keener than those occupying the same position in Saxon land',[200] a superiority which he attributed to bilingualism. Rendel thought that 'the leading distinction' between Wales and England was that in Wales 'the weekly waged and humble classes are within the Christian fold to a very much larger extent than in England'.[201] Reichel in 1905 was adamant, upon the experience of twenty-one years, that the best students came from farms not towns, and he was always prone to associate industrial conurbations with smoke, strikes and socialism. Carried away by his fresh-air theories, he proclaimed that 'in every state of human society the best was grown in the country air, whether it was muscle, brain or morale'.[202] Welshmen added their tributes. J. C. Davies, director of education for Denbighshire, informed the University Court in 1926 that the rural districts were 'predominantly Welsh with a high type of Welsh culture'. It was here, said William George on the same occasion, that the 'old Welsh culture was found at its best'.[203] In 1935 Ifor L. Evans, new to his Aberystwyth principalship, tended to speak with unguarded eloquence. The assimilation of a huge immigrant population was but 'a passing phase'. The rural areas, where one looked for 'the Welsh personality', were more important than the industrial areas 'for they were Wales itself'.[204] To many Evans's words must have appeared extravagant especially in view of his upbringing at Aberdare where, as in other valley towns, there were lively Welsh communities constantly refreshed when he was a lad by internal immigrants bringing with them the religious, cultural values of the countryside.

A mood of gloomy introspection was frequently to be observed in the University Court during the inter-war years. Had the University really done enough to avert depopulation? Extra-mural classes could perhaps combat more effectively 'the dullness and monotony of rural life',[205] but even here care was needed. The orthodoxy then current was that adult classes, rather in the spirit of the charity school movement of the eighteenth century, should educate men and women in their natural environment as members of the class to which they belonged, 'out of which they can only be in exceptional circumstances lifted',[206] as J. E. Lloyd wrote in *The Times Educational Supplement* in 1916. Economic remedies were sought and eyes turned to the woollen industry. By the late 1920s the University Council had constituted a Rural Textile Industries Committee and was able, with a modest Treasury grant, to appoint an advisory officer who before long had visited every mill in Wales and who became secretary of a co-operative society, the Welsh Textile Association Limited, which firms in the Welsh woollen industry were invited to join. Later a Swiss woman was recruited to invent new designs and combinations of colour on a hand loom. The Association acted as agent for sales at home and abroad. It has to be conceded, however, that at a time of economic privation the scheme touched but the hem of the problem of the Welsh textile industry.[207] The case for extended afforestation in Wales appeared irrefutable. There was but one small department in the University, at Bangor, where initial developments had been encouraging. After the war, however, the newly created Forestry Commission decided that advisory work should be performed by its own officers. Despite eloquent appeals in 1931, the Commission refused to relent and only grants from local authorities and the University Council enabled the department at Bangor to weather the 1930s.[208]

Fisheries had by no means been neglected at Aberystwyth and Bangor. In 1912 Aberystwyth received a small government grant to study crustaceans in the waters of Cardigan Bay and the problem of lead pollution upon local salmon and trout. The College became involved, too, in the lobster hatcheries in the River Beaulieu in Hampshire. At Bangor the College acquired a marine biological station on Ynys Seiriol (and a small boat appropriately called the 'Puffin'), but although it had to be abandoned in 1900 and could not be resited elsewhere because of financial problems, yet good work had been done to improve mussel and oyster cultivation in the Menai Straits. The College's most notable contribution was to preserve the Conwy mussel and sparling fisheries before the Great War.[209] Pride of place, however, had naturally been given at the two colleges to agriculture, the premier industry of Wales. In order to wean farmers from primitive methods and to induce them to profit from advances in applied chemistry, instruction was for years provided at various centres, usually at a more elementary level than would be countenanced within a university institution. To convince a farmer rooted in ancestral traditions that a mere academic, especially a monoglot Englishman, had anything to teach him was not easy. But by dint of persuasion and persistence, by distributing countless pamphlets in Welsh and above all by practical demonstration, the farming community warmed to the staff of the two colleges and later of Cardiff, where such developments were naturally more modest. In time it became clear that distinguished scientific research at Bangor and Aberystwyth raised the standard of arable and especially of pastoral farming, for the Welsh farmer was primarily a stockman. Ifor Evans was fully entitled in 1935 to draw attention to Stapeldon's outstanding work at Aberystwyth.[210] The mountains of Wales, he said, were becoming habitable by the creation of grasslands, but J. F. Rees could not abide his claims that the future of Wales lay in the rural areas. Economic isolation was one of the evils of the day and above the roar of Cardiff's traffic Rees deplored the talk of 'going back to the land'. It was a will o' the wisp, he said, adding in words which historians are prone to avoid, that 'the past was gone'.[211] It was hard to control large economic and social forces; an occasional touch on the tiller was perhaps possible, but little else. Moreover it had long been evident that the spread of education had inevitable social consequences. William McCormick suggested in 1907 to the Raleigh Committee, of which he was a member, that local rates for elementary and secondary education meant that country people were 'paying to depopulate themselves'.[212] In the 1930s a Cardiganshire alderman, Gwernant Williams, was robustly hard-headed: 'if you want to keep your children in the country, don't give them any education at all'. It seemed that 'getting on' meant 'getting out', and once out the native was unlikely to return.[213] Thomas Jones was characteristically plain-spoken. The idea that there were a lot of able Welshmen eager to return to Wales to undertake burdens of administration on patriotic grounds was 'moonshine'. It would, for instance, have been fatuous for Lloyd George to have spent his days in Llanystumdwy.[214] D. J. Williams attacked him predictably and fiercely, and there was more than a suggestion that Lloyd George's brother, William, had chosen the better part by remaining at home.[215] D. Emrys Evans saw the depth of the tragedy: 'Inbreeding may indeed impair the vigour of a stock; bleeding will destroy it.'[216]

X

University and Nation 2

Despite the manifold services outlined in the previous chapter, questions frequently arose as to whether the University was a recognizably Welsh institution. The period before the First World War has been eloquently described by K. O. Morgan as 'the Edwardian high noon'. Wales was 'a land of especial achievement and success'. Economically and socially it was 'exceptionally thriving': by 1913 the south Wales coalfield was 'at its zenith'; in west Wales 'the curse of McKinley' was past and the tinplate industry displayed 'new buoyancy'. The emergent middle class was thriving, the professions flourished and it was an age of 'increasingly passionate national awareness'.[1] Yet, there is to be detected an underlying unease made more manifest in the age of interrogation following the Great War. As he reflected upon educational achievements in Wales during his lifetime, and few were better equipped to do so, Percy Watkins believed that the years between the Aberdare Report and the creation of the Central Welsh Board (1896) 'represent the finest flowering period of statesmanship and effective performance in the whole history of Welsh Education'.[2] A. H. Williams characterized the period between 1895 and 1914 as one of disillusionment.[3] It is a large subject, but if we may legitimately speak of an Edwardian high noon, we must also note that critics often viewed the University in the cold light of a grey dawn. Two matters caused particular disquiet, language and religion.

It is true that the number of Welsh speakers, monoglot and bilingual, reached its peak in 1911, namely 977,366. Nevertheless, whereas 54.4 per cent spoke Welsh in 1891, 49.9 per cent did so in 1901, 43.5 per cent in 1911 and only 37.1 per cent in 1921.[4] John Morris-Jones was deeply moved by the beauty of utterance of Anglesey labourers at prayer during the religious revival of 1904–5, drawing, as it seemed, upon hidden, long-forgotten sources. He did not hesitate, however, to tell quarrymen in 1905 that they were not as cultured as their fathers thirty years earlier.[5] Early on there had been a tendency to ask whether the University through its Colleges was discharging its responsibility towards the language, literature and history of Wales. In O. M. Edwards's *Wales* in 1895 York Powell, Professor of History at Oxford, charged the University with giving Welsh language and literature a subordinate place in its matriculation scheme. The claim for a Welsh University, he said, had been based on nationality, the essence of which was the Welsh tongue and Welsh literature. 'Why have a Welsh university at all', he asked, 'if these are thrust into a corner as unimportant subjects?' Such neglect would mortally wound Welsh nationality and the University would forfeit 'the immense advantage it may draw from such grand instruments of culture and education in the truest sense of Welsh literature and Welsh history'.[6] The *Western Mail* pointed to York Powell's strictures and added some of its own. There was nothing distinctively Welsh about any of the constituent colleges; Bangor, it alleged, had gone 'holus bolus' against Welsh aspirations.[7] Such attacks took little account of the intricate process of breaking away from the demands of the London syllabus.

By 1900 J. Arthur Price was critical of the apparent neglect of Welsh history in the University. He had heard that the author of *Aylwin*, Theodore Watts-Dunton, had done more to draw the attention of the educated public to Wales than had all the professors: 'How long shall the reproach last?'[8] Criticism bubbled up at the Caernarfon Eisteddfod in 1906, in one instance in a spontaneous, unforeseen fashion. It seems that O. M. Edwards was presiding at one of the meetings. His progress was at best halting, for he was no natural orator, until he chanced to say, in praise of some merit or other of the Eisteddfod, that it was a pity that the University was not imbued with a similar spirit, so that those dry bones be made alive.[9] There was a roar of approbation. At the Cymmrodorion meeting at the same Eisteddfod, W. Llywelyn Williams wondered whether the consequences of the university movement were commensurate with so much zeal and sacrifice. The University should 'instantly reflect every phase and change in the national life'. It was training men to 'get on' and not 'quite the class of men the nation needed'.[10] If the University was to accomplish its 'high mission' it should be brought into association with the National Eisteddfod. Dyfed, the archdruid, declared at a St David's Day dinner in the following year that the time was not opportune because the national colleges 'lacked that strong sympathy and intellectual grasp'[11] of national ideals which would alone make close co-operation possible. Earlier the Revd H. M. Hughes of Cardiff told the Welsh Congregational Union at Blaenau Ffestiniog that the University of Wales was anti-national. Its Senate, hitherto unreformed, knew 'very little of the true life of Wales'. Its members were rootless Englishmen without 'an atom of sympathy'[12] with the great revival of 1859, the true parent of the University, a view strongly contested by the editor of the *Western Mail*, who drew attention to the Anglican tradition of education from the Society for the Promotion of Christian Knowledge to the founding of Lampeter and beyond.[13]

There was more to come in the post-war period. Sir Alfred Zimmern in *My Impressions of Wales*, largely based upon a sharply curtailed period at Aberystwyth, believed that Welsh civilization had come unduly under the influence of England and that the Colleges, not one of them half a century old, were 'victims of an academic tradition . . . which divorces them from the native associations and culture of the countryside' without establishing 'living contacts with the thought of a wider world'. Wales in general, and particularly her Colleges, should 'cultivate what is truly Welsh . . . [and] . . . seek to open more windows on the world'.[14] In 1925 William George argued that Haldane's concept of a democratic government for the University was neither democratic nor efficient. The sight of professors in their robes twice a year was insufficient to create a bond between the University and the people; the only beneficiaries of such arrangements were shareholders of railway companies. The University was not responding to the challenge of protecting and stimulating the study and use of the Welsh language. English was its official language, all its proceedings were in English and all its intra-mural teaching, with a 'partial exception within purely Welsh departments'. Only one of the four principals was a Welsh-speaking Welshman, staff were largely non-Welsh, except at Aber-ystwyth where the number of 'Cymry' on the staff was greater than elsewhere. William George recommended the creation of a

Welsh Academy to guard and guide the interests of the language.
The Board of Celtic Studies could be the nucleus of such a body,
which in fact came into being in 1959, though without direct,
formal association with the Board.[15] There was further criticism
in 1929 when the Court supported the Academic Board's reply
to the representations of Morgan Watkin (Cardiff) and Mary
Williams (Swansea) that students be allowed to answer
examination questions in English or Welsh. The view then taken
was that to permit choice was incompatible with university
organization, that it would seriously prejudice the value attached
to a Welsh degree and inevitably limit the University's selection
of external examiners, though it was recognized that circumstances might later change.[16] The initiative in successfully
pressing for the degree ceremony to be conducted in Welsh was
taken by students in 1921. So bad was the general situation,
Saunders Lewis concluded in 1945, that the dignity of the nation
called for the establishment of a Welsh-speaking college within
the University. His arguments, based partly upon the status of
Flemish in Ghent, of Irish in Galway and of Hebrew in
Jerusalem, were not widely accepted.[17]

Fears of progressive anglicization sometimes disturbed the true
spirit of concord. There were jibes at the 'starchy fellows' on
College staffs who bought their clothes at the Army and Navy
Stores in London rather than at local emporia. The wife of a
Cardiff member of staff caused more than a puff of smoke when
in an advertisement for domestic help she specified that a Welsh
girl need not apply.[18] Persons of judgement of course knew that it
would have been impossible for many years to recruit even a
small number of Welsh people to staff the colleges. T. Witton
Davies of Bangor said in 1906 that 'Welshmen ought to be very
thankful that distinguished English scholars have settled amongst
us and helped us by their knowledge and experience to develop
our educational system'.[19] Others, too, including John Morris-
Jones, were always ready to defend their English colleagues from
foolish onslaughts. Of Reichel it was said by Marchant Williams
that he would never blend into the Welsh scene any more than
water and oil would mix. Reichel emerged from such assaults
undaunted and undiminished. Marchant attacked the Scots in
turn, for who could escape his ire? True, North Britons in

England did not emerge unscathed. More than once it was suggested that chairs of moral philosophy south of the Tweed were created to reduce unemployment amongst graduates from the banks of the Clyde. In Wales it was speedily recognized that the Scots, from their own experience, had a special understanding of impoverished Welsh students. In 1906 T. Witton Davies said that English professors were 'a constantly diminishing number thanks to the marvellous progress of Welsh education', roundly adding that the Revd H. M. Hughes of Cardiff and others who claimed to speak for Welsh education would serve their cause the better if they agitated for higher salaries and 'make it worth the while of brilliant Welshmen to make their home among their own people instead of accepting much better paid positions across the border'.[20] He could give instances of professors and ministers who made financial sacrifices by remaining in Wales.

Aberystwyth was frequently regarded (and not simply by Aberystwyth people) as being rather more Welsh than Bangor, and both much more so than Cardiff. Aberystwyth had been fortunate, too, in enlisting the services of many non-Welsh staff who identified themselves with the College, C. H. Herford, H. J. Fleure, R. G. Stapledon and W. A. Ashby amongst them. It would also be less than just not to recall members of the Cardiff staff who endeavoured to understand Welsh aspirations. Gilbert Norwood, Professor of Greek, was always profoundly indebted to Thomas Powel, Professor of Celtic, who had welcomed him to Wales upon his appointment in 1908 and 'who gave him insight into the Welsh national spirit'. Norwood remained on intimate terms with W. J. Gruffydd, who presented him for an honorary degree in 1933. Indeed, Gruffydd went so far as to say that in his experience there was as much goodwill towards Welsh matters amongst Englishmen who had come to Wales as amongst Welshmen, some of whom he regarded as being fundamentally ignorant of the culture of Wales and not much better, we must imagine, than the Welsh 'friendlies' who had fought for Edward I.[21] It was said of Cyril Brett, Professor of History who died at the age of fifty-four, that 'though in many respects a typical English Conservative of the old school, he particularly endeared himself to his Welsh colleagues'. Further, 'he had an instinctive understanding of Welsh students, and . . . was the most popular teacher on the staff of the University College'.[22]

The noblest example, perhaps, was R. M. Burrows, Norwood's predecessor. The great mixed population of Cardiff, he thought, would 'never realise that Cardiff was Welsh and that it was their duty and their privilege to throw in their lot with Welsh national aspirations until those amongst whom they had come granted them the full rights of nationality in no grudging spirit'. The erection of race barriers and claims to privileges of race would inevitably impede assimilation and the creation of the 'new Wales'. The Boer War was still fresh in the mind and the newcomer was not to be regarded as an *uitlander* and an alien. On the other hand, Wales could not be expected to welcome the newcomers as Welshmen unless they were in entire sympathy with its fundamental purposes, its zeal for education and 'the tenacity with which it has preserved that most priceless of all possessions, its language and those things which must be pondered on, understood, drawn into the blood'. In the College at Cardiff and in the University of Wales staff and students were 'learning to understand one another under the banner of great national institutions'.[23] Had Burrows remained in Cardiff after 1908 it is possible that he might have modified his opinions. J. S. Mackenzie, Professor of Philosophy, had in turn reflected much on national characteristics, though it must be added that his analysis in *Arrows of Desire* of the 'races' of Britain seems today less than satisfactory.[24]

It was not expected that most members of staff would acquire a sound knowledge of Welsh in an age devoid of the teaching aids which have now partially smoothed the path of the serious learner. Yet it was a delicate matter. J. E. Lloyd noted that 'the key to a knowledge of the people lay in mastering their language, for this hung as a veil between them and all strangers, however benevolent and understanding'.[25] Clearly, the need was more urgent at Bangor and Aberystwyth where a high proportion of students habitually spoke Welsh, and especially at Bangor which had chosen as Principal one who sprang from the Anglo-Irish ascendant minority instead of Henry Jones, a true son of the people. Reichel soon made headway, greatly impressing his colleagues, though he was never very fluent (any more than in

English, except when pressed). He frequently recalled with amusement his attempt to practise his early Welsh upon an innocent roadmaker near the College, who speedily excused himself on the ground that he did not understand English. How many members of staff learnt Welsh it is impossible to say, for academics are seldom disposed to reveal that they are less than masters. Teachers of languages had an initial advantage. Alfred Zimmern certainly made an effort during his short stay at Aberystwyth. R. S. Conway at Cardiff and E. V. Arnold at Bangor used Welsh illustrations in their lectures.[26] The greatest triumph was that of O. H. Fynes-Clinton, the son of a Yorkshire rector and educated almost entirely in England, whose study, *The Welsh Vocabulary of the Bangor District*, appeared in 1913. W. J. Gruffydd believed that this study of a rich dialect in an area forty miles square had not been surpassed by scholars of other nations. Ifor Williams paid him this tribute: 'No Cymro born and bred could have loved the Welsh language more than did this shy, reserved Englishman, and few worked harder, more steadfastly, or with more zest in its service.' He added that Fynes-Clinton's work 'preserves for all time the exact fashion of one Celtic speech'.[27] It was not then considered strange that a Professor of French should have embarked upon such a substantial enterprise, for he was effectively asserting a central principle, the unity of knowledge. Nor should we be surprised that on the wall overlooking the terrace of the new College building at Bangor, in addition to the leek were placed the rose, the thistle and the shamrock, emblems of the other nations of the British Isles.[28] It was a just tribute to their contribution and a permanent reminder that universities cannot survive in isolation but depend one upon another if they are to attain their true purpose.

The state of religion, as of language, perplexed discerning observers. On the surface it seemed that the long-awaited revival of 1904–5, to some a tempestuous interlude, would lead to sustained spiritual regeneration. Church membership reached its statistical peak in 1907 and the churches were full of energy. Yet, as R. Tudur Jones has noted in his admirable study of the crisis in the religious life of Wales between 1890 and 1914, there was a dispiriting feeling that sheer activity concealed a remorseless decline.[29] Had Welsh Liberal Nonconformity after all introduced the Trojan horse of infidelity? At Cardiff, as we have seen, a harmless mathematician was bullied for 'atheism', and around Viriamu Jones there hovered a faint aroma, dangerously seductive, some thought, of unorthodoxy.[30] Henry Jones did little to appease his denouncers who accused him of denying the divinity of Christ, by declaring: 'I do not deny the divinity of any man.'[31] At Aberystwyth, Thomas Jones injured his fortunes by refusing to play the denominational card. The redoubt was stoutly defended. In 1907 the *South Wales Daily News* reported that the history professor at Aberystwyth, Edward Edwards, elected to the diaconate, was the fifth member of staff to be called to an office in his Church, not to speak of the College Registrar, J. H. Davies, a deacon at Llangeitho.[32] The charges, however, persisted. In 1916 Theodore H. Robinson, lecturer in Semitic languages at Cardiff, told Haldane that 'we are, a good many of us, in the theological colleges in Wales, under suspicion of heterodoxy'. Haldane goodhumouredly replied that people were prone to look for aberrations, 'and you are very fond of aberrating in Wales'.[33] Following reports that Cardiff medical students, in the company of city medicos, had on one occasion consumed whisky and beer at a 'smoker' on College premises, the College was called 'the tippling college'. The Principal's proposal to establish a University and City Club, optimistically intended to be 'the intellectual centre of the Principality',[34] caused uproar at the Association of East Glamorgan Baptists, not at all impressed by the long-felt need for a cheap social, non-political club. E. H. Griffiths, it seemed, had blundered again, certainly in the eyes of 27,557 Baptists. Few took seriously the charges that students returned home as self-proclaimed agnostics, but as late as March 1934 the Revd Moelwyn Hughes, a prominent Calvinistic Methodist minister and the writer of at least two memorable hymns, delivered a thunderbolt from the pulpit of London's City Temple. Teachers and professors at the Welsh colleges were showing 'definite pagan tendencies',[35] felicities which he repeated at an Association meeting at Llanstephan. These assaults by a well-known divine were understandably interpreted as a crack of the whip. J. F. Rees, roused to unwonted ire, felt under a cloud and said that if Moelwyn Hughes wished 'to strike at any person, or any institution, let him do it openly and take the consequences'.[36]

By 1914 it was clear that the University regarded itself as the fountain-head of national culture.[37] It was to be expected, therefore, that educational matters beyond its walls were constantly within its purview. The unity of Welsh education, so dear to Viriamu Jones, had early suffered a serious reverse. Nevertheless, this combustible issue flared up periodically. In 1918 it appeared to have been extinguished, for A. T. Davies failed to persuade Lloyd George and H. A. L. Fisher of the need to establish a co-ordinating National Council of Education, to fuse together the Central Welsh Board and the University.[38] One of the recommendations of W. N. Bruce's report in 1920 upon the reorganization of secondary education was to form an Advisory Council. In 1928 the University Court, however, rejected the offer of the President of the Board of Education to create such a body. A parliamentary bill, supported by Megan Lloyd George to the same end came to nothing in 1929, and after successive conferences the matter was discussed for the last time at the University Court in 1936.[39] A little earlier W. J. Gruffydd had attacked the proposal, adding for full measure that it had been stirred up for years by William George, who, in turn, rebuked 'this somewhat erratic genius'.[40] The Council of the University was evidently less hostile, but not so the Academic Board which stressed the importance of academic independence and of maintaining existing relations with the University Grants Committee. Indeed, the latest scheme had been further complicated because it involved the appointment of a Secretary of State for Wales (an office which did not materialize until 1964). In the last analysis the campaign in the 1920s for a National Council of Education was fatally flawed by internal dissension. Without the unequivocal co-operation of the University its fate was settled. The University, it was alleged, 'was more concerned with its academic reputation than its national role'.[41]

Committed defenders of the secondary schools began to wonder whether Viriamu Jones had suffered total defeat. As time passed it became clear that the chief instrument in advancing the fortunes of the youth of Wales was not the Central Welsh Board but the University, which laid down conditions for matriculation and whose staff were the examiners. There was an allied consideration. The word 'intermediate' in the Welsh Intermediate

Act (1889) appeared to indicate a stage between elementary and university education, thus consigning technical education, where it existed at all, to an inferior status. In fact it limped far behind that of Scotland, and, to a lesser extent, that of England, a situation abhorrent to O. M. Edwards, who wanted the University to lead on a broad front. The aim of establishing a National Council stemmed principally from a desire to correct a distorted sense of values and to seek justice for the whole educational system, since it was evident that the great majority of secondary students were ill-suited to pursue university studies. Charges of arrogance, not altogether unfounded, were levelled against the University. An anonymous pamphleteer accused it in 1917 of endeavouring 'to evade all demands'[42] for reform. Ten years later there were signs of petulance when the Central Welsh Board convened a conference to discuss an important report on Welsh education without having allowed the University Court to take the initiative. The 'educational Parliament' seemed to be too attentive to its own interests in relation to secondary schools. F. A. Cavanagh, Professor of Education at Swansea, agreed that hundreds of children were annually prepared for matriculation without having the smallest intention of proceeding to a university, yet he would not concede that any responsibility lay with universities. Gladys Perrie Williams declared that since the proportion of pupils entering the University of Wales was so small 'this ruthless sacrifice of the many to the few seems incredible', and all the more strange in a land 'where the spirit of democracy is so prominent'.[43] Others, such as Gwenan Jones and Olive Wheeler, thought that Welsh education had taken a wrong path. Matriculation courses imposed by the University did not encourage the use of Welsh, and the needs of Wales, especially the rural areas, were not being met.

Nevertheless it would be wrong to suppose that the University was regarded with hostility by parents. Neither they nor employers considered the School Certificate to be an acceptable alternative. If the London 'matric' (with its insistence on both Latin and mathematics) could not be attained, then nothing less would do than the Welsh 'matric'. Parents favoured an academic curriculum because it would enable their graduate sons and daughters to rise in the social scale, whether in Wales, in

Wolverhampton or in the Great Wen itself. When Tom Ellis's widow remarked to Herbert Lewis in 1930 that the membership tickets read out in her London chapel on Sunday nights were 'larger than ever',[44] we may be certain that many of them belonged to newly arrived teachers. It must be acknowledged, too, that although a substantial majority of assistant teachers in the secondary schools of Wales were Welsh, the proportion of English headmasters was high, unduly so, many believed. When the new headmaster of Haverfordwest grammar school was appointed in 1925 it was noted with considerable displeasure that not a single graduate of the University of Wales had been shortlisted. Inevitably, there followed many bleak reflections upon the comparative value of the Welsh degree.[45] In general, however, relations between the University and the schools were cordial. The academic staff was well represented both on the Central Welsh Board and on the local education authorities; they were invited to distribute prizes and usually made solid, well-reported contributions to debates on educational matters. The teaching staff looked back with gratitude upon their college days, associations of former students flourished, particularly at Aberystwyth, and the Guild of Graduates was a further bond.

The University's debt to the common people of Wales had not been forgotten, especially at Aberystwyth, during the passionate debate to determine the nature of the University of Wales. R. D. Roberts and others were entirely convinced that it was practicable and necessary to allow students enmeshed in the toils of poverty to pursue degree courses without attending a constituent college. The overwhelming majority, however, believed that having long sought freedom from the London external examinations it was quixotic to create a similar system in Wales and to provide two dissimilar degrees within one institution. The dispute paralysed the university movement between 1888 and 1891, but at length Roberts's arguments were cast aside. In the University charter limited recognition was given to work performed outside the Colleges, but there was no question of awarding external degrees. In some quarters there was a sense of betrayal. One newspaper, later quoted in the American *Y Drych*, recalled that when news reached the Chicago Eisteddfod in 1893 of the granting of the University charter, it was received to the sound of trumpets, these being no more than slender pieces of pomp which left the people of Wales with mere bones.[46]

Between 1893 and 1914 the progress of adult education was at best fragmentary. In the early days the Colleges had encouraged their staff to deliver extension lectures, but after 1893 there was a decline, partly because of the increasing demands of internal teaching and partly because of new, even troublesome, administrative duties inevitable in a federal university. There was, however, one development of note, namely university settlements. The initial inspiration, Thomas Jones believed, came from Aberystwyth where civic enthusiasm was engendered, less by any formal teaching than by 'intense social life'[47] which prompted lively discussions concerning the great problems of society. A workmen's institute was maintained at Trefechan and during vacations students of the college worked in Bermondsey and Canning Town. Their activities found a responsive echo in Cardiff. R. S. Burrows was influenced, as Viriamu Jones had been, by T. H. Green and the Idealist school of philosophy. J. S. Mackenzie, like Henry Jones and Thomas Jones, was deeply affected at Glasgow by the Scottish Idealists led by Edward Caird. In order to create an enlightened, united society, education and liberal culture were to reach out beyond the walls of universities and colleges to the underprivileged, thus dissolving class antagonisms. Evolution, not revolution, was the watchword. To Burrows, university settlements were a partial answer to social discontent. At East Moors, Cardiff, he became warden of a settlement where he and his wife (daughter of a bishop of Chichester) took up residence. Burrows was a great friend not only of President Venizelos of Greece but also of the underprivileged at Cardiff, and students, who have an unusually keen eye for such matters, commemorated him in rhyme:

> Burrows lives in the slums
> And has gamins for chums
> And practises just what he preaches.[48]

Burrows and Mackenzie, anxious to balance the technical provisions of the county councils by lectures in arts subjects, managed to persuade the College Senate in 1901 to establish a

University Extension Committee. In north Wales R. H. Tawney began a three-year tutorial class at Wrexham which left a permanent impress upon the young A. H. Dodd. Bangor was the first of the Welsh Colleges to initiate a tutorial class, for in 1910 J. F. Rees was tutor to a highly successful class at Blaenau Ffestiniog. Soon both Aberystwyth and Bangor, though not Cardiff, appointed full-time tutors. In 1913 Bangor began its celebrated summer school which attracted students associated with several English universities and colleges. Something of the exuberant idealism of the proceedings may be gathered from Professor George Unwin's remark, upon hearing that the Great War had broken out, that he was returning to Manchester 'to stop the war'.[49] In 1909 R. D. Roberts had succeeded in persuading the University to establish a committee to examine the most effective means of co-ordinating the work of adult education under the aegis of the University. Nevertheless, when Roberts died in 1911 little real progress had been made.

In the mean time the Workers' Educational Association, founded in England in 1903, made its first appearance in Wales, at Barry in 1906. By 1910 there was a Welsh district, of which J. S. Mackenzie was chairman. He was succeeded in 1915 by Daniel Lleufer Thomas, who proposed to blend the rural popular culture of the *gwerin*, based upon the chapel and eisteddfod, with the traditions of the mechanics' institutes in England and Scotland and of the Christian Socialists and Pre-Raphaelites. He particularly deplored the rootless materialism which was undermining the ideals of religion and of nationality. In co-operation with the WEA the task of the University was 'to effect a reconciliation of individualism and socialism'.[50] In 1914 O. M. Edwards acknowledged that in founding the University in 1893 the 'one possible and acceptable scheme' had been adopted. Yet there was 'an ideal of a very different University in the minds of some of the acutest educationalists of Wales'. He added that 'for this University of Dreams there was no temple of stone, nor any castles. Its classes were to be established in every town, village and glen in Wales.' Edwards thought that the Welsh people had been too timid but he discerned in the work of the WEA 'signs of a kind of reunion between the common people of Wales and the University'.[51]

Such views would have been regarded as sentimental meanderings by workers then fighting for emancipation during a period of intense industrial strife. The leaders of the National Council of Labour Colleges in 1909 drew their inspiration from Karl Marx and as syndicalists they advocated the transfer of the means of production and distribution from their owners to unions of workers. One revolutionary socialist in south Wales declared that he strongly favoured voting a generous grant to the National Library of Wales because he recognized the value to workers of research conducted in a great library for 'the founder of my faith – Karl Marx – devoted forty years of his life to such research in the British Museum'.[52] Soon Central Labour College classes were being run in south Wales by the Miners' Federation and the National Union of Railwaymen. The University and the WEA were regarded as agencies to buttress the ruling class. According to one of Thomas Jones's well-informed correspondents (in this instance anonymous, but quite possibly Hector Hetherington) the notion that there was something to be said for the other side was anathema to an 'aggressive class movement'. It seemed that 'in itself the profession of impartiality is sufficient to discredit the University'.[53] In 1918 Elizabeth P. Hughes indicated to Lloyd George that education provided by the WEA would encourage Welsh colliers 'to give of their best to the Empire rather than anything dangerous'.[54]

It is evident that between the WEA and the Labour College there was a deep ideological divide, most marked as may be imagined in the teaching of economics. Serious impediments to the work of the WEA were naturally brought to the attention of the Haldane Commission. Amongst them was the difficulty of arousing the interest of employers in the Association. Characteristically, D. Lleufer Thomas spoke in conciliatory terms of the Central Labour College. Although co-operation seemed out of the question, collision was to be avoided. He deplored the fact that the University's extra-mural activities had 'dwindled to very small proportions'.[55] Yet it was evident that workers had a thirst for knowledge. Robert Richards, for example, reported that whilst theology had fallen out of fashion there was considerable discussion in the quarries during the dinner hour concerning economics, now perceived to be the sovereign remedy.

Quarrymen were 'exceedingly keen'; notes of Richards's lectures would be discussed next day in the *caban* 'and the following week I used to have all kinds of questions on what I had said the previous week'.[56] Haldane, who knew of miners trudging three to four miles to a class, had no need to be convinced of the value of adult education. It was natural, therefore, that in consequence of his report the new charter provided for a University Extension Board to review, co-ordinate, assist and supplement the extra-mural work of the Colleges and to co-operate with bodies outside the University to promote adult education in Wales.[57] Already each College had a Joint Committee and the creation of a new College, Swansea, which had a zestful commitment to adult education, added to the effectiveness of the work of the University.

It is true that immediate post-war developments at Cardiff were not encouraging. Alfred Zimmern was scathing in his attack upon a university which could 'even display, on occasion, a deliberate preference for the unlettered, if titled, capitalist over the zealous and lettered proletarian'.[58] There were also misgivings at Aberystwyth and Bangor concerning the founding of Coleg Harlech in 1927, largely the creation of Thomas Jones, because of the fear of socialist influences. The Bangor Registrar, W. P. Wheldon, perhaps still smarting at his failure to be appointed Principal in succession to Reichel, told T. J. that 'quite a number of mandarins in this part of the world are ridiculously sensitive to the possibility of propaganda in adult education'.[59] Coleg Harlech, however, did more than survive early buffets. By the outbreak of war it was no nearer to becoming part of the structure of the University of Wales, but it had amply demonstrated, as T.J. had hoped on opening day, that the College was not a luxury but a necessity. Of the University's Extension Board he had sharp things to say. No one would mistake it for 'a power-house', adding that 'for the source of heat and light of a national movement it has a low candle-power'.[60]

An authoritative *Survey of Adult Education in Wales* (1940) gave a more encouraging picture. A North Wales District of the Workers' Educational Association had been formed in 1925 under an energetic secretary, R. Silyn Roberts. The Aberystwyth area, as large as the medieval diocese of St David's but far less densely populated than the Cardiff area, nevertheless had as many students as Cardiff in 1939. Criticism that Aberystwyth compared unfavourably in numerical terms with Bangor was for a time true, but not in 1939. It offered far fewer tutorial classes in the 1930s than the other areas, partly on financial grounds and partly because its numerous extension courses more effectively met the needs of the countryside. Aberystwyth had one advantage denied to the other colleges, for it had a full-time director of extra-mural studies, the Revd Herbert Morgan, who had a rare capacity to inspire colleagues and students. Bangor appointed its first director, Alun Llywelyn-Williams, soon after the war, but Cardiff and Swansea were in this respect somewhat laggard. During the inter-war years the National Library was mainly responsible for lending books to classes, but there was a serious lack of appropriate text-books in Welsh. The Extension Board in conjunction with the University Press Board arranged for a series of books to be published called 'Cyfres y Brifysgol a'r Werin' (the University and Common People Series), authoritatively and, in the main, attractively written to meet the needs of adult students. By 1940, nineteen volumes had appeared, almost all upon arts subjects. Between 1921 and 1939 the number of classes held under the auspices of the four Colleges had increased from 82 to 201. It is certain that the lives of many were enriched. They would doubtless have echoed the words of Albert Mansbridge to quarrymen at Bangor in 1912: 'If a tutorial class did anything worth doing, it was to give men a great reverence for things they did not know.'[61]

Since Welshmen had long delighted in theological controversy, thereby whetting an appetite for speculative thought, it was hoped that the study of theology would greatly prosper within the University. The results had been disappointing. The *Welsh Outlook* compared them adversely with those of London and Manchester, indicating that of the forty-two theologians who had responded to a manifesto by German theologians in 1915 not one was a Welshman.[62] Two years later Reichel, in a considered judgement, gave out that only one theological work of outstanding merit was the fruit of 'our own university system',[63] namely *Christianity in Early Britain* (1912) by Hugh Williams. The University's wartime Dean of Divinity, Owen Prys, told

Haldane that Wales was distinguished for her preachers, not her theological scholars whom he clearly preferred, for 'our main cause is to serve the churches'.[64] Principal Thomas Rees of Bala-Bangor agreed that Wales had 'nothing approaching'[65] the Scottish record nor that of the Tübingen school. In Wales three-quarters of students in theological colleges were ill-prepared upon arrival, having spent several years in employment, and were further obliged for financial reasons to preach on Sundays, thus unduly scattering their attention during long weekends. The teaching staff were overwhelmed by teaching duties, usually at a non-graduate level, whereas in Scotland, as Reichel noted, 'few years pass without some substantial addition to theological learning'.[66] Much of it emanated, it was true, from the country manse, rather than the universities, because the minister was a graduate fired by a zeal for theological research by his university professor, himself a scholar of the highest rank. In Wales this was not possible until the staffs of theological colleges were able to undertake systematic original work. One of the consequences of the Haldane Report and the establishment of Schools of Theology at Bangor and Cardiff was to stimulate biblical studies, but theology, as usually interpreted, did not fulfil in the Welsh Colleges the traditional role of 'queen of the sciences'. Nevertheless, the bringing together of denominational colleges in close association with University Colleges promoted a deeper understanding of opposing and often passionately held convictions, whilst the preaching engagements of ministerial students throughout the land were timely reminders to the churches of their continuing links with the colleges which they had done much to found.

Amongst the Welsh public at large there was a lamentable lack of interest in art and architecture, a serious defect which the University authorities wished to remedy. There were, of course, fine inherited examples of architectural achievement, churches, castles, country houses, farmhouses and bridges. Yet when new colleges were built at Cardiff and Bangor there was no native tradition to which architects could turn, and in competitions for public buildings Englishmen triumphed. The deficiencies of domestic and decorative art in Wales had long troubled Thomas Ellis. The days he had spent at the Paris Exhibition in 1887 were a revelation; here were to be seen in separate rooms, not only the native work of large nations but also that of small countries such as Denmark, Greece and Finland, not unlike Wales in many ways, but which, he characteristically added, had 'enjoyed the priceless gift of self-government'.[67] He might also have spoken at length, had he wished, of the absence in Wales of patronage indispensable to artists and architects. Not even the more fervent patriot, said Ellis, could claim that there was a native school of art. A year earlier he had pleaded for a Welsh School of Architecture for it saddened him that communities who built chapels on hills and in valleys 'are too often at the mercy of Architects who have neither training, nor skill nor taste, nor imagination, nor knowledge of material nor true tests of good workmanship'.[68] The theme was taken up by D. Lleufer Thomas in 1917. He deplored the absence of a School of Architecture and Town Planning in Cardiff which might follow the fine example set by Liverpool.[69] Educationists were alarmed by the distressing lack of taste in everyday life. Olive Wheeler, Professor of Education at Cardiff, recalled in 1930 the parlour of a small house known to her. It had numerous antimacassars, the walls were covered with pictures of Methodist ministers, the fourteen china dogs each had a different facial expression and although the countryside was carpeted with flowers there was not a single natural flower in the room. Children raised in such surroundings would have a distorted view of life and 'would come to think of the universe as a conglomeration of useless articles'.[70]

The notion that environment affected one's view of life was scarcely new. The future Lord Pontypridd said in 1906 that he never passed the tower of St John's church at Cardiff without being moved and he hoped that the new college building, which should be 'novel and commanding',[71] would be educational in itself. Kenyon felt the same about Bangor; a shade ecstatically, he thought that the completed building would have as deep an influence upon students as the teaching received within. M. F. Rathbone believed that there was a sound basis upon which to build. The native stone masons and stone cutters, the smiths and the joiners of north Wales were, to her certain knowledge, 'notable craftsmen', and it was 'out of the native crafts that a truly national art will grow'. She also held that 'in a people so susceptible to music and poetry, the eye only needs training to appreciate beauty in concrete form and colour'.[72] The University Court did more than bewail the 'general indifference to the place of beauty in life which is prevalent in our country'.[73] It determined to give a lead. Already in 1929 there was a special session of the Court (which Haldane would have welcomed) to consider means of cultivating a greater sense of beauty in art and nature in national education. (Sir) Clough Williams-Ellis, the celebrated architect, resented the 'affronts to man's most sensitive organ – the eye'.[74] H. M. Vaughan, author and landowner, believed that an appreciation of the beautiful was inborn in certain individuals, no matter how lowly and illiterate, and lay in wait to be awakened. He hoped to see two artistic movements, one spreading upwards from the *gwerin*, the other downward from the University, leading to a revival of good taste amongst the Welsh people. He and others argued for the creation of a chair and directorship of art in the University.[75]

There was little progress. True, after considerable delay a Faculty of Architecture was established in 1938, the University permitting the granting of an initial degree in architecture following a study of six years, the first to be spent at a constituent college, the remainder at Cardiff Technical College. The purpose was evidently to avoid needless duplication of facilities, but the Privy Council indicated, quite reasonably, that the University should control the appointments of the head of department and of other teachers of architecture at the Technical College. The Court, upon the advice of the Academic Board, responded by passing a special statute in accord with the recommendation of the Privy Council, whose salutary intervention was welcomed by those who upheld the 'sound maxim that the University cannot properly concern itself with teaching or teachers outside its own boundaries'.[76] It need scarcely be added that a degree in architecture was not awarded before the Second World War. As to the teaching of art, it was recommended in 1933, after inspection by two experts, one of whom was Herbert Read, that courses in the department of arts and crafts at Aberystwyth should be recognized at the initial stage of the BA degree.[77] At Bangor annual art lectures endowed by a former College Treasurer, T. Rowland Hughes, began in 1924. Nothing came of a proposal to institute a University lectureship in fine art (modest enough in the eyes of those who had advocated a chair and a directorship), mainly because the Academic Board believed that the funds available would be better employed in stimulating artistic activities in the Colleges. After endless discussions there was little to show, except the provision of public lectures in the main towns of Wales. In fairness it must be stressed that it was difficult to treat art upon the same terms as music, which had been given a special statutory position by charter following the Haldane recommendations. The University had already diverged from those recommendations in respect of agriculture and the Medical School and caution was necessary if anything approaching justice was to be done for music, clearly accorded primacy.[78]

The masters of pulpit oratory had long employed their formidable dramatic talents to terrorize their countrymen and to rescue them from the snares of Satan. Gradually, despite severe misgivings and censure, these gifts found expression on the stage. A well-known continental producer, Dr Stefan Hock, held that only two peoples in Europe were actors by nature, those of Sicily and Wales, a large, unqualified claim which cannot profitably be pursued.[79] It may be said, however, with confidence that the dramatic movement made an immediate appeal to staff and students in Wales before the First World War, so much so that Kenyon wrote in 1914 that the movement was particularly to be identified with the University.[80] Plays were regularly produced at Aberystwyth and Bangor and the first drama in Welsh to be publicly performed was W. J. Gruffydd's *Beddau'r Proffwydi* at the Theatre Royal, Cardiff, in 1913, staged and acted entirely by members of the College.[81] In the 1920s the honorary degree of magister was conferred upon three playwrights. R. G. Berry, educated at Bangor (where he was a victim of the intermediate examination in mathematics of the London University), was a Congregationalist minister with an engaging gift of satire. Both J. O. Francis, who wrote plays in English with a Welsh rural setting, and D. T. Davies, writing in Welsh and praised for his interpretation of social life in Wales, were educated at Aberystwyth and were considered to be the most skilful craftsmen of their day. There was much dramatic activity throughout Wales and at Swansea, for example, the staff of the College presented frequent productions of plays in Welsh. Several works were translated by members of the University staff from Russian, French and Norwegian. At Bangor the College Dramatic Society performed one of Ibsen's plays in Welsh in 1926 to great acclaim. Kate Roberts thought that there was an excessive dependence upon translated works, but Thomas Parry at Bangor stoutly defended the practice at a time when a Welsh tradition had far from established itself.[82] The two best dramatists of the century writing in Welsh, Saunders Lewis and John Gwilym Jones, had a close, if intermittent, association with the University, but their major contributions belong to a later period. In the main, amateurism prevailed. There was no attempt by the authorities to create chairs and departments of drama. It is remarkable that the only Principal known to have raised his voice on the subject was Maurice Jones of Lampeter, who appealed for a school of dramatic production in Wales: 'I consider that this is essentially a matter for the University, and [that] there should be in each of the constituent colleges a teacher of drama, who would supervise the production of plays and the setting up of a school of acting.'[83]

The appointment in 1919 of Walford Davies, then a large, burly figure in air force blue, to the Gregynog chair of music at Aberystwyth and to the directorship of the University Council of Music had aroused great expectations. One of his first papers was delivered to the Cymmrodorion Society at 10 Downing Street (an unusual meeting-place for the Society) under the chairmanship of Lloyd George. Wales, Davies said, 'speaks Welsh, English and Music – and the greatest of these is Music'.[84] Before, at Aberystwyth, he had stated his aims: to reinvigorate the work of the Colleges, though without direct interference; to enliven musical education from the earliest childhood to adulthood; to wean choral singing from its competitive tradition to an appreciation of the riches of European music, and to encourage the development of instrumental music.[85] It was difficult to object to any of these aims. For example, the work of the Colleges in music, other than at Cardiff, had not been impressive in its higher reaches. Yet it was perhaps unwise of Walford Davies to speak, as he did, of his Welsh 'mission', for some were not prepared to listen with bated breath to an evangelistic message from an Oswestry man but one-eighth Welsh. D. Vaughan

Thomas, rejected in favour of Walford, knew from within what were the special needs of Wales. Moreover, the folk-song movement, founded in 1906 by A. P. Graves (father of Robert) and Reichel, owed much to J. Lloyd Williams and a group of students, Y Cantorion (The Songsters), at Bangor. They had gathered a number of traditional songs at a crucial time because the religious revival of 1904–5, like other revivals, was inimical to popular songs sung in fairs, taverns and 'merry nights' (*nos-weithiau llawen*). W. S. Gwynn Williams, editor of *Y Cerddor Newydd*, and decidedly hostile to Walford Davies, whom he believed to be under the thrall of continental composers, wrote that 'we must never forget that Welsh music, to be of any intrinsic value, must be definitely nationalistic in character, and not merely a copy of some foreign school, however wonderful that school may be'.[86] There were also disparaging remarks concerning 'Teutonism', a phrase acceptable enough when Reichel, years earlier, had spoken of the Welshman as 'the Teuton of the Celts',[87] but less so in the aftermath of the Great War.

Gwynn Williams doubtless drew support from the Haldane Report in which the section on music was clearly influenced by Hadow, abidingly fascinated by the relation between music and nationality. The Council of Music and its Director could do for Welsh music what Mussorgsky and other enthusiasts had done for Russia. The material available in Wales was no less rich than the Russian: 'the great fabric of Russian music . . . is a standing example of the value of the national movement wisely conceived and skilfully treated'. The report had, however, insisted that the great masterpieces of other countries should by no means be excluded. Rather, they should be employed 'to educate the national genius and train it to deliver the national message'.[88] Walford Davies was in entire agreement with Hadow. Whilst the folk-song movement was 'bringing us back to simple melodic meanings', he countered with alacrity to the charge that Wales could not be made musical by Bach. The Hungarian, Béla Bartók, a recent visitor to Aberystwyth, although brought up on Mozart had never baffled the Hungarians. Every Welshman who wished to write Welsh music 'would have to drink first . . . at the springs of the great masters'.[89] He did not silence his critics.

Davies was determined through various agencies to penetrate all layers of Welsh society. In schools there was to be daily choral singing, if possible in the afternoon 'when mental effort is hard, and cheery doings are a God-send'.[90] College trios, familiar to generations of school pupils and which he greatly encouraged, had by 1939 given over 3,000 lecture-recitals. For students he prepared a hymnal, *Hymns of the Kingdom* (to which title a confused patriot wished to have added *and the Principality*).[91] Not the least of his triumphs was to engage the attention of Cardiff businessmen for two hours at the Park Hotel where he lectured 'On the Use of the Domestic Piano'.[92] When he retired from the Gregynog chair at Aberystwyth in 1926 he became organist at St George's chapel, Windsor. In 1935 he succeeded Elgar as Master of the King's Musick. Nevertheless, he remained Director of the Council of Music (at Cardiff) until his death in 1941. To Gregynog he returned whenever possible for there he found solace. He was perhaps at his best as a trainer of choirs. At the Welsh week at Wembley in August 1924 he demonstrated a remarkable gift for conducting large choirs. Five years later he spoke of the need to organize 'untutored enthusiasm' and it is likely that the Council of Music, under his direction, was at its most successful in educating adults. Each class, he held, should '*hear* music . . . *make* music, and, under guidance, *try to understand it*'.[93] To the distressed areas of south Wales – the Three Valleys Festival is a notable example – he brought a shaft of light in the darkest of days; gramophone and radio were his ready instruments, and 'he knew instinctively that most members of his audiences were waiting to be awakened'.[94] He broadened musical awareness and pointed the way to the post-war period, when Wales, in musical terms, became one of the emerging nations.

Although relations with the National Eisteddfod were not always harmonious, there was a natural tendency to look upon the Eisteddfod as 'an elder sister of the university'.[95] It could not be forgotten that when the pioneer college was battling for survival it was given £250 in 1873 out of the Mold Eisteddfod's surplus and £600 from the surplus of the Caernarfon Eisteddfod in 1877. State grants to the Colleges were bound to affect contributions, yet Bangor received 100 guineas towards its building fund out of the profits of the memorable Eisteddfod held there in

1902, and Swansea £1,000 in 1926 as 'a capital nucleus' of a department of music. In the summer following its arrival, the University charter was lent for display at the Eisteddfod, an eloquently symbolic act.[96] Both institutions, J. E. Lloyd informed ill-humoured critics of the University, were of modern growth, 'the joint action of two forces which at first flowed in separate and even divergent channels'. The modern Eisteddfod, though of ancient ancestry, was the offspring of the patriotic movement, 'the protest of romanticism against the doctrines of the French Revolution'. In its recent form it was the product of the last half of the nineteenth century. The University, however, owed its origin to the religious awakening of the eighteenth century. Both movements had united in mid-Victorian times 'to create the Wales we know'. Neither the Eisteddfod nor the University could have succeeded without the cordial co-operation of the leaders of both movements, both 'ignored all distinctions of party and creed' (a generous assessment not easy to sustain) and both were victims of the perfervid criticisms of idealistic patriots. Lloyd believed, from his own experience as adjudicator, that the standards in the Eisteddfod had recently been raised, largely, we must assume, because of academic influences, so that an essay which won a £25 prize at the Eisteddfod could not fail to win the approval of examiners as a thesis for the MA degree of the University.[97] These assertions were sometimes too easily made. When O. M. Edwards told J. H. Davies at the Haldane Commission's hearings that in the opinion of an Oxford professor (York Powell) Eisteddfod productions were 'very much on a par' with Oxford prize essays, Davies replied: 'He was rather fortunate, then.'[98] Yet it would not be long before a schoolmaster's Eisteddfod essay on the history of the Puritan movement in Wales would earn him a master's degree and thereafter the lasting gratitude of serious students of the subject.[99]

The *Western Mail* did not care for Lloyd's historical survey; 'the plausible varnish of the learned professor'[100] had obscured the services of the largely Anglican Society for the Promotion of Christian Knowledge and of literary-minded clergy in Wales. No one, however, could cavil at Lloyd's insistence that the Colleges had nourished the eisteddfod spirit or that students who had won their spurs at college eisteddfodau went on to further triumphs upon a national platform. Thus T. H. Parry-Williams, whilst still a student, won both chair and crown at the National Eisteddfod in 1912, a phenomenal achievement which he repeated in 1915. R. Williams Parry, a student at both Aberystwyth and Bangor, was chaired in 1910, for his *awdl*, 'Yr Haf', and his two volumes of poetry, though slim, place him securely amongst the greatest of Welsh poets. Thomas Gwynn Jones, a stirring example of victory over adversity, received no formal university education but nevertheless began a distinguished career at Aberystwyth in 1913, eleven years after winning a chair at the National Eisteddfod for his *awdl*, 'Ymadawiad Arthur', fittingly regarded as a landmark in the history of Welsh poetry in the twentieth century. A fundamental contribution was to establish and uphold literary standards. The adjudications of John Morris-Jones, who readily assumed the mantle of mentor, were heard with a rapt reverence. If Thomas Charles Edwards, Aberystwyth's first Principal, was the bridge between one book and many, as Lloyd George once said, Morris-Jones was the formidable instrument in transferring the authority of the pulpit to that of literary criticism.[101] In the inter-war years a constellation of poets was educated at the University Colleges.

The University resolutely believed that it was its duty to make representations to public bodies concerning Welsh interests. In 1935 the University's Advisory Board of Law submitted a memorandum to the Royal Commission on the Despatch of Business at Common Law relating to the administration of justice in Wales. Amongst other matters it recommended that in appointing High Court Judges to go on circuit in Wales and Monmouthshire preference should be given to those who had a knowledge of Welsh and that 'a Welsh witness is entitled to claim as of right to give his evidence in Welsh'.[102] Nine years earlier there had begun a long struggle for elementary justice concerning broadcasting in Wales. The Court received resolutions from Cardiff's Court and Aberystwyth's Council to the effect that a broadcasting station should be established to provide primarily for the needs of Wales, her individuality and national culture. Subsequent discussions led to the appointment of a deputation (including W. N. Bruce, Lloyd George, Walford Davies and

W. J. Gruffydd) to wait upon the British Broadcasting
Corporation. The essence of the matter was that Wales was linked
to south-west England and that the Western Region, as it was
called, was, in Saunders Lewis's words, 'an impossible unit'. He
added that 'the subservience of cultural unity to technical
conveniences is fantastic'.[103] The Cardiff station, moreover, had a
very limited range. The details of the protracted discussions need
not concern us here. Sometimes they were farcical. For example,
the BBC declared that it was prepared occasionally to extend the
Saturday 'Welsh Interlude', usually from 6.45 to 7 p.m., by five
minutes provided it was not immediately followed by 'In Town
Tonight'.[104] Scotland, it should be added, had been recognized in
1924 as being in no sense a 'region' of England. In 1929 'grave
dissatisfaction'[105] was expressed by the University Court concerning broadcasts to schools, Reichel declaring that the
problems arising from two languages and the claims of Wales
were much stronger than those of Scotland. At length the
Corporation's powerful first Director-General, John Reith,
agreed in 1933 to be advised on matters relating to broadcasting
in Wales by a University Committee appointed by the University
Council. Two years later the Corporation announced that it was
prepared to separate Wales from south-west England and to
provide a relay station to serve north Wales. Not until December
1938 was the Pro-Chancellor able to tell the Court that the
University Committee's repeated meetings with the Corporation
and its 'perseverance and importunity'[106] had led to the
establishment of a broadcasting station for Wales. Whilst it may
justly be conceded that the Corporation had problems concerning wavelengths, they were certainly not insuperable and should
not have caused an inordinate delay of eleven years after the issue
was first raised by the University. Saunders Lewis was right to say
that the University Committee had been obliged to assume a task
more appropriately performed at Westminster.[107] There was also
the civil service, unduly tardy in allowing Welsh studies due
recognition in examinations for the administrative grade. The
University presented its case with compelling logic. The Commissioners, 'of course unintentionally', were 'encouraging, by
economic stimulus, the neglect of Welsh studies'.[108] The Commissioners cogitated for five years and in July 1936 the Court was

told that they were now prepared to include 'Welsh Civilization' as a subject for the junior grade of the administrative class.[109] In view of such excessive delays in dealing with reasonable requests, it is not surprising that some sober men began to wonder whether Welsh matters were best discharged at the heart of a declining Empire.

The responsibility of the University and its Colleges for Welsh studies was never questioned. 'The first service which a national university should render to the country it represents', said Lord Sankey in 1934, 'is the preservation of the national language, literature and history.'[110] Whatever contribution might be made in Oxford, Dublin, Scotland, Liverpool and on the continent, the prime duty lay within Wales itself. 'An institution which exists to maintain the traditions of our civilization', declared D. Emrys Evans, 'would be false to its own character if it ignored those traditional elements which lie at its doors. To ignore them is to conspire to destroy them.'[111] Saunders Lewis proclaimed that his action at Penrhos aerodrome on 8 September 1936 was in order to save the honour of the University of Wales, 'for the language and literature of Wales are the very *raison d'être* of this University'.[112] In 1925 a Departmental Committee was appointed by the President of the Board of Education to inquire into the position of Welsh in the educational system of Wales. The illustrious chairman was John Owen, Bishop of St David's, who died before the completion of the report, *Welsh in Education and Life* (1927).[113] The University of Wales presented an impressive memorandum to the Committee. One of the most valuable contributions, which lies buried in appendices, consists of penetrating observations by professors of Welsh upon the study of Welsh in their departments and by J. Lloyd Williams upon the cultural value of the language in music. The memorandum begins with a forthright declaration of principle: 'The Welsh language and its literature is necessarily the speciality of the University of Wales; this is a branch of learning in which the University possesses overwhelming initial advantages.' Moreover,

> it is obviously the duty of the University, as the highest educational institution in Wales, to spare no effort to further the native language and literature. This duty it owes to its own reputation,

and to the Welsh nation, whose educational needs it was erected to satisfy. The University of Wales should be able at the least to establish itself as the most important centre of Welsh scholarship, and as a result of the work of its members in this field it should not fail to secure recognition from all countries.[114]

In practical terms it was necessary to increase staff in the departments of Welsh. Their task was 'singularly complex', for they had 'to search for the raw material, work it into presentable shape, and dictate it to their class or else edit and print it'. They were, in short, researchers, editors and publishers before they were able to teach effectively, a situation 'without parallel' in any other department of the University. The publication of suitable text-books was fundamental, if only to escape the treadmill of mechanical dictation. In Ireland and in some other countries governments subsidized publication of academic works which in Wales the University Press Board would gladly produce. The teaching of Welsh history was to be encouraged, though in surprisingly narrow terms, 'on lines that would assist the work of the Welsh departments themselves'. Again, whilst it was indeed true that in some departments of Welsh the language was not employed for all purposes, there was an unanswerable case for its extended use in other departments on the arts side because students who pursued subjects other than Welsh had 'little incentive to consider a knowledge of Welsh as a desirable part of their general culture'. Welsh was 'a cultural instrument, and until it is recognised as such the Welsh people must remain in intellectual thraldom'.[115] If Welsh were more widely used in the University its study would be promoted and its place in national life secured. Schools would soon follow suit and the number of subjects taught through the medium of Welsh would multiply.

There were other considerations. The University should be active in the training of teachers for elementary and secondary schools. Welsh should be recognized as a subject of educational value by bodies such as the Law Society and joint stock banks in their preliminary examinations. The civil service and the Army Council had already done so. Finally, the orthography of the Welsh language needed to be standardized following the confusions of the nineteenth century.[116] The University should have a central role in creating a body, perhaps an Academy of Letters, to 'guide the language in its progressive adaptation to modern needs'.[117] These recommendations were almost all incorporated in the report, long and justly regarded by many as an inspiring affirmation.

The Academic Board appeared at its best when it prepared a quinquennial submission on the subject to the University Grants Commission in 1934. Broadly speaking, it reinforced the arguments presented in the 1927 report. Every other subject in the curriculum was studied at other universities, but 'if the University of Wales should fail in its duty towards Welsh, no other university would be able to make good the loss'. The field of Welsh research was 'vast', a word it used advisedly, for only at the beginning of the century was the field 'even surveyed'. Almost all work of significance in this area had been undertaken by the University. It was true that the work completed by staff and former students which appeared in lists of published research during the last three decades was greater in quantity than in other subjects, but only because it had been undertaken in 'practically a virgin field'.[118] Teachers were devoting a disproportionate amount of time to purveying factual information and there would be no improvement unless departments of Welsh were given resources, on the surface disproportionate, in order to remedy the distressing deficiencies of the past.[119]

In the mean time, Welsh scholars were not neglecting the common reader. In 1920 there began a series, 'Cyfres y Werin', edited by Ifor L. Evans and Henry Lewis, both academics of distinction. Their declared purpose was to follow the example of Gruffudd Robert of Milan, a Roman Catholic of the sixteenth century permanently exiled from his native land, where he was later honoured by Methodist and Anglican alike as one of the princes of Welsh Renaissance scholarship. In the preface to his celebrated Welsh grammar, prepared in adverse circumstances, Gruffudd Robert stated his purpose: 'to teach, help, divert and lead to perfection my own countrymen in all things which may enrich them and which are of good report in the eyes of the world'.[120] Evans and Lewis published fifteen volumes at modest prices between 1920 and 1927. Only the first concerned Welsh literature. The others were translations of European masterpieces, by Ibsen, Maupassant and Gogol, for example. This outward-looking series was succeeded in 1928, as we have seen, by 'Cyfres y Brifysgol a'r Werin'.[121] In the first issue of *Y Beirniad* (The Critic), 1911, the editor, John Morris-Jones, made it clear that the new journal was intended not solely for University people but for a national readership. He took the opportunity to inform critics of the University that greater attention was given at the colleges to Welsh language and literature than at any time since the fifteenth and sixteenth centuries when poets instructed their disciples in the skills and mysteries of syntax and *cynghanedd*.[122] In 1925 W. J. Gruffydd said that in the nineteenth century the literature of Wales had descended into 'its very nadir'. The revival which had taken place, 'unparalleled in recent history', was due to the University, the 'fount and source' of this awakening. 'Through the poets and writers, trained and inspired by the new learning, the large ideas of the greater world have flowed into the common life of the Welsh democracy.'[123]

Retrospect

As the university movement gained momentum during the third quarter of the nineteenth century the intention was to found a unitary university in Wales or, if that was not immediately possible, a university college which would blossom into a university after a period of apprenticeship. The tiny college opened at Aberystwyth in 1872 faced many perils. The Aberdare Report (1880) demolished all hope of establishing a unitary university of Wales and cast serious doubt concerning the future of the college which, nevertheless, survived and joined Cardiff (1883) and Bangor (1884) to form the University of Wales in 1893, to which was added Swansea in 1920.

The failure to found a unitary university in Wales has aroused retrospective ire. The triplication and at length the quadrupling of departments and of administrative offices essential to each separate college has been condemned as a severe, needless impost upon exiguous resources. Frequent, long journeys and the expanding tentacles of bureaucracy also drew adverse comment. Yet such hostile reflections gave scant weight to the circumstances of the time. In 1893 a federal university in Wales was inevitable.

The spirit of goodwill was soon put to the test. Decisions which accorded precedence to one college touched exposed nerves. The fitting choice of Aberystwyth for the installation of the University's first chancellor was readily accepted at Bangor but not at Cardiff. Understandable hesitation to determine the creation of a central registry led to protracted delays before Cardiff was justly chosen in the teeth of Aberystwyth's unrelenting opposition. Freedom from the London system had aroused expectations of relative independence in devising courses, but the Court's formal responsibility in such matters devolved in practice upon the University Senate which enmeshed the colleges in rules of frustrating complexity. Several of those who had been active promoters of the charter allowed it to be known in the early 1900s that at a time, perhaps not far distant, it would be realistic to regard the federal university as a mere staging post before the colleges went their separate ways. Henry Jones suggested in unguarded moments that Wales might well emulate Scotland, which sustained four universities. Some nourished intemperate ambitions, especially at Cardiff, when Birmingham became a unitary university in 1900, soon to be followed by the disintegration of the Victoria University whose constitution had been well-thumbed in Wales before 1893. It was not surprising that the attempt to strengthen central authority by imposing a working head upon the colleges failed totally.[1]

The unanimous conclusion of the Haldane Report, as of the Raleigh Committee, was that the University of Wales should remain a federal university. Later generations, especially in 1964, turned to the Haldane Report for inspiration and reassurance when the unity of the University seemed imperilled from within.[2] As to the application of the federal principle, the report appeared on the surface to speak with two voices. Greater academic freedom was certainly allowed to the Colleges to devise their own courses without interference and to dispense with external examiners until the degree examinations. On the other hand, the authority of the newly created University Council was initially considered to be oppressive. Henceforth, the main government grants were dispatched, not to each college separately, but to the Council, charged with equitable division upon the basis of declared needs and according to an ingenious formula. A new department could not henceforth be established except with the approval of the Council, expected to seek the prior advice of the Academic Board which not infrequently found it difficult to adjudicate between various claims and which appeared to lack the power and the will to exercise a decisive influence upon major academic matters.[3]

It is ironical that the rebirth of the University (for it was nothing less) was soon followed, not by the spirit of concord, but by the furious controversy concerning the Medical School. Whilst the University cannot be absolved from the charges of tergiversation, the dispute was clouded by the School's relations with the Cardiff Infirmary so that it was not exclusively a federal problem. The episode was a salutary reminder to the University and its Colleges that they should be circumspect in their dealings with one another.[4] When confronted with such combustible issues as the Officers' Training Corps and the case of Saunders Lewis, the University was careful not to invade the rights of Colleges.[5] Many felt that it should have intervened to protect Saunders Lewis and there was widespread disapproval, which has persisted to this day. Geraint H. Jenkins, for example, speaks of the University's 'inertia',[6] whilst also acknowledging that on constitutional grounds no other course was possible. In a democracy constitutions may be changed but not ignored. That was the University's unalterable conviction.

The Kilbrandon Commission declared that 'even at its best federalism is an awkward system to operate. It depends a great deal on co-operation between governments.' The impression formed was that 'even in countries where it has worked satisfactorily this is not because of its intrinsic merits but because those concerned with government have been successful in overcoming its drawbacks'.[7] Those who know the University well need not read these remarks with pursed lips. A federal system does have drawbacks, as became clear in England by the end of the nineteenth century. Essential ingredients are a broad basis of consent and effective government by men of goodwill. Kilbrandon further observed that as a general rule 'power in federations gravitates towards the centre'[8] (Canada being 'an interesting exception'). Such tendencies were to be seen in the University of Wales, when the working head controversy was conducted with some bitterness, especially during the early 1900s. The Colleges firmly opposed undue centralization, as it appeared to them, and it is evident that a loose federation was the only acceptable form of government in the University of Wales. Kilbrandon further observed that federal countries in the modern world were 'hampered by an inflexible system of government'.[9] We are not here concerned with Kilbrandon's recommendations but simply to recognize problems which have afflicted the University. In 1914 David Davies hoped that Sir William James Thomas might make his gift to establish a Medical School to the University, not to the Cardiff College. If this were done he would act likewise in relation to his endowment of colonial history at Aberystwyth. The principle would thus be established that all special subjects would come under the direct control of the University, thereby avoiding overlapping in the Colleges.[10] However, there was little prospect that the future lay in this direction. It is true that provision was made in the supplemental charter (in line with the Haldane Report) that staff could be appointed by the University to teach in more than one College, but it remained a dead letter. The right to appoint teachers belonged to the Colleges. In 1928 it was decided that a teacher in one College might pay a brief visit to another College to lecture on his speciality. This, however, was an entirely different matter. As Viriamu Jones had indicated many years earlier, teaching in a federal university could only be systematically conducted in the colleges. Thus it was neither financially possible nor deemed academically desirable to establish University institutes or schools in a constituent College, though the University retained a general oversight of the Schools of Theology at Bangor and Cardiff and of the Advisory Board of Law (which mainly concerned Aberystwyth, where there was the only department of law in the University). The separate School of Medicine was *sui generis*. Care was taken to state clearly that the Director of the University Council of Music should consult the constituent colleges 'without prejudice to their autonomy'.[11] D. Emrys Evans rightly stressed that 'federalism is a specific which may be taken in varying doses'.[12] An inability to adjust to changing needs and circumstances is a recipe for damaging, and perhaps destructive, conflicts. That the University has, by and large, been flexible and adaptable is one of the principal reasons why it has survived far longer than its leaders would have conceived possible (or even desirable) in the first decade of the century. The other governing consideration is that the University, principally through its Court, has believed that in its federal form it reflects the aspirations of the Welsh people.

The question naturally arises as to the measure of support which the University might reasonably count upon, both within and without. The Cardiff Senate was almost alone in seeking separation in 1916, and the College has from time to time harboured more critics of the federal system than the other colleges. Its standpoint has not always been sympathetically considered. Isambard Owen believed that when a college had a thousand students it might reasonably expect to be granted university status. Manchester had 1,308 students when it became independent in 1903, Liverpool but 600. Cardiff had more than a thousand students for almost all the inter-war years, reaching a peak of 1,292 in 1934. It was natural, therefore, that it should look quizzically in 1938 at Bristol, Reading and Sheffield, which had respectively 1,005, 584 and 767 students, for they were universities, not university colleges. Again, Cardiff was the closest approximation in Wales to a 'civic' university or college in England, where cities with a population of over 300,000 claimed that a university was a proud emblem of wealth and status. Indeed, it has been suggested that the absence of a university was a 'civic disgrace'.[13] In 1901 cities and towns with colleges soon to become universities varied in population from 339,000 at Bristol to 704,000 at Liverpool. It is likely that E. H. Griffiths had mused much upon such matters before his arrival at Cardiff in 1902. Thereafter he would have felt justifiable resentment that Cardiff's basic grant of £4,000 was the same as that of Aberystwyth and Bangor, whereas the formula applied to 'civic' institutions, based upon rateable value, seemed especially tempting. On the other hand Cardiff's population in 1901 of 180,000 was scarcely large enough to seek independence according to the English pattern.[14] Nor could Griffiths forget that the College's constituency by charter embraced the whole of south Wales and also Monmouthshire. Swansea, despite its strong territorial claims upon south-west Wales, thus became the University College of Swansea, the only college during this period not to include 'Wales' in its title. Further, federalism grated upon each College to some degree at some stage, but none had greater cause for indignation than Cardiff when the University displayed infirmity of purpose in relation to the School of Medicine, the College's own offspring. Again, there was the seductive possibility that the industrialists of south Wales might seriously support a unitary university at Cardiff free from all association with Aberystwyth which by title, 'The University College of Wales', carried with it a certain metropolitan air decidedly unpalatable to those who were not even quite sure where it was.[15] A comparison with Dundee offers an instructive parallel. Dundee had begun spectacularly well in 1880, attracting huge sums from the Baxter manufacturing company. After 1890, when the College was formally united with St Andrews, business enthusiasm waned. There were two principal reasons. First, industrialists no longer felt that they were benefiting from the work of the College. Second, since Dundee was now part of a larger whole, businessmen lost a sense of pride of possession and the hope that they would in time have in their midst a city university with which they could identify.[16] From time to time speculation arose as to the fate of the other colleges if Cardiff became an independent university. The notion was floated in wartime that Bangor and Aberystwyth might respond to the challenge by uniting 'to create a *real* University of *Wales*'.[17] It was never seriously considered. In 1916 E. H. Griffiths was asked whether Swansea would 'readily acquiesce in being absorbed into a new university, with its headquarters at Cardiff'.[18] He replied that he had been impressed by the remarks of the Vice-Chancellor of Leeds concerning possible co-operation with Bradford: 'You never find two big towns comparatively near each other who want to support each other; it is the very contrary.'[19] Although Leeds and Bradford were geographically closer than Swansea and Cardiff the basic point lost none of its force; there was not the slightest prospect that Swansea would consent to be 'absorbed' by or united with Cardiff. Indeed, Reichel was convinced that the jealousy of large towns such as Swansea, Merthyr and Newport would prevent the Cardiff College from doing anything effective outside the Cardiff district.[20] Moreover, if the example of Birmingham in 1900 had, on the one hand, encouraged English and Welsh colleges to seek independence it had also prompted wariness against the proliferation of degree-awarding bodies. If there was to be a University of Bangor, why, asked the *Welsh Leader* in 1905 in its jocular way, should there not be a University at Bala and yet another at Strata Florida?[21]

After the prolonged dispute with the University, Cardiff had lost favour with Whitehall. There was less prospect of independence in the inter-war years than in the first decade of the century. True, College spokesmen not infrequently proclaimed in the 1920s that the federal University could not long survive. In the 1930s there were minatory rumblings off-stage, but few paid much attention. Finally, the Cardiff College, situated in a city leavened by more than a sprinkling of Welsh patriots and with just claims to be designated the capital of Wales, did not care to lay itself open to the charge of attempting to dismember the national University. This remained a fundamental dilemma.

The problem of adequate financing by the state had from the first proved formidable. Aberystwyth for years struggled without state aid despite constant remonstrances that universities in Scotland and Ireland received substantial subventions. As late as 1920 Sir William McCormick would not acknowledge anything approaching parity with Scotland, whose four universities had long preceded the Act of Union of 1707 which granted them legislative protection. Ireland, particularly, stuck in the gullet, for it seemed that rebellion was rewarded with unfettered generosity. When introducing the Irish Universities Act in 1908, Augustine Birrell announced that not much could be expected from private beneficence in Ireland unless government aid was given at once: 'we have got to do our duty first'.[22] In Wales, as E. H. Griffiths noted, 'help was not to be given except as a consequence of local generosity'.[23] Here, as we have seen, the doctrine of self-help, so beloved of the Victorian mind, had been honourably espoused. During the 1880s each of the Welsh colleges was given £4,000, but successive governments had correctly foreseen that once such a precedent was conceded claims would speedily follow from universities and colleges south of the Tweed. For a brief period Wales was betwixt and between for she was accorded special treatment until 1889 when grants were also made to English institutions. The additional sum of £3,000 allowed to the University itself in 1893 was but a quarter of the amount recommended by O. M. Edwards. Income from other sources was scarcely sufficient to dispel in the colleges the ever-present spectre of insolvency until the Raleigh Committee reported in 1909.[24]

Here we may justifiably pause to consider the role of Liberal governments in advancing the cause of higher education in Wales. Gladstone, it is true, was not always consistent. In 1870 he had told Henry Richard and Osborne Morgan that Wales because of 'its clearly marked nationality',[25] which it was impossible to ignore, could not be placed on the same footing as an English town. In the following year, however, he caved in to his Chancellor, Robert Lowe, and refused a grant to Aberystwyth. Nevertheless, it was in the early months of his second administration in 1880 that the Aberdare Committee was appointed. It had far-reaching consequences. Aberystwyth, it must be allowed, had to wait before receiving the same grant as Cardiff and Bangor, and then from a Tory government in 1885. The Liberals, returned to power in 1892, depended crucially upon the loyalty of Welsh members and the scene was set for the granting of the Royal Charter. Prudential factors played their part, yet it is clear that Gladstone had a greater attachment to Wales than may be discerned in Roy Jenkins's *Gladstone* (1995). A. J. Mundella spoke of his 'thorough affection for Welsh people', and a Treasury official of standing remarked, 'Upon my word, I believe he is half a Welshman.'[26] From 1895 to 1905 there was little hope of progress and although the new Liberal government did not instantly attend to the urgent needs of the University and its Colleges, the appointment of the Raleigh Committee led in 1909 to nearly a twofold increase in grants. Lloyd George was roundly cheered in Wales for his role in creating a new spirit of confidence. On the eve of the Great War, however, serious difficulties had again emerged. The financial issue overshadowed all others. To Isambard Owen it was 'the dominant question'.[27] The Treasury Advisory Committee was not able to recommend the allocation of additional sums until the University dealt appropriately with such matters as the duplication of departments, the Medical School and local government grants. In short the University was asked to reform itself. This it signally failed to do and as a condition of increased grants it accepted the appointment of a royal commission. The hand of Lloyd George is again to be seen in the choice of Haldane as chairman and of the other eight distinguished members, of whom two were Welshmen. The Premier discussed the report at Downing Street with a large representation of the University and of interested bodies on two occasions and at a time when he was deeply engaged upon high matters of state. His authority was decisive in the adoption of the report. Civil servants obeyed his commands without question, though after he left office they were prone to challenge his pronouncements concerning financial commitments. On public occasions he said that as Prime Minister he must think of Britain as a whole. Nevertheless, he clearly felt it his duty to repair the inadequacies of the past and place the University, by no means rich in endowments, on more just, secure foundations. It was he, too, who insisted upon the pooling of local government grants, to the undoubted benefit of Colleges in less densely populated areas. The University represented the whole of Wales.[28]

The financing of the Welsh Colleges was a perpetual concern. After 1889 they were more dependent on state grants than colleges which had sprung up in England during the nineteenth century. Other than from Welshmen in dispersion it was not realistic to expect large sums from beyond Offa's Dyke. Of the city companies, heavy with gold and silver, only the Drapers' Company, mindful of its ancient association with the Welsh woollen industry, made significant contributions. Generous though he was towards a multitude of good causes Andrew Carnegie drew the line at helping the University of Wales. We may be sure that he felt, as did Austen Chamberlain in 1904, that those who had drawn great wealth above and below ground in Wales had not discharged their responsibilities. A few had contributed handsomely, and no one could expect them to emulate the prodigious generosity of the two Wills brothers who handed over a million pounds to Bristol University in the early twentieth century. In his evidence to the Haldane Commission the Cardiff Registrar said that the total sum subscribed to the College since its foundation (including the Treasury grant for the new building) was appreciably less than the coalowners' contributions to their own college at Trefforest.[29] Again, gifts were almost always to the Colleges, not to the University, the £50,000 by Dan Radcliffe being the largest of the exceptions. There was also a pronounced tendency to support scholarship and building funds rather than to found chairs. In 1938–9 Cardiff had but one endowed chair, Swansea not one, whereas in the Faculty of Arts alone at Liverpool there were fourteen.

By the second decade of the century the conviction grew in government circles that local authorities in Wales should make a significant contribution to the University, to be matched by an equivalent sum by the state. A pound for pound was accepted, and for a time the arrangement worked reasonably well.[30] After

1929, local authorities were not fully honouring their pledge, to the unalloyed dismay of the University, which was, however, bound to recognize that local authorities were hard pressed during the despairing 1930s. Nor were ordinary people now responding with their erstwhile alacrity. Gone were the days when William Rathbone had marvelled at their generosity in the Commons in 1889. Ten years earlier, Lyon Playfair, the member for the Universities of Edinburgh and St Andrews, had said that he knew of no instance in Scotland where poor people had subscribed, as in Wales, for scholarships to send their sons to university.[31] Naturally the sums collected were small, but as Rathbone sagely remarked, in proportion to their means they put to shame the wealthier classes 'by the largeness of their contribution'.[32] Within their religious communities there were constant calls upon meagre resources, to build, extend and repair chapels, to sustain the ministry and foreign missions. If the oft-reiterated claim that the Colleges were founded by the pennies of the poor is not literally true, yet it captured an aspect of the truth, for ordinary people inspired their wealthier countrymen to contribute. They also established a tradition of self-sacrifice.

The setting and maintaining of standards was vital. In the early days the level of attainment at matriculation was lamentable and so continued until the Welsh Intermediate Act bore fruit. This took time. As to appointments it was inevitable that for many years there would be a heavy dependence upon graduates of Oxford, Cambridge and the Scottish Universities. The Scots in particular had an intuitive understanding of the challenge facing struggling students in a largely Nonconformist country. The Welsh Colleges were rightly, and frequently, praised for having given priority to appointing the best staff. Expensive buildings could come later. As time passed there was impatience in some quarters to see Welshmen in post. H. A. L. Fisher counselled caution in 1917 against the temptation to shield 'native talent from Saxon competition'.[33] In 1920 Haldane urged the reconstituted Court 'not to appoint a Welshman as your teacher, but to appoint the best teacher'.[34] This had always been Reichel's view and it is difficult to imagine that any of the College Principals would have acted otherwise. J. H. Davies was troubled that there were not many Welshmen in chairs at Cardiff, but in such matters we see at best through a glass darkly. The few bad appointments seem mainly to have been errors of judgement, not the result of canvassing, fast declining at university level. The fiercest contest for a principalship was at Aberystwyth in 1919, and between the partisans of two Welshmen. It must also be added that there was genuine regret in all Colleges when outstanding men who were not Welsh at length departed for other universities, understandably attracted by higher emoluments.[35]

Whatever the defects of the London external system of examination its supreme merit was the preservation of common standards in Britain and beyond. This was of inestimable benefit to the infant colleges. It was not easy for the new University of Wales to win its spurs. The principal reason for refusing to countenance external degrees was that two values would be attached to the same degree. At a time when some ministers of religion not renowned for scholarly achievements returned home 'doctored' from the States there was an added imperative to strive for the highest standards. The serious 'leakage' at Cardiff in 1908 was dealt with speedily and firmly by the University. There was no repetition. As Isambard Owen once observed, 'university credit is as delicate a matter as commercial credit'.[36] Hence the insistence upon securing the services of the most reputable scholars as external examiners and at considerable expense. The light from outside was a sure safeguard. It was also an essential prerequisite to the recognition of the University beyond the confines of Wales. The first Principals had no illusions as to the immensity of the task. T. F. Roberts in 1894 said that one could not speak lightly of higher studies. It was necessary to 'pass through a prolonged period of silent self-discipline carried on under principles derived from international experiences'.[37] When he retired in 1927 Reichel reaffirmed his belief in 'The International of the Intellect'.[38] Viriamu Jones had faith from the first in the capacity of the Welsh people 'to make their University respected among the universities of the world'.[39] Part of that continuing process is outlined in the sections of this volume devoted, and necessarily devoted, to the Colleges.

Some had looked back wistfully to a nebulous past. One witness in 1880 told the Aberdare Committee that the Welsh had 'cultivated learning from time immemorial', the arts and the sciences before the Christian era. During the early years of Christianity in these islands Wales was celebrated for its colleges at Llanilltud Fawr and Bangor Is-coed. 'Our history', he averred, 'gives us a claim to have a national existence again in connexion with learning.'[40] In 1883 those who hoped that a college in north Wales would be placed at Rhyl said without hesitation that there had been 2,400 resident students at Bangor Is-coed during the early Christian era in Wales.[41] Not surprisingly, scholars at the new Colleges were soon to demolish reassuring fictions. New myths replaced the old, the purity of rural life, for example, the law-abiding land of white gloves ('gwlad y menyg gwynion'), notions that the poor had founded the Colleges and that the Welsh had a special aptitude for a wide variety of subjects. Of this we may be certain: the prime purpose was to open the window of opportunity to a rising generation whose forebears had been denied the benefits of higher education. Some speculated dreamily at the number who might have graduated through the centuries had Owain Glyn Dŵr succeeded in his aims. Whether the economy of an independent Wales could have sustained two universities of the front rank is another matter,[42] but Scotland remained a shining example of what had been achieved from the late Middle Ages onwards. In 1868 Matthew Arnold urged that university education should be taken to the people. In 1931 Ernest Barker noted at Cardiff that the main difference between the ancient and modern universities was that the former were not bound by territorial limitations in respect of students whereas the latter were mainly influenced by regional considerations, drawing students from their own area.[43] In Wales it was certain that a federal rather than a unitary solution ensured that far more students received university education. In 1963 Thomas Parry told the Aberystwyth Court of Governors that:

> . . . the pressure for university places can to a considerable extent be attributed to England's effort to catch up with Wales and Scotland. Wales has been conscious of the value of higher education for three generations, and Scotland for a longer period. I remember being very perplexed to hear friends of mine who are Vice-Chancellors of Universities in England discuss the difficulties of 'first generation students', that is students whose parents had

not themselves received university education, and I realised that ever since our University was established we in Wales had had hundreds of 'first generation students'. Those of us in this room who are the sons and daughters of small farmers, farm servants, miners, steelworkers, quarrymen, and shopkeepers might very well never have gone to a university, had we been born in England.[44]

The question of social origins is one of great complexity, especially if comparisons are attempted with other modern universities. Nomenclature is itself an obstacle, for students upon arrival did not declare that their parents were large or small farmers, prosperous shopkeepers or upon the verge of bankruptcy. It would not be rash to surmise that on average students in the University of Wales were poorer than those at Liverpool. However, it would be imprudent to say the same with regard to Nottingham, for example, or Sheffield. In 1917 H. A. L. Fisher, perhaps as an antidote to too much rhetoric on the subject, did well to remind his Bangor audience of the contributions of workmen to the founding of Sheffield University, of which he, like Viriamu Jones, had been head.[45] However, Thomas Parry's observations were broadly accurate. The high proportion of students in Wales who had received their education in public elementary schools by comparison with students from other parts of Britain is perhaps the surest indication that the lower middle class and the working class tended to be more heavily represented in the University of Wales than elsewhere. Women were welcomed from the outset, though their numbers declined sharply in times of privation between the wars. Very few were appointed to chairs and they did not fill offices on Councils and Courts according to their just deserts.[46]

In 1863 Thomas Nicholas declared that young Welshmen were not enjoying the fruits of the industrial revolution: 'in time past the ministry seemed to be the only outlet to native talent'.[47] Now a thousand avenues of honourable employment lay before them. A century later the Robbins Report observed that through the ages only a minority had attended universities to pursue pure knowledge or pleasure. It quoted an apparently authentic analect of Confucius to the effect that 'it was not easy to find a man who had studied for three years without aiming for pay'.[48] Nicholas

would have been disappointed that comparatively few Welsh
graduates had turned to industry or the higher branches of the
civil and Indian services and that so many almost inevitably
became teachers and preachers, matters which indeed caused
concern to University authorities in the 1920s and 1930s. Robert
Anderson thought it perfectly reasonable for Wales to produce
teachers and preachers if this were her prime social requirement.
Michael Sanderson, on the other hand, was critical of the
University for not attending to the industrial needs of Wales.[49]
No one, however, who has read earlier portions of the present
volume can imagine that Bangor had deliberately ignored the
quarrying industry or that Cardiff was other than cast down by
the failure to forge sturdy links with the industrialists of south
Wales. The two colleges were thwarted at practically every turn.
Circumstances, not choice, were the determinants. When modest
sums were available for developing agriculture (Wales's chief
industry) or forestry (to a lesser extent) the results were highly
creditable.

Informed opinion in Wales had long held that it was the duty
of the University to attend to the needs of the people who had
brought it into being. Thus, Abel Jones Parry, a Baptist minister
of Swansea, told the Aberdare Committee that 'its very existence
would raise the intellectual tone of the whole nation'.[50] He clearly
had in mind J. H. Newman's words in 1852:

> . . . a University training is the great ordinary means to a great but
> ordinary end; it aims at raising the intellectual tone of society, at
> cultivating the public mind, at purifying the national taste, at
> supplying true principles to popular enthusiasm, at giving
> enlargement and sobriety to the ideas of the age, at facilitating the
> exercise of political power, and refining the intercourse of private
> life.[51]

These words had of course influenced men closely associated
with the newer colleges. At Dundee there are signs that its great
benefactor J. B. Baxter wished to counteract the materialism of
business. Alfred Marshall held that the businessmen of Bristol
should receive 'that true literary education which refines the
mind and broadens its interests in human life'.[52] Moreover it is

incontrovertible that there was need to educate a number of Welshmen as to the nature of a university. In 1876 David Davies, Aberystwyth's generous supporter, thought that the College was 'to be pure and simple a mercantile College or school purely Elementary'.[53] In 1882 Lord Aberdare, seldom inclined to over-estimate his countrymen, chose St David's Day at Manchester to unburden himself: 'The Welsh needed to have a far higher sense of what education consisted in, and that was one of the main difficulties.'[54] Nearly forty years later a member of the Holywell District Education Committee proclaimed that 'a skilled village blacksmith is of more value to the community than a cart-load of University men'.[55] In 1924 A. H. Trow said of a former Professor of Botany at Bangor that amongst his distracting duties was the need 'to educate public opinion in North Wales as to the true aims and functions of University education'.[56] Reichel was always alert to the need to correct ignorant, complaisant men. In Australia he had heard a colonial governor expressing the hope that university professors might be so occupied with teaching that they would have no time for research.[57] Attention has elsewhere been drawn to Reichel's dismay when confronted by the ineffable parochialism of a member of his College Council, reputed to be an educationist, when an appointment was being made.[58]

The University and the Colleges were in turn subjected to criticism, not all of it genial. Occasionally members of staff were thought to be aloof and to have no wish to blend into their surroundings. From time to time there were ill-founded accusations that the colleges bred atheists. Those who considered themselves authorities on the Welsh language did not care to have imposed upon them a reformed orthography by academic 'cocks o' the walk' led by John Morris-Jones. Even Herbert Lewis, normally a stout defender of national institutions, concluded that graduates of the University had stamped upon them a uniform pattern, quite unlike the colourful, untutored men he had known in his youth. Thomas Jones, in turn, was disappointed that graduates were not participating as fully as he would have expected in local government.[59] An allied complaint sometimes erupted. The University was not producing leaders as in the days of yore. Such a charge was scarcely reasonable. Lloyd George, a

force of nature, had never been to a university, nor later had
Aneurin Bevan and Dylan Thomas. Perhaps it was in self-defence
that a Cardiff Principal made unwarrantable claims that average
intelligence had risen in recent times, owing, we are to gather, to
the spread of education.[60] Maurice Jones of Lampeter went
further. The Wales of 1923 was immensely superior to the Wales
of 1893 'in intelligence and intellectual capacity',[61] but her
University was still too young to produce giants. University and
College Courts prided themselves on being democratic bodies,
especially after 1920. Some members spoke up on matters of
which they had little direct knowledge and it was mainly for this
reason that Emrys Evans and others had scant patience with
Haldane's ill-starred proposal that Court meetings of the
University should become festivals where specialists and non-
specialists would rub shoulders.[62]

It must be allowed that there had been disappointments.
Schemes to unify intermediate and higher education under the
control of the University Court were doomed once the Central
Welsh Board was established; successive debates concerning a
National Council for Education in Wales simply confirmed the
original objections. In time it was apparent that the 'educational
Parliament' had cast its net too wide and that some of the
responsibilities it had assumed were later best performed by
other agencies such as the Welsh Arts Council. Nor can it be said
that relations with training colleges were always as cordial as they
might have been. There was criticism, too, that the University
exercised excessive influence upon the curricula of secondary
schools, to the detriment of pupils not at all academically
inclined. External degrees continued to be frowned upon. There
was little progress in the teaching of art, none in drama and
architecture. Theology, 'the queen of the sciences', was not as
comfortably enthroned in Wales as had once been hoped, and
certainly not by comparison with Scotland. Teaching through the
medium of Welsh was almost entirely confined to the departments of Welsh, which had taken unexpectedly long to respond
to the challenge. English, in tune with the spirit of the age, was
the formal instrument of communication and of administration.
Saunders Lewis's views on such subjects were widely regarded as
chimerical.[63]

Yet when necessary qualifications have been made, contemporaries, English perhaps even more than Welsh, were profoundly impressed by the zest in Wales for education. Nowhere, it seemed, was education a matter of greater public concern. True, universities in England did not regard their courts as superfluous. James Mountford, Vice-Chancellor of Liverpool, for example, possibly with his Aberystwyth experience in mind, said that a university court 'in a real sense . . . embodies that informed public opinion to which the university is in long run accountable'.[64] If Emrys Evans was not always able to view the democratically elected University Court as a reservoir of informed opinion, there was, nevertheless, a widespread conviction that the University belonged to the people, who, as innumerable newspaper reports testified, felt that they had a freeborn right to call Principals and Registrars to account if, in words so frequently quoted, they forgot the rock from which they were hewn. But there was more than a zeal for education and for all its temporal blessings. Viriamu Jones recognized the cause and consequence of the march of democracy. 'Equality of rights for all men, equality of opportunity for all men – these are the phrases of the platform, and they embody the tendency of our legislation.' But in Wales there were 'certain special causes contributing to a warmer glow of educational opportunity'. The religious revival of the eighteenth century 'was an awakening of national life. It developed a spiritual life that found a natural outcome in a real reverence for knowledge, a reverence that penetrated to the humblest homes.'[65] The university movement in Wales cannot be properly understood without due regard to this sense of reverence, which moved and inspired such men as T. F. Roberts and Rendel at Aberystwyth, Rathbone and Reichel at Bangor, Viriamu and W. J. Gruffydd at Cardiff, Henry Lewis and Stephen J. Williams at Swansea.

As time passed, it seemed that the aspirations of a Welsh chemist at Chester were being fulfilled. Leaving a legacy to the University and to one of its Colleges he believed that there was 'a large body of ability' in Wales 'hidden from the surface and waiting for an opportunity to show itself'.[66] Indeed, the discovery of latent powers was a theme repeated throughout the decades. There was further satisfaction that denominationalism in its

ranker forms was waning. The various religious bodies genuinely
believed that they were the appointed guardians of neglected
facets of divine truth but they had so trumpeted against one
another as to imperil concerted action in a noble cause. It is a
melancholy fact that not a single bishop sat on the University
Court in 1893 nor for years afterwards. As late as 1923 Wales's
first archbishop, A. G. Edwards, declared that the contributions
which the University Colleges could make to the national life
were 'far-reaching and profound'. They could 'help to eradicate
. . . the party and sectarian spirit which had imperilled it in the
past and to give that breadth of view which might promote
unity'.[67] In thirty years there had, of course, been substantial
progress. True, the scene had been clouded by disestablishment
and especially disendowment (from which the University later
benefited) and by ruffled relations with Lampeter, Wales's oldest
degree-awarding body. Yet no fair-minded person could forget
the remarkable services of prominent Anglicans between 1893
and 1939 to the University and its Colleges. Every Pro-
Chancellor was a churchman, and by election of the Court. After
the Great War a deeper understanding among staff and students
of various persuasions, more than faltering convictions, led to a
new spirit of co-operation.

An impartial view leads us to conclude that many alert,
articulate Welshmen took pride in their University. Its scholars
were attentive to various aspects of Wales, her land and people,
epitomized in a special way by H. J. Fleure's appointment in
1917 as Professor of Geography and Anthropology. The geology
of Wales was first systematically examined by University men.
Botanists such as J. Lloyd Williams were excited by their discoveries and there were gleams of promise in studies of marine
life. Generations of farmers, after initial hesitation, had cause to
bless the application of chemistry to soils bereft of essential
minerals. At Cardiff, Marquand's investigations into the plight of
distressed areas were proof that not all economists were immured
in lonely towers. The Medical School won plaudits for its
endeavours to heal diseases and injuries by no means confined to
industrial areas. The purpose of the Colleges, said J. F. Rees, was
to produce a stream of educated people. Maurice Jones did not
doubt that they had brought forth men who had 'blessed their

country immeasurably'.[68] Graduates, too, were bound together by the Guild of Graduates and Old Students' Associations, and members of staff by their participation in the work of University Boards after 1920. Not for nothing did the young Iorwerth Peate hope that the University as a corporate body would encourage his countrymen to develop a breadth of outlook and a true understanding one of another.[69] Out of a small purse provision was made for lectures on art by eminent men in colleges and towns. Although the architecture of public buildings in Wales had been much disparaged, the University could in good heart point to the new College at Cardiff and to the Registry, both in Cathays Park (to some the manifestation of an alien grandeur) and especially to the new College at Bangor, the finest college building in the University. Dramatic productions, popular amongst staff and students, were a prelude to exciting developments in the future. The greatest advance in the arts was in music, stemming largely from the folk-song movement and from the special recommendation of the Haldane Report. Extra-mural classes flourished, notably in the post-war years. It was taken as axiomatic that the University had a special responsibility for furthering studies in the language, literature and history of Wales. A few believed that there had been an overaddiction to philology, but firm foundations had to be laid. The vigorous, penetrating study of the inherited culture was a key which unlocked the treasuries of the past, the indispensable nourishment for fresh advance.[70]

In the sixteenth century Thomas Churchyard reflected upon the Council in Wales and the Marches which most commonly met at Ludlow: 'It stands for Wales.'[71] Nothing more certainly demonstrated the absence of indigenous Welsh secular institutions. Viriamu Jones described the University as 'the first of our national institutions'.[72] The federal structure represented the elements of particularism in Welsh life, but above all the revitalized force of nationhood. To Haldane in 1920 'the University of Wales could not be at its greatest until it was a University that stood for Wales as a nation'.[73] T. F. Roberts saw the single University as 'co-extensive with the whole national area'.[74] Henry Jones's invitation to his countrymen to pay heed to Scotland with its four universities was not generally well received, for Scotland had additional marks of separate identity. In 1917 the chairman of the Monmouthshire Education Committee urged that 'A National University . . . commands as one of its chief assets the priceless gift of national allegiance.'[75] In the same year D. Lleufer Thomas declared that 'A national case is much stronger than a particularist one.'[76] It was in this spirit that during degree ceremonies new graduates are enjoined to be constant in their care for the success and honour of 'our University and nation'. To those who devised the formula these were not empty words.

The unprecedented expansion of recent years (which would have astounded the founders of the University) and the arrival of a Welsh Assembly may prompt renewed questions as to the future of the federal University. Each generation, as Lleufer Thomas told the Haldane Commission, must judge such matters in its own way. History, we have learnt, does not teach lessons. Illumination is another matter, and a perusal of these pages may generate the hope that a re-examination will be conducted in a spirit of goodwill and without contention.

Appendix 1

Authorities and Officers of the University

Protector

His Majesty King Edward VII, 1901–10
His Majesty King George V, 1920–36
His Majesty King Edward VIII, 1936
His Majesty King George VI, 1937–52

Chancellor

The Right Hon. Henry Austin, 1st Baron Aberdare, 1895
H.R.H. Albert Edward, Prince of Wales (His Majesty King Edward VII), 1895–1901
His Majesty King George V, 1920–21
H.R.H. Albert Edward, Prince of Wales (His Majesty King Edward VIII), 1921–36
H.R.H. The Duke of Kent, 1937–42

Senior Deputy-Chancellor

Sir Isambard Owen, 1895–1910
The Right Hon. Lloyd, 4th Baron Kenyon, 1910–20

Pro-Chancellor

The Right Hon. Lloyd, 4th Baron Kenyon, 1920–7
The Hon. William Napier Bruce, 1927–34
The Right Revd The Bishop of Monmouth, 1934–41

Vice-Chancellor

John Viriamu Jones, 1895–6, 1898–1900
Sir Harry Rudolf Reichel, 1896–7, 1900–1, 1905–7, 1911–13, 1917–21, 1926–7
Thomas Francis Roberts, 1897–8, 1901–3, 1907–9, 1913–15
Ernest Howard Griffiths, 1903–5, 1909–11, 1915–17
Albert Howard Trow, 1921–3, 1927–9
John Humphreys Davies, 1923–5
Sir Thomas Franklin Sibly, 1925–6
Sir Henry Stuart Jones, 1929–31
Charles Alfred Edwards, 1931–3

Sir Emrys Evans, 1933–5
Sir Frederick Rees, 1935–7
Ifor Leslie Evans, 1937–9

Warden of the Guild of Graduates

Sir Owen Morgan Edwards, 1895–6
Thomas Edward Ellis, 1896–9
Sir John Edward Lloyd, 1899–1901
Daniel Evan Jones, 1901–3
Sir Thomas Marchant Williams, 1903–7
Edward Edwards, 1907–9
Charles Morgan, 1909–11
Edgar Jones, 1911–13
Frederick Daniel Chattaway, 1913–15
Albert Howard Trow, 1915–17
Sir John Morris-Jones, 1917–19
John Humphreys Davies, 1919–21
Professor Emeritus Edward Ernest Hughes, 1921–5
Frances Mary Rees, 1925–30
The Revd Principal John Morgan Jones, 1930–3
Professor Henry Lewis, 1933–6
Professor Emeritus T. Hudson-Williams, 1936–7
Herbert Morgan, 1937–40

Registrar

Ivor James, 1895–1905
J. Mortimer Angus, 1905–21
D. Brynmor Anthony, 1921–45

Secretary to the University Council

Jenkin James, 1921–45

Representative in Parliament

The Right Hon. Sir J. Herbert Lewis, 1918–22
Thomas Arthur Lewis, 1922–3
George Maitland Lloyd Davies, 1923–4
Ernest Evans, 1924–43

Appendix 2

Professors and other Heads of Departments

(L. Lecturer: I.L. Independent Lecturer)

University College of Wales, Aberystwyth

Greek
T. C. Edwards, 1872–91
T. F. Roberts, 1891–1909
J. W. Marshall, 1909–23
E. D. T. Jenkins, 1923–38 (I.L.)

Latin
J. Hoskyns-Abrahall, 1872–3
J. M. Angus, 1873–1905
E. Bensly, 1905–19
H. J. Rose, 1919–27
J. F. Mountford, 1927–32
E. J. Wood, 1932–8

Greek and Latin
E. D. T. Jenkins, 1938–47

Comparative Philology
J. Hoskyns-Abrahall, 1872–3
J. M. Angus, 1873–1905
Edward Anwyl, 1905–14

English Language and Literature
T. C. Edwards, 1872–5
J. R. Buckley, 1875–6
W. J. Craig, 1876–9
M. W. MacCallum, 1879–86
C. H. Herford, 1887–1901
G. C. Macaulay, 1901–6
J. W. E. Atkins, 1906–40

Welsh Language and Literature
D. Silvan Evans, 1875–83
J. E. Lloyd, 1885–91 (L.), 1891–2
Edward Anwyl, 1892–1914

T. H. Parry-Williams, 1920–52

Welsh Literature
T. Gwynn Jones, 1913–19 (Reader),
  1919–37

Celtic Philology and Palaeography
Timothy Lewis, 1920–42 (Reader)

French Language and Literature
G. Thibaut, 1872–5
H. Ethé, 1875–94
W. Borsdorf, 1894–1903
L. E. Kastner, 1903–9
J. L. André Barbier, 1909–44

Italian
G. Thibaut, 1872–5
H. Ethé, 1875–1900

German
G. Thibaut, 1872–5
H. Ethé, 1875–1914
M. Brebner, 1914–20 (L.)
David Evans, 1920–36 (I.L.),
  1936–52

Hebrew
G. Thibaut, 1872–5
H. Ethé, 1875–1914
Norman Jones, 1914–16 (L.)

History
J. Hoskyns-Abrahall, 1872–3
J. M. Angus, 1873–5

C. J. Cooper, 1875–6 (L.)
W. J. Craig, 1876–9
M. W. MacCallum, 1879–85
J. E. Lloyd, 1885–91 (L.), 1891–2
Edward Edwards, 1892–5 (L.),
    1895–1930
R. F. Treharne, 1930–67

Colonial History
T. Stanley Roberts, 1915–34
E. Jones Parry, 1935–46 (L.)

Welsh History
E. A. Lewis, 1931–42

Logic and Philosophy
T. C. Edwards, 1872–83
J. Brough, 1883–5(L.), 1885–1911
W. Jenkyn Jones, 1911–32
R. I. Aaron, 1932–69

Education
H. Holman, 1892–3 (L.), 1893–4
Foster Watson, 1894–6 (L.),
    1896–1913
C. R. Chapple, 1913–39

Political Economy
C. J. Cooper, 1875–6 (L.)
W. J. Craig, 1876–9
M. W. MacCallum, 1879–85
Edward Edwards, 1892–1902 (L.)

Political Science
W. Jenkyn Jones, 1902–9 (L.),
    1909–11

Economics and Political Science
E. A. Lewis, 1912–31
R. B. Forrester, 1931–51

International Politics
A. E. Zimmern, 1919–21
C. R. Webster, 1922–32
Jerome D. Greene, 1932–4
E. H. Carr, 1936–46

Music
Joseph Parry, 1874–80
D. Jenkins, 1899–1910 (L.), 1910–15
H. Walford Davies, 1919–26
D. J. De Lloyd, 1927–48

Law
T. A. Levi, 1901–40

Constitutional and Comparative Law
W. Jethro Brown, 1901–6

*Mathematics, Natural Philosophy, and
    Astronomy*
H. N. Grimley, 1872–9
R. W. Genese, 1879–1909

Pure Mathematics
R. W. Genese, 1909–19
W. H. Young, 1919–23
G. A. Schott, 1923–6
V. C. Morton, 1926–33 (I.L.),
    1933–61

Applied Mathematics:
G. A. Schott, 1909–10 (L.), 1910–33
Thomas Lewis, 1933–50 (I.L.)

Physics
F. W. Rudler, 1877–9
T. S. Humpidge, 1879–84
D. E. Jones, 1884–90 (L.), 1890–1
D. Morgan Lewis, 1891–1919
Gwilym Owen, 1919–37
E. J. Williams, 1938–45

Chemistry
H. N. Grimley, 1872–4
L. Lyell, 1874–5
F. W. Rudler, 1875–6 and 1877–9
R. D. Roberts, 1876–7
T. S. Humpidge, 1879–87
H. Lloyd Snape, 1888–1901
J. J. Sudborough, 1901–11
A. Findlay, 1911–19
B. Mouat Jones, 1919–21

T. Campbell James, 1921–44

Zoology
L. Lyell, 1874–5
F. W. Rudler, 1875–6
W. Keeping, 1876–9
T. S. Humpidge, 1879–83
J. R. Ainsworth Davis, 1883–91 (L.),
   1891–1908
H. J. Fleure, 1908–10 (L.), 1910–18
R. D. Laurie, 1918–22 (I.L.),
   1922–40

Geography
J. Hoskyns-Abrahall, 1872–3
L. Lyell, 1874–5
F. W. Rudler, 1875–6
R. D. Roberts, 1876–7
W. Keeping, 1877–9
T. S. Humpidge, 1879–83
H. J. Fleure, 1908–18 (L.)

Geography and Anthropology
H. J. Fleure, 1918–30
C. D. Forde, 1930–45

Botany
L. Lyell, 1874–5
F. W. Rudler, 1875–6
W. Keeping, 1876–9
T. S. Humpidge, 1879–83
J. R. Ainsworth Davis, 1883–91 (L.),
   1891–4
J. H. Salter, 1894–9 (L.), 1899–1903
R. H. Yapp, 1903–14
J. Lloyd Williams, 1914–26
W. Robinson, 1926–30
Lily Newton, 1930–58

Geology
L. Lyell, 1874–5
F. W. Rudler, 1875–6
W. Keeping, 1876–9
T. S. Humpidge, 1879–83
J. R. Ainsworth Davis, 1883–91 (L.),
   1891–1908
O. T. Jones, 1909–10 (L.), 1910–19

W. J. Pugh, 1919–31
H. P. Lewis, 1931–47

Agriculture
T. Parry, 1891–1901 (L.)
D. D. Williams, 1901–7 (L.)
C. Bryner Jones, 1907–19
Abel E. Jones, 1919–24
J. Jones Griffith, 1924–42

Agricultural Chemistry
J. A. Murray, 1892–1907 (L.)
J. Jones Griffith, 1907–21 (L.),
   1921–4 (I.L.)
T. W. Fagan, 1925–30 (I.L.), 1930–9

Agricultural Botany
R. G. Stapledon, 1912–19 (Adviser),
   1919–42

Dairying
B. L. Brown, 1901–7 (Instructress)
M. Fisk, 1908–19 (Instructress)
D. M. Evans, 1919–29 (Instructress)
G. T. Morgan, 1930–7 (L.)
John Lewis, 1937–40 (L.)

Agricultural Economics
A. W. Ashby, 1929–46

Welsh Plant Breeding Station: Director
R. G. Stapledon, 1919–42

Extra-mural Studies: Director
H. Morgan, 1920–40

Registrar
E. P. Jones, 1872–92
T. Mortimer Green, 1892–1905
J. H. Davies, 1905–19
J. Morgan Jones, 1936–44

Librarian
E. P. Jones, 1872–1902
J. D. Williams, 1902–32
A. Ap Gwynn, 1932–68

University College of South Wales and Monmouthshire, Cardiff

Greek
T. F. Roberts, 1883–91
G. C. Richards, 1891–7
R. M. Burrows, 1897–1908
Gilbert Norwood, 1908–26
H. J. W. Tillyard, 1926–46

Latin
J. R. Wardale, 1883–8
G. Hartwell Jones, 1889–93
R. S. Conway, 1893–1902
D. A. Slater, 1903–14
O. L. Richmond, 1914–19
G. A. T. Davies, 1919–23
G. E. K. Braunholtz, 1924–5
W. W. Grundy, 1925–36
Roland G. Austin, 1936–54

English
W. P. Ker, 1883–9
C. E. Vaughan, 1889–98
H. Littledale, 1899–1921
Cyril Brett, 1921–36
E. C. Llewellyn, 1936–64

Welsh
Thomas Powel, 1883–4(L.), 1884–1918
W. J. Gruffydd, 1919–46

French
Paul Barbier, 1883–1920
Morgan Watkin, 1920–43

German
L. Müller, 1883–5 (L.)
F. T. Arnold, 1886–1926 (L.)
M. D. I. Lloyd, 1926–35(I.L.)
O. H. Edwards, 1935–41 (I.L.)

Semitic Languages
J. Lloyd Williams, 1885–91 (L.)
D. Tyssil Evans, 1891–1915 (L.)
Theodore H. Robinson, 1915–27
  (L.), 1927–44

History
W. P. Ker, 1883–9
C. E. Vaughan, 1889–98
A. G. Little, 1898–1902
Herbert Bruce, 1902–35

History of Wales
William Rees, 1930–53

Industrial Relations
H. A. Marquand, 1930–45

Economics and Political Science
S. J. Chapman, 1899–1901 (L.)
C. J. Hamilton, 1901–5 (L.)
H. Stanley Jevons, 1906–10 (L.),
  1910–11
W. J. Roberts, 1911–43

Philosophy
A. S. Pringle-Pattison, 1883–7
W. R. Sorley, 1887–94
J. S. Mackenzie, 1894–1915
H. J. W. Hetherington, 1915–20
J. W. Scott, 1920–44

Education (Men)
Thomas Raymont, 1890–1904 (L.),
  1904–5
William Phillips, 1905–32

Education (Women)
H. Millicent Mackenzie, 1891–1904
  (L.), 1904–15
Barbara Foxley, 1915–25
Olive A. Wheeler, 1925–32

Education (Men and Women)
Olive A. Wheeler, 1932–51

Archaeology
R. E. Mortimer Wheeler, 1921–4 (L.)
Cyril Fox, 1924–6 (L.)
V. E. Nash-Williams, 1926–53 (L.)

Music
Clement Templeton, 1883–7 (L.)
Joseph Parry, 1888–1903 (L.)
David Evans, 1903–10 (L.), 1910–39
J. Morgan Lloyd, 1939–45

Mathematics
H. W. Lloyd Tanner, 1883–1909
R. H. Pinkerton, 1888–1922
G. H. Livens, 1922–50

Physics
J. Viriamu Jones, 1883–1901
A. L. Selby, 1890–8 (L.), 1898–1926
H. R. Robinson, 1926–30
R. T. Dunbar, 1930–54

Chemistry
C. M. Thompson, 1883–1921
W. J. Jones, 1921–51

Biology
W. N. Parker, 1883–1900

Zoology
W. N. Parker, 1900–22
W. M. Tattersall, 1922–43

Botany
A. H. Trow, 1892–1905 (L.), 1905–19
R. C. McLean, 1919–55

Physiology
J. Berry Haycraft, 1893–1919
T. Graham Brown, 1919–47

Anatomy
A. W. Hughes, 1893–7
A. F. Dixon, 1897–1902
D. Hepburn, 1903–27
C. McLaren West, 1927–51

Geology
F. T. Howard, 1891–6 (L.)
W. S. Boulton, 1897–1905 (L.),
   1905–13

T. Franklin Sibly, 1913–18
A. Hubert Cox, 1918–49

Engineering
A. C. Elliott, 1890–1913
F. Bacon, 1913–20
W. T. David, 1920–2
A. J. Sutton Pippard, 1922–8
W. Norman Thomas, 1928–50

Mining
Sir W. Galloway, 1891–1902
S. Warren Price, 1902–35 (L.)
T. David Jones, 1935–47

Metallurgy
A. A. Read, 1894–1910 (L.), 1910–33
W. R. D. Jones, 1933–61

Pharmacology
D. R. Paterson, 1894–1906 (I.L.)
W. Mitchell Stevens, 1906–31 (I.L.)

Bacteriology
W. G. Savage, 1899–1903 (I.L.)
H. A. S Cholberg, 1903–10 (I.L.)

Pathology
E. Emrys-Roberts, 1910–23
E. H. Kettle, 1924–7
J. H. Dible, 1928–9
J. B. Duguid, 1929–31 (Acting Head)

Hygiene and Public Health
E. L. Collis, 1919–31

Medicine
A. M. Kennedy, 1921–31

Surgery
A. W. Sheen, 1921–31

Obstetrics and Gynaecology
E. J. MacLean, 1922–31

Tuberculosis
S. Lyle Cummins, 1921–31

Registrar
Ivor James, 1883–95
J. Austin Jenkins, 1895–1910
Percy E. Watkins, 1910–13
D. J. A. Brown, 1913–36
Louis S. Thomas, 1936–49

Librarian
Miss Dyer, 1884–8

G. V. Waite, 1888–91
Jessie Waite, 1891–1900
E. M. Breese, 1900–14
Gwladys I. Johns, 1914–16
G. M. Hughes, 1916–19
The Revd John Jenkins, 1919
S. O. Moffet, 1919–51

University College of North Wales, Bangor

Greek
W. Rhys Roberts, 1884–1904
T. Hudson-Williams, 1904–40

Latin
E. V. Arnold, 1884–1924
H. J. Thomson, 1924–48

English Language and Literature
H. R. Reichel, 1884–90
W. Lewis Jones, 1897–1919
H. G. Wright, 1919–54

Welsh Language and Literature
J. Morris-Jones, 1889–94 (L.),
    1894–1929
Ifor Williams, 1920–47

Modern Languages
E. J. Trechmann, 1884–8 (L.)
Frederick Spencer, 1889–1903

French
O. H. Fynes-Clinton, 1903–37
P. Mansell Jones, 1937–51

German
T. Rea, 1903–9 (L)
E. L. Milner-Barry, 1909–17
F. W. Stokoe, 1919–21 (L.)
Edna Purdie, 1921–33 (I.L.)
Kathleen Cunningham, 1933–50
    (I.L.)

Hebrew
T. Witton Davies, 1899–1921
Edward Robertson, 1921–34
H. H. Rowley, 1934–45

History
H. R. Reichel, 1884–99
J. E. Lloyd, 1899–1930
A. H. Dodd, 1930–58

Welsh History
R. T. Jenkins, 1930–46 (I.L.)

Philosophy
Henry Jones, 1884–91
E. Keri Evans, 1891–5
James Gibson, 1895–1932
C. A. Campbell, 1932–8
D. James Jones, 1938–47

Economics:
Robert Richards, 1921–2 (I.L.)
R. D. Richards, 1923–5 (I.L.)
Henry Higgs, 1925–9 (I.L.)
J. M. Rees, 1929–37 (I.L.), 1937–52

Education
J. A. Green, 1894–1906
R. L. Archer, 1906–42

Music
E. T. Davies, 1920–43 (I.L.)

Mathematics
G. B. Mathews, 1884–96
G. H. Bryan, 1896–1926
W. E. H. Berwick,1926–41

Physics
Andrew Gray, 1884–99
E. Taylor Jones, 1899–1925
E. A. Owen, 1926–54

Electrical Engineering
W. E. Williams, 1920–42 (I.L.)

Chemistry
J. J. Dobbie, 1884–1903
K. J. P. Orton, 1903–30
J. L. Simonsen, 1930–43

Biology
R. W. Phillips, 1884–8 (L.), 1888–94

Botany
R. W. Phillips, 1894–1923
D. Thoday, 1923–49

Zoology
P. J. White, 1895–1929

F. W. Rogers Brambell, 1930–68

Forestry
Fraser Story, 1904–20
T. Thomson, 1920–43 (I.L.)

Agriculture
T. Winter, 1894–1912
R. G. White, 1912–45

Agricultural Chemistry
G. W. Robinson, 1922–6 (I.L.),
 1926–50

Agricultural Botany
R. Alun Roberts, 1926–45 (I.L.)

Registrar
W. Cadwaladr Davies, 1884–92
J. E. Lloyd, 1892–1920
W. P. Wheldon, 1920–33
E. H. Jones, 1933–41

Librarian
W. Lewis Jones, 1890–1911
J. E. Lloyd, 1914–26
T. Richards, 1926–46

University College of Swansea

Classics
D. Emrys Evans, 1921–7
S. K. Johnson, 1927–33
R. B. Onians, 1933–5
B. Farrington, 1936–56

English Language and Literature
W. D. Thomas, 1921–54

Welsh Language and Literature
Henry Lewis, 1921–54

Modern Languages
Mary Williams, 1921–31

French
Mary Williams, 1931–48

German
F. W. Halliday, 1931–48 (I.L.)

History
E. Ernest Hughes, 1920–6 (I.L.),
 1926–44

Philosophy
A. E. Heath, 1925–52

Economics
K. S. Isles, 1937–9

Education
F. A. Cavanagh, 1921–33
W. M. Williams, 1934–42

Mathematics
A. R. Richardson, 1920–41

Physics
E. J. Evans, 1920–44

Chemistry
J. E. Coates, 1920–48

Botany
Florence A. Mockeridge, 1921–36
   (I.L.), 1936–54

Geology
A. E. Trueman, 1920–30 (I.L.),
   1930–1

Geology and Geography
A. E. Trueman, 1931–3
T. N. George, 1933–46

Metallurgy
C. A. Edwards, 1920–47

Engineering
F. Bacon, 1920–43

Extra-mural Studies
P. S. Thomas, 1937–41 (Senior Tutor)

Librarian
Olive M. Busby, 1921–59

Registrar
Edwin Drew, 1920–52

Welsh National School of Medicine

Medicine
A. M. Kennedy, 1931–50

Surgery
A. W. Sheen, 1931–5
Lambert Rogers, 1935–60

Obstetrics and Gynaecology
G. I. Strachan, 1931–53

Pharmacology
W. Mitchell Stevens, 1931–3 (I.L.)
R. St A. Heathcote, 1933–8 (I.L.),
   1938–51

Pathology
J. B. Duguid, 1931–3 (Acting Head),
   1933–48

Tuberculosis
S. Lyle Cummins, 1931–8
W. H. Tytler, 1938–49

Preventive Medicine
E. L. Collis, 1931–3
R. M. F. Picken, 1933–49

Child Health
A. G. Watkins, 1932–50 (I.L.)

Secretary
S. C. Edwards, 1931–48

Appendix 3

Students

(a) *Social Origins*

The statistics which follow should be read in conjunction with those treated in *The University Movement in Wales* (UMW), pp.202–5. Both the table prepared by J.E. Lloyd and the statement made in evidence by J.H. Davies were included in the Raleigh Report's volume of evidence (Ral., *Rept.*), at pp.41 and 120.

i **Bangor**

Occupation of Parents of Present Students, Session 1906–7

Professions:	
Clergy and Ministers	27
Professors and Lecturers	4
Schoolmasters	18
Doctors	4
Lawyers	5
Surveyors	3
Engineers	4
Chemists	4
Journalists	3
	72
Commercial Class:	
Merchants, Builders, etc.	21
Commercial Travellers and Agents	15
Retail Tradesmen	33
Clerks and Officials	14
	83
Agriculture:	
Farmers	50
Working Men:	
Artisans, Mechanics and Workmen	59
Quarrymen	32
Labourers	4
Soldiers	2
Sailors	2
	99

ii Aberystwyth

J. H. Davies in evidence said that he had analysed the occupations of 'new students this session' (1907–8). Out of 181 he had been able to account for 160. Only two students were the sons of people living on their means. He proceeded:

> Fourteen are children of professional people, such as lawyers and doctors; 13 are children of civil servants and clerks; there are a good number of the children of Inland Revenue officers; 10 are children of teachers; 5 are children of clergy of the Church of England; 13 are children of Nonconformist ministers; 5 are children of sea captains; 23 are children of farmers; 39 of tradesmen – that would be small tradesmen; and 36 belonging to the working classes – that is, miners, tin-workers, colliers, or agricultural labourers. Large classes are farmers, tradesmen and working men. They account for 98 out of the 160, and they are divided as follows between England and Wales; there are 14 boys from Wales, the sons of farmers, and 9 women; and no men or women from England, children of farmers; 7 boys from Wales, who are the sons of tradesmen, and 15 women the children of tradesmen; 4 from England and 13 women, the children of tradesmen. Of the men, 29 from Wales are the children of parents who belong to the working classes, and 5 women; and no men from England, and 2 women from England, both normals, are the children of people belonging to the working classes. There is one rather striking disproportion that I should like to call your attention to, namely, the fact that of the so-called lower class, the working class, there are 29 men from Wales and only 5 women. The only way I can account for that is this: all the women have to live in the hall of residence; the lowest fee at which a woman can get rooms there is £31 10s. a session. If you add to that £11 for the College fee, it means £42 10s., and I think we find that it is quite impracticable for the children of people such as miners, agricultural labourers and tin-workers, and colliers, to pay that price for their daughter's education. In the cases where they have done it, they are mostly normals, and people who have got scholarships. This is all I have to say about the students.

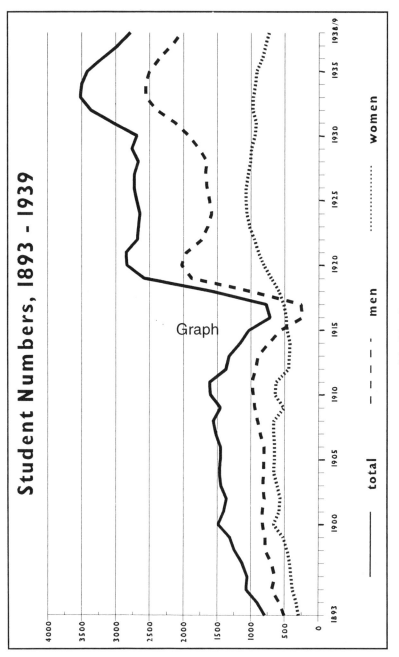

(b) *Numbers*

(c) *Examination results, Pass and Honours graduates*

i 1897–1907

Combined total as reported to the Raleigh Committee:

Arts	903
Science	298

Honours graduates:

Arts	535
Science	81

ii 1925–1929, 1935–1939

The following analysis is based on annual reports to the University Court for two quinquennial periods:

Pass degree candidates
in the Faculties of Arts (including Law and Music) and of Science (including Mathematics)

	Arts	*Science*
1925–9	724	519
1935–9	998	645

Honours degree candidates

	No. presented	I	II.i	II.ii	III	Percentage Classified
1925–9						
Arts	1009	20.5	38.5	26.7	14.3	92.2
Science	502	35.6	32	18.5	13.9	93
1935–9						
Arts	1399	19.9	38.1	31.7	10.3	95.6
Science	759	25.8	35.6	26	12.6	95

The few who were not classified either failed or did not attend.

iii   Certificates and Diplomas, 1923–1939

Certificates in Education, 1923–8 Diploma in Education, 1929–39	3231
Diploma in Public Health Parts I and II	102
Tuberculous Diseases Diploma	106
Degrees in Medicine and Divinity MB, B.Ch. BD	 170 102
The Degrees of Magister and of Doctor	
Ll M	2*
MA	486**
M.Mus.	4
M.Sc.	506
Ph.D.	170
DD	-
D.Litt.	4
D.Mus.	2
D.Sc.	34
MD	12

* including one distinction
** including 107 distinctions

This survey begins in 1923 because the information to the University Court then began to be presented in a standard form.

A Certificate, later Diploma, in Education rose from 81 in 1923 to a peak of 292 in 1933. Throughout the 1930s the number never fell below 218 (in 1930), partly reflecting socio-economic pressures confronting students.

The figures relating to the Diploma in Public Health include, as reported, those who passed Part I and Part II, from 1 in 1923 to 16 in 1939. The successful candidates for the Tuberculous Diseases Diploma increased from 5 in 1923 to 16 in 1939.

There was a steady rise in the MB and B.Ch. graduates, from 1 in 1923 to 25 in 1939.

The highest number who qualified for the BD degree was 11 in 1933 and also in 1938. In 1923 and 1927 there was not a single graduate.

Distinctions were awarded to 22 per cent of those who qualified for the MA degree. Distinctions were not given at all for the M.Sc. degree. On the other hand, 25 per cent of the candidates for the MA degree did not qualify, as opposed to 7 per cent of M.Sc. candidates. The preponderating majority of Ph.D. graduates were scientists, all 16, for example, in 1930; 93 per cent of candidates were successful. For the role of the University in introducing the Ph.D. degree, see above (p. 46). Doctors of Science were appreciably more numerous than Doctors of Literature. Throughout the seventeen years examined here there were only two Doctors of Music. No candidate was successful for the degree of Doctor of Divinity, thus reinforcing observations made above (376–7).

(d) *Occupations and destination*

i Occupations

The best analysis of the various vocations pursued by former students was submitted by J. E. Lloyd to the Raleigh Committee.

Professions:		
Clergy and ministers		210
Law:		
Barristers	1	
Solicitors	9	10
Medicine		34
Education:		
Professors, lecturers and teachers in universities, university colleges and higher educational institutions (including technical colleges)	58	
Head teachers and assistant teachers in secondary schools	233	
Head teachers and assistant teachers in elementary schools	483	
		774
Army officers		3
Chemists, analysts, etc.		8
Architects, surveyors and estate agents		25
Journalists		3
Trade and commerce		16
Agriculture		179
Engineering:		
Electrical engineers	35	
Mechanical engineers	6	41
		1306

Note: The total number of students registered since the opening of the College (excluding those now in residence) is 2,075
Not accounted for   772
Explained by:
    (a) Number of occasional students
    (b) Deaths
    (c) Women married
    (d) Cases where no information is obtainable.

ii Destination

The late Professor E. G. Bowen very kindly indicated that he would allow me to include any of the maps in his pamphlet *The Guild Today* published in 1973 by the Guild of Graduates, of which he was warden. Figure 5 reproduced here throws light upon a proposal made by Ernest Hughes of Swansea that the Guild should establish branches 'in Wales and the Borderland'. Hughes appeared to infer that most Welsh graduates in 1920 were in this area. Bowen set out to 'test the validity of this view point', and it is as well to quote his words verbatim:

> I have endeavoured to plot from the available records the distribution of Welsh graduates in the year 1920 before there were graduates from Swansea and before the full effect of the ex-service impact was felt outside. The map (Fig. 5) is revealing in so far as it makes clear that a very large proportion of Welsh graduates were still in Wales, more particularly around the three Collegiate centres, but with very few, indeed, in the Border counties. It is clear also that Welsh graduates were chiefly found in the major centres of population in the country as a whole. Areas particularly well-marked are the Lancashire and Yorkshire industrial areas, the Midland conurbation, and, of course, the London area. Branches of the Guild should have been envisaged by Professor Hughes in these areas as well as 'in Wales and the Borderland'.

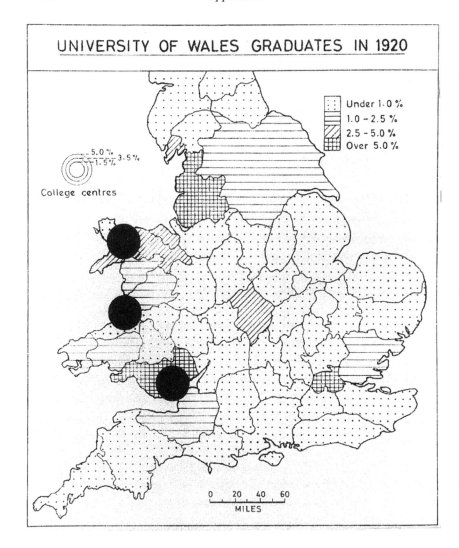

UNIVERSITY OF WALES GRADUATES IN 1920

Under 1·0 %
1.0 – 2.5 %
2.5 – 5.0 %
Over 5.0 %

5.0 %
1.5 %
3.5 %

College centres

0   20   40   60
MILES

Abbreviations

Aber.	E. L. Ellis, *The University College of Wales, Aberystwyth, 1872–1972* (Cardiff, University of Wales Press, 1972).
Bangor	J. Gwynn Williams, *The University College of North Wales: Foundations, 1884–1927* (Cardiff, University of Wales Press, 1985)
'Cardiff'	'University College, Cardiff: A Centenary History, 1883–1983', ed. S. B. Chrimes (unpublished).
DNB	*Dictionary of National Biography.*
DWB	*Dictionary of Welsh Biography Down to 1940*, ed. J. E. Lloyd and R. T. Jenkins (Cardiff, 1959).
Evans, *Univ. of Wales*	D. Emrys Evans, *The University of Wales: A Historical Sketch* (Cardiff, University of Wales Press, 1953).
Hald., *Rept.*	*Royal Commission on University Education in Wales, Final Report* (London, HMSO, 1918), Cd. 8991.
Hald., *App.* I	*Appendix to First Report, Minutes of Evidence* (London, HMSO, 1917), Cd. 8507.
Hald., *App.* II	*Appendix to Second Report, Minutes of Evidence* (London, HMSO, 1917), Cd. 8699.
Hald., *App.* III	*Appendix to Final Report, Minutes of Evidence* (London, HMSO, 1918), Cd. 8993.
Lamp.	D. T. W. Price, *A History of Saint David's University College, Lampeter,* i: *To 1898* (Cardiff, University of Wales Press, 1977); ii: *1898–1971* (1990).
Man. Guard.	*Manchester Guardian*
NLW	National Library of Wales
NW Chron.	*North Wales Chronicle*
PRO	Public Record Office
Ral., *Rept.*	*Report of the Committee on the University of Wales and the Welsh University Colleges* (London, HMSO, 1909), Cd. 4571.
Ral., *Evid.*	*Minutes of Evidence* (London, HMSO, 1909), Cd. 4572.
Swansea	David Dykes, *The University College of Swansea* (Alan Sutton, 1992).
SWDN	*South Wales Daily News.*

SWN	*South Wales News* from 1919.
TJ MSS	The Thomas Jones Manuscripts at the National Library of Wales.
UMW	J. Gwynn Williams, *The University Movement in Wales* (Cardiff, University of Wales Press, 1993).
Univ. Cncl. Mins.	Minutes of the Council of the University of Wales.
Univ. Ct. Mins.	Minutes of the Court of the University of Wales.
W. Mail	*Western Mail*

Notes

Introduction

1. J. Gwynn Williams, *The University Movement in Wales* (Cardiff, 1993), henceforth *UMW*.
2. Ibid., 28.
3. Ibid., 29.
4. Ibid., 26.
5. Ibid., 188.
6. Ibid., ch. VII.
7. Above, 132–3.
8. Ibid., 151.
9. Ibid., 84.
10. Ibid., 145.
11. *The Report on the Proposed University of Wales by Owen M. Edwards* (1893), facs. with introduction by J. Gwynn Williams (Aberystwyth, 1993), 6.

I University Development, 1893–1914

1. *Man. Guard.*, 31 Oct. 1895; K. V. Jones, *Life of John Viriamu Jones* (London, 1915), 237.
2. *Man. Guard.*, 23 May 1896.
3. *Yr Herald Cymraeg*, 5 Nov. 1895.
4. *Man. Guard.*, 29 May 1896.
5. University College of Wales *Magazine*, 15 (1892), 1. *Baner*, 25 Mar. 1896.
6. *Welsh Leader*, 6 July 1905, 658.
7. *Univ. Ct. Mins.*, 13 Mar., 16 Oct. 1896.
8. T. F. Roberts to Rendel, 7 Oct. 1897, NLW MSS 19441E, fo. 13.
9. *Man. Guard.*, 31 Oct. 1896, *Border Counties Advertizer*, 4 Nov. 1896; Cardiff College *Calendar* 1895–6 (1896), 231; Rept. to Bangor's Court, 1895–6.
10. *Man. Guard.*, 23 Apr. 1897.
11. Ibid., 27 Nov. 1896.
12. Memorandum: 'To the Lords Commissioners of her Majesty's Treasury, 16 Nov. 1896'. *Aber.*, 122.
13. T. Kelly, *For Advancement of Learning: The University of Liverpool* (Liverpool, 1981), 64.
14. Memorandum, op. cit.
15. *Univ. Ct. Mins.*, Oct. 1896, 5.
16. Ibid.
17. Lewis Morris to T. F. Roberts, 10 Nov. 1896. See *Aber.*, 123.
18. *Young Wales*, 3 (1897), 39.
19. Rendel to T. F. Roberts, 14 Oct. 1896, College Archives, *Aber.* 123, *Man. Guard.*, 31 Oct. 1896, *Border Counties and Oswestry Advertizer*, 4 Nov. 1896.
20. *Univ. Ct. Mins.*, Oct. 1896, 5. For installation, see *UMW*, 160–4.
21. See, for example, Aber., *Calendar*, 1914–15 (1914), 387.
22. Humphreys-Owen to his wife, 5, 15, 23 Feb. 1896, NLW Glansevern. Not numbered.

23. Charter, art. xix (5).
24. *Univ. Ct. Mins.*, May 1895, 4–5.
25. Ibid.
26. Ibid.
27. *Univ. Ct. Mins.*, Apr. 1897, 64 ff.
28. Ibid., 66; Univ. Registry Archives, H 906–7, 909.
29. *SWDN*, 23 Apr. 1897.
30. *Man. Guard.*, 24 Apr. 1897.
31. 27 Apr. 1897.
32. *Man. Guard.*, 24 Apr. 1897.
33. Ibid., 26 Apr. 1897.
34. Ibid., 15, 22 Apr. 1897.
35. *Univ. Ct. Mins.*, Apr. 1897, 64 ff.
36. Ibid., Nov. 1901, 15.
37. T. F. Roberts to Rendel, 10 Feb., 26 May 1897, NLW MSS 19441E, fos. 6–7. *Aber.*, 121.
38. *SWDN*, 31 May 1902; *Univ. Ct. Mins.*, 30 May 1902, 9–13. Univ. Registry Archives, H911, 913, *Man. Guard.*, 29 May 1902.
39. *Cambrian News*, 5 June 1902; *Aber.*, 142.
40 John Rhys to William Jones, 24 May 1902, Bangor MSS 5469, no. 22.
41. *UMW*, 167.
42. *Univ. Ct. Mins.*, May 1902, 12–13.
43. H. R. Reichel to T. F. Roberts, 28 May 1902, Univ. Coll. of Wales, G. History file.
44. T. F. Roberts to Rendel, 2 June 1902, NLW MSS 19441E, Rendel II, fo. 52. *Aber.*, 143.
45. J. Rhys to William Jones, 19 July 1902, Bangor MSS 5469, fo. 22.
46. *The Report on the Proposed University of Wales by Owen M. Edwards* (1893), facs. with introduction by J. Gwynn Williams (Aberystwyth, 1993), 6.
47. Kelly, *Advancement of Learning*, 127.
48. Ibid.
49. 'In the Privy Council. Case of the Yorkshire College, Leeds', 1901. PRO, PC 8/605.
50. Ibid.
51. Ibid., 5, para. 4.
52. Ibid., 7.
53. Ibid., Liverpool's 'Objections to Separation'.
54. Ibid., 19, 23.
55. Ibid., 20.
56. Ibid., 24.
57. Ibid., 19.
58. *The Collected Papers of Thomas Frederick Tout . . .*, ct. n 60 i (Manchester, 1932), 49.
59. *Man. Guard.*, 6 Apr. 1907.
60. Ibid. For a good discussion, see T. W. Moody and J. C. Beckett, *Queen's Belfast, 1845–1949* (London, 1958), i, 381–4.
61. W. C. Davies and W. L. Jones, *The University of Wales* (London, 1905), 205–6. Also *Man. Guard.*, 25 Aug. 1905.
62. Ibid., 207.
63. *Univ. Ct. Mins.*, Nov. 1904, 176.
64. Reichel to T. F. Roberts, 23 Nov. 1904. Library, Univ. Coll. of Wales, History file.
65. *In Memoriam, Herbert Isambard Owen* (reprinted from *Welsh Outlook*, Mar. 1927), 11.
66. *Man. Guard.*, 23 Oct. 1908. For (Sir) Henry Lewis's view on 10 July 1908, see Bangor, Belmont MSS 296.
67. *NW Chron.*, 3 Oct. 1905.
68. For example, *Welsh Leader*, 9 Mar. 1905, 385. For his attack on 'my old friend Wheldon', *NW Chron.*, 3 Oct. 1905.
69. Negley Harte, *The University of London, 1836–1986* (London, 1986), 175.
70. Ibid.

71. Jones's speech at Cardiff was published under the title, *The University of Wales: The Line of its Growth* (Bangor, 1905). For his remarks at Bangor, see *Man. Guard.*, 3 July 1905.
72. Ibid., 34.
73. Ibid., 30.
74. Ibid., 21.
75. Reichel to Roberts, 6 Oct. 1905. Library, Univ. Coll. of Wales, History File.
76. Ibid., Reichel to Roberts, 10 Oct. 1905.
77. *Welsh Leader*, 12 Oct. 1905, 49.
78. *Univ. Ct. Mins.*, June 1905, 8–9; Nov. 1905, 8.
79. Reichel to T. F. Roberts, 6 Oct. 1905. Library, Univ. Coll. of Wales, History File.
80. *Man. Guard.*, 16 Nov. 1905.
81. *Univ. Ct. Mins.*, Nov. 1905, 154.
82. Reichel to T. F. Roberts, 16 Oct. 1905. Library, Univ. Coll. of Wales, History File.
83. *Univ. Ct. Mins.*, May 1903, 29 ff.
84. A. Stuart Gray, *Edwardian Architecture* (London, 1985), 386. *The Builder*, 152 (1937), 305.
85. *Univ. Ct. Mins.*, Nov. 1904, 171–2.
86. Edgar Chappell, *Cardiff's Civic Centre* (Cardiff, 1946), 39–40.
87. Ibid., 40.
88. *Univ. Ct. Mins.*, May 1903, 33. J. B. Hilling, *Cardiff and the Valleys* (London, 1973), 145. Gray, *Edwardian Architecture*, 232.
90. *Journal of the Roy. Inst. of Brit. Architects*, 21 Mar. 1937, 517.
91. *UMW*, 154.
92. Ibid., 153.
93. *Man. Guard.*, 14 Mar. 1896.
94. *Univ. Ct. Mins.*, Feb. 1896, 5. Hald., *App.* I, Q. 4734.
95. *Man. Guard.*, 18 Feb. 1896.
96. Ibid., 19 Feb. 1896.
97. Above, 369–70.
98. Gareth Elwyn Jones, *Controls and Conflicts in Welsh Secondary Education, 1889–1944* (Cardiff, 1982), 34.
99. Ibid., 23–4.
100. Above, 160.
101. *Univ. Ct. Mins.*, Jan. 1904, special meeting to discuss Swansea's petition. See also Nov. 1904, 153 ff.
102. Supplemental charter, 1906, art. ii.
103. *The Nationalist,* Dec. 1907, 28.
104. *Bangor*, 148–50.
105. Above, 35, 99.
106. *Bangor*, 149 and n. 99.
107. *Man. Guard.*, 23 Oct. 1908.
108. Statute xxiii(5); my italics.
109. *Univ. Ct. Mins.*, Nov. 1907, 196–7, 225–6; May 1908, 42–7; Nov. 1908, 179–81.
110. *Bangor*, 150, n. 104. D. Gerwyn Lewis, *The University and the Colleges of Education in Wales 1925–1979* (Cardiff, 1980), 25–6.
111. O. M. Edwards, *The Report on the Proposed University of Wales* (1893), 49.
112. Evans, *Univ. of Wales*, 50.
113. *Univ. Ct. Mins.*, Apr. 1897, 5.
114. Hald., *App.* I, 304, app. x; *Univ. Ct. Mins.*, Apr. 1898, 14 ff.
115. *Wales*, 2 (1895), 140.
116. *Univ. Ct. Mins.*, May 1899, 16.
117. Reichel to J. Herbert Lewis, 5 Mar. 1907, NLW, Penucha MSS For salaries, see *Man. Guard.*, 7 Apr. 1906, *Bangor*, 124.
118. 3 Mar. 1904, Printed statement of meeting with Austen Chamberlain, PRO, ED 24/570. There is a xerox copy of a detailed report in the Bangor Archives, GC 49.

119. Reichel to Herbert Lewis, 17 Feb. 1907, NLW, Penucha MSS.
120. Same to same, 24 Feb. 1907, ibid.
121. Reichel to T. F. Roberts, 21 Apr. 1906, Library, Univ. Coll. of Wales, History file.
122. *Man. Guard.*, 28 Apr. 1906.
123. Reichel to Herbert Lewis, 12 Apr. 1906, NLW, Penucha MSS.
124. Same to same, 24 Feb. 1907; E. H. Griffiths, 27 Feb. 1907, Library, Univ. Coll. of Wales, History file.
125. See below for full reference, and *Bangor*, 127, n. 25.
126. *Aber.*, 155, n. 94.
127. Above, 43–4.
128. *Rept.*, xxv. It is unfortunate that the tabular statement in app. I(ii), 106–7, does not give the promised percentages of those who attained a degree.
129. Ibid., xxvi.
130. Ibid., xxvii.
131. Ibid.
132. Ibid.
133. Ibid., xxviii
134. Ibid., xxx.
135. Ibid.
136. Ibid.
137. Ibid., xxxi.
138. Treasury minute preceding *Report*.
139. T. Raleigh, *Annals of the Church in Scotland: Preliminary Reminiscences by Sir Harry Reichel* (London, 1921), xlvi; *Bangor*, 128–9.
140. *Bangor*, 129.
141. *Man. Guard.*, 14 Nov. 1908.
142. Raleigh, *Annals*, xlvi.
143. Ibid.
144. *Univ. Ct. Mins.*, Nov. 1904, 181.
145. *Bangor*, 122.
146. Ibid., 123.
147. Raleigh, *Annals*, xlvi; Ral., *Evid.*, 114–15.
148. Renate Simpson, *How the Ph.D. came to Britain* (Guildford, 1982), 97–9.
149. *Univ. Ct. Mins.*, Nov. 1910, 160 ff.
150. Ibid., May 1911, 93. Univ. Coll. of N. Wales, Welsh Library, GC 37.
151. *W. Mail*; Bangor Archives, GC 37.
152. *The University of Wales and the Nation* (Cardiff, 1910).
153. *Univ. Ct. Mins.*, May 1911, 93.
154. 25 Nov., Bangor, Belmont MSS 298.
155. A. C. Wood, *A History of the University College, Nottingham, 1881–1948* (Oxford, 1953), 53–5.
156. A. H. Trow and D. J. A Brown, *A Short History of the College, 1883 to 1933* (Cardiff, 1933), 46–7.
157. *Univ. Ct. Mins.*, Oct. 1896, 4.
158. Ibid., Nov. 1910, 157.
159. *Young Wales*, 8 (1902), 94–5.
160. Raleigh, *Evid.*, Q. 1048.
161. Ibid., QQ. 428, 431.
162. *Univ. Ct. Mins.*, Nov. 1910, 226–7.
163. Ibid.
164. *Univ. Ct. Mins.*, May 1899, 16, Isambard Owen to Treasury, 14 Feb. 1899.
165. *Univ. Ct. Mins.*, Nov. 1900, 7.
166. Ral., *Evid.*, Q. 142.
167. Reichel to Herbert Lewis, 7 March 1907, NLW Penucha MSS.
168. Ral., *Evid.*, Q. 148. Moderations was the first public examination in some faculties for the Oxford BA degree.

169. Ibid., QQ. 497–8.
170. *Univ. Ct. Mins.*, Nov. 1910.
171. Ibid., Nov. 1913, 206.
172. *A Brief Survey of the Work of the University of Wales, 1909–14* (Wrexham, 1914), 9.

II The Colleges, 1893–1914

1. Rendel to T. F. Roberts, 25 Oct. 1906, NLW MSS 19442E, fo. 142.
2. *UMW*, 138.
3. Rendel to Roberts, 14 June 1905. NLW MSS 19442E, Rendel II, fos. 96–7, 98a, 107, 3 Sept. 1903. Ibid., fo. 68.
4. *Aber.*, 167.
5. Ruth Evans, *Sir John Williams, 1840–1926* (Cardiff, 1952), 11.
6. Quoted in *Aber.*, 189.
7. Ibid., 124.
8. Ral., *Rept.*, xv.
9. Board of Education, *Reports for the Year 1913–14 from . . . Universities and University Colleges in Great Britain . . . in Receipt of Grant from the Board of Education,* ii (London, 1915), Cd. 8138, 423 [1013].
10. Ivor Thomas, *Top Sawyer* (Golden Grove Edition, 1988), 55–61.
11. J. Roger Webster, *Old College, Aberystwyth* (Cardiff, 1995), back cover.
12. *Aberystwyth, 1277–1977*, ed. Ieuan Gwynedd Jones (Llandysul, 1977), 94.
13. Webster, *Old College*, 83–4.
14. A. Stuart Gray, *Edwardian Architecture*, 362.
15. Webster, *Old College*, 63–5, Ill. 2.
16. Above, 347 ff.
17. D. B. Hague, in *Aberystwyth, 1277–1977* (Llandysul, 1977), 93; Sir Peter Swinnerton Dyer to writer; Morton, quoted by Lord Elwyn-Jones, *In My Time, an Autobiography* (London, 1983), 23.
18. *UMW*, 42.
19. *Aber.*, 150–4.
20. W. Ll. Davies, *The National Library of Wales: A Survey of its History, its Contents and its Activities* (Aberystwyth, 1937), 42.
21. Univ. Coll. of Wales, *Reports* (1863–91), 19, 21–2, 56.
22. David Jenkins, *Trans. Hon. Soc. of Cymmrodorion*, 1982, 147.
23. *Aber.*, 138.
24. Ibid., 126.
25. *W. Mail*, 2 Oct. 1901.
26. R. Evans, *Sir John Williams*, 77.
27. Ibid.
28. T. F. Roberts to Rendel, 5 May 1904, NLW, Rendel MSS 19441E, fo.77.
29. Davies, *National Library*, passim.
30. O. M. Edwards to J. E. Lloyd (no date), Bangor, Lloyd MSS 314, fos. 90–1.
31. *DNB, 1931–1940*, 424.
32. R. T. Jenkins, *Edrych Yn Ôl* (Denbigh, 1968), 135.
33. *Aber.*, 171.
34. *DWB*, 12–13.
35. Ibid.; Brynley F. Roberts, *Syr Edward Anwyl (1866–1914)*, 1968, pt. II (1969), 211–64.
36. For Holman, see *The College by the Sea*, ed. Iwan Morgan (Aberystwyth, 1928), 175–7.
37. John Andrews, 'Law in Aber', *Cambrian Law Review*, 7 (1976), 7–10.
38. *Aber.*, 91.
39. Owen M. Edwards to T. F. Roberts, 28 Jan. 1901, Univ. Coll. of Wales Archives, T. F. Roberts Letters.

40. *DNB, 1961–1970*, 599.
41. *Aber.*, 169; for J. Lloyd Williams, *Y Bywgraffiadur Cymreig, 1941–1950* (London, 1970), 62.
42. Below, n. 113; *Bangor*, 84, n. 34; Richard J. Collyer, *Man's Proper Study* (Llandysul, 1982), 21.
43. *Aber.*, 157–8; *Bangor*, 110, n. 139.
44. *Bangor*, 59.
45. *NW Chron.*, 17 May 1884; *Bangor*, 64.
46. *Bangor*, 433.
47. Ibid., 60.
48. Draft application for post of Principal at Aberystwyth, 27 Oct. 1919. Bangor Archives, Lloyd MSS, U 235.
49. *Bangor*, 104.
50. Ibid., 104–11.
51. *The University College of North Wales, Bangor* (n. pl., 1930), 6, a brief survey of 44 pages.
52. Ibid., 7. For the new building, see *Bangor*, 238–86.
53. *Bangor*, 270. For Hare's various styles, see ibid., 268–9.
54. Ibid., 244.
55. University College of N. Wales, *Magazine* (Mar. 1911), 19.
56. *NW Chron.*, 29 Dec. 1906.
57. *The Builder*, 21 Jan. 1921, 93. Obituary of Hare.
58. *Bangor*, 279.
59. Ibid., 281.
60. *Nature*, 1928, 850.
61. *Bangor*, 155.
62. Ibid., 157.
63. Ibid., 159.
64. Ibid.
65. Ibid., 160–6.
66. Ibid.
67. Ibid., 130.
68. Univ. Coll. of N. Wales, *Magazine*, Dec. 1904, 7.
69. *Bangor*, 134, n. 48.
70. Ibid., 89–91.
71. Ibid., 134–7.
72. Ibid., 137–8.
73. *Mind*, 27 (1918), 354. *Bangor*, 92, 110, 141.
74. *Bangor*, 144–6, 177–80. *Board of Education Reports . . . 1913–14 from . . . University Colleges,* ii (1915), Cd. 8138.
75. Quoted in *Univ. of Wales*, 32.
76. 'Cardiff', 33, n. 46.
77. Ibid., 83.
78. K. V. Jones, *Viriamu Jones*, 297.
79. Neville Masterman, *J. Viriamu Jones* (Llandybïe, 1957), 6.
80. E. B. Poulton, *John Viriamu Jones* (Oxford, 1911), 37. *Reichel*, ed. J. E. Lloyd, 30.
81. K. V. Jones, *Viriamu Jones*, 360.
82. Ibid.
83. Poulton, *J. V. Jones*, 305.
84. Ibid., 309.
85. *DNB, 1931–1940*, 377–8.
86. South Wales Institute of Engineers, *Report of the Proceedings*, 12 Nov. 1903 (London, 1904), 9.
87. *SWDN*, 25 Sept. 1902.
88. Thomas Jones, *College Principals*, recorded talk on the Welsh Home Service, 18 Dec. 1953.

89. Percy E. Watkins, *A Welshman Remembers* (Cardiff, 1944), 102.
90. David Williams, *Thomas Francis Roberts, 1860–1919* (Cardiff, 1961), 24. *UMW*, 108.
91. Watkins, *Welshman Remembers*, 98.
92. K. V. Jones, *Viriamu Jones*, 195–201.
93. Jennifer M. Freeman, *W. D. Caröe . . . his Architectural Achievement* (Manchester, 1990).
94. *SWDN*, 14 Oct. 1909.
95. Ibid.
96. Ibid.
97. Freeman, *Caröe*, 209.
98. Edgar Chappell, *Cardiff's Civic Centre* (Cardiff, 1946), 40.
99. *The Builder*, 17 Oct. 1903, 376.
100. Freeman, *Caröe*, 210–11.
101. *The Builder*, 17 Oct. 1903, 376, for references to external features.
102. Quoted by Dewi-Prys Thomas in Gwyn Jones and Michael Quinn (eds.), *Fountains of Praise* (Cardiff, 1983), 67.
103. Ibid., 65.
104. Ibid., 69.
105. Ibid.
106. Ibid., 70.
107. Ibid., 58.
108. *The Builder*, 17 Oct. 1903, 376.
109. Freeman, *Caröe*, 209.
110. *The Builder*, 17 Oct. 1903, 375.
111. 'Cardiff', 77.
112. A. Harvey, *1866–1966, One Hundred Years of Technical Education* (Cardiff, n.d.), 12–14.
113. In 1890 the Local Taxation (Customs and Excise) Act aimed to control the multitude of public houses by withdrawing licences from those considered unsatisfactory. The intention of compensating brewers out of public funds angered Victorian opinion and it was decided to give moneys equal to the proposed compensation to the new county councils which tended to devote it to the promotion of technical and agricultural education.
114. Howard Spring, *Heaven Lies About Us: The Autobiography of Howard Spring* (London, 1972), 50, 54. Harvey, *One Hundred Years*, 17; 'Cardiff', 77.
115. Harvey, *One Hundred Years*, 16–18.
116. Masterman, *Viriamu Jones*, 12.
117. *DNB, 1931–1940*, 377–8.
118. *DNB, 1961–1970*, 459.
119. H. K. M. Lloyd in 'Cardiff', 391. See also 338–9, 365–6.
120. *UMW*, 106.
121. Viriamu Jones to Lyon Playfair, 12 May 1886, PRO ED 199/74.
122. Trow and Brown, *Short History*, 51.
123. 'Cardiff', 126.
124. *DNB, 1922–1930*, 328.
125. Trow and Brown, *Short History*, 53.
126. Ibid.
127. 'Cardiff', 345, 396.
128. D. Williams, *T. F. Roberts*, 24.
129. Ibid.
130. Above, 372; Peter Walcot in 'Cardiff', 223.
131. G. Hartwell Jones, *A Celt Looks at the World* (Cardiff, 1946), 41.
132. *Bangor*, 230.
133. Quoted by Kelly, *Advancement of Learning*, 218.
134. *DNB, 1922–1930*, 467–9.

135. *W. Mail*, 11 Oct. 1922, 'C. E. Vaughan, by an old Student'.
136. R. G. Thomas, in 'Cardiff', 228.
137. Above, 46–7.
138. D. A. Jackson, in 'Cardiff', 237.
139. Ibid., 238.
140. *DWB*, 771–2.
141. The most recent assessment is by T. Robin Chapman, *W. J. Gruffydd* (Cardiff, 1993).
142. G. O. Pierce, *A Matter of Primary Urgency* (Cardiff, 1979), 12. This is an admirable account of the development of Welsh history at the College.
143. *DNB, 1931–1940*, 679.
144. *Bangor*, 221.
145. *DNB, 1931–1940*, 578–9. For Sorley, see ibid., 827–8.
146. 'Cardiff', 303.
147. Trow and Brown, *Short History*, 89.
148. *DWB*, 738. Rhian Davies, *Never so Pure a Sight* (Llandysul, 1994), passim. (bilingual volume).
149. J. B. Thomas, 'The Origins of Teacher Training at University College, Cardiff', *Journal of Educational Administration and History*, 16 (Jan., 1984), 11.
150. *Bangor*, 143.
151. Ibid., 145.
152. Trow and Brown, *Short History*, 79–83.

III   War

1. *The German Menace Before the War* (Cardiff, 1915), 13–14. *Bangor*, 329.
2. *Man. Guard.*, 15 Dec. 1916.
3. *Y Beirniad*, 4 (1914), 217–24.
4. The Welsh translation was entitled, *Datguddiadau'r Tywysog Lichnowsky*.
5. *Bangor*, 331.
6. *Man. Guard.*, 7 Dec. 1916.
7. *Univ. Ct. Mins.*, June 1920, 212–13.
8. 'The University of a Small Nation', *The Contemporary Review* (Feb. 1916), 243.
9. *Cap and Gown,* 11 (Dec. 1914), 20.
10. Ibid. (May 1915), 28.
11. Kenyon, *A Brief Survey of the Work of the University of Wales . . . 1909–14* (Wrexham, 1914), 10.
12. *Dragon*, 37 (1914–15), 259–60.
13. *Bangor*, 325.
14. *Cap and Gown*, 11 (Dec. 1914), 25.
15. Ibid., 1.
16. *Bangor*, 326.
17. *Aber.*, 174–5.
18. *SWDN*, 23 Oct. 1914.
19. Ibid., also 27, 28 Oct. 1914.
20. *Univ. Ct. Mins.*, Nov. 1914, 204 ff.
21. *How They Educated Jones* (Cardiff, 1974), 72.
22. Ibid., 91.
23. *Univ. Ct. Mins.*, July 1915, 219–20.
24. A War Book I, 98, NLW, deposited by George Eyre Evans. Lewis Valentine to writer; *Bangor*, 334.
25. *Bangor*, 327.
26. M. Sanderson, *The Universities and British Industry, 1850–1970* (London, 1972), 227, 229.
27. Above, 222.

28. *Parliamentary Debates*, 5th Ser., LXXXII, 22 May 1916, 1844.
29. *Bangor*, 327.
30. *W. Mail*, 12 June 1920.
31. *W. Mail*, 22 Oct. 1915.
32. Ibid., 13 Oct. 1917, 10 Mar. 1931.
33. *Univ. Ct. Mins.*, July 1915, 132. Kelly, *Advancement of Learning*, 111–14.
34. Above, 61–2.
35. T. Gwynn Jones, MS Journal, 12. Seen by courtesy of Dr David Jenkins, Aberystwyth.
36. *Aber.*, 173.
37. R. T. Jenkins, *Edrych yn ôl*, 115. *SWDN*, 24 Oct. 1914.
38. *Dragon*, 39 (1916–17), 126–7. Ill. 24, 'The Call'.
39. *W. Mail*, 22 Oct. 1915.
40. *Dragon*, 37 (1914–15), 93.
41. Ibid., 94.
42. Ibid.
43. *Aber.*, 176.
44. Hald., *App.* II, 104, Q. 6819. E. Ashby and M. Anderson, *The Rise of the Student Estate* (London, 1970), 56. The authors then thought that Marion Soar was 'clearly a young lady flourishing forty years before her time'!
45. *Univ. Concl. Mins.*, Nov. 1923, 491.
46. *Man. Guard.*, 27 Oct. 1915.
47. *Bangor*, 339. Lewis Valentine, *Dyddiadur Milwr*, ed. John Emyr (Llandysul, 1988).
48. Quoted by A. J. P. Taylor, *English History, 1914–1945* (Oxford, 1965), 54.
49. E. Morgan Humphreys, *Gwŷr Enwog Gynt* (Aberystwyth, 1950), 72.
50. Taylor, *English History*, 116.
51. 25 Feb. 1916.
52. *Dragon*, 39 (1916–17), 165.
53. Information from my wife, whose father, the Revd H. M. Stafford Thomas, was a fellow prisoner.
54. *Univ. Ct. Mins.*, July 1934, 47.
55. David Williams, *T. F. Roberts*, 44. For the background, see David Jenkins, *T. Gwynn Jones* (Denbigh, 1973), 241 ff.
56. *Y Tro Olaf* (Denbigh, 1939), 130.
57. *Y Tyst*, 28 Jan. 1971, 21.
58. *Dragon*, 37 (1914–15), 92.
59. *North Wales Observer*, 28 May 1915; *NW Chron.*, 28 May 1915.
60. *Liverpool Echo*, 22 Mar. 1915.
61. *Bangor*, 333.
62. *Address to the Court* of the College (Cardiff, 1918), 7.
63. K. O. Morgan, *Rebirth of a Nation: 1880–1980* (Oxford and Cardiff, 1981), 166.
64. *Bangor*, 331–2.
65. Univ. Coll. Cardiff Archives, OTC, 1910–14, G560, C156.
66. *Cap and Gown* (Dec. 1914), 25.
67. Ibid.
68. *SWDN*, 12 May 1915.
69. Ibid., 7 June 1915.
70. *Bangor*, 333.
71. *Aber.*, 174, n. 46.
72. Ibid.
73. *Windsor Magazine* (June 1915), 39.
74. *Welsh Outlook*, 4 (1917), 444. By 1917 the number of students had fallen to eight; *Lamp.*, 42.
75. *Dragon*, 37 (1914–15), 256.
76. *Bangor*, 330 and n. 18.
77. *Dragon*, 37 (1914–15), 258.

78. *Dragon*, 38 (1915–16), 178–9.
79. R. Williams Parry to Thomas Jones, 25 Mar. 1917. NLW, R. W. Parry Collection, no. 273.
80. 'Personal Reminiscences . . . of H. Lloyd Williams', Univ. Coll. of N. Wales Archives, 129–30. *Bangor*, 335.
81. *W. Mail*, 30 July 1923.
82. *Dragon*, 40 (1917–18), 74.
83. NLW, O. M. Edwards Miscellaneous Box 9, 1917.
84. Dr David Jenkins to writer; *Aber.*, 243.
85. *Cap and Gown* (Mar. 1915), 33.
86. Hywel Davies in *The College by the Sea*, 249.
87. D. Densil Morgan, 'Ffydd yn y Ffosydd: Bywyd a Gwaith D. Cynddelw Williams', *National Library of Wales Journal*, 29 (Summer 1995), 77–9.
88. *Proceedings of the British Academy*, 53 (1967), 367; *Bangor*, 392.
89. Bangor 336, and n. 40.
90. *University of Wales, Roll of Service, 1914–18* (Bangor, 1921).
91. *DNB, 1981–1985*, 209–10.
92. *Welsh Outlook*, 3 (1916), opp. p. 152.
93. 'Futility'. *Bangor*, 338.
94. Univ. Coll. of N. Wales *Magazine* (Mar. 1915), 28–9.
95. Communication from Mary Glynne.
96. *Old Bangorian*, jubilee number (1934), 23.
97. *Bangor*, 337–8.
98. *Seren Gomer* (1928), 244: Book of Job 2: 13. *Bangor*, 337.

IV The Haldane Commission

1. *Welsh University and Colleges, Grants in Aid* (London, HMSO, Apr. 1916), [62] i, 1. (Submitted in 1914, published in 1916.)
2. Ibid., 4.
3. Ibid., 10.
4. Ibid., 4.
5. Ibid., 5.
6. See chapter V.
7. *Welsh University . . . Grants in Aid*, 16.
8. Ibid., 33.
9. Ibid., 34.
10. *W. Mail*, 22 Mar. 1915.
11. Ibid., 8 Apr. 1915.
12. Ibid.
13. *W. Mail*, 20, 24 Apr. 1915.
14. *The Times Educational Supplement*. Special Welsh section, 6 June 1916, 76–84, which provides a useful background by including extracts from previous issues. See especially 6 July 1915.
15. Hald., *Rept.*, 22–3.
16. *W. Mail*, 22 Oct. 1915.
17. Henry Jones to Reichel. TJ MSS, U, iii, 16.
18. *Times Educ. Suppl.*, 2 Nov. 1915.
19. *Man. Guard.*, 28 Oct. 1915.
20. *W. Mail*, 16 Apr. 1915. We may be certain that neither T. F. Roberts nor Reichel would have been so injudicious.
21. Arnold J. Toynbee, *Acquaintances* (Oxford, 1967), 153.
22. Henry Jones to Reichel, 5 Mar. 1916, TJ MSS, U, iii, 27/2.
23. William George to D. Lloyd George, 28 Jan. 1916, House of Lords, Lloyd George Papers I/2/2/46.

24. Henry Jones to Reichel, 5 Mar. 1916, TJ MSS, U, iii, 27/2; *The Case for Welsh Disestablishment* (London, 1913).
25. Eric Ashby and Mary Anderson, *Portrait of Haldane at Work on Education* (London, 1974), 124.
26. Caroline Bingham, *The History of the Royal Holloway College, 1886–1986* (London, 1987), 93.
27. Herbert Lewis to Lloyd George, 4 Jan. 1916. NLW, Penucha Papers 8/1; attached to letter of 4 Jan. 1916.
28. Reichel to Henry Jones, 22 Nov. 1915, TJ MSS, U, iii, 18.
29. Herbert Lewis to Lloyd George, 4 Jan. 1916, Penucha Papers 8/1.
30. M. F. Rathbone to Thomas Jones, 11 Feb., 17 Mar. 1916, TJ MSS, W, xvi, 11.
31. *UMW*, 164.
32. Reichel to Henry Jones, 22 Nov. 1915, TJ MSS, U, iii, 18. Reichel here quotes Roberts's views.
33. Hald., *App.* III, Q. 12436.
34. Herbert Lewis, 'Diary Note', 29 Nov. 1915, NLW, Penucha Papers, D68/15.
35. D. Jenkins, *Thomas Gwynn Jones* (Denbigh, 1973), 255.
36. *Times Educ. Suppl.*, 6 June 1916.
37. *Liverpool Express*, 28 Jul. 1916.
38. Herbert M. Vaughan, *The South Wales Squires* (London, 1926), 166.
39. *Welsh Outlook*, 2 (1915), 414.
40. Quoted in *Times Educ. Suppl.*, 2 May 1916.
41. Ibid.
42. *Times Educ. Suppl.*, 2 May 1916.
43. *Welsh Outlook*, 3 (1916), 140.
44. *Liverpool Express*, 28 July 1916. H.M. Vaughan, *Squires*, 166.
45. *Y Beirniad,* 6 (1916), 175.
46. *W. Mail*, 24 Jan. 1917.
47. Ibid., 19 Mar. 1917. Indeed, Haldane later told William George that he had raised the matter simply in order to elicit views, Hald., *App.* III, Q. 13974.
48. *Welsh Outlook*, 3 (1916), 140.
49. Reichel to Henry Jones, 8 June 1916, TJ MSS, U, iii, 41.
50. M. F. Rathbone to Thomas Jones, 11 May 1916, TJ MSS, W, xvi, 22.
51. Same to same, 13 Jan. 1916, TJ MSS, W, xvi; 4 Oct. 1915, J, i, 73.
52. J. Morris Jones to J. H. Davies, 24 Apr. 1916, NLW, J. H. Davies MSS.
53. M. F. Rathbone to Thomas Jones, 15 Oct. 1915, TJ MSS, J, i, 75.
54. Thomas Jones, *A Theme with Variations* (Newtown, 1933), 68–85.
55. M. F. Rathbone to Thomas Jones, 10 Sept. 1916, TJ MSS, J, ii, 24–5.
56. Henry Jones to Thomas Jones, 9 Sept. 1916, TJ MSS, U, i.
57. Same to same, 7 Dec. 1919, TJ MSS, U, i. See also above, 351. Jones's early experiences at Aberystwyth seem, in any case, to have led him to mistrust many people south of the Dyfi, with the exception of Viriamu Jones and Thomas Jones!
58. Hald., *App.* I, 177.
59. Hald., *App.* II, 205.
60. *Rept.*, 30; *App.* II, Q. 10756.
61. *App.* II, Q. 10757.
62. *App.* I, 135, Q. 2142.
63. Ibid., 58, III.
64. Hald., *Rept.*, 30, *App.* II, Q. 10124.
65. Hald., *App.* I, 219, IV.
66. Ibid., 259, para. 11.
67. Ibid., para. 12.
68. Ibid., II, QQ. 7494, 7498.
69. Ibid., I, Q. 3605.
70. Ibid., 4740.
71. Ibid., 195, para. 2.

72. Ibid., Q.3886; Ral., *Evid.*, Q.221. This unusual combination was taken by a woman student.
73. Hald., *App.* II, 106, Q.6861.
74. Kate Roberts and Gwladys Williams (later Lady Goronwy Edwards) to writer.
75. Hald., *App.* I, 12, QQ. 28, 243.
76. Ibid., I, 233, QQ. 3892, 3998.
77. Ibid., 259, para. 12.
78. *Times Educ. Suppl.*, 24 Oct. 1918, 454.
79. Hald., *App.* I, 161, Q. 2638.
80. Ibid., 60–1, QQ. 939–40; 261, Q. 4519.
81. *Rept.*, 31; *App.* III, 172, para. 9; *App.* I, 128, Q. 2078.
82. *App.* I, 91, Q. 1434.
83. Ibid., 90, para. 1(e).
84. Ibid., 33.
85. Ibid., II, 103–4.
86. *Rept.*, 31.
87. *App.* I, 14, Q. 62.
88. Ibid., Q. 4639.
89. Ibid., 156, para. 2(2), 197, para. 16 (ii).
90. *Rept.*, 24, para. 68.
91. Ibid., 57.
92. Ibid., 58.
93. Above, 19–20.
94. *Rept.*, 58; J. C. Beaglehole. *The University of New Zealand* (Auckland, 1937), ch. x.
95. *Rept.*, 58–9.
96. Ibid., 59.
97. Ibid., 60.
98. Ibid.
99. Ibid.
100. Ibid., 60–1.
101. *App.* III, Q. 14004.
102. *Rept.*, 63.
103. Ibid.
104. Ibid., 64.
105. Evans, *Univ. of Wales*, 98.
106. *Rept.*, 64–7.
107. Ibid.
108. Ibid., 69.
109. *App* I, Q. 944.
110. Ibid., Q. 2906.
111. Ibid., Q. 2390.
112. *Rept.*, 100.
113. Ibid.
114. Ibid., 70–1.
115. Ibid., 71.
116. Ibid., 93–8.
117. See ch. V.
118. *Rept.*, 75–8, 100.
119. *Rept.* 82.
120. *Rept.*, 101.
121. *App.* II, 169–72.
122. Ibid., Q. 8232.
123. Ibid., 170–1; *Rept.*, 84.
124. *Rept.*, 92.
125. Ibid., 90.
126. Ibid., 84.

127. Ibid., 87.
128. Ibid., 91.
129. Ibid., 92.
130. Ibid., 88.
131. Ibid., 32.
132. Ibid., 89.
133. Ibid., 89–90.
134. Ibid., 94.
135. Ibid.
136. Ibid.
137. Above, 26–7.
138. H. J. W. Hetherington, *The Life and Letters of Sir Henry Jones* (London, 1924), 39. *Bangor*, 361.
139. *Rept.*, 94.
140. Above, 161.
141. *App.* I, Q. 93.
142. Ibid., QQ. 2644, 2654, 2781, 3020.
143. *Rept.*, 96–7.
144. Henry Jones to Thomas Jones, 1 May 1916, TJ MSS. U, iii, 35.
145. Ibid., same to Reichel, 18 Apr. 1916.
146. Ibid., same to same, 1 May 1916.
147. *Y Beirniad*, 6 (1916), 171; above, 128–9.
148. Hald., *App.* II, Q. 8898.
149. Ashby and Anderson, *Portrait*, 105.
150. Hald., *App.* III, 11540 ff.
151. Ashby and Anderson, *Portrait*, 105.
152. *Parliamentary Debates*, 5th Ser., XXX, 24 July 1918, 1136.
153. *Welsh Outlook*, V (1918), 324.
154. *Times Educ. Suppl.*, 28 Mar., 1918, 137–8.
155. Above, 122–3.
156. 'The Shorthand Notes of a Deputation to the Prime Minister from the University of Wales'. There are copies at the University Registry and in various collections.
157. M. F. Rathbone to Thomas Jones, 11 Feb. 1916, TJ MSS, W, xvi.
158. *W. Mail*, 20 July 1922.
159. Ibid.
160. Lloyd George Papers, House of Lords, A 11/1/16; *Liverpool Mercury*, 2 Mar. 1903.
161. *North Wales Observer*, 19 Nov. 1908.
162. Lloyd George Papers, House of Lords, A 9/2/46, A 8/3/5, 12.
163. *Bangor*, 185.
164. *Man. Guard.*, 3 Mar. 1910.
165. *Bangor*, 185. Bangor MSS, Belmont 298, 21 Jan. 1910.
166. *Man. Guard.*, 14 Nov. 1908.
167. *Bangor*, 265; Belmont MSS 297, 11 Sept. 1908. *The University College of North Wales*, handbook (1934), 58. No place of publication noted.
168. Above, 15.
169. Lloyd George Papers, House of Lords, A 8/2/4; *SWDN*, 18 Jan. 1896.
170. *NW Observer, NW Chron.*, 19 Nov. 1908.
171. *Liverpool Courier*, 10 July 1907; Belmont MSS 297, 15 Oct. 1908.
172. Herbert Lewis Diary, 26 Feb., 11 Mar. 1909. NLW, Penucha MSS.
173. *Man. Guard.*, 25 June 1910.
174. *NW Chron.*, 16 Apr. 1908.
175. 'Notes of a Deputation', 1918, 16.
176. T. Gwynn Jones, unpublished journal. See ch. III, n. 35.
177. *Liverpool Courier*, 10 July 1907.
178. Belmont MSS 299, 2 Sept. 1911.
179. C. Addison, *Four and a Half Years, a Personal Diary*, i (London, 1934), 70.

180. Belmont MSS 299, 2 Sept. 1911.
181. Above, 120–2.
182. 4 Jan. 1916 NLW, Penucha Papers 8/1. It is remarkable that all Lewis's suggestions, except one, were accepted.
183. John Williams to [? Thomas Jones], in Welsh, 14 Jan. 1916, TJ MSS, J, ii, 1.
184. 'Notes of a Deputation', 16.
185. Ashby and Anderson, *Portrait*, 123.
186. Fisher, Diary, 14 Aug. 1918. Bodleian Library, Fisher MSS, 9.
187. In all forty, of whom twenty-five represented the University of Wales and its Colleges.
188. 'Notes of a Deputation', 5–9.
189. Ibid., 16.
190. Herbert Lewis diary, 14 Aug. 1918, NLW, Penucha Papers.
191. 'Notes of a Deputation', 17.
192. Ibid.
193. Ibid., 13.
194. Ibid., 21.
195. Ibid., 21.
196. Ibid., 18–19.
197. 'The Organization of Higher Education in Wales', by A. T. Davies, July 1918. PRO, ED 24/2027, TJ MSS, J, iv, 67. *Aber.*, 195–6.
198. Ibid., para. 7.
199. Fisher, Diary, 14 Aug. 1914, Bodleian Library, Fisher MSS, 9.
200. A. H. Kidd, 1 Aug. 1918. Comments upon A. T. Davies's memorandum (n. 197, above), PRO, ED 24/2027.
201. 'Notes of a Deputation', 20.
202. Ibid.
203. Aug. 1919.
204. Kenyon to A. H. Kidd, 9 Aug. 1919, PRO, ED 24/2027.
205. Fisher to Lloyd George, 15 Aug. 1919, ibid.
206. *Univ. Ct. Mins.*, Dec. 1919, 9.
207. Ibid., July 1919, 149–50.
208. Ibid., Dec. 1919, 9, 77–8. Reichel to Lloyd George, 6 Dec. 1919, PRO, ED 24/2027.
209. Ashby and Anderson, *Portrait*, 94; *Bangor*, 366 and n. 101.
210. Herbert Lewis to Fisher, 3 Feb. 1920, PRO, ED 24/2027 and an unsigned memorandum of 4 Mar. 1920 reporting the views of Sir William McCormick.
211. Above, 220–1.
212. ED 24/2027, 4 Mar. 1920.
213. Ibid.
214. Deputation to Prime Minister, 10 Downing Street, 19 Mar. 1920. Transcript of shorthand notes of F. Primrose Stevenson, TJ MSS, V, no. 4, 4.
215. Ibid., 10.
216. Ibid., 10.
217. Ibid., 11, 13.
218. Ibid., 9.
219. Ibid., 3, 9. Also, important memo from Fisher to Lloyd George, 15 Aug. 1919, ED 24/2027.
220. Deputation (above, n. 214), 17.
221. Ibid., 14.

V   **The Founding of the University College, Swansea, and the Welsh National School of Medicine**

1. *Swansea*, 56. These are the words of Lewis Llewelyn Dillwyn.
2. *W. Mail*, 10 July 1885, quoted in *Aber.*, 87.
3. Hald., *App.* II, 29.
4. Above, 33.
5. Hald., *App.*, II, Q. 5271.
6. Ibid., 18–45.
7. Ibid., 27.
8. Ibid., 35–42.
9. Ibid., 43.
10. Ibid., 37. W. Mansergh Varley, Principal of the Swansea Technical College.
11. Ibid., Q. 5281.
12. Ibid., QQ. 5283, 5309. See also Q. 5189.
13. There is a good discussion of Swansea's application for affiliation in *Man. Guard.*, 28 Nov. 1904. See also *Univ. Ct. Mins.*, 25 Nov. 1904, 153 ff.
14. Hald., *App.* II, Q. 7061.
15. Hald. *App.* I, Q. 146.
16. Ibid., QQ. 5183, 4653.
17. Hald., *App.* II, 323–8.
18. *Swansea*, 65.
19. *W. Mail*, 12 June 1920.
20. Hald., *App.* II, 337–8.
21. Hald., *Rept.*, 74.
22. Ibid.
23. Ibid.
24. Ibid.
25. *Univ. Ct. Mins.*, Apr. 1919, 55–64; *Swansea*, 75–8.
26. *Univ. Ct. Mins.*, Apr. 1919, 55–7.
27. Ibid., 58.
28. Ibid., 63.
29. Ibid., 64.
30. Ibid., July 1919, 9–10.
31. *UMW*, 31.
32. J. V. Jones to Lyon Playfair, 12 May 1896, PRO, ED 119/74. Playfair was Vice-President of the Committee of Council on Education.
33. Ibid.
34. Treasury reply, 15 July 1896, ED 119/74.
35. Ivor J. Davies, *Memories of a Welsh Physician* (Cardiff, 1959), 14.
36. Printed in University *Calendars*, immediately following the original charter.
37. Hald., *Rept.*, 100.
38. Deputation, 1920, see above, ch. IV, n. 214.
39. *Royal Commission on University Education in London: Final Report* (London, 1913), Cd. 6717, 108.
40. Trow and Brown, *Short History*, 62. See *W. Mail*, 20 May 1927, for a useful survey.
41. *Univ. Ct. Mins.*, Nov. 1923, 34; Oct. 1925, 7–20.
42. Ibid., 16 Oct. 1925, app. 1 ff.
43. Ibid., 7 ff.
44. *W. Mail*, 9 Jan. 1925.
45. Ibid.
46. Hald., *Rept.*, 44, *App.* I, Q. 4592.
47. *W. Mail*, 9 Jan. 1925.
48. Lynn Thomas accused him of having made a 'complete volte-face'. *W. Mail*, 6 July 1925.
49. Ibid., 8 Jan. 1925.

50. Ibid.
51. Ibid., 5 Jan. 1925.
52. 18 Oct. 1918, Univ. Coll., Cardiff, Council Mins., which included E. H. Griffiths's well-argued case on the future of the Medical School.
53. *Univ. Ct. Mins.*, Oct. 1925, app., 16.
54. *SWN*, 14 and 17 Oct. 1925.
55. *Univ. Ct. Mins.*, Oct. 1925, app., 4.
56. Glamorgan Record Office, Medical Board Minute Book, 1921–30, meeting of 10 Jan. 1928, 172; *W. Mail*, 17 Oct. 1928.
57. *Univ. Ct. Mins.*, Oct. 1925, app., 8.
58. David Davies to Thomas Jones, 27 Apr. 1914, TJ MSS, J, xv, 101.
59. Reichel to W. N. Bruce, 28 May 1919, PRO, ED 24/2027.
60. Trow and Brown, *Short History*, 62. It is clear that Kenyon was in close touch at this stage with the Privy Council, PRO, PC 8/1027.
61. 'Observations on Statement forwarded to the Prime Minister', by W. N. Bruce, 30 May 1919, PRO, ED 24/2027.
62. Ibid., A. H. Kidd to the President of the Board of Education, 18 June 1919. *W. Mail*, 29 Jan. 1925, for Reichel's admission of a change of opinion.
63. A. T. Davies to R. Mayor, 9 Dec. 1922.
64. Note to Secretary, 3 Jan. 1923, communicating Kenyon's views. ED 119/75.
65. *Univ. Ct. Mins.*, Oct. 1925, 11.
66. Evans, *Univ. of Wales*, 105.
67. *Univ. Ct. Mins.*, Jan. 1927, 9, 32–9.
68. Ibid., 6, 35–7.
69. *SWN*, 19 Feb. 1926.
70. *Univ. Ct. Mins.*, Dec. 1926, 73.
71. Ibid., Jan. 1927, 5–6.
72. *W. Mail*, 15 Jan. 1927.
73. *Univ. Ct. Mins.*, Jan. 1927, 4–6.
74. Hald., *Rept.*, 44.
75. Ivor Davies, *Welsh Physician*, 60.
76. *W. Mail*, 20 May 1927. For these tensions see Arnold S. Aldis, *Cardiff Royal Infirmary, 1883–1983* (Cardiff, 1984), 33–4.
77. Ibid., 12 Oct. 1925.
78. Ibid., 30 May 1927.
79. Ibid., 19 Dec. 1928.
80. Ibid., 9 Oct. 1928.
81. Ibid., 19 Dec. 1928.
82. Ibid., 12 Oct. 1928, 17 June 1929.
83. Ivor Davies, *Welsh Physician*, 63.
84. *Univ. Ct. Mins.*, July 1929, 27, 155–62.
85. *W. Mail*, 15 Jan. 1927.
86. *SWN*, 1 June 1928.
87. H. R. Reichel in *NW Chron.*, 25 Oct. 1929.

VI University Development, 1920–1939

1. Haldane to his mother, 26 Nov. 1920. National Library of Scotland, Edinburgh, Haldane Letters, 6003 fo. 224.
2. *Univ. Ct. Mins.*, Nov. 1920, 10.
3. *W. Mail*, 9 June 1921.
4. *SWN*, 26 Nov. 1920.
5. *W. Mail*, 20 Jan. 1923. It appears, however, that he was not a good rider, for the press tended to congregate at the first fence, where he not infrequently fell.
6. *W. Mail*, 1 Dec. 1927. See also Reichel's moving tribute, *In Memoriam, Lloyd Tyrrell*

Kenyon, Baron Kenyon (Newtown, 1928). For Kenyon's attitude to disendowment, see Bangor Archives, Belmont MSS 301, under 9 and 15 Apr. 1914.

7. *SWN*, 3 Jan. 1928.
8. *Lamp.*, 42.
9. Evans, *Univ. of Wales*, 95.
10. *W. Mail*, 17 Jan. 1921.
11. Art. 6 of the new supplemental charter.
12. *Univ. Ct. Mins.*, Nov. 1923, 14 ff.
13. Ibid., Dec. 1925, 17; Dec. 1929, 100.
14. Evans, *Univ. of Wales*, 84.
15. Hald., *App.* I, Q. 3605.
16. *Univ. Ct. Mins.*, Nov. 1920, 7.
17. M. F. Rathbone to Thomas Jones, 13 July 1922, TJ MSS, W, xvi.
18. *Univ. Cncl. Mins.*, Nov. 1931, 158–9. A further example of the bishop's grasp of financial affairs may be seen in his letter to the University Registrar, 15 Nov. 1934, at the University Registry, H673.
19. The annual reports of the UGC are of first importance for the years which follow.
20. *Univ. Ct. Mins.*, July 1922, 16.
21. UGC *Reports*, passim.
22. *Univ. Cncl. Mins.*, Oct. 1925, 385–7.
23. *Univ. Ct. Mins.*, Nov. 1923, 29–30. Rept. of Council to Court, 1922–3.
24. Ibid., Dec. 1935, 17–18.
25. Ibid., Apr. 1939.
26. Evans, *Univ. of Wales*, 127.
27. Above, 194.
28. Elwyn Davies, former secretary of the University Council, in conversation with writer.
29. *Univ. Ct. Mins.*, July 1938, 16.
30. Ibid.
31. *SWN*, 15 Mar. 1923.
32. UGC, *Returns from Universities and University Colleges in receipt of Treasury Grant . . . 1938–39* (London, HMSO, 1940), 5.
33. *Bangor*, 293.
34. Art. xv (1).
35. *Trans. Hon. Soc. Cymmrodorion* (1917–18), 137.
36. *Univ. Cncl. Mins.*, Jan. 1922, app. x, 2–3.
37. Ibid., 1–2.
38. Ibid., Oct. 1924, 22.
39. Elwyn Davies to writer.
40. *Academic Board Mins.*, July 1932, 373.
41. Ibid., Nov. 1935, 82–3.
42. Evans, *Univ. of Wales*, 96.
43. *Univ. Cncl. Mins.*, May 1935, 146.
44. W. J. Gruffydd, *A New University of Wales* (Penmark Press, 1945), 4.
45. *Reports* of the University Commission appointed by the Court of the University of Wales (Cardiff, 1964), 94, my italics.
46. K. O. Morgan, *Welsh History Review*, 17, no. 2 (1994), 256.
47. Ifor L. Evans to D. Emrys Evans, 10 Dec. 1943, Univ. Coll. of Wales, Archives, CA/PC2/D/4. I am grateful to Dr Ian Salmon for drawing my attention to this letter which I would otherwise not have seen.
48. *Cap and Gown*, jubilee no., 30 (May 1933), 20.
49. Statute xxviii, 2(a).
50. Art. xxv.
51. Statute xxvii, 2(a).
52. *Univ. Ct. Mins.*, Nov. 1922, app. xiii, 1.
53. Ibid., Nov. 1923, app. xvii, 89.

54. *Univ. Press Board Mins.*, 17 Oct. 1934, app., 315.
55. Ibid., 5 June 1929, app., 109.
56. Ibid., 13 Dec. 1929; 4 Mar. 1930; 6 Mar. 1931, app., 192. The annual grant was reduced to £650 during the 1939–40 session, *Annual Rept. of Press Board*, 2.
57. *English Historical Review*, 49 (1934), 547–8.
58. *Univ. Press Board Mins.*, 19 Sept. 1938, 170–1; 2 May 1940, 227.
59. Ibid., Apr. 1939, 194.
60. Ibid., Annual Reports for 1931–2, 1934–5, 1938–9; Mins., 2 May 1937, app. A.
61. Ibid., Mins., May, July 1922; T. H. Parry-Williams, *Gwasg Prifysgol Cymru: Rhai Atgofion* (Cardiff, 1972), 16.
62. There is a good survey by E. G. Bowen, *The Guild Today* (Cowbridge, 1973), and another by T. I. Ellis, *The Guild of Graduates* (Guild of Graduates, 1969). See also *UMW*, 151.
63. *Wales,* i (1894), 26–7.
64. *Univ. Ct. Mins.*, Dec. 1938, 122–3.
65. *Guild Annual,* 1928, 7.
66. Bowen, *Guild Today*, 13; *Guild Annual*, 1939, 11; Henry Lewis to J. E. Lloyd, 29 Mar. 1936. Bangor, Lloyd MSS, 317.
67. Above, 34–5.
68. D. Gerwyn Lewis, *The University and the Colleges of Education in Wales, 1925–78* (Cardiff, 1980), 47–79, for an authoritative treatment.
69. Evans, *Univ. of Wales*, 107.
70. Hald., *App.* III, 150–2.
71. Ibid., Q. 13, 732.
72. Ibid., *Rept.*, 92.
73. *Lamp.*, ii, 18–19, 46–51.
74. Ibid., 59.
75. Ibid., 89.
76. Ibid., 68.
77. Ibid., 78–80, 103.
78. Ibid., 53–4.
79. *Univ. Ct. Mins.*, July 1924, 22.
80. Ibid., July 1926, 19.
81. Academic Board Mins., July 1929, in *Univ. Cncl. Mins.*, July 1929, 28–9.
82. *Lamp.*, ii, 72–3.

VII   The Colleges, 1920–1939

1. Thomas Jones to J. H. Davies, 31 May 1916, NLW, J. H. Davies Correspondence.
2. M. F. Rathbone to Thomas Jones, 3 Oct. 1915, TJ MSS, J, i, 72.
3. For H. J. Fleure's tribute, see his letter to Thomas Jones, 27 Feb. 1915, TJ MSS, J, i, 25.
4. David Williams, *Thomas Francis Roberts* (Cardiff, 1961), 46.
5. There is an excellent biography by E. L. Ellis, *T.J.: A Life of Dr Thomas Jones, CH* (Cardiff, 1992).
6. D. Lleufer Thomas to Thomas Jones, 3 Oct. 1919, TJ MSS, X, v, 40.
7. R. Silyn Roberts to Thomas Jones, 9 Nov. 1919, ibid., fo. 147. H. A. L. Fisher to same, 9 Nov. 1919, ibid., fo. 173. A. L. Smith to same, 13 Nov. 1919, fo. 177.
8. 18 Dec. 1953, BBC Welsh Home Service.
9. T. I. Ellis, *John Humphreys Davies* (Liverpool, 1963), 62. It must be conceded that some considered Davies to be rather sly. *Barn*, 26 (Dec. 1964), 48.
10. Ellis, J. H. Davies, 223.
11. *DNB, 1931–1940*, 496–8.
12. D. Jenkins, *T. Gwynn Jones*, 303.
13. Thomas Jones, 18 Dec. 1953, BBC; see n. 8.
14. Ibid.

15. H. D. Henderson to Thomas Jones, 9 Nov. 1926, TJ MSS, J, xvi, 29.
16. T. H. Parry-Williams, *Bwrdd Gwasg Prifysgol Cymru*, 13–15.
17. Tribute by D. Emrys Evans at the University Court, 17 July 1952, and included in *Ifor L. Evans, Principal 1934–1952* (University College of Wales, 1952), 20–1.
18. Quoted in *Aber.*, 247.
19. Ibid., 228–9. Wheldon left Bangor in 1933.
20. David Davies to John Williams, 5 Dec. 1918, NLW, Llandinam MSS, Wilson chair, box 2. *Aber.*, 188.
21. *DNB, 1951–1960*, 1096–7; *Aber.*, 197–8, 217.
22. *Aber.*, 239.
23. *DNB, 1981–1985*, 75.
24. *DWB*, 943–4.
25. D. I. Allsobrook, *Music for Wales* (Cardiff, 1992), 62; *Aber.*, 185.
26. Walford Davies to J. H. Davies, 12 Nov. 1925, 5 Oct. 1926, NLW, J. H. Davies Correspondence.
27. *Aber.*, 233–5.
28. D. Jenkins, *T. Gwynn Jones*, 264–71.
29. *Y Traethodydd*, 130 (1975), 294.
30. John Andrews in *Cambrian Law Review*, 7 (1976), 8.
31. *Aber.*, 236.
32. *Nature*, 156 (1945), 655. *Professor E. J. Williams, F.R.S., 1903–1945*, ed. J. Tysul Jones (Llandysul, 1970).
33. *DNB, 1961–1970*, 368–9.
34. Ibid.
35. *DNB, 1951–1960*, 920–1; Univ. Coll. of Wales, Cncl. Mins., 25 Jan., 6 Mar. 1919; *Aber.*, 236–9.
36. Quoted in *Aber.*, 239, n. 45.
37. *DNB, 1951–1960*, 34–6.
38. *Bywgraffiadur Cymreig, 1941–1950* (London, 1970), 34–6.
39. UGC *Returns*, 1929–30, 8 ff.; 1935–6, 7 ff.; 1938–9, 7 ff.
40. *Bangor*, 368.
41. For the most recent assessment of Reichel, see *Bangor*, 63–5, 304, 433–7.
42. Ibid., 433–7.
43. Ibid., 424–6.
44. Ibid., 428.
45. Ibid.
46. Univ. Coll. of N. Wales, Bangor's *Gazette*, 5 (May 1966), 5–6.
47. *Bangor*, 369.
48. Recollections of A. H. Dodd, Bangor Archives, Dodd MSS, VI, 108; *Bangor* 373–7.
49. *NW Chron.*, 5 Nov. 1926.
50. *Bangor*, 379–385.
51. *DNB, 1961–1970*, 1006–7; *Bangor*, 385.
52. *DNB, 1961–1970*, 129–30.
53. *Obituary Notices of Fellows of the Royal Society*, 7 (1951), 485.
54. *Bangor*, 389–90.
55. *Welsh Leader*, 2 (1905), 690.
56. *Bangor*, 392–3.
57. Above, 204; *Bangor*, 397–8.
58. Quoted from *The Times* by Jenny Rees, *Looking for Mr Nobody* (London, 1997), 29–30.
59. *Bangor*, 395.
60. *DNB, 1961–1970*, 898–9.
61. R. Tudur Jones, *Theology in Bangor, 1922–1972* (Cardiff, 1972), 158.
62. *Bangor*, 369–70, 399.
63. Hald., *App.* III, 185.
64. UGC, *Returns*, 1938–9, 25.

65. *The University College of North Wales, Bangor* (n.pl., 1934), 60–1; *Bangor*, 431.

66. UGC, *Returns*, 1920–1939, statistical tables, passim.

67. *Association of Past Students of the University College of South Wales and Monmouthshire, College Jubilee Number* (1933), 24.

68. Ibid. See also *DNB, 1931–1940*, 377–8, and *Nature*, 1932, 461.

69. *Address to the Court of Governors*, 14 Feb. 1918 (Cardiff, 1918), 11.

70. Quoted in *Aber.*, 208, n. 73. See also undated note from Percy Watkins to Thomas Jones. TJ MSS, J, xiv, 131. Ellis, *T.J.*, 202–3.

71. Printed application, supported by the Duke of Argyll and others, May 1919, NLW; Chapman, *W.J. Gruffydd*, 69.

72. 'Cardiff', 118, nn. 71 and 72; conversation with Professor Gwyn Jones; *W. Mail*, 17 Feb. 1929.

73. Jenkin Jones to Thomas Jones, 15 Jan. 1929, TJ MSS, J, xv, 15.

74. Mabel Howell to same, 13 Dec. 1928, ibid., 7.

75. Ellis, *T.J.*, 320.

76. Appointment files, 1928–9 Univ. of Wales, Cardiff Archives, 27/5/C1–3. Richards had been director of the Government School of Medicine, 1919–24.

77. Morgan Watkin to Thomas Jones, 11 Jan. 1929, TJ MSS, J, xv, 10.

78. Same to same, 1 Jan. 1929, ibid., 27.

79. Letter of 12 Dec. 1929, 28/5/C/1 file.

80. Ibid., letters of 21 Feb. 1929 from Ernest Barker and William Beveridge. David Williams, foreword, xiv, to J. F. Rees, *The Problem of Wales and Other Essays* (Cardiff, ?1963).

81. Letter of 21 Feb. 1929, Cardiff file, 28/5/C/1; O. M. Edwards to J. E. Lloyd, Bangor, 30 Jan. 1910, Lloyd MSS, 314, no. 96.

82. Geraint H. Jenkins, *The University of Wales, an Illustrated History* (Cardiff, 1993), 110, 132; 'Cardiff', 100; below, Note on Sources.

83. 'Cardiff', 431–4, 450.

84. Ibid., 361.

85. Ibid., 365–6.

86. Sir Charles Evans, 1918–96.

87. 'Cardiff', 324, 335.

88. Trow and Brown, *Short History*, 52. *DNB, 1961–1970*, 845–6. In the departmental survey of engineering ('Cardiff', 279–81) there is no mention of Pippard.

89. Trow and Brown, *Short History*, 54.

90. 'Cardiff', 390–2.

91. Ibid., 345–7, 349.

92. Ibid., 227–9; Cecil Price, *Gwyn Jones*, Writers of Wales Series (Cardiff, 1976).

93. Quoted by Aneurin Lewis, in an admirable departmental survey, 'Cardiff', 270.

94. Chapman, *W.J. Gruffydd,* passim.

95. *DNB, 1931–1940*, 578–9; *DNB, 1961–1970*, 510–12.

96. 'Cardiff', 224–5.

97. Ibid, 233.

98. Ibid., 241.

99. Ibid., 265.

100. Quoted by Gwynedd O. Pierce in his obituary to William Rees, *Welsh History Review*, 9 (1979), 489.

101. Gwynedd O. Pierce, *A Matter of Primary Urgency* (Cardiff, 1979), 4.

102. Jacquetta Hawkes, *Mortimer Wheeler, Adventurer in Archaeology* (London, 1982), 79–80, 83, 90, 102.

103. 'Cardiff', 219–21.

104. Ibid., 296.

105. *DNB, 1951–1960*, 164–6.

106. *DNB, 1971–1980*, 549–50.

107. *Byw. Cym.*, 13–14.

108. Ral., *Rept.*, xxiii.

109. 'Cardiff', 278–80.
110. Ibid., 104. UGC, *Returns*, 1920–1, 15; 1934–5; 1938–9, 10. *Univ. Ct. Mins.*, Dec. 1935, 79.
111. *Welsh Outlook*, 7 (1920), 133.
112. Sir William McCormick in *W. Mail*, 12 June 1920; *UMW*, 90.
113. *Swansea*, 89.
114. Ibid., 139–40, 192–3.
115. Ibid., 82.
116. Ellis, *T.J.*, 217.
117. *DNB, 1941–1950*, 785–6.
118. Ibid.
119. Lewis Jones to Thomas Jones, 'Sunday', TJ MSS, J, xvi, 122.
120. T. J. Rees to same, 27 Dec. 1926, ibid., 133.
121. Ibid., 123.
122. *Swansea*, 84.
123. Ibid., 111.
124. *Biographical Memoirs of Fellows of the Royal Society*, 6 (1960), 33–5.
125. *Swansea*, 96.
126. Ibid., 96, 104; Evans, *Univ. of Wales*, 118.
127. Above, 220.
128. Information from Sir John Meurig Thomas.
129. *DNB, 1951–1960*, 994–5.
130. *Swansea*, 114–16, 125.
131. Inaugural address, 1920.
132. Hald., *Rept.*, 75.
133. Inaugural address, 1920.
134. *Swansea*, 87, 99, 127–8, 148–9.
135. Ibid., 99–100, 117.
136. Ibid., 106, 117.
137. There is a clear, balanced survey ibid., 136–9.
138. Univ. of Wales, Swansea, Cncl. Mins., 15 Mar. 1937.
139. *Saunders Lewis, Letters to Margaret Gilchrist*, ed. Mair Saunders Jones, Ned Thomas and Harri Pritchard Jones (Cardiff, 1993), 513.
140. Ibid., 513
141. *Swansea*, 138–9.
142. It was a misfortune that the vacancy was not publicly advertised. *Swansea*, 139.
143. *W. Mail*, 14 Jan. 1926.
144. Ibid., 30 Nov. 1922; above, 220.
145. *Univ. Cncl. Mins.*, Oct. 1927, 56, App. F.
146. C. A. Edwards, presenting the College's *Seventh Annual Report* to its Court of Governors, TJ MSS., J, xvi; UGC *Returns*, 1938–9, 20–1.
147. Edwards, TJ MSS., J, xvi; *Univ. Ct. Mins.*, Dec. 1939, 41–4.
148. Charter, *Univ. Ct. Mins.*, Dec. 1929, 44–54; Dec. 1932, 112–20.
149. *The Times*, 31 Mar., 1945; *The Lancet*, 1 (1945), 484.
150. 'Cardiff', 319–20.
151. Obituary, *Journal of Obstetrics and Gynaecology of the British Empire*, 60 (1953), 930–1. I am indebted to Professor Brian Hibbard for much information concerning Maclean and Strachan.
152. *Univ. Ct. Mins.*, July 1926, 15.
153. *Proceedings of the Cardiff Medical School,* 1954–5 (1956), 41–3.
154. I am grateful to Sir Dillwyn Williams for writing to me concerning Kettle.
155. *Univ. Ct. Mins.*, July 1935, 29, 178–83; Dec. 1937, 17, 125; *Univ. Cncl. Mins.*, July 1938, 9.
156. UGC, *Returns*, 1932–3, 10; 1938–9, 10.
157. *Univ. Ct. Mins.*, Dec. 1934, 25. Between 1933 and 1936 only one student entered the School from north Wales. Information from Mr John Lancaster, librarian.

158. *Univ. Ct. Mins.*, Dec. 1934, 129; Dec. 1935, 147.
159. Ibid., Dec. 1933, 102.
160. *SWDN*, 19 Feb. 1902.
161. *Univ. Ct. Mins.*, Dec. 1935, 24; UGC, *Returns*, 1938–9, 20–1.
162. *The Lancet* (14 Oct. 1933); *Univ. Ct. Mins.*, Dec. 1934, 129.

VIII   Student Life

1. Above, 11.
2. Reply of College Council to Treasury Minute of 3 Mar. 1896, separately printed and undated. College Archives.
3. Ral., *Evid.*, 119; I. C. Peate, *Rhwng Dau Fyd* (Denbigh, 1976), 59; D. Emrys Evans, Report to Bangor Court, Bangor MS 14191; *Univ. Ct. Mins.*, Dec. 1939, 76.
4. *Univ. Ct. Mins.*, Dec. 1939, 75–9.
5. Hald., *App.* II, 43, para. 6.
6. J. R. Webster, *Old College, Aberystwyth*, 69.
7. *Univ. Ct. Mins.*, Dec. 1928, 169.
8. J. B. Thomas, 'The Origins of Teacher Training at University College, Cardiff', *Journal of Educational Administration and History*, 16, no. 1 (Jan. 1984), 11.
9. *Royal Commission on the Civil Service*, 1913, XVII, Cd. 6740, 513, Q. 20996.
10. Ibid.
11. Ibid., 1914, XVI, Cd. 7340, 446, Q. 23990.
12. Reichel, presenting Percy Watkins for an honorary degree, *Univ. Ct. Mins.*, Mar. 1930, 53.
13. Aberdare, *Rept., Evidence*, 127.
14. Ral., *Evid.*, Q. 34.
15. Ibid.
16. G. S. M. Ellis, *The Poor Student and the University* (London, 1925), 8–9.
17. UGC, *Returns*, 1938–9, 5.
18. *Royal Commission on the Civil Service*, 1914, XVI, Cd. 7340, Q. 25838.
19. Ral., *Evid.*, 4, Q. 37.
20. *Dragon*, 19 (1897), 192.
21. Above, 150, 158.
22. 'Interview between the Chancellor of the Exchequer and the Deputation for the Welsh University Colleges', Bangor Archives, GC 49.
23. H. Spring, *Heaven Lies About Us: The Autobiography of Howard Spring* (London, 1972), 50.
24. *SWDN*, 7 Mar. 1903; Caradog Pritchard, *Afal Drwg Adda* (Denbigh, 1973), 106.
25. David Hughes Parry, *O Bentref Llanaelhaearn i Ddinas Llundain*, i (Caernarfon, 1972), 52.
26. Hald., *App.* I, 107–8.
27. *SWDN*, 11 May 1914.
28. Above, 270.
29. Ral., *Evid.*, Q. 286.
30. *Royal Commission on the Civil Service*, 1913, XVII, Cd. 6740, Q. 21051.
31. *Univ. Coll. of N. Wales* (1934), 58. See note.
32. *Univ. Ct. Mins.*, Dec. 1938, 236. Raymond Williams (to writer) indicated that in retrospect he would prefer to have gone to one of the Welsh colleges first, proceeding thereafter to Cambridge for postgraduate studies.
33. *Royal Comm. on Civil Service*, 1914, XVI, Cd. 7340, QQ. 22,423, 22,426.
34. G. S. M. Ellis, *Poor Student*, 18.
35. *Committee to Enquire into the Position of Natural Sciences in the Educational System of Great Britain*, 1918, IX, Cd. 9011, 30.
36. *The University of Wales* (reprint of lecture given to the Hon. Soc. of Cymmrodorion, Jan. 1920), 7.

37. *Univ. Ct. Mins.*, Dec. 1938, 9–12.
38. G.S.M. Ellis, *Poor Student*, 9; Ral., *Evid.*, Q. 34; Kate Roberts, *Erthyglau ac Ysgrifau Llenyddol*, ed. David Jenkins (Swansea, 1978), 38–40.
39. *W. Mail*, 3 May 1930; Lord Elwyn-Jones, *In my Time, An Autobiography* (London, 1983), 23.
40. Arthur Bigge to Kenyon, 15 Dec. 1902, Kenyon Papers, Bangor College Archives; the University College Magazine, Nov. 1885, in manuscript, Cardiff College Archives; Ral., *Evid.*, Q. 1337.
41. *R. S. Thomas Autobiographies*, translated from the Welsh by Jason Walford Davies (London, 1997), 37; information from Mrs Huana Morgan; K. V. Jones, *Viriamu Jones*, 124.
42. *Man. Guard.*, 20 Apr. 1911; *Welsh Review,* ed. Gwyn Jones, 1, no. 1 (Feb. 1939), 329.
43. E. H. Jones in *W. Mail*, 10 Feb. 1934. T. Mervyn Jones, *Going Public* (Cowbridge, 1987), 54.
44. Quoted in *Aber.*, 254.
45. Undated newspaper cutting in Cardiff College Archives, but probably June 1901.
46. Thomas Jones in *W. Mail*, 19 July 1922; *Bangor*, 411, and student recollections.
47. Ral., *Evid.*, 764.
48. Recollections of Dr Harry Evans and of Mrs Huana Morgan; *Aber.*, 250–1.
49. Ral., *Evid.*, Q. 453.
50. *Aber.*, 153.
51. *Univ. Ct. Mins.*, Dec. 1939, 79; *Fountains of Praise*, 98.
52. *College by the Sea*, ed. I. Morgan, 234.
53. W. Gareth Evans, *Education and Female Emancipation: The Welsh Experience, 1847–1914* (Cardiff, 1990), 213–14.
54. Ibid., 217.
55. *Man. Guard.*, 11 Oct. 1897; Carol Dyhouse, *No Distinction of Sex? Women in British Universities, 1870–1939* (London, 1995), 95.
56. Above, 67–8.
57. Dyhouse, *No Distinction*, 121.
58. *SWDN*, 9 Oct. 1895.
59. Aberdare, *Evid.*, QQ. 8332–3.
60. W. G. Evans, *Education and Emancipation*, 172.
61. Univ. Coll. of N. Wales, *Students' Handbook*, 1914–15, 54; Bangor Senate Mins., VI, 371 (17 Mar. 1919).
62. Dyhouse, *No Distinction*, 203.
63. 'Cardiff', 432.
64. *Aber.*, 125.
65. *Bangor*, 310–11.
66. Conversations with Kate Roberts and Gwladys Williams (later Lady Goronwy Edwards).
67. Information from Professor Gwyn Jones.
68. *Aber.*, 160–1; *Univ. Ct. Mins.*, May 1908, 12.
69. *Man. Guard.*, 27 Nov. 1909; *SWDN*, 3 June 1910.
70. D. Hughes Parry, *O Bentref Llanaelhaearn*, 60–1. *Cambrian News*, 22, 29 Mar. 1912.
71. *The Barrian* (magazine of the notable Barry School), 18 (1932), 31.
72. Ibid., 21 (1935), 13.
73. Roy Jenkins in *Fountains of Praise*, 98.
74. *College by the Sea*, 250.
75. Conversation with Lewis Valentine.
76. *College by the Sea*, 145.
77. *The Undergrad.* (Nov. 1924), 5–6.
78. *Welsh Outlook,* 1 (1914), 363.
79. *Aber.*, 212–13; *Swansea*, 134; *Cap and Gown* (Mar. 1914), 27.
80. Quoted by Glyn Penrhyn Jones, *Newyn a Haint yng Nghymru* (Denbigh, 1962), 108, 117–23.

81. *Aber.*, 72.
82. *Man. Guard.*, 11 Dec. 1896.
83. BBC talk, Welsh Home Service. See ch. II, n. 88.
84. P. H. Burton, *Early Days: My Life and the Theatre* (New York, 1969), 37.
85. *Bangor*, 317, 319, 420–1; *Aber.*, 215, 276, 290, 323; 'Cardiff', 442; *Fountains of Praise*, 96.
86. In writing this paragraph I am much indebted to Dr Gareth Williams who provided me with valuable notes.
87. *Aber.*, 214.
88. *Cap and Gown* (Dec. 1923), 29; (Mar. 1924), 30, 48–50; (Apr. 1925), 60.
89. Ibid., 1923, 4.
90. Ibid., 1928, 17–18.
91. Above, 112–13.
92. *Aber.*, 252.
93. Ibid., 253.
94. *W. Mail*, 25 Apr. 1935.
95. *Univ. Ct. Mins.*, Dec. 1935, 36.
96. Ibid., 32–6. Helen M. Jones (later Ramage) said that the majority of students were opposed to the OTC. See also ibid., July 1936, 186–7.
97. *W. Mail*, 24 May 1935.
98. Burton, *Early Days*, 33.
99. *Yr Efrydydd*, 1 (1921), 2.
100. Burton, *Early Days*, 38.
101. Univ. Coll. Cardiff, *Magazine* (May 1904), 51.
102. *Cap and Gown* (Nov. 1925), 45–6.
103. Information from Dr Christopher Hill.
104. Information from Mr T. A. Lewis.
105. Moelwyn Merchant, *Fragments of a Life* (Llandysul, 1990), 21.
106. Ibid.
107. Ibid., 22–3.
108. Bangor, *Students' Handbook*, 1928–9, 15–16.
109. *Dragon*, 25 (1913–14), 180.
110. *NW Chron.*, 6 May 1943.
111. *Y Wawr*, 1 (1913), 2–3.
112. *Dragon*, 36 (1913–14), 159.
113. Ibid., 45 (1922–3), 80.
114. *Aber.*, 215.
115. Univ. Coll. Cardiff *Magazine*, 1 (1903), 25.
116. *Cap and Gown* (Mar. 1910), 116.
117. Ibid., May 1910, 212–13; Nov. 1922, 49–50.
118. May 1935, 34–6; Jan. 1936, 11.
119. *NW Chron.*, 6 Aug. 1943.
120. Quoted in J. E. Jones, *Tros Gymru* (Swansea, 1970), 25, 'yn genedlaetholwr Cymreig rhonc'.
121. Ibid., 30.
122. *Bangor*, 414.
123. *Seren Cymru*, 15 Apr. 1921.
124. J. E. Jones, *Tros Gymru*, 40; *Ysgrifau Beirniadol*, 9 (1976), 368.
125. *Efrydiau Athronyddol*, 38 (1974), 32.
126. This passage is in the main based on conversations with Dr Eirwen Gwynn, Dr Isaac Thomas and the late Stephen J. Williams. See also Gwynfor Evans, *Bywyd Cymro*, ed. Manon Rhys (Caernarfon, 1982), 46–7.
127. Thomas Jones, *Leeks and Daffodils* (Newtown, 1942), 33.
128. *Sir Harry Reichel*, ed. J. E. Lloyd, 75.
129. Recollections of A. H. Williams, Mrs Huana Morgan and an 'old student' of Cardiff in *W. Mail*, 11 Oct. 1922.

130. *Dragon*, 42 (1920–1), 66; *College by the Sea*, 251.
131. *NW Chron.*, Feb. 1885.
132. Alfred Zimmern to J. H. Davies, 3 Apr., 25 June, J. H. Davies Correspondence. The years are not stated, but are almost certainly 1920.
133. *Gwanwyn yn y Ddinas* (Denbigh, 1975), 73.
134. *Magazine* (Feb. 1900), 116–17.
135. *Univ. Cncl. Mins.*, Oct. 1931, 38–9.
136. Bruce Truscott, *Red Brick University* (London, 1943), 85–6.
137. Ibid., 86.
138. *Aber.*, 236.
139. Glyn Daniel, *Some Small Harvest . . .* (London, 1986), 48; Burton, *Early Days*, 33.
140. Mervyn Jones, *Going Public*, 51; information from Mr Moses J. Jones; R. T. Jenkins, *Edrych yn Ôl*, 134; *Univ. Ct. Mins.*, July 1936, 26. Swansea's *Old Students Association* publication, 1937, 17.
141. These statistics are based on Ral., *Evid.*, 114; *Univ. Ct. Mins.*, Dec. 1939.
142. J. F. Rees to Thomas Jones, 18 Oct. 1934, TJ MSS, W, xvi, 175.
143. *The Passman* (London, 1918); *Bangor*, 372.
144. Ral., *Evid.*, Q. 316.
145. Hald., *App.* I, 306.
146. App. III (b), below.
147. *Univ. Ct. Mins.*, July 1936, 23–8.
148. Aberystwyth *Calendar*, 1886–7, 30–1.
149. Journal of Henry Lewis, 29 Mar. 1908, Bangor archives, Belmont MSS 296.
150. *Bangor*, 302–3.
151. *W. Mail*, 11 Oct. 1922.
152. *Univ. Ct. Mins.*, July 1936, 172–3.
153. Ibid., 26.
154. *Swansea*, 121; *W. Mail*, 16 Oct. 1936.
155. *Swansea*, 121.
156. Ibid., 120–1.
157. App. III (d), below; *Univ. Ct. Mins.*, Dec. 1939.
158. H. Laski, *The American Democracy* (New York, 1948), 346–7; *Bangor*, 458.
159. *Aber.*, 251.
160. *Bangor*, 458.
161. *Dragon*, 38 (1915–16), 19.
162. Quoted in *Aber.*, 213; Thomas Jones, *A Theme with Variations* (Newtown, 1933), 66–95.
163. *Welsh Outlook*, 6 (1919), 106.
164. Undated memorandum from Lord Davies to the College's Discipline Committee. Aberystwyth College Archives.
165. Conversation with Kate Roberts.
166. *Welsh Outlook*, 12 (1924–5), 186–90.
167. *Aber.*, 213–14.
168. *The Collected Papers of Thomas Frederick Tout*, i, 49.
169. The *Supplement* was published under the auspices of *Cap and Gown*. For Marquand and the Prince of Wales, see 1–2.
170. *Dawn*, 3, no. 1 (1924), 13–14.
171. *Cap and Gown*, jubilee no., 30 (May 1933), 22.
172. D. Emrys Evans to Ifor L. Evans, 17 Mar. 1938, quoted in *Aber.*, 253.
173. Hald., *App.* I, Q. 2625.
174. Evans, *Univ. of Wales*, 140–1.
175. *Trans. Hon. Soc. of Cymm.* (1917–18), 142, n. 1.

IX   University and Nation 1

1.   Articles in *Baner*, 14, 28 May, 4 June 1964. A translation was deposited in Univ. Coll. Cardiff Library, Accession no. 147069.
2.   Ibid., 28 May 1964.
3.   Ibid.
4.   Above, 316.
5.   *Baner*, 28 May 1964.
6.   Ibid., Saunders Lewis in *Baner* (Dec. 1964), 33.
7.   *Cambrian News*, 13 Oct. 1876.
8.   *Baner*, 28 May 1964.
9.   Ibid.
10. Thomas Nicholas, *Middle and High Schools and a University for Wales* (London, 1863), 26.
11. Ieuan Gwynedd Jones, *Explorations and Explanations* (Llandysul, 1981), 293–4.
12. *UMW*, 68; Aberdare, *Evid.*, Q. 336.
13. *Baner*, 28 May 1964.
14. Aberdare, *Rept.* 19, 889.
15. I. Gwynedd Jones, *Explorations*, 293–4; *UMW*, 211.
16. Aberdare, *Rept.*, xvii.
17. Wales, I (1894), 27.
18. *Baner*, 28 May 1964.
19. Evans, *Univ. of Wales*, 44.
20. Preamble to 1893 Charter.
21. Ibid.
22. *Baner*, 28 May 1964.
23. 'The People's University in Retrospect', *The University of Wales Review* (The Welsh Anvil), Summer 1964, 7.
24. T. Nicholas, *A University for Wales* (London, 1864), 7. *UMW*, 29, 211, n. 93.
25. Aberdare, *Rept.*, xlvi ff.
26. Introduction to Univ. Coll. of Wales *Magazine*, 1 (Nov. 1878), 4.
27. *Young Wales*, 2 (1896), 129–30.
28. Ibid., 131.
29. Ibid., 154.
30. *North Wales Observer*, 28 Oct. 1893.
31. *UMW*, 43.
32. Ibid., 57–8, 66, 99–100.
33. J. Rhys and D. Brynmor-Jones, *The Welsh People* (London, 1906), 474, n.1.
34. *Welsh Leader*, 3 Mar. 1904, 374–5. Here J. Morris-Jones speaks eloquently of his own experiences and those of Henry Jones.
35. *Parliamentary Papers*, IX (1919), Cd. 24, *Wages and Conditions of Employment in Agriculture in Wales*, 51. I am obliged to Dr D. W. Howells for this reference.
36. *UMW*, 150.
37. Ibid., 190–1.
38. W. H. G. Armytage, *Civic Universities* (London, 1955), 256.
39. At Bangor, Marion C. Soar, below.
40. *Bangor*, 408.
41. 'Hall Notes', *Dragon*, 42 (1919–20), 115; Dr Eirwen Gwynn to writer.
42. UGC, *Returns*, 1924–5, 1933–4, 1938–9, for tables of comparative statistics.
43. Quoted by C. Dyhouse, *No Distinction*, 138.
44. *Fountains of Praise*, 190.
45. Quoted by Dyhouse, *No Distinction*, 152.
46. Hald., *App*, I, Q. 113.
47. *Univ. of Wales Calendar*, 1946–7, 4. She was appointed for six years from Oct. 1944. It is worth noting, too, that it was by the intervention of the Privy Council that a woman became a member of the University Appointments Board. *Univ. Ct. Mins.*, Dec. 1937, 26.

48. Hald., *Rept.*, 68, 75.
49. Hald., *App.* III, Q. 12416; *Rept.*, 68.
50. *Univ. Cncl. Mins.*, Apr. 1936, 118; Hald., *App.* II, 5856.
51. L. Doreen Whiteley, *The Poor Student and the University* (London, 1933), 24.
52. *Dragon*, 39 (1916–17), 127. M. F. Rathbone to Thomas Jones, TJ MSS, W, xvi; Dyhouse, *No Distinction*, 117.
53. Cardiff, 433.
54. *South Wales Echo*, 30 Nov. 1925.
55. P. Ellis Jones, 'The Women's Suffrage Movement in Caernarvonshire', *Trans. Caerns. Hist. Soc.* (1987), 77, 80–1, 94, 112; *Our Mother's Land*, ed. Angela John (Cardiff, 1991), 162–3.
56. Quoted by Dyhouse, *No Distinction*, 18.
57. *SWN*, 15 July 1927.
58. J. W. Mackail, quoted by W. G. Evans, *Education and Emancipation*, 248.
59. *Bangor*, 310.
60. *Dragon*, 26 (1903–4), 163.
61. Ibid., 42 (1920), 183; Mervyn Jones, *Going Public*, 50.
62. *Swansea*, 100.
63. *Univ. Ct. Mins.*, July 1933, 51.
64. *Dragon*, 31 (1908–9), 54.
65. Aberystwyth *Calendar*, 1886–7 (1886), 30–1.
66. *Man. Guard.*, 21 June 1902; Ral., *Evid.*, Q. 316; *Trans. of the Liverpool Welsh National Society* (1886–7), 5–6.
67. *Trans. of Liverpool Welsh Nat. Soc.* (1892–3), 98–108.
68. *UMW*, 117, 222, n. 9.
69. *Patriotism, Local and Imperial, an Address to the Manchester Welsh National Society* (Bangor, 1921), 9; *Bangor*, 225, 159.
70. *NW Chron.*, 7 Nov. 1907.
71. *Patriotism, Local and Imperial*, 9.
72. *Man. Guard.*, 22 Feb. 1906.
73. *Patriotism and Cosmopolitanism* (n.pl., 23 Oct. 1908), 10.
74. *Welsh Outlook,* 3 (1916), 76.
75. *W. Mail*, 14 and 16 Jan. 1904.
76. In F. Spencer, *Chapter on the Aims and Practice of Teaching* (Cambridge, 1897), 148.
77. *The Importance of Teaching the History of the British Empire*. Paper read before the Imperial Conference on Education at Toronto, 10 Aug. 1920 (no place or date of publication), 7.
78. David Davies to T. Francis Roberts, 3 Mar. 1906, Aberystwyth College Archives, T. F. Roberts letters.
79. Hald., *App.* III, 209.
80. *Welsh in Education and Life . . .* (London, 1927), 81.
81. *Aber*, 162.
82. Ibid.
83. *W. Mail*, 5 Mar. 1906.
84. J. Herbert Lewis to D. Lloyd George, 21 Jan. 1918, NLW, Penucha Papers D79. This view is questioned, and not without cause, by Aled Eurig, *Llafur*, 4, no. 4 (1987), 58, 67, n. 2.
85. *Parliamentary Debates* (Commons) XCIX, 29 Nov. 1917, 2416.
86. Ibid. (Lords) 5th Ser., XXVII, 23 Jan. 1918, 1129 ff.
87. H. J. Fleure to Mrs [Herbert] Jones, 15 Dec. 1918; Ifor Williams to same, 27 Nov. 1918. NLW Penucha Papers.
88. *English History, 1914–45*, 156, n.1.
89. *Parliamentary Debates* (Commons) XCIX, no. 151, 29 Nov. 1917, 2420.
90. Ernest Evans to J. Herbert Lewis, 18 July 1929, NLW, J. Herbert Lewis Letters, no. 374.
91. *W. Mail*, 8 and 18 May 1906.

92. Ibid., 12 May 1906, 18 Dec. 1928; *Univ. Ct. Mins.*, Dec. 1928, 24.
93. *Univ. Ct. Mins.*, July 1936, 39–40.
94. *W. Mail*, 23 July 1936.
95. *Univ. Ct. Mins.*, July 1938, 46.
96. Ibid., Dec. 1930, 16.
97. *W. Mail*, 28 July 1934.
98. *Univ. Ct. Mins.*, July 1926; 19, Dec. 1926, 28; J. Lloyd Williams to J. H. Davies, 28 Sept. 1925, NLW, J. H. Davies correspondence.
99. *Fountains of Praise*, 30.
100. *Bangor*, 219.
101. J. H. Davies to Thomas Jones, 4 May 1915, TJ MSS, J, i, 46.
102. Ibid.,
103. T. Robin Chapman, *W. J. Gruffydd* (Cardiff, 1993), 32.
104. *Bangor*, 222.
105. Ibid., 370.
106. PRO, ED 82; *W. Mail*, 13 Aug. 1915.
107. Above, 364.
108. *Thomas Charles Edwards Letters*, ed. T. I. Ellis, 291.
109. P. Watkins, *A Welshman Remembers* (Cardiff, 1944), 96.
110. A. T. Davies to R. Mayor, 29 Dec. 1922, PRO, ED 119/75.
111. A. H. Kidd to S. Gawler, 30 May 1922, PRO, ED 24/2029.
112. *Bangor*, 221.
113. J. W. Marshall to J. E. Lloyd, 23 Aug. 1891, Bangor Archives, Lloyd MSS, 314, no. 314.
114. S. R. Jenkins to same, 2 Nov. 1901, ibid., U, 234.
115. J. R. Ainsworth Davies to same, 30 Oct. 1901, ibid.
116. Same to same, 7 June 1901, ibid.
117. Same to same, 7 Nov. 1901, ibid.
118. Edward Lloyd to same, 8 Nov. 1901, ibid.
119. G. Hartwell Jones, *A Celt Looks at the World* (Cardiff, 1946), 42; *UMW*, 52–3.
120. Jack Tanner in *Man and Superman*, quoted by Armitage, *Civic Universities*, 230.
121. Above, 350.
122. Henry Jones, *Old Memories* (London, 1924), 182, 185.
123. Lord Penrhyn to R. Williams Bulkeley, 20 Dec. 1892, Bangor Archives, Penrhyn Papers; *Bangor*, 186.
124. *Bangor*, 187.
125. *DNB, 1941–1950*, 200.
126. Watkins, *Welshman Remembers*, 95–6.
127. Hald., *App.* II, QQ. 10, 494–5.
128. Ibid.
129. Memorandum by H. A. L. Fisher, 22 July 1918, PRO, ED 24/2027.
130. A. C. Wood, *A History of the University College Nottingham, 1881–1948* (Oxford, 1953), 33.
131. A. H. Kidd to Fisher, 18 June 1919, PRO ED 24/2027.
132. A. H. Williams to writer.
133. *Welsh Outlook*, 4 (1917), 164. Strictly speaking Reichel was referring to North Wales, but his remarks were of general application.
134. Henry Jones to Thomas Jones, 11 Mar. 1917, NLW, TJ MSS, U, i, 21/2.
135. *W. Mail*, 15 Oct. 1934.
136. *Nodiadau'r Golygydd W. J. Gruffydd: Detholiad o Nodiadau Golygyddol 'Y Llenor' gyda Rhagymadrodd a Sylwadau gan T. Robin Chapman* (Llandybïe, 1986), 137–9.
137. *The University in Wales* (Newtown, 1920), 17.
138. Reichel to J. E. Lloyd, 27 Oct. 1901, Bangor Archives, Lloyd MSS, U, 234.
139. Armytage, *Civic Universities*, 219–20.
140. Deputation to Prime Minister, Aug. 1918. See above, 157 ff.
141. W. C. Davies and W. L. Jones, *The University of Wales* (London, 1905), 209. Such a

sum, Lockyer thought, would not be considered extravagant when the needs of Birmingham University were calculated at £5 million. Ibid.

142. Armytage, *Civic Universities*, 228.
143. *Aber.*, 128; *Bangor*, 197, 275; 'Cardiff', 409.
144. *Aber.*, 130.
145. *Address* by E. H. Griffiths to the College, 9 Jan. 1902 (Cambridge, ?1902), 13. (There is no title.)
146. Ibid.
147. A. J. Balfour to Lord Kenyon, 14 June 1904, Bangor Archives, Kenyon Papers.
148. 'Interview between the Chancellor of the Exchequer and the Deputation for the Welsh University College', 3 Mar. 1904, Bangor archives, GC 49.
149. M. Sanderson, *The Universities and British Industry*, 134.
150. *Bangor*, 193.
151. Ral., *Evid.*, 18–19; Hald., *App.* III, Q. 14260.
152. L. A. Duff Assheton Smith to Lord Penrhyn, 14 Dec. 1902 and undated letter to same, Bangor Archives, Penrhyn Papers.
153. Above, for example, 213.
154. The Coal Mines Regulation Act (1887) Amendment Act (1903); *W. Mail*, 26 Sept. 1903.
155. *Address to Court of Governors . . . Feb. 14th 1918* (Cardiff, 1918), 10.
156. Hald., *App.* I, Q. 638. In fact, Chamberlain, by the time Birmingham's charter was granted, had exceeded this target by £80,000. Sanderson, *British Industry*, 70.
157. Sanderson, *British Industry*, 139.
158. T. J. Williams, Hald., *App.* II, QQ. 5207–8, 5257.
159. Ibid., Q. 10172.
160. Ibid.
161. Ral., *Evid.*, 108. K. G. Robbins, 'Academic Life and Public Expectations', an inaugural lecture at Lampeter, 27 November 1992, n. 17; Martin Daunton, *Coal Metropolis: Cardiff, 1870–1914* (Leicester, 1977).
162. Trow and Brown, *Short History*, 39; *W. Mail*, 10 May 1938.
163. Ral., *Evid.*, Q. 1152.
164. *Address to Court*, 14 Feb. 1918, 10.
165. Hald., *App.* II, Q. 10173.
166. *W. Mail*, 21 Nov. 1923 for Llewellyn, and *W. Mail*, 30 Apr. 1932 for Glanely's outburst.
167. Hald., *App.* II, QQ. 10211, 10216.
168. Ibid., 70, para. 1
169. Ibid., Q. 10209.
170. Ibid., I, Q. 661.
171. Ibid., Q. 660.
172. Ibid., II, 10241.
173. Ibid., 10235–6.
174. Ibid., 10065.
175. Hald., *App.* III, Q. 11840. Henry Jones to Thomas Jones, 10 July 1918, TJ MSS, U, i, 45.
176. *UMW*, 102.
177. J. F. Rees to Thomas Jones, 1 Oct. 1929, ibid., W, xvi, 169.
178. 'Cardiff', 25.
179. Ral., *Evid.*, 73.
180. Trow and Brown, *Short History*, 54.
181. *Univ. Coll for N. Wales*, handbook (1930), 34 ff.
182. Ibid., 35.
183. Jaroslav Pelikan, *The Idea of the University: A Reexamination* (New Haven, 1992), 139.
184. Sanderson, *British Industry*, 122.
185. *Universities, Society and the Future*, ed. Nicholas Phillipson (Edinburgh, 1983), 208.

186. *Univ. Ct. Mins.*, Dec. 1937, 239.
187. Above, 372.
188. Wynford Davies, *Rhiwbina Garden Village: A History of Cardiff's Garden Suburb* (Bridgend, ?1985), 12.
189. Ibid., 17.
190. D. Morgan Rees, industrialist, 21 Apr. 1919. NLW, printed application of W. J. Gruffydd for the principalship of Cardiff.
191. *DNB, 1971–1980*, 549–50.
192. *Univ. Cncl. Mins.*, Feb. 1936, 133.
193. Gwynne Meara, *Juvenile Unemployment in South Wales* (Cardiff, 1936).
194. It reported annually to the University Court.
195. *Tir Newydd*, rhif 8 (Liverpool, May 1937), 11.
196. *W. Mail*, 1 Dec. 1934.
197. *Wales, 1880–1914*, ed. T. Herbert and Gareth E. Jones (Cardiff, 1988), 24, 25, 29.
198. Ibid.
199. *Bangor*, 305.
200. *Book of North Wales* (London, 1903), 213; *Welsh Leader*, 1 (1904), 374–5.
201. Rendel to T. F. Roberts, 18 Oct. 1906, NLW, Rendel MSS 19442E, 140.
202. *Man. Guard.*, 7 July 1905.
203. *Univ. Ct. Mins.*, Dec. 1926, 32–3.
204. *W. Mail*, 11 Feb. 1935.
205. J. C. Davies, *Univ. Ct. Mins.*, Dec. 1934, 25.
206. *Times Educ. Supplement*, 19 Oct. 1916, 174.
207. *Univ. Cncl. Mins.*, June 1928, 310; Nov. 1930, 191; Apr. 1931, 328–9.
208. *Univ. Cncl. Mins.*, Apr. 1931, 358 ff.; *Bangor*, 389–90. Thomas Waterhouse of Holywell was an active member.
209. Sanderson, *British Industry*, 132–3; *Bangor*, 164–5, 197–8.
210. *W. Mail*, 11 Feb. 1935; above, 221–3.
211. Ibid., 24 Oct. 1934.
212. Ral., *Evid.*, Q. 233.
213. Quoted in G. E. Jones, *Controls and Conflicts in Welsh Secondary Education 1889–1944* (Cardiff, 1982), 197.
214. *The Native Never Returns* (London, 1946?), 24.
215. *Saunders Lewis, ei feddwl a'i waith*, ed. Pennar Davies (Denbigh, 1950), 7–17. D. J. Williams, 13–14, was, however, too severe upon the University, as may be gathered from chs. IX and X of this volume.
216. *The University of Wales Today* (BBC script of talk delivered on 10 and 14 Feb. 1938), 5.

X   University and Nation 2

1. K. O. Morgan, *Rebirth of a Nation: Wales 1880–1980* (Oxford and Cardiff, 1981), 122, 125–6, 131.
2. Percy Watkins, *A Welshman Remembers* (Cardiff, 1944), 58.
3. A. H. Williams, *Cymru Oes Victoria* (Cardiff, 1973), 42–3.
4. John Williams, *Digest of Welsh Historical Statistics*, i (Cardiff, 1985), 86. The census of 1921 demonstrated 'an absolute drop since the preceding census'. Morgan, *Rebirth*, 198.
5. *Man. Guard.*, 17 and 20 Mar. 1905.
6. *Wales*, ii (1895), 93–4.
7. *W. Mail*, 14 Feb. 1895.
8. Ibid., 12 Oct. 1900.
9. W. J. Gruffydd, *Nodiadau Golygydd*, ed. T. R. Chapman, 121–2.
10. *W. Mail* and *SWDN*, 21 Aug. 1906.
11. *W. Mail*, 4 Mar. 1907.

12. Ibid., 12 May 1906. For H. M. Hughes see *DWB*, 378. In 1930 the University conferred upon him an honorary LLD.
13. Ibid.
14. *My Impressions of Wales* (London, 1921), 29, 31, 41–2.
15. *W. Mail*, 28 Feb. 1924, 11 Dec. 1925.
16. *Univ. Ct. Mins.*, July 1929, 168–70.
17. Ibid., Feb. 1921, 15; Saunders Lewis, *Ysgrifau Dydd Mercher* (Llandysul, 1945), 103–5.
18. *Man. Guard.*, 27 Apr. 1906; *The Nationalist*, Jan. 1908, 4–5.
19. *W. Mail*, 14 July 1906. For Marchant's attack on Reichel, see, *Welsh Leader*, 1 (1904), 322.
20. *W. Mail*, 14 July 1906.
21. *W. Mail*, 18 May 1922; W. J. Gruffydd, *Nodiadau Golygydd*, 126–8.
22. *W. Mail*, 15 June 1936.
23. Ibid., 5 Mar. 1906.
24. *Arrows of Desire* (London, 1920), ch. 7, 'The Sister Nations', 162–99.
25. *Sir Harry Reichel*, ed. J. E. Lloyd, 11.
26. D. Tecwyn Evans, *Atgofion Cynnar* (Tywyn, Meirionnydd, 1951), 119. For Zimmern, see, for example his letter to Thomas Jones, 28 July 1920, TJ MSS, W, xx, 227. For R. S. Conway and E. V. Arnold, *The Restored Pronunciation of Greek and Latin* (Cambridge, 1895), 3.
27. *Y Beirniad*, 4 (1914), 63–4; *NW Chron.*, 22 Aug. 1941.
28. J. E. Lloyd, *The University of North Wales: A Short Guide* (Cardiff, n.d.), 10.
29. R. Tudur Jones, *Ffydd ar Argyfwng Cenedl, Cristionogaeth a Diwylliant yng Nghymru, 1890–1914*, ii (Swansea, 1982), 279, 281.
30. Above, 338.
31. *Y Cymro*, 8 Feb. 1922; H. J. W. Hetherington, *The Life and Letters of Sir Henry Jones* (London, 1924), 43.
32. *SWDN*, 3 June 1907.
33. Hald., *App.* I, QQ. 1058–9.
34. *W. Mail*, 13 and 21 June 1906.
35. Ibid., 3 Mar. 1934. For an earlier fusillade on this theme by the Revd H. Barrow Williams (Calvinistic Methodist), Llandudno, see *SWDN*, 14 May 1914.
36. *W. Mail*, 3 Mar. 1934.
37. This is the prevailing theme of Kenyon in *A Brief Survey of the Work of the University of Wales . . . 1909–14* (Wrexham, 1914), especially 3–5.
38. Above, 160.
39. *Univ. Ct. Mins.*, July 1928, 29–30; July 1936, 21–2, 162–70.
40. *W. Mail*, 17 and 19 July 1935.
41. G. E. Jones, *Controls and Conflicts,* 97.
42. Ibid., 51.
43. G. Perrie Williams, *Welsh Education in Sunlight and Shadow* (London, 1918), 22. For the views of Cavanagh, Gwenan Jones and Olive Wheeler, see G. E. Jones, *Controls and Conflicts*, 121–2, 156.
44. Mrs Peter Hughes Griffiths to Herbert Lewis, 29 Dec. 1930, NLW, Herbert Lewis Letters, no. 493.
45. G. E. Jones, *Controls and Conflicts*, 123 ff.
46. *UMW*, 156, 174; *Y Drych*, 21 Sept. 1893.
47. Hald., *App.* III, QQ. 11845, 11858.
48. *W. Mail*, 15 May 1920 for a fine tribute to Burrows.
49. *Survey of Adult Education in Wales* (Cardiff, 1940), 17. *Bangor*, 208.
50. Quoted by Richard Lewis, *Leaders and Teachers, Adult Education and the Challenge of Labour in South Wales, 1904–1940* (Cardiff, 1993), 107.
51. *Welsh Outlook*, 20 (1933), 289, translating O. M. Edwards in *Cymru* (Mar. 1914).
52. Hald., *App.* III, Q. 11926, n. 1.
53. TJ MSS, J, xiv, 117, fo. 5 (no writer's name, n.d.).

54. Deputation to the Prime Minister, 14 Aug. 1918, 15.
55. Hald., *App.* III, QQ. 12213, 12182.
56. Hald., *App.* II, Q. 5841.
57. Hald., *Rept.*, 90, 101.
58. *My Impressions of Wales*, 32.
59. Quoted by Peter Stead, *Coleg Harlech, the First Fifty Years* (Cardiff, 1977), 33.
60. Ibid., 25.
61. *Liverpool Daily Post and Mercury*, 12 Feb. 1912; *Survey of Adult Education in Wales* (1940), passim.
62. *Welsh Outlook*, 2 (1915), 85.
63. *The Development of Theological Education in the University of Wales*, delivered 27 Mar. 1917 (Bangor, 1917), 7.
64. Hald., *App.* I, QQ. 4352–3.
65. Ibid., QQ. 4402, 4470.
66. *Development of Theological Education*, 7.
67. Thomas Ellis, *Speeches and Addresses* (Wrexham, 1912), 30.
68. Ibid., 31.
69. Hald., *App.*, III, 60.
70. *W. Mail*, 3 May 1930.
71. *SWDN*, 6 Feb. 1906.
72. Hald., *App.* I, 189.
73. *Univ. Ct. Mins.*, Dec. 1931, 14.
74. Ibid., Dec. 1929, 100.
75. Ibid., 97–9.
76. Evans, *Univ. of Wales*, 90; *Univ. Ct. Mins.*, July 1938, 27.
77. *Univ. Cncl. Mins.*, July 1933, 26–7; *Bangor*, 371, and n. 117.
78. Hald., *Rept.*, 84–8.
79. O. Llew Owain, *Hanes y Ddrama yng Nghymru* (Liverpool, 1948), 2.
80. Kenyon, introduction to *A Brief Survey of the Work of the University of Wales, 1909–14*, 5.
81. Owain, *Hanes*, 112–13.
82. Ibid., 151, 184; *Bangor*, 417.
83. Owain, *Hanes*, 175.
84. 'Our Mother-Tongue: A Musical Policy for Wales', *Trans. Hon. Soc. Cymm.*, 1921–2 (1923), 1, 9.
85. D. I. Allsobrook, *Music for Wales* (Cardiff, 1992), 71–2.
86. Ibid., 89; *Bangor*, 232–3.
87. Above, 328.
88. Hald., *Rept.*, 87–8.
89. *W. Mail*, 20 May 1922.
90. Allsobrook, *Music for Wales*, 109.
91. Thomas Jones, *Leeks and Daffodils* (Newtown, 1942), 76.
92. Allsobrook, *Music for Wales*, 137–8.
93. Ibid., 142–3.
94. Ibid., 161.
95. *Univ. Ct. Mins.*, July 1932, 15.
96. *Univ. Ct. Mins.* June 1894; C. A. Edwards, *7th Annual Report* to Swansea Ct. of Governors, TJ MSS, J, xvi.
97. *W. Mail* and *SWDN*, 21 Aug. 1906. Lloyd's speech was delivered to the Cymmrodorion Society meeting at the Caernarfon Eisteddfod.
98. Hald., *App.* II, Q. 8356.
99. Thomas Richards, *The History of the Puritan Movement in Wales* (London, 1920). Nor should be forgotten, for example, the scholarly triumphs of Charles Ashton, *DWB*, 16.
100. *W. Mail*, 23 Aug. 1906.
101. Ibid., 20 July 1922, at the College's Jubilee celebrations.
102. *Univ. Ct. Mins.*, July 1936, 193. See also ibid., 45; Dec. 1935, 37; July 1935, 22.

103. *Univ. Cncl. Mins.*, Nov. 1934, 84. See also *Univ. Ct. Mins.*, July 1927, 12–13; July 1928, 35. There is a stimulating treatment of broadcasting in Wales by John Davies, *Broadcasting and the BBC in Wales* (Cardiff, 1994).
104. *Univ. Cncl. Mins.*, Nov. 1935, 70–1.
105. *Univ. Ct. Mins.*, July 1929, 33.
106. Ibid., Dec. 1938, 11. In addition, see ibid., Dec. 1933, 20; July 1935, 27.
107. *Hai ati Wŷr Ieuainc,* detholwyd gan Margaret Dafydd (Cardiff, 1986), 43.
108. *Univ. Ct. Mins.*, July 1938, 28, app. XII, 178.
109. Ibid., July 1938, 44.
110. *Jubilee Addresses* at the University College of North Wales, Bangor, 3 Nov. 1934, 9 (no place or date of publication).
111. *University Education*, an address delivered on 27 Apr., 1938 at Bangor, 9 (no place or date of publication).
112. 'The Caernarfon Court Speech' in *Presenting Saunders Lewis,* ed. A. R. Jones and Gwyn Thomas (Cardiff, 1983), 115.
113. *W. Mail*, 14 Feb. 1927; *SWN*, 10 Feb. 1927.
114. *Univ. Ct. Mins.*, July 1926, 136.
115. Ibid., 137.
116. Ibid., 138.
117. Ibid., 139.
118. *Mins. of the Academic Board*, May 1934, 186.
119. Ibid.
120. *Cyfres y Werin* (Cardiff, [1920]), Cyfarchiad, 'At Werin Cymru', not paginated.
121. Above, 376.
122. *Y Beirniad,* 1 (1911), 1–2.
123. *W. Mail*, 28 Feb. 1924.

Retrospect

1. Above, 25–7. On federalism in higher education.
2. *University Commission, Final Reports*, 56–7.
3. Above, 195–7.
4. Ch. V.
5. Above, 290–1.
6. *Cof Cenedl*, 10 (1995), 142, 'diymadferthwch'.
7. *Royal Commission on the Constitution* (Kilbrandon), 1967–73, I, *Report*, Cmd. 5460 (1973), 156.
8. Ibid.
9. Ibid., 157.
10. A. H. Kidd, 29 June 1914, internal memo, PRO, ED 119/81.
11. Statute XXIX(5)a of 1920 charter.
12. Evans, *Univ. of Wales*, 42.
13. Sanderson, *British Industry*, 79.
14. Ibid.
15. Above, 350–1.
16. Sanderson, *British Industry*, 171–2.
17. M. F. Rathbone to Thomas Jones, 3 Oct. 1915, TJ MSS, J, i, 72.
18. Hald., *App.* I, Q. 32.
19. Ibid.
20. Reichel to Thomas Jones, 8 June 1916, TJ MSS, U, iii, 41.
21. *Welsh Leader,* 2 (1905), 657.
22. *Principal's Statement . . . October, 1911 on State Assistance* to Cardiff Court of Governors, 6.
23. Ibid., 7.
24. Above, 43–6.

25.   *UMW*, 44.
26.   *NW Chron.*, 25 Oct. 1884.
27.   Hald., *App.* I, 259.
28.   Above, 156.
29.   Hald., *App.* I, 28.
30.   Above, 163, 191.
31.   *UMW*, 184.
32.   *Bangor*, 49.
33.   *Man. Guard.*, 6 Oct. 1917.
34.   *The Ideal of the University*, reprint of Haldane's address to the University Court, 25 Nov. 1920, 6 (no place of publication).
35.   Above, 220–1.
36.   Ibid., 192.
37.   *The University of Wales in its Relation to the National Life* (Liverpool, 1894), 4–5.
38.   Quoted by Evans, *University of Wales*, 139.
39.   K. V. Jones, *Life*, 385.
40.   Aberdare, *Evid.*, Q. 19042.
41.   *Bangor,* 36.
42.   Rees Davies, *The Revolt of Owain Glyn Dŵr* (Oxford, 1995), 172.
43.   *Bangor*, 10–11; *W. Mail*, 16 Mar. 1931.
44.   *University Commission, Final Reports*, 83.
45.   4 Oct. 1917, *Address*, separately printed (Bangor, 1917), 13–14.
46.   Above, 320 ff.
47.   *UMW*, 28.
48.   Robbins, *Higher Education Report* (London, 1963), Cmnd. 2154, 6.
49.   Above, 353.
50.   *UMW*, 75.
51.   Quoted by Sanderson, *The Universities in the Nineteenth Century*, 124.
52.   Ibid., 161–2.
53.   *UMW*, 171.
54.   Quoted in 'Cardiff', 32, n. 37.
55.   *Welsh Outlook*, 7 (1920), 45.
56.   *Univ. Ct. Mins.*, July 1924, 34.
57.   *The University in Wales* (1920), 17.
58.   Above, 342.
59.   Thomas Jones, *Old and Young* (Cardiff, 1945), 11, reprinted from *Welsh Review* (June, 1945).
60.   *W. Mail*, 30 Jan. 1931.
61.   *SWN,* 20 July 1923.
62.   Above, 187.
63.   *Efrydiau Athronyddol*, 37 (1974), 32; above, 364.
64.   Quoted in G. C. Moodie and Rowland Eustace, *Power and Authority in British Universities* (London, 1974), 95.
65.   K. V. Jones, *Life*, 374.
66.   *Man. Guard.*, 1 Nov. 1907.
67.   *W. Mail*, 11 June 1923.
68.   *SWN*, 20 July 1923; *Cap and Gown*, jubilee no., 30 (1933), 19.
69.   *Dragon*, 45 (1922–3), 80.
70.   Above, ch. X, passim.
71.   Quoted by A. H. Dodd, *Studies in Stuart Wales* (Cardiff, 1952), 75.
72.   *Man. Guard.*, 31 Oct. 1895.
73.   *The Ideal of the University*, reprint of Haldane's address to the Univ. Ct., 25 Nov. 1920 (no place of publication), 6.
74.   *Y Cymmrodor*, 11 (1893), 245.
75.   Hald., *App.*, III, 112, para. 2.
76.   Ibid., I, Q. 1927.

A Note on Sources

My debt to numerous university and college histories in England, Scotland and Ireland is far greater than may be gathered from direct references in notes. W. H. G. Armytage, *Civic Universities: Aspect of a British Tradition* (London, 1955), remains important for its discussion of the motives which led to the foundation of new institutions in England and Wales. I have also derived much benefit from the following: R. D. Anderson, *Educational Opportunity in Victorian Scotland: Schools and Universities* (Oxford, 1983) and *The Student Community at Aberdeen, 1860–1939* (Aberdeen, 1988); R. B. McDowell and D. A. Webb, *Trinity College Dublin, 1592–1952: An Academic History* (Cambridge, 1982); Thomas Kelly, *For Advancement of Learning: The University of Liverpool, 1881–1981* (Liverpool, 1981); T. W. Moody and J. C. Beckett, *Queen's Belfast, 1845–1949: The History of a University*, 2 vols. (The Queen's University, Belfast, 1959).

The first history of the University of Wales was prepared by W. Cadwaladr Davies and W. Lewis Jones twelve years after the grant of a royal charter. Entitled *The University of Wales and its Constituent Colleges* (London, 1905), it repays reading today. The authors speak with pride of the university movement, yet W. L. Jones did not forbear to criticize the federal system as it had then developed (above, p. 23). The movement itself was examined in greater detail in *The University Movement in Wales* by the present writer (above, p. 430). The first sixty years were treated with characteristic discernment in a comparatively short book by D. Emrys Evans who drew upon his experience as student, professor, principal and vice-chancellor.

The University's oldest college was exceptionally well served by E. L. Ellis, *The University College of Wales, Aberystwyth, 1872–1972*, which first demonstrated the importance of sources at the National Library of Wales and at the Public Record Office. I was much illumined by two succeeding volumes, D. T. W. Price,

A History of Saint David's University College, Lampeter, Vol. I, *To 1898*, Vol. II, *To 1971* (Cardiff, 1977 and 1990), and David Dykes, *The University College of Swansea* (Alan Sutton, 1992). The present writer wrote *The University College of North Wales: Foundations 1884–1927* (Cardiff, 1985) . Details of these works may be found in the List of Abbreviations. On no account should the reader pass by Geraint H. Jenkins's engaging *The University of Wales: An Illustrated History, 1893–1993* (Cardiff, 1993).

In 1934, to celebrate fifty years, the Cardiff College produced *A Short History of the College, 1883–1933* (Cardiff, 1933) by A. H. Trow and D. J. A. Brown. It still has its uses, but it is not a systematic history; simply to devote four hundred words or so under the title 'Academic Achievement' was manifestly inadequate. In good time for the centenary the College enlisted the services of a distinguished medievalist, S. B. Chrimes, to write an authoritative history. Surrounding this unpublished work there remains an aura of mystery which should now be dispelled. The bound volume (remaining in typescript) has many merits, for the author was especially sure-footed in dealing with constitutional and financial matters. His decision to set aside more than half the volume to 'The Academic Departments and Other Organisations', written by a member of each department, led to mixed results. Some are very good and deserve a wide readership; others are less than satisfactory. In general, however, it is fair to say that no other college has a comparable compilation. Having consulted seasoned historians, the College concluded that the volume could not be published in this form. It should perhaps be added that the author was disinclined to place the College in its social setting, to examine sources beyond its walls or to contemplate the use of oral history (which he regarded as so much tittle-tattle). At all events, and at a late stage, Professor Gwyn Jones, who kindly discussed the circumstances with me, was recruited, together with Michael Quinn, to prepare *Fountains of Praise: University College, Cardiff, 1882–1983* (Cardiff, 1983), a very attractive volume, but not the systematic history originally planned. The Welsh School of Medicine likewise has not been favoured with the history it richly deserves and I do not view with equanimity my brief, untutored efforts which scarcely repair the omission.

Two specialist investigations which include treatment of aspects of university education in Wales are rewarding: Michael Sanderson, *The University and British Industry, 1850–1970* (London, 1972), and Carol Dyhouse, *No Distinction of Sex? Women in British Universities 1870–1939* (London, 1995). On matters pertaining directly to Wales I have greatly profited from the following: W. Gareth Evans, *Education and Female Emancipation: The Welsh Experience, 1847–1914* (Cardiff, 1990); Richard Lewis, *Leaders and Teachers: Adult Education and the Challenge of Labour in South Wales, 1906–1940* (Cardiff, 1993); David Ian Allsobrook, *Music for Wales, Walford Davies and the National Council of Music, 1918–1941* (Cardiff, 1992); Gareth Elwyn Jones, *Controls and Conflicts in Welsh Secondary Education, 1889–1944* (Cardiff, 1982). Of articles, the one which has influenced me most is Sheldon Rothblatt's valuable contribution, 'Historical and comparative remarks on the federal principle in higher education', in *History of Education*, 16, no. 3 (1987), 151–80.

To volumes of autobiography and biography there is happily no end, though only three Principals have received anything approaching adequate treatment: Katherine Viriamu Jones, *Life of John Viriamu Jones* (London, 1915); *Sir Harry Reichel 1856–1931*, ed. J. E. Lloyd (Cardiff, 1934); T. I. Ellis, *John Humphreys Davies, 1871–1926* (Liverpool, 1963). It is a matter of abiding regret that, during this period at least, Aberystwyth's three first Principals are the only Principals to have left a substantial body of correspondence, the others (or their executors) apparently being unduly cautious in matters of legitimate concern to posterity. Aberystwyth, too, has an unrivalled collection of reminiscences in *The College by the Sea*, edited by Iwan Morgan (Aberystwyth, 1928). I have not thought it necessary to list here the many volumes of autobiography which appear in notes. As might be expected, College magazines contain much useful material. Under 'Acknowledgments' I have gratefully named those who so willingly imparted knowledge which might otherwise have been for ever lost. I am sorry that long ago I did not listen with greater attention to the reminiscences of my elders. I have since learnt the value of oral history.

Mr Hugh Flynn Hughes, as archivist, eased my entry into the records of the University Registry by preparing a serviceable schedule. These are largely formal, as might be expected; lively correspondence is to be sought elsewhere. A strong case can be made for transferring a high proportion of Registry records, other than those needed for day-to-day administration, to the National Library of Wales upon the strict understanding that most Senate papers, for example, in the pre–1920 period, cannot be expected to survive responsible winnowing.

Minutes of the Court before 1920 and thereafter of Court and Council are of first importance. Printed and widely distributed, they may be consulted in several libraries. They are buttressed by reports of such bodies as the Academic, Appointments, Extramural and Press Boards. The Registry has a good collection of press cuttings, as has Cardiff (until 1937) and Bangor (until 1927), though not Aberystwyth (for reasons that are not entirely clear). Of all the colleges, Bangor has the largest number of relevant deposits (Isambard Owen, J. E. Lloyd, Henry Lewis and Thomas Richards, for example), but it was natural that many of those who served Aberystwyth well should have placed their papers at the National Library, Rendel, Humphreys-Owen, Herbert Lewis and J. H. Davies amongst them. The most rewarding for University matters (as for much else) is the splendid Thomas Jones collection generously presented by Baroness White and her brother, the late Tristan Lloyd Jones. At the Public Record Office the archives of the Department of Education and Science (and, marginally, of the Privy Council Office) are essential for an understanding of official attitudes during crucial periods. I have, of course, consulted archives of individual colleges as the need arose, and also the following: those of the Cardiff Royal Infirmary at the Glamorgan Record Office; of W. E. Gladstone at the British Library; of R. B. Haldane at the National Library of Scotland, Edinburgh; of Lloyd George at the House of Lords; of A. J. Mundella at Sheffield University and of William Rathbone at Liverpool University.

The official annual publications I have most frequently consulted are the *Reports . . . from those Universities and University Colleges in Great Britain which are in receipt of Grants from the Board of Education* before 1914 and the University Grants Committee's *Returns from Universities and University Colleges in*

Receipt of Treasury Grants, from 1919 onwards. The Reports of the Raleigh Committee (1909) and of the Haldane Commission (1918) are indispensable, particularly the latter, whose volumes of evidence, in addition, provide a wonderful vantage point almost midway through this period to examine the past and to peer into the future.

The following unpublished theses have proved most useful:

Bryn L. Davies, 'An Assessment of the Contribution of Sir Hugh Owen to Education in Wales', Ph.D., University of Wales, 1971.

Clive Hughes, 'Army Recruitment in Gwynedd, 1914–1916', MA University of Wales, 1983.

Gwilym Arthur Jones, 'The Life and Work of Sir Isambard Owen (1850–1927)', MA University of Wales, 1967.

Roger J. Webster, 'The Place of Secondary Education in Welsh Society, 1800–1918', Ph.D., University of Wales, 1959.

Index